INTERNATIONAL LAW STUDIES

Volume 79

International Law and the War on Terror

Fred L. Borch & Paul S. Wilson
Editors

Naval War College
Newport, Rhode Island
2003

INTERNATIONAL LAW STUDIES

Volume 79

Library of Congress Cataloging-in-Publication Data

International law and the war on terror / Fred L. Borch & Paul S. Wilson, editors.
       p. cm. -- (International law studies, v. 79)
Includes bibliographical references and index.
  ISBN 1-884733-28-X (hardcover : alk. paper)
1. Terrorism. 2. War (International law) I. Borch, Frederic L.,1954–
II. Wilson, Paul S., 1964– III. Series.
K5256.I584 2003
345´.02--dc22

                                         2003019449

Table of Contents

International Law and the War on Terrorism

FOREWORD. ix
INTRODUCTION xi
PREFACE xiii

I   Welcoming Address
            Rear Admiral Rodney P. Rempt. 1

PART I: JUS AD BELLUM

II   Counter-Terrorism and the Use of Force in International Law
           Michael Schmitt 7

III   Jus Ad Bellum and International Terrorism
           Rein Müllerson 75

IV   Commentary—Jus ad Bellum
           Robert Turner 129

V   Commentary—Jus ad Bellum
           William Dalton 137

VI   Discussion—Jus ad Bellum
           Application of Force to al Qaeda and Taliban Members. . . 139
           Legitimacy of the Use of Force 143
           Regime Change in Iraq 146

PART II: JUS IN BELLO

VII   Unlawful Combatancy
           Yoram Dinstein 151

VIII	The Laws of War in the War on Terror
	Adam Roberts 175

IX	Commentary—Jus in Bello
	Charles Garraway. 231

X	Commentary—Jus in Bello
	Leslie Green 235

XI	Commentary—Jus in Bello
	Tony Montgomery. 243

XII	Discussion—Jus in Bello
	The Overlap Between Jus ad Bellum and Jus in Bello 247
	The Power of the Security Council. 248
	The Nature of the Current Conflict in Afghanistan 249
	Shielding Military Targets with Noncombatants. 250
	The Currency of the Law of Armed Conflict. 251
	Unprivileged Combatants 251

PART III: MARITIME AND COALITION OPERATIONS

XIII	The Legality of Maritime Interception/Interdiction Operations Within the Framework of Operation ENDURING FREEDOM
	Wolff von Heinegg. 255

XIV	The Limits of Coalition Cooperation in the War on Terrorism
	Ivan Shearer. 275

XV	Commentary—Maritime and Coalition Operations
	Kenneth O'Rourke. 297

XVI	Commentary—Maritime and Coalition Operations
	Paul Cronan. 301

XVII	Commentary—Maritime and Coalition Operations
	Neil Brown 303

XVIII	Commentary—Maritime and Coalition Operations
	Jean-Guy Perron 309

XIX	Discussion—Maritime and Coalition Operations	
	Abduction or Extradition of Terrorists.	313
	Application of the Laws of Armed Conflict	319
	Terrorism as a Criminal or International Law Problem . . .	320

PART IV: BRINGING TERRORISTS TO JUSTICE: THE PROPER FORUM

XX	International Criminal Law Aspects of the War Against Terrorism	
	Michael Newton.	323
XXI	Terrorism: The Proper Law and the Proper Forum?	
	Christopher Greenwood.	353
XXII	Commentary—Bringing Terrorists to Justice	
	Manuel Supervielle	371
XXIII	Commentary—Terrorism and the Problem of Different Legal Regimes	
	Daniel Helle.	375
XXIV	Discussion—Bringing Terrorists to Justice	
	The Distinction Between Armed Conflict and Armed Attack.	381
	September 11th—Armed Attack, Armed Conflict or Criminal Act?.	381
	Military Commissions	386
	The Challenges Associated with Defining and Addressing Terrorism	387

PART V: THE ROAD AHEAD

XXV	International Law and the War on Terrorism: The Road Ahead	
	John Murphy	391
XXVI	Al Qaeda And Taliban Detainees—An Examination of Legal Rights and Appropriate Treatment	
	James Terry.	441
XXVII	Commentary—The Road Ahead in Afghanistan	
	James Terry.	455

XXVIII	Commentary—The Road Ahead
	Nicholas Rostow 461
XXIX	Commentary—The Road Ahead
	Michael Saalfeld 467
XXX	Commentary—The Road Ahead
	Ronald Winfrey 473
XXXI	Commentary—The Road Ahead
	Jane Dalton 477
XXXII	Discussion—The Road Ahead
	Iraq 483
	Terrorism 486

Appendix A—Contributors 491
Index 501

Foreword

The International Law Studies "Blue Book" series was initiated by the Naval War College in 1901 to publish essays, treaties and articles that contribute to the broader understanding of international law. This, the seventy-ninth volume of the series, contains edited proceedings of a scholarly colloquium entitled *International Law and the War on Terrorism* hosted here at the Naval War College on June 26–28, 2002.

The colloquium's mission was to examine international law and its continuing relevance after the events of September 11th, 2001 and the subsequent military operations against al Qaeda and the Taliban. In doing so, the colloquium participants focused on the basis for the use of force against organizations such as al Qaeda and the Taliban, the rules applicable to military operations against such organizations, the challenges associated with maritime and coalition operations in the war on terrorism, the proper forum for bringing terrorists to justice, and finally, the path before us in this war on terrorism.

Renowned international scholars and practitioners, both military and civilian, representing government and academic institutions from throughout the world participated in the colloquium, which was co-sponsored by the Center for National Security Law of the University of Virginia, Charlottesville, Virginia, the Israeli Yearbook on Human Rights, Tel Aviv, Israel, the Roger Williams University Ralph R. Papitto School of Law, Bristol, Rhode Island, the Pell Center for International Relations and Public Policy of Salve Regina University, Newport, Rhode Island, and the International Law Department of the Center for Naval Warfare Studies, United States Naval War College.

On behalf of the Secretary of the Navy, the Chief of Naval Operations, and the Commandant of the Marine Corps, I extend to all the co-sponsors, the contributing authors, and the co-editors, our thanks and gratitude for their invaluable contributions to this project and to the future understanding of the laws of war.

RODNEY P. REMPT
Rear Admiral, U.S. Navy
President, Naval War College

Introduction

The events of September 11th brought home to the United States that, perhaps unlike any time in its past, the "tyranny of distance" could not be relied upon to protect its citizens from harm. The destruction of the World Trade Center and the attack on the Pentagon wrought countless millions in damages to those affected and to the economy of the United States as a whole. More importantly, the attacks caused the deaths of some 3,000 and injury to countless others. Many of the victims were, of course, from countries other than the United States. With the benefit of hindsight, it seem clear that an act of the magnitude of September 11th would eventually strike the United States. Still, terrorism on this scale is clearly new to the United States and the world and brings with it challenges to the law of armed conflict paradigm that has lasted since the closure of World War II. This changed environment and its impact on the existing laws of armed conflict require careful study and debate to develop insight into the future legal framework for responding to terrorism. This was the purpose of the colloquium that this book, volume 79 of the International Law Studies ("Blue Book") series, memorializes.

In June, 2002, the Naval War College conducted a symposium on International Law and the War on Terrorism. The colloquium, organized by Lieutenant Colonel Steven Berg, JAGC, US Army, was made possible with the support of the Center for National Security Law of the University of Virginia, Charlottesville, Virginia, the Israeli Yearbook on Human Rights, Tel Aviv, Israel, the Roger Williams University Ralph R. Papitto School of Law, Bristol, Rhode Island, and the Pell Center for International Relations and Public Policy of Salve Regina University, Newport, Rhode Island. Without the support and assistance of these organizations, the colloquium would not have been the success that it was, and this volume would not be before you as it is. Their support is greatly appreciated.

Colonel Frederick L. Borch, JAGC, US Army, and Major Paul S. Wilson, JAGC, US Army, both of our International Law Department, collaborated as editors of this volume. Their dedication and perseverance are responsible for the production and completion of this product.

A special thank you is necessary to Dr. Alberto Coll, the current Dean of the Center for Naval Warfare Studies and Rear Admiral Rodney P. Rempt, the President of the Naval War College for their leadership and support in the planning and conduct of the colloquium and the funding for the printing of this book.

The "Blue Book" series is published by the Naval War College and distributed throughout the world to academic institutions, libraries, and both US and foreign military commands. This volume on International Law and the War on Terrorism is a fitting and necessary addition to the series as the world continues to grapple with the senseless acts of terrorism common in our world today.

DENNIS L. MANDSAGER
Professor of Law & Chairman
International Law Department

Preface

The September 11, 2001 attacks on the World Trade Center and the Pentagon catapulted the United States—indeed the world—into a new war on terrorism. On September 14th, the US Congress passed a joint resolution authorizing President George W. Bush "to use all necessary and appropriate force against those nations, organizations, or persons he determines planned, authorized, committed or aided the terrorist attacks ... or harbored such organizations or persons." On September 28th, the UN Security Council adopted Resolution 1373. It not only condemned terrorism as a threat to international peace and security, but implicitly recognized that al Qaeda's use of commercial aircraft as weapons constituted an "armed attack" within the meaning of Article 51 of the UN Charter. In any event, on October 7, 2001, less than a month after the terrorist attacks on America, US forces began operations against al Qaeda and Taliban forces in Afghanistan.

For lawyers and academics practicing and studying international law and the Law of Armed Conflict, "9/11" and subsequent legal actions taken by the US Congress, the United Nations, and the North Atlantic Treaty Organization, meant a greatly renewed interest in a subject that had not received enough attention over the last 10 years. The same was true of military actions taken by the United States and its allies, as the nature of the fighting against the Taliban and al Qaeda in Afghanistan raised new jus in bello issues. Recognizing that a forum in which scholars and practitioners could meet and examine legal issues in the war on terrorism would be exciting, instructive, and rewarding, the International Law Department began planning a conference in November 2001. The result was a June 26–28, 2002 symposium called "International Law and the War on Terrorism," and this book records the events occurring during those three days, bringing together the perspectives and ruminations of the roughly 100 conference participants.

Almost from the beginning of the symposium, a major theme emerged: that while al Qaeda's attacks on the World Trade Center and Pentagon represented a type of armed conflict not anticipated by those participating in the conference, the Law of Armed Conflict was capable of addressing the myriad legal issues raised by terrorism after 9/11. This is not to say that the scholars and practitioners agreed on all jus ad bellum or jus in bello issues discussed; they did agree, however, that the Law of Armed Conflict and other existing laws as they now exist provide an adequate framework for regulating armed conflict with terrorism.

The first session, titled "Jus ad Bellum," had two presenters. Prof. Michael N. Schmitt, George C. Marshall European Center, Garmisch, Germany, began with a paper titled "Counter-Terrorism and the Use of Force in International Law." Schmitt explored the circumstances under which a victim state may react forcibly to an act of terrorism, and concluded that "in most respects the law on the use of force has proven adequate" in countering terrorist attacks. That is, while the current "normative system developed for state-on-state conflict," it nonetheless has shown itself to be sufficiently flexible to respond to terrorist attacks by non-state actors.

In the absence of a post-9/11 resolution from the UN Security Council, Prof. Schmitt asserted that the sole basis for the United States and its coalition partners to take action was self-defense. No advance Council authorization is required for force used in self-defense; all the U.N. Charter requires is 'notice.' It follows that while a state's use of force in self-defense does not deprive the Council of its 'right' to respond to any terrorist attack, the Council's failure to take action does not deprive a state of its inherent right to exercise individual or collective self-defense. In Prof. Schmidt's view, it is "tragically self-evident" that the al Qaeda attacks on September 11, 2001 were of sufficient "scale and effects" to qualify as an "armed attack" within the meaning of Article 51 of the UN Charter. Consequently, US and coalition operations against al Qaeda in Afghanistan were a legitimate exercise of individual and collective self-defense. Self-defense requires 'necessity" ("a sound basis for believing that further attacks will be mounted") and 'imminency' ("self-defense may be conducted against an ongoing terrorist campaign"); the use of force also must be proportional. Schmitt concluded his paper with an examination of the legality of using force against the Taliban. While he determined that the legal authority for acting in self-defense against al Qaeda was much clearer than the legal basis for using force against the Taliban, Schmitt nonetheless was satisfied that the principle of state responsibility established in the *Corfu Channel* case justified US and coalition military operations against Taliban forces in Afghanistan.

Prof. Rein Müllerson, Kings College, Univ. of London, followed Schmitt with an oral presentation of his paper, "Jus ad Bellum and International Terrorism." In examining terrorism and the law of war, Müllerson concluded that not all terrorist attacks are contrary to jus ad bellum; if they lack a link to a state or are "relatively insignificant" in size and scope, the attacks fall outside the scope of jus ad bellum. However, any terrorist attack that does "come under" jus ad bellum (like 9/11, which Müllerson believes is an armed attack) by definition also violates jus in bello. The fact, says Müllerson, that those drafting Article 51 in 1945 contemplated that only states would be conducting armed attacks does not mean that a non-state entity cannot launch an armed attack. To conclude otherwise is both illogical and ignores "current realities." Müllerson further argued that the September 11th attacks are crimes against humanity as defined by Nuremberg Tribunals and "the statutes of international criminal tribunals recently adopted." Like Prof. Schmidt, Prof. Müllerson also arrives at the same "bottom line:" that our existing international legal framework provides more than adequate authority to use force against terrorists.

After comments from Prof. Robert Turner and Mr. Harvey Dalton, and questions from the audience, the conference shifted from jus ad bellum to an examination of jus in bello issues. Leading off this session was Prof. Yoram Dinstein, Visiting Professor, DePaul Univ. College of Law, who talked about "Unlawful Combatancy." Calling this topic "a matter a of great practical significance in present-day international law," Dinstein began with the basics: that combatants are individuals who are either members of the armed forces (except religious or medical personnel) or persons who take an active part in hostilities; that noncombatants are civilians (who are not allowed to actively participate in the fighting); and that one *cannot be both* at the same time. As the US, its friends, and allies are involved in a war with terrorists who are almost by definition *unlawful* combatants, Prof. Dinstein devoted the remainder of his remarks to explaining the distinction between lawful and unlawful combatants. In Dinstein's view, combatants must satisfy "seven cumulative conditions" to qualify as *lawful* combatants and enjoy immunity from prosecution or punishment for killing and wounding the enemy or destroying and damaging his property. They must:

(1) Be subordinate to a responsible command (thus excluding "one-man" armies);

(2) Wear a fixed distinctive emblem recognizable at a distance (so that the principle of distinction may be observed);

(3) Carry arms openly (so that they will not be confused with civilians);

(4) Fight in accordance with the jus in bello (so that in claiming the law's protections if captured, a combatant must be willing himself to respect this same law);

(5) Act within a hierarchic framework, embedded in discipline and subject to supervision by upper echelons;

(6) Belong to a party to the conflict; and finally

(7) Not have any allegiance (or nationality) to the Detaining Power (so that a German soldier in the French Foreign Legion would be entitled to POW status if captured while fighting in Indo-China but would not be entitled to such status if fighting in a war against Germany.)

Based on these seven cumulative conditions, Prof. Dinstein concluded that both the Taliban and al Qaeda failed to qualify for POW status, but for very different reasons. The Taliban fighters were members of regular armed forces professing allegiance to a government unrecognized by the Detaining Power. This meant that they could qualify for POW status in the same manner as De Gaulle's Free French forces were entitled to be POWs when captured by the Germans in World War II. That was not the principal reason, however, that captured Taliban fighters were not POWs. Rather, because they did not comply with virtually all of the seven factors earlier identified by Dinstein as required for POW status (e.g. the Taliban wore no uniform of any kind, much less any distinctive insignia), they were not entitled to claim POW status. Al Qaeda combatants, however, belong in an entirely different category. In contrast to the Taliban, al Qaeda combatants were irregular forces who failed to wear uniforms and who "displayed utter disdain toward the jus in bello." This contempt for the Law of War meant that no al Qaeda fighters were entitled to POW status. Prof. Dinstein concluded his remarks with the warning that the "constraints of the conditions of lawful combatancy must not . . . be seen as binding only on one Party to the conflict." Some American combatants, notably special forces troops and CIA agents in the field, were not wearing uniforms while in combat. Dinstein cautioned that had any US combatants in civilian clothing been captured by al Qaeda or Taliban forces, they would not have been entitled to POW status.

Sir Adam Roberts followed Prof. Dinstein. Sir Adam, a professor of international relations at Oxford, began by asking these questions: Are the laws of war "formally applicable" to the war on terrorism? If counter-terrorism operations involve "situations different" from those envisaged by the laws of war, should we still try to apply that body of law? Are terrorists entitled to POW status? If not, what "international standards apply to their treatment?" Finally, Sir Adam asked whether the laws of war should be "revised" to take into account the "special circumstances" of the war on terrorism. Sir Adam concluded that there were "particular difficulties" in applying the laws of war to counter-terrorism. That is, while Operation ENDURING FREEDOM might look like an "ordinary" international armed conflict, "a war that has as a purpose the pursuit of people deemed to be criminals involves many awkward issues for which the existing laws of war are not a perfect fit." With that said, the UN Security Council, states, and non-governmental organizations have all assumed that the laws of war do apply. Consequently, this reality—and considerations of "reciprocity" and "prudence"—require that the US and its coalition partners apply the law of war "to the maximum extent possible." Professor Roberts also concluded that the US decision to deny POW status to al Qaeda combat captives was sound both as a matter of law and policy. However, he faulted the Bush administration for failing to highlight that the detainees would be accorded humane treatment in accordance with Common Article 3. Sir Adam also stressed that the United States missed an opportunity to show the world that it is scrupulous in observing the laws of war when it did not announce that all Taliban and al Qaeda detainees would be treated in accordance with Articles 45 and 75 of the 1977 Geneva Protocol I. The latter articles elaborate a range of minimum rules of protection for all those who are not entitled to POW status. Since the US treatment of the detainees comported with these two Protocol provisions, and since most nations are signatories to Protocol I, announcing that it would adhere to these Protocol provisions would have been smart public relations. Finally, Prof. Roberts opined that "there is a case for consideration of further revision" of the law of war. While rejecting the idea that existing laws of war are inadequate in the face of the "terrorist challenge," Roberts did believe that "some modest evolutionary changes" should be examined. In Sir Adam's view, legal issues involving "targeting, cluster bombs, and the classification and treatment of detainees" were appropriate topics, as was "the whole difficult problem of . . . suicide bombers who by definition cannot be deterred by normal means."

After commentary from Col. Charles Garraway, Prof. Leslie C. Green, and Lt. Col. Tony E. Montgomery, and questions from the audience on jus in bello issues, the conference participants shifted their focus to a third topic: coalition operations. Prof. Wolff Von Heinegg, a member of the international law faculty at Europa-University in Frankfurt, Germany, presented an article on the legality of maritime interception and interdiction operations (MIO) in Operation ENDURING FREEDOM, the name given to the military operation launched in the aftermath of 9/11. In von Heinegg's view, MIO seek to disrupt supplies for terrorist groups (especially by preventing materiel support for, and financing of, international terrorism), eliminate terrorist command and training facilities, and capture international terrorists for the purpose of prosecuting them.

Von Heinegg first observed that the Security Council has neither required flag states to permit MIO against ships flying its flag, nor authorized the US and its coalition partners to conduct MIO. It follows that the legal basis for MIO must be individual or collective self-defense as permitted by customary international law and reflected in Article 51 of the UN Charter. But von Heinegg also argued that Resolution 1373, because it obligates all UN member states to prevent and suppress within their territories all acts of international terrorism, provides an additional legal basis for MIO. In Prof. von Heinegg's view, the clear language of Resolution 1373 acts to waive any member states's objection to MIO conducted against terrorists. The right of self-defense and Resolution 1373, taken together, provide the legal authority for the "the US and its coalition partners [to] control international shipping and aviation in order to verify the innocent status of such shipping and aviation." With that said, because the principle of proportionality applies to a state's right of self-defense, "indiscriminate implementation and enforcement of MIO covering vast sea areas" would be impermissible as disproportionate. Consequently, all MIO must be based upon "sufficient intelligence indicators . . . of conspiracies to commit, or acts of, international terrorism." Prof. von Heinegg concluded his presentation by explaining that the US and its coalition partners "are entitled to establish maritime interdiction areas" (i.e. to restrict "neutral" or third party state access to certain sea areas) for the purpose of identifying ships carrying terrorists or materiel for them. He also briefly examined the limitations imposed on MIO "by the law of naval warfare and by the law of maritime neutrality."

Ivan Shearer, Challis Professor of International Law at the University of Sydney, Australia, followed Von Heinegg with a paper titled "The Limits of Coalition Cooperation in the War on Terrorism." In Shearer's view, there were a number of obstacles to successful coalition warfare against international terrorism. First, as there is no universal definition of terrorism, each state is free to adopt its own definition. These varying domestic law definitions of terrorism are certain to make coalition efforts against terrorists more problematic, especially regarding extradition for prosecution. Second, while there are international norms of human rights, how each state interprets these norms in the detention and prosecution of terrorists is very much controlled by domestic law. For example, Article 5 of the Universal Declaration of Human Rights provides that "no one shall be subjected to . . . cruel, inhuman, or degrading treatment of punishment." But how this provision is viewed in the United States is quite different from how Article 5 is interpreted in the European Union. A third potential obstacle is extradition. Since there is no customary international law requirement for a state to honor an extradition request from another, bi-lateral and multi-lateral extradition treaties have been negotiated. Many of these existing treaties prohibit the extradition of their own citizens. They also prohibit the extradition of "politically motivated offenders." In Shearer's view, these two provisions are certain to create obstacles to the successful prosecution of terrorists. Fourth, the death penalty poses a very real obstacle, especially since it has been retained in the United States. The countries of the European Union, Australia, Canada, and New Zealand, for example, will only extradite a terrorist to the United States on the condition that any death penalty, if imposed, will not be carried out. Finally, Prof. Shearer addressed the role of the International Criminal Court (ICC) in coalition operations against terrorism. He noted that terrorism is not a crime within the jurisdiction of the ICC; it was specifically excluded out of fear that its inclusion as a crime might politicize the ICC. That said, Shearer concluded that as some acts of terrorism—such as a widespread or systematic attack against any civilian population—might constitute a crime against humanity and, as the ICC has subject-matter jurisdiction over this offense, some terrorists could be prosecuted in that forum.

After commentary by Commanders Neil Brown (UK) and Kevin O'Rourke (US), Wing Commander Paul Cronan (Australia), and Lt. Col. Jean-Guy Perron (Canada), and questions and comments from the audience and presenters, the conference moved to its next topic: The "proper" forum for "bringing terrorists to justice." Lt. Col. Michael Newton, an Army judge advocate and faculty member at the U.S. Military Academy, and Christopher Greenwood, a professor at the London School of Economics and Political Science, presented papers on this subject.

The thrust of Newton's presentation was that existing international law provides a sufficient framework to prevent and punish terrorism. Newton recognized, however, that the current state of the law, predicated as it is on "the voluntary efforts of sovereign states to implement and enforce international norms . . . is not a panacea" for combating terrorism. Nonetheless, after examining the Nuremberg trials, the UN tribunals for Rwanda and the Former Yugoslavia, and the International Criminal Court, Newton concludes that the creation of "a new superstructure of supranational justice"—an international terrorist tribunal—would not "materially enhance" the law. In his view, establishing an international court to prosecute terrorists is "abdicating state responsibility to an internationalized process [and this] would be the first step toward paralyzing politicization of the fight against terrorism."

Prof. Chris Greenwood responded that he believed that the national courts were the best forum in which to prosecute terrorists. He objected to the idea that al Qaeda members were guilty of war crimes prior to the commencement of international armed conflict in Afghanistan in mid-October 2001; rejecting the idea that there could be a war between a non-state actor and the United States prior to that time.

After commentary by Col. Manuel E.F. Supervielle, by Mr. Daniel Helle, and questions and comments from the audience, the conference moved to its final topic: "The Road Ahead." Prof. John Murphy, Mr. James P. Terry, and Dr. Nicholas Rostow made presentations. Murphy, a professor of law at Villanova University, discussed "the application of legal lessons learned [and] review of the role of international conventions on terrorism." Prior to examining these issues, however, Murphy identified a number of "trends" in terrorism. These include the "globalization" of terrorism," as reflected in the worldwide expansion of the al Qaeda network of terrorists now operating in as many as 60 different countries, and the reality that September 11, 2001 signals "the increased willingness of terrorists to kill large numbers of people and to make no distinction between military and civilian targets." Another trend is that terrorists appear to be increasingly "smarter and more creative . . . and better equipped to take advantage of the information on weapons, targets, and resources available on the internet," and that some terrorist organizations are cooperating with each other (*e.g.* the IRA traveled to Colombia to assist the FARC in planning an urban bombing campaign). But Murphy also noted a "positive" trend in terrorism: the relative decline of state-sponsored terrorism when compared to the 1970s and 1980s.

With this as background, Prof. Murphy examined how international law has addressed these developments. He first stressed that international terrorism had been treated primarily as a domestic criminal law matter prior to September 11, 2001. Now, however, it seems clear that the scope and scale of al Qaeda's attacks on the World Trade Center and Pentagon—and the US and coalition response to it in Afghanistan—have given the law of armed conflict a much greater role in combating international terrorism. But Murphy reminded the audience that international criminal law—in the form of 12 UN-related antiterrorism conventions—will also have an important role in the future.

In his view, these anti-terrorism conventions have taken a piecemeal approach to terrorism because it has been impossible to develop a comprehensive convention against terrorism, primarily because agreeing upon a definition of terrorism has not been possible. In any event, while a comprehensive treaty might have been preferable, these individual conventions have provided much coverage, especially those negotiated in the 1990s like the *International Convention for the Suppression of the Financing of Terrorism*; in Prof. Murphy's view, all that is missing is a convention directed toward the use of weapons of mass destruction by terrorists. In short, while recognizing that responding with military force in self-defense may be increasingly necessary in the war against terrorism, Prof. Murphy's paper highlighted that international criminal law conventions will remain important and valuable tools in the struggle as well.

Jim Terry, a retired Marine Corps lawyer now serving as a Deputy Assistant Secretary at the U.S. State Department, next offered a series of observations on the Road Ahead in Afghanistan. Recognizing that the United States must use all available instruments of power, Terry provided a fascinating road map of those actions that should take place in Afghanistan over the course of the next few years. Terry noted particularly that within the next two years, the United States must help Afghanistan: move toward increased stability and prosperity; develop an emerging economy, facilitate the establishment of a national military and police force, and be prepared for the process to be long and hard.

Jim Terry then presented a legal analysis of the "legal rights" of, and "appropriate treatment" of al Qaeda and Taliban detainees held by the United States in Guantanamo Bay, Cuba. In Terry's view, two questions are central to this analysis: After the United States and its allies commenced military operations against Afghanistan in mid-October 2001, did the 1949 Geneva Conventions apply to the conflict? If so, were members of al Qaeda as a group, and the Taliban individually or as a group, entitled to POW status if captured?

Terry explained that the US government view was that the al Qaeda organization was not part of "the armed forces of a Party," or the "militias and volunteer corps forming part of such armed forces." It followed that al Qaeda was a non-state actor and its members did not qualify for POW status. As for the Taliban, Mr. Terry agreed that, as the Taliban were the *de facto* government of Afghanistan, it followed that there was an international armed conflict between the U.S. and its allies and Afghanistan. However, the Taliban's failure to require its fighters to wear uniforms or other distinctive insignia, or be subject to a command structure that enforced the law of war, meant that captured Taliban combatants also were not entitled to POW treatment. But, explained Mr. Terry, "Part II of Geneva Convention III [Relative to the Treatment of POWs]" requires humane treatment, including food, medical

Preface

attention, the opportunity to worship, and other benefits. In short, while not legally entitled to POW status, the detainees were entitled to much the same treatment afforded POWs. Jim Terry closed with a brief discussion about military commissions, and how Taliban and al Qaeda personnel who committed violations of the law of war would be subject to trial and punishment by such commissions.

Nick Rostow, General Counsel to the US Mission to the United Nations, presented "a few words about the UN and terrorism before September 11, 2001, the impact of September 11th and where the UN seems to be headed from here." Rostow repeated a remark made recently by the Secretary General: "Terrorism against innocent civilians is clearly a bad thing and yet most of you wouldn't be here except for acts of what are now called terrorism or what the colonial powers regarded as terrorism." In Rostow's view, this comment "aptly captures the tension at the UN" when it comes to terrorism. With that said, Nick Rostow believed that the events of September 11th "changed the focus of both the Security Council and the General Assembly," and there was every reason to think that the UN would "finally . . . make progress toward addressing terrorism on the world stage."

Comments from Messrs. Michael Saalfeld and Ronald Winfrey, and Capt. Jane Dalton followed, with discussion from conference participants. When the symposium closed shortly thereafter, all who attended better understood the complexity and difficulty involved in the challenges facing lawyers and operators in the war on terrorism.

* * * * * * * * * *

In editing the papers presented and transcribing the hundreds of pages of oral commentary, we have striven to be accurate and yet retain the tenor of the conference. We could not have brought this 79th volume of the International Law Studies to print without the unsung, but outstanding efforts of Ms. Susan Meyer and Mr. Matthew Cotnoir in Desktop Publishing. Nor would this volume be complete without the incredible efforts of Ms. Pat Goodrich, Ms. Wilma Haines, Ms. Kathleen Koegler, Ms. Erin Poe, Ms. Margaret Richard, and Mr. Jeremiah Lenihan in proofreading and correcting the multiple errors we surely made. Finally, a special note of thanks to Captain Jack Grunawalt, JAGC, USN (Ret.) for his willingness to again support the International Law Studies series in an effort to insure it remains the standard that it is. It is only due to these individuals' efforts that the International Law

Department is able to bring you this volume. However, there are sure to be errors, and these are our responsibility alone.

Last but not least, we dedicate this book to Janet and Pauline, without whose support and love we would be lost.

Fred L. Borch
Colonel, U.S. Army
Judge Advocate General's Corps

Paul S. Wilson
Major, U.S. Army
Judge Advocate General's Corps

I

Welcoming Address

Rear Admiral Rodney Rempt

Welcome to the US Naval War College in Newport, Rhode Island as we undertake what should prove to be very fruitful discussions and debate about the defense of our nation and the critical operational and legal issues that confront the United States today. In particular, welcome to our College's conference on International Legal Issues in the Global War on Terrorism. It is exceedingly helpful to have scholars of international renown and practitioners charged with dealing with these particularly thorny issues come together to identify and discuss the bases for the conduct by the US and its coalition partners of military operations against terrorists and those who support them. As it is in many such cases, over the next few days participants in this conference will plow new ground and review history at the same time. Such goals are an important purpose of the US Naval War College and it is important that you strive to do this while you are here.

Our academic environment permits us to exchange thoughts, analyze ideas and be forward leaning. From conferences such as these, policy is developed and written, and significant consequences can emerge. As we exchange ideas amongst ourselves, I encourage you to press the envelope and challenge each other with creative new thinking because frankly our world is currently engaged in a rapid paradigm shift. Current norms must be flexible and adaptive or they must be discarded as new norms press to the front as we peer into the

Welcoming Address

future in an effort to vigilantly protect our citizens, our property, indeed our very way of life from cowards who call themselves terrorists.

Your presence here for these several days is extremely important. Bringing together international scholars and practitioners to examine and study the basis for how the United States and other nations partner together in this common cause of conducting military operations against terrorists and those state agencies and organizations that support them is of vital importance to the United States and to the international community at large.

As an example, a current discussion of great interest deals with Iraq. In some sense, Iraq presents a simple situation. Iraq has a very unstable ruler who is closing in on his goal of greater access to weapons of mass destruction. While not currently a policy maker, I recognize that if the need arises to deal with Saddam Hussein militarily, we must be clear as to the international basis for the use of force against him. What would be the legal basis for a regime change? How do we proceed on the best possible terms to address the circumstances that we face? The question is not whether it is desirable to oust Saddam Hussein from Iraq. Instead, since we are a nation founded upon the rule of law, the question is how do we pursue what is determined to be in the national interest while remaining squarely within the parameters of customary international law and the treaties and conventions of which we are currently signatories?

You must look at how the law of armed conflict applies to our combat operations in Afghanistan, the Philippines and elsewhere around the world as it seems clear that we will be conducting combat operations for the foreseeable future in many of these areas. So the question is how to proceed in an area and in a situation that is starkly new in our nation's history. In addressing this question you must analyze and debate many other difficult questions.

Specifically, we need answers to the following tough questions: Do members of terrorist organizations ever qualify as prisoners of war under the Geneva Conventions? Do members of the Taliban qualify for such protection? Should the Geneva Conventions be amended, updated, changed? In this single series of questions, I have, in some sense, questioned the continuing validity of the Geneva Conventions. The root question is how do the legal conventions we have in place apply to the circumstances confronting the United States and the international community? The current international legal regime applicable to the law of armed conflict remains heavily influenced by World War I and World War II. If our society is truly entering a new era, should this continue to be the case? Or must international law change to reflect the new reality of non-state actors and other amorphous groups?

2

Other difficult questions to be considered include: what is the legal status of members of the US Central Intelligence Agency and Federal Bureau of Investigation who engaged directly in combat activities in the armed conflict in Afghanistan? Are these personnel combatants, privileged combatants, unlawful combatants, civilians, or are they entitled to some other status? Did these personnel uphold or violate the law of armed conflict? Similarly, what are the standards for the treatment of captured terrorists? How long may they be detained? What if these terrorists are US citizens? What due process are they entitled to receive?

From these questions must be asked: what are the lessons learned from the Global War on Terrorism? What action should the legal community take regarding future military operations against terrorists and those states supporting terrorist activity? These are not the only difficult questions as there are many others. These are, however, a small sampling of the types of issues I expect you will consider during the next few days. These are questions of great significance, not only to lawyers but more importantly to commanders and policy makers.

Two weeks ago, the Naval War College hosted our Current Strategy Forum. It brought together the best of military and civilian leadership, academia, and the defense industry to address the strategic challenges confronting our nation. The present conference is a like effort to bring together the best minds in international law to further define and seek answers to the critical questions that must be identified and resolved for our military and our nation's future. Your work here is important to how our nation proceeds in its war against terror in the future.

Again, welcome to this conference. I wish you an enjoyable and productive stay here at the Naval War College. Your challenge awaits you.

Panel I

Wednesday—June 26, 2002

9:00 AM–12:00 PM

Jus ad Bellum

Moderator:
    Lieutenant Andru Wall,
    Judge Advocate, US Navy
    International Law Department
    US Naval War College

Presenters:
    Professor Michael Schmitt
    George C. Marshall European Center

    Professor Rein Müllerson
    Kings College, University of London

Commentators:
    Professor Robert Turner
    Center for National Security Law
    University of Virginia School of Law

    Mr. William Dalton
    Office of the General Counsel
    US Department of Defense

II

Counter-Terrorism and the Use of Force in International Law

Michael Schmitt[1]

The terrorist attacks of September 11th undoubtedly ushered in a new era in international security affairs. Although terrorism has been a tragically prominent feature of the global condition for most of the past half century, these operations were quantitatively and qualitatively different than those of the past. They involved extensive and sophisticated long-term planning by a group that cuts across lines of nationality and which operates from within many countries.[2] The scale of the destruction in both human and physical terms was shocking; the fact that the attacks and their aftermath were broadcast live only served to further exacerbate their psychological impact.

---

1. Professor of International Law, George C. Marshall European Center for Security Studies, Garmisch-Partenkirchen, Germany. The views expressed herein are those of the author in his personal capacity and do not necessarily represent those of any United States or German government agency.
2. For an excellent discussion of how the attacks were a turning point in the evolution of international terrorism, see Paul J. Smith, *Transnational Terrorism and the al Qaeda Model: Confronting New Realities*, PARAMETERS, Summer 2002, at 33. See also, Michael Howard, *What's in a Name? How to Fight Terrorism*, FOR. AFF'S, January/February 2002, at 8, which argues that declaring a "war" on terrorism was a "terrible and irrevocable error." *Id.* at 8.

That all 19 terrorists directly involved executed them with great precision despite the certainty of their own deaths may well portend a terrifying face of 21st century terrorism—a genre of terrorism likely to prove extraordinarily difficult to counter by traditional means.

Combating this aggravated form of terrorism will require new cooperative security strategies. Certainly, the Global War on Terrorism articulated by the United States represents one such strategy.[3] As time passes and opportunities and threats become clearer, the worldwide war on terrorism will evolve responsively. Other governments and intergovernmental organizations are already developing parallel and complimentary strategies.

Lest the lawlessness inherent in terrorism spread to its victims, counter-terrorism strategy must be formulated with great sensitivity to the international law governing the use of force. Some have suggested that this body of law, including that facet regarding the right to self-defense, is not up to the task[4]

---

3. The extent to which the GWOT represents a fundamental shift in US strategies for dealing with threats is apparent in President Bush's discussion of preemptive strategies. *See* Remarks by the President at 2002 Graduation Exercise of the United States Military Academy, June 1, 2002, *available at* http://www.whitehouse.gov/news/releases/2002/06/20020601-3.html (Jun. 18, 2002). Released on September 17, 2002, the US National Security Strategy incorporates such strategies. *See* U.S. National Security Strategy, at 4, *available at* http://www.whitehouse.gov/nsc/nss.html (Nov. 4, 2002).

4. *See* Michael J. Glennon, *The Fog of Law: Self-Defense, Inherence, and Incoherence in Article 51 of the United Nations Charter*, 25 HARV. J. L. & PUB. POL. 539 (2002). Professor Glennon argues that:

> The international system has come to subsist in a parallel universe of two systems, one *de jure*, and the other *de facto*. The *de jure* system consists of illusory rules that would govern the use of force among states in a platonic world of forms, a world that does not exist. The *de facto* system consists of actual state practice in a real world, a world in which states weigh costs against benefits in regular disregard of the rules solemnly proclaimed in the all-but-ignored *de jure* system. The decaying *de jure* catechism is overly schematized and scholastic, disconnected from state behavior, and unrealistic in its aspirations for state conduct.

Id. at 540.

Others counter that effective responses to terrorism and state "supporters" thereof are proving entirely consistent with existing prescriptive norms.[5] This article explores those norms, specifically the relevant jus ad bellum,[6] in the context of the response to the 9/11 attacks. Under what circumstances can a victim state react forcibly to an act of terrorism? Against whom? When? And with what degree of severity? It concludes that a natural evolution in the community understanding of limitations on the use of force has occurred over the past decades, such that claims of international law's present insufficiency are overblown. However, assertions that the law as traditionally understood supports a full range of forceful responses to terrorism equally overstate reality. As is usually the case, the truth lies between the extremes.

The Relevant Facts

In order to effectively appraise the international law governing the use of force in counter-terrorism today, and to acquire a sense for its normative vector, it is necessary to first paint the factual backdrop. Law tends to be reactive and responsive to the factual context in which it operates. Obviously, this is the case for customary international law, which relies, inter alia, on state practice for its emergence. The same is true, however, for convention-based law. Despite declarations that international agreements, such as the UN Charter, should be interpreted in accordance with the ordinary meaning of their text, it is undeniable that community understanding of law shifts over time to remain

---

5. *See, e.g.*, Jack M. Beard, *America's New War on Terror: The Case for Self-Defense Under International Law*, 25 HARV. J. L. & PUB. POL. 559 (2002).

> [T]he case for America's forcible response to the September 11 attacks as being fully consistent with the inherent right of self-defense under customary international law and Article 51 of the U.N. Charter is very strong. The unanimous condemnation of the attacks by the U.N. General Assembly, the affirmation of the right of self-defense by the Security Council, the growing consensus in the international community to hold states accountable for terrorist actions, and the repeated condemnation by the Security Council of the Taliban Regime's support of terrorists in particular, clearly help establish an appropriate framework under international law for the exercise of self-defense by the United States.

Id. at 589–90.

6. That component of international law that governs when it is that a state may resort to force in pursuit of its national interests, such as defending itself from armed attack.

coherent and relevant to both current circumstances and the global community's normative expectations.[7]

Sadly, the facts of 9/11 are all too familiar. On 11 September 2001, terrorists seized control of four passenger aircraft in the United States. Two were flown into the Twin Towers of the World Trade Center in New York City, a third was driven into the Pentagon in Washington D.C. and the fourth crashed in Pennsylvania following an unsuccessful attempt by passengers to regain control from the highjackers. Roughly 3000 people of over 80 nationalities perished.

Investigation quickly led authorities to focus their attention on Osama bin Laden and his al Qaeda terrorist organization.[8] Al Qaeda operates from more than 60 countries through a compartmentalized network using operatives of numerous nationalities. By October, the British government felt sufficiently confident in intelligence reports at its disposal to release certain facts and conclusions regarding the group. These were subsequently confirmed by the United States. Specifically, 10 Downing Street announced that al Qaeda had planned and conducted the attacks, that it continued to have the resources to mount further operations, that US and UK citizens were potential targets and that "Usama Bin Laden and Al-Qa'ida were able to commit these atrocities

---

7. Pursuant to Article 31 of the Vienna Convention on the Law of Treaties:

> 1. A treaty shall be interpreted in good faith in accordance with the ordinary meaning to be given to the terms of the treaty in their context and in light of its object and purpose . . . ;
>
> 2. There shall be taken into account together with the context: . . .
>
> b. any subsequent practice in the application of the treaty which establishes the agreement of the parties regarding its interpretation. . . .

Vienna Convention on the Law of Treaties, May 23, 1969, art. 31, 1155 U.N.T.S. 331, 8 I.L.M. 679 (1969). This point was reiterated by the International Court of Justice in *Competence of the General Assembly for the Admission of a State to the United Nations*. There, the Court noted "the first duty of a tribunal which is called upon to interpret and apply the provisions of a treaty is to endeavour to give effect to them in their natural and ordinary meaning in the context in which they occur." 1950 I.C.J. 4, 8.

8. For background on bin Laden, see PETER L. BERGEN, HOLY WAR, INC.: INSIDE THE SECRET WORLD OF OSAMA BIN LADEN (2001); Michael Dobbs, *Bin Laden: Architect of New Global Terrorism*, WASH. POST, Sep. 16, 2001, at A8.

because of their close alliance with the Taleban regime, which allowed them to operate with impunity in pursuing their terrorist activity."[9]

Of particular relevance to the use of force issue is the fact that al Qaeda was hardly venturing into terrorism for the first time on September 11th. The organization had allegedly been involved in the 1993 World Trade Center bombing, the 1998 bombings of the US embassies in Kenya and Tanzania (attacks for which Osama bin Laden has been indicted[10]), and the attack on the USS *Cole* in 2000; the group had also claimed responsibility for the 1993 attack on US special forces in Somalia, as well as three separate 1992 bombings intended to kill US military personnel in Yemen. Moreover, the US Department of State alleges the existence of al Qaeda ties to plots (not executed) to kill the Pope, attack tourists visiting Jordan during the millennium celebration, bomb US and Israeli embassies in various Asian capitals, blow up a dozen passenger aircraft while in flight and assassinate President Clinton.[11]

That al Qaeda represents a continuing threat is apparent not only from its track record, but also from statements periodically issued by Osama bin Laden himself. The British government's October Press Release cited a number of his most virulent:

> The people of Islam have suffered from aggression, iniquity and injustice imposed by the Zionist-Crusader alliance and their collaborators . . . . It is the duty now on every tribe in the Arabian peninsula to fight jihad and cleanse the land from these Crusader occupiers. Their wealth is booty to those who kill them. (1996)

> [T]errorising the American occupiers [of Islamic Holy Places] is a religious and logical obligation. (1996)

> We—with God's help—call on every Muslim who believes in God and wishes to be rewarded to comply with God's order to kill Americans and plunder their money whenever and wherever they find it. We also call on Muslims . . . to

---

9. United Kingdom Press Release, 10 Downing Street Newsroom, *Responsibility for the Terrorist Atrocities in the United States*, Oct. 4, 2001, at paras. 21–22, *available at* http://www.number-10.gov.uk/news.asp?NewsId=2686 (Jun. 18, 2002). As to US confirmation of the facts, see David E. Sanger, *White House Approved Data Blair Released*, N.Y. TIMES, Oct. 6, 2001, at B6.
10. Indictment, United States v. Usama bin Laden *et al.*, S(2) 98 Cr. 1023 (LBS) (S.D.N.Y. Nov. 4, 1998).
11. Department of State, Patterns of Global Terrorism, app. B: Background Information on Terrorist Groups, al-Qa'ida, April 30, 2001, *available at* http://www.state.gov/s/ct/rls/pgtrpt/2000/2450.htm (Jun. 18, 2002).

launch the raid on Satan's US troops and the devil's supporters allying with them, and to displace those who are behind them. (1998)

[A]cquiring [chemical or nuclear] . . . weapons for the defence of Muslims [is] a religious duty. (1998)

Thus, in al Qaeda we have a determined terrorist organization that has committed multiple acts of terrorism over the course of a decade—acts which resulted in the deaths of thousands and caused property and financial damage measured in the billions of dollars—and views its continuing campaign in terms of *jihad*.

The US reaction was swift. Within a week, President Bush formally proclaimed a national emergency[12] and called up members of the reserve component of the armed forces.[13] He also established the Office of Homeland Security and the Homeland Security Council in order to facilitate a coordinated response to the terrorist threat.[14] For its part, Congress passed a joint resolution that authorized the President to "use all necessary and appropriate force against those nations, organizations, or persons he determines planned, authorized, committed, or aided the terrorist attacks that occurred on September 11, 2001, or harbored such organizations or persons, in order to prevent any future acts of international terrorism against the United States by such nations, organizations or persons."[15] Essentially, the United States was placed on a war footing. Indeed, the President characterized the attacks as "an act of war against our country."[16] Thus, the US government quickly moved beyond a criminal law enforcement paradigm in determining how to respond to the attacks.

Almost immediately, the spotlight focused on Taliban connections to al Qaeda, which was "headquartered" in Afghanistan. Although the United

---

12. Proclamation No. 7463, 66 Fed. Reg. 48,199 (Sep. 18, 2001).
13. Exec. Order No. 13,223, 66 Fed. Reg. 48,201 (Sep. 18, 2001). A number of other steps were taken. For instance, President Bush gave the Treasury Department greater power to undermine financial support for terrorism through freezing assets and imposing financial sanctions on those who refused to cooperate in the effort. Exec. Order No. 13,224, 66 Fed. Reg. 49,079 (Sept. 23, 2001).
14. Exec. Order No. 13,228, 66 Fed. Reg. 51,812 (Oct. 10, 2001).
15. Authorization for Use of Military Force, Pub. L. No. 107-40, 115 Stat. 224 (2001).
16. President George W. Bush, Address Before a Joint Session of the Congress on the United States Response to the Terrorist Attacks of September 11, 37 WEEKLY COMP. PRES. DOC. 1347 (Sep. 20, 2001).

States did not formally recognize the Taliban as the legitimate government of the country, the Taliban controlled the greatest amount of territory, including that where al Qaeda was based.[17] Working through the Pakistani government, which maintained diplomatic relations with the Taliban, the United States issued a series of demands. These were set forth publicly in late September during a Presidential address to a joint session of Congress. Specifically, the United States insisted that the Taliban:

> Deliver to United States authorities all the leaders of Al-Qa'ida who hide in your land. Release all foreign nationals, including American citizens, you have unjustly imprisoned. Protect foreign journalists, diplomats, and aid workers in your country. Close immediately and permanently every terrorist training camp in Afghanistan, and hand over every terrorist and every person in their support structure to appropriate authorities. Give the United States full access to terrorist training camps, so we can make sure they are no longer operating.[18]

President Bush made it quite clear that there would be no negotiation and that he expected immediate compliance. Moreover, he unambiguously laid out the consequences of non-compliance: "They will hand over the terrorists, or they will share in their fate."[19]

Despite the "no-negotiations" stance, the Taliban expressed a desire to resolve the matter. These entreaties were rebuffed and on October 6 the President issued a final public warning to cooperate.[20] The following day the United States and United Kingdom launched the first phase of Operation ENDURING FREEDOM, consisting of airstrikes against both al Qaeda and Taliban targets. The scope and nature of the campaign quickly expanded to encompass ground and maritime operations.

---

17. For background on the Taliban, see AHMED RASHID, TALIBAN: MILITANT ISLAM, OIL AND FUNDAMENTALISM IN CENTRAL ASIA (2001); PETER MARSDEN, THE TALIBAN: WAR, RELIGION AND THE NEW ORDER IN AFGHANISTAN (1998).
18. Address Before a Joint Session of the Congress, *supra* note 16.
19. *Id.*
20. President George W. Bush, Radio Address, 37 WEEKLY COMP. PRES. DOC. 1429, 1430 (Oct. 6, 2001).

As required by Article 51 of the United Nations Charter, the United States promptly notified the Security Council that it was acting in individual and collective self-defense.[21] In the report, the United States asserted that it had "clear and compelling information that the Al-Qaeda organization, which is supported by the Taliban regime in Afghanistan, had a central role in the attacks" and that there was an "ongoing threat" made possible "by the decision of the Taliban regime to allow the parts of Afghanistan that it controls to be used by [al Qaeda] as a base of operations." The purpose of the military operations was to "prevent and deter further attacks on the United States." Ominously, the United States warned, "We may find our self-defense requires further actions with respect to other organizations and other States."[22] In an address to the nation, the President echoed the threat contained in the Article 51 notification: "Every nation has a choice to make. In this conflict, there is no neutral ground. If any government sponsors the outlaws and killers of innocents, they have become outlaws and murderers, themselves. And they will take that lonely path at their own peril."[23]

Because it had participated in the strikes, the United Kingdom also transmitted the requisite report to the Security Council. It announced that the attacks were conducted in self-defense against "Usama Bin Laden's Al-Qaeda terrorist organization and the Taliban regime that is supporting it." The avowed purpose was "to avert the continuing threat of attacks from the same source."[24] Thus, although limiting the scope of its operations to al Qaeda and

---

21. U.N. CHARTER, art. 51. Article 51 provides that:

Nothing in the present Charter shall impair the inherent right of individual or collective self-defence if an armed attack occurs against a Member of the United Nations, until the Security Council has taken measures necessary to maintain international peace and security. Measures taken by Members in the exercise of this right of self-defence shall be immediately reported to the Security Council and shall not in any way affect the authority and responsibility of the Security Council under the present Charter to take at any time such action as it deems necessary in order to maintain or restore international peace and security.

22. Letter from the Permanent Representative of the United States of America to the United Nations Addressed to the President of the Security Council (Oct. 7, 2001), U.N. Doc. S/2001/946, *available at* http://www.un.int./usa/s-2001-946.htm (Jun. 18, 2002) [hereinafter US Letter].
23. President George W. Bush, Address to the Nation Announcing Strikes Against Al Qaeda Training Camps and Taliban Military Installations, 37 WEEKLY COMP. PRES. DOC. 1432, (Oct. 7, 2001).
24. Letter from the Charge d'Affaires of the Permanent Mission of the United Kingdom of Great Britain and Northern Ireland to the United Nations addressed to the President of the Security Council (Oct. 7, 2001) *available at* http://www.ukun.org/xq/asp/SarticleType.17/Article_ID.328/qx/articles_show.htm (Jun. 18, 2002).

the Taliban, like the United States it suggested that action was necessary to prevent further attacks.

The international reaction to the affair was almost universally one of outrage over the terrorist acts and support for the United States. On September 12th, the Security Council passed Resolution 1368 condemning the attacks as "horrifying," labeling them a threat to international peace and security, and reaffirming the "inherent right of self-defence as recognized by the Charter of the United Nations."[25] Resolution 1373, passed on September 28th, likewise cited the right to self-defense and laid out steps to combat terrorism, such as suppressing the financing of terrorism, denying safe haven to terrorists and their accomplices, and cooperating in law enforcement efforts.[26] Interestingly, the General Assembly did not refer to self-defense in its own resolution on the attacks.[27]

Following commencement of the military campaign, the Security Council passed a number of relevant resolutions. For instance, on November 14th it issued Resolution 1378, which expressed support for "international efforts to root out terrorism, in keeping with the Charter of the United Nations"; reaffirmed Resolutions 1368 and 1373 (which had cited the right to self-defense); condemned the Taliban for "allowing Afghanistan to be used as a base for the export of terrorism by the Al Qa'ida network and other terrorist groups and for providing safe haven to Osama Bin Laden, Al-Qa'ida and others associated with them"; and expressed support for the "efforts of the Afghan people to replace the Taliban."[28] On December 20th it passed Resolution 1386, which (as with Resolution 1373) expressed support for rooting out terrorism in accordance with the Charter, reaffirmed Resolutions 1368 and 1373, and

---

25. S. C. Res. 1368, pmbl., U.N. SCOR, 56th Sess, U.N. Doc. S/1378/(2001). It is interesting that the Security Council did not reference self-defense in response to the 1998 attacks on the East African embassies even though the United States formally invoked Article 51. According to Article 39 of the UN Charter, the Security Council has cognizance over "any threat to the peace, breach of the peace, or act of aggression" and decides upon measures necessary to "maintain or restore international peace and security." U.N. CHARTER, art. 39. Therefore, labeling the acts as a threat to international peace and security is normatively significant in that it empowers the Council to act.
26. S. C. Res. 1373, pmbl. U.N. SCOR, 56th Sess., U.N. Doc. S/1373/(2001).
27. G.A. Res. 56/1, U.N. GAOR, 56th Sess., Agenda Item 8 (Sep. 18, 2001).
28. S. C. Res. 1378, U.N. SCOR, 56th Sess., U.N. Doc. S/1378/(2001).

authorized the establishment of the International Security Assistance Force [ISAF].[29] Reaffirmation of the international counter-terrorist effort, of previous resolutions, of its prior condemnation of the Taliban and al Qaeda and of the fact that terrorism constitutes a threat to international peace and security occurred yet again on January 20th, 2002 with Resolution 1390.[30] In it, the Security Council employed its Chapter VII authority to impose sanctions on the Taliban and al Qaeda, including a freezing of assets, a prohibition of travel and an arms embargo.

In none of the resolutions did the Security Council explicitly authorize the United States, any coalition of forces, or a regional organization to use force pursuant to Article 42 of the Charter, as the Council is entitled to do in the face of a "threat to the peace, breach of peace or act of aggression."[31] However, it is important to note that the Security Council twice referred to the inherent right to individual and collective self-defense prior to coalition combat operations against the Taliban and al Qaeda, that no effort was made to condemn the forceful response once launched, and that the Council repeatedly reaffirmed the right to self-defense and expressed support for the international effort to "root out terrorism" as those operations were ongoing.

Beyond the United Nations, the most powerful military alliance in the world articulated its position in even more unequivocal terms. The day after the terrorist attacks, NATO's North Atlantic Council, consisting of Permanent Representatives of all 19 NATO member states, announced that if the attacks originated from outside the United States, they would be "regarded as

---

29. S. C. Res. 1386 U.N. SCOR, 56th Sess., U.N. Doc. S/1386/(2001). Pursuant to the Agreement on Provisional Arrangements in Afghanistan pending the Re-establishment of Permanent Government Institutions (Bonn Agreement of Dec. 5, 2001), ISAF is to assist in maintenance of security in the vicinity of Kabul. ISAF executed a military technical agreement (MTA) with the Interim Administration in Afghanistan on 4 January 2002. For the text of the Bonn Agreement, see http://www.uno.de/frieden/afghanistan/talks/agreement.htm (Jun. 18, 2002). The MTA text is at http://www.operations.mod.uk/isafmta.pdf (Jun. 18, 2002).
30. S. C. Res. 1390, U.N. SCOR, 57th Sess., U.N. Doc. S/1390/(2002). The operation itself is described by the British Ministry of Defence at http://www.operations.mod.uk/fingal/ (Jun. 18, 2002).
31. U.N. CHARTER, art. 42. The text reads:
> Should the Security Council consider that measures provided for in Article 41 would be inadequate or have proved to be inadequate, it may take such action by air, sea, or land forces as may be necessary to maintain or restore international peace and security. Such action may include demonstrations, blockade, and other operations by air, sea, or land forces of Members of the United Nations.

an action covered by Article 5 of the Washington Treaty."[32] Article 5, based on Article 51 of the UN Charter, provides for collective self-defense if any of the member states suffers an "armed attack."[33] Within three weeks, and following briefings in which US officials provided "clear and compelling" evidence that the attacks were not the work of domestic terrorists, the North Atlantic Council made precisely that finding and invoked Article 5.[34] There was no mention of whom the defense, which began five days later, could be directed against. This was a normatively significant omission given that one of the entities the United States and United Kingdom struck on October 7th was a non-state actor, whereas the other was a government supportive of that group, but which did not control it.

Similarly, the Organization of American States invoked the collective self-defense provisions of the Rio Treaty[35] following its finding that "these terrorist attacks against the United States are attacks against all American States."[36] Australia did likewise, citing Article IV of the ANZUS Treaty in offering to

---

32. North Atlantic Treaty Organization (NATO), Press Release No. 124, statement by the North Atlantic Council (Sep. 12, 2001) *available at* http://www.nato.int/docu/pr/2001/p01-124e.htm, (Jun. 18, 2002).
33. The Parties agree that an armed attack against one or more of them in Europe or North America shall be considered an attack against them all and consequently they agree that, if such an armed attack occurs, each of them, in exercise of the right of individual or collective self-defence recognised by Article 51 of the Charter of the United Nations, will assist the Party or Parties so attacked by taking forthwith, individually and in concert with the other Parties, such action as it deems necessary, including the use of armed force, to restore and maintain the security of the North Atlantic area.

North Atlantic Treaty, Aug. 24, 1959, art. 5, T.I.A.S. 1964, 34 U.N.T.S. 243.
34. Secretary General Lord Robertson, statement at NATO Headquarters (Oct. 2, 2001) *available at* http://www.nato.int/docu/speech/2001/s011002a.htm, (Jun. 18, 2002).
35. The High Contracting Parties agree that an armed attack by any State against an American State shall be considered as an attack against all the American States and, consequently, each one of the said Contracting Parties undertakes to assist in meeting the attack in the exercise of the inherent right of individual or collective self-defense recognized by Article 51 of the Charter of the United Nations.

Inter-American Treaty of Reciprocal Assistance, Sep. 2, 1947, art. 3.1, 62 Stat. 1681, 21 U.N.T.S. 77.
36. Terrorist Threat to the Americas, Resolution 1, Twenty-Fourth Meeting of Consultation of Ministers of Foreign Affairs Acting as Organ of Consultation In Application of the Inter-American Treaty of Reciprocal Assistance, OEA/Ser.F/II.24, RC.24/RES.1/01 (Sep. 21, 2001).

deploy military forces.[37] Russia, China and India agreed to share intelligence with the United States, while Japan and South Korea offered logistics support. The United Arab Emirates and Saudi Arabia broke off diplomatic relations with the Taliban, and Pakistan agreed to cooperate fully with the United States. Twenty-seven nations granted overflight and landing rights and 46 multilateral declarations of support were obtained.[38]

Once the campaign against al Qaeda and the Taliban began, offers or expressions of support flowed in from many sources. The United Kingdom, as noted, participated directly in the initial strikes, whereas many other states, such as Georgia, Oman, Pakistan, the Philippines, Qatar, Saudi Arabia, Tajikistan, Turkey and Uzbekistan, provided airspace and facilities. China, Egypt, Russia and the European Union publicly backed the US/UK operations. The Organization for the Islamic Conference simply urged the United States to limit the campaign to Afghanistan,[39] while the Asia-Pacific Economic Cooperation Forum condemned terrorism of all kinds. Neither organization criticized the operations. Australia, Canada, the Czech Republic, Germany, Italy, Japan, the Netherlands, New Zealand, Turkey, and the United Kingdom offered ground troops.[40] By May 2002, the forces of several nations, in particular sizable British, Australian, Canadian and American contingents, were engaged in dangerous "mop-up" actions.[41]

---

37. Prime Minister John Howard, Government Invokes ANZUS Treaty—Press Conference (Sep. 14, 2001), *available at* http://australianpolitics.com.au/foreign/anzus/01-09-14anzus-invoked.shtml, (Jun. 18, 2002). *See also* White House, Fact Sheet: Operation ENDURING FREEDOM Overview (Oct. 1, 2001) *available at* http://www.state.gov/s/ct/rls/fs/2001/5194.htm (Jun. 18, 2002). Article VI of the ANZUS Treaty provides: "Each Party recognizes that an armed attack in the Pacific Area on any of the Parties would be dangerous to its own peace and safety and declares that it would act to meet the common danger in accordance with its constitutional processes." Security Treaty (Australia, New Zealand, United States), Sep. 1, 1951, art. IV, 3 U.S.T. 3420, 3422, 131 U.N.T.S. 83, 84.
38. Fact Sheet, *supra* note 37.
39. *See* Sean D. Murphy, *Terrorism and the Concept of "Armed Attack" in Article 51 of the U.N. Charter*, 43 HARV. INT'L L. J. 41, 49 (2002); Sean D. Murphy, *Contemporary Practice of the United States Relating to International Law*, 96 AM. J. INT'L. LAW 237, 248 (2002).
40. Murphy, *Contemporary Practice 2002*, *supra* note 39, at 248. The European Council "confirm[ed] its staunchest support for the military operations ... which are legitimate under the terms of the United Nations Charter and of Resolution 1368." Declaration by the Heads of State of Government of the European Union and the President of the Commission: Follow-up to the September 11 Attacks and the Fight Against Terrorism, Oct. 19, 2002, SN 4296/2/01 Rev. 2.
41. Perhaps best illustrative of the coalition nature of the campaign were operations that month from Manas airport, near Bishket, Kyrgyz Republic. Although typically a sleepy airfield, it was hosting US and French fighter-bombers; Australian and French tankers; transport aircraft from Spain, the Netherlands, Denmark and Norway; and a South Korean medical team. *Americans in a Strange Land*, THE ECONOMIST, May 4, 2002, at 41.

Since the counter-terrorism operations began, controversy has surfaced regarding a number of legal issues. Most notable among these has been the detention, treatment and proposed prosecution of the detainees held at US Naval Base Guantanamo Bay. Also a point of contention, albeit more muted, is the extent of collateral damage and incidental injury from the strikes conducted against al Qaeda and Taliban targets. And looming on the horizon is a very divisive issue, i.e., carrying the fight beyond the borders of Afghanistan. Yet, except in legal circles, and particularly the sub-circle of academia, there has been minimum controversy about the lawfulness of the operations conducted within Afghanistan under the jus ad bellum. On the contrary, and as illustrated in the events described above, support for the US and coalition military response has been strong. The extent to which this support is grounded in either the *lex lata* or *lex ferenda* is the subject of the remainder of this article.

The Normative Framework for the Use of Force

The UN Charter expresses the basic prohibition on the use of force in international law. It provides, in Article 2(4), that "[a]ll Members shall refrain in their international relations from the threat or use of force against the territorial integrity or political independence of any state, or in any other manner inconsistent with the Purposes of the United Nations."[42] Within the four corners of the Charter, there are but two exceptions to this prohibition. The first, set forth in Article 39, empowers the Security Council to determine the existence of a threat to the peace, breach of peace or act of aggression and decide what measures are necessary to maintain or restore international peace and security. By Article 42, the Council may turn to military force to resolve these situations in what are generally labeled "enforcement operations."[43] States would provide troops under a UN flag, as a coalition of the willing or individually. Regional

---

42. U.N. CHARTER, art. 2(4). On this article, see Albrecht Randelzhofer, *Article 2, in* THE CHARTER OF THE UNITED NATIONS: A COMMENTARY 72 (Bruno Simma ed., 1995).
43. U.N. CHARTER, art. 42.

organizations are also authorized to engage in "enforcement" activities, but only with the approval of the Security Council.[44]

The second exception is found in Article 51. It provides

> Nothing in the present Charter shall impair the inherent right of individual or collective self-defense *if an armed attack occurs* against a Member of the United Nations, until the Security Council has taken measures necessary to maintain international peace and security. Measures taken by Members in the exercise of this right of self-defense shall be immediately reported to the Security Council and shall not in any way affect the authority and responsibility of the Security Council under the present Charter to take at any time such action as it deems necessary in order to maintain or restore international peace and security.

Thus, states victimized by an armed attack may not only defend themselves, but also receive assistance from others in mounting that defense. They need not await a Council authorization to act, but are required to report actions taken to the Security Council, which may itself determine that it needs to respond in some fashion.

Some commentators assert that additional exceptions to the prohibition on the use of force lie outside the Charter. Most frequently cited is a right to humanitarian intervention, a topic rendered timely by NATO's 1999 intervention in the Federal Republic of Yugoslavia on behalf of the Kosovar Albanians.[45] However, no such purported exception, or at least none that has

---

44. The Security Council shall, where appropriate, utilize such regional arrangements or agencies for enforcement action under its authority. But no enforcement action shall be taken under regional arrangements or by regional agencies without the authorization of the Security Council, with the exception of measures against any enemy state, as defined in paragraph 2 of this Article, provided for pursuant to Article 107 or in regional arrangements directed against renewal of aggressive policy on the part of any such state, until such time as the Organization may, on request of the Governments concerned, be charged with the responsibility for preventing further aggression by such a state.
U.N. CHARTER, art. 53.1.
45. On this issue, see Adam Roberts, *The So-Called 'Right' of Humanitarian Intervention*, 3 Y.B. INT'L HUM. L. 3 (2000).

garnered any significant support, would apply in the case of counter-terrorist operations.[46]

Despite the seeming expansiveness of the Charter prohibition, there has been, as will be discussed, growing support for, or at least a diminishing degree of criticism of, forceful counter-terrorist operations. Tellingly, they are almost always justified in terms of the right to self-defense, rather than as an exception to the general prohibition on the use of force. Perhaps more normatively significant is the fact that acceptance by other states of their legitimacy, when expressed, is also usually framed in self-defense terms. Thus, while it is apparent that such activities are increasingly acceptable politically, it is more appropriate to consider that acceptance as bearing on the evolution of the norms regarding self-defense, than as exemplars of an emergent exception to a prohibition generally characterized as comprehensive in nature.

Returning to the Charter, a more apropos inquiry is whether counter-terrorist operations can fall within the Chapter VII enforcement framework. That international terrorism may constitute a threat to international peace and security, as understood in the Charter use of force context, is unquestionable. For instance, in 1992 the Security Council, reacting to attacks against Pan Am Flight 103 (the *Lockerbie* case) in 1988 and UTA Flight 722 the following year, affirmed "the right of all states . . . to protect their nationals from acts of international terrorism that constitute threats to international peace and security" and expressed concern over Libya's failure to fully cooperate in establishing responsibility for the acts.[47] The same year, and in response to Libya's failure to render the requisite cooperation, the Council re-emphasized that "suppression of acts of international terrorism, including those in which States are directly or indirectly involved, is essential for the maintenance of

---

46. It has been suggested that the Article 2(4) prohibition does not apply in any event to limited strikes against terrorists based in another country. Such operations, so the reasoning goes, do not "violate the territorial integrity or political independence" of the state in which they occur since they are not directed against that state's personnel or property, are not intended to affect its political independence in any way, and are limited temporally to the period necessary to eradicate the terrorist threat. Gregory M. Travalio, *Terrorism, International Law, And The Use Of Military Force*, 18 WIS. INT'L L. J. 145, 166–67 (2000), *citing,* inter alia, Jordan J. Paust, *Responding Lawfully to International Terrorism*, 8 WHITTIER L. REV. 711, 716–7 (1986); JOHN NORTON MOORE ET AL., NATIONAL SECURITY LAW 131 (1990); LOUIS HENKIN, HOW NATIONS BEHAVE 141–45 (1979); Jean Kirkpatrick and Allan Gerson, *The Reagan Doctrine, Human Rights and International Law*, in RIGHT V. MIGHT 25–33 (Council on Foreign Relations 1989). This article rejects the approach, favoring, as discussed infra, one that acknowledges an infringement on sovereignty, but balances it against other state rights.
47. S. C. Res. 731, U.N. SCOR, 47th Sess., U.N. Doc. S/731/(1992).

international peace and security." It further reaffirmed that "in accordance with the principle in Article 2, paragraph 4, of the Charter . . . every State has the duty to refrain from organizing, instigating, assisting or participating in terrorist acts in another State or acquiescing in organized activities within its territory directed towards the commission of such acts, when such acts involve a threat or use of force." Finally, the Council styled the failure of Libya to cooperate a threat to international peace and security.[48]

Similarly, following the 1998 US Embassy bombings in Nairobi and Dar-es-Salaam, the Security Council condemned "such acts which have a damaging effect on international relations and jeopardize the security of States." As it did in 1992, the Council also reiterated the duty to refrain from "organizing, instigating, assisting or participating in terrorist acts in another State or acquiescing in organized activities within its territory directed towards the commission of such acts."[49] The following year, the Council approved Resolution 1269 (1999), which, without being tied to any particular incident, "[u]nequivocally condemn[ed] all acts, methods and practices of terrorism as criminal and unjustifiable, regardless of their motivation, in all their forms and manifestations, wherever and by whomever committed, *in particular those which could threaten international peace and security.*"

Indeed, the Security Council characterized the pre-September 11th situation in Afghanistan as one implicating international peace and security. In October 1999, it "strongly condemn[ed] the continuing use of Afghan territory, especially areas controlled by the Taliban, for the sheltering and training of terrorists and planning of terrorist acts, and reaffirm[ed] its conviction that the suppression of international terrorism is essential for the maintenance of international peace and security."[50] It did precisely the same in December 2000. In July 2001, the Council made its position completely unambiguous by determining that "the situation in Afghanistan constitutes a threat to international peace and security in the region."[51] By September 2001, therefore, it was abundantly clear that international terrorism, as well as allowing one's territory to be used as a base of terrorist activities, could rise to the level of a "threat to the peace." This being so, the Council is entitled, pursuant to

---

48. S. C. Res. 748, U.N. SCOR, 47th Sess., U.N. Doc. S/748/(1992).
49. S. C. Res. 1189, U.N. SCOR, 53d Sess., U.N. Doc. S/1189/(1998). *See also* S. C. Res. 1044, U.N. SCOR, 51st Sess., U.N. Doc. S/1044/(1996) regarding assassination attempts against the President of Egypt, which styled "the suppression of acts of international terrorism . . . an essential element for maintenance of international peace and security."
50. S. C. Res. 1267, U.N. SCOR, 54th Sess., U.N. Doc. S/1267/(1999).
51. S. C. Res. 1363, U.N. SCOR, 56th Sess., U.N. Doc. S/1363/(2001).

Article 39, to decide on the appropriate measures to take to "maintain or restore international peace and security," and such measures include the use of force.

In the aftermath of the attacks, the Security Council labeled them threats to the peace. On September 12, 2001, it "[s]trongly condemn[ed] in the strongest terms the horrifying terrorist attacks which took place on September 11, 2001 in New York, Washington D.C. and Pennsylvania and, regard[ed] such acts, like any act of international terrorism, as a threat to international peace and security."[52] On September 28, it did so again in nearly identical language.[53] Meeting at the ministerial level on November 12, 2001, the Council issued Resolution 1377, in which it declared "that acts of international terrorism constitute one of the most serious threats to international peace and security in the twenty-first century."[54] In subsequent resolutions on the situation in Afghanistan, it adopted the practice of reaffirming all previous resolutions, thereby continuing to characterize the September 11 attacks, as well as any other act of international terrorism, as a threat to international peace and security. Such a finding is the sine qua non of an authorization for a forceful response pursuant to Chapter VII (with the exception of self-defense).

Thus, it is unquestionable that the Security Council could have elected to mount enforcement operations—either under the UN banner or by granting a mandate to member states or an intergovernmental organization—in an effort to restore and maintain international peace and security.[55] Since the demise of the Cold War, the Council has not hesitated to exercise its enforcement authority, sometimes in quite creative fashion. Chapter VII enforcement operations have been conducted in response to such diverse situations as the Iraqi invasion of Kuwait, the failed-state disorder in Somalia, fighting resulting from the breakup of Yugoslavia and internal violence in Indonesia. It has even, in the case of Operation DENY FLIGHT, authorized a regional security organization, NATO, to maintain a no-fly zone. And when that same organization mounted Operation ALLIED FORCE to stop human rights abuses against the Kosovar Albanians by forces of the Federal Republic of Yugoslavia, ad

---

52. S. C. Res. 1368, U.N. SCOR, 56th Sess., U.N. Doc. S/1368/(2001).
53. S. C. Res. 1373, U.N. SCOR, 56th Sess., U.N. Doc. S/1373/(2001).
54. S. C. Res. 1377, U.N. SCOR, 56th Sess., U.N. Doc. S/1377/(2001). In the resolution, it adopted the Declaration on the Global Effort to Counter Terrorism.
55. For an article arguing that there is "a continuing process of attempting to widen customary rights while eroding the effective powers of international organizations," of which Operation ENDURING FREEDOM is an excellent example, see Eric P.J. Myjer and Nigel D. White, *The Twin Towers Attack: An Unlimited Right to Self-Defence?*, 7 J. CONF. & SEC. L 5 (2002).

bellum-based criticism of the bombing centered on the fact that the NATO members had *not* turned to the Council for authorization to conduct their humanitarian intervention, rather than on the operation itself. Perhaps best illustrative of the flexibility with which the Council has interpreted its Chapter VII authority is creation of international tribunals to try those charged with human rights and humanitarian law violations during both international and non-international armed conflicts.[56]

In fact, the Security Council has used its Chapter VII authority to respond to terrorism in the past by imposing sanctions on both Libya and Sudan for allowing terrorist organizations to operate from their territory.[57] Yet the Security Council was never asked to issue a mandate in response to the 9/11 attacks and in no resolution did it do so. Although some commentators have searched for an implied use of force authorization in the post-attack Security Council resolutions,[58] such efforts are unnecessary. There was no reason for the Council to issue one. The sole basis for conducting Coalition operations was self-defense, which does not require advance Council authorization. All the Charter requires is notice whenever such activities are undertaken. By the terms of Article 51, an operation in self-defense does not deprive the Council of its "right" to respond to the situation, but, by the same token, that fact does not deprive states of their inherent right to exercise individual or collective self-defense, a form of armed self-help.[59]

---

56. *See, e.g.*, Statute of the International Tribunal for the Former Yugoslavia, *available at* http://www.un.org/icty/index.html (Jun. 18, 2002) [established by S. C. Res. 827, U.N. SCOR, 47th Sess., U.N. Doc. S/827/(1993)]; Statute of the International Tribunal for Rwanda, *available at* http://www.ictr.org/ (Jun. 18, 2002) [established by S. C. Res. 955, U.N. SCOR, 50th Sess., U.N. Doc. S/955/(1994)]; Statute of the Special Court for Sierra Leone, *available at* http://www.sierraleone.org/specialcourtstatute.html (Jun. 18, 2002) [established by S. C. Res. 1315, U.N. SCOR, 55th Sess., U.N. Doc. S/1315/(2000)]. Note that the authority of the Council to establish such tribunals was unsuccessfully challenged in an interlocutory appeal before the Appeals Chamber of the International Criminal Court for Yugoslavia. Prosecutor v. Tadic, Case IT-94-1-T, Decision on Jurisdiction (Aug. 10, 1995). *See* George H. Aldrich, *Comment: Jurisdiction Of The International Criminal Tribunal For The Former Yugoslavia*, 90 AM. J. INT'L L. 64 (1996).
57. S. C. Res. 748 U.N. SCOR, 47th Sess., U.N. Doc. S/748/(1992) (Libya); S. C. Res. 1054, U.N. SCOR, 51st Sess., U.N. Doc. S/1054/(1996) (Sudan).
58. *See, e.g.*, Carsten Stahn, *Addendum: Security Council Resolutions 1377 (2001) and 1378 (2001)*, ASIL Insights, Dec., 2001, http://www.asil.org/insights/insigh77.htm (Jun. 18, 2002).
59. Report of the International Law Commission, 32d Sess., II(2) Y. B. INT'L L. COMM. 1, 54 (1980).

Self-Defense

As noted, Security Council Resolutions 1368 and 1373 cited the inherent right to self-defense in the specific context of international terrorism. Further, both the United States and the United Kingdom notified the Security Council that they were conducting operations against the Taliban and al Qaeda pursuant to their right of individual and collective self-defense. They received verbal and actual support from an array of states and intergovernmental organizations, and there was no significant criticism of either the general premise that states may respond to international terrorism in self-defense or of its invocation in this particular case. However, the operations that have been mounted against the Taliban and al Qaeda raise a number of issues regarding the precise (or not so precise) parameters of the right to self-defense and the nature of its evolution. Before turning to them though, it is useful to survey several of those surrounding self-defense generally.[60]

One involves ascertaining whether an action constitutes an "armed attack," for under Article 51 the right to defend oneself surfaces only in the face of such an attack. Not all uses of force rise to this level. For instance, it is arguable that certain operations that do not involve physical force, such as a computer network attack, might be a "use of force" [and thereby contrary to Article 2(4)], but not an "armed attack."[61] Similarly, the International Court

---

60. One important issue is whether or not Article 51 represents the entire body of the law of self-defense. In the Nicaragua case, the International Court of Justice held that the customary international law right of self-defense "continues to exist alongside treaty law," specifically Article 51 of the Charter. To begin with, the article itself refers to the "inherent right" of individual and collective self-defense. More to the point in this inquiry is the fact that Article 51 leaves unanswered certain aspects of its exercise. As the Court pointed out, for instance, although Article 51 sets a threshold of "armed attack" for vesting of the right, there is no definition of that term. The Charter also fails to articulate the well-accepted requirements that acts of self-defense be proportional and necessary. Military and Paramilitary Activities in and against Nicaragua (Nicaragua v. US), Merits, I.C.J. Reports 1986, para. 176 [hereinafter Nicaragua]. See also Legality of the Threat or Use of Nuclear Weapons (Advisory Opinion), I.C.J. Reports 1996, para. 41 [hereinafter Nuclear Weapons]. Customary international law can prove useful in filling voids in the understanding of self-defense. This fact renders the current campaign normatively significant in that pervasive state practice over time, when the product of a sense of legal obligation, matures into received customary international law. The Afghanistan operations therefore represent important data points in the development of the right of self-defense.
61. See Michael N. Schmitt, *Computer Network Attack and the Use of Force in International Law: Thoughts on a Normative Framework*, 37 COLUM. J. TRANSNAT'L L. 885, 896 (1999).

of Justice, applying customary international law, held in the *Nicaragua* case that:

> the prohibition of armed attacks may apply to the sending by a State of armed bands to the territory of another State, *if* such an operation, because of its *scale and effects*, would have been classified as an armed attack rather than as a mere frontier incident had it been carried out by regular armed forces. But the Court does not believe that the concept of "armed attack" includes only acts by armed bands where such acts occur on a *significant scale* but also assistance to rebels in the form of the provision of weapons or logistical or other support. Such assistance may be regarded as a threat or use of force, or amount to intervention in the internal or external affairs of other States.[62]

It is therefore the "scale and effects" of the act that are determinative in assessing whether an armed attack is taking place such that a right to respond in self-defense vests. By the Court's standard, acts of a "significant scale" suffice. That said, the Court's reference to a *mere* frontier *incident*, as well as the acceptance of actions by *other than* a state's armed forces, imply that the requisite significance of the scale and effects is rather low. Border incidents are characterized by a minimal level of violence, tend to be transitory and sporadic in nature, and generally do not represent a policy decision by a state to engage an opponent meaningfully. They are usually either "unintended" or merely communicative in nature. By negative implication, it would not take much force to exceed this threshold.

It is possible, then, that a state employing violence will have "used force,"[63] and in doing so committed an international wrong, or even engaged in activity constituting a threat to the peace, breach of the peace or act of aggression (thereby allowing the Security Council to take cognizance of the matter under Chapter VII), but not have conducted an armed attack as that term is

---

62. Nicaragua, *supra* note 59, para. 195 (emphasis added).
63. Note that Article 2(4) prohibition on the use of force applies only to states.

understood normatively in the context of self-defense.[64] Analogously, actions by non-state actors (the applicability of self-defense in such situations is discussed infra) might be criminal in nature and/or represent threats to the peace, breaches of the peace or acts of aggression, but not be of a scale sufficient to implicate the international law right of self-defense. Despite the gaps, however, it would appear that the level of violence necessary to rise to the level of an armed attack is markedly low.

Once an armed attack has been launched, the victim state may respond with force in self-defense. However, customary international law imposes certain requirements on self-defense. In the 19th century *Caroline* case, Secretary of State Daniel Webster set out the standard that has since achieved nearly universal acceptance. According to Secretary Webster, there must be a "necessity of self-defence, instant, overwhelming, leaving no choice of means, and no moment for deliberation" and the defensive acts must not be "unreasonable or excessive."[65] This standard has matured into the requirements that self-defense be necessary and proportionate. The International Court of Justice confirmed their existence in both the *Nicaragua* case[66] and the *Nuclear Weapons* advisory opinion.[67] In the latter case, the Court noted "this dual

---

64. In ascertaining whether an armed attack has occurred, resort is sometimes made to the term "aggression," which was defined in General Assembly's Definition of Aggression Resolution. However, aggression is not wholly synonymous with armed attack. As Randelzhoffer has noted,

> The travaux preparatoires of the Definition illustrate that a definition of 'armed attack' was not intended. In the special committee that worked out the Definition, the United States, supported by other Western states, strongly opposed tendencies to include the 'armed attack'. [Cf the statements made by the US representative (U.N. Doc. A/AC.134/S. C. 113, S. C. 105, p. 17 and S. C. 108, p. 43), the representative of Japan (U.N. Doc. A/AC.134/S. C. 112), and the UK (U.N. Doc. A/AC.134/S. C. 113)]. Like the Soviet Union [see stmt by the Soviet Representative (U.N. Doc. A/AC.134/S. C. 105, p. 16)], they also expressed the view that the notions of 'act of aggression' and 'armed attack' are not identical [see the statement by the US representative (U.N. Doc. A/AC.134/S. C. 105, p. 17)].

Albrecht Randelzhofer, *Article 51*, in THE CHARTER OF THE UNITED NATIONS: A COMMENTARY 661, 668 (Bruno Simma ed., 1995).
65. Letter from Daniel Webster to Lord Ashburton (Aug. 6, 1842), 29 BRITISH AND FOREIGN STATE PAPERS 1129, 1138 (1840–1).
66. Nicaragua, *supra* note 60, para. 176.
67. Nuclear Weapons, *supra* note 60, para. 41. *See also* RESTATEMENT (THIRD) OF THE FOREIGN RELATIONS LAW OF THE UNITED STATES 905 (1987). Ian Brownlie labels proportionality "the essence of self-defence." IAN BROWNLIE, INTERNATIONAL LAW AND THE USE OF FORCE BY STATES 279 n. 2 (1963).

condition applies equally to Article 51 of the Charter," thereby verifying the applicability of the requirements in both customary and conventional law.[68]

The principle of necessity requires that the resort to force occur only when no other reasonable options remain to frustrate continuation of the armed attack. Obviously, directly reacting with force to an armed attack that is underway would seldom be deemed unnecessary. More normatively complex is the situation where an armed attack has taken place, but for some reason has paused. Perhaps it has achieved its intended objectives. Or cooler heads may have prevailed in the attacking state's government. Maybe the government that ordered the attack has been ousted and a successor government opposed to the conflict is now in power. Whatever the case, necessity mandates other than forceful responses whenever feasible.

Transposing the standard to terrorism, the question is generally whether law enforcement operations are likely to be sufficient to forestall continuation of the armed attack. Such operations may be undertaken by the victim state, the state where the terrorists are based, or, for that matter, any other state. Similarly, if a state in which the terrorists are located conducts military operations with a high probability of success, there would be no necessity basis for self-defense by the victim state.

The proportionality principle simply requires that the response in self-defense be no more than necessary to defeat the armed attack and remove the threat of reasonably foreseeable future attacks. Yet, it is sometimes wrongly suggested that the size, nature and consequences of the response must be proportional to the size, nature and consequences of the armed attack. As to the size of the attack, it would be absurd to suggest that there must be an equivalency of force between the armed attack and self-defense. On the contrary, the attacker typically seizes the initiative, thereby acquiring an advantage. To successfully defend against an opponent enjoying such an advantage may take much greater force than that used to mount the attack.

Requiring equivalency of nature is equally inappropriate. The International Court of Justice suggested as much by implication in its *Nuclear Weapons* opinion. When assessing the proportionality of the use of nuclear weapons, the Court opined that "(t)he proportionality principle may . . . not in itself exclude

---

68. Nuclear Weapons, *supra* note 60, para. 41.

the use of nuclear weapons in self-defense in all circumstances."[69] While representing a non-decision on the issue at hand, the Court had admitted the possibility that use of a nuclear weapon might be legitimate in the face of a non-nuclear attack. Scaled down from the nuclear level, such a criterion remains equally malapropos. By way of illustration, in responding to a maritime attack the most productive tactic may be to disrupt land-based maritime command and control assets. Likewise, in an effort to cause an attacker to desist by altering his cost-benefit calculations, it may be more effective to concentrate on targets of particular value to him rather than those directly involved in the attack.[70] In fact, doing so may well result in a lesser level of violence than would be necessary to definitively defeat the attacking units themselves. Surely international law does not mandate tit-for-tat exchanges.

At first glance, a standard of proportionality vis-à-vis the harm caused (or possible) to the victim might seem more reasonable. In other words, the state engaging in self-defense should not be entitled to cause more harm than it has suffered. But such a standard ignores the fact that international law grants states the right to self-defense in order that they not be rendered helpless in the face of an attack. To suggest that a state cannot use the destructive force necessary to cause an attacker to discontinue (or to prevent future attacks) because the resulting destruction outweighs that the victim state originally suffered is to effectively deprive the victim of the right to self-defense.

Finally, there have been suggestions that self-defense operations are disproportionate if they cause more collateral damage and incidental injury than the civilian casualties and damage to civilian objects originally suffered by the victim state. Such assertions have been made in the context of the current

---

69. *Id.*, para. 42. There are, as noted in the discussion of self-defense, competing views of proportionality. India argued that the principle meant a nuclear weapon could not be used except in response to a nuclear attack. But even in such a case, so India argued, the use of nuclear weapons would be malum in se. Thus, any nuclear reprisal would be unlawful. Written statement of the Government of India, June 20, 1995 (Legality of the Threat or Use of Nuclear Weapons), at 2–3. Other approaches include proportional to the harm caused, vice technique employed to cause the harm, and proportional to the force needed to cause the other side to desist. Compare the approach of the Netherlands and United States, both of which argued that the legality would be situational, with that of India. Observations of the Government of the Kingdom of the Netherlands, June 16, 1995 (Legality of the Threat or Use of Nuclear Weapons), at 12; Written statement of the Government of the United States of America, June 20, 1995 (Legality of the Threat or Use of Nuclear Weapons), at 30.

70. In a slightly different context, this approach lies at the heart of compellance strategies. On the issue of affecting an enemy's decision-making, see Jeanne M. Meyer, *Tearing Down the Façade: A Critical Look at the Current Law on Targeting the Will of the Enemy and Air Force Doctrine*, 51 A. F. L. REV. 143 (2001).

counter-terrorist operations, in which the number of civilian casualties allegedly exceeds the number of fatalities resulting from the 9/11 attacks.[71] Claims of this nature confuse the self-defense proportionality requirement of the jus ad bellum with the jus in bello proportionality principle that forbids attacks "expected to cause incidental loss of civilian life, injury to civilians, damage to civilian objects, or a combination thereof, which would be excessive in relation to the concrete and direct military advantage anticipated."[72] But even by the in bello standard, the correct phenomena to compare are incidental injuries/collateral damage and military advantage. The issue is whether or not the military advantage accruing from an attack justifies the civilian casualties and damage to civilian objects; there is no balancing of the civilian suffering on the opposing sides of the conflict.

Restated in the context of terrorism, the proportionality standard allows only that degree of force necessary to fend off a terrorist attack and protect oneself from a future continuation thereof. But the force necessary to achieve this purpose may far exceed that employed in the attack. Terrorists often operate in loose networks from dispersed locations, receiving logistic support in ways intended to mask their nature. Further, they may be fanatical devotees willing to die for their cause; this makes it extremely difficult to meaningfully affect their cost-benefit calculations. Taking them on is a daunting task that typically requires extremely aggressive measures.

Beyond necessity and proportionality, the *Caroline* standard has also often been deemed to impose an imminency requirement, i.e., that the attack be ongoing, or at least so imminent that the victim state has to react almost reflexively to counter it. This requirement has generated enormous debate about precisely when it is that an attack becomes imminent enough to merit

---

71. Estimates of civilian casualties vary widely. Compare, e.g., Marc W. Herold, *A Dossier on Civilian Victims of United States' Aerial Bombing of Afghanistan: A Comprehensive Accounting*, Dec. 10, 2001, *available at* http://www.cursor.org/stories/civilian_deaths.htm (Jun. 18, 2002) (approximately 4000 by Jan. 1, 2002) with Carl Connetta, *Operation Enduring Freedom: Why a Higher Rate of Civilian Bombing Casualties*, Jan. 18, 2002, *available at* http://www.comw.org/pda/0201oef.html#ref7 (Jun. 18, 2002) (1000–13000 over the same period). A Human Rights Watch Report is forthcoming on the subject (unreleased as of Jun. 19, 2002).
72. Protocol Additional (I) to the Geneva Convention of 12 August 1949, and Relating to the Protection of Victims of International Armed Conflicts, arts. 51.5(a) & 57.2(a)(iii) & (b), Dec. 12, 1977, 1125 U.N.T.S. 3, 16 I.L.M. 1391 (1977), *reprinted in* ADAM ROBERTS & RICHARD GUELFF, DOCUMENTS ON THE LAWS OF WAR 419 (3d ed. 2000). On proportionality, *see* William J. Fenrick, *The Rule of Proportionality and Protocol Additional I in Conventional Warfare*, 98 MIL. L. REV. 91 (1982); Judith G. Gardam, *Proportionality and Force in International Law*, 87 AM. J. INT'L L. 391 (1993).

"pre-emptive" action in self-defense. This is the issue of the appropriateness of "anticipatory self-defense."[73]

Certain commentators who read *Caroline* narrowly suggest a high standard of imminence.[74] Such a reading logically flows from Webster's "instant, overwhelming, leaving no choice of means, and no moment for deliberation" verbiage. However, the nature of combat has evolved dramatically since the time of the *Caroline* correspondence. In the 21st century, the means of warfare are such that defeat can occur almost instantaneously. Indeed, the linear blitzkrieg strategies of the Second World War appear slow and unwieldy by today's standards, in which the battlespace is four-dimensional and effects are generated in fractions of a second.

In such an environment, the most apropos approach is to concentrate on the underlying intent of the right to self-defense. Its primary purpose is to afford states a self-help mechanism by which they may repel attackers; it recognizes that the international community may not respond quickly enough, if at all, to an armed attack against a state. Yet, the limitations of necessity, proportionality and imminency play to the community's countervailing aversion to the use of violence by states. Thus, there is a balancing between the state's right to exist unharmed and the international community's need to minimize the use of force, which is presumptively destabilizing.

The most responsive balance between these two interests lies in permitting a use of defensive force in advance of an attack if "the potential victim must immediately act to defend itself in a meaningful way and if the potential aggressor has irrevocably committed itself to attack."[75] This standard combines an exhaustion of remedies component with a requirement for a reasonable expectation of future attacks—an expectation that is more than merely speculative.

---

73. Yoram Dinstein has rejected the terminology "anticipatory" in favor of "interceptive" on the basis that the former term suggests that preventive actions in the face of a "foreseeable" armed attack are legitimate. For Professor Dinstein, the question is whether or not the "other side has committed itself to an armed attack in an ostensibly irrevocable way." As he explains, "[t]he crucial question is who embarks upon an irreversible course of action, thereby crossing the Rubicon. This, rather than the actual opening of fire, is what casts the die and forms what may be categorized as an incipient armed attack. It would be absurd to require that the defending state should sustain and absorb a devastating (perhaps a fatal) blow, only to prove an immaculate conception of self-defence." YORAM DINSTEIN, WAR, AGGRESSION AND SELF-DEFENSE 172 (3rd ed. 2001).
74. *See, e.g.*, Oscar Schachter, *The Right of States to Use Armed Force*, 82 MICH. L. REV. 1620, 1634–35 (1984).
75. Schmitt, *supra* note 61, at 932.

However, what if an attack is "complete" at the time of the proposed response in self-defense? To some extent, this question bears on the necessity requirement; the termination of the initial action may allow for other than forceful resolution of the situation, thereby rendering a use of force in self-defense unnecessary. But the query also touches upon the imminency requirement. Must defense against a future attack be measured by the same standard of imminency as defense against an initial one?

The answer is "yes," but the mere fact that an entity has attacked once makes it easier to conclude that it will do so again. After all, the "potential" attacker's mens rea has now been tangibly demonstrated. Much more to the point, it may also be reasonable to conclude that the first attack was part of an overall campaign that in itself constitutes a single extended armed attack. By this understanding, an after-the-fact reaction to an initial attack constitutes a response to an on-going armed attack in which there is but a tactical pause. The approach reflects the reality of combat, in which pauses are the norm, not the exception. They may be necessary for logistical purposes, as a result of weather, due to enemy responses, pending acquisition of further intelligence, to leverage surprise, etc. The question is whether the attack that has occurred is part and parcel of a related series of acts that will continue to unfold.

Treating a series of actions as a unitary whole makes particular sense in the context of terrorism. Terrorist campaigns generally consist of a series of actions that occur periodically over extended periods of time. Moreover, given their nature, they are very difficult to defend against while underway—the potential target is usually only revealed by the attack itself, all of society represents a potential target thus rendering effective on-the-spot defense problematic, the actual violence may occur after the terrorists have left the scene (as in a bombing), the terrorists may be willing to die in the attack, and the identity and location of the terrorists may not be uncovered until after the completion of a particular action. In fact, in the majority of cases it is only after the attack that the victim state can mount its response. Therefore, unless one is willing to deny victim states a consequential right of self-defense against terrorists, it is reasonable to interpret self-defense as permitting the use of force against terrorists who intend, and have the capability to, conduct further attacks against the victim. By this interpretation, it is not the imminency of an isolated action that is relevant, but rather the relationship between a series of attacks. Once the first of the related attacks has been launched, the question becomes whether the victim state has sufficient reliable evidence to conclude that further attacks are likely, not whether those further attacks are themselves imminent.

Self-Defense Against al Qaeda

"Armed attacks" by terrorists. That the attacks of 9/11 were of sufficient "scale and effects" to amount to an armed attack is tragically self-evident. However, the self-defense operations launched against the al Qaeda terrorist network in Afghanistan raise a number of other interesting issues. The first is whether an "armed attack" can be carried out by a terrorist group or, stated conversely, whether self-defense can be conducted against one.

Some commentators have suggested that until 9/11, the understanding of self-defense against an armed attack was essentially limited to aggression by states.[76] But Article 51 makes no mention of the nature of the entity that must mount the attack that in turn permits a forceful response in self-defense. This omission is particularly meaningful in light of the fact that Article 2(4)'s prohibition on the use of force specifically applies only to actions by Members of the United Nations, all of which are states. That one key provision on the use of force [2(4)] includes a reference to states, whereas another (51) does not, implies that the latter was not meant to be so limited. This distinction makes sense in the Charter context. The Charter was meant to govern state behavior, but in doing so it both limits what states may do and empowers them. Thus, in 2(4) it restricts a state's resort to force, but in 51 authorizes it to use force in the face of armed attack. It would make no sense to limit the authorization to attacks by states because at the time the Charter was drafted, that was the greater threat.

Article 39 is similarly devoid of reference to state action when charging the Security Council with responsibility for deciding on the measures to take in the face of a threat to the peace, breach of the peace or act of aggression. In the various resolutions regarding the events of 9/11 (and those resulting from it), the Council characterized the situation as a threat to international peace and security. Moreover, it specifically noted that as a general matter terrorism constituted such a threat. While Article 39 does not directly address self-defense and armed attacks, both it and Article 51 fall within Chapter VII, which is entitled "Action with Respect to Threats to the Peace, Breaches of the Peace, and Acts of Aggression." Considering these related points vis-à-vis

---

76. *See, e.g.*, Antonio Cassese, *Terrorism is also Disrupting Some Crucial Legal Categories of International Law*, European Journal of International Law Discussion Forum, *available at* http://www.ejil.org/forum_WTC/ny-cassese.html (Jun. 18, 2002). *See also* Giorgio Gaja, *In What Sense Was There an "Armed Attack"?*, European Journal of International Law Discussion Forum, *available at* http://www.ejil.org/forum_WTC/ny-gaja.html (Jun. 18, 2002).

Articles 39 and 51, it is reasonable to conclude that the entire chapter deals with actions that threaten international peace and security, *whatever the source.*

Moreover, recall that Security Council Resolutions 1368 and 1373, which both cited the inherent right of self-defense, were issued before the counter-terrorist campaign began and at a time when suspicion was focused on an international terrorist group as the culprit. In particular, recall that Resolution 1368 passed the very day after the attack, when no one was discussing the possibility that a state may have been behind the actions. This indicates that the Council's understanding of self-defense includes defending against armed attacks by non-state actors.

State practice in the aftermath of 9/11 further supports the applicability of self-defense to acts by non-state actors. No voices were raised claiming that either the customary right of self-defense or Article 51 was limited to the context of state actions. On the contrary, there were very visible illustrations, such as NATO's invocation of Article V for the first time in its existence, of the fact that most states viewed 9/11 as an armed attack meriting actions in self-defense; in no case was there any suggestion that the right was dependent on identifying a state as the attacker. Lest there be any question on this point, once the self-defense actions commenced against both a state *and* a non-state actor on October 7th, the dearth of controversy over using self-defense against non-state actors persisted.[77] In fact, post-October 7th Security Council resolutions went so far as to urge member states to "root out terrorism, in keeping with the Charter of the United Nations."[78]

Necessity and the impact of law enforcement alternatives. It is interesting to note that support for using force was widely evident despite the fact that a logical alternative to self-defense existed—criminal law enforcement.[79] After all, the September 11th terrorist acts constituted a variety of criminal offences under the laws of a number of jurisdictions. Because it allows for universal

---

77. Ireland's Ambassador to the United Nations, who was acting as President of the Security Council, noted the unanimous support of the Council following the briefing on the United States' and United Kingdom's operations in self-defense. Christopher S. Wren, *U.S. Advises U.N. Council More Strikes Could Come*, N.Y. TIMES, Oct. 9, 2001, at B5.

78. S. C. Res. 1378, U.N. SCOR, 57th Sess., U.N. Doc. S/1378/(2002); S. C. Res. 1386, U.N. SCOR, 56th Sess., U.N. Doc. S/1386/(2001); S. C. Res. 1390, U.N. SCOR, 57th Sess., U.N. Doc. S/1390/(2002). Specific reference was made to Osama bin Laden and the al Qaeda network in the January resolution.

79. For a pre 9/11 discussion of the alternatives, and the appropriateness of each, see Walter Gary Sharp, *The Use of Armed Force Against Terrorism: American Hegemony or Impotence?*, 1 CHI. J. INT'L L. 37 (2000).

jurisdiction, of particular significance is the offense of crimes against humanity.[80] Further, relevant international law instruments that bear on the incident (or analogous terrorist incidents) include, inter alia, the Hague Convention for the Suppression of Unlawful Seizure of Aircraft, the Tokyo Convention on Offences and Certain Other Acts Committed on Board Aircraft, the Montreal Convention for the Suppression of Unlawful Acts against the Safety of Civil Aviation, and the International Convention for the Suppression of Terrorist Bombings.[81] Although these treaties do not directly criminalize the actions, they often require criminalization at the domestic level and/or set forth mutual law enforcement cooperation and extradition procedures.[82] Under US federal law, the acts violated certain sections of the Antiterrorism Act of 1990[83] and the US statutes implementing the Montreal Convention.[84] Of course, specific elements of the attacks violated the criminal law of the US states (and the District of Columbia) where they occurred, such as the prohibitions on murder and the various forms of accomplice participation.

---

80. A crime against humanity involves the commission of certain acts, including murder and "other inhumane acts ... causing great suffering, or serious injury to body or to mental or physical health" when committed as part of a widespread or systematic attack directed against any civilian population." Rome Statute for the International Criminal Court, art. 7.1, *reprinted in* 37 I.L.M. 999 (1998), M. CHERIF BASSIOUNI, THE STATUTE OF THE INTERNATIONAL COURT: A DOCUMENTARY HISTORY 39 (1999), *available at* http://www.un.org/law/icc/statute/romefra.htm (Jun. 18, 2002). Widespread consensus exists that the attacks of 9/11 constituted crimes against humanity. For an analysis of its applicability to the 9/11 attacks, see Cassese, *supra* note 76.
81. Hague Convention for the Suppression of Unlawful Seizure of Aircraft, Dec. 16, 1970, art. 1, 22 U.S.T. 1641, 10 I.L.M. 133 (1971); Tokyo Convention on Offences and Certain Other Acts Committed on Board Aircraft, Sept. 14, 1963, 20 U.S.T. 2941, 704 U.N.T.S. 219; Montreal Convention on the Suppression of Unlawful Acts Against The Safety of Civil Aviation, Sept. 23, 1971, 24 U.S.T. § 565, T.I.A.S. No. 7570; Convention for the Suppression of Unlawful Seizure of Aircraft, Dec. 16, 1970, art. 1, 22 U.S.T. 1641, 860 U.N.T.S. 105, 107. On the applicability, or difficulties thereof, of the treaties to the 9/11 attacks, see Arnold N. Pronto, *Comment*, ASIL INSIGHTS, Sep. 2001, *available at* http://www.asil.org/insights/insigh77.htm (Jun. 18, 2002).
82. Professor M. Cherif Bassiouni has convincingly argued that the international law governing this topic is not comprehensive. "[G]overnments have avoided developing an international legal regime to prevent, control, and suppress terrorism, preferring instead the hodgepodge of thirteen treaties that currently address its particular manifestations." M. Cherif Bassiouni, *Legal Control of International Terrorism: A Policy-Oriented Assessment*, 43 HARV. INT'L L. J. 83 (2002).
83. Antiterrorism Act of 1990, 18 U.S.C. §§ 2331 et seq. (2000).
84. 18 U.S.C. § 32 (2000). *See* Jordan J. Paust, *Addendum: Prosecution of Mr. bin Laden et al. for Violations of International Law and Civil Lawsuits by Various Victims*, ASIL INSIGHTS, Sep. 21, 2001, *available at* http://www.asil.org/insights/insigh77.htm (Jun. 18, 2002). Professor Paust also discusses the possibility of civil suits against the perpetrators.

It is apparent, therefore, that the international community does not view the applicability of a criminal law enforcement regime as precluding a response in self-defense to an armed attack by terrorists. That said, the prospect of law enforcement bears on the issue of whether particular acts of self-defense are necessary. Recall that necessity requires an absence of reasonable alternatives to the defensive use of force. In this context, then, the state may only act against the terrorists if classic law enforcement reasonably appears unlikely to net those expected to conduct further attacks *before* they do so. One must be careful here. There is no requirement for an expectation that law enforcement will fail; rather, the requirement is that success not be expected to prove timely enough to head off a continuation of the terrorist campaign. Of course, if no further attacks are anticipated, the necessity principle would preclude resort to armed force at all, since self-defense contains no retributive element.

In this case, the necessity of resort to force was obvious despite the nearly global law enforcement effort to identify and apprehend members of the al Qaeda network and prevent further attacks. Recall that al Qaeda had been implicated in numerous prior acts of terrorism, most notably the 1998 East African embassy bombings, and was at the time of the 9/11 attacks already the target of a massive international law enforcement effort. Nevertheless, law enforcement failed to prevent the tragic events of September 11th. That is hardly surprising. Al Qaeda is a shadowy, loose-knit terrorist organization in which cells operate with substantial autonomy from scores of countries. The complexity of coordinating law enforcement efforts in the face of widely divergent capabilities, domestic laws and national attitudes was daunting. Further, al Qaeda was headquartered in Afghanistan, then ruled by a government seemingly oblivious to international pressure to deny al Qaeda its main base of operations. Simply put, there was no guarantee that even a law enforcement effort that was proving successful against much of the organization could effectively eradicate the threat of another major attack. At the same time, aggressively attacking the senior leadership and denying it a base of operations promised great returns in alleviating the threat, far greater than would likely be realized by law enforcement in a comparable period. And it must be remembered that the clock was ticking. As the United States and its coalition partners planned their response, warnings of imminent attacks flowed through intelligence channels with great frequency.

Proportionality. The second core requirement of self-defense, that of proportionality, also limits when a state may resort to self-defense in responding to a terrorist act. Whereas necessity asks whether the use of force is appropriate, proportionality asks how much may be applied.

Like necessity, proportionality is affected by the prospect of law enforcement activities. Even if armed force is necessary, the extent of that force may be diminished by on-going or future law enforcement activities. In counter-terrorist operations, law enforcement and military force can act synergistically, thereby reducing the level of force that needs to be applied (and affecting its nature). For instance, law enforcement disruption of a number of terrorist cells within an organization may lessen the extent (number, location, etc.) of military strikes that need to be conducted. That is exactly what happened in the aftermath of 9/11. Thousands of potential terrorists were arrested or detained worldwide, thereby dramatically reducing the need to resort to force in countering future terrorism.

Were the strikes against al Qaeda proportionate, particularly in light of the extensive parallel law enforcement campaign? Clearly, they were. Al Qaeda forces in Afghanistan numbered in the thousands and were widely dispersed. Moreover, to be disproportionate, the use of force would have had to be excessive in relation to the degree of force actually needed to prevent *continuation* of al Qaeda's terrorist campaign. As of June 2002, al Qaeda forces remain in the field, periodically engaging coalition forces, albeit in small unit fashion. Further, intelligence sources have reported that mid-level al Qaeda operatives have pulled the organization back together again and are forging alliances with other terrorist groups. The organization reportedly "is as capable of planning and carrying out potent attacks on U.S. targets as the more centralized network once led by Osama bin Laden."[85] So, despite the success of international law enforcement and military efforts, al Qaeda remains a very viable threat, continuing to operate from bases in any number of countries. The group may have been gravely wounded, but it would be highly premature to contend the wounds are fatal.

That said, the increasing effectiveness of international counter-terrorist law enforcement efforts and the fact that the fight may now need to be taken outside the borders of Afghanistan do raise questions regarding the proportionality of future military efforts. Using an extreme example for the sake of illustration, one might question the proportionality of a large scale military operation mounted into an uncooperative state which refuses to hand over a small number of low-level operatives. The action might be necessary in the sense that diplomacy and law enforcement offered slim prospects of taking

---

85. David Johnson et al., *Qaeda Lieutenants Form Terror Alliance*, INT'L HERALD TRIBUNE, June 17, 2002, at 1.

them out of the terrorist network, but the extent of the use of force would appear to be more than reasonably required to accomplish the objective.

Imminency. As noted above, it would make little sense to evaluate each terrorist attack individually in every case. Doing so would deny the reality that most conflict, even conventional conflict between states, is a series of engagements, with contact repeatedly made and broken. This being so, in many situations it may be reasonable to conclude that an attack was merely the opening shot in an overall campaign that in itself constitutes a single on-going armed attack.

That is exactly the case with regard to the 9/11 attacks. Al Qaeda had been involved in terrorism against US assets for a decade, terrorism that resulted in extensive property damage, loss of life and injury. Although there was often a hiatus between attacks, they did occur with some regularity. In light of this record, it is absurd to suggest al Qaeda would terminate the campaign after achieving its most significant victory; logic would impel just the opposite conclusion. Additionally, not only did al Qaeda's own statements style continued attacks as a religious duty, one of the organization's central objectives, withdrawal of US and coalition forces from Islamic territory, remained unfulfilled. Since 9/11, multiple al Qaeda related plots have been uncovered or foiled, most recently that involving use of a "dirty (radiological) bomb" against a US population center.[86] Thus, it is not necessary to speculate on whether further attacks were likely and imminent on October 7th; they clearly were (and remain so).

Cross-border counter-terrorist operations. While it is appropriate to extend self-defense to acts committed by non-state actors, and though the availability of criminal law enforcement responses does not preclude doing so, since non-state actors possess no territory as a matter of international law (they may in *fact*), can the victim state enter another state's territory in order to conduct self-defense operations? The answer requires balancing the rights and duties of the respective states involved. The state in which the terrorists are located has a right of territorial integrity. This well-established customary international law right creates corresponding duties in other states. For instance, Article 2(4) of the UN Charter prohibits the threat or use of force against the "territorial integrity . . . of any State."[87] Commentators generally agree that

---

86. On the continuing operations of the organization, see David Johnston et al., *Qaeda's New Links Increase Threats From Far-Flung Sites,* N.Y. TIMES, June 16, 2002, at 1.
87. U.N. CHARTER, 2(4).

the prohibition extends to any non-consensual penetration of a state's territory, not simply those intended to seize parts of that territory.[88] Non-compliance may amount to an act of aggression.[89]

However, the state victimized by terrorism has a right to self-defense. No one would dispute that a state forfeits a degree of its right to territorial integrity when it commits acts that vest the right to self-defense in another state, at least to the extent necessary for self-defense to be meaningful. Thus, an armed attack by state A may justify the crossing of state B's military forces into state A to put an end to the attack.

Lest the right to self-defense be rendered empty in the face of terrorism, in certain circumstances the principle of territorial integrity must yield to that of self-defense against terrorists. Putting aside the issue of when the acts of terrorists may be ascribed to a state, thereby justifying self-defense directly against that state, the balancing of self-defense and territorial integrity depends on the extent to which the state in which the terrorists are located has complied with its own responsibilities vis-à-vis the terrorists.

As John Basset Moore noted in the *Lotus* case, "it is well settled that a State is bound to use due diligence to prevent the commission within its dominions of criminal acts against another nation or its people. . . ."[90] This principle has been reflected in numerous pronouncements on terrorism. For instance, the 1970 Declaration on Friendly Relations urges each state to "refrain from . . . acquiescing in organized activities within its territory directed toward

---

88. Randelzhoffer, Article 2(4), *supra* note 42, at 117. *See also* Declaration on Principles of International Law Concerning Friendly Relations and Cooperation Among States in Accordance with the Charter of the United Nations:

> Every State has a duty to refrain in its international relations from the threat or use of force against the territorial integrity or political independence of any state, or in any other manner inconsistent with the purposes of the United Nations. Such a threat or use of force constitutes a violation of international law and the Charter of the United Nations and shall never be employed as a means of settling international issues.

G.A. Res. 2625 (XXV), U.N. GAOR, 25th Sess., anx, U.N. Doc. A/Res/2625 (1970), *reprinted in* 65 AM. J. INT'L L. 243 (1971) and in KEY RESOLUTIONS OF THE UNITED NATIONS GENERAL ASSEMBLY, 1946–1996 (Dietrich Rauschning, Katja Wiesbrock & Martin Lailach eds., 1997), at 3 [hereinafter Declaration on Friendly Relations]. The resolution was adopted by acclamation.
89. Aggression is the use of "armed force by a State against the . . . territorial integrity . . . of another State." Definition of Aggression, anx, art. 1, G.A. Res. 3314 (XXIX), U.N. GAOR, 29th Sess., Supp. No. 31, at 142, U.N. Doc. A/9631 (1975), 13 INT'L LEG. MAT'L 710 (1974). Additionally, pursuant to Article 3, aggression includes "[t]he invasion or attack by the armed forces of a State of the territory of another State. . . ."
90. S.S. Lotus (Fr. v. Turk.) 1927 P.C.I.J. (ser. A) No. 10, at 4, 88 (Moore, J., dissenting).

the commission of [terrorist acts in another state],"[91] a proscription echoed in the 1994 Declaration on Measures to Eliminate Terrorism.[92] In the context of the instant case, recall the 1999, 2000 and 2001 Security Council resolutions condemning the Taliban's willingness to allow territory they controlled to be used by al Qaeda.

Should a state be unable or unwilling to comply with this obligation, the victim state is then permitted to enter the territory of the state where the terrorists are located for the limited purpose of conducting self-defense operations against them. This is only logical, since the unwillingness or inability of state A to comply with the requirements of international law cannot possibly be deemed to deprive state B of its authority to defend itself against an armed attack, the seminal right of the state-centric international normative architecture. Of course, all requirements of self-defense must be met. There must be an on-going armed attack (or armed campaign), no reasonable alternative to the penetration of state A's territory for the purpose of using force against the terrorists can exist, and the force used has to be limited to that necessary to accomplish the defensive objectives. Once those objectives are attained, state B must immediately withdraw because at that point there is no right of self-defense to justify its "violation" of state A's territorial integrity. Further if, during the self-defense operations, state A takes actions that comply with its obligation to deny use of its territory to terrorists, state B's right of self-defense will diminish accordingly. Finally, state A may not interfere with the self-defense operations, as state B is simply exercising a right under international law. Since state B's use of force is lawful, any other state's use of force against it would constitute an "armed attack."[93]

In fact, there have been numerous instances of states exercising this self-help right of self-defense. In the aftermath of the coalition operations against

---

91. Declaration on Friendly Relations, *supra* note 88.
92. Declaration on Measures to Eliminate International Terrorism, G.A. Res. 49/60, U.N. GAOR 6th Comm., 49th Sess., 84th plen. mtg., U.N. Doc. A/49/743 (1994); Declaration to Supplement the 1994 Declaration on Measures to Eliminate International Terrorism, G.A. Res. 51/210, U.N. GAOR 6th Comm., 51st Sess., 88th plen. mtg., U.N. Doc. A/51/631 (1996).
93. Professor Robert Turner perceptively offered an analysis along these lines in the aftermath of the September 11th attacks. Robert F. Turner, *International Law And The Use Of Force In Response To The World Trade Center And Pentagon Attacks*, JURIST, available at http://jurist.law.pitt.edu/forum/forumnew34.htm (Jun. 18, 2002). On the subject of self-help, see also Guy B. Roberts, *Self-Help in Combating state-Sponsored Terrorism: Self Defense and Peacetime Reprisals*, 19 CASE W. RES. J. INT'L L. 243 (1987); Franz W. Paasche, *The Use of Force in Combating Terrorism*, 25 COLUM. J. TRANSNAT'L L. 377 (1987); Oscar Schachter, *The Extra-Territorial Use of Force against Terrorist Bases*, 11 HOUS. J. INT'L L. 309 (1989).

al Qaeda, the most often cited has been US General John Pershing's unsuccessful 1916 foray into Mexico after Pancho Villa and his bandits killed 18 Americans in New Mexico. At the time, Mexico was in the midst of a revolution and, thus, incapable of effectively controlling Villa. Note that the Mexican government asked the US forces to withdraw three months after they entered Mexican territory, a demand refused on the basis of Mexico's inability to police Villa. Similarly, during the Vietnam conflict, the United States conducted aerial and ground attacks against enemy forces that had sought refuge in Cambodia. Although criticized widely, such criticism was arguably more the product of general anti-war fervor, than concern over the legality of the operations.[94] In another example, Israel conducted airstrikes against PLO facilities in Tunisia during 1985 on the grounds that the PLO was using Tunisia as a base of operations for terrorist attacks on Israel—with the acquiescence of the Tunisian government.[95] The Security Council, with the United States abstaining, condemned the bombings as an "act of armed aggression perpetrated by Israel against Tunisian territory in flagrant violation of the Charter of the United Nations, international law and norms of conduct" in a 14–0 vote.[96] Whether concern centered on the alleged violation of international law or on the fact that the operation posed a "threat to the peace and security in the Mediterranean region"[97] (and on general hostility to Israel) remains an open question.

Political unacceptability instead of normative concern also drove most international criticism of South Africa's operations against African National Congress groups based in Angola during the 1970s.[98] Similarly, the international community was unsupportive as Turkey mounted regular incursions into Northern Iraq against Kurdish terrorists throughout the 1990s. As in the South African case, opposition arguably was driven by factors other than the legal acceptability of crossing into Iraq. At the time there was de minimus concern over violation of Iraq's territorial integrity, as Iraqi forces and

---

94. On the Cambodian incursions, see Timothy Guiden, *Defending America's Cambodian Incursion*, 11 ARIZ. J. INT'L & COMP. L. 215 (1994); John Fried, *United States Military Intervention in Cambodia in the Light of International Law*, reprinted in 3 THE VIETNAM WAR AND INTERNATIONAL LAW 100 (Richard Falk, ed. 1972); *International Law and Military Operations Against Insurgents in Neutral Territories*, 68 COLUM. L. REV. 1127 (1968).
95. See statement of [then] Israeli Ambassador to the UN, Benjamin Netanyahu, U.N. Doc. S/PV.2615, at 86–7 (Oct. 4, 1985).
96. S. C. Res. 573, U.N. SCOR, 40th Sess., U.N. Doc S/573/(1985).
97. Id.
98. See W. Michael Reisman, *International Legal Responses to Terrorism*, 22 HOUS. J. INT'L L. 3, 53 (1999); G.A. Res. 45/150, U.N. GAOR, 3d Comm., 45th Sess., 69th plen. mtg., U.N. Doc. A/Res/45/150 (1990).

government officials were already excluded from the area due to their suppression of the Kurds. Rather, criticism most likely derived from irritation over interference with the relief and no-fly operations in northern Iraq[99] and concern over a track record of human rights abuses against the Kurds during Turkish military operations conducted in Southeastern Turkey.[100]

Most recently, the United States launched raids on terrorist facilities in Afghanistan and Sudan following the 1998 bombings of the US embassies in Nairobi and Dar-es-Salaam.[101] Although the cruise missile strike against the al Shifa pharmaceutical plant in Sudan (it was allegedly involved in chemical weapons production) was criticized, most censure surrounded the alleged invalidity of the claim of a connection between the plant and international terrorism, not the violation of Sudanese territory;[102] the attacks against al Qaeda training bases in Afghanistan evoked little condemnation. Nor did the 1999 pursuit of Hutu guerrillas in the Democratic Republic of Congo by Ugandan forces following a massacre of foreign tourists,[103] although the internationalization of the conflict did draw international concern and resulted in the dispatch of a peacekeeping force by the Security Council.[104]

Of greatest normative relevance on the issue of cross-border counterterrorist operations is the famous *Caroline* incident cited above in regard to the core requirements of self-defense.[105] Recall the facts. In 1837 a rebellion was underway in Canada against the British. Some of the rebels were based in the United States. The British attempted to negotiate with the American side, in particular the Governor of New York, to no avail. At that point they

---

99. First Operation PROVIDE COMFORT, later NORTHERN WATCH. The author was staff judge advocate of the operations during this period.
100. *See, e.g.,* Department of State, 1999 Country Reports on Human Rights Practices: Turkey, *available at* http://www.state.gov/www/global/human_rights/1999_hrp_report/turkey.html (Jun. 18, 2002).
101. Ruth Wedgwood, *Responding to Terrorism: The Strikes Against bin Laden*, 24 YALE J. INT'L L. 559 (1999); Leah M. Campbell, *Defending Against Terrorism: A Legal Analysis of the Decision to Strike Sudan and Afghanistan*, 74 TUL. L. REV. 1067 (2000).
102. On the confusion surrounding whether the facility was involved in terrorist activities, see Vernon Loeb, *U.S. Wasn't Sure Plant Had Nerve Gas Role; Before Sudan Strike, CIA Urged More Tests*, WASH. POST, Aug. 21, 1999, at A1.
103. Reisman, *supra* note 98, at 54.
104. In S. C. Res. 1291, U.N. SCOR, 55th Sess., U.N. Doc. S/1291/(2000), the Council authorized the United Nations Organization Mission in the Democratic Republic of the Congo. For details and background, see http://www.un.org/Depts/dpko/monuc/monuc_body.htm (Jun. 18, 2002).
105. On the *Caroline* incident in the context of the issue at hand, see Reisman, *supra* note 98, at 42–47. On the facts, see R.Y. Jennings, *The Caroline and McLeod Cases*, 32 AM. J. INT'L L. 82 (1938).

mounted a small raid (80 men) into the United States where they seized the *Caroline*, a vessel used by the rebels and their supporters. The ship was set ablaze and sent over Niagara Falls.

The incident generated a fascinating correspondence over the next several years between the British Foreign Office and the United States Department of State. The issue in dispute, though, was not whether the British could legitimately cross into the United States for the limited purpose of attacking the rebels. Instead, controversy focused on the *circumstances* permitting them to do so and how. As Lord Ashburton, the Foreign Minister, wrote to his US counterpart, Daniel Webster:

> I might safely put it to any candid man, acquainted with the existing state of things, to say whether the military commander in Canada had the remotest reason, on the 29th day of December, to expect to be relieved from this state of suffering by the protective intervention of any American authority. How long could a Government, having the paramount duty of protecting its own people, be reasonably expected to wait for what they had then no reason to expect?[106]

Ashburton's premise that crossing the border was proper in the absence of effective action by the authorities where the rebels were based went unchallenged, with Webster simply asserting that the action had been excessive in the particular circumstances of the case.[107]

---

106. Letter from Lord Ashburton to Daniel Webster (July 28, 1842), 30 BRITISH AND FOREIGN STATE PAPERS 195.

107. A necessity of self-defence, instant, overwhelming, leaving no choice of means, and no moment for deliberation. It will be for it to show, also, that the local authorities of Canada, even supposing the necessity of the moment authorized them to enter the territories of The United States at all, did nothing unreasonable or excessive; since the act, justified by the necessity of self-defence, must be limited by that necessity, and kept clearly within it. It must be shown that admonition or remonstrance to the persons on board the Caroline was impracticable, or would have been unavailing; it must be shown that day-light could not be waited for; that there could be no attempt at discrimination between the innocent and the guilty; that it would not have been enough to seize and detain the vessel; but that there was a necessity, present and inevitable, for attacking her in the darkness of the night, while moored to the shore, and while unarmed men were asleep on board, killing some and wounding others, and then drawing her into the current, above the cataract, setting her on fire, and, careless to know whether there might not be in her the innocent with the guilty, or the living with the dead, committing her to a fate which fills the imagination with horror. A necessity for all this, the Government of The United States cannot believe to have existed.

Jennings, *supra* note 105, at 89 (quoting Daniel Webster).

Therefore, quite aside from the trinity of self-defense criteria, *Caroline* supports the principle that a state suffering attack from non-state actors in another may, after seeking assistance from that state (assuming the requested state is capable of doing so), enter its territory for the limited purpose of preventing further attacks, although its actions must be necessary and proportional. State practice seems guardedly consistent. Objections to such limited cases as have occurred are usually attributable to political, vice normative, motivations. Of course, in fairness, the same could be said regarding the relative absence of criticism when penetrating the territory of ostracized states, such as Afghanistan, in operations against organizations which enjoy no consequential support from members of the international community, such as al Qaeda. The better interpretation, however, is that, as a general matter, state practice, beginning with the *Caroline* case, supports the approach posited.

Do US and coalition operations in Afghanistan comport with this standard? Recall the Security Council's pre and post 9/11 demands that the Taliban cease allowing territory they controlled to be used as a terrorist base and that they cooperate in bringing Osama bin Laden and al Qaeda to justice. Recall also the US demands that the Taliban unconditionally surrender bin Laden and other al Qaeda leaders and grant the United States sufficient access to terrorist bases to ensure their inoperability. In reply, the Taliban regime first stated it wished to see the evidence linking bin Laden to the 9/11 attacks.[108] As the likelihood of US strikes drew closer, the Taliban indicated that they had Osama bin Laden and might be willing to negotiate, possibly about turning him over to a third country. The United States again stated that only an unconditional surrender of bin Laden and other al Qaeda leaders would suffice.[109] After the coalition attacks commenced, the Taliban renewed the offer. However, the US administration maintained its no-negotiation stance.[110]

Were the US demands, particularly in that they were unconditional, sufficient? It might be argued that no demand at all was necessary, for on multiple occasions the Security Council had insisted that the Taliban comply with the

---

108. Murphy, *Contemporary Practice 2002*, *supra* note 39, at 244. The situation caused divisions within the Taliban and Afghan religious leadership. Clearly, unanimity did not exist as to how to respond to the US demands. John F. Burns, *Afghans Coaxing bin Laden, But U.S. Rejects Clerics' Bid*, N.Y. TIMES, Sep. 21, 2001, at A1.
109. Murphy, *Contemporary Practice 2002*, *supra* note 39, at 244.
110. Elisabeth Bumiller, *President Rejects Offer By Taliban For Negotiations*, N.Y. TIMES, Oct. 15, 2001, at A1.

measures sought by the United States. Consider, for instance, the following unambiguous language in Security Council Resolution 1333 (2000):

> [The Security Council] *Demands* . . . that the Taliban comply without further delay with the demand of the Security Council in paragraph 2 of resolution 1267 (1999) that requires the Taliban to turn over Usama bin Laden to appropriate authorities in a country where he has been indicted, or to appropriate authorities in a country where he will be returned to such a country, or to appropriate authorities in a country where he will be arrested and effectively brought to justice;
>
> *Demands further* that the Taliban should act swiftly to close up all camps where terrorists are trained within the territory under its control, and calls for the confirmation of such closures by the United Nations, inter alia, through information made available to the United Nations by Member States in accordance with paragraph 19 below and through such other means as are necessary to assure compliance with this resolution. . . .[111]

Extended non-compliance with the Security Council demands arguably provided a good faith basis for determining that further exhortations would prove fruitless. However, the Council's insistence was made in the context of cooperative law enforcement (albeit in the face of a threat to international peace and security) rather than self-defense. Therefore, the most defensible position is that while non-compliance strengthened the political case for action by the Security Council under Chapter VII, a separate demand was required for action by a state pursuant to the right to self-defense.

As noted, the United States made one. Unconditionality was certainly reasonable in the circumstances. The United States had just suffered a horrendous terrorist attack, with every reason to believe more were imminent. The Taliban request for evidence of al Qaeda's complicity might have made sense but for the previous Security Council resolutions, which clearly rendered the request superfluous. Moreover, the United States government, which had been conducting talks with the Taliban since 1996 over the presence of al Qaeda in Afghanistan, had previously provided evidence of al Qaeda responsibility for the 1998 bombings of the two US embassies in East Africa—at the request of Taliban officials.[112] The provision of that evidence, and the continuing talks, had no discernible affect on the Taliban's continued harboring of the terrorist organization.

---

111. S. C. Res. 1333, U.N. SCOR, 55th Sess., U.N. Doc. S/1333/(2000).
112. UK Press Release, *supra* note 9, at paras. 14–15.

Additionally, unless the Taliban regime controlled al Qaeda absolutely, which it did not, post 9/11 negotiations would merely have extended the window of vulnerability for the United States. If the right to self-defense was to be meaningful in these circumstances, the United States needed to act as quickly as possible. This meant that either the Taliban should have complied with the demands promptly or acknowledged they lacked the capability to do so and stood aside as the United States entered Afghanistan to engage al Qaeda.

In other words, the adequacy of a request to the state in which terrorists are located, as well as the sufficiency of the response thereto, must be assessed contextually. Have there been prior requests? For what? What is the nature of relations between the requesting and requested state? Between the terrorist group and the state in which it is located? What capability does the requested state have to counter or control the terrorists? What is its track record in doing so? What are the nature and the imminency of the threat by the terrorists against the requesting state? Under the circumstances, the US decision to attack al Qaeda on October 7th, despite Taliban quibbling over the US request to turn over members of the organization, was reasonable and legally defensible.

There are two other circumstances in which it is unquestionable that one state can enter the territory of another to conduct defensive counter-terrorist operations. The first is upon invitation, though any such operation would have to comply with the relevant provisions of human rights and humanitarian law, as well as any conditions imposed by the host state.[113] Obviously, that did not occur in the case of Afghanistan. More problematic is the situation in which the terrorist group acts on behalf of the state such that its attacks can be deemed those of the state itself. As in traditional armed attacks by a state actor, the sole question regarding the penetration of the attacker's territory is whether cross-border operations are necessary, proportional and in response to an armed attack. To the extent the state could be attacked in self-defense, so too can the terrorist group that actually executed the armed attack. The issue of Taliban support for al Qaeda is considered in the following section.

Summarized, the campaign against al Qaeda in Afghanistan is a legitimate exercise of the right to individual and collective self-defense. The right extends to armed attacks from whatever source, the 9/11 attacks met the threshold requirement of being "armed," crossing into Afghanistan was appropriate

---

113. On the conduct of forces in another country, see THE HANDBOOK OF THE LAW OF VISITING FORCES (Dieter Fleck ed., 2001).

once the Taliban failed to police the territory they controlled, the attacks were necessary and proportionate, and they occurred in the face of an imminent, credible continuation of an al Qaeda campaign that had been underway for a period measured in years.

Operations Against the Taliban

In his address to a Joint Session of Congress on 20 September, President Bush uttered his ominous warning that "[e]ither you are with us, or you are with the terrorists. From this day forward, any nation that continues to harbor or support terrorism will be regarded by the United States as a hostile regime."[114] When the attacks began, the United States cited the Taliban's decision to "allow the parts of Afghanistan that it controls to be used by [al Qaeda] as a base of operation," a policy which the Taliban refused to alter despite repeated entreaties to do so, as justification for their actions.[115] It should be noted that in June 2001 the United States had already warned the Taliban regime that it would be held responsible for any terrorist acts committed by terrorists that it was sheltering.[116]

The United Kingdom has released the most extensive information to date regarding the relationship between al Qaeda and the Taliban.[117] Al Qaeda provided troops, weapons and financing to the Taliban for its conflict with the Northern Alliance. The organization was also reportedly involved in the planning and execution of Taliban operations, assisted in training Taliban forces, and had representatives assigned to the Taliban command and control structure. Additionally, al Qaeda was a source of "infrastructure assistance and humanitarian aid."[118] In return, the Taliban granted al Qaeda safe haven and a base for its terrorist training camps; essentially, al Qaeda enjoyed free rein to do as it pleased in Taliban controlled territory. Further, the two groups cooperated closely in the drug trade, with the Taliban providing security for al Qaeda's drug stockpiles.[119] Was this relationship such that conducting

---

114. President George W. Bush, Address Before a Joint Session of the Congress, *supra* note 16, at 1349.
115. US Letter, *supra* note 22.
116. UK Press Release, *supra* note 9, para. 16.
117. *See id.* generally. *See also* the update to the UK press release. United Kingdom Press Release, 10 Downing Street Newsroom, *Responsibility for the Terrorist Atrocities in the United States*, Nov. 14, 2001, *available at* http://www.pm.gov.uk/news.asp?NewsId=3025 (Jun. 18, 2002).
118. UK Press Release, *supra* note 9, para. 12.
119. *Id.*, para. 13.

military operations against the Taliban on October 7th was a legitimate exercise of the use of force by the United States and United Kingdom?

State Responsibility. Unfortunately, there has been much confusion surrounding the relationship between Taliban obligations and the attacks mounted against them on October 7th. In the discussion of self-defense against al Qaeda, it was noted that the Taliban had a duty to keep their territory from being used as a base of terrorist operations. Failure to comply with that duty in part justified penetrating Afghan territory when attacking al Qaeda, albeit only to conduct operations against al Qaeda. If the Taliban were incapable of stopping al Qaeda, then they would incur no responsibility for their failure to address the situation.

On the other hand, if capable, but unwilling, the Taliban would be responsible for their failure under the international law of state responsibility.[120] The duty to desist from assisting terrorists in any way is manifest. In 1996 the General Assembly articulated this duty in the Declaration on the Strengthening of International Security. Specifically, it stated that:

> States, guided by the purposes and principles of the Charter of the United Nations and other relevant rules of international law, must refrain from organizing, instigating, assisting or participating in terrorist acts in territories of other States, or from acquiescing in or encouraging activities within their territories directed towards the commission of such acts.[121]

In doing so, it echoed earlier exhortations in the 1970 Friendly Relations Declaration[122] and its 1965 progenitor, Resolution 2131 (1965).[123] Similar

---

120. On the issue of state responsibility, see Gregory Townsend, *State Responsibility for Acts of De Facto Agents*, 14 ARIZ. J. INT'L & COMP. L. 635 (1997); Ian Brownlie, *International Law and the Activities of Bands*, 7 INT'L & COMP. L. QTRLY 712 (1958).
121. Declaration on Measures to Eliminate International Terrorism, G.A. Res. 49/60, U.N. GAOR, 6th Comm., 49th Sess., 84th plen. mtg., U.N. Doc. A/49/743 (1994); Declaration to Supplement the 1994 Declaration on Measures to Eliminate International Terrorism, G.A. Res. 51/210, U.N. GAOR, 6th Comm., 51st Sess., 88th plen. mtg., U.N. Doc. A/51/631 (1996).
122. "Every state has the duty to refrain from organizing, instigating, assisting or participating in acts of civil strife or terrorist acts in another state or acquiescing in organized activities within its territory directed towards the commission of such acts, when the acts referred to in the present paragraph involve a threat or use of force." Declaration on Friendly Relations, *supra* note 88, prin. 1.
123. "No state shall organize, assist, foment, finance, incite, or tolerate subversive, terrorist or armed activities directed toward the violent overthrow of another regime...." G.A. Resolution 2131, U.N. GAOR, 20th Sess., Supp. No. 14, at 107, U.N. Doc. A/6221 (1965).

prohibitions can be found in Article 2(4) of the International Law Commission's 1954 Draft Code of Offenses against the Peace and Security of Mankind.[124]

Case law supports these declarations. Most notably, in the *Corfu Channel* case the International Court of Justice held that "every State has an obligation to not knowingly allow its territory to be used in a manner contrary to the rights of other States."[125] *Corfu Channel* involved an incident in which two British destroyers struck mines in Albanian waters while transiting the Corfu Strait in 1946. Though the evidence was insufficient to demonstrate that the Albanians laid the mines, the Court nevertheless held that they had the obligation to notify shipping of the danger posed by the mines. Albania's failure to do so represented an internationally wrongful act entailing the international responsibility of Albania. Other case law and arbitral decisions are in accord.[126]

Applying the *Corfu Channel* principle to the case of terrorism, states that permit their territory to be used as a base of operations for terrorist acts against other countries have committed an international wrong. There is no question that Taliban acquiescence in allowing Afghan territory to be used by al Qaeda,

---

124. The organization, or the encouragement of the organization, by the authorities of a State, of armed bands within its territory or any other territory for incursions into the territory of another state, or the toleration of the organization of such bands in its own territory, or the toleration of the use by such armed bands of its territory as a base of operations or as a point of departure for incursions into the territory of another State, as well as direct participation in or support of such incursions.

Draft Code of Offenses Against the Peace and Security of Mankind, art. 2(4), *available at* http://www.un.org/law/ilc/texts/offfra.htm (Jun. 18, 2002).

125. Corfu Channel Case (Merits), 1949 I.C.J. Rep. 4, 22.

126. *See* discussion in JAMES CRAWFORD, THE INTERNATIONAL LAW COMMISSION'S ARTICLES ON STATE RESPONSIBILITY: INTRODUCTION, TEXT AND COMMENTARIES 77–85 (2002). Article 2 of the International Law Commission's Articles on State Responsibility (adopted by the Commission in 2001) provides that "There is an internationally wrongful act of a State when conduct consisting of an act or omission: (a) is attributable to the State under international law; and (b) constitutes a breach of an international obligation of the State." International Law Commission, Articles on State Responsibility, *reprinted in id.* at 61. These elements have been articulated in a number of tribunals. Among those referenced specifically by Professor Crawford are: Phosphates in Morocco, Preliminary Objections, 1938, P.C.I.J., Series A/B, No. 74, p. 10; United States Diplomatic and Consular Staff in Tehran, I.C.J. Reports 1980, p. 3; Military and Paramilitary Activities in and against Nicaragua (Nicaragua v. US), Merits, I.C.J. Reports 1986, p. 14, 117–118, para. 226; Gabcikovo-Nagymaros Project (Hungary/Slovakia), I.C.J. Reports 1997, p. 7, 54, para. 78.

assuming arguendo that their conduct is attributable to the "State" of Afghanistan,[127] created responsibility under international law for that wrongful act. Does this responsibility justify the October 7th attacks by the United States and the United Kingdom?

Despite occasionally loose discussion of the subject in the aftermath of 9/11, the existence of state responsibility for an international wrong does not justify the use of force in self-help to remedy the wrong. Traditional reparations for an international wrong come in the form of restitution, compensation or satisfaction.[128] It is also permissible to take countermeasures in response to an internationally wrongful act.[129] Countermeasures are "measures which would otherwise be contrary to the international obligations of the injured State vis-à-vis the responsible State if they were not taken by the former in response to an internationally wrongful act by the latter in order to procure cessation and reparation."[130] Various requirements, such as the existence of an on-going wrong,[131] proportionality of the countermeasure to the injury suffered,[132] and a call on the state committing the wrong to comply with its obligations[133] apply to the taking of countermeasures.

But it is generally agreed that countermeasures employing armed force are prohibited.[134] Article 50 of the Articles on State Responsibility specifically provides that "Countermeasures shall not affect . . . the obligation to refrain from the threat or use of force as embodied in the Charter of the United Nations."[135] This provision tracks the holding in *Corfu Channel*. There the

---

127. The Commentary to the ILC Articles on State Responsibility describes a "state" as "a real organized entity, a legal person to act under international law." Crawford, *supra* note 126, at 82 (para. 5 of commentary to art. 2).
128. Articles on State Responsibility, *supra* note 126, arts. 34–37. Restitution is reestablishing "the situation which existed before the wrongful act was committed" (art. 35); compensation is covering any financially assessable damage not made good by restitution (art. 36); satisfaction is "an acknowledgement of the breach, an expression of regret, a formal apology or another appropriate modality" that responds to shortfalls in restitution and compensation when making good the injury caused (art. 37).
129. *Id.*, art. 49.1.
130. Crawford, *supra* note 126, at 281.
131. Articles on State Responsibility, *supra* note 126, art. 52.3(a).
132. *Id.*, art. 51.
133. *Id.*, art. 52.1.
134. Certain countermeasures employing force are permissible. An example would be sending agents into a state to apprehend a terrorist who that state wrongfully refused to extradite. Mary Ellen O'Connell, *Lawful Responses to Terrorism*, JURIST, *available at* http://jurist.law.pitt.edu/forum/forumnew30.htm (Jun. 18, 2002).
135. Articles on State Responsibility, *supra* note 126, art. 50.1(a).

International Court of Justice held that Albania's failure to comply with its responsibility did not justify the British minesweeping of the Strait, an act that therefore constituted a violation of Albanian sovereignty. Thus, breach of the obligation not to allow Afghanistan to be used as a base for terrorist activities did not, alone, justify use of force against the Taliban.

An identical analysis would apply in assessing whether the actions of al Qaeda in conducting the 9/11 (and other) attacks can be attributed to the Taliban under the law of state responsibility. The International Law Commission's Articles on State Responsibility set forth the standards for imputing an armed group's acts to a state for the purpose of assessing state responsibility. Two are relevant here.

Article 8 provides that the "conduct of a person or group shall be considered an act of a State under international law if the person or group of persons is in fact acting on the instructions of, or under the direction or control of, that State in carrying out the conduct."[136] This was the issue in the *Nicaragua* case, where Nicaragua argued that the United States was responsible under international law for violations of humanitarian law committed by the Contras, the anti-Sandinista rebel group it supported. After finding that the United States had provided "subsidies and other support", the Court held that:

> United States participation, even if preponderant or decisive in the financing, organizing, training, supplying and equipping of the contras, the selection of its military or paramilitary targets, and the planning of the whole of its operation, is still insufficient in itself, . . . for the purpose of attributing to the United States the acts committed by the contras in the course of their military or paramilitary operations in Nicaragua. All the forms of United States participation mentioned above, and even the general control by the respondent state over a force with a high degree of dependency on it, would not in themselves mean, without further evidence, that the United States directed or enforced the perpetration of the acts contrary to human rights and humanitarian law alleged by the applicant State. . . . For this conduct to give rise to legal responsibility of the United States, it would in principle have to be proved that that State had effective control of the military or paramilitary operations in the course of which the alleged violations were committed.[137]

Aside from the Contras, certain individuals, not of US nationality, were paid by the United States and directly instructed and supervised by US

---
136. *Id.*, art. 8.
137. Nicaragua, *supra* note 60, para. 115.

military and intelligence personnel. For instance, they carried out such operations as mining Nicaraguan ports. The Court easily found their actions imputable to the United States, either because they were paid and instructed by the US, and were therefore agents thereof, or because US personnel had "participated in the planning, direction, support and execution" of particular operations.[138]

The evidence released to date regarding Taliban ties to al Qaeda does not suggest that al Qaeda was under the direction or control of the Taliban in conducting the 9/11 attacks or any other acts of international terrorism. In fact, some have suggested precisely the opposite—that it was the Taliban that was dependent on al Qaeda, both financially and militarily. While that may be a more accurate characterization, such dependency bears little direct connection to al Qaeda's international terrorist campaign.

Article 11 sets forth a second possibly relevant standard. It provides that "[c]onduct which is not attributable to a State under the preceding articles shall nevertheless be considered an act of that State under international law if and to the extent that the State acknowledges and adopts the conduct as its own."[139] This principle lay at the core of the International Court of Justice's *Diplomatic and Consular Staff* case.[140] There the Court held that the Iranian government violated its responsibility to prevent the 1979 seizure by militant students of the US Embassy in Tehran and subsequently failed to meet its obligation to act promptly in ending the seizure.[141] Following the takeover, the Iranian government, including its leader, the Ayatollah Khomeni, expressed approval of the student actions. Indeed, in a decree issued within two weeks of the seizure, Khomeni declared that "the hostages would remain as they were until the U.S. had handed over the former Shah for trial" and that "the noble Iranian nation will not give permission for the release . . . until the American Government acts according to the wish of the nation."[142] For the International Court of Justice, "[t]he approval given . . . by the Ayatollah Khomeni and other organs of the Iranian state, and the decision to perpetuate them, translated continuing occupation of the Embassy and detention of the hostages into acts of that State."[143]

---

138. *Id.*, para. 86.
139. Articles of State Responsibility, *supra* note 126, art. 11.
140. United States Diplomatic and Consular Staff in Tehran (Iran v. USA), 1980 I.C.J. 3.
141. According to the court, Iranian authorities were "fully aware of their obligations to protect the premises of the U.S. Embassy and its diplomatic and consular staff from any attack [,] . . . had the means at their disposal to perform their obligations [but,] . . . completely failed to comply." *Id.*, para. 68.
142. *Id.*, para. 73.
143. *Id.*, para. 74.

Therefore, while the Iranian government breached its own obligations when the Embassy was taken, it became responsible for the seizure itself (or at least the continuing occupation thereof) when it supported the student actions and took steps to continue the occupation.

Are the Taliban responsible for the 9/11 attacks under the principle of attribution of state responsibility? The level of Taliban support falls far below that of the Iranian government in the Embassy case. It did not express open and public support for the attacks, nor did it ever assume control of the terrorist campaign in the way that the Iranian government took control over release of the US hostages. Further, although its military did conduct combat operations against US and coalition forces in concert with al Qaeda, that was only after October 7th, following air attacks on its own facilities and personnel.

By either of these two standards of state responsibility, it is difficult to attribute al Qaeda's terrorist attacks to the Taliban. That said, any such assessment is fact-dependant; unfortunately, many of the relevant facts tying the Taliban to al Qaeda and vice versa remain either unreleased or as yet undiscovered. However, what must be remembered in discussions over the state responsibility of the Taliban is that the existence of responsibility in the general sense is a question quite distinct from that of whether an armed attack has been committed by that state, so as to justify self-defense by the state attacked. This is a very fine point. The principles of state responsibility determine when a state may be held responsible for an act and thus subject to reparations or countermeasures. But as noted, forcible countermeasures are not an acceptable remedy for violations of state responsibility. That is so whether the issue is harboring a terrorist group or being responsible for an act committed by one.

Nevertheless, certain acts that generate state responsibility may at the same time justify a violent response. Although forcible countermeasures are impermissible to make whole the victim or cause the wrongdoer to desist in breaching an international obligation, the application of force against the

---

144. This reality explains why the prohibition on forcible countermeasures is reasonable; the ban is compensated for in those cases where one might most want to engage in them—when victimized by an armed attack—by the existence of the right to self-defense. Conversely, the various limits on self-defense are compensated for by the fact that once the need for self-defense vanishes, the state that committed the wrongful attack remains liable for the consequences under the law of state responsibility. The classic example is the Iraqi invasion of Kuwait in 1990. In S. C. Res. 681, U.N. SCOR, 46th Sess., U.N. Doc. S/681/(1991), the Security Council found that "Iraq . . . is liable under international law for any direct loss, damage, including environmental damage and the depletion of natural resources, or injury to foreign Governments, nationals and corporations, as a result of Iraq's unlawful invasion and occupation of Kuwait." It subsequently established the United Nations Compensation Commission to handle claims in S. C. Res. 692, 46th Sess., U.N. Doc. S/692/(1991).

wrongdoer may be justified as an act of self-defense in the face of an imminent or on-going armed attack.[144] Restated in the context of the present case, the proper query in assessing the lawfulness of attacking the Taliban on October 7th is *not* whether the Taliban are in any way responsible under principles of state responsibility for the acts of 9/11. Rather, it is whether or not the Taliban can be determined to have committed the armed attack under the law of self-defense.

Self-Defense. No evidence has been released to suggest that Taliban forces played a direct role in the attacks of 9/11 or any other al Qaeda operation. Was the Taliban relationship with al Qaeda nevertheless such that the terrorist acts constructively amounted to a Taliban *armed attack*?

The precise degree of association between a non-state organization and state sponsor necessary for attribution of an armed attack to the state is a matter of some controversy.[145] However, on September 11th, the most widely accepted legal standard on the issue was that set forth in the *Nicaragua* case. That case was discussed earlier vis-à-vis the nature of an armed attack, as well as state responsibility. However, the International Court of Justice also addressed the issue of imputing an armed attack to a state.

In the case, the United States argued that Nicaragua had conducted an armed attack against El Salvador through support to guerillas attempting to overthrow the El Salvadoran government. This being so, US activities directed against Nicaragua were, so the argument went, legitimate exercises of the right of collective self-defense with El Salvador. The Court rejected the assertion, setting a high standard for attributing the actions of a non-state actor to a state in the context of an armed attack.

> There appears now to be general agreement on the nature of the acts which can be treated as constituting armed attacks. In particular, it may be considered to be agreed that an armed attack must be understood as including not merely action by regular armed forces across an international border, but also "the sending by or on behalf of a State of armed bands, groups, irregulars or mercenaries, which carry out acts of armed force against another State of such gravity as to amount to" (inter alia) an actual armed attack conducted by regular forces, "or its substantial involvement therein". This description,

---

145. For instance, Oscar Schachter has argued "When a government provides weapons, technical advice, transportation, aid and encouragement to terrorists on a substantial scale, it is not unreasonable to conclude that an armed attack is imputable to the government." Oscar Schachter, *The Lawful Use of Force by a State Against Terrorists in Another Country, reprinted in* HENRY H. HAN, TERRORISM AND POLITICAL VIOLENCE 250 (1993). *See also* Alberto Coll, *The Legal and Moral Adequacy of Military Responses to Terrorism*, 81 PROC. AM. SOC. INT'L L. 297 (1987).

contained in Article 3, paragraph (g), of the Definition of Aggression annexed to General Assembly resolution 3314(XXIX), may be taken to reflect customary international law.[146]

By this standard, the state to which the acts are to be attributed must be "substantially involved" in an operation that is so grave it would amount to an armed attack if carried out by regular members of its armed forces. Recall from the earlier discussion of the holding that armed attacks are measured in terms of their scale and effects, and that the Court specifically held that the provision of "weapons or logistical or other support" was insufficient. Further, to constitute an armed attack by the state, that state must have "sent" the group into action or it must be acting on the state's behalf. These criteria resemble the requirement under state responsibility that the group in question act on the instructions of, or under the direction or control of, the state to which responsibility is to be imputed. In this sense, the principles of state responsibility can assist in determining whether specific conduct is an armed attack.

It should be noted that the Court was not unanimous in its findings. Most notably, Judge Stephen Schwebel of the United States dissented, arguing that there had been an armed attack:

> The delictual acts of the Nicaraguan government have not been confined to provision of very large quantities of arms, munitions and supplies (an act which of itself might be viewed as not tantamount to an armed attack); Nicaragua (and Cuba) have joined with the Salvadoran rebels in the organization, planning and training for their acts of insurgency; and Nicaragua has provided the Salvadoran insurgents with command-and-control facilities, bases, communications and sanctuary, which have enabled the leadership of the Salvadoran insurgency to operate from Nicaraguan territory. Under both customary and conventional international law, that scale of Nicaraguan subversive activity not only constitutes unlawful intervention in the affairs of El Salvador; it is cumulatively tantamount to an armed attack upon El Salvador.[147]

What seems to run through both the Court's and Judge Schwebel's position is that the state must at least exercise significant, perhaps determinative, influence over the group's decision-making, as well as play a meaningful role in the specific operations at hand, before an armed attack will be imputed to it. The facts asserted by Judge Schwebel suggest that Nicaragua not only provided the means to conduct operations against El Salvador, but it did so in a

---

146. Nicaragua, *supra* note 60, at 195.
147. *Id.*, (Schwebel dissent) at 258–259, para. 6.

manner that would allow operations it helped plan to be mounted. Further, by organizing and planning the actions, Nicaragua occupied a central position in the decision-making hierarchy. By contrast, the Court focused almost exclusively, as it did regarding the issue of state responsibility, on the extent of control the state has over the specific actions of the group.

There seems to be little evidence that the Taliban "sent" al Qaeda against any particular targets or even that they provided the materiel and logistic support that the *Nicaragua* Court found insufficient to amount to an armed attack. In essence, the key contribution made by the Taliban was granting al Qaeda a relatively secure base of operations. By the classic *Nicaragua* test, or even the lower standard advocated by Judge Schwebel, it would be difficult to argue that the Taliban, through complicity with al Qaeda, launched an armed attack against the United States or any other country. Harboring terrorists is simply insufficient for attribution of an armed attack to the harboring state. Rather, the situation appears to have been a marriage of convenience—convenient for al Qaeda's conduct of external terrorist acts and convenient for the Taliban's control over territory within Afghanistan and their battles with internal enemies.

One further judgment of relevance is that rendered by the Appeals Chamber of the International Criminal Tribunal for the Former Yugoslavia in *Prosecutor v. Tadic*. There the issue was whether acts of Bosnian Serb forces could be attributed to Yugoslavia. The Chamber held that the degree of control necessary for attribution would vary according to the factual circumstances of the case. Refusing to apply the *Nicaragua* approach in its entirety, the Chamber adopted a standard of "overall control going beyond the mere financing and equipping of such forces and involving also participation in the planning and supervision of military operations" for acts by an "organized and hierarchically structured group."[148] It felt the dual requirements of effective control of the group and the exercise of control over a specific operation were excessive, except in the cases of individuals acting alone or disorganized groups.

By way of caveat, it must be noted that *Tadic* involved neither state responsibility nor the criteria for attribution of an armed attack. Rather, the issue was whether the Bosnian Serb actions could be attributed to Yugoslavia such that there was an international armed conflict. The existence of such a conflict was a prerequisite for applicability of various aspects of humanitarian law to

---

148. International Criminal Tribunal for Yugoslavia, Case IT-94-1, Prosecutor v. Tadic, 38 I.L.M. 1518 (1999), at paras. 120 & 145.

the defendants before the tribunal. Because there was no jurisprudence on the issue, the Chamber turned to the law of state responsibility by way of analogy.

Again, and though the opinion is only relevant by analogy to the issue at hand, it would appear that Taliban relations with al Qaeda did not rise to this level. Thus, al Qaeda actions do not appear imputable to the Taliban as a matter of state responsibility, as an armed attack or in the context of having caused an international armed conflict (although no doubt exists that its harboring of the terrorists was an internationally wrongful act). It must be emphasized, however, that this assessment is entirely fact-dependant, and that there is a relative paucity of reliable open-source information on the subject.

To summarize, al Qaeda conducted an armed attack against the United States on September 11th. That attack activated the right of self-defense, one that continues as long as the terrorist campaign against the United States can reasonably be characterized as ongoing. Once attacked, the United States properly demanded that the Taliban turn over al Qaeda leaders and allow the United States to verify that no further operations were ongoing from the country. When the Taliban failed to comply, the United States and its partners acquired the right to enter Afghanistan for the limited purpose of putting an end to al Qaeda operations. Had it done so, and had the Taliban interfered, the interference would have amounted to a separate attack of its own. However, from the evidence available, it does not appear that the Taliban were sufficiently entwined with al Qaeda terrorist operations for the 9/11 attacks to be imputed to it, thereby justifying the immediate use of force against the Taliban. Were the attacks against the Taliban therefore illegal? That is a very uncertain matter.

The Evolving Standard of Self-Defense

There is little doubt that the response to the tragic events of September 11th has tested accepted understandings of the international law regarding the use of force. Many would dispute certain of the legal conclusions set forth above—that a terrorist group can mount an "armed attack"; that a series of terrorist attacks can be treated as a single on-going attack; or that the United States and the United Kingdom were justified in forcibly crossing into Afghan territory on October 7th. Indeed, this article has concluded that use of force directly against the Taliban is difficult to fit within traditional understandings of attribution of an armed attack.

Such unease has led some to pronounce the traditional normative system dead in fact, if not in law. For instance, Michael Glennon has opined that:

> the rules concerning the use of force are no longer regarded as obligatory by states. Between 1945 and 1999, two-thirds of the members of the United Nations—126 states out of 189—fought 291 interstate conflicts in which over 22 million people were killed. This series of conflicts was capped by the Kosovo campaign in which nineteen NATO democracies representing 780 million people flagrantly violated the Charter. The international system has come to subsist in a parallel universe of two systems, one de jure, the other de facto. The de jure system consists of illusory rules that would govern the use of force among states in a platonic world of forms, a world that does not exist. The de facto system consists of actual state practice in a real world, a world in which states weigh costs against benefits in regular disregard of the rules solemnly proclaimed in the all-but-ignored de jure system. The decaying de jure catechism is overly schematized and scholastic, disconnected from state behavior, and unrealistic in its aspirations for state conduct.
>
> The upshot is that the Charter's use-of-force regime has all but collapsed. . . . I suggest that Article 51, as authoritatively interpreted by the International Court of Justice, cannot guide responsible U.S. policy-makers in the U.S. war against terrorism in Afghanistan or elsewhere.[149]

Professor Glennon's thoughtful analysis exaggerates the de jure-de facto divide. In fact, what has been happening over the past half-century is a regular evolution in the global community's understanding of the use of force regime. This evolution has been, as it always is and always must be, responsive to the changing circumstances in which international law operates. Practice does not contradict law so much as it informs law as to the global community's normative expectations. It is a phenomenon that is particularly important in international law because of the absence of highly developed constitutive entities and processes.

Consider the changing context in which use of force norms have operated. In the immediate aftermath of the Second World War an understandable preference for collective remedies to threats to international peace and security, remedies that would be executed through inclusive international institutions, emerged—hence the United Nations and its restrictive use of force regime. With the outbreak of the Cold War, and its resulting bipolarity, that system fell into desuetude as the veto power of the permanent five members

---

149. Glennon, *supra* note 4, at 540–41.

[P-5] rendered the Security Council impotent. States were therefore compelled to engage in various forms of coercive self-help to perform tasks that would otherwise have been the preferred prerogative of the Council.[150]

The demise of the Cold War removed two contextually determined constraining influences on the use of force. First, the Security Council was reinvigorated because the zero-sum paradigm of the Cold War no longer held; for the first time in nearly 50 years, the P-5 could share common cause (or at least not find themselves inevitably in opposition). This meant that the Council could assume its intended role in the maintenance of international peace and security. The Council promptly did so, authorizing one major international effort to counter aggression, the 1990–91 Gulf War, and multiple peace enforcement operations.

Second, the Cold War had imposed an implicit limitation on unilateral uses of force—that they not threaten the fragile peace between East and West. Thus, for example, whereas intervention was deemed inappropriate as a general matter during the Cold War (it risked sparking a broader conflict), intervention within a zone of influence appeared more palatable (or as "the other fellow's business"). With this second constraint removed, states today are more willing to accept unilateral uses of force, as there is less chance of spillover effects (as reflected by Operation ALLIED FORCE).

What happened is that the operational code regarding the use of force shifted with the emergence of new geo-political circumstances. Circumstances determine the viability of normative strategies for advancing shared

---

150. For instance, Michael Reisman has identified nine basic categories of unilateral uses of force that enjoyed a significant degree of community support: "self-defense, which has been construed quite broadly; self-determination and decolonization; humanitarian intervention; intervention by the military instrument within spheres of influence and critical defense zones; treaty-sanctioned interventions within the territory of another state; use of the military instrument for the gathering of evidence in international proceedings; use of the military instrument to enforce international judgments; and counter measures, such as reprisals and retorsions." W. Michael Reisman, *Criteria for the Lawful Use of Force in International Law*, 10 YALE J. INT'L L. 279, 281 (1985). *See also* W. Michael Reisman, *Article 2(4): The Use of Force in Contemporary International Law*, PROC. AM. SOC. INT'L L. LAW 74, 79–84 (1984–85); W. Michael Reisman, *War Powers: The Operational Code of Competence*, 83 AM. J. INT'L L. 777 (1989).

community values.[151] It is not that new law emerges or that old law fades away, as much as it is that the understanding of the precise parameters of the law evolves as it responds to fresh challenges or leverages new opportunities. That international law is understood in light of the circumstances in which it finds itself is a strength, not a weakness.

This is certainly true regarding responses to terrorism. During much of the Cold War, the pressing problem of violence outside the classic state-on-state paradigm was guerilla warfare by insurgents against a government. Both sides had their clients, whether states or rebel groups, and in many cases the conflicts were proxy in nature. The geopolitical and normative appeal of proxy wars was that they tended to facilitate avoidance of a direct superpower clash. Thus, as demonstrated in *Nicaragua*, a very high threshold was set for attributing rebel acts to their state sponsors or for characterizing assistance to a rebel group as an "armed attack" legitimizing a victim state's forceful response. This was a very practical approach. The bipolar superpowers were surely going to engage in such activity regardless of the normative limits thereon, so a legal scheme that avoided justifying a forceful response by the other side contributed to the shared community value of minimizing higher order violence. The result was creation of a legal fiction that states that were clearly party to a conflict, were not.

To some extent, this paradigm was illustrated by community reactions to counter-terrorist operations. Consider Operation EL DORADO CANYON, the 1986 air strikes against terrorist and Libyan government facilities by US forces in response to the bombing of the La Belle discothèque in Berlin. The Libyan leader, Muammar el Qadhafi, had previously praised terrorist actions.

---

151. Such as physical survival and security for individuals and the tangible or intangible objects on which they rely, human dignity, social progress and quality of life, and "the right of peoples to shape their own political community." These aims derive from those expressed in the Preamble to the UN Charter:

> To save succeeding generations from the scourge of war, which twice in our life-time has brought untold sorrow to mankind, and to reaffirm faith in fundamental human rights, in the dignity and worth of the human person, in the equal rights of men and women and of nations large and small, and to establish conditions under which justice and respect for the obligations arising from treaties and other sources of international law can be maintained, and to promote social progress and better standards of life in larger freedom.

U.N. CHARTER, pmbl. The final aim was articulated in W. Michael Reisman, *Allocating Competences to Use Coercion in the Post-Cold War World: Practices, Conditions, and Prospects*, in LAW AND FORCE IN THE NEW INTERNATIONAL ORDER 26, 45 (Lori Damrosch & David J. Scheffer eds., 1991).

Moreover, in advance of the attacks the United States intercepted communications to the Libyan People's Bureau in West Berlin containing an order to attack Americans. Additional intercepts immediately preceding and following the La Belle bombing provided further evidence of Libyan complicity.[152]

Despite Libya's support of terrorism, international reaction to the US operation, which was justified on the basis of self-defense, was overwhelmingly negative.[153] Many of the United States' closest allies were critical, with the exceptions of the United Kingdom and Israel. The General Assembly passed a resolution condemning the action, while Secretary-General Javier Perez de Cuellar issued a statement "deploring" the "military action by one member state against another."[154] Viewed in the then-existing international security context, this was an unsurprising reaction. If state sponsorship of terrorism (a particularly ill-defined term given the bipolarity of the period) rose to the level of an armed attack justifying a forceful response in self-defense, then, given both sides' propensity to support opponents of their foe, the risk of a superpower affray grew.

However, the geopolitical context has changed dramatically in the last decade. Today there is but one superpower. Additionally, any antagonism that exists between it and other significant world players, such as Russia and China, is unlikely to erupt into open conflict. On the contrary, in many cases the former antagonists are cooperating against common threats, a trend illustrated by the recent creation of the NATO-Russia Council.[155]

Yet, as the likelihood of inter-state conflict receded, the relative importance of the terrorist threat grew correspondingly. For the major players on the world scene, it was no longer attack by another state that dominated strategic risk assessment, but rather the spread of instability, particularly through the mechanism of non-international armed conflict, and the related menace

---

152. Marian Nash Leich, *U.S. Practice* 80 AM. J. INT'L. L. 612, 633 (1986); Gregory Intoccia, *American Bombing of Libya: An International Legal Analysis*, 19 CASE WES. RES. J. INT'L L. 177 (1987); Jeffrey A. McCredie, *The April 14, 1986 Bombing of Libya: Act of Self-Defense or Reprisal?*, 19 CASE WES. RES. J. INT'L L. 215 (1987); David Turndorf, *The U.S. Raid on Libya: A Forceful Response to Terrorism*, 14 BROOK. J. INT'L L. 187 (1988).
153. See Reisman, *International Legal Responses*, supra note 98, 33–34, for a detailed description of the international reaction. See also Stuart G. Baker, *Comparing the 1993 U.S. Airstrike on Iraq to the 1986 Bombing of Libya: The New Interpretation of Article 51*, 24 GA. J. INT'L & COMP. L. 99 (1994).
154. *Israelis Praise It While Arabs Vow to Avenge It*, CHICAGO TRIBUNE, Apr. 16, 1986, at A9.
155. The NATO-Russia Council, approved in May 2002, is specifically tasked with countering terrorism. See Declaration by Heads of State and Government of NATO Member states and the Russian Federation, May 28, 2002, available at http://www.nato.int/docu/basictxt/b020528e.htm (Jun. 18, 2002).

of terrorism, either domestic or international. Not surprising, normative understandings shifted accordingly.

That shift was dramatically illustrated by the deafening silence, described at the outset of this article, over the issue of the lawfulness of the US and UK attacks of October 7th. Of course, some academic voices pointed to the normative faultlines in the operations, but academe was by no means united on the subject. Media criticism was rare, as was that by important non-governmental organizations. Most significantly, there was almost no state censure of the actions; on the contrary, states scrambled to join the cause.

This reaction was a logical continuation of a trend evident in two earlier post-Cold War responses to terrorism. In 1993, a plot to assassinate former President George Bush during a visit to Kuwait was foiled. Investigation suggested Iraqi government involvement. In response, the United States launched cruise missiles against Iraqi intelligence facilities. President Clinton justified the action in the following terms:

> This Thursday, Attorney General Reno and Director of Central Intelligence Woolsey gave me their findings. Based on their investigation there is compelling evidence that there was, in fact, a plot to assassinate former President Bush and that this plot, which included the use of a powerful bomb made in Iraq, was directed and pursued by the Iraqi intelligence service.
>
> These actions were directed against the Iraqi Government, which was responsible for the assassination plot. Saddam Hussein has demonstrated repeatedly that he will resort to terrorism or aggression if left unchecked. Our intent was to target Iraq's capacity to support violence against the United States and other nations and to deter Saddam Hussein from supporting such outlaw behavior in the future. Therefore, we directed our action against the facility associated with Iraq's support of terrorism, while making every effort to minimize the loss of innocent life.[156]

Of course, Iraq is a unique case given that an international armed conflict with the United States had occurred in 1991 (and arguably continues today). Nevertheless, the international community generally supported the strikes, or

---

156. President William Clinton, Address to the Nation on the Strike on Iraqi Intelligence Headquarters, 29 WEEKLY COMP. PRES. DOC. 1180–81 (Jun. 26, 1993). For an excellent analysis on the state of international law regarding counter-terrorism in the wake of the US strikes, see Robert J. Beck and Anthony Clark Arend, *"Don't Tread On Us": International Law and Forcible State Responses To Terrorism*, 12 WIS. INT'L L. J. 153 (1994). *See also* Robert F. Teplitz, *Taking Assassination Seriously: Did the United States Violate International Law in Responding to the Iraqi Plot to Kill George Bush*, 28 CORNELL INT'L L. J. 569 (1995).

at least muted its criticism thereof. Of the P-5, only China expressed concern. By contrast, support was voiced by, inter alia, the United Kingdom, Israel, Russia, Germany, Italy, Japan and South Korea, as well as the three Islamic states then sitting on the Security Council, Pakistan, Djibouti and Morocco. Egypt, Jordan and Iran criticized the attack, but on the basis of the civilian casualties caused.[157]

What is normatively remarkable is that the attack was somewhat questionable as a traditional exercise of self-defense, the legal basis asserted by the United States. It was in response to a plot that had already been foiled; indeed, some of those directly responsible for executing it were behind bars. Additionally, there was no assertion that this was but one phase in a continuing campaign by the Iraqis against the United States. Interestingly, the Security Council appeared more interested in the facts of the case, which it reportedly found sufficient to establish Iraqi involvement, than in the legal sufficiency of the US actions.[158]

A more viable argument legally would have been that an international armed conflict was still in existence between the United States and Iraq, punctuated only by a cease-fire agreement, the terms of which had been breached by Iraqi complicity in the plot. Curiously, that argument never surfaced. Instead, Article 51 was the sole legal justification asserted, an assertion that was relatively uncontested. It is also important to note that, aside from the strict legal stylization, the strikes were characterized as deterrent in purpose, a warning to Iraq to desist from any further involvement in acts of terrorism. This purpose has pervaded virtually every justification for striking back at terrorists over the past two decades.

The relative lack of criticism is all the more striking when contrasted with that generated by the 1986 attacks against Libya. Some 50 Americans were injured and two died in the La Belle Disco attacks. Further, prior to the attacks Qadhafi had threatened that the Libyans were "capable of exporting terrorism to the heart of America," a threat repeated on multiple occasions.[159] There was no reason at the time to believe the Libyans would desist in their support of terrorism against the United States; indeed, such support continued after

---

157. Baker, *supra* note 152, at 99–101.
158. On the extent to which the Council was satisfied with the US evidence, see *U.S. Photo Evidence Convinces the U.N.*, TORONTO STAR, June 28, 1993, at A13.
159. *Text of the State Department Report in Libya Under Qaddafi*, N.Y. TIMES, Jan. 9, 1986, at A6.

the strikes, most notably with the bombing of Pan Am 103 over Lockerbie.[160] Thus, the severity of the terrorist attack and the likelihood more were forthcoming make the Libya case more egregious than the plot against George Bush. Nevertheless, international reaction differed dramatically.

Further evidence of the trend came in 1998 in response to the bombings of the US embassies in Nairobi and Dar es Salaam. Almost 300 people, including 12 Americans, perished in the attacks, which were tied to Osama bin Laden and al Qaeda. In response, the United States launched cruise missile attacks against terrorist training camps in Afghanistan and a pharmaceutical plant suspected of involvement in chemical weapons production in Sudan. On the day they were conducted, President Clinton announced his rationale for ordering the attacks:

> First, because we have convincing evidence these groups played the key role in the Embassy bombings in Kenya and Tanzania; second, because these groups have executed terrorist attacks against Americans in the past; third, because we have compelling information that they were planning additional terrorist attacks against our citizens and others with the inevitable collateral casualties we saw so tragically in Africa; and fourth, because they are seeking to acquire chemical weapons and other dangerous weapons.[161]

Formal legal justification for the actions came in the required notification of the Security Council that actions in self-defense had been taken.

> These attacks were carried out only after repeated efforts to convince the Government of the Sudan and the Taliban regime in Afghanistan to shut these terrorist activities down and to cease their cooperation with the bin Laden organization. That organization has issued a series of blatant warnings that "strikes will continue from everywhere" against American targets, and we have convincing evidence that further such attacks were in preparation from these same terrorist facilities. The United States, therefore, had no choice but to use

---

160. The accused bombers were tried in Her Majesty's Advocate v. Abdelbaset ali Mohamed al Megrahi and Al Amin Khalifa Fhimah, Scot. High Court of Justiciary at Camp Zeist, Case No. 1475/99. Megrahi was found guilty and sentenced to life imprisonment in January 2001; the Court accepted the allegation that he was a member of Libya's Jamahariya Security Organization. In March 2002, Megrahi's appeal was denied. Abdelbaset Ali Mohmed Al Megrahi v. Her Majesty's Advocate, Appeal Court, High Court of Justiciary, Appeal No: C104/01. Negotiations over Libyan compensation for the victims' families have been ongoing for some time. *See, e.g.,* Rob Crilly, *Libya Denies Offer of (Pounds) 1.8bn Deal for Lockerbie Families,* THE HERALD (Glasgow), May 30, 2002, at 2.

161. President William Clinton, Remarks on Departure for Washington, D.C., from Martha's Vineyard, Massachusetts, 34 WEEKLY COMP. PRES. DOC. 1642 (Aug. 20, 1998).

armed force to prevent these attacks from continuing. In doing so, the United States has acted pursuant to the right of self defence confirmed by Article 51 of the Charter of the United Nations. The targets struck, and the timing and method of attack used, were carefully designed to minimize risks of collateral damage to civilians and to comply with international law, including the rules of necessity and proportionality.[162]

International reaction to the two strikes was telling. Although Iran, Iraq, Libya, Pakistan,[163] Russia and Yemen condemned them, Australia, France, Germany, Japan, Spain and the United Kingdom were supportive.[164] In other words, support or condemnation tended to track political alignment with the United States. More normatively significant is the difference in the reaction to the two strikes. The League of Arab States' Secretariat condemned the strikes against the Sudanese pharmaceutical factory, but not those against the terrorist bases in Afghanistan.[165] Similarly, Sudan, the Group of African States, the Group of Islamic States and the League of Arab States individually asked the Security Council to consider the attacks against the pharmaceutical plant and send a fact-finding mission to Sudan, but did not do likewise vis-à-vis the strikes into Afghanistan.[166]

The best explanation for the difference is revealed in the brouhaha that followed the strikes on the Sudanese factory. Almost immediately questions began to surface in the press regarding the accuracy of US claims that the plant

---

162. Letter from the Permanent Representative of the United States of America to the President of the Security Council (Aug. 20, 1998), U.N. Doc. S/1998/780 (1998), *available at* http://www.undp.org/missions/usa/s1998780.pdf (Jun. 18, 2002).
163. Pakistan protested the violation of its airspace. Letter from the Permanent Representative of Pakistan to the President of the Security Council, Aug. 24, 1998, U.N. Doc. S/1998/794 (1998).
164. The international reaction is well-described in Sean D. Murphy, *Contemporary Practice of the United States Relating to International Law*, 93 AM. J. INT'L L. 161, 164–5 (1999).
165. Letter from the Charge d'Affaires of the Permanent Mission of Kuwait to the United Nations Addressed to the President of the Security Council, Aug. 21, 1998, U.N. Doc. S/1998/789 (1998).
166. Letter from the Permanent Representative of the Sudan to the United Nations Addressed to the President of the Security Council, Aug. 21, 1998, U.N. Doc. S/1998/786, annex (1998); Letter from the Permanent Representative of Namibia to the United Nations Addressed to the President of the Security Council, Aug. 25, 1998, U.N. Doc. S/1998/802 (1998) (Group of African states request); Letter from the Charge d'Affaires A.I. of the Permanent Mission of Qatar to the United Nations Addressed to the President of the Security Council, Aug. 21, 1998, U.N. Doc. S/1998/790 (1998) (Group of Islamic states request); Letter from the Charge d'Affaires of the Permanent Mission of Kuwait to the United Nations Addressed to the President of the Security Council, Aug., 21, 1998, U.N./ Doc. S/1998/791 (1998) (League of Arab States request).

was tied to chemical weapon production. In the end, the United States never made a convincing case that the plant was engaged in the activities alleged.[167] Moreover, even if the assertions had been accurate, the causal relationship between the plant and the attacks against the embassies was indirect at best. By contrast, little doubt existed that terrorists were operating from bases in Afghanistan with the seeming acquiesence of the Taliban or that the organization targeted was tied to the bombings.

The reaction of the politically relevant actors such as states, non-governmental organizations, and the media in this case reflects a general sense that it was not the fact that the United States struck back which caused concern as much as it was that the United States "got it wrong" in the Sudanese case. In other words, if a state is going to take the dramatic step of conducting military operations against terrorists, it needs to have sufficient evidence of the connection between the target and the act that was committed, as well as a reasonable belief that future acts are on the horizon.

What is the relationship between these incidents and the law of self-defense as it applies to international terrorism? As Professor Reisman has perceptively noted, "law is not to be found exclusively in formal rules but in the shared expectations of politically relevant actors about what is substantively and procedurally right."[168] Though such New Haven School pronouncements often evoke controversy, there can be little doubt that the received law—customary, conventional and case law—is informed by state practice and the practice of other politically relevant actors on the international scene. Their normative expectations as to how law should foster shared community values are determinative of international law's vector. In the context of counter-terrorist operations conducted in self-defense, a number of conclusions as to possible criteria bearing on the international community's assessment of lawfulness can be suggested from both the legal analysis offered earlier and the short discussion of the evolving international reaction to counter-terrorist operations.

Armed attack. A community consensus now appears to exist that armed attacks may be conducted by terrorist organizations. At the same time, such attacks constitute violations of international and domestic criminal law. Thus,

---

167. Tim Weiner & Steven Lee Myers, *After the Attacks: The Overview, Flaws in the U.S. Account Raise Questions on Strike in Sudan*, N.Y. TIMES, at A2 (Aug. 19, 1998).
168. W. Michael Reisman, *The Raid on Baghdad: Some Reflections on its Lawfulness and Implications*, 5 EUR. J. INT'L L. 120, 121 (1994). He further notes "a prerequisite for appraisal of the lawfulness of an incident . . . is identification of the yardstick of lawfulness actually being used by the relevant actors." *Id.*

the target state may respond to them with armed force in self-defense and/or engage in law enforcement activities. To amount to an armed attack, the "scale and effects" must be "significant," although in a series of related attacks significance is a cumulative calculation. This is a somewhat ambiguous standard, but factors such as the nature and capabilities of the organization conducting the attack, the extent of human injury and physical damage caused (or likely to have been caused if the attack is foiled or otherwise unsuccessful), the relation of the attack to previous attacks and the method and means used to conduct it bear on the appraisal.

Necessity. For compliance with the necessity requirement of self-defense, there must be a sound basis for believing that further attacks will be mounted and that the use of armed force is needed to counter them. This requires the absence of a reliable means other than force to counter the prospective attacks. The relative success of any law enforcement efforts (or likelihood thereof) will affect the extent to which resort to armed force is necessary. Similarly, if self-defense operations involve crossing into another state's territory, that state must be unable or unwilling to prevent the terrorists from continuing to threaten the victim state.

As an aside, the option of seeking Security Council action under Chapter VII has no relation to the necessity assessment. Although it is sometimes asserted that states should turn to the Council for assistance if the opportunity presents itself, Article 51 contains no such legal obligation.

Proportionality. Self-defense operations against terrorists and states involved in terrorism are limited to the nature, targets, level of violence and location required to defeat an on-going attack or, if that attack has ended, prevent any further reasonably foreseeable attacks. That said, those who act in self-defense should be sensitive to the other face of proportionality, its jus in bello face.

Imminency. Self-defense may only be conducted against an attack that is imminent or ongoing. An attack is imminent when the potential victim must immediately act to defend itself and the potential aggressor has irrevocably committed itself to attack. In the context of terrorism, this point may occur well before the planned attack due to the difficulty of locating and tracking terrorists. Imminency is not measured by the objective time differential between the act of self-defense and the attack it is meant to prevent, but instead by the extent to which the self-defense occurred during the last window of opportunity.

More significant are responses to on-going attacks. The acceptability of viewing separate acts of terrorism conducted by the same organization (or closely related organizations acting in concert) as a single on-going attack appears clear in the aftermath of the response to 9/11. Thus, whereas Operation EL DORADO CANYON was widely characterized as punitive in nature, the US counter-terrorist strikes in 1993, 1998 and 2001 were generally seen as appropriately preventive. In other words, the understanding of armed attack has evolved from one looking at particular operations in isolation, and asking whether each is imminent or ongoing in and of itself, to one where terrorists are viewed as conducting campaigns. Once it is established that an ongoing campaign is underway, acts of self-defense are acceptable throughout its course, so long as the purpose is actually to defeat the campaign. In this sense, deterrent self-defense has become, or is at least in the process of becoming, accepted. As noted, almost all justifications, official and otherwise, of counter-terrorist strikes cite the purpose of preventing and deterring future terrorism.

Purpose. The sole acceptable purpose for self-defense operations is to defeat an on-going attack or prevent one that is imminent. The motivation cannot be retribution, general deterrence (deterring terrorism generally vice deterring specific acts and actors), punishment or any other motive. Of course, although each of these may be the logical consequence of a defensive action or, perhaps, a secondary goal, they are impermissible as the primary purpose of the actions.

Conducting self-defense in another state. It is permissible to cross into the territory of another state to conduct defensive counter-terrorist operations when that state has granted consent to do so or when it is unable or unwilling to effectively prevent terrorist activities on its soil. In the latter two cases, a request from the victim state to take the steps that are necessary must precede nonconsensual entry into the country. Operations may only be conducted against the terrorists and their assets; however, if the host state forcibly interferes with them, then that state may have committed an armed attack against the force carrying out the counter-terrorist actions.

Conducting self-defense against a state sponsor. The formal rules regarding the extent of support to a terrorist organization necessary to attribute an armed attack to a state appear to differ from the normative expectations of the global community. Those rules require a high degree of control over a specific operation, such that the terrorist organization is sent by or on behalf of a state to conduct the attack. Mere harboring does not suffice.

However, normative expectations are clearly in the process of rapid evolution. Seemingly authoritative articulations of the standard, such as that by the International Court of Justice in *Nicaragua*, are increasingly out of step with the times. Although no definitive conclusions can be drawn yet regarding the extent and nature of the relationship between the state and terrorist group deemed sufficient to impute an armed attack, several factors seem to have informed the community's general support (or at least lack of criticism) for the strikes against the Taliban. Of particular importance is the fact that the Security Council had made repeated demands that the Taliban put an end to the use of its territory by terrorists, all to no avail. The existence of these warnings by an authoritative international body rendered the Taliban the masters of their own fate. Refusal to cooperate even after the unthinkable happened on September 11th, despite demands and an opportunity to do so, only served to exacerbate their culpability.

Moreover, the terrorists being harbored were of a particularly nasty sort. They had conducted multiple operations in the past that resulted in hundreds of casualties, and had now mounted an attack in which the death toll was measured in the thousands. Their attack also had global impact; financial reverberations were felt throughout the world economy, citizens of over 80 countries were killed, and a pervasive sense of fear infected millions. Clearly, the scale and effects of al Qaeda's attacks bore directly on the community's assessment of Taliban actions (or the lack thereof).

Additionally, the relationship between al Qaeda and the Taliban was extremely close, actually symbiotic in many ways. Although no evidence has been released of direct complicity in the 9/11 attacks, it is difficult to imagine a more cooperative host for al Qaeda than the Taliban, cooperation that was the inevitable result of the Taliban's own dependence on al Qaeda.

Finally, the Taliban were viewed as illegitimate in many ways. Only three countries—Saudi Arabia, the United Arab Emirates and Pakistan—recognized them as the proper government of Afghanistan, by no stretch of the term could they be described as democratic and their human rights record was horrendous.[169] To describe the Taliban as internationally ostracized would be an understatement. Thus, conducting assaults against them seemed to do less violence to countervailing international law principles such as territorial integrity than would similar actions against other governments and states.

Drawing these strands together, relevant factors in assessing the lawfulness of a response against a state sponsor include the severability (or lack thereof) between it and the terrorist group; the frequency, source and timing of warnings to desist from cooperation with the group; the scale and nature of the

---

169. *See, e.g.*, Department of State, Human Rights Country Report: Afghanistan, Mar. 4, 2002, *available at* http://www.state.gov/g/drl/rls/hrrpt/2001/sa/8222.htm (Jun. 18, 2002). *See also* the various reports by Human Rights Watch, *available at* http://hrw.org/reports/world/afghanistan-pubs.php (Jun. 18, 2002).

cooperation; the extent to which the state is perceived as generally law abiding and legitimate or not; the inclusivity of the threat in terms of states threatened; and the severity of the acts committed by the terrorist group with which the state has chosen to associate itself. Further, it appears that self-defense vis-à-vis state involvement (like that against the terrorists themselves) is heading in deterrent directions. Although each determination will be fact-specific, it is clear that the bar is being measurably lowered.

Evidence. As illustrated in the case of the 1998 strikes against the Sudanese pharmaceutical plant, the international community expects states carrying out counter-terrorist strikes to act only on the basis of reliable information. The United States learned its lesson well; in the recent attacks, the United States provided briefings on al Qaeda and Taliban activities to the Security Council, North Atlantic Council and other intergovernmental organizations, as well as numerous states bilaterally.

The incidents considered above highlight the core facts that need to be demonstrated: that the target of the self-defense operations conducted the attack, either directly or constructively, and that the self-defense complies with the requirements of necessity, proportionality and imminency. A much more difficult question is that of how heavy the burden of proof should be.

Because the issue at hand involves the most significant act of international intercourse, the use of armed force, a high standard of proof is obviously required. A preponderance of the evidence standard (i.e., evidence that the fact in issue is more likely than not) is clearly insufficient to justify acts of such import. On the other hand, a beyond a reasonable doubt standard would prove impractical in all but the rarest of cases. The shadowy world of international terrorism simply does not lend itself to immediate access to credible information. By this standard, states would almost never have sufficient evidence to mount a timely and decisive response to a terrorist act.

Mary Ellen O'Connell has suggested a "clear and convincing" standard.[170] Although acknowledging that no accepted standard exists, she draws on domestic law evidentiary standards and an assortment of decisions by international courts, including the *Nicaragua* case,[171] as well as the work of other

---

170. Mary Ellen O'Connell, *Evidence of Terror,* 7 J. CONF. & SEC. L. 19, 22–28 (2002).
171. Professor O'Connell notes that the Court referred to the need for "sufficient proof" [at 437, para. 101], which she argues equates by implication to convincing proof. *Id.* at 24.

scholars.[172] Her suggested standard is consistent with the US notification of self-defense to the Security Council, in which the United States adopted a "clear and compelling" evidentiary standard;[173] this was also the verbiage used to describe the evidence presented to the North Atlantic Council.[174] Application of such a standard, or an analogous one, meets the dual requirements of practicality and rigor—practicality in the sense that an evidentiary burden should not render a state paralyzed as it seeks the requisite quality of evidence, but rigor in that the burden should be heavy enough to preclude states from reacting precipitously to terrorist attacks. Ultimately, an adequacy assessment will rest on the international community's determination of whether a reasonable international actor would have acted in self-defense on the basis of the evidence in question. All such assessments are inherently subjective and contextual.

Once a state possesses the requisite evidence must it disclose it? Professor Jonathan Charney argues that it must.

> To limit the use of force in international relations, which is the primary goal of the United Nations Charter, there must be checks on its use in self-defense. Disclosure to the international community of the basis for such action would help to serve this purpose. The alleged credibility of conclusory statements by a state's leadership should not be a sufficient basis for actions in self-defense since it would encourage abuse. When attacks on a state are so grave as to justify actions in self-defense, the supporting evidence would normally be readily available. Disclosure of that evidence should be required even if the state would wish to claim that classified information would be disclosed. The use of force in self-defense is limited to situations where the state is truly required to defend itself from serious attack. In such situations, the state must carry the burden of presenting evidence to support its actions, normally before these irreversible and irreparable measures are taken.[175]

---

172. *Id.* at 25, citing Christopher Greenwood, *International Law and the United States' Air Operation Against Libya*, 89 W. VA. L. REV. 933, 935 (1987) ["sufficiently convincing"]; Jules Lobel, *The Use of Force to respond to Terrorist Attacks: The Bombing of Sudan and Afghanistan*, 24 YALE J. INT'L L. 537, 538 (1999) [clear and stringent evidentiary standard]; LOUIS HENKIN, HOW NATIONS BEHAVE (2d ed. 1979) [the attack must be "clear, unambiguous, subject to proof, and not easily open to misinterpretation or fabrication"].
173. US Letter, *supra* note 22.
174. Robertson statement, *supra* note 34.
175. Jonathan I. Charney, *Editorial Comments: The Use of Force Against Terrorism and International Law* 95 AM. J. INT'L. L. 835, 836 (2001).

This is a noble proposal, but unfortunately an impractical one. In the vast majority of cases, the information necessary to establish the material facts will be extraordinarily sensitive. Releasing it may endanger the lives of human sources, jeopardize on-going intelligence operations of use in targeting the terrorists or foiling future attacks, surrender the element of surprise, and reveal critical information regarding the extent to which the battlefield, and the enemy's command and control, is transparent to the state engaged in self-defense operations. An absolute disclosure standard is not one the international community will ever adopt in the case of self-defense against terrorism.

A more reasonable standard would require disclosure to the extent practicable in the circumstances. Professor Charney's concern about abuse of the right to self-defense is well founded; however, that concern must be balanced against the need to be able to conduct self-defense, and otherwise safeguard oneself from terrorists, effectively. Moreover, the situation is not always a strict disclosure/no disclosure conundrum. For instance, it may serve both purposes to disclose the necessary information in closed session, as was done when the United States briefed its NATO allies. The subsequent support of states that have received such briefings serves as a safeguard against abuse, albeit a less than perfect one. Additionally, it may be possible to disclose information after the fact, as was done by the United States in 1997 regarding Operation EL DORADO CANYON.[176] Doing so will allow states to build a track record of credibility in their claims, a particularly valuable safe-guard in those cases where immediate disclosure is impossible.

Conclusion

It has been asked whether the attacks of September 11th ushered in a dramatically new era in international law. This article has suggested that in most respects the law on the use of force has proven adequate vis-à-vis international terrorism. Where it has not, the emerging normative expectations represent less a new era than the logical and constant evolution of the existing legal system in the face of changing global realities. That evolution has resulted in some degree of softening in the community understanding of when self-defense is appropriate.

Such a softening is appropriate in the face of the new threat environment. Terrorism today represents a particularly pernicious prospect. Unfortunately,

---

176. *See* Bill Gertz, *U.S. Intercepts from Libya Play Role in Berlin Bomb Trial*, WASH. TIMES, Nov. 19, 1997, at A13. The United States provided intercepted communications gathered by the National Security Agency.

the attacks that occurred in September 2001 may represent only the tip of the iceberg. Thousands of individuals trained under bin Laden are at large worldwide.[177] More ominously, the threat of terrorism using weapons of mass destruction looms ever larger. The normative system developed for state-on-state conflict, in which the risk of super power confrontation was always present, is predictably shifting to remain responsive to community values in the face of the changing threat.

Consider the apparent relaxation in the requirements for attribution of an armed attack. Although it may make striking at a state in self-defense more acceptable, thereby heightening the likelihood of state-on-state conflict, it may have just the opposite effect by serving as an effective deterrent to state sponsorship without risking the higher order conflict that was the danger during the Cold War. Similarly, characterizing terrorist attacks as part of a campaign rather than a series of individual actions actually gives the state acting in self-defense an opportunity to seek resolution of the situation without being compelled to immediately resort to force lest the imminency pass. This permits greater community involvement in the decision-process and greater opportunity to gather and assess evidence.

The final normative verdict on the US and coalition attacks against al Qaeda and the Taliban is uncertain. The attacks against al Qaeda appear novel, but consistent with the community expectations existing on September 10th. By contrast, the attacks against the Taliban represent a less than crystalline glimpse of the direction in which the international law regarding responses to terrorism may be heading. But given the existing security landscape, the vector appears positive.

---

177. According to the Egyptian Minister of Interior, "as many as 80,000 people may have been trained in Afghanistan under bin Laden." 1 THE TERRORIST THREAT (no. 2), Apr. 2002, at 2.

III

Jus ad Bellum and International Terrorism

Rein Müllerson[1]

Legal Regulation of the Use of Force: The Failure of Normative Positivism

The central tenet in international law is the legal regulation of the use of force. The nature, content and effectiveness of this area of international law mirrors, much more clearly than any other branch, the very character of international law. In order to grasp the essence of the current debate in this area of international law it is helpful to have a brief review of the evolution of the proscription on the use of force.

Thucydides' *History of the Peloponnesian War* demonstrates a complete absence of any legal (or even legal-moral-religious) restriction on the recourse to war. As Thucydides writes, "the Athenians and the Peloponnesians began the war after the thirty-year truce" since "Sparta was forced into it because of her apprehensions over the growing power of Athens."[2] This sounds somewhat familiar and contemporary as there was a violation of the balance of power that caused Sparta to ally with smaller Greek city-states—forming the Peloponnesian League to counter militarily the Delian League headed by

---

1. Professor of International Law, King's College, London; *Institut de droit International*, Membre.
2. THUCYDIDES, THE PELOPONNESIAN WAR 11–12 (W. W. Norton & Company, 1998).

Athens. But differently from today's or even from yesterday's world, Greek city-states did not need to justify their recourse to arms. Athenians believed it to be "an eternal law that the strong can rule the weak" as "justice never kept anyone who was handed the chance to get something by force from getting more."[3] Their ambassadors explained to the Melians that "those who have power use it, while the weak make compromises. . . . Given what we believe about the gods and know about men, we think that both are always forced to dominate everyone they can. We didn't lay down this law, it was there—and we weren't first to make use of it."[4] "[E]ach of us must exercise what power he really thinks he can."[5]

Starting from Saint Augustine, through Saint Thomas Aquinas and other Christian theologians, various concepts of just wars developed. War had to be declared and waged by proper authorities, had to have just cause and just intention. What causes were just was, of course, open to debate. During this period, natural law doctrines in international relations dominated and were indistinguishable from religious and moral reasoning. This period continued beyond the times of Hugo Grotius. Legal limits on the use of force came from the interpretation of religious texts or Roman private law and not from what states or other political entities actually did. If international law at all governed (i.e., limited or justified) the use of armed force it was because its arguments were drawn from and supported by religious texts and their interpretation.

Christianity was not the only religion that had something to say about the use of force, as interpreters of the Old Testament and the Koran, similarly, tried to distinguish between just and unjust causes of resorting to arms. There are some striking similarities, though no doubt there are significant differences too, between the main monotheistic religions in that respect. For example, the Spanish Dominican professor, Franciscus Victoria, explained that, as the Indians in America, though not Christians, were nevertheless humans and therefore endowed with reason, it was not possible to use force against them without just cause and "difference in religion is not a cause of just war."[6] At the same time, "the Indians had violated the fundamental right of the Spaniards to travel freely among them, to carry on trade and to propagate Christianity."[7] Hence, though force could not be used to proselytise, it could be

---

3. *Id.* at 30.
4. *Id.* at 229.
5. *Id.* at 227.
6. YORAM DINSTEIN, WAR, AGGRESSION AND SELF-DEFENSE 61–62 (3rd ed. 2001) [hereinafter DINSTEIN].
7. *Id.* at 61.

used when proselytes refused to be proselytised. In 1948, Sheikh Shaltut of Al-Azhar University in Cairo justified the Muslim conquests of Byzantine and Persia on the grounds of the response by the Byzantines and Persians to communications calling them to convert to Islam. He wrote that "Moslems only attacked people when they showed a spirit of hostility, opposition and resistance against the mission and a contempt for it."[8] As Ann Elisabeth Mayer comments, "here religious reasons, resistance to converting to Islam and contempt for Islamic missionaries, apparently justify recourse to military force—at least where the states attacked are perceived to be a danger to Muslims or the spread of Islam."[9] Here too, only those who refused to adhere to the true faith were killed and their lands conquered.

After Emerich de Vattel, positivism gradually started to prevail in international law and the differentiation between just and unjust wars based on religious laws or the laws of nature (the human nature or the nature of the state) lost its meaning. Although this was not a return to the naked power politics of Ancient Greece it was only thinly veiled power politics where any offense, real or perceived, may have been good enough to justify the use of military force. In such a situation the *Caroline* incident and the subsequent exchange of letters between US Secretary of State Daniel Webster and the British Minister to Washington was more an aberration than a pattern of behavior.[10] As will be discussed below, the *Caroline* formula holds interest for explaining some of today's conflicts but in the middle of the 19th century, it was at best *opinio juris* of two states that was not confirmed by any practice. Recall that in 1914 during the Vera Cruz incident, triggered by the arrest by Mexican authorities of several crewmembers from the USS *Dolphin*, the United States used military force against Mexico when Mexican authorities refused to honor the US flag with a 21 gun salute as an official apology.[11] Similarly, Great Britain and Germany used gunboats to force Venezuela to pay its debts to nationals of these states.[12]

Positivism, that is the resort to the use of force without limits resulted in a system where any offense against a state or its honor could be responded to

---

8. Sheik Shaltut, Al-Azhar University Cairo, Egypt, *quoted in* ANN ELISABETH MAYER, WAR AND PEACE IN THE ISLAMIC TRADITION AND INTERNATIONAL LAW, IN JUST WAR AND JIHAD. HISTORICAL AND THEORETICAL PERSPECTIVES ON WAR AND PEACE IN WESTERN AND ISLAMIC TRADITION 204 (J. Kelsay and J. T. Johnson eds., 1991).
9. *Id.* at 205.
10. *See* R. Y. Jennings, *The Caroline and McLeod Cases*, 32 AM. J. INT'L L. 82 (1938).
11. IAN BROWNLIE, INTERNATIONAL LAW AND THE USE OF FORCE BY STATES, 36–37 (1963) [hereinafter BROWNLIE].
12. *Id.* at 35.

with force. At the beginning of the 20th century, this positivism, became diluted by normativism. International law regulating the use of force evolved not to what states did to each other but what they had agreed they should or should not do (normative positivism). Using customary law terminology, it was not so much state practice as their *opinio juris* that mattered. Here, the term *opinio juris* is used in a wider sense and it includes authoritative statements by states as to what international law is, including those laws enshrined in international treaties.[13]

This has been a controversial development. It may be said that there has always been an immense gap between words and deeds, but words as well as the notions and ideas expressed in those words, when repeated long enough and desired by many, often change reality. Though this gap may be still immense, the world's views on the use of force is not what it was hundreds of years ago. A learned few may change laws, while laws may also change the views of many and even force those whose views remain unchanged to act within the law. Here the relationship between law and behavior is a kind of chicken-and-egg question as it is impossible to say whether European neighbors (e.g., the United Kingdom, Germany and France) who warred against each other for ages do not do it now because they finally concluded that they needed effective norms and institutions to protect their citizens from the scourges of war. Alternatively, it may well be that Europe remains at peace because of these very norms and institutions. Obviously, the change in viewpoint and the creation of norms and institutions occurred simultaneously.

Europe is not the only, though the most prominent place (having also been one of the bloodiest and having become the most peaceful), where such changes have taken place. The American continent also has moved in the same direction.

Beginning in the 20th century, the development of the League of Nations Covenant, the Kellogg-Briand Pact of 1928, the UN Charter and other important international treaties, worked to severely restrict use of military force in relations between states. Unfortunately, this normative system has been violated so many times, often with impunity, that it is hardly possible to call it an effective (even relatively effective) legal regime. This system does, however, reflect the world's desire to avoid the repetition of the two world wars that brought untold sorrow to Europe and mankind. This system now shapes the mentality of many people and therefore conditions their attitude towards the use of force amongst states.

---

13. Whether a treaty that is formally in force but that is not implemented in practice is law or not is another issue. The same question may be asked about *opinio juris* not confirmed by practice.

The current UN Charter paradigm concerning the use of force can be called normative positivism since it is based on the consent of states and not upon what states (or at least most of them) do in practice. It is normative since it is not premised on the actual practice of states. It is positivist since it does not make distinctions between just, unjust, more justified, and less justified causes for the use of force.

The Charter paradigm sees the use of force between states as an almost absolute evil (after the two world wars it is understandable) without distinguishing between causes for the resort to force. This paradigm, as understood by the founding fathers of the UN, did not provide for the use of force at all except in response to the illegal use of force (even the collective security paradigm was meant to provide for the possible pre-emptive use of force in collective self-defense). As the UN Charter was drafted, humanitarian crises or even civil wars were not considered to constitute threats to international peace and security, the magical talisman for Security Council approval. The Cold War period supported formal normative positivism as what was just for the West (e.g., containment of the Soviet expansion) was most unjust from the point of view of the Soviet Union and its satellites. Similarly, what was just in the eyes of the Soviet leaders (e.g., advancement of socialism throughout the world) was the thing most feared by the West. Accordingly, in this bipolar world order, international law on the use of force had to be based on the formal norms that the two antagonistic groups were able to agree upon. That it was difficult, if not impossible, for these competing titans to agree on the proper invocation of the use of force, except in self-defense, is not surprising.

Clearly, the world has now changed, though no change is ever absolute. There are still, and there will remain in the foreseeable future, states with competing interests. Additionally, religion may perhaps have replaced ideology as one of the main sources of confrontation, but is not religion one of the forms of ideology?

With respect to the use of force amongst states, a significant transition has occurred towards morality or ethics and away from strict positivistic formalism. Recent uses of force not sanctioned by the UN Security Council have been justified by references to morality. For example, references to "humanitarian intervention" have been used to legitimate if not legalize certain uses of force. None other than Kofi Annan, Secretary-General of the United Nations and the chief custodian of its Charter, speaking in Stockholm on the Kosovo Intervention, stated that "there is emerging international law that countries cannot hide behind sovereignty and abuse people without expecting the rest of the world to do something about it."[14] Although the current legal regime may still be a far cry from the doctrine of just war, neither can it be claimed to be one of "formal positivism" on which the UN Charter was premised. The Security Council itself has expanded the concept of threats to international peace and security, legitimizing use of force that would not have been justified in the eyes of the drafters of the UN Charter. Just war considerations have led to this flexing of the Charter paradigm and are now even reflected in the new National Security Strategy of the United States. In that document, President George W. Bush stated that "the reasons for our [preemptive] actions will be clear, the force measured and the *cause just*" (emphasis added).[15]

Changes in the World's Political Configuration and Jus ad Bellum. Jus ad Bellum in Treaties and Practice

In 1963, British scholar Ian Brownlie published an excellent monograph still considered today as perhaps the best study of the history of the legal regulation of the use of force—*International Law and the Use of Force by States*.[16] Almost forty years later, a highly decorated and respected Professor Brownlie (CBE, QC, Member of the International Law Commission), emphasizing the continuing relevance of the ideas and conclusions developed in this book, observed: "whilst there have been obvious changes in the political configuration of the world, especially in the 1990s, these changes have not had any particular effect on the law."[17] What does this mean? Is it true? If it is true, what are the implications of the gap between the "obvious changes in the political configuration of the world" and the absence of any particular effect of these changes on international law? Does this not mean that the world and the law exist as if in parallel universes without impacting one another at all?

---

14. Tim Burton & Robert Anderson, *UN Warns Yugoslavia Over Human Rights*, FINANCIAL TIMES, May 26, 1999, at 2.
15. The National Security Strategy of the United States of America 16 (Sep. 17, 2002) *available at* http://www.whitehouse.gov/nsc/nss.html (Nov. 26, 2002).
16. *See generally* BROWNLIE, *supra* note 11.
17. Ian Brownlie, A Europaeum Lecture on International Law and the Use of Force by States at HEI, Geneva (Feb. 1, 2001) [hereinafter Brownlie Lecture].

Law, as one of the main stabilizing factors in society, is indeed a relatively conservative phenomenon[18] and changes in all legal systems typically lag behind transformations in "real" life. This phenomenon, a reflection of both the positive and negative sides of conservatism generally, is not of course wholly negative. Law not only cannot, but must not, vacillate in synchronicity with every change in society, reacting immediately to all political turmoil and social upheavals. In such an environment, law could not fulfill its stabilizing functions. At the same time, when economic, social or political transformations reflect longer-term trends that are substantial and lead to changes in political configuration of society, the conservative nature of the law's change may create serious problems for both law and society.

International law has relatively recently (during the last quarter of the previous century) overcome some radical and rapid changes. However, it is true that such changes have mainly occurred not at the core of international law but instead in some, albeit important, but quite specific areas of international law. For example, the development of international space law occurred so quickly that it led to the emergence of the concept of "instant custom."[19] The law of the sea that had slowly developed over the centuries was codified in 1958 but so many of its basic norms were outdated even before the four Geneva Conventions entered into force that the 1982 Law of the Sea Convention was adopted to codify new developments. Equally, international environmental law has emerged and rapidly developed within only a few decades.[20]

Despite this seemingly rapid evolution of international law in these three areas though, the treaties concerning the use of force have undergone little, if any, change since the adoption of the UN Charter in 1945. Even General

---

18. Of course, law may be used not only for the stabilization of existing relations and situations or for the enhancement of tendencies that are already discernible. Law can perform creative functions as well. Through treaty making or decisions of international bodies, international law may help to create new relations and situations. However, even in such cases (or maybe especially in such cases), international law also tends to freeze (crystallize, to use the widely accepted, but incorrect in my opinion, term to describe the process of custom formation) relations that are created with the assistance of such legal mechanisms.

19. BIN CHENG, "United Nations Resolutions on Outer Space: 'Instant' International Customary Law," INTERNATIONAL LAW: TEACHING AND PRACTICE 273 (Bin Cheng ed., 1982).

20. See, e.g., Convention on International Trade in Endangered Species of Wild Fauna and Flora, (Mar. 3, 1973), 27 U.S.T. 1087; Convention for the Protection of the Marine Environment of the North-East Atlantic, Sept. 22, 1992, art. 23, *reprinted in* 3 Y.B. INT'L ENVTL. L. 759, (1992); Protocol to the 1979 Convention on Long-Range Transboundary Air Pollution concerning the Control of Emissions of Volatile Organic Compounds or their Transboundary Fluxes, art. 3, para. 3, 31 I.L.M. 573, (1992).

Assembly resolutions on international law have not contained anything that could be remotely defined as "progressive development of international law."[21] Why? Why have treaties on the use of force been so conservative while in other areas they have demonstrated, responding to societal change (including international society), considerable ability for change? Perhaps the law on the use of force has changed but some experts and even states have not yet noticed?

The aforementioned branches of international law (space law, the law of the sea, environmental law) have undergone significant changes following, or in parallel with, equally manifest transformations in these respective areas of human activity. In the legal regime regulating the use of force, so central to international law that novelties in it may affect the very foundations of the overall legal system, significant changes have occurred only after the most terrible conflicts that shocked the conscience of humankind. In such cases, changes in the geo-political environment, in international law generally and in jus ad bellum in particular have not only coincided in time and space, but have all been caused by the same set of factors, simply reflecting different facets of the same process.

For example, the absence, existence, content or enforceability of rules concerning preservation of living resources in the Northern Atlantic are important political and economic issues for many countries. However, whether these issues are resolved in one way or other will not alter the structure or basic characteristics of international society or international law. At the same time, this is not the case depending upon how the following question is answered: Is the UN Security Council the only organization that can decide how and when to use force (not involving self-defense) or can states, for example, reclaim unpaid debts by using gunboat diplomacy? Radical changes in jus ad bellum reflect serious transformations taking (or that have taken) place in the very structure and characteristics of international society. Such transformations create shock waves necessary for overcoming states' inertia and the traditional conservatism found in legal regimes.

---

21. For example, the 1987 Declaration on the Enhancement of the Effectiveness of the Principle of Refraining from the Threat or Use of Force in International Relations swearing allegiance to the UN Charter and confirming what had been already said in many previous UN resolutions, did not touch upon any controversial issue. *See generally* G.A. Res. 42/22, U.N. GAOR, 42d Sess., U.N. Doc. A/Res/42/22 (1987). *See also* TREVES, *La Declaration des Nations Unies sur le renforcement de l'efficacité du principe du non-recours à la force* 33 AFDI (1987); CHRISTINE GRAY, INTERNATIONAL LAW AND THE USE OF FORCE 5 (2000).

The Thirty Years War and its subsequent peace led to the emergence of the Westphalian international system. This system has served as the basis for the development of the modern international system as well as the development of international law, to include its fundamental principles such as sovereign equality of states and non-intervention in the internal affairs of such states. World War I provided the impetus for considerable innovations in international legal treaties generally and in the use of force in particular. The "cooling-off" periods provided for in the Statute of the League of Nations and the 1928 Briand-Kellogg Pact outlawing wars of aggression have been significant landmarks in the development of legal texts on the use of force in international relations.[22] Moreover, after the horror and tragedy caused by World War II, significant changes occurred in both jus ad bellum (the UN Charter) and jus in bello (the 1949 Geneva Conventions). It is reasonable then, to conclude that only multi-state wars and the shocks felt in their aftermath are able to change international law on the use of force. Changes in jus ad bellum have always been accompanied by changes in the geo-political configuration of the world; or rather have been caused by the latter (e.g., the rise of nation-states instead of feudal multi-layered authority in Europe; the effect of the two world wars; the emergence and subsequent collapse of the Cold War bipolar world). If bilateral wars have usually ended with bilateral treaties on "eternal peace and friendship," multi-state wars have ended with attempts to create general norms that purport to regulate, limit or even completely prohibit the use of force between states.

Geo-political restructuring does not seem, by itself to cause changes to the law regulating the use of force. These changes must also be accompanied by significant events operating to shock the conscience of the world, causing states to come together to ensure such events do not happen again. Such conferences took place after the Thirty Years War, the Napoleonic Wars, WW I and WW II. However, even after WW II, the consensus on the prohibition to use force was only temporary, conditional on unrealistic expectations (unrealistic understood only with hindsight) that the Chapter VII collective security mechanism would work. Unfortunately, bilateral treaties espousing "eternal friendship" as well as the general limitations on the use of force have been honored more in the breach than in the observance. Things are not completely hopeless and at least in one region, Western Europe, where both

---

22. *See* League of Nations, arts. 10–13; General Treaty Providing for the Renunciation of War as an Instrument of National Policy, art. 1 (Aug. 27, 1928), 46 Stat. 2343, 94 L.N.T.S. 57.

World Wars started as well as where many earlier bloody conflicts occurred, the consensus to ban the aggressive use of force has been quite genuine and the Europeans have made it work, at least in their mutual relations.[23]

Since the end of the 1980s the geo-political structure has undergone dramatic changes but this has happened without any single shocking event that would have implicated the vital interests of the most powerful states to the extent, or in the manner, of the two World Wars of the last century. Rather, changes have been more gradual, and some of the most significant ones have not been bloody. Neither the genocide in Rwanda, nor the crimes against humanity committed in the former Yugoslavia, nor even the September 11th terrorist attacks (though the last directly affecting by far the most powerful state in the world), have forced the states to sit down and draft new rules corresponding to a changed political environment requiring new legal responses for such new threats. These developments have not impacted the evolution of international law treaties concerned with the core of international law itself—jus ad bellum, as the two World Wars did. However, due to the character of the main victim-state and the particularly tragic nature of the attacks witnessed by millions on television screens on 9/11, terrorists may well become victims of their own "spectacular success" for these events may have shocked the world enough to open the way to radical reappraisal through customary process of some basic principles of the jus ad bellum.

Consequently, a new geo-political environment now exists. New threats exist that can be effectively dealt with only by using, inter alia, military force in circumstances not foreseen in 1945 and therefore not provided for (at least explicitly) in the UN Charter. However, states have not been, and will hardly be, able to draft new rules corresponding to the new geo-political environment and allowing for an adequate response to these new threats. No consensus exists on responses to new global threats such as civil wars, humanitarian emergencies, international terrorism and the proliferation of weapons of mass destruction (including into the hands of terrorists). Achieving consensus on

---

23. The European experience, as well as various examples from other parts of the world, shows that there is no such thing as inherently peaceful nations or regions (or vice versa, inherently bellicose ones). Smaller and weaker nations have historically been more peaceful only due to their inability to successfully carry out more aggressive foreign policy. As the European experience testifies, institutions and rules that become a part of political culture are necessary to make peace durable. Peaceful relations between nations, like human rights in society, are not natural or inherent. Rather, war and human wrongs are natural. For nations and peoples to enjoy peace and human rights it is necessary to fight and constantly work for them as they are the rather fragile results of the long and difficult development and acculturation of humankind.

these issues is dependent, inter alia, on the co-existence in the contemporary world, of three different categories of states and societies—pre-modern, modern and postmodern—each with different characteristics, values, interests and perceptions of security threats. Of course, societies and states with different levels of societal development have co-existed in the world before but never before have they co-existed in the world that is so interdependent and shrinking.

Accounting for the fact that the treaties attempting to regulate the use of force which were adopted after WW I and WW II, created unrealistic expectations and noting the absence of consensus on important new issues concerning the use of force, the difficulty of drafting new rules of jus ad bellum may, however, not be so dramatic. The customary process may be not only more natural and flexible, but in today's circumstances, more rapid at consolidating emerging trends into law. Such a process, inevitably, has its shortcomings though.

Brownlie observes that the main reason for a huge gap between the dynamics of political change and the consistency in law lies in the fact that "individual States continue to have a fairly conservative view of the law." And he is critical of those academics, who think that that the law has changed, and especially of those who, for instance, "believe that there is a right to use force for humanitarian purposes."[24]

However, even if many states are conservative or inertial, given an absence of political will to draft new rules on the use of force and intervention, it does not necessarily follow that law too is as inertial as are these states. Recent practice in customary international law and its effect on jus ad bellum proves this point.

To an extent, this has been a kind of partial effect: a part of international law on the use of force, that was understood by most states and by most commentators, has ceased to exist as a reliable normative guide (if it had ever existed as a reliable guide).[25] Moreover, new norms that would have enjoyed general consensus have not (yet?) emerged, though there are new trends enjoying at least relative consensus.

---

24. See Brownlie Lecture, *supra* note 17.
25. A different, though related, question: to what extent did the Charter paradigm on the use of force correspond to the reality existing during the Cold War? During the Cold War, the Charter paradigm on the use of force competed (usually not very successfully) with rules of the game expressed, for example, in the Brezhnev, Johnson or Reagan doctrines, with concepts of wars of national liberation, as well as with various ad hoc practices that did not find legitimization in any laws or doctrines.

Therefore, I agree with Ian Brownlie, but only to an extent. Legal treaties and even some states' practice have not undergone any changes since the establishment of the UN Charter. However, the position on, and the practice of, the jus ad bellum by other states as well as actions undertaken by the Security Council in recent years, is in many ways quite different from the Charter paradigm of the legal regulation of the use of force.

What are these "obvious changes in the political configuration of the world," that, from Professor Brownlie's point of view, have had no effect on the law, but that in my opinion have had at least a partial effect and should have a complete effect on the jus ad bellum?

Most obvious is the conclusion of the Cold War. Initially, the end of the Cold War raised the expectation that the UN Charter, and especially its Chapter VII, would start working as planned when originally drafted. The Gulf War of 1990–91 provided support for this expectation. However, though the Security Council became considerably more active in the 1990s, the Chapter VII paradigm did not become reality. Instead, a new interpretation of "threats to international peace and security" and delegation of Security Council powers to individual states and regional organizations became widespread.[26] The Council also started to ex post facto legitimize cases of the use of force by individual states or groups of states[27] and the latter started to use Security Council's findings to carry out acts that, though arguably necessary for the implementation of the relevant resolutions of the Security Council, were nevertheless neither expressly nor implicitly authorized by the Security Council.[28]

---

26. DANESH SAROOSHI, UNITED NATIONS AND THE DEVELOPMENT OF COLLECTIVE SECURITY (1999); Christine Gray, *From Unity to Polarization: International Law and the Use of Force against Iraq*, 13 EUR. J. INT'L L. 1–19 (2002), *available at* http://www.ejil.org/journal/Vol13/No1/art1-03.html (Nov. 26, 2002).

27. *See, e.g.*, Security Council Resolution 866 stating that the UN peace keeping mission in Liberia is the "first peace-keeping mission undertaken by the United Nations in cooperation with a peace-keeping mission already set up by another organization." S. C. Res. 866, U.N. SCOR, 48th Sess., U.N. Doc. S/866/(1993). *See also* S. C. Res. 1181, U.N. SCOR, 53d Sess., U.N. Doc. S/1181/(1998) (authorizing the same thing in Sierra Leone).

28. For example, neither Operation PROVIDE COMFORT—the humanitarian aid mission in northern Iraq nor Operation ALLIED FORCE—the NATO led campaign for humanitarian intervention against the former Yugoslavia were undertaken pursuant to authorization although the Security Council had certainly expressed its concerns with situations in these areas. *See, e.g.*, S. C. Res. 1203, U.N. SCOR, 53d Sess., U.N. Doc. S/1203/(1998) and S. C. Res. 688, U.N. SCOR, 46th Sess., U.N. Doc. S/688/(1991).

Secondly, the Cold War had frozen or at least limited the development of certain trends beginning before the two World Wars. Among these trends are the trends of globalization and its nemesis—fragmentation, both of which have a considerable impact on the issue of the use of force. Fragmentation often manifests itself in wars of secession, conflicts between different religious or ethnic groups. Globalization (which ironically leads also to the globalization of fragmentation itself), internationalizes such conflicts and other developments and processes, which in different circumstances may have had only a local or regional effect. Today, "internal" wars are neither politically nor even legally speaking internal affairs of the state in which they occur. Also, such internal wars often extend to neighboring states. This internationalizes the conflict.

The legal regime regulating the use of force is only one, though perhaps the most controversial, of the areas covered by international law demonstrating that traditional distinctions between domestic and international affairs are, if not disappearing, then at least becoming more confused. Strictly interstate jus ad bellum does not relate well to a changed international system where non-state, sub-state and super-state actors play important roles. Mary Kaldor is right that "the new wars involve transnational networks, which include both state and non-state actors—mercenary groups, warlords, as well as parts of state apparatus."[29] Based on this, Richard Falk is also correct that:

> at this stage it is unreasonable to expect the US government to rely on the UN to fulfil its defensive needs. The UN lacks the capability, authority and will to respond to the kind of threat to global security posed by this new form of terrorist world war. The UN was established to deal with wars among states, while a transnational actor that cannot be definitively linked to a state is behind the attacks on the United States. Al Qaeda's relationship to the Taliban in Afghanistan is contingent, with al Qaeda being more the sponsor of the state than the other way around.[30]

This is one of the reasons why Eric Myjer and Nigel White are worried that "the response to the Twin Towers attack may contribute to a development of international law, which would place self-defense outside the context and thereby outside the limit of the Charter of the United Nations."[31] This potential danger becomes real if the Charter norms are interpreted out of the current context.

---

29. MARY KALDOR, *The Power of Terror* [hereinafter The Power of Terror], RE-ORDERING THE WORLD—THE LONG TERM IMPLICATIONS OF SEPTEMBER 11TH (Mark Leonard ed. 2002) 21–22 [hereinafter RE-ORDERING THE WORLD].
30. Richard Falk, *Defining a Just War*, THE NATION, October 29, 2001 at 11.
31. Eric Myjer & Nigel White, *The Twin Towers Attack: An Unlimited Right to Self-Defence*, 7 J. CONFLICT AND SEC. 1 at 17 (2002) [hereinafter Myjer & White].

The end of the Cold War ended the Soviet-NATO confrontation and extended democracy and civil liberties to Eastern and Central Europe. It also lifted the lid on the multitude of suppressed hatreds and simmering conflicts. As Bernard Lewis observes:

> The ending of the Cold War, and the collapse of the bi-polar discipline which the two superpowers, sometimes acting in competition, sometimes in accord, had managed to impose, confronted the people of the Middle East, like those of other regions liberated from superpower control or interference, with an awful choice. They could move, however slowly and reluctantly, to settle their disputes and live peacefully side by side, as happened in some parts of the world; or they could give free rein to their conflicts and hatreds, and fall into descending spiral of strife, bloodshed and torment, as happened in others.[32]

Today, both scenarios are being realized in different parts of the world. In some parts of the world proliferation of weapons of mass destruction, terrorist attacks, humanitarian crises, inter-ethnic and inter-religious conflicts have all increased manifold after the end of the Cold War and these developments, unavoidably, affect how and whether military force is used in various regions.

Bassam Tibi is right that:

> with the restraining power of bipolarity no longer maintaining a global order of checks and balances, the aspirations of ethnicities and religio-political ideologies that had lain low during the Cold War now boiled to the surface. It was only after the Cold War that the factors underlying these conflicts came to be perceived. Previously, ethnicity, religion, and culture were considered to be the terrain of anthropologists, and of little interest of international politics.[33]

These factors were of even less interest for international law than for international politics. However, without taking these factors into account, international lawyers may indeed conclude today that international law is essentially the same as it was in 1945 notwithstanding that it is a very different world.

Morover, with the end of the Cold War, the polarity of the world changed. Instead of being distinctively bipolar, the world is now unipolar, especially in

---

32. BERNARD LEWIS, THE MIDDLE EAST. 2000 YEARS OF HISTORY FROM THE RISE OF CHRISTIANITY TO THE PRESENT DAY at 371–72 (1995).
33. BASSAM TIBI, THE CHALLENGE OF FUNDAMENTALISM. POLITICAL ISLAM AND THE NEW WORLD DISORDER at 64 (1998) [hereinafter Tibi].

the military field.[34] This means that state practices on the use of force (even if not opinio juris) will be determined for the foreseeable future mainly by the United States, acting either with its allies or unilaterally. Historically speaking, there is a tendency to counterbalance such dominance by one "hyperpower" and it would be natural that in the future the geo-political environment will change again. No balance, or imbalance for that matter, of power has yet been permanent. Nor is such a power arrangement likely to become permanent.

However, in the foreseeable future it is likely that the world will remain militarily unipolar (which does not at all mean that the United States militarily can do as it wishes) and US dominance will remain significant in most other instruments of power as well. For liberal democratic societies as well as for societies aspiring to become such, it would be counterproductive to try to counterbalance US dominance in either the political and military-strategic domain.[35] At the same time, it might well be necessary to join the United States in an effort to influence its policy choices to further enhance its role in the world as raw power does not always mix well with sophistication and moderation. Audrey Cronin of Georgetown University, writing insightfully on

---

34. Stephen Brooks and William Wohlforth, on the basis of thorough analysis of various indicators, write: "If today's American primacy does not constitute unipolarity, then nothing ever will." See Stephen Brooks & William Wohlforth, *American Primacy in Perspective*, 81 FOR. AFF'S 21 (2002).

35. Until September 11, 2001 Russia seemed to be trying to create a multi-polar world. The Concept of National Security of Russia signed by President Putin in January 2000 stated that Russia "will advance the ideology of the creation of a multipolar world." See Decree of the President of the Russian Federation, 24 (Jan. 10, 2000). However, things have changed considerably since then. In their Joint Declaration, the United States and Russia, speaking of the need to promote stability, sovereignty and territorial integrity in Central Asia and the South Caucasus, stated that they "reject the failed model of Great Power rivalry that can only increase the potential of conflict in those regions." See Joint Declaration on New US-Russia Relationship 38 WEEKLY COMP. PRES. DOC. 21, 894–897 (May 24, 2002), *available at* http://frwebgate.access.gpo.gov/cgi-bin/multidb.cgi (Nov. 27, 2002). Dmitri Trenin writes that "a confrontation with NATO is something Russia cannot afford and should never attempt. . . . Rather, it is in Russia's supreme national security interest to strive toward full demilitarisation of its relations with the West." See DIMITRI TRENIN, THE END OF EURASIA, at 285 (2002). Trenin concludes that "Russia stands on the boundary between the post-modern and modern and even pre-modern world. It must make its choice. The only rational option is to fully stress Russia's European identity and engineer its gradual integration into a Greater Europe." *Id.*, at 311. Though there are various political forces in Russia vying to steer its foreign policy in opposite directions, it seems that President Putin has reasonably chosen supporting the United States on many strategic issues. In his keynote public address to the Russian Foreign Ministry on 12 July 2002, President Putin emphasized that cooperation with the United States is the key to Russian political and economic revival. B.B.C. *Worldwide Monitoring, Putin Notes Importance of Diplomacy in Helping Russian Business* (B.B.C. Radio Broadcast, July 12, 2002).

terrorism, observes that "the United States is ill-equipped by culture, history and bureaucratic structure to respond effectively to this new kind of strategic threat"[36] and that "US political and cultural sophistication lag behind its military technological capabilities."[37]

However, Europe can fulfill its potential in the current and future fight against terrorism and other threats by becoming militarily stronger and mentally tougher. Robert Kagan may have a point that Europeans "hope to constrain American power without wielding power themselves. In what may be the ultimate feat of subtlety and indirection, they want to control the behemoth by appealing to its conscience."[38] Subtlety and sophistication without power though are often impotent while single-mindedness without subtlety and sophistication often leads to unexpected and unwanted consequences. Regardless, today's liberal democracies can hardly afford the luxury of becoming disunited versus a less centralized but no less serious threat than the one that existed during the Cold War.

Subtlety and Sophistication or Single-Mindedness?

The war against terrorism is in many ways different from traditional wars. "War" cannot be used, in this context, as a legal term and "war" or rather "armed conflicts" are only a part of this wider war on terror to be fought by economic, financial, educational and other means.[39] Audrey Cronin is right that "military responses, while disruptive in the short run, tend to drive terrorists underground, to encourage innovation, to engender sympathy and, sometimes, even build support for the "underdog." The point is not that swift and decisive uses of force are irrelevant; far from it. Instead, the argument is that effective counter-terrorism policy must be placed in a larger strategic context, in which the longer-term consequences are understood and calculated."[40]

---

36. Audrey Cronin, *Rethinking Sovereignty: American Strategy in the Age of Terrorism*, 44 SURVIVAL 2, at 127 (2002) [hereinafter Cronin].
37. *Id.* at 132.
38. Robert Kagan, *Power and Weakness*, 113 POL'Y REV. 7 (2002) [hereinafter Kagan].
39. Granville Byford makes an important point writing that "wars have typically been fought against proper nouns (Germany, say) for good reasons that proper nouns can surrender and promise not to do it again. Wars against common nouns (poverty, crime, drugs) have been less successful. Such opponents never give up. The war on terrorism, unfortunately, falls into the second category." *See* Graham Byford, *The Wrong War*, 81 FOR. AFF'S, 34 (2002) [hereinafter Byford].
40. Cronin, *supra* note 36, at 127.

The use of force against terrorists in the new geo-political environment identifies some questions that before the end of the Cold War and September 11, 2001 seemed far from the law regulating the use of force. Today, because of the radical change of the political and military-strategic context in which jus ad bellum functions and the need to extend the application of jus ad bellum rules to areas such as humanitarian intervention, intervention in failed states or against "rogue" regimes that develop weapons of mass destruction (WMD), or self-defense against terrorist attacks by non-state actors, these questions are no longer distant from the law governing the use of force.

Flatland Thinking and the Fight Against Terrorism

The current debate about terrorism and responses to it reveal a dichotomy (sometimes almost an abyss) in thinking and acting between hawks and doves, left and right, liberals and conservatives, human rights activists and military (or political) leaders, and pacifists and militarists. This is not the natural dichotomy between terrorists, their supporters and civilized society, rejecting terrorism whatever its form. No, this dichotomy, to borrow the simple but effective words of President Bush, is "you're either with us or against us" in this war against terrorism.

This division is clearly reflected in the different approaches to combating crime, including the crime of terror, and other forms of anti-social behavior. Liberals often speak of changing social, economic or political conditions causing high crime rates or terrorism while conservatives (often) call for zero tolerance, longer prison terms or wider use of the death penalty. As American philosopher Ken Wilber writes:

> liberals tend to believe in exterior causes, whereas conservatives tend to believe in interior causes. That is, if an individual is suffering, the typical liberal tends to blame external social institutions (if you are poor it is because you are oppressed by society), whereas the typical conservative tends to blame internal factors (you are poor because you are lazy).[41]

Real life situations are fluid and dynamic and a pure liberal or conservative approach as the only answer for all circumstances is bound to fail. Wilber calls both of these approaches "flatland" thinking and acting. "Truly integral politics would . . . encourage both interior development and exterior

---

41. KEN WILBER, A THEORY OF EVERYTHING: AN INTEGRAL VISION FOR BUSINESS, POLITICS, SCIENCE AND SPIRITUALITY 84 (2001).

development—the growth and development of consciousness and subjective well-being, as well as the growth and development of economic, social, and material well-being."[42] What seems difficult, if sometimes not impossible, is to be conservative (or at least admit that those who are conservative may have a valid point) when the situation requires tough and resolute actions against terrorists and those who support them and to be more liberal in thought and deed when studying and addressing contextual issues giving rise to terrorists and their supporters (such contextual issues are often invoked as a pretext or justification for terrorist acts).

This dichotomy manifests itself in individual answers to the following questions. Whether the national policy should be to pursue vigorously terrorists, using all necessary means, dead or alive, or whether to "drain the swamp," i.e., to deal with what some call root causes of terrorism (e.g., poverty, social inequality, injustice in various forms or religious fundamentalism and extremism)? What are the root-causes of terrorism? How does a government guarantee security in a liberal society without sacrificing fundamental human rights? Is the US strategy in its war on terrorism correct or inappropriate?

These are not easy questions and often contain real dilemmas as choosing one option may foreclose another. However, this is not always the case as when choices must be made the response must not always be dictated by the same set of reasons (e.g., either exclusively by humanitarian concerns or exclusively by security rationale). When comparing Benjamin Netanyahu's views on terrorism[43] to that of some Amnesty International representatives, it is easy to feel frustrated by the simplicity and singlemindedness of either position. Those who are tough on crime, on terrorism, on "rogue" states may view talk about human rights, economic assistance, state building and other similar issues, as at best an annoyance, at worst as pouring water on the mill of terror.[44] On the

---

42. *Id.* at 88.
43. *See generally,* BENJAMIN NETANYAHU, FIGHTING AGAINST TERRORISM. HOW DEMOCRACIES CAN DEFEAT THE INTERNATIONAL TERRORIST NETWORK (2001) [hereinafter FIGHTING AGAINST TERRORISM].
44. For example, the American Civil Liberties Union has harshly criticized US Attorney General John Ashcroft for his testimony where he equated "legitimate political dissent with something unpatriotic and un-American." The statement by Laura W. Murphy, Director of ACLU Washington Office emphasized that "the Attorney General swore an oath to guard the Bill of Rights and the Constitution, including the First Amendment. For him to openly attack as "aiding the enemy" those who question government policy is all the more frightening in light of his constitutional duty to protect each and every American's right to speak and think their mind." (Laura Murphy, Statement on Attorney General John Ashcroft's Testimony (ACLU Washington National Office, Dec. 10, 2001)).

other hand, human rights activists, leftist liberals and sophisticated academics often seem to be blind to real life hard choices.

The former Prime Minister of Israel Ehud Barak analyzing the 11 September attacks writes:

> This kind of terror cannot be defeated without determined patience, strategic goals and tactical flexibility. You have to think and act, not by the book, but "out of the box," open eyed, your mind free from any dogma or conventional wisdom. The approach must be systematic: intensive worldwide intelligence-gathering; a wide operational and logistical deployment; economic sanctions and no softness in applying them; diplomatic ultimatums and no backing down from them.[45]

Beyond this, writes Barak, a systematic battle will require fully streamlined immigration rules and procedures, internationally coordinated anti-money laundering legislation, and, importantly, the reassessment of the generation-old American practice not permitting pre-emptive strikes against terrorists and terror operatives.[46] These measures are clearly important and necessary to fight terrorists but are they sufficient? The short answer is they are not. It is rather futile to use only military or law-enforcement measures in the war against terrorism. It would be counterproductive and look very much like a Sisyphean toil. As Professor Lawrence Freedman observes, "if raids failed to differentiate between the guilty, the half-committed and the innocent then the main result would be to generate many new recruits and supporters."[47] Juxtapose this insightful comment with the recent Israeli attack which killed the Hamas military commander Sheikh Salah Shehada and 14 others, including 9 children, while wounding more than 140 people.[48] Is it Barak then, or Freedman who is correct?

If Barak were only a former general it might be possible to understand his exclusive attention to military and law-enforcement measures. But Barak was also Prime Minister of Israel, a country constantly facing terrorist attacks. For a politician, such one-sidedness and single-mindedness may be fatal. And this

---

45. Ehud Barak, *Security and Counter-Terrorism* in RE-ORDERING THE WORLD, *supra* note 29, at 93.
46. *Id.*
47. Lawrence Freedman, *A New Type of War*, WORLDS IN COLLISION. TERROR AND THE FUTURE OF GLOBAL ORDER 40 (Ken Booth et al. eds., 2002) [hereinafter WORLDS IN COLLISION].
48. Brian Knowlton, *Heavy Handed Israeli Attack is Condemned*, INT'L HERALD TRIBUNE, Jul. 24, 2002, at 1.

is Ehud Barak and not Benjamin Netanyahu, whose views on terrorism are much more simplistic.[49]

However, human rights activists and those with a liberal agenda are not doing any better. For example, Daniel Warner, the acting Secretary General of the Institute of International Studies in Geneva, writes:

> But what is terrorism? It is the activity of the dispossessed, the voiceless, in a radically asymmetrical distribution of power. . . . Terrorism has causes. Growth in inequalities of wealth and lack of political access lead to frustration, which eventually leads to aggression, violence and terrorism. The greater the levels of frustration, the greater the levels of violence. The higher the levels of repression, the higher the levels of reaction.[50]

This is the corresponding liberal approach to terrorism and while there is some truth in this approach, such a view is also one-sided and simple. It is often useless to argue what the root causes of terrorism are because there are different views on this issue that are firmly entrenched. It is also useless because it is often quite impossible to distinguish clearly between causes of, circumstances conducive to and pretexts or justifications for various phenomena, including terrorism. "To a Western observer," writes Bernard Lewis,

> schooled in the theory and practice of Western freedom, it is precisely the lack of freedom—freedom of the mind from constraint and indoctrination, to question and inquire and speak; freedom of the economy from corrupt and pervasive mismanagement; freedom of women from male oppression; freedom of citizens from tyranny—that underlies so many of the troubles of the Muslim world. But the road to democracy, as the Western experience amply demonstrates, is long and hard, full of pitfalls and obstacles.[51]

Thomas Friedman believes that, "the anti-terror coalition has to understand what this war is about. It is not fighting to eradicate "terrorism." Terrorism is just a tool. It is fighting to defeat an ideology: religious totalitarianism."[52] Whether religious totalitarianism is a cause or a circumstance conducive to

---

49. Although most, if not all, of the remedies Netanyahu proposes may be necessary indeed, they are limited to law-enforcement measures, economic or diplomatic sanctions and the use of military force. See FIGHTING AGAINST TERRORISM, *supra* note 43, at 129–148.
50. Daniel Warner, *For The West, A War On Terror Makes No Sense*, INT'L HERALD TRIBUNE, Sep. 21, 2001, at 11.
51. Bernard Lewis, *What Went Wrong?*, 289 THE ATLANTIC MONTHLY 1, at 6 (2002).
52. Thomas Friedman, *World War III is Against Religious Totalitarianism*, INT'L HERALD TRIBUNE, Nov. 28, 2001, at 7.

terrorism is beyond the point. It is a factor closely linked to terrorism, especially to its modern version.

Poverty, discrimination, repression, inequality and religious intolerance all contribute to the creation and sustainment of terrorism. However, not all poor and oppressed are terrorists and most of the terrorists are not at all poor and oppressed. The false dilemma—whether to concentrate on changing the conditions that may be conducive to terrorism or to respond forcefully to acts of terror—is answered differently at different times. This is a false dilemma between liberals who see the problems arising from external factors and the conservatives blaming only internal factors—the mindset of perpetrators of criminal acts. Addressing both sets of factors is equally important and necessary. Responses to terrorism should involve various methods, addressing all the causes and conditions favorable to its creation and development. As Audrey Cronin writes, "the United States, working in tandem with key allies from the UK to Japan, must disable the enabling environment of terrorism."[53] It is also, however, necessary to use military and/or law-enforcement measures against terrorists and their accomplices as it is impossible to appease terrorists and hopeless to try to meet their demands believing this would end their terrorist acts.[54] Terrorists understand strength and power even if they do not necessarily respect (or may even hate) that power. Terrorists also despise weakness and see it in every concession and moderation.

Successful domestic societies use both criminal justice and social programs in efforts to lower the crime rate. Similarly, in international society it would be inadequate to resort to only one category of measures. Conditions conducive to terrorism have to be addressed and terrorists and those who support them must be arrested and tried. Moreover, where necessary, military force, as a measure of self-defense or collective security, must be used against them.

Richard Falk correctly distinguishes between two fallacies: "just as the pacifist fallacy involves unrealistic exclusion of military force from an acceptable response, the militarist fallacy involves excessive reliance on military force in a manner that magnifies the threat it is trying to diminish, almost certain to

---

53. Cronin, *supra* note 36, at 133.
54. In a way, terrorists act counterproductively to the content of their demands since to meet their demands, even if these demands were justified if not made by terrorists, would encourage further terrorism. For example, Palestinian terrorists demand the end of the Israeli occupation and dismantlement of the settlements in the occupied territories. Ending this occupation would be seen by terrorists, however, as a victory of their means. Surrendering to their demands then would only tempt them to increase their demands underpinned by terrorist threats.

intensify and inflame anti-Americanism."[55] Only when these fallacies combine can they become mutually supportable and achieve success.

Post-Modern Societies and Pre-Modern Threats

The post September 11th world reveals another unfortunate and widening rift related to the gap between liberals and conservatives, the gap between the United States and Western Europe in their attitudes towards the war against terrorism and terrorists. One explanation for the different visions on terrorism may be the huge difference in their military capabilities. Robert Kagan puts it only as a rhetorical question: "If Europe's strategic culture today places less value on power and military strength and more value on such soft-power tools as economics and trade, isn't it partly because Europe is militarily weak and economically strong?"[56] However, these differing visions are not only due to the gap in military capabilities on both sides of the Atlantic. Kagan insightfully notes that along with natural consequences of the transatlantic power gap, there has also opened a broad ideological gap:

> Europe, because of its unique historical experience of the past half-century—culminating in the past decade with the creation of the European Union—has developed a set of ideals and principles regarding the utility and morality of power different from the ideals and principles of Americans, who have not shared that experience. If the strategic chasm between the United States and Europe appears greater than ever today, and grows still wider at a worrying pace, it is because these material and ideological differences reinforce one another.[57]

Although by their internal characteristics European states and the United States belong to the same category of liberal democratic states with highly developed market economies, their place and role in the international system are rather different indeed. As international actors they belong not only to different weight categories but also even to different worlds.

---

55. Richard Falk, *Defining a Just War*, THE NATION, Oct. 29, 2001, at 3–4.
56. Kagan, *supra* note 38, at 9.
57. *Id.* at 3.

Robert Cooper, a senior British diplomat, writes of pre-modern, modern and post-modern states that co-exist side-by-side in today's world.[58] He speaks of the existence of:

> two new types of state: first there are now states—often former colonies—where in some sense the state has almost ceased to exist: a "premodern" zone where the state has failed and a Hobbesian war of all against all is underway (countries like Somalia and, until recently, Afghanistan). Second, there are post imperial, postmodern states that no longer think of security primarily in terms of conquest. And thirdly, of course there remain the traditional "modern" states who behave like states always have, following Machiavellian principles and *raison d'état* (one thinks of countries such as India, Pakistan and China).[59]

In the post-modern world—the world of the European Union—there are no security threats in the traditional sense (at least threats that would originate from within this world) and instead of power (or balance of power), law prevails. In this world, the traditional distinctions between domestic and foreign affairs have broken down; there is not only the legal promise not to use force but the use of such force between post-modern states has become almost unthinkable as their security is based on transparency, mutual openness, interdependence and mutual vulnerability. This is a new paradigm of international relations, which Western European nations have created only recently after centuries of wars, anarchy and the traditional struggle to balance power. The two World Wars served as the main catalyst for the creation of this new Kantian world, albeit in one region only. "Within the confines of Europe," writes Robert Kagan, "the age-old laws of international relations have been repealed. Europeans have stepped out of the Hobbesian world of anarchy into the Kantian world of perpetual peace."[60]

It is, of course, debatable to what extent this peace is perpetual but Kagan is right in emphasizing: "Consider again the qualities that make up the European strategic culture, the emphasis on negotiation, diplomacy, and commercial ties, on international law over the use of force, on seduction over coercion, on multilateralism over unilateralism."[61] These are admirable qualities indeed

---

58. *See generally* ROBERT COOPER, THE POST-MODERN STATE AND THE WORLD ORDER (2nd ed., 2000) [hereinafter WORLD ORDER]; Robert Cooper, *The New Liberal Imperialism*, OBSERVER, (Apr. 7, 2002); Robert Cooper, *The Post-Modern State* in RE-ORDERING THE WORLD, *supra* note 29, at 12.
59. Robert Cooper, *The Post-Modern State* in RE-ORDERING THE WORLD, *supra* note 58, at 12.
60. Kagan, *supra* note 38, at 11.
61. *Id.* at 10.

and hopefully they may serve as an example for other states and other regions of the world. Kagan may be right that "the transmission of the European miracle to the rest of the world has become Europe's new *mission civilatrice.*"[62] There is nothing wrong with such a mission as the expansion of human rights ideas, economic aid, assistance in state-building and other similar policies as well as the very lessons of European experience (negative and positive) may help other societies avoid disasters that the Europeans experienced, without necessarily repeating all the mistakes made in Europe.

No society can or should repeat the development or evolution of other societies, especially if their historic, cultural and religious traditions are rather different. Nevertheless if countries like Rwanda or Burundi of today do not learn something from the past experience of countries like Sweden or Finland, the Rwandas and Burundis of tomorrow will not be much different from those of 1994. Some aspects of the European experience, for example, its painful and long process of secularization, may be especially important in the context of today's major terrorist threats. Chris Brown insightfully writes that:

> the subjection of all accounts of the ultimate ends of life to the same rationality, which has induced a self-consciously ironic dimension to even deeply held religious and social beliefs; the notion that representative forms of democracy are the only legitimate basis for political power; the spread of a human rights culture in which the privileges once extended only to rich and powerful white males are understood as legitimate only if universally available—this actually rather disparate set of ideas and propositions has come to be seen not as disparate, and thereby separable, but as a package that, taken as such, gives meaning to the notion of modernity within Western society and, with the onset of globalisation, within a nascent global society.[63]

However, fundamentalists of various kinds "want a world with modern technology, but with scientific rational confined to the technical."[64] It may not be accidental that amongst terrorists, especially Islamist terrorists, there are many young men educated either in madrasas or technical institutions (not necessarily in flight schools).

Today there are huge differences between the realities of Europe and the situation in most other parts of the world. Still it happens that in their dealings with actors from different parts of the world, the Europeans often try to use

---

62. *Id.* at 12.
63. C. Brown, *Narratives of Religion, Civilization and Modernity*, [hereinafter Brown] in WORLDS IN COLLISION, *supra* note 47, at 299.
64. *Id.*

post-modern rules of the game that (even amongst each other) are of recent origin. Europeans too often follow their newly acquired post-modern mindset when confronting modern or even pre-modern actors. These standards may not apply.

The United States, because of its unique position in the world, Cooper believes, combines characteristics of modern and post-modern society. Defining the United States as a "partially post-modern" state, he writes:

> Outside Europe, who might be described as postmodern? Canada certainly; the USA up to a point perhaps. The USA is the more doubtful case since it is not clear that the US government or Congress accepts either the necessity and desirability of interdependence, or its corollaries of openness, mutual surveillance and mutual interference to the same extent as most European governments now do. . . . The knowledge that the defence of the civilised world rests ultimately on its shoulders is perhaps justification enough for the US caution.[65]

A recent film[66] captures the essence of a post-modern society. In it violence was unthinkable, everybody was terribly polite and political correctness had reached quite absurd levels. A villain (played by Wesley Snipe) from the earlier "modern" age returns to help the leader of the city deal with some difficult problems left over from previous times. When the "villain," quite predictably acts like a villain, the authorities must bring a "modern" police officer (played by Sylvester Stallone) back to deal with the "modern" villain. Using physical force and all necessary means, he succeeds in eliminating the "modern" threat to the benevolent "post-modern" world.

By analogy, what was Europe when facing President Milosevic, Radovan Karadjic or General Mladic? Ultimately, Europe was forced to rely on the United States to face real (and not fictional) villains in its own backyard. At the same time many Europeans continued to criticize the United States for not being nice enough towards such "modern" and "pre-modern" villains for not treating them in accordance with European post-modern rules. Is there not some truth then in the notion that post-modern values can flourish in places of the world today where societies are at different levels of development because the United States has performed for the Europeans the role of a modern cop? As Kagan points out, "Europe's new Kantian order could flourish only under the umbrella of American power exercised according to the rules

---

65. WORLD ORDER, *supra* note 58, at 27.
66. DEMOLITION MAN (Warner Brothers 1996).

of the old Hobbesian order" and that "most Europeans do not see the great paradox: that their passage into post-history has depended on the United States not making the same passage."[67] Though the Vietnam and Mogadishu syndromes seriously affected the US ability to act adequately and decisively in some pre-modern situations (e.g., in Rwanda or Haiti) there is nevertheless the ring of truth in Kagan's words.

It is also not by chance that al Qaeda and many other terrorist organizations have been able to operate freely in Western European countries (and in the United States) exploiting in their fight against modern (or post-modern) liberties and freedoms, the very same liberties and freedoms, using technological achievements of the West to undermine its cultural achievements (democracy, human rights, tolerance) that have made these technological achievements possible.[68]

In the world that is far from post-modern, post-modern states must have to retain and rely upon not only some of their modern capabilities (police, prisons, military power) but also some of the norms of the modern world based on power politics. Adequate armed forces and intelligence services combined with the readiness to use them are necessary even for post-modern states. Robert Cooper is absolutely right that "in the coming period of peace in Europe, there will be a temptation to neglect our defenses, both physical and psychological. This represents one of the great dangers for the post-modern state."[69] Chris Brown, observing that fascism and national socialism did not collapse of their own contradictions, emphasizes that "the opponents of Islamo-fascism have to be prepared to fight for what they believe in, and the intelligent use of military force will, inevitably, be one component of the struggle."[70]

---

67. Kagan, *supra* note 38, at 16.
68. Bassam Tibi has written that:

    Muslim fundamentalists very much favour the adoption of modern science and technology by contemporary Islam. But they restrict what may be adopted to select instruments, that is, to the products of science and technology, while fiercely rebuffing the rational worldview that made these achievements possible. The late great Berkeley scholar Reinhardt Bendix showed that 'modernisation in some sphere of life may occur without resulting in [a full measure of] modernity,' and added that 'more or less ad hoc adoption of items of modernity [actually] produces obstacles standing in the way of successful modernisation.'

Tibi, *supra* note 33, at 74.
69. WORLD ORDER, *supra* note 58, at 39.
70. Brown, *supra* note 63, in WORLDS IN COLLISION, *supra* note 47, at 300.

A dangerous side of European reliance on its post-modern values in the wider world is illustrated by the disastrous standoff between the post-modern Dutch peacekeepers and pre-modern Mladic thugs at Srebrenica in 1995, which ended with thousands of Muslim men dead. This is not to criticize the young Dutch soldiers but instead the softness of Western and especially European leaders and societies as a whole when confronting pre-modern villains.

Therefore, is not there some truth in Robert Cooper's words when he emphasizes that "when dealing with more old-fashioned kinds of states outside the post-modern continent of Europe, we need to revert to the rougher methods of an earlier era—force, pre-emptive attack, deception, whatever is necessary to deal with those who still live in the nineteenth century world of every state for itself?"[71] Among ourselves, he continues, "we keep the law but when we are operating in the jungle, we must also use the laws of the jungle," emphasizing the need to get used to the idea of double standards.[72]

The language used by Cooper may be too provocative and should not be taken literally. International law and not the law of the jungle has to play a role even in dealings with modern and post-modern states and other actors from that world. However, double standards, or even treble standards for that matter, may be acceptable if we openly recognize, for example, that certain categories of weapons are much more dangerous in the hands of regimes like Saddam Hussein's than in the hands of more responsible and civilized actors, or that not all ideologies are of equal value (we have already made exceptions for fascism and recently for communism too), that some of them are so intolerant that they constitute a threat to international peace and security. The principles and rules of international law applicable in the non-Kantian world must be different from those applicable in the post-modern environment. It follows then that contemporary jus ad bellum cannot be based on the values and principles applicable in the post-modern Kantian world where the usefulness and applicability of jus ad bellum is unthinkable. What then is the contemporary jus ad bellum and what should it be? As further discussed infra, the sovereignty of those states that massively violate human rights or failed states that are unable to guarantee a minimum of order and justice and especially those states that are unwilling or unable to prevent their territory from being used for carrying out terrorist attacks against other states and their nationals cannot be respected in the same way as the sovereignty of other states. As Kofi

---

71. Robert Cooper, *The New Liberal Imperialism*, OBSERVER, Apr. 7, 2002, at 3.
72. Id.

Annan, the UN Secretary General, said during the NATO operation in Kosovo: "[T]here is emerging international law that countries cannot hide behind sovereignty and abuse people without expecting the rest of the world to do something about it."[73]

The Charter Paradigm and the Use of Force at the Turn of the Century

The question of the current state of the law on the use of force is approachable from different angles:

(a) What does the text of the UN Charter say?

(b) What did the drafters of the Charter mean in 1945?

(c) What may be reasonable or plausible interpretations of the Charter principles and rules concerning the use of force?

(d) What do the current circumstances require?

(e) What is the prevalent (if any) consensus on use of force today?

Different authors have used in their study of the use of force all of these approaches. States have also relied, in various degrees and combinations depending on circumstances, on all these possible interpretations of jus ad bellum.

Today, however, we have a rather schizophrenic situation in jus ad bellum. The more one thinks of it, the less one seems to understand it. The more one tries to understand it, the less certain one becomes about what it requires. Therefore, it is wise in many cases to avoid definitive conclusions like "international law certainly allows it," or vice versa, that "it certainly prohibits it." Most conclusions of that nature are not only vulnerable to convincing criticism but also cannot be verified as correct.

It would be equally wrong to say either that there have been no changes whatsoever in the legal regime regulating the use of force, or, on the contrary, to interpret too creatively certain tendencies in the rather confused international practice in order to conclude, for example, that there undoubtedly is a right to use force to save lives in foreign countries. Today, there are not many areas in

---

73. Tim Burton & Robert Anderson, *UN Warns Yugoslavia Over Human Rights*, FINANCIAL TIMES, May 26, 1999, at 2.

jus ad bellum where the word "undoubtedly" is used. Instead, it is better to speak of trends, legitimization and more justifiable or less justifiable practices. It follows that it is better to avoid definitive terms such as lawful or illegal.

For some, the UN Charter seems to have acquired certain characteristics of the Holy Books—either the Bible or the Koran. One cannot change it, one has to believe in it and even swear allegiance to it, but at the same time, one can hardly live by it. However, a Charter fundamentalism may be almost as dangerous as Biblical or Koranic fundamentalisms. Literal and non-contextual interpretation of any text—be they religious or secular texts—is bound to lead to social impasse. If in the case of holy texts such interpretation sometimes guides towards and justifies violence, in the case of the UN Charter, it may be one of the causes of the inability to adequately respond to violence.

However, it is often said that the prohibition on the use of force [Article 2(4) of the Charter] is a jus cogens norm[74] and therefore treaties and practice not only cannot deviate from it but even when such practice is widespread, it does not undermine or change the fundamental norm. In such a case, how can one question what the Charter says on the use of force?

Many things might be said about jus cogens in support of this concept as well as by way of criticism.[75] It is necessary here to emphasize what Oscar Schachter has written about principles of international law. He distinguishes between the core and penumbra of applicability of such principles.[76] While the core may be jus cogens, the penumbra need not necessarily be of such a character.

If we take by way of comparison and illustration, for example, one of the basic human rights norms—the right to life—we see that the core of it—the prohibition of arbitrary deprivation of life and especially the prohibition of genocide (e.g., Article 6 of the International Covenant on Civil and Political Rights)—is undoubtedly jus cogens in the sense that no deviation from it is permitted under any circumstances. When deviations do occur, they do not undermine the basic prohibition since there is strong and general *opinio juris* supporting this core of the norm. However, when considering, for instance, the issue of the death penalty it is much less clear. Contradictory practices as well as contradictory opinions (including *opinio juris*) exist on this matter. Sensitive areas such as abortion and euthanasia—both hotly debated right to life issues—make the problem of the jus cogens character of the right to life

---

74. *See, e.g.*, 1966 Y.B. OF THE INT'L L. COMM 247–48 (1966).
75. *See, e.g.*, REIN MÜLLERSON, ORDERING ANARCHY 156–61 (2000).
76. OSCAR SCHACHTER, INTERNATIONAL LAW IN THEORY AND PRACTICE 20 (1991) [hereinafter SCHACHTER].

(its absolute and non-derogable character) as a whole uncertain and complicated.

Similar situation exists in the legal regulation of the use of force. Of course, there are areas of jus ad bellum where legal rules are rather certain. The Charter and customary international law prohibition against the use of force, for example, for territorial aggrandizement or political subjugation of other states (as well as the affirmative right to use force in self-defense) remain valid and relatively non-controversial. The Iraqi aggression against Kuwait and the world community's responses to it have confirmed and reinforced these aspects of the prohibition on the use of force. As Anne-Marie Slaughter and William Burke-White, referring to the numerous resolutions of the General Assembly and the Security Council, write, "when interstate aggression happens, the vast majority of the world's nations routinely and automatically condemn it as illegal."[77] However, when considering issues like the use of force for humanitarian intervention different practices and conflicting views exist. Michael Glennon's point that "there is, today, no coherent international law concerning intervention by states. States disagree profoundly on fundamental issues—issues on which consensus is necessary for a treaty or customary rule to work."[78] Though consensus does not exist in some domains of jus ad bellum, it is somewhat difficult to accept this negative evaluation of the role of the UN Security Council in the changes that are taking place in jus ad bellum.

Glennon writes:

> By intervening in the internal affairs of states, the Security Council itself contributed to the erosion of the Charter's constraints on use of force, beginning with Southern Rhodesia and continuing with legally questionable interventions in South Africa, Iraq, Somalia, Rwanda, and Haiti. Governments that have come to justify humanitarian intervention by states acting in the face of Security Council paralysis rely on the Council's own record.[79]

Glennon believes that "there can be little doubt that the Security Council has acted in a manner inconsistent with the limits placed on its authority by Article 39 and Article 2(7) of the Charter."[80] In support of this thesis he quotes Sean

---

77. Anne Slaughter & William Burke-White, *An International Constitutional Moment*, 43 HARV INT'L L. J. 1 (2002) [hereinafter Slaughter & Burke-White].
78. MICHAEL GLENNON, LIMITS OF LAW, PREROGATIVES OF POWER. INTERVENTIONISM AFTER KOSOVO 2 (2001).
79. *Id.* at 114.
80. *Id.* at 120.

Murphy who wrote: "by considering essentially internal human rights violations and deprivations to be "threats to the peace," the Security Council is expanding the scope of its authority beyond that originally envisioned in Chapter VII of the Charter."[81]

However, these are two rather different statements. Murphy's understanding corresponds to Schachter's explanation that "no text adopted by governments can or should foreclose choices imposed by changing conditions and by new perceptions of ends and means. The Charter is a living instrument. It is, like every constitutional instrument, continuously interpreted, moulded and adapted to meet the interests of the parties."[82] Had not the Security Council reacted to changing circumstances, had it continued to apply the interpretation of the Charter held by its drafters in 1945, the Council would have remained completely inadequate. As the Permanent Court of International Justice observed in 1923, "the question whether a certain matter is or is not solely within the jurisdiction of a state is an essentially relative question; it depends upon the development of international relations."[83] The Council has not yet come close to intervening in any state's internal affairs. While the Council, using its wide discretionary powers, have found threats to international peace and security (e.g., Haiti) where no such threat seemed to exist, given the egregious behavior of these states towards their people, their behavior could not be viewed as within the "internal affairs of the state" any longer.

Michael Schmitt is correct when emphasizing that:

> Professor Glennon's thoughtful analysis exaggerates the *de jure-de facto* divide. In fact, what has been happening over the past half-century is a regular evolution in the global community's understanding of the use of force regime. This evolution has been, as it always is and always must be, responsive to the changing circumstances in which international law operates. Practice does not contradict law so much as it informs law as to the global community's normative expectations.[84]

---

81. SEAN MURPHY, HUMANITARIAN INTERVENTION: THE UNITED NATIONS IN THE EVOLVING WORLD 196 (1996).
82. SCHACHTER, *supra* note 76, at 118–19.
83. *See* Nationality Decrees in Tunis and Morocco Case, P.C.I.J., Series B, No. 4, at 24, 2 I.L.R. 349 (1923).
84. Michael Schmitt, *Counter-Terrorism and the Use of Force in International Law*, *supra* Chap. II this volume.

Although the end of the Cold War and the accelerating pace of events have required more changes in the law of jus ad bellum[85] than in the previous fifty years, neither the existing Charter interpretation nor a completely new set of rules is either possible or even desirable. International lawyers, be they in the service of their governments or academics, must avoid extreme choices between, using the words of Ronald Dworkin, "the dead but legitimate hand of the past and the distinctly illicit charm of progress."[86] Past decisions have to be interpreted and reinterpreted in the light of current needs and tendencies.

Terrorism: Jus ad Bellum or Jus in Bello?

Since terrorism is basically about means and methods and not about the purpose for the use of force[87] why is it a jus ad bellum issue at all? Should not it be,

---

85. Slaughter and Burke-White even write that "[T]o respond adequately and effectively to the threats and challenges that are emerging in this new paradigm, we need new rules. Just as in 1945, the nations of the world today face an international constitutional moment." Slaughter & Burke-White, *supra* note 77, at 2.

86. RONALD DWORKIN, LAW'S EMPIRE 348 (1998). While Dworkin writes that judges have to choose between these extremes, his whole book seems to indicate that the proper choice has to be somewhere in between and not always either the legitimate hand of the past or the illicit charm of progress.

87. Granville Byford draws our attention to the fact that many historical figures who today are admired (at least, but not exclusively, by their own people) have committed acts that today would be defined as terrorism or crimes against humanity. He, for example, refers to Henry V who killed his prisoners before the Battle of Agincourt but was still lionized by Shakespeare. Byford, *supra* note 39, at 36. Tamerlane enjoyed building huge pyramids from human skulls but today on his monument in the centre of Uzbek capital Tashkent the following words are ascribed to him: "Power is in Justice." Even in the second half of the twentieth century (the UN Charter period) several future Israeli leaders used terror tactics in their fight for Israeli statehood and even the accusations of terrorism against Nelson Mandela's ANC were not all groundless. The Irish Republican Army has had sympathizers in various US governments and the list can be continued. Byford, therefore, proposes, in order to untangle the knot, "to think of a graph with the morality of means running along one axis and the morality of the ends running along the other." (*Id.* at 38). Byford correctly observes that even in today's world in certain conditions noble aims cannot be achieved without the recourse to violence. However, what was acceptable or even heroic in the past may well be criminal today, and secondly, if violence (even considerable) may be necessary and acceptable for the achievement of even noble aims, this does not mean that terrorism is acceptable too. No graph that would justify terror violence depending on the high morality of pursued aims should be acceptable. We have had it enough already and it is called: one man's terrorist is another man's freedom fighter.

as some argue,[88] an issue of criminal justice, or if it has anything to do with the legal regulation of use of force at all, then a jus in bello topic only? However, something cannot be a jus in bello issue without first coming under jus ad bellum and terrorism belongs to the domain of jus ad bellum as terrorist attacks may constitute a specific, non-traditional (i.e., what the drafters of the UN Charter did not have in mind in 1945) form of an armed attack that gives rise to the right of self-defense and/or collective security measures involving use of force under Chapter VII of the UN Charter.

Of course, if a terrorist attack is covered by jus ad bellum, if it constitutes an armed attack or a threat to international peace and security against which Chapter VII collective security measures involving use of force are applied, it is automatically also contrary to jus in bello. Such a conclusion follows from the very definition of terrorism as a crime.[89] Note here that not every terrorist attack is contrary to jus ad bellum (either because it does not have any foreign element or because of the relatively insignificant nature of the attack). However, every terrorist attack that comes under jus ad bellum, by definition violates jus in bello. For terrorists, attacks against civilians and civilian objects are not collateral to the recourse to military force but one of the necessary elements of it. Jason Vest notes that a defining characteristic of fourth-generation warfare is "the emphasis on bypassing an opposing military force and striking directly at cultural, political, or population targets."[90] This is what terrorists do and this kind of tactic is, *ab initio*, contrary to jus in bello and (as discussed infra)

---

88. Abdullahi Ahmed An-Na'im, for example, writes that "the answer is simply that the attacks were international crimes of the utmost seriousness that must be vigorously investigated in order to hold those responsible accountable under the law. . . . If there is the political will to treat the attacks as a matter for law enforcement, not military retaliation, I believe there are enough normative and institutional resources to begin the process of criminal accountability under international law." *See* Abdullahi An-Na'im, *Upholding International Legality against Jihad*, WORLDS IN COLLISION, *supra* note 47, at 169. It is interesting that though An-Na'im writes that in the case of the 9/11 attacks pursuing extradition would have been unrealistic, he nevertheless accuses the United States of failing to do so. This is like asking the current Iraqi regime to extradite Saddam Hussein. Such a request does not correspond with the seriousness of the matter. Moreover, in the case of crimes of that magnitude, history since the Nuremberg trials have shown, that military and criminal justice measures are almost necessarily interlinked.

89. One may ask whether those who commit acts of terror in armed conflicts are terrorists or war criminals. They are both, of course. In time of war, acts of terror (e.g., deliberately attacking civilians, killing POWs, using indiscriminate force etc.) are either grave breaches under the Geneva Conventions or other acts defined as war crimes. *See, e.g.*, Article 130, Geneva Convention (III) Relative to the Treatment of Prisoners of War, 1949, *reprinted in* THE LAWS OF ARMED CONFLICTS: A COLLECTION OF CONVENTIONS, RESOLUTIONS AND OTHER DOCUMENTS 435 (D. Schindler & J. Toman eds., 3rd ed., 1988).

90. Jason Vest, *Fourth-Generation Warfare*, 288 THE ATLANTIC MONTHLY 5, at 2–3 (2001).

necessarily changes some modalities of defensive responses. Still, Caleb Carr has ably demonstrated in his book *The Lessons of Terror* that terror tactics were historically used as a supposedly effective method of waging wars (however, Carr convincingly argues that even in the past, though such tactics may have provided some short-term tactical advantages, they have always been counter-productive in the long run).[91]

Of course, a direct armed attack by armed forces of state A against state B may be also committed as a terrorist attack if the attack is carried out in flagrant violation of jus in bello requirements and if at least one of the purposes of the use of such modalities of attack is spreading terror among the population of the victim state or forcing the government to change its policies or surrender.

Terror Attacks and the Necessity of Self-Defense

Terrorism has different causes and circumstances exist that may enhance or diminish its likely emergence and flourishing. These circumstances must, of course, be addressed. However, leaving terrorist attacks without a tough and physical response, addressing only the so-called "underlying causes" demonstrates weakness thereby only encouraging new attacks. The use of force as a law-enforcement measure or as a military response, though not the only or even perhaps the most important means of dealing with terrorism, is nonetheless necessary as both a special and general deterrent. Authorization for military responses to terrorist attacks may combine both the element of self-defense and that of necessity. Of course, these two are closely linked any way as the seminal *Caroline case* speaks of the "necessity of self-defense."[92] In fact, though the *Caroline case* is often used in the practice and teaching of international law as a self-defense precedent that clarifies issues such as necessity, immediacy and proportionality, the International Law Commission (ILC) has dealt only with the case as one dealing with the concept of necessity.[93] The 1980 Report of the ILC, for example, observes that:

---

91. *See* CALEB CARR, LESSONS OF TERROR. A HISTORY OF WARFARE AGAINST CIVILIANS—WHY IT HAS ALWAYS FAILED, AND WHY IT WILL FAIL AGAIN (2002).
92. R. Y. Jennings, *The Caroline and McLeod Cases*, 32 AM. J. INT'L. L. 82 (1938) [hereinafter Jennings].
93. *See* International Law Commission *Commentaries to the Draft Articles on Responsibility of States for Internationally Wrongful Acts*, para. 5, UN GAOR, 56th Sess., Supp. No. 10, UN Doc. A/56/10 (2001) [hereinafter *Commentaries*].

in the past, there has been no lack of actual cases in which necessity was invoked precisely to preclude the wrongfulness of an armed incursion into foreign territory for the purpose of carrying out one or another of the operations referred above. To cite only one example of the many involving situations of this kind, there was the celebrated "Caroline" case."[94]

Unlike in the first half of the 19th century when the *Caroline* incident occurred, the right to self-defense today includes measures undertaken against non-state entities.[95] Accordingly, a situation can exist today when self-defense against terrorist attacks may be carried out, by necessity and under certain circumstances, in the territory of a third state even without the latter's consent. Hence, the concept of self-defense characterizes the use of force vis-à-vis a terrorist organization, while the concept of necessity characterizes the use of such force in the territory of another state. Necessity, unlike the inherent right to self-defense, is not a right (though both are considered as circumstances precluding wrongfulness), but as a justification used in exceptional circumstances, or as the ILC comments, "under certain very limited conditions."[96]

When terrorists operate from the territory of a state and that state is unable or unwilling to end the terrorist acts, military action by other states directed at the terrorists within the state where the terror operations are originating from can be justified as a state of necessity. This is what Roberto Ago's comment to the draft article in the ILC Report called "the existence of conduct which, although infringing the territorial sovereignty of a State, need not necessarily be considered as an act of aggression, or not, in any case, as a breach of an international obligation of jus cogens."[97] This is instead a self-defense operation against the terrorist organization that is by necessity carried out in the territory of a third state; preferably, of course, with the latter's consent. However, if the territorial state, which has itself been unable to prevent terrorists

---

94. 1980 Y.B. INT'L L. COMM. Vol II, Part 2 at 44 (1980), U.N. Doc. A/CN.4/SER.A/1980/Add. 1.
95. In the Caroline incident, the British in 1837 crossed the Niagara River and destroyed the steamship Caroline which was being used by private persons to help rebels fight the British. The British were not attacked by the United States or by irregulars acting on behalf of the United States. Therefore, the ensuing discussion between US Secretary of State Daniel Webster and UK Envoy Lord Alexander Ashburton might as well have been about the actions of non-state entities in the territory of another state. *See generally* Jennings, *supra* note 93.
96. *See Commentaries, supra* note 93 at para. 14.
97. *See* 1973 Y.B. INT'L L. COMM. Vol II, at 249 (1973), U.N. Doc. A/CN.4/SER.A/1973/Add. 1.

attacking other states or their nationals and interests, resists the victim-state (or its allies) in their efforts to eliminate the terrorists, it itself becomes an accomplice to the terrorist organization. The Entebbe raid in 1976 illustrates this point nicely. When Ugandan forces attacked the Israeli commandos attempting to liberate the hostages (something the Ugandan authorities had failed to do), Ugandan forces became legitimate targets of Israeli countermeasures.

Once again, of course, the requirements of necessity and proportionality play an important role in determining the character of self-defense measures. Indeed, the character of terrorist attacks themselves, often of uncertain origin and magnitude, puts an even higher emphasis on the need to observe the principles of necessity and proportionality in the use of military force in response to such attacks. They are especially important in helping to avoid escalation of terrorist related conflicts.

This portion of this article concentrates only on the self-defense paradigm response to terrorists attacks—leaving for another day the discussion of the collective security paradigm. These two paradigms are not exclusive and ideally, responses to terrorist attacks should involve the use of force across both paradigms.

An armed attack, in the form of a terrorist attack or not, is an *erga omnes* violation of international law and the victim state is not the only injured state.[98] A terrorist act(s) that is tantamount to an armed attack concerns the entire international community and therefore any such attack should ideally trigger the UN collective security mechanism at the same time as the right of the victim state to use force, either alone or together with its allies, in self-defense occurs. Indeed, although dealing primarily with terrorists and support for such terrorists, Security Council Resolution 1373 states that all states shall "take the necessary steps to prevent the commission of terrorist acts." While different from, and falling short of authorizing the "use of all necessary means," the interpretation of this language may well lead to similar conclusions.

Interestingly, the Security Council, while taking measures necessary to maintain international peace and security, at the same time recognized in its Resolution 1368 and reaffirmed in Resolution 1373 the inherent right to

---

98. International Law Commission, *Draft Articles on Responsibility of States for Internationally Wrongful Acts, Report of the International Law Commission on the Work of its Fifty-third Session*, Art. 48(1b), U.N. GAOR, 56th Sess., Supp. No. 10, U.N. Doc. A/56/10 (2001) [hereinafter *Draft Articles*].

individual and collective self-defense.[99] Accordingly, though the Council was acting within the collective security paradigm in these resolutions, it did not consider that these measures in any way interfered with or superceded the right to use force in individual or collective self-defense.

In the current fight against terrorism the use of military force in self-defense in Afghanistan by the United States, United Kingdom, Canada and other allies is combined with collective security such as those that are the basis for the International Security Assistance Force (ISAF).[100] These are not the only collective security measures being used by the Security Council. As an example, it has also used financial measures against al Qaeda, other terrorist organizations and individuals linked to them. Chapter VII non-military measures are beyond the scope of this article and will not therefore be addressed. However, their use does help make the point that only combinations of various means and methods of fighting terrorism can lead ultimately to success.

Specific Characteristics of Self-Defense Against Terrorist Attacks.

Terrorist attacks have some characteristics which traditional armed attacks, as a rule, do not have: (i) attacks are usually carried out not by a state's armed forces but by non-state groups which may or may not have links with some states (except that terrorist groups have to operate on the territory of at least some states and this is one of the essential differences between piracy and terrorism, though in some respect they may be comparable); (ii) the identity of the attackers and their affiliation with other entities (including states) is usually not clear; and, (iii) the means and methods used by terrorists are, by definition, contrary to international humanitarian law since they intentionally

---

99. Myjer and White point to the fact that references to the right to self-defense were only in the Preambles of the Security Council Resolutions 1368 and 1373 and therefore, in their opinion, the Council did not unequivocally determine that there had been an armed attack against the United States on 11 September 2001. They believe that "at an early stage therefore the Security Council should have made it clear without a shadow of doubt whether it was of the opinion that there solely is an article 39 situation, or a Chapter VII self-defence situation." *See* Myjer & White, *supra* note 31, at 10. However, on 12 September when the Security Council passed Resolution 1368 it may not yet have been clear who was behind these attacks (e.g., had they been committed by a US terrorist group, then such an attack would not have given rise to the right to self-defense under international law notwithstanding the magnitude of the attack). Therefore, the Security Council could not have used such specific language. Moreover, a reference to the right to self-defense in the preamble of a resolution wholly devoted to a terrorist attack is a sufficient indication that the Council believed that there was at least a prima facie self-defense situation.

100. S. C. Res. 1386 U.N. SCOR, 56th Sess., U.N. Doc. S/1386/(2001).

target non-combatants and attack prohibited objects. These particular features of terrorist attacks condition the character of responses to them.

First, what is the status of terrorist organizations in international law? Does Article 51 apply to attacks carried out by non-state entities? Michael Byers writes that "it will probably be argued that the atrocities of 11 September did not constitute an armed attack since they did not involve the use of force by a state, and that the relevant framework of analysis is instead international criminal law."[101] Eric Myjer and Nigel White write that "the categorization of the terrorist attacks on New York and Washington as an "armed attack" within the meaning of article 51 is problematic to say the least.... Self-defence, traditionally speaking, applies to an armed response to an attack by a state."[102] Pierre-Marie Dupuy writes that "the shock of 11 September should cause a re-examination of norms conceived solely on the basis of relations between states."[103] However, such a re-examination has already been ongoing for some time and international law is no longer as state-centric as it was, for example, in 1945 when the UN Charter was adopted. Not only are individuals held criminally responsible directly under international law for genocide, war crimes and crimes against humanity, but the Security Council has gone so far as to impose sanctions against non-state entities such as the Ian Smith regime in Southern Rhodesia, UNITA in Angola and Bosnian Serbs.[104]

There is little doubt that the drafters of Article 51 contemplated armed attacks committed only by states even though the article itself does not explicitly say so. However, it is not only the absence of any direct reference to an armed attack by a state in Article 51 but more importantly, the need to interpret the Charter in the context of current realities that indicates that the right of self-defense may arise also in the case of attacks by non-state entities.[105] As Yoram Dinstein writes:

---

101. Michael Byers, *Terrorism, the Use of Force and International Law after 11 September*, 51 ICLQ 411 (2002).
102. Myjer & White, *supra* note 31, at 7.
103. Pierre-Marie Dupuy, *The Law After the Destruction of the Towers*, EUR J. INT'L L. DISCUSSION FORUM at 1 (2002) *available at* http://www.ejil.org/forum_WTC/ny-dupuy.html (Nov. 30, 2002).
104. For example, Security Council Resolution 924 imposed sanctions against Bosnian Serbs. *See* S. C. Res. 924, U.N. SCOR, 49th Sess., U.N. Doc. S/924/(1994). Similarly, Resolution 864 found that "as a result of UNITA's military actions, the situation in Angola constitutes a threat to international peace and security." An arms embargo was imposed against a non-state entity—UNITA. *See* S. C. Res. 864, U.N. SCOR, 48th Sess., U.N. Doc. S/864/(1993).
105. *See, e.g.*, Ruth Wedgwood, *Responding to Terrorism: The Strikes against bin Laden*, 24 YALE J. INT'L L. 559 (1999).

[I]t should be pointed out that, for an armed attack to justify countermeasures of self-defence under Article 51, it need not be committed by another state. Ordinarily, the perpetrator of the armed attack is indeed a foreign state as such. Yet, in exceptional circumstances, an armed attack—although mounted from the territory of a foreign state—is not launched by that state.[106]

Referring to the case when the Security Council had employed the term "armed attacks" characterizing raids by mercenaries from the territory of Angola and condemning Portugal for not preventing these raids, Dinstein emphasizes that "armed attacks by non-state actors are still armed attacks, even if commenced only from—and not by—another State."[107]

Giorgio Gaja, analyzing the 11 September attacks against the United States in light of the references to the right to self-defense in Security Council resolutions and the NATO decision activating Article 5 of the Washington Treaty, cautiously opines that "depending on the factual circumstances, the definition of the terrorist acts of September 11th as "armed attack" may not necessarily imply that the concept actually refers to acts that are not attributable to a state."[108] However, the US demands addressed to the Taliban (which itself was a non-recognized authority that various Security Council resolutions had called "the Afghan faction known as the Taliban, which also calls itself the Islamic Emirate of Afghanistan")[109] to surrender Osama bin Laden and other al Qaeda terrorists seem to indicate that the United States, at least initially, did not consider that Afghanistan (or even the Taliban for that matter) was directly responsible for the attacks.[110] Only the refusal of the Taliban regime to comply with the US demands and their active defense of the Qaeda network led to the use of force in self-defense against both al Qaeda and the Taliban.

---

106. *See* DINSTEIN, *supra* note 6, at 192.
107. *Id.* at 214.
108. Giorgio Gaja, *In What Sense was There an "Armed Attack?"*, EUR J. INT'L L. DISCUSSION FORUM at 1 (2002), *available at* http://www.ejil.org/forum_WTC/ny-gaja.html (Nov. 30, 2002).
109. *See, e.g.*, S. C. Res. 1267, U.N. SCOR, 54th Sess., U.N. Doc. S/1267/(1999).
110. The Unites States insisted that the Taliban: "Deliver to United States authorities all the leaders of Al Qaeda who hide in your land. Release all foreign diplomats, including American citizens, you have unjustly imprisoned. Protect foreign journalists, diplomats, and aid workers in your country. Close immediately and permanently every terrorist training camp in Afghanistan, and hand over every terrorist and every person in their support structure to appropriate authorities. Give the United States full access to terrorist training camps, so we can make sure they are no longer operating." President George W. Bush, Address Before a Joint Session of the Congress on the United States Response to the Terrorist Attacks of September 11, 37 WEEKLY COMP. PRES. DOC. 1347 (Sep. 20, 2001).

The current war against terrorism, of course, differs from previous wars in the sense that though there was a clear victim of the attack—the United States (or rather several victims because, e.g., hundreds of British and other nationals were also attacked), there was no prima facie perpetrator. This is one of the peculiarities of 21st century wars, that is not without precedent. Acts of so-called indirect aggression[111] do not always have an obvious author since it may be difficult to attribute acts of paramilitary or irregular forces to a specific state. However, indirect aggression, as enshrined in the 1974 Definition of Aggression, presumes the existence of an aggressor state, which instead of using its regular armed forces perpetrates acts of aggression through irregular armed bands, guerrilla forces, etc. In such a case, irregulars are agents of an aggressor state.

Contemporary terrorism is even more complicated. Acts of indirect aggression are usually, though not necessarily always, carried out against neighboring states and notwithstanding that there may be difficulties in attributing acts of irregulars to the state from the territory of which these attacks are launched, the identity of the state is not, as a rule, in question (what may be questioned is whether that state is an aggressor or not). Attacks like those of September 11th may not even have a prima facie culprit, state or non-state.

However, this does not mean that an aggressor does not exist. Such a conclusion would not only be contrary to common sense, it is not one required by contemporary international law.

In a sense, military responses to terrorist attacks do not raise legal, philosophical, moral or even political issues as complicated as, for example, humanitarian intervention does. First of all, notwithstanding its specific and even non-traditional features, terrorist attacks originating from abroad can still be qualified as armed attacks giving rise to the inherent right to self-defense. Together with military operations to rescue one's nationals abroad, such anti-terrorist operations may be qualified as special (non-traditional) self-defense operations. Secondly, military responses to terrorist attacks are today politically less controversial than, for example, the use of force to protect human rights in foreign countries. Although some states still refuse to condemn specific terrorist attacks and even try to find justifications for some of them

---

111. *See* Article 3(a) of the Definition of Aggression of 1974 which states that "the sending by or on behalf of a state of armed bands, groups, irregulars or mercenaries, which carry out acts of armed force against another state of such gravity as to amount to the acts listed above, or its substantial involvement therein," is an act of aggression. *See* 1974 U.N. Definition of Agression, 29 U.N. GAOR, Supp. 31, art. 3(a), U.N. Doc. A/RES/3314 (XXIX) (1975) [hereinafter Definition of Aggression].

(e.g., most Arab states still refuse to condemn, without any qualification, Palestinian terrorism), the traditional support for the idea that a just cause (e.g., national-liberation struggle) justifies the use of terrorist methods is becoming weaker.[112]

If the right to the use of force in self-defense is dependent on the existence of an armed attack (or arguably in the case of so-called anticipatory or interceptive self-defense in anticipation of such an attack), the modalities of the exercise of this right depend on the characteristics of the armed attack.[113] Therefore, we have to consider the specific and distinctive features of terrorist attacks that would condition specific methods and means of defensive responses.

In the case of responses to terrorist attacks, the question of immediacy may have to be addressed differently. As the source of attacks may not be immediately obvious and preparations for responses that often have to be secret may take time (gathering intelligence data, building coalitions etc.), the period between the attack and responsive measures may be rather substantial. In that respect, the situation may be compared to one that existed, for example, after the Iraqi invasion of Kuwait. Although for almost half a year there were no active military operations going on after the Iraqis had occupied Kuwait, the right by Kuwait and its allies to use force in self-defense was not extinguished (maybe only suspended for a while due to the active involvement of the Security Council). The Gulf War did not start on January 15th, 1991 when the Coalition launched Operation DESERT STORM. It started on August 1st, 1990 when the Iraqi troops attacked and occupied Kuwait. Similarly, the war against terrorist attacks started on September 11th at 8:45 when the first aircraft hit the World Trade Center, if not earlier had the United States been able to use its right to anticipatory or interceptive self-defense.

---

112. In 1978 the statement by Ambassador Harriman of Nigeria, who was Chairman of the Ad Hoc Committee on the Drafting of an International Convention Against the Taking of Hostages, disputed the use of the word 'terrorist' describing the Palestinian struggle against Israel: "Here I wish to reiterate that my Government does not believe that any liberation movement should damage its prestige by taking hostages, and that the noble fights for liberation should be based on very high values. I believe that the PLO at no stage in its war for liberation has abused privilege; at no stage has it terrorised; it is at war." Ambassador Harriman is *quoted in* William O'Brien, *Reprisals, Deterrence and Self-Defense in Counterterror Operations*, 30 VA. J. INT'L L. 449 (1990). If at that time, the Soviet Union, a permanent member of the Security Council, wholeheartedly subscribed to this statement, today Russia, which is facing separatist terrorism in Chechnya, as well as Central Asian successor states to the Soviet Union, adamantly reject such assessments of 'liberation' movements.
113. DINSTEIN, *supra* note 6, at 192–221.

The question of immediacy is close also to two other issues: use of force in anticipation of an attack and defensive reprisals. Often military responses to terrorist attacks have to draw a fine balance between two controversial modalities of the use of military force in self-defense—the Scylla of anticipatory self-defense and the Charybdis of reprisals. As Gregory Travalio writes, "if the anticipated action by terrorists is not sufficiently imminent, the right to use force is not available for purposes of deterrence. On the other hand, if past terrorist actions by a group are too remote in time, the response by force is likely to be characterized as an illegal reprisal."[114] Because terrorist warfare usually consists of a series of relatively small-scale attacks that often need to be prevented by measures that combine some elements of retaliation (since a response comes after the attack) and anticipation (since a response comes in anticipation of a new attack), the exercise of the right to self-defense against terrorist attacks requires at least some (sometimes quite considerable) practical use of concepts of a anticipatory self-defense and defensive reprisals.

The need to use preventive force against terrorists becomes even more obvious when we take into consideration the fact that terrorists do not attack military targets that are usually well defended and that, at least in principle, should be ready to defend themselves when attacked. Anne-Marie Slaughter and William Burke-White observe that "in our previous understanding of war, it was possible to attack the vital life within a nation by first destroying the army that protected it."[115] Today, terrorists avoiding military objectives intentionally target defenseless civilians and civilian objects, i.e., non-combatants; they choose soft targets that would be almost inevitably destroyed if attacks were not prevented. Therefore, in many cases preventive, anticipatory or interceptive self-defense is the only effective method of preventing terrorists from achieving their goals.

Interceptive self-defense seems to indicate that only when an attack is already launched is it legitimate to intercept (e.g., intercepting missiles on their boost trajectories but not destroying them in their launching silos). In the case of traditional inter-state conflicts this is probably a prudent interpretation of the right to self-defense. However, today and in the context of self-defense against terrorist attacks (especially if the latter have access to WMD), preventive or anticipatory measures seem justified. As terrorism is usually a continuous process being carried out in the murky underworld, it would be too late or

---

114. Gregory Travalio, *Terrorism, International Law, and the Use of Military Force*, 18 WIS. INT'L L. J. 165 (2000) [hereinafter Travalio].
115. Slaughter & Burke-White, *supra* note 77, at 3.

risky to rely only on the interception of individual attacks that have been already irrevocably launched without attempting to destroy terrorist bases, supply lines, training camps and other similar facilities.

The necessity to use military force in self-defense against terrorist attacks shows that the dividing line drawn, for example, by the International Court of Justice in the *Nicaragua Case* between armed attacks and "less grave forms" of the use of force,[116] is no longer tenable, if it ever was.[117] Dinstein, referring to J.L. Hargrove and J.I. Kunz, has rightly emphasized that "in reality, there is no cause to remove small-scale armed attacks from the spectrum of armed attacks. Article 51 in no way limits itself to large, direct or important armed attacks."[118] The same criticism also applies to Article 3(g) of the Definition of Aggression, which emphasizes that actions by armed bands, groups, irregulars or mercenaries "sent by or on behalf of a state," which carry out acts of armed force against another state "of such gravity as to amount to an actual armed attack conducted by regular forces" could be considered as acts of aggression.[119] Why only attacks of such gravity? Why this difference? It is the requirement of proportionality between a legitimate purpose for the use of force and the character and scale of force necessary to achieve that purpose that has to take care that relatively minor incidents involving the use of military force do not escalate (sometimes unintentionally) into whole-scale wars.

Antonio Cassese recently observed that:

> As to the specific question of how to react to terrorist attacks, some states (notably Israel, the United States and South Africa) argued in the past that they could use force in self-defence to respond to such attacks by targeting terrorist bases in the host country. This recourse to self-defence was predicated on the principle that such countries, by harbouring terrorist organisations, someway promoted or at least tolerated terrorism and where therefore "accomplices": they were responsible for the so-called indirect armed aggression. However, the majority of states did not share let alone approve this view. Furthermore, armed reprisals in response to small-scale use of force short of an "armed attack" proper, have been regarded as unlawful both against states and against terrorist

---

116. Military and Paramilitary Activities in and against Nicaragua (Nicaragua v. US), Merits, I.C.J. Reports 1986, para. 191 [hereinafter Nicaragua].
117. Many authors have criticized this distinction drawn by the ICJ between armed attacks and "mere border incidents." *See, e.g.,* ROSALYN HIGGINS, PROBLEM AND PROCESS: INTERNATIONAL LAW AND HOW WE USE IT, 250–51, (1994); DINSTEIN, *supra* note 6 at 192.
118. DINSTEIN, *supra* note 6 at 192.
119. Definition of Aggression, *supra* note 112, art. 3(g).

organisations. The events of 11 September have dramatically altered this legal framework."[120]

This traditional attitude that may have been prevailing before 9/11 was predicated on the paradigm of traditional state-to-state conflicts but today it does not correspond to the character and seriousness of terrorist threats.

In the case of terrorist attacks the immediate gravity of a single attack may not be very significant indeed either because this is a link in a chain of attacks, or even more importantly, because in the case of a terrorist attack the immediate target is not the only and even the most important objective. As Michael Reisman writes:

> terrorism, like any other act of unauthorised violence, has three expanding circles of effects including: an immediate effect of killing or injuring people, who are deemed, either for all purposes or in that context, to constitute an internationally prohibited target; an intermediate effect of intimidating a larger number of people and thereby influencing their political behaviour and that of their government; and an aggregate effect of undermining inclusive public order.[121]

This means that legal frames of responses to terrorist attacks cannot be tailored on the basis of the experience of the World Wars (or even the Gulf War for that matter) only.

In order to provide for effective responses to terrorist attacks, international law cannot prohibit the use of military force in self-defense in cases that the ICJ may have defined as "less grave forms."[122] At the same time, responses to terrorist attacks may combine significant elements of deterrence, anticipation and reprisal. The changing character of jus ad bellum, it seems, will most probably lead in the short run towards the emergence of a kind of flexible (soft) jus ad bellum—jus ad bellum in which the concept of legitimacy instead of legality is central, where the impact of a few specially interested states (or their organizations such as NATO, G8 or G9) is crucial, where the legitimizing role of the Security Council (especially its P5) remains noticeable, where the practice of some states and *opinio juris* of other states may considerably differ and where

---

120. Antonio Cassese, *Terrorism Is also Disputing some Crucial Categories of International Law*, 12 EUR. J. INT'L L. 996 (2001).
121. W. Michael Reisman, *International Legal Responses to Terrorism*, 22 HOUS. J. INT'L L. 1, 6–7 (1999).
122. Nicaragua, *supra* note 118, at para. 191.

the frontiers between interstate and intrastate conflicts is becoming more and more blurred. Such a flexible set of guidelines enjoying consensus of the majority of states and being supported by the world public opinion creates relative predictability and is therefore preferable to "hard," definitive and clear rules that are not observed in practice.

Terrorist Organizations and States Supporting Them

Another specific feature of military responses to terrorist attacks arises from the link between terrorist organizations and states in the territory, or from the territory, of which they operate. Somewhat different is the situation when a state supports terrorists (e.g., financially, logistically, politically, ideologically or otherwise) but its territory is not used as a basis for launching terrorist attacks. Differences, however, do not mean that the latter can eschew responsibility for its support of terrorists.

The fact that non-state entities are directly responsible under international law for armed attacks and that states have the right to use force in self-defense against such entities does not mean that the states from which these terrorists operate are not themselves responsible under international law. Depending on the degree of support given to, or control exercised by, a state over a terrorist organization such a state may be directly responsible for armed attacks carried out by terrorists.

It has been argued, however, that a mere tolerance of the presence of terrorist groups in the territory of a state or even encouragement of their activities is an insufficient connection to constitute an armed attack by that state.[123] It has been asserted that the state must exercise actual control over a terrorist organization to have the latter's acts attributed to the state.[124]

In the *Nicaragua* Case the ICJ held, for example, that assistance in the form of providing weapons, logistical or other support did not amount to an armed attack.[125] The Court found that by training, arming, equipping, financing and supplying the Contra forces or otherwise encouraging, supporting and aiding military and paramilitary activities in and against Nicaragua" the United States had been "in breach of its obligation under customary international law not to intervene in the affairs of another state."[126] The Court also said that only "by

---

123. *See, e.g.,* RICHARD ERICKSON, LEGITIMATE USE OF FORCE AGAINST STATE SPONSORED TERRORISM, 134 (U.S. Air War College 1989).
124. Francis A. Boyle, *Military Responses to Terrorism: Remarks of Francis A. Boyle*, 81 PROC. AM. SOC'Y INT'L L. 288 (1987).
125. Nicaragua, *supra* note 119, at para. 195.
126. *Id.,* para. 292 (3).

those acts of intervention referred to in subparagraph (3) (i.e., aiding the contras and otherwise encouraging and supporting military and paramilitary activities in and against Nicaragua)," which involved "the use of force," had the United States acted "in breach of its obligation under customary international law not to use force."[127] Here the Court clearly made a distinction between the breach of the non-use of force principle and the concept of armed attack since it did not consider that any support by the United States to the Contras constituted an armed attack. However, it is not clear at all as to the kind of force (used by whom?) the Court spoke of in paragraph 292 (4). If it is force used by the Contras against the Sandinista government then should not it be quite obvious that the US support as a whole should have been in breach of the non-use of force principle?

Judge Stephen Schwebel in his dissenting opinion concluded that "the Judgement of the Court on the critical question of whether aid to irregulars may be tantamount to an armed attack departs from accepted—and desirable—law."[128] Judge Sir Robert Jennings expressed a similar view stating that:

> it may be readily agreed that the mere provision of arms cannot be said to amount to an armed attack. But the provision of arms may, nevertheless, be a very important element in what might be thought to amount to armed attack, where it is coupled with other kinds of involvement. Accordingly, it seems to me that to say that the provision of arms, coupled with logistical or other support is not armed attack is going much too far.[129]

Although it seems that during the Cold War, state practice did not consider assistance in the form of arming and financing armed groups that operated in other countries as armed attacks by supporting states (because both parties of the Cold War used to support financially and militarily their proxies), today there are rather strong arguments in favor of reconsidering such a condescending posture towards states that support terrorist groups. That international law has not always had such a complacent attitude towards attributability to states of acts of non-state entities was recently reinforced by the International Criminal Tribunal for the Former Yugoslavia (ICTY).

The Appeals Chamber of the ICTY in its Judgement of 15 July 1999 in the *Dusco Tadic* case found that "a first ground on which the *Nicaragua* test as such may be held to be unconvincing is based on the very logic of the entire

---

127. *Id.*, para. 292 (4).
128. Nicaragua, *supra* note 119, at Dissenting Opinion of Judge Schwebel, para. 155.
129. Nicaragua, *supra* note 119, at Dissenting Opinion of Judge Jennings, para. 543.

system of international law on State responsibility."[130] The Chamber stated that under this logic

> States are not allowed on the one hand to act *de facto* through individuals and on the other to disassociate themselves from such conduct when these individuals breach international law. The requirement of international law for the attribution to States of acts performed by private individuals is that the State exercises control over the individual. The degree of control may, however, vary according to the factual circumstances of each case. The Appeals Chamber fails to see why in each and every circumstance international law should require high threshold for the test of control.[131]

The Chamber found that "the "effective control" test propounded by the International Court of Justice is at variance with international and State practice."[132] References to state practice collected over many years, inter alia, in various ILC reports on the Draft Articles on State Responsibility seem to support the position of the Appeals Chamber of the ICTY.

Although one of the important features of the changing international landscape is the increasing role (both positive and negative) of non-state actors, the world still is, and in the foreseeable future will remain, divided between sovereign states. Therefore, terrorists necessarily act (preparing for their attacks, training, receiving financial and other support) from the territory of some states even when they do not act on behalf of, or are not even supported, by any state. Such states are either unable or unwilling[133] to prevent non-state terrorist organizations using their territory for the purposes of carrying out attacks against other states. Thereby they are committing, using the language of the Draft Articles on State Responsibility recently adopted by the ILC,[134] internationally wrongful acts either by action (condoning or supporting terrorists)

---

130. *See* Prosecutor v. Tadic, Judgement of 15 July 1999 in the Appeals Chamber, at para 116, (ICTY Appeals Chambers, Jul. 15, 1999).
131. *Id.*, para. 117.
132. *Id.*, para. 124.
133. The term 'unwilling' should here include not only tolerance of the presence of terrorist organizations and sympathy for their cause but also active support, assistance as well as various degrees of control.
134. *See generally Draft Articles, supra* note 99.

or by omission (not preventing attacks from its territory against another state).[135] At the same time, as Gregory Travalio writes,

> although this may not necessarily preclude the use of military force in response to a terrorist attack emanating from such a state, the impotence of a state to control international terrorist organisations would not be an armed attack against another state, and, therefore the use of force in response is not expressly sanctioned by Article 51.[136]

However, this only means that the use of force is not sanctioned against such an impotent state. This does not mean that use of force would be unlawful against the terrorist group which is present and operates in the territory of that state. If a state is impotent to prevent the presence of terrorist groups in its territory and their attacks against third states it must not prevent a victim state or its allies from exercising their right to individual or collective self-defense in response to armed attacks by terrorists. In such a case, the state from the territory of which a terrorist group operates is under the obligation not to hinder the victim state in the exercise of its right to individual or collective self-defense in the territory that it is unable to control. If such a state tries to prevent the exercise of the right to use force in self-defense against the terrorist organization, it becomes an accomplice of the terrorist organization and in that case it is not important whether the state supports terrorists, or vice versa the latter, as it seems to have been the case with al Qaeda in Afghanistan, control the state. Otherwise, the impotence of territorial states would lead to impunity of terrorist organizations.

Conclusion

Simplifying a bit, the law of self-defense has, at least until recently, corresponded to the strictly inter-state nature of international society mostly in its bilateral manifestation. The law of collective security corresponds to rather feeble shoots of the supra-state elements in international society. But what about uses of force against terrorists or to protect fundamental human rights? These seem to be contrary to the very nature of a strictly inter-state system. However, the contemporary international system itself is less and less strictly

---

135. Article 2 of the Draft Articles states "'there is an internationally wrongful act of a State when conduct consisting of action or omission' is attributable to the State and constitutes a breach of an international obligation of the State." *Id.* at art. 2.

136. *See* Travalio, *supra* note 115, at 153.

an inter-state one. One of the consequences of such a change in the international system is the impossibility of seeing states as "black boxes." If states traditionally collided as "billiard balls" (from the point of view of international law) in the "armed attack—self-defense" paradigm they could eventually disengage and continue, at least for a while, to co-exist more or less peacefully (often until the next conflict) without changing their internal, or even external, characteristics. Historically, this is what usually happened. The relatively recent Iraq-Iran war, for example, ended in such a way. However, even in the inter-state "armed attack—self-defense" paradigm it may be necessary, in order to break the cycle of violence, to change internal characteristics of some of the participants in the conflict. The de-nazification of Germany or demilitarization and democratization of Japan after WW II may serve as examples of such necessary changes. Even today there are potential, simmering or actual conflicts between states that could find peaceful and durable solution only if participating states (all or some) radically change their policies, including internal ones. For example, Iraq was defeated in 1991 as a result of Operation DESERT STORM but notwithstanding measures requested from, and sanctions undertaken against it, the regime in power in Iraq is the same as it was in 1990 and the threats it constitutes to the regional and world security are therefore the same too. To fight against terrorists without addressing circumstances conducive to the rise of terrorism or intervening for the sake of human rights without being ready to undertake considerable efforts focused on state-building will be in most cases simply a Sisyphean toil. As Dmitri Trenin, writing on the future place and role of Russia in the world and referring, inter alia, to the Russian problems with Islamic militants, observes,

> there is no acceptable alternative to fighting Islamic terrorism. At the same time, cultural and humanitarian dialogue across that divide is a must, and the development of economic links, including new communications along both East-West and North-South axes, is one of the few instruments available to encourage modernization and help resolve or manage the various conflicts.[137]

I prefer to discuss the use of force against terrorists and not against terrorism. Fighting terrorism or waging a war against terrorism (which in any case is a non-legal concept) goes far beyond jus ad bellum or jus in bello, for that matter. Fighting terrorism implies, besides fighting terrorists through military, financial or law-enforcement means, also addressing the conditions conducive

---

137. DIMTRI TRENIN, THE END OF EURASIA. RUSSIA ON THE BORDER BETWEEN GEOPOLITICS AND GLOBALIZATION, 196 (2002).

to the emergence and flourishing of terrorism. One of the peculiar features of the fight against terrorism is that tough military or, depending on circumstances, law enforcement measures, practically always have to be paralleled by the search for political solutions to problems exploited by terrorists or by changes in the social and economic conditions that are conducive to terrorism.

Looking at the character and causes of some of the most violent contemporary conflicts, states, and the societies they represent, have to become in some important respects more similar to each other than they are today. Cultural diversity is, of course, a source of the rich tapestry of the world. However, when huge developmental gaps are taken for cultural differences, denying at the same time, that certain cultural factors condition the existence of these gaps, that such factors may be also a serious source of the wealth of some societies and the poverty of others, serious sources of conflicts cannot be ignored. If people, for example, in Saudi Arabia or other Islamic states have only two choices—the corrupt and authoritarian regimes or Islamic fundamentalism—these societies will remain a fertile soil for terrorism. Of course, all religions have always had and many still have this totalitarian exclusivist trend. As Hamid Enayat has written, "if Islam comes into conflict with certain postulates of democracy it is because of its general character as a religion. . . . An intrinsic concomitant of democracy . . . involves a challenge to many a sacred axiom."[138] And Rabbi David Hartman writes: "[a]ll faiths that come out of the biblical tradition—Judaism, Christianity and Islam—have the tendency to believe that they have the exclusive truth."[139] However, in contradistinction to Christianity, Islam has not gone through what Francis Fukuyama has called the Protestantisation of Catholicism[140] or the secularization of religious worldviews. Bassam Tibi writes:

> [i]n the Middle East as well as in other parts of the World of Islam, there has never been a process of structural change underlying a substantive shift in worldview from a religious one to a secular one, as did occur in the historical process that took place in Europe. Given the community and dominance of the Muslim's worldview there has never been a genuine process of secularisation in the Middle East underlain by secular ideologies.[141]

---

138. HAMID ENAYAT, MODERN ISLAMIC THOUGHT, 126 (1982).
139. Id.
140. FRANCIS FUKUYAMA, TRUST: THE SOCIAL VIRTUES AND THE CREATION OF PROSPERITY, 41 (1995).
141. Tibi, *supra* note 33, at 97.

Secularization of religious worldview has helped Western societies to change (modernize) in response to natural and social challenges. Returning to basics is never an adequate response to any new challenge and only adequately responding to constant challenges are societies able to develop and flourish. Modernization, including democratization, the development of human rights, including freedom of expression, and equality between sexes, is a *conditio sine qua non* of the development of Islamic and other societies in the so-called developing world. Karim Raslan, a Malaysian lawyer, writes that:

> [t]he moral bankruptcy of militant Islam as embodied by the Taliban, as well as its abject failure in socio-economic terms, should embolden the leaders of moderate, predominantly Muslim nations such as Turkey, Indonesia and Malaysia in their struggle against religious obscurantism and backwardness. Needless to say, Saudi Arabia, as an absolute monarchy with no concern for civil liberties, does not constitute a model Islamic polity.[142]

He also correctly points out that reforms must be driven from within the Islamic world. It is doubtful whether those Islamic scholars who, as Karim Raslan writes, try to "extract the prophetic truths from the Koran to show the inherent compatibility of modern-day concerns with sacred texts,"[143] can do what Christian scholars failed in doing. Bassam Tibi has written that:

> [t]he predicament of Islamic fundamentalists vis-à-vis modernity has in fact become an expression of their ambiguity: on the one hand they seek to accommodate instrumentally all or most of the material achievements of modernity (that is, science and technology) into Islamic civilisation; on the other hand, they reject vehemently the adoption of the man-centred rationality that has made these achievements possible.[144]

As a result of that we have post-modern weapons in pre-modern hands. Bassam Tibi further writes that "secular cultural modernity is worth defending against the predations of religious fundamentalisms," and he and Ernest Gellner share the conviction that "reason and enlightenment need also be protected from the intellectual adventures of postmodernism."[145] I agree.

---

142. Karim Ralsan, *Now a Historic Chance to Welcome Muslims into the System*, INT'L HERALD TRIBUNE, Nov. 27, 2001, at 8.
143. *Id.*
144. Tibi, *supra* note 33, at 118.
145. *Id.* at 47.

Western political correctness that is not unrelated to the post-colonial sense of guilt and shame for injustices committed against non-Western peoples sometimes reminds of the ostrich who, facing a threat, hides its head in sand. Something like that happens when some Western liberals discuss, or face, threats from culturally and religiously different sources. It is correct, (and also politically correct), to say that poverty and injustice are conducive to terrorism (whether they are root-causes or not, is another matter). However, it is also correct (but politically incorrect), to say that often poverty and injustice are due not only and not so much to the colonial or neo-colonial inheritance, but are of endogenous, and not exogenous, origin. Chris Brown writes that:

> the West's handling of the religious dimension of the current conflict has been based on a rather irritating, if perhaps politically understandable, double standard. Christians such as Tony Blair and George W. Bush—undeniably sincere in their beliefs, but living in a world where religious conviction is tinged with irony—cannot express their own deeply held convictions in explicitly Christian terms for fear of alienating the decidedly un-ironic beliefs of their coalition partners in Pakistan and the Arab world. The sensibilities of the latter—however irrational—have to be respected; and, indeed, respect in this case seems to mean actually pandering to irrational. The implicit assumption seems to be that it would be both unfair and unsafe to subject Muslim beliefs, attitudes and behaviour to the kind of robust criticism common in Western societies.[146]

Brown calls it "reverse racism" that is expressed, for example, in the words of British correspondent of *The Independent* Robert Fisk who, as a Westerner, was beaten up in Afghanistan, but who seemed to understand and justify the behavior of his tormentors "given the indignities and violence to which they had been subjected."[147] As New Yorkers seem not to be justified in beating up Muslims, the obvious explanation, writes Brown, is that Muslims as individuals cannot be held morally responsible for their acts in the way New Yorkers can."[148] Politicians and diplomats may be justified (naturally not always lest it become a bad habit) in avoiding straight talk when building shaky but necessary coalitions but journalists and especially academics have to try to uncover truths however unpleasant or inconvenient they may be. Pretending that religious

---

146. Brown, *supra* note 63, in WORLDS IN COLLISION, *supra* note 47, at 295.
147. Robert Fisk, *My Beating by Refugees is Symbol of the Hatred and Fury of the Filthy War*, THE INDEPENDENT, Dec. 10, 2001, at 1.
148. Brown, *supra* note 63, in WORLDS IN COLLISION, *supra* note 47, at 295.

fundamentalism has nothing to do with the religion of which it is one of the trends does not help.

The war against terrorism requires moral clarity, intellectual sophistication and military toughness—qualities that are not always in harmonious relationship. This makes that war especially difficult. However, only addressing all the conditions that are conducive to the emergence and flourishing of terrorism, searching for solutions to political situations and crises that are exploited by terrorists but that often are real and serious, using available and creating new criminal justice mechanisms and, finally, when necessary intelligently resorting to military coercion, is it possible to control terrorism.

IV

Panel I
Commentary—Jus ad Bellum

Robert Turner[1]

Starting with the issue of the Taliban, Mike Schmitt continues to be troubled about the legality of using force against the Taliban. I began at this position also. Indeed, at one point I authored an opinion for an editorial page stating that if the Taliban resisted when the United States used force against al Qaeda, it would be legally permissible to use force against the Taliban. Subsequently, I have re-thought this view and I now think the appropriate way to deal with this issue is to recognize that the Taliban was not in fact either de jure or de facto the lawful government of Afghanistan.

To begin with, at the height of the "Taliban Regime," only three countries in the world, Saudi Arabia, United Arab Emirates, and Pakistan, conducted diplomatic relations with the Taliban. This means that 189 countries did not. When the UN Security Council ordered countries to either break relations with the Taliban or not to have dealings with the Taliban, the number of states with diplomatic relations with the Taliban became one, Pakistan. As an aside, I believe that Pakistan was probably encouraged by a number of states to

---

1. Professor Robert Turner co-founded the Center for National Security Law at the University of Virginia School of Law in April 1981 and is its Associate Director. He is a former holder of the Charles H. Stockton Chair of International Law at the US Naval War College in Newport, Rhode Island.

retain such a relationship with the Taliban in order to have a state capable of communicating demands to the Taliban. However, almost all states that comprise the world community did not recognize the Taliban as the government of a sovereign state. Moreover, at the time the United States initiated the use of military force against the Taliban, the UN Security Council, on behalf of the international community, had taken the position that the Taliban did not comprise the government of a state. In fact, the Security Council consistently has referred to them as the "faction in Afghanistan known as the Taliban" so as to ensure there is a clear international understanding that the Taliban do not comprise the recognized government of the country of Afghanistan.[2]

The easiest way then, to resolve the issue of whether the Taliban was the recognized government of Afghanistan or not is to conclude that the Taliban was a religious force that had seized control over substantial parts of Afghanistan and was trying to enforce its moral rules upon the people. I do not believe that the Taliban viewed itself as the government of Afghanistan. My strong guess is that military leaders of the Taliban militia did not hold commissions issued in the name of the government of Afghanistan nor did they think of themselves as the armed forces of Afghanistan but rather as the enforcement arm of a religious organization or entity. Before Operation ENDURING FREEDOM began, I do not think the United States government, its citizens, or the citizens of Afghanistan perceived that the United States was going to war with Afghanistan. I think the perception and the reality were that the United States was using force inside Afghanistan to bring to an end a very abusive, illegitimate, totalitarian regime, controlling the people of that country. The United States was liberating the people of Afghanistan not oppressing them.

On a related note, an argument exists based on humanitarian intervention grounds for the US intervention in Afghanistan. After all, if one takes the position that international law makes it unlawful for sovereign states to intervene to prevent the genocide in World War II or the slaughter of two-million Cambodians, then international law itself has become part of the problem, not the solution. Indeed my friend Rudy Rummel in his book *Death by Government* points out that during the 20th century, probably three to four times more people were slaughtered by their own governments than died in hostilities throughout the entire century.[3]

Now let me raise a trivial point and one I have previously discussed with Professor Schmitt. Mike refers to the September 11th attacks as "causing

---

[2]. *See, e.g.,* S. C. Res. 1193 U.N. SCOR, 53d Sess., U.N. Doc. S/1193/(1998), para. 7.
[3]. RUDY RUMMELL, DEATH BY GOVERNMENT (1994).

property and financial damage measuring in the hundreds of millions of dollars." The reality is that this cost must be in the many billions of dollars. Counting only the value of the human lives lost in the attack on the World Trade Center, the cost would surely be in the billions of dollars. This is to say nothing of the incredible clean-up efforts currently underway or the impact of the attacks on financial institutions throughout the world. Added to this, of course, are the countless costs such as the lost time of business executives to airport security, the cost of strengthening cockpit doors, the loss to the airline industry.

These costs are only financial in nature though. How much more difficult to attempt to quantify the emotional costs in fear, anger and grief? I recently lectured on terrorism at the Naval Justice School, and my son came with me. During my presentation, my nine-year-old son drew a picture of the World Trade Center with some very poignant words about terrorism. This type of emotional cost cannot be measured in dollars but it is nonetheless tremendous. When all of these costs are quantified, we may well be talking in the trillions of dollars.

More substantively, I have a nuanced difference with Mike Schmitt regarding the definition of what an "armed attack" truly is. I think Professor Schmitt is taking a literalist approach to the UN Charter regarding the definition of an armed attack. It is true that Article 51 refers to the inherent right of self defense if an armed attack occurs against a member of the United Nations.[4] However, Professor Schmitt also makes the point that only members of the United Nations are cloaked with the inherent right of self-defense pursuant to Article 51. While perhaps true with respect to Article 51 in the literal sense, this is false in reality inasmuch as the inherent right to self-defense is a cornerstone of customary international law. As an example, when non-UN member North Korea invaded non-UN member South Korea, the United Nations Security Council acted and authorized the use of force in collective self-defense. Clearly, South Korea had this right before the action of the Security Council. Undoubtedly, the prohibition on the use of aggressive force contained in Article 2(4) of the UN Charter is binding but the more important point is

---

4. U.N. CHARTER, art. 51, provides that "[n]othing in the present Charter shall impair the inherent right of individual or collective self-defence if an armed attack occurs against a Member of the United Nations until the Security Council has taken measures necessary to maintain international peace and security."

that Article 51 of the Charter does not *create* the right of self-defense.[5] While Article 51 was one of the most important parts of the charter, it was also an afterthought.

The prohibition against the aggressive use of force is embodied in Article 2(4) of the UN Charter. With the conclusion of the Act of Chapultepec in 1945[6] which embodied the principle of collective self-defense, the United States and its Latin American neighbors wanted the UN Charter to clearly state that if the Security Council was blocked from taking action by a veto or some other reason, the traditional right of collective self-defense as embodied in the Act of Chapultepec remained unimpaired and available. This was the ultimate purpose of Article 51 of the United Nations Charter.

Although the drafters of the UN Charter had in mind World War I and World War II, the French version of Article 51 uses the term armed aggression and not armed attack and I believe this to be the more appropriate focus of Article 51. The question is whether there is a wrongful act involving the use of lethal force that creates a right to use force in self-defense. Mind you, the proportionality doctrine applies in this analysis and a small incursion will not authorize a nuclear response or any disproportional response.

This view is quite clearly supported by a review of the notes exchanged at the time of the Kellogg Briand Pact of 1928. Prior to entry into force of this Pact, a number of countries were prepared to include reservations to their ratification reserving the right to self-defense. The US response was to send out a diplomatic note saying the right to self-defense is imprescriptable. This right pre-exists treaties, is inherent in treaties, and cannot be taken away, even by treaty. Interestingly, the Russian text of Article 51 also does not refer to the inherent right of individual or collective self-defense but instead to the

---

5. In 1928, Secretary of State Frank Kellogg stated "that right is inherent in every state and is implicit in each treaty. Every nation is free at all times and regardless of treaty provisions to defend its territory from invasion and it alone is competent to decide whether circumstance require recourse to war in self-defense." Frank B. Kellogg, Address Before the American Society of International Law (Apr. 28, 1928) *in* 22 PROC AM. SOC'Y INT'L L. 141, 143 (1928). This quote constituted official US recognition at the time that the right of self-defense cannot be restricted by treaty.

6. Inter-American Reciprocal Treaty of Assistance and Solidarity (Act of Chapultepec, Mexico); March 6, 1945 This act provided:

[t]hat every attack of a State against the integrity or the inviolability of the territory, or against the sovereignty or political independence of an American State, shall, conformably to Part III hereof, be considered as an act of aggression against the other States which sign this Act. In any case invasion by armed forces of one State into the territory of another trespassing boundaries established by treaty and demarcated in accordance therewith shall constitute an act of aggression.

imprescriptable right of individual or collective self-defense. Thus, given the US position and indeed that of the nations that became signatories to the Kellogg Briand Pact, the individual and collective right to self-defense is indeed imprescriptable.

So, to state that after entry into effect of the UN Charter, self-defense is only permissible in response to an armed attack, misses the point that lethal force continues to be available to states, members and non-members, in self-defense and in collective self-defense supporting the victims of aggression of the illegal use of lethal force by other states. Accordingly, I do not believe the standard to invoke either self-defense or collective self-defense to be quite as difficult to achieve as perhaps Professor Schmitt indicates.

Additionally, I believe that the International Court of Justice in the *Military and Paramilitary Activities Case In and Against Nicaragua*[7] quite simply, reached the wrong conclusion. This case had more political involvement than most cases and in my view does not reflect the law. Although Article 59 of the Statute of the ICJ provides that ICJ decisions have "no binding force except between the parties and in respect to that particular case,"[8] such decisions are often very useful for international lawyers trying to understand the developing law. However, with the exception of the brilliant dissent authored by Judge Schwabel, the ICJ decision in the *Nicaragua* Case is mostly cited in disagreement. In my opinion, this particular case has absolutely no precedential value.

The *Caroline* Case I think is better viewed as a description of anticipatory self defense than of self defense.[9] Others may disagree but if you really look at the facts, the steamboat was being fitted out with the intention of providing support to rebels in Canada. The British crossed the Canadian-US border, set the *Caroline* afire, cut it adrift, and apparently not realizing there were people onboard sent it over the falls. I think the *Caroline* Case may be too strong a test for self-defense. Regardless of which term is used, there ought to be an overwhelming presumption against the legality of initiating force prior to an attack by another country. But, particularly in an environment of weapons of mass destruction, the idea that the law ought to say a Saddam Hussein gets one more free kick before a state can defend itself strikes me as not very well thought out.

---

7. Military and Paramilitary Activities in and against Nicaragua (Nicaragua v. US), Merits, 1986 I.C.J. 14 [hereinafter Nicaragua Case].
8. Article 59, states: The decision of the Court has no binding force except between the parties and in respect of that particular case. I.C.J. Statute, Article 59.
9. See R.Y. Jennings, *The Caroline and McLeod Cases*, 32 AM. J. INT'L L. 82 (1938).

On a related note, Professor Schmitt seemed to struggle a bit with justification for the attacks on the al Qaeda terrorist group. This is so because Article 2(4) of the UN Charter only talks about states. This seems to be a somewhat easier problem to resolve though. The Charter is designed to primarily defend the rights of states although it also set the stage for a tremendous growth of international humanitarian law involving individuals. I think the best view is that terrorists such as al Qaeda members are just like pirates in the sense that they are the common enemy of mankind. I think this should be the official US position, that terrorists occupy the same legal status as pirate. Note that this does not mean that terrorists are not protected by international law. Just as you cannot murder pirates, you cannot murder, maim, or torture terrorists. Both of these groups are entitled to some fundamental due process protections once they have either surrendered or are under your control. However, as long as they continue to engage in piracy or ongoing acts of terrorism, they are lawful targets.

With respect to Rein Müllerson's paper, his notion that the UN Charter continues to be updated by evolving customary international law makes great sense. I also share his view that al Qaeda is more the marionette than the Taliban. Professor Müllerson's comments on post-modern societies in Europe and the tension created between post-modern European societies and the still modern society of the United States were also quite intriguing. The tension between these two models presents serious problems.

Sun Tzu teaches us that the acme of skill is not to win one hundred victories and one hundred battles but to subdue the enemy without fighting.[10] The best way to do that with thugs such as Osama bin Laden and Saddam Hussein is to demonstrate to them that the perceived benefits of their behavior are greatly outweighed by the perceived cost. To do this, the world must unite against them.

We had to use force in 1991, but at that point we reestablished the credibility of the world community through the Security Council. Sadly, since then, we have largely frittered away that credibility in a variety of rather tragic incidents. At least prior to 9/11, we missed several opportunities to respond firmly to threats to the peace and particularly the problem of terrorism. And sadly, time is not on the side of the United States nor the other peace loving countries. In this era of weapons of mass destruction, this ostrich-like idea that the United States should not do anything until Saddam Hussein obtains weapons of mass destruction and delivery systems is fatally flawed. Should the United

---

10. SUN TZU, THE ART OF WAR (Samuel Griffith trans., 1963).

States really wait to act until after Saddam Hussein blows up his neighbors or destroys Israel? This approach is not helpful to the cause of peace.

I do not share Professor Mike Glennon's view that there is no coherent international law regarding the intervention of states. The basic prohibition against the aggressive use of force by states is well understood. As an example, even before the United Nations Charter, when Adolf Hitler invaded Poland, he claimed he was defending Germany from Poland. This was a lie but why did Hitler bother to lie? Hitler understood that, by itself, aggression was unlawful and that the world community viewed aggression as unlawful. Similarly, when Kim Il Sung invaded South Korea in 1950, he claimed that North Korea was simply defending itself against attacks by South Korea. This too was a lie. These two events highlight the reality that even the worst tyrants understand that it is illegal to engage in major acts of aggression. They mask it.

When the Sandinistas attempted to overthrow the government of El Salvador, they did a brilliant job of turning the world against the defensive response of the United States. But they did not come out and claim a right to overthrow the government of El Salvador. They did it in secret because they knew to do so was unlawful. If you read the American and Nicaraguan briefs before the world court, it would be hard to distinguish them. They basically gave the same summary of the law.[11] And each party charged the other with providing money, support and advice and said this is illegal. The question dealt with whether the US involvement was a defensive response, or was it an act of aggression directed against Nicaragua? I think the evidence now clearly shows it was a defensive response.

---

11. See Nicaragua Case, *supra* note 7.

V

Panel I
Commentary—Jus ad Bellum

William Dalton[1]

I note with interest and some curiosity that the two presenters for this panel employ a UN Charter paradigm when discussing the war on terrorism. The inherent right of collective and individual self-defense embodied in customary international law might well be a more appropriate analytical starting point when discussing Operation ENDURING FREEDOM, however. This seems to be a fundamental question worthy of debate and discussion. Many of the questions raised by Rear Admiral Rempt this morning are also of a fundamental nature. Such questions as what is the nature of terrorism, are terrorists lawful combatants, do terrorists comply with the law of armed conflict; do they wear a distinctive uniform, are they under military command, are all questions of great import as the United States prosecutes this Global War on Terrorism.

In my view, terrorists do not qualify as lawful combatants. Instead, they are unlawful combatants and international thugs. Given this starting point, why are nations constrained in pursuing and eliminating international terrorists? Why are preemptive strikes not routinely taken? One basic reason states operate within the framework of international law is the existence and strength accorded state sovereignty. The UN Charter prohibits states from engaging in

---

1. William Dalton is a retired Navy captain and now serves as the Assistant General Counsel for Intelligence with the US Department of Defense.

aggressive wars against one another.[2] Numerous mutual agreements exist pursuant to this same charter that recognize, with the exception of variations of self-defense, that the Security Council is the only organization that may authorize the aggressive use of force. This inability to use aggressive force, properly or improperly, constrains how states respond to international terrorism. This is quite an interesting dilemma; one almost certainly not considered when the Charter itself was written.

When looking at the *Caroline* Case, Secretary Webster was really applying a domestic concept of self-defense—the defender having his back to the wall and having to respond immediately.[3] Groups engaging in terrorist acts against the United States need time to plan, to organize, to mount such attacks. When applying the imminency requirement necessary for anticipatory self-defense to international terrorism, there must be a lessening of the immediacy of the threat. In other words, the requirement to have an immediate threat before anticipatory self-defense can be invoked must be moderated.

On a different matter, in looking at the close relationship between the Taliban and al Qaeda, it is clear that a mutual dependency existed between the two organizations. Each of these organizations enjoyed a mutual benefit from the other. The Taliban enjoying the purchasing power of al Qaeda funds and al Qaeda enjoyed the safe haven of Afghanistan provided by the Taliban. In order to allay the threat presented by al Qaeda it was necessary to prosecute the Taliban as well because as long as the Taliban provided safe haven to al Qaeda, al Qaeda continued to be an imminent threat to the coalition partners. So it was as a matter of military necessity in applying anticipatory self-defense that action was undertaken against the Taliban. In my mind, this made the Taliban a perfectly legitimate target. Note also, that this analysis applies to the current situation with Iraq. The key here is that of necessity. At some point, it will become necessary to respond to the Iraqi regime. At some point the threat will be so imminent and so serious that the international community will have to respond. Clearly then, the key to the overall war on terrorism is this notion of imminency and the exercise of the extraordinary right of self-defense.

---

2. Article 2(4) of the United Nations Charter prohibits the aggressive use of force by member states; Article 51 recognizes the customary international law right of self-defense.
3. *See* R.Y. Jennings, *The Caroline and McLeod Cases*, 32 AM. J. INT'L L. 82 (1938).

VI

Panel I
Discussion—Jus ad Bellum

On the Application of Force to al Qaeda and Taliban Members

Leslie Green
I do not believe that we have distinguished sufficiently between al Qaeda members and Taliban members. Bear in mind that many of the volunteers from the United Kingdom or from other countries who went to join the Taliban had no desire to take part in al Qaeda terrorist activities. These volunteers were concerned with spreading a fundamentalist type of Islam. They were proselytizing, in many cases assisting Islamic colleagues in places such as Chechnya.

The Taliban may indeed not have been the government of the people of Afghanistan. They were, however, the de facto authority in control of most of the territory comprising Afghanistan. If this be the case though, once al Qaeda has been dealt with, the issue of what are we doing in Afghanistan must be raised. Otherwise, we might be supporting a government in frustrating a revolution or a civil war.

Finally, the word terrorism is used with too much abandon. This pejorative has been too widely used and attributed to non-terrorist groups. Governments have always argued that those trying to overthrow them are terrorists. Historically, governments have also taken the position that if the group was fighting a government that was not liked, the group consisted of freedom fighters, fighting for their liberation. Care should be taken to not become involved in what are simply civil wars even when carried out by political ideologies that do not appeal to us. Such civil wars do not rise to the level of terrorist movements simply because we do not like them.

Rein Müllerson

There are many governments which use the mantra of the Global War on Terrorism to fight their opponents who may not be terrorists at all. This danger, of course, always exists and can be seen today in both Russia and Central Asia. Our task is to distinguish between those using terror tactics and those who are not. It is true that in Afghanistan, and also in Chechnya and other places, religious fundamentalists have used terror tactics. So one has to make distinctions between freedom fighters genuinely struggling for independence and common terrorists. Though I believe in many cases, if not in most cases, terrorists are independence fighters and independence fighters are terrorists too since they use terror tactics in order to achieve their aims. There should not be any difference whether their aims are noble, lawful or not. If they use terror tactics, they are terrorists.

Now about the distinctions between al Qaeda and the Taliban. Of course, there are these distinctions. Al Qaeda is a worldwide net, and the Taliban was an endogenous organization operating only in the territory of Afghanistan. And the United States made these distinctions I believe. The United States demanded that the Taliban surrender Osama bin Laden and other leaders of al Qaeda to it and that the Taliban dismantle the bases used by al Qaeda. The Taliban did not comply with these requests and so the United States used force in self-defense against both al Qaeda and the Taliban.

Perhaps a fine distinction between al Qaeda and the Taliban may be that you could initially attack only al Qaeda and then based upon the reaction of the Taliban, attack them as well. That is to say, if the Taliban come to the assistance of al Qaeda then they too could be properly targeted. This seems to me to be too formalistic, however, and international law does not require making this distinction.

Robert Turner

When asked, "who was the government of Afghanistan on 11 September?," I would respond by querying whether Somalia had a government a decade ago. It is clearly possible to have states that are so dysfunctional and so split that no authority constitutes the legitimate government. The UN Security Council, acting on behalf of the world community, has taken the position that the Taliban was *not* the government of Afghanistan, referring to it only as a faction.[1] Moreover, the Security Council had ordered all states to immediately cease supporting terrorism, declaring such support a threat to the peace.[2] Given that the Security Council had de-legitimized any Taliban claim to act on behalf of the government of Afghanistan, it is hard to argue the case that the Taliban was the government of Afghanistan. In my view then, the Taliban was never the legitimate government of Afghanistan. This of course does not necessarily mean that a true, legitimate government actually existed within Afghanistan.

I am not of the same opinion as Michael Schmitt that the case for using force against the Taliban would be easier to understand if the Taliban was the legitimate government of Afghanistan. Subparagraph 4 of Article 2 of the UN Charter protects states against intervention by other states.[3] The *Lotus* case tells us that international law is permissive.[4] The UN Charter and the Kellogg Briand Pact say states cannot use armed force in their political diplomatic relations against each other to solve problems.[5] States may use force to defend themselves against attacks by other states.[6] However, a large body of international law on state responses to attacks by non-state entities such as terrorist groups does not currently exist.

States are not guarantors of the security of their neighbors but they do have a legal obligation to take reasonable steps to insure that their territory is not used to launch armed attacks against other states.[7] Having been placed on notice that terrorist activity is originating from within their territory and thereafter demonstrating an unwillingness or inability to control such activity, a state is deprived to some degree of its right against non-intervention by the aggrieved state. In this case, in the absence of other effective remedies, the aggrieved state may enter the host state for the express purpose of self-defense against the terrorist threat. The aggrieved state may not generally attack the

---

1. *See generally* S. C. Res. 1214, U.N. SCOR, 53d Sess., U.N. Doc. S/1214/(1998), and S. C. Res. 1373, U.N. SCOR, 54th Sess., U.N. Doc. S/1373/(2001).
2. *Id.*
3. Article 2(4) specifically provides that "[a]ll Members shall refrain in their international relations from the threat or use of force against the territorial integrity or political independence of any state, or in any other manner inconsistent with the Purposes of the United Nations." U.N. CHARTER, art. 2(4).
4. Lotus Case (Fr. v. Turk.), P.C.I.J. (ser. A) No. 10 (1923), 2 Hudson, World Court Reports 20 (1929).
5. Kellogg Briand Pact, 27 Aug 1928, 46 Stat. 2343, 94 U.N.T.S. 57.
6. U.N. CHARTER, art. 51.
7. Oscar Schachter, *International Law: The Right of States to Use Armed Force*, 82 MICH. L. REV. 1620, 1626 (1984); JOHN F. MURPHY, STATES SUPPORT OF INTERNATIONAL TERRORISM at 89 (1989).

host state's government or attempt to overthrow it. However, when that government is actively engaged in supporting the terrorist, then it too becomes a lawful target. Under this rationale, the Taliban were clearly a legitimate target of the United States, after September 11th.

A note of caution is appropriate though. The general principle that states may not use armed force as a means of resolving differences with other states in a non-defensive setting is thoroughly agreed upon and is tremendously important to uphold. Taking the position, as some do, that there is no international law governing use of force is not only silly but it is harmful to the notion of the rule of law that prohibits states from engaging in aggressive wars.

Michael Schmitt
Once the Taliban refused to comply with the demands of the United States, it relinquished the exclusive right to act against al Qaeda. At that point, the Taliban right to territorial integrity was subordinated to the right to self-defense possessed by the United States. This type of distinction is of critical importance because many states provide support to different rebel groups. This difference needs to be maintained to prevent the argument that any state providing support to a rebel group in another state is engaging in an armed attack thereby authorizing the state to invoke self-defense as a basis for action. The US support of the Iraqi resistance is a great example of this. Clearly, the United States does not want to be in a position where international law permits Saddam Hussein to claim a right of self-defense against the United States simply because the Unites States is funding the acts of the Iraqi resistance.

Recognizing that the right to self-defense may only have applied initially against al Qaeda, as soon as the Taliban interfered with the US exercise of that right the Taliban properly became targetable as well. Such interference would have been wrongful and would constitute an armed attack by the Taliban, justifying the application of force against the Taliban by United States and coalition forces. I remain somewhat surprised that US and UK forces engaged the Taliban on the first day of Operation ENDURING FREEDOM instead of waiting until Taliban forces proved they were hostile to the exercise of US self-defense. Certainly, had coalition forces waited until the demonstration of such hostility by the Taliban, their claim that their actions against the Taliban were legitimate because they had been attacked and were exercising the right of self-defense would ring truer.

Wolff von Heinegg

I would caution against a rush to abolish recognized principles and rules of international law just to serve certain purposes. So for example, if it is agreed the Taliban is the de facto regime, the Taliban should be treated as such and the protections of the Third Geneva Convention should be applied to Taliban members.[8]

Christopher Greenwood

The Taliban cannot be considered anything other than the de facto government of Afghanistan immediately before the use of force in October. They controlled 80% of the territory of the country. They controlled virtually all the levers of power within the state and all of the ordinary organs of government from the central bank to the air traffic controllers. The border authorities were taking their instructions from the Taliban. I know it was not the kind of government the civilized world is used to. However, in functioning terms it was the government of Afghanistan. And therefore its acts are imputable to Afghanistan. I agree with Professor Schmitt that this makes the actions of the coalition easier rather than more difficult to justify. However, I do not believe that the question of whether it is convenient to us or not that these people were the government of Afghanistan has any real bearing on the question of whether they were in fact the government. It seems to me that we have become all too ready to accept interpretations of the law on the basis of the convenient result which they produce. As lawyers we should have the integrity to say this is what we think the law is. If the consequences of that are inconvenient, let us look to see what we can do about that. We should not, however, allow the wish to be father to the thought.

Legitimacy of the Use of Force

Robert Turner

As is well established, there are two instances where force may be appropriately used pursuant to the UN Charter: when authorized by the Security Council and in different variations of self-defense.[9] Interceptive self-defense or anticipatory self-defense is the theory that force may be used in order to protect against the prospective loss of lives caused by an armed attack. It is true

---

8. *See generally* Geneva Convention Relative to the Treatment of Prisoners of War of August 12, 1949, 6 U.S.T. 3516.
9. *See* U.N. CHARTER arts. 42 and 51.

historically, pre-UN Charter, that if a state was slaughtering its own citizens, another state would have no legitimate basis for intervening as these were purely matters internal to the affairs of the state. However, the growth of international humanitarian law subsequent to the Charter clearly recognizes that individuals have internationally respected rights and that when a state does engage in an act like genocide, it is not an internal matter. It is a matter of legitimate global concern and international law should apply and prohibit such state acts. To promote such international law, states must act as if it is their customary practice to recognize a limited right of the world community to intervene, to stop massive slaughter of innocent people.

Wolff von Heinegg

There is no need to refer to humanitarian intervention as a legal justification for the attacks on Afghanistan. There seems to be a general consensus that the fight against terrorism justifies the action taken in and against Afghanistan and probably in and against all other states similarly situated. Referring to humanitarian intervention as a basis for action against Afghanistan is counterproductive, lessening state credibility in the fight against international terrorism.

In looking at the action taken against Afghanistan, the strongest and best legal justification is self-defense. If it is proved that the acts of September 11th are attributable to the Taliban and thus to Afghanistan, every measure of self-defense may be taken. This is a very important point as it addresses the traditional concept of self-defense and what we are today ready to acknowledge to be within the competency of the Security Council. If the Security Council in Resolution 1373 requires states to take very concrete measure against international terrorism, every state is obliged to do just that. Such obligations are conferred upon states by the Security Council for the purpose of peace and international security. Benefiting from these measures is the entire international community and not just the United States or Germany. So these obligations laid down by the Security Council, for example in 1373, can be qualified obligations. When a state does not comply with such resolutions, it violates its obligations towards the community of states as a whole. This violation, when it constitutes a threat like permitting al Qaeda to continue operations in Afghanistan, can then be acted upon by the affected community of states as a whole. Clearly in a situation like this, there is no need to advocate humanitarian intervention as the basis for such actions when the self-defense position is so strong.

Michael Schmitt

It is important that Security Council Resolution 1368 and 1373 not be interpreted as use of force authorizations, which they clearly were not. To do so would seem to somehow imply that the Security Council needs to act before the right of self-defense matures and can be exercised. The law of self-defense provides all the answers necessary for determining whether the right to act exists for the United States as well as the international community. Security Council Resolution 1373 is relevant on the issue of whether or not the Taliban is in compliance with their obligations under international law to remove the al Qaeda threat on the territory that it controls. The resolution though, was not needed before the right to act in self-defense could be invoked by aggrieved states.

Christopher Greenwood

The self-defense case for the use of force by the Americans and their allies in Afghanistan is an extremely powerful one and should not be watered down in any way by trying to squeeze interpretations out of Security Council Resolutions or referring to humanitarian law as the basis for intervention in Afghanistan. This is a classic example of how to undercut a strong case. Although I am a supporter of humanitarian intervention, I do not believe that Afghanistan is a particularly good example of this. Instead of straining to understand actions in Afghanistan as for humanitarian purposes, we should instead stay focused on the self-defense reasons for such actions.

If a neutral state allowed a belligerent to conduct military operations from its territory or from its waters and refused to put a stop to that, then the receiving belligerent is entitled to take military action in the neutral's territory to put a stop to them. If the neutral state intervened to protect the belligerent it had been sheltering, then it exposed its own armed forces to attack. In the present case, this argument is particularly strong as the Taliban regime was subject to sanctions imposed by the United Nations beforehand for their support for al Qaeda. The Taliban made it crystal clear that they would resist vigorously any attempt by any part of the international community to deal with the al Qaeda presence in their territory. This is an important point as we do not want to give credence to a theory that as soon as any state has a group of terrorists which have operated from its territory, it exposes itself to armed attack. That very broad brush approach opens up the most horrific possibilities because at some time or other virtually every state however hard it had tried otherwise, had ended up with terrorists operating from its territory.

On Regime Change In Iraq

Robert Turner

Saddam Hussein's *non*-nuclear options are the options that truly frighten me. As we all know, Saddam Hussein is trying to obtain nuclear weapons and delivery systems. However, he is also playing with smallpox that is immune to known cures as well as with the bubonic plague. Saddam does not stop there either; he is playing with all sorts of biological systems that could be spread without leaving fingerprints and that could cause a major loss of life around the world.

As long ago as October 1990 I advocated the intentional killing of Saddam Hussein and I continue to feel that way.[10] Attacking regime elites who threaten international peace is clearly not "assassination" but is instead a legitimate act of self-defense which the United States should avail itself of. The same argument can be made for targeting and eliminating Osama bin Laden.

The consequences of military action in the Middle East are frightening, as there is the very real possibility that conflict with Iraq may spread and ignite the entire region. However, the penalties for inaction are even greater. Time is not on our side. The best way for the United States to deter Saddam and his procurement of weapons of mass destruction is by presenting a united front with the world community that demands the unfettered access of UN weapons inspectors.

One viable justification for attacking Iraq might well be a request from Israel for assistance under Article 51 given that Saddam Hussein has repeatedly admitted to not only encouraging people to engage in terrorism, but to providing money to pay the families of people who commit suicide bombings. Clearly, soliciting such acts against the sovereign territory of Israel violates international law and Israel and its allies are entitled to act in defense of Israeli citizens.

Moreover, given that the UN Security Council Resolutions of 1990 and 1991 remain valid, the conditions contained in them have not been met by Saddam Hussein, and since Saddam Hussein continued to aggressively pursue the development of weapons of mass destruction in violation of international law, it seems clear that sufficient authority exists to effect a regime change in Iraq. Saddam Hussein is acting aggressively, in violation of international law, and I believe it is legal for the world community to use force against Iraq to stop that threat. Furthermore, I also believe that it is legal to specifically use force against Saddam Hussein as an individual if that is the best method available to end the threat to world peace.

---

10. Robert F. Turner, *Killing Saddam: Would it be a Crime?*, WASH. POST, Oct. 7, 1990 at D1

Michael Schmitt

There is a colorable argument that an international armed conflict currently exists with Iraq and that the conflict is merely in a state of ceasefire. Given this, to the extent that Iraq has in some form materially breached the ceasefire agreement then recommencement of hostilities would be appropriate. This position certainly has merit.

Yoram Dinstein

Under the jus in bello, there is nothing inherently wrong in the targeting of enemy combatants. Enemy military personnel can be attacked either collectively or individually. Saddam Hussein, being the commander-in-chief of the Iraqi forces, is a legitimate military objective for attack by the United States.[11] Obviously, such an attack—like all other attacks—has to be carried out by lawful combatants on the American side, i.e., members of the armed forces wearing uniform, carrying their arms openly, etc.

---

11. *See* Yoram Dinstein, *Legitimate Military Objectives under the Current Jus in Bello, in* LEGAL AND ETHICAL LESSONS OF NATO'S KOSOVO CAMPAIGN (Andru Wall ed., 2003) (Vol. 78, US Naval War College International Law Studies).

Panel II

Wednesday—June 26, 2002

1:30 PM–4:30 PM

Jus in Bello

Moderator:
    Colonel David Graham
    Judge Advocate, US Army
    Chief, International & Operational Law Division
    Department of the Army

Presenters:
    Professor Yoram Dinstein
    International Human Rights Law Institute
    DePaul University College of Law

    Professor Sir Adam Roberts
    Oxford University

Commentators:
    Colonel Charles Garraway
    Army Legal Services
    United Kingdom

    Professor Leslie Green
    Professor Emeritus
    University of Edmonton

    Lieutenant Colonel Tony Montgomery
    Judge Advocate, US Air Force
    Deputy Staff Judge Advocate
    US Special Operations Command

VII

Unlawful Combatancy

Yoram Dinstein[1]

Combatants and Civilians

Under the jus in bello, combatants are persons who are either members of the armed forces (except medical and religious personnel) or—irrespective of such membership—who take an active part in hostilities in an international armed conflict.[2] The jus in bello posits a fundamental principle of distinction between combatants and non-combatants (i.e., civilians).[3] The goal is to ensure in every feasible manner that inter-state armed conflicts be waged solely among the combatants of the belligerent parties. Lawful combatants can attack enemy combatants or military objectives, causing death, injury and destruction. By contrast, civilians are not allowed to participate in the

---

1. Professor Yoram Dinstein is the Charles H. Stockton Professor of International Law, US Naval War College, Newport, Rhode Island.
2. *See* A.P.V. ROGERS & P. MALHERBE, MODEL MANUAL ON THE LAW OF ARMED CONFLICT 29 (ICRC, 1999).
3. *See* Advisory Opinion on Legality of the Threat or Use of Nuclear Weapons, [1996] I.C.J. REPORTS 226, 257.

fighting. As a complementary norm, civilians "enjoy general protection against dangers arising from military operations."[4]

It is not always easy to define what an active participation in hostilities denotes. Sometimes, the reference is to "direct" participation in hostilities.[5] But the adjective "direct" does not shed much light on the extent of participation required. For instance, a person who gathers military intelligence in enemy controlled territory and a driver delivering ammunition to firing positions are generally acknowledged as actively taking part in hostilities (although merely assisting in the general war effort does not suffice).[6]

A civilian may convert himself into a combatant. In fact, every combatant is a former civilian: nobody is born a combatant. In the same vein, a combatant may retire and become a civilian. But at any given point a person is either a combatant or a civilian: he cannot (and is not allowed to) be both at the same time, nor can he constantly shift from one position to the other.

Whether on land, by sea or in the air, one cannot fight the enemy and remain a civilian. Interestingly, this general norm first began coalescing in the law of sea warfare. By the time of the Declaration of Paris of 1856, Article 1 proclaimed: "Privateering is, and remains, abolished."[7] Privateers were private persons (at times known as corsairs, not to be confused with pirates) who obtained official letters of marque from a government, allowing them to attack enemy merchant ships.[8] As the language of the Declaration of Paris indicates, it merely confirms the abolition of privateering as "an already established situation" under customary international law.[9] The law of land (and air) warfare ultimately adjusted to proscribe parallel modes of behavior.

Combatants can withdraw from the hostilities not only by retiring and becoming civilians, but also by becoming hors de combat. This can happen either by choice (through laying down of arms and surrendering) or by force of

---

4. Protocol Additional to the Geneva Conventions of 12 August 1949, and Relating to the Protection of Victims of International Armed Conflicts (Protocol I), 1977, *reprinted in* THE LAWS OF ARMED CONFLICTS: A COLLECTION OF CONVENTIONS, RESOLUTIONS AND OTHER DOCUMENTS 621, 651 (D. Schindler & J. Toman eds., 3rd ed., 1988) (Article 51(1)) [hereinafter LAWS OF ARMED CONFLICT].
5. See ROGERS & MALHERBE, *supra* note 2, at 29. *Cf.* Article 51(3) of Protocol I, LAWS OF ARMED CONFLICT, *supra* note 4, at 651.
6. See ROGERS & MALHERBE, *supra* note 2, at 29.
7. Paris Declaration Respecting Maritime Law, 1856, LAWS OF ARMED CONFLICT, *supra* note 4, at 787, 788.
8. *See* Ulrich Scheuner, *Privateering*, 3 ENCYCLOPEDIA OF PUBLIC INTERNATIONAL LAW 1120, 1120–1121 (R. Bernhardt ed., 1997).
9. *Id.* at 1122.

circumstances (by getting wounded, sick or shipwrecked). A combatant who is hors de combat and falls into the hands of the enemy is in principle entitled to the status of a prisoner of war. Being a prisoner of war means denial of liberty, i.e., detention for the duration of the hostilities (which may go on for many years). However, that detention has only one purpose: to preclude the further participation of the prisoner of war in the ongoing hostilities. The detention is not due to any criminal act committed by the prisoner of war, and he cannot be prosecuted and punished "simply for having taken part in hostilities."[10] While his liberty is temporarily denied, the decisive point is that the life, health and dignity of a prisoner of war are guaranteed. Detailed provisions to that end are incorporated in Geneva Convention (III) of 1949.[11]

Lawful and Unlawful Combatants

Entitlement to the status of a prisoner of war—upon being captured by the enemy—is vouchsafed to every combatant, subject to the *conditio sine qua non* that he is a lawful combatant. The distinction between lawful and unlawful combatants complements the fundamental distinction between combatants and civilians: the primary goal of the former is to preserve the latter.[12] The jus in bello can effectively protect civilians from being objects of attack in war only if and when they can be identified by the enemy as non-combatants. Combatants "may try to become invisible in the landscape, but not in the crowd."[13] Blurring the lines of division between combatants and civilians is bound to result in civilians suffering the consequences of being suspected as covert combatants. Hence, under customary international law, a sanction (deprivation of the privileges of prisoners of war) is imposed on any combatant masquerading as a civilian in order to mislead the enemy and avoid detection.

An enemy civilian who does not take up arms, and does not otherwise participate actively in the hostilities, is guaranteed by the jus in bello not only his life, health and dignity (as is done with respect to prisoners of war), but even his personal liberty which cannot be deprived (through detention) without

---

10. ALLAN ROSAS, THE LEGAL STATUS OF PRISONERS OF WAR: A STUDY IN INTERNATIONAL HUMANITARIAN LAW APPLICABLE IN ARMED CONFLICTS 82 (1976).
11. Geneva Convention (III) Relative to the Treatment of Prisoners of War, 1949 [hereinafter GC III] *reprinted in* LAWS OF ARMED CONFLICT, *supra* note 4, at 423.
12. *See* Theodor Meron, *Some Legal Aspects of Arab Terrorists' Claims to Privileged Combatancy*, 40 NORDISK TIDSSKRIFT FOR INT'L RET 47, 62 (1970).
13. Denise Bindschedler-Robert, *A Reconsideration of the Law of Armed Conflicts*, THE LAW OF ARMED CONFLICTS: REPORT OF THE CONFERENCE ON CONTEMPORARY PROBLEMS OF THE LAW OF ARMED CONFLICT, 1, 43 (1971).

cause. But a person is not allowed to wear simultaneously two caps: the hat of a civilian and the helmet of a soldier. A person who engages in military raids by night, while purporting to be an innocent civilian by day, is neither a civilian nor a combatant. He is an unlawful combatant.

Upon being captured by the enemy, an unlawful combatant—like a lawful combatant (and unlike a civilian)—is subject to automatic detention. But in contradistinction to a lawful combatant, an unlawful combatant fails to enjoy the benefits of the status of a prisoner of war. Hence, although he cannot be executed without trial, he is susceptible to being prosecuted and severely punished for any acts of violence committed in the course of the hostilities in which he has participated. The legal position was summed up by the Supreme Court of the United States, in the *Quirin* case of 1942 (per Chief Justice Stone):

> [b]y universal agreement and practice, the law of war draws a distinction between the armed forces and the peaceful populations of belligerent nations and also between those who are lawful and unlawful combatants. Lawful combatants are subject to capture and detention as prisoners of war by opposing military forces. Unlawful combatants are likewise subject to capture and detention, but in addition they are subject to trial and punishment by military tribunals for acts which render their belligerency unlawful.[14]

With the exception of the last few words, this is an accurate reflection of the jus in bello.

What can unlawful combatants be prosecuted and punished for? The *Quirin* judgment refers to "trial and punishment by military tribunals for acts which render their belligerency unlawful." Admittedly, sometimes the act which turns a person into an unlawful combatant constitutes by itself an offence (under either domestic or international law) and can be prosecuted and punished as such before a military tribunal. But on other occasions the judicial proceedings may be conducted before regular courts and, more significantly, they are likely to pertain to acts other than those that divested the person of the status of lawful combatant. Even when the act negating the status as a lawful combatant does not constitute a crime per se (under either domestic or international law), it can expose the perpetrator to ordinary penal sanctions (pursuant to the domestic legal system) for other acts committed by him that are branded as criminal. Unlawful combatants "may be punished under the internal criminal legislation of the adversary for having committed hostile acts

---

14. Ex parte Quirin, 317 U.S. 1, 30–31 (1942).

in violation of its provisions (e.g., for murder), even if these acts do not constitute war crimes under international law."[15]

At bottom, warfare by its very nature consists of a series of acts of violence (like homicide, assault, battery and arson) ordinarily penalized by the criminal codes of all countries. When a combatant, John Doe, holds a rifle, aims it at Richard Roe (a soldier belonging to the enemy's armed forces) with intent to kill, pulls the trigger, and causes Richard Roe's death, what we have is a premeditated homicide fitting the definition of murder in virtually all domestic penal codes. If, upon being captured by the enemy, John Doe is not prosecuted for murder, this is due to one reason only. The jus in bello provides John Doe with a legal shield, protecting him from trial and punishment, by conferring upon him the status of a prisoner of war. Yet, the shield is available only on condition that John Doe is a lawful combatant. If John Doe acts as he does beyond the pale of legal combatancy, the jus in bello simply removes the protective shield. Thereby, it subjects John Doe to the full rigor of the enemy's domestic legal system, and the ordinary penal sanctions provided by that law will become applicable to him.

There are several differences between the prosecution of war criminals and that of unlawful combatants.[16] The principal distinction is derived from the active or passive role of the jus in bello. War criminals are brought to trial for serious violations of the jus in bello itself. With unlawful combatants, the jus in bello refrains from stigmatizing the acts as criminal. It merely takes off a mantle of immunity from the defendant, who is therefore accessible to penal charges for any offence committed against the domestic legal system.

It is also noteworthy that, unlike war criminals (who must be brought to trial), unlawful combatants may simply be subjected to administrative detention without trial. Detention of unlawful combatants without trial was specifically mentioned as an option in the *Quirin* case (as quoted above), and the option has indeed been used widely by the United States in the war in Afghanistan (see infra).

Detention of unlawful combatants is also the subject of special legislation of Israel, passed by the Knesset in 2002.[17] This Detention of Unlawful Combatants Law defines an unlawful combatant as anyone taking part—directly or indirectly—in hostilities against the State of Israel, who is not entitled to

---

15. Rosas, *supra* note 10, at 305.
16. See Yoram Dinstein, *The Distinction between Unlawful Combatants and War Criminals*, INTERNATIONAL LAW AT A TIME OF PERPLEXITY 103–116 (Essays in Honour of Shabtai Rosenne, Y. Dinstein ed., 1989).
17. See Detention of Unlawful Combatants Law, 2002, 1834 *Sefer Hahukim* [S.H.] 192.

prisoner of war status under Geneva Convention (III).[18] Detention is based on the decision of the chief of staff of the armed forces, on grounds of state security, but it is subject to judicial review by a (civilian) district court (both initially and every six months thereafter).[19] The law emphasizes that detention is just one option, and that an unlawful combatant can equally be brought to trial under any criminal law.[20] An important point addressed by the law is the maximum duration of the detention. An unlawful combatant can be held in detention as long as the hostilities of the force to which he belongs have not been terminated.[21]

The Entitlement to Prisoner of War Status under Customary International Law

Article 1 of the Regulations Respecting the Laws and Customs of War on Land, Annexed to Hague Convention (II) of 1899 and Hague Convention (IV) of 1907, proclaims:

> [t]he laws, rights, and duties of war apply not only to armies, but also to militia and volunteer corps fulfilling the following conditions:
>
> 1. To be commanded by a person responsible for his subordinates;
> 2. To have a fixed distinctive emblem recognizable at a distance;
> 3. To carry arms openly; and
> 4. To conduct their operations in accordance with the laws and customs of war.[22]

Article 2 adds a provision entitled "Levée en masse," which reads in the revised 1907 version:

> [t]he inhabitants of a territory which has not been occupied, who, on the approach of the enemy, spontaneously take up arms to resist the invading troops without having had time to organize themselves in accordance with Article 1,

---

18. *Id.* (Section 2).
19. *Id.* (Sections 3, 5).
20. *Id.* (Section 9).
21. *Id.* (Sections 7–8).
22. Regulations Respecting the Laws and Customs of War on Land, Annexed to Hague Convention (II) of 1899 and Hague Convention (IV) of 1907, *in* LAWS OF ARMED CONFLICT, *supra* note 4, at 63, 75.

shall be regarded as belligerents if they carry arms openly and if they respect the laws and customs of war.[23]

Article 3 prescribes further: "[t]he armed forces of the belligerent parties may consist of combatants and non-combatants. In the case of capture by the enemy, both have a right to be treated as prisoners of war."[24] As far as civilians who are not employed by the armed forces, yet accompany them, Article 13 stipulates:

> [i]ndividuals who follow an army without directly belonging to it, such as newspaper correspondents and reporters, sutlers and contractors, who fall into the enemy's hands and whom the latter thinks expedient to detain, are entitled to be treated as prisoners of war, provided they are in possession of a certificate from the military authorities of the army which they were accompanying.[25]

The Hague formula thus establishes four general—and cumulative—conditions for lawful combatancy: (i) subordination to responsible command, (ii) a fixed distinctive emblem, (iii) carrying arms openly, and (iv) conduct in accordance with the jus in bello. In the special setting of a "levée en masse," conditions (i) and (ii) are dispensed with, and only conditions (iii) and (iv) remain valid. These provisions of the Hague Regulations (like others) "are considered to embody the customary law of war on land."[26]

The Geneva Conventions of 1949 retain the Hague formula, making it even more stringent. Article 4(A) of Geneva Convention (III) sets forth:

> A. Prisoners of war, in the sense of the present Convention, are persons belonging to one of the following categories, who have fallen into the power of the enemy:
>
> (1) Members of the armed forces of a Party to the conflict, as well as members of militias or volunteer corps forming part of such armed forces.
>
> (2) Members of other militias and members of other volunteer corps, including those of organized resistance movements, belonging to a Party to the conflict and operating in or outside their own territory, even if this territory is occupied, provided that such militias or volunteer corps, including such organized resistance movements, fulfil the following conditions:

---

23. Id. at 75–76.
24. Id. at 76.
25. Id. at 79.
26. See G.I.A.D. Draper, The Status of Combatants and the Question of Guerilla Warfare, 45 BRIT. Y.B. INT'L L. 173, 186 (1971).

(a) that of being commanded by a person responsible for his subordinates;

(b) that of having a fixed distinctive sign recognizable at a distance;

(c) that of carrying arms openly;

(d) that of conducting their operations in accordance with the laws and customs of war.

(3) Members of regular armed forces who profess allegiance to a government or an authority not recognized by the Detaining Power.

(4) Persons who accompany the armed forces without actually being members thereof, such as civilian members of military aircraft crews, war correspondents, supply contractors, members of labour units or of services responsible for the welfare of the armed forces, provided that they have received authorization from the armed forces which they accompany, who shall provide them for that purpose with an identity card similar to the annexed model.

(5) Members of crews, including masters, pilots and apprentices, of the merchant marine and the crews of civil aircraft of the Parties to the conflict, who do not benefit by more favourable treatment under any other provisions of international law.

(6) Inhabitants of a non-occupied territory, who on the approach of the enemy spontaneously take up arms to resist the invading forces, without having had time to form themselves into regular armed units, provided they carry arms openly and respect the laws and customs of war.[27]

This language is replicated in Article 13 of both Geneva Convention (I)[28] and Geneva Convention (II).[29] Article 4(B) of Geneva Convention (III) goes on to create two further categories of persons that should be treated as prisoners of war: one relating to occupied territories (members of armed forces who have been released from detention in an occupied territory and are then

---

27. Geneva Convention III, art. 4, in LAWS OF ARMED CONFLICT, *supra* note 4, at 430, 431.
28. Geneva Convention (I) for the Amelioration of the Condition of the Wounded and Sick in Armed Forces in the Field, 1949, *in* LAWS OF ARMED CONFLICT, *supra* note 4, at 373, 379–380.
29. Geneva Convention (II) for the Amelioration of the Condition of Wounded, Sick and Shipwrecked Members of Armed Forces at Sea, 1949, *in* LAWS OF ARMED CONFLICT, *supra* note 4, at 401, 408.

reinterned),[30] and the other pertaining to neutral countries (members of armed forces of belligerents who reach neutral territory and have to be interned there as required by international law).[31] Article 4(C) states that nothing in the above provisions affects the status of medical personnel and chaplains[32] who, under Article 33 of Geneva Convention (III) cannot be taken prisoners of war, but may be retained by the Detaining Power with a view to assisting prisoners of war.[33]

The first and foremost category of persons entitled to the status of prisoners of war covers members of the armed forces of the belligerent Parties, including all their different components. These are the regular forces of the belligerents. It does not matter what the semantic appellation of regular forces is (they may function, e.g., under the technical designation of militias); how they are structured; whether military service is compulsory or voluntary; and whether the units are part of standing armed forces or consist of reservists called to action. The distinction is between regular forces of all types, on the one hand, and irregular forces in the sense of partisans or guerrilla forces, on the other.

On the face of it, the Geneva Conventions do not pose any conditions to the eligibility of regular forces to prisoners of war status. Nevertheless, regular forces are not absolved from meeting the cumulative conditions binding irregular forces. There is simply a presumption that regular forces would naturally meet those conditions. But the presumption can definitely be rebutted. The issue came to the fore in the *Mohamed Ali* case of 1968, where the Privy Council held (per Viscount Dilhorne) that it is not enough to establish that a person belongs to the regular armed forces, in order to guarantee to him the status of a prisoner of war.[34] The Privy Council pronounced that even members of the armed forces must observe the cumulative conditions imposed on irregular forces, although this is not stated *expressis verbis* in the Geneva Conventions or in the Hague Regulations.[35] The facts of the case related to Indonesian soldiers who—at a time of a "confrontation" between Indonesia and

---

30. This special category makes it "impossible for an occupying Power to deprive prisoners of war of the benefit of the convention through the subterfuge of release and subsequent arrest." Raymond Yingling & Robert Ginnane, *The Geneva Conventions of 1949*, 46 AM. J. INT'L L. 393, 405–406 (1952).
31. Geneva Convention III, art. 4(B), in LAWS OF ARMED CONFLICT, *supra* note 4, at 431–432.
32. *Id.* at 432.
33. *Id.* at 442–443.
34. Mohamed Ali v. Public Prosecutor, [1969] 1 A.C. 430, 449.
35. *Id.* at 449–450.

Malaysia—planted explosives in a building in Singapore (then a part of Malaysia) while wearing civilian clothes. The Privy Council confirmed the appellants' death sentence for murder, on the ground that a regular soldier committing an act of sabotage while not in uniform loses the entitlement to a prisoner of war status.[36] The earlier *Quirin* judgment—concerning German members of the armed forces who took off their uniforms when on a sabotage mission in the United States (where they had landed by submarine)—is to the same effect.[37]

The second category of prisoners of war under the Geneva Conventions pertains to irregular forces: guerrillas, partisans and the like, however they call themselves. This is the most problematic category, given the proliferation of such forces in modern warfare. The Geneva Conventions repeat the four Hague conditions verbatim. However, two additional conditions are implied from the *chapeau* of Article 4(A)(2): (v) organization, and (vi) belonging to a party to the conflict. One more condition is distilled in the case law from the text of the Geneva Conventions: (vii) lack of duty of allegiance to the Detaining Power.

Each of the four Hague conditions, and the additional three conditions, deserves a few words of explanation:

The first condition—of subordination to a responsible commander—is designed to exclude the possibility of activities of individuals (known in French as "franc-tireurs") on their own. The operation of small units of irregular forces is permissible, provided that the other conditions are fulfilled, but there is no room for individual initiatives. John Doe or Richard Roe—especially in an occupied territory—cannot legitimately conduct a private war against the enemy.

The second condition—of having a fixed distinct emblem recognizable at a distance—is predicated on two elements. The emblem in question must meet the dual requirement of distinction (i.e., it must identify and characterize the force using it) and fixity (to wit, the force is not allowed to confuse the enemy by ceaselessly changing its distinctive emblem). The most obvious fixed distinct emblem of regular armed forces is that of a particular uniform. But irregular armed forces need not have any uniform, and suffice it for them to possess a less complex distinctive emblem: part of the clothing (like a special shirt or particular headgear) or certain insignia.[38]

---

36. *Id.* at 451–454.
37. Ex parte Quirin, *supra* note 14, at 35–36.
38. JEAN DE PREUX, COMMENTARY III: GENEVA CONVENTION RELATIVE TO THE TREATMENT OF PRISONERS OF WAR 60 (1960).

The fixed distinctive emblem must be worn throughout every military operation against the enemy in which the combatant takes part (throughout means from start to finish, namely, from the beginning of deployment to the end of disengagement), and the emblem must not be deliberately removed at any time in the course of the operation.[39] Still, combatants are not bound to wear the distinctive emblem when discharging duties not linked to military operations (such as training or administration).[40]

The condition of having a fixed distinctive emblem raises a number of questions owing to its language. Thus, it is not easy to fully understand the obligation that the distinctive emblem will be recognizable at a distance. The phraseology must be reasonably interpreted. Combatants seeking to stay alive do not attempt to draw attention to themselves. On the contrary, even soldiers in uniform are prone to use camouflage. This is a legitimate ruse of war,[41] as long as the combatant merely exploits the topographical conditions: the physical as distinct from the demographic landscape of civilians.[42] Another question is germane to night warfare. Needless to say, if the combatant does not carry an illuminated distinctive emblem, that emblem will not be recognizable at a distance in the dark. Again, it is important that the terse and imperfect wording would not overshadow the thrust of the condition, which is crystal clear. Just as regular forces wear uniforms, so must irregular forces use a fixed emblem which will distinguish them—in ordinary circumstances and in a reasonable fashion—from the civilian population. The issue is not whether combatants can be seen, but the lack of desire on their part to create the false impression that they are civilians.

It should be added that when combatants go to (or from) battle in a vehicle or a tank—and, similarly, if they sail in a vessel or fly in an aircraft—it is not enough for each individual person to carry the distinctive emblem: the vehicle or other platform must itself be properly identified.[43] By the same token, the external marking of the vehicle or platform does not absolve the combatants on board from having their personal distinctive emblems. As for members of the crew of a military aircraft, there is a specific provision to that effect in Article 15 of the (non-binding) 1923 Hague Rules of Air Warfare, where it is explained that this is

---

39. Howard Levie, PRISONERS OF WAR IN INTERNATIONAL ARMED CONFLICT 47 (Howard S. Levie ed., 1978), (Vol. 59, US Naval War College International Law Studies).
40. WALDEMAR SOLF, Article 44, NEW RULES FOR VICTIMS OF ARMED CONFLICTS: COMMENTARY ON THE TWO 1977 PROTOCOLS ADDITIONAL TO THE GENEVA CONVENTIONS OF 1949 241, 252 (M. Bothe et al. eds., 1982).
41. Article 37(2) of Protocol I, in LAWS OF ARMED CONFLICT, supra note 4, at 645.
42. Bindschedler-Robert, supra note 13, at 43.
43. DE PREUX, supra note 38, at 60.

required in case the members of the crew "become separated from their aircraft."[44]

The third condition—of carrying arms openly—brings up similar issues as the second. Does this mean that a combatant is barred from carrying a handgun in a holster or hand grenades in a pouch? The question is patently rhetorical. Once more, what counts is not the ambiguous language but the gist of the condition. A lawful combatant must abstain from purporting to be an innocent civilian, with a view to facilitating access to the enemy by stealth. He must carry his arms openly in a reasonable way, depending on the nature of the weapon and the circumstances at hand.

The fourth condition—conduct in accordance with the jus in bello—is the key to lawful combatancy. Unless a combatant is willing himself to respect the jus in bello, he is estopped from relying on that body of law when desirous of enjoying its benefits.[45]

These are the original Hague conditions, endorsed by the Geneva Conventions. As mentioned, the following additional conditions are derived from the Conventions:

The fifth condition—organization—actually reinvigorates the first condition in a somewhat different way. Lawful combatants must act within a hierarchic framework, embedded in discipline, and subject to supervision by upper echelons of what is being done by subordinate units in the field.

The sixth condition—belonging to a party to the conflict—got a practical expression in the 1969 judgment of an Israeli military court in the *Kassem* case.[46] Here a number of people who belonged to an organization calling itself the "Popular Front for the Liberation of Palestine" crossed the Jordan River from the East Bank (the Kingdom of Jordan) to the West Bank (Israeli occupied territory) for sabotage purposes. When captured and charged with security offences, they claimed entitlement to prisoners of war status. The Israeli Military Court held that irregular forces must belong to a party to the conflict.[47] Since no Arab government at war with Israel had assumed responsibility for the activities of the Popular Front—which was indeed illegal in the Kingdom of Jordan—the condition was not fulfilled.[48] The judgment was criticized by Georg Schwarzenberger on the ground that the Geneva Conventions

---

44. Hague Rules of Air Warfare, 1923, art. 15, *in* LAWS OF ARMED CONFLICT, *supra* note 4, at 207, 209.
45. *See* Levie, *supra* note 39, at 50–51.
46. Military Prosecutor v. Kassem, 42 INT'L L. R. 470 (Israel, Military Court, 1969).
47. *Id.* at 476.
48. *Id.* at 477–478.

were not meant to limit the scope of lawful combatancy under preexisting rules of international law.[49] However, even prior to the Geneva Conventions, the premise was that the Hague conditions apply only to combatants acting on behalf of a state party to the conflict.[50] It is evident that the members of an independent band of guerrillas cannot be regarded as lawful combatants, even if they observe the jus in bello, use a fixed distinctive emblem, and carry their arms openly. One way or another, "a certain relationship with a belligerent government is necessary."[51] One can, of course, argue whether Palestinian guerrillas factually belonged at the time to a party to the conflict. But the condition itself is irreproachable.

The seventh and last condition—of non-allegiance to the Detaining Power—is not specifically mentioned in the Geneva Conventions, and is derived from the case law. The principal authority is the 1967 Judgment of the Privy Council in the *Koi* case,[52] in which captured Indonesian paratroopers—landing in Malaysia—included a number of Malays convicted and sentenced to death for having unlawfully possessed arms in a security zone. The question on appeal before the Privy Council was whether they were entitled to prisoners of war status. The Privy Council held (per Lord Hodson) that nationals of the Detaining Power, as well as other persons owing it a duty of allegiance, are not entitled to such status.[53] This was viewed by the Privy Council as a rule of customary international law.[54] Although the condition does not appear in the text of Article 4(A), the Privy Council found other provisions of Geneva Convention (III)—specifically Articles 87 and 100[55]—in which it is clearly stated that prisoners of war are not nationals of the Detaining Power and do not owe it any duty of allegiance.[56]

The requirement of nationality (or allegiance) has to be approached carefully. The fact that a combatant belonging to state A—captured by state B—is a national of state C, does not make any difference. A German soldier in the French Foreign Legion was entitled to a prisoner of war status in the Indo-

---

49. Georg Schwarzenberger, *Human Rights and Guerrilla Warfare*, 1 ISR. Y.B. HUM. RTS. 246, 252 (1971).
50. Lester Nurick & Roger Barrett, *Legality of Guerrilla Forces under the Laws of War*, 40 AM. J. INT'L L. 563, 567–569 (1946).
51. Bindschedler-Robert, *supra* note 13, at 40.
52. Public Prosecutor v. Koi, A.C. 829 (1967).
53. *Id.* at 856–858.
54. *Id.* at 856–857.
55. Geneva Convention III, arts. 87 & 100, *in* LAWS OF ARMED CONFLICT, *supra* note 4, at 460, 464.
56. *Koi*, *supra* note 52, at 857.

China War. But such a soldier would not have been entitled to the same status if fighting in a war against Germany.

The *Koi* case occasions also a question of the law of evidence. Under Article 5 (para. 2) of Geneva Convention (III), should any doubt arise as to whether certain persons belong to any of the categories enumerated in Article 4, they enjoy the Convention's protection until their status is determined by a competent tribunal. Opinions in the Privy Council were divided as to whether the mere allegation by a defendant that he is a foreign national generates doubt in accordance with Article 5: the majority held that that was the legal position, but a minority dissented.[57] The more central issue is that of the burden of proof. The minority opined that the burden of proof lies on the defendant, who must show that he is entitled to prisoner of war status (and consequently that he is not a national of the Detaining Power).[58] The majority did not address the point. But the correct position apparently is that, once a defendant persuades the court that he is a member of the enemy armed forces, the burden of proof that he owes allegiance to the Detaining Power (and is therefore not entitled to prisoner of war status) falls on the prosecution.[59] Incontestably, the defendant first has to establish that he is a member of the enemy armed forces.

It is not easy for irregular forces to observe cumulatively the seven conditions catalogued or—for that matter—even the core four Hague conditions. These conditions are actually patterned after the operations of regular forces (to which they do not explicitly allude). Regular forces are organized, are subject to hierarchical discipline, and naturally belong to a party to the conflict; they have a proud tradition of wearing uniforms and carrying their arms openly; they are trained to observe the *jus in bello*; and the issue of allegiance scarcely arises. However, with irregular forces (to whom the conditions expressly refer), the position is not so simple. Even if other problems are ignored, the difficulty to meet both the (ii) and (iii) conditions (of a fixed distinctive emblem and carrying arms openly) is blatant, "since secrecy and surprise are the essence" of guerrilla warfare.[60] Most of the partisan (resistance) movements of World War II did not fulfil all the cumulative conditions.[61] From a

---

57. *Id.* at 855, 865.
58. *Id.* at 864.
59. Richard Baxter, *The Privy Council on the Qualifications of Belligerents*, 63 AM. J. INT'L L. 290, 293 (1969).
60. Richard Baxter, *So-Called 'Unprivileged Belligerency': Spies, Guerrillas, and Saboteurs*, 28 BRIT. Y.B. INT'L L. 323, 328 (1951).
61. Jean Pictet, *The New Geneva Conventions for the Protection of War Victims*, 45 AM. J. INT'L L. 462, 472 (1951).

practical standpoint, many believe that "obedience to these rules would be tantamount to committing suicide, as far as most guerrillas would be concerned."[62] Still, these are the norms of the Hague Regulations, the Geneva Conventions, and customary international law.

Under the Hague Regulations, the Geneva Conventions, and customary international law, the only time that the cumulative conditions are eased is that of "levée en masse." It must be accentuated that this category applies only to the inhabitants of unoccupied areas, so that there is no "levée en masse" in occupied territories. The idea (originating in the French Revolution[63]) is that at the point of invasion—and in order to forestall occupation—the civilian population takes arms spontaneously, without an opportunity to organize. This is an extraordinary situation in the course of which—for a short while and as an interim stage in the fighting—there is no need to meet all seven cumulative conditions to the status of lawful combatancy. The Hague Regulations and Geneva Conventions enumerate only two cumulative conditions: carrying arms openly and respect for the jus in bello (conditions (iii) and (iv)). It follows that there is no need to meet the two other Hague conditions of subordination to a responsible commander and using a fixed distinctive emblem (conditions (i) and (ii)). Given the postulate that there was no time to organize, condition (v) is inapplicable. Condition (vi) is also irrelevant: when the civilian population resists invasion, the problem of belonging to a party to the conflict is moot. On the other hand, it is arguable that condition (vii) of nationality (or allegiance) remains in place. In any event, the transitional phase of "levée en masse" lapses *ex hypothesi* after a relatively short duration. One of three things is bound to happen: either the territory will be occupied (despite the "levée en masse"); or the invading force will be repulsed (thanks to the "levée en masse" or to the timely arrival of reinforcements); or the battle of defense will stabilize, and then there is ample opportunity for organization.

Both the Hague Regulations and the Geneva Conventions equate the position of certain civilians—employed by or accompanying the armed forces—to that of lawful combatants as far as prisoners of war status is concerned. Evidently, the fact that a civilian is employed by or accompanies the armed forces does not turn him into a combatant. Hence, the question of the fulfilment of most of the cumulative conditions does not arise. Yet, in all instances condition (iv) must be regarded as paramount: anybody seeking the privileges of the

---

62. Gerhard von Glahn, *The Protection of Human Rights in Time of Armed Conflicts*, 1 ISR. Y.B. HUM. RTS. 208, 223 (1971).
63. On the origins of the institution, see Walter Rabus, *A New Definition of the 'Levée en Masse,'* 24 NETH INT'L L. REV. 232 (1977).

jus in bello must himself respect the laws from which he proposes to benefit. Condition (vii) of nationality—or allegiance—is also relevant to civilians. Should the civilian bear light arms for self-defense, condition (iii) relating to carrying the arms openly will apply.

Who should observe the seven conditions: the individual or the group of which he is a member? The issue does not arise with respect to regular troops. The assumption is that these forces collectively fulfil all the conditions, and to the extent that there is doubt in the concrete case, it affects John Doe but not an entire army. In the *Mohamed Ali* and *Koi* cases, there was no doubt that members of the armed forces of Indonesia generally wear uniforms and do not owe allegiance to Malaysia, although the defendants in the dock failed to meet these conditions (and were therefore denied prisoners of war status). However, where irregular forces are concerned, the question whether the conditions of lawful combatancy are met may relate both to a guerrilla movement collectively and to each of its members individually. The answer to the question is contingent on the various conditions.

The addressee of conditions (i), (v) and (vi) is clearly the group collectively, and not any of the members individually. It is necessary to ascertain that the group as a whole is organized, has a responsible commander and belongs to a party to the conflict. Should that be the case, the same yardsticks must be applied to all members of the group.[64] The reverse applies to condition (vii), directed at each member of the group rather than the group as a collective: the link of nationality is determined individually. In between are the other conditions: (ii), (iii) and (iv). Condition (ii) on a fixed distinctive emblem requires some preliminary action on the part of the group, which must adopt its identifying emblem; if it does not do that, no member of the group is capable of meeting the condition. Still, even if the group adopts a fixed distinctive emblem, that does not mean that John Doe will use it at the critical time (just as the defendants in the *Mohamed Ali* case did not wear their uniforms at the critical time). If John Doe fails to do that, his misconduct does not contaminate the entire group, but the personal consequences are liable to be dire.

As for conditions (iii) and (iv)—carrying arms openly and observance of the jus in bello—the present writer believes that the correct approach is that their fulfilment should be monitored primarily on an individual basis and only secondarily on a group basis. That is to say, if observance of these conditions in the individual case comes to a test in reality, John Doe has to answer for his actual behavior. However, if no opportunity for such individual verification

---

64. See Draper, *supra* note 26, at 196.

presents itself—for instance, when John Doe is captured in possession of arms but before setting out to accomplish any hostile mission—it is possible to establish how the group behaves in general and extrapolate from the collectivity to the individual. If the group as a whole has a record of disrespect for the jus in bello, there is no need to accord John Doe prisoner of war status. Conversely, if the group as a whole generally acts in compliance with the jus in bello, John Doe should be allowed to benefit from doubt. It has been contested that—even if John Doe actually observes the jus in bello—he should not be deemed a lawful combatant when the group as a whole generally acts in breach of that body of law.[65] This is unassailable in extreme cases, like al Qaeda. But if the conduct of the members of the group is uneven, John Doe should be judged on the merits of his own case and not on the demerits of his comrades at arms.

The Legal Position under Protocol I of 1977

The legal position is radically changed pursuant to Additional Protocol I of 1977. Article 43 of the Protocol promulgates:

> 1. The armed forces of a Party to a conflict consist of organized armed forces, groups and units which are under a command responsible to that Party for the conduct of its subordinates, even if that Party is represented by a government or an authority not recognized by an adverse Party. Such armed forces shall be subject to an internal disciplinary system which, *inter alia*, shall enforce compliance with the rules of international law applicable in armed conflict.
>
> 2. Members of the armed forces of a Party to a conflict (other than medical personnel and chaplains covered by Article 33 of the Third Convention) are combatants, that is to say, they have the right to participate directly in hostilities.
>
> 3. Whenever a Party to the conflict incorporates a paramilitary or armed law enforcement agency into its armed forces it shall so notify the other Parties to the conflict.[66]

By itself, Article 43 appears to follow in the footsteps of the Hague and Geneva rules, as reflected in customary international law. Indeed, it reaffirms four of the seven conditions for (lawful) combatancy: condition (i) concerning the existence of a command responsible for the conduct of its subordinates; condition (iv) about compliance with the rules of the jus in bello; condition

---

65. *See id.* at 197; *see also* Meron, *supra* note 12, at 65.
66. Protocol I, art. 43, *in* LAWS OF ARMED CONFLICT, *supra* note 4, at 647.

(v) stressing the need for organization and discipline; and condition (vi) pertaining to the need to belong to a Party to the conflict.[67]
Unfortunately, Article 44 goes much further:

> 1. Any combatant, as defined in Article 43, who falls into the power of an adverse Party shall be a prisoner of war.
>
> 2. While all combatants are obliged to comply with the rules of international law applicable in armed conflict, violations of these rules shall not deprive a combatant of his right to be a combatant or, if he falls into the power of an adverse Party, of his right to be a prisoner of war, except as provided in paragraphs 3 and 4.
>
> 3. In order to promote the protection of the civilian population from the effects of hostilities, combatants are obliged to distinguish themselves from the civilian population while they are engaged in an attack or in a military operation preparatory to an attack. Recognizing, however, that there are situations in armed conflicts where, owing to the nature of the hostilities an armed combatant cannot so distinguish himself, he shall retain his status as a combatant, provided that, in such situations, he carries his arms openly:
>
> during each military engagement, and
>
> during such time as he is visible to the adversary while he is engaged in a military deployment preceding the launching of an attack in which he is to participate.
>
> Acts which comply with the requirements of this paragraph shall not be considered as perfidious within the meaning of Article 37, paragraph 1(c).
>
> 4. A combatant who falls into the power of an adverse Party while failing to meet the requirements set forth in the second sentence of paragraph 3 shall forfeit his right to be a prisoner of war, but he shall, nevertheless, be given protections equivalent in all respects to those accorded to prisoners of war by the Third Convention and by this Protocol. The protection includes protections equivalent to those accorded to prisoners of war by the Third Convention in the case where such a person is tried and punished for any offences he has committed.
>
> 5. Any combatant who falls into the power of an adverse Party while not engaged in an attack or in a military operation preparatory to an attack shall not

---

67. *See* Jean de Preux, *Article 43*, COMMENTARY ON THE ADDITIONAL PROTOCOLS OF 8 JUNE 1977 TO THE GENEVA CONVENTIONS OF 12 AUGUST 1949 505, 517 (Y. Sandoz et al. eds., ICRC, 1987).

forfeit his rights to be a combatant and a prisoner of war by virtue of his prior activities.

6. This article is without prejudice to the right of any person to be a prisoner of war pursuant to Article 4 of the Third Convention.

7. This article is not intended to change the generally accepted practice of States with respect to the wearing of the uniform by combatants assigned to the regular, uniformed armed units of a Party to the conflict.

8. In addition to the categories of persons mentioned in Article 13 of the First and Second Conventions, all members of the armed forces of a Party to the conflict, as defined in Article 43 of this Protocol, shall be entitled to protection under those Conventions if they are wounded or sick or, in the case of the Second Convention, shipwrecked at sea or in other waters.[68]

The language of this verbose text is quite convoluted, not to say obscure. But when a serious attempt is made to reconcile its disparate paragraphs with one another, a distressing picture emerges. Notwithstanding the provision of Article 43, Article 44(2) does away—for all intents and purposes—with condition (iv): whether or not in compliance with the jus in bello, all combatants (i.e., those taking a direct part in hostilities) are entitled to the status of lawful combatancy and to the attendant privileges of prisoners of war. Paragraph (3) of Article 44, while paying lip service to the principle of distinction, retains only a truncated version of condition (iii): the duty to carry arms openly is restricted to the duration of the battle itself and to the preliminary phase of deployment in preparation for the launching of an attack, while being visible to the enemy. The issue of visibility to the enemy is complex, implying that if the combatant neither knows nor should know that he is visible, the obligation does not apply.[69] It is not clear whether visibility is determined solely by the naked eye or it also includes observation by means of binoculars and even infra-red equipment.[70] More significantly, there is no agreement as to when deployment begins: at the original assembly point (from which the combatants proceed to their destination) or only moments before the attack is launched.[71] But these and other points are quite moot, since—in a most enigmatic

---

68. Protocol I, art. 44, in LAWS OF ARMED CONFLICT, *supra* note 4, at 647–648.
69. *See* Jean de Preux, *Article 44*, COMMENTARY ON THE ADDITIONAL PROTOCOLS, *supra* note 67, at 519, 535.
70. *See* Solf, *supra* note 40, at 254–255.
71. *See* DE PREUX, *supra* note 69, at 534–535.

fashion[72]—Paragraph (4) mandates that, albeit technically deprived of prisoners of war status, transgressors must be accorded every protection conferred on prisoners of war. Thus, in terms of practicality, condition (iii)—however circumscribed—is vitiated by Article 44. As far as condition (ii) is concerned, the sole reference to it is made in Paragraph (7), articulating an intention to not affect the practice of wearing uniforms by regular armies. Thereby, Article 44 only underscores the elimination of condition (ii) where it really counts, namely, when irregular forces take part in hostilities. In fact, the consequence is "to tip the balance of protection in favor of irregular combatants to the detriment of the regular soldier and the civilian."[73] In the final analysis, it is the civilians who will suffer. "Inevitably, regular forces would treat civilians more harshly and with less restraint if they believed that their opponents were free to pose as civilians while retaining their right to act as combatants and their POW status if captured."[74]

As pointed out above, the seven cumulative conditions of lawful combatancy are onerous for irregular forces. Hence, it would have made sense to alleviate the conditions to some extent. For instance, conditions (ii) and (iii) could become alternative rather than cumulative in their application, considering that when one is fulfilled the other may be looked at as redundant.[75] Still, the pendulum in Article 44 has swung from one extreme to the other, reducing *ad absurdum* the conditions of lawful combatancy. The outcome is that, for contracting parties to the Protocol, the general distinction between lawful and unlawful combatants becomes nominal in value.

Objections to the new legal regime created in Article 44 are among the key reasons why the leading military power of the day—the United States—declines to ratify Protocol I (while recognizing that many of its other provisions reflect customary international law),[76] and this negative assessment is shared by an array of other states.

---

72. See Ruth Lapidoth, *Qui a Droit au Statut de Prisonnier de Guerre?*, 82 REV. GNR'L DE DROIT INT'L PUBLIC 170, 204 (1978).
73. Guy Roberts, *The New Rules for Waging War: The Case against Ratification of Additional Protocol I*, 26 VA. J. INT'L L. 109, 129 (1985–1986).
74. Abraham Sofaer, *The Rationale for the United States Decision*, 82 AM. J. INT'L L. 784, 786 (1988).
75. See W.J. Ford, *Members of Resistance Movements*, 24 NETH INT'L L. REV. 92, 104 (1977).
76. See INTERNATIONAL AND OPERATIONAL LAW DEP'T, THE JUDGE ADVOCATE GENERAL'S SCHOOL, U.S. ARMY, JA-422, OPERATIONAL LAW HANDBOOK, 11 (2003).

The War in Afghanistan

The war in Afghanistan, waged by the United States and several allied countries against the Taliban regime and the al Qaeda terrorist network—following the armed attacks of 11 September 2001—raises multiple issues germane to the status of lawful/unlawful combatancy:

1. The first problem relates to the standing of Taliban fighters. On the one hand, the Taliban regime—on the eve of the war—was in de facto control of as much as 90% of the territory of Afghanistan. On the other hand, the regime was unrecognized by the overwhelming majority of the international community. This lack of recognition does not by itself alter the legal position of combatants under customary international law. According to Article 4(A)(3) of Geneva Convention (III), members of regular armed forces professing allegiance to a government unrecognized by the Detaining Power (the paradigmatic case being that of the "Free France" forces of General De Gaulle in World War II, unrecognized by Nazi Germany[77]) are entitled to prisoners of war status. Yet, inasmuch as the underlying idea is the equivalence of armed forces of recognized and unrecognized governments, the latter—no less than the former—are bound by the seven cumulative conditions of lawful combatancy. The proper question, therefore, is not whether the Taliban regime was recognized, but whether the Taliban forces actually observed all these conditions.

In light of close scrutiny of the war in Afghanistan by the world media—and, in particular, the live coverage by television of literally thousands of Taliban troops before and after their surrender—it is undeniable that, whereas Taliban forces were carrying their arms openly (condition (iii)) and possibly meeting other conditions of lawful combatancy, they did not wear uniforms nor did they display any other fixed distinctive emblem (condition (ii)). Since the conditions are cumulative, members of the Taliban forces failed to qualify as prisoners of war under the customary international law criteria. These criteria admit of no exception, not even in the unusual circumstances of Afghanistan as run by the Taliban regime. To say that "[t]he Taliban do not wear uniforms in the traditional western sense"[78] is quite misleading, for the Taliban forces did not wear any uniform in any sense at all, Western or Eastern (nor even any special headgear that would single them out

---

77. See DE PREUX, *supra* note 38, at 62.
78. Robert Cryer, *The Fine Art of Friendship: Jus in Bello in Afghanistan*, 7 J. CONF. & SEC L. 37, 70 (2002).

from civilians). All armed forces—including those belonging to the Taliban regime—are required to wear uniforms or use some other fixed distinctive emblem. If they do not, they cannot claim prisoners of war status.

The legal position seems singularly clear to the present writer. But since some observers appear to entertain doubt in the matter (perhaps because the case of governmental forces not wearing any uniform is so extraordinary), the issue could be put to judicial test. Article 5 (Second Paragraph) of Geneva Convention (III) enunciates:

> Should any doubt arise as to whether persons, having committed a belligerent act and having fallen into the hands of the enemy, belong to any of the categories enumerated in Article 4, such persons shall enjoy the protection of the present Convention until such time as their status has been determined by a competent tribunal.[79]

Ex abundante cautela, the United States might be well advised to have the status of Taliban forces determined by a competent tribunal. A competent tribunal for this purpose can be a military commission.[80]

2. The legal position of al Qaeda fighters must not be confused with that of Taliban forces. Al Qaeda fighters constitute irregular forces. They easily satisfy the requirement of belonging to a Party to the conflict (condition (vi)): in reality, in the relations between al Qaeda and the Taliban regime there were times when it appeared that "the tail was wagging the dog," in other words, that the party to the conflict (Afghanistan) belonged to al Qaeda rather than the reverse. Incontrovertibly, al Qaeda is a well-organized group (condition (v)), with subordination to command structure (condition (i)), and in the hostilities in Afghanistan its members carried their arms openly (condition (iii)). However, apart from the fact that al Qaeda (like the Taliban regime) has declined to use a uniform or possess a fixed distinctive emblem (condition (ii)), the group has displayed utter disdain towards the *jus in bello* in brazen disregard of condition (iv).[81] Al Qaeda's contempt for this paramount prerequisite qualification of lawful combatancy was flaunted in the execution of the original armed attack of 9/11. Not only did the al Qaeda terrorists, wearing civilian clothes, hijack US civilian passenger planes. The most striking aspects

---

79. Geneva Convention III, art. 5, in LAWS OF ARMED CONFLICT, *supra* note 4, at 432.
80. *See* Kenneth Anderson, *What to Do with Bin Laden and Al Qaeda Terrorists? A Qualified Defense of Military Commissions and United States Policy on Detainees at Guantanamo Bay Naval Base*, 25 HARV. J.L. & PUB. POL'Y 591, 619–620 (2002).
81. *See* Christopher Greenwood, *International Law and the 'War against Terrorism,'* 78 INT'L AFF'S 301, 316 (2002).

of the shocking events of 9/11 are that (i) the hijacked planes (with their explosive fuel load) were used as weapons, in total oblivion to the fate of the civilian passengers on board; and (ii) the primary objective targeted (the World Trade Center in New York City) was manifestly a civilian object rather than a military objective.[82] The net result was a carnage in which some 3,000 innocent civilians lost their lives. No group conducting attacks in such an egregious fashion can claim prisoner of war status for its fighters . Whatever the lingering doubt which may exist with respect to the entitlement of Taliban forces to prisoners of war status, there is—and there can be—none as regards al Qaeda terrorists.

3. The al Qaeda involvement raises another issue. Whereas the Taliban forces were composed of Afghan (and some Pakistani) nationals, al Qaeda is an assemblage of Moslem fanatics from all parts of the world. Most of them are apparently Arabs, but some have come from Western countries, and there were at least two cases of renegade American nationals. Without delving into the question of how the United States should have handled the situation from the standpoint of its domestic—constitutional and criminal—legal system, the salient point is that, under the jus in bello, irrespective of all other considerations, nobody owing allegiance to the Detaining Power can expect to be treated as a prisoner of war (condition (vii)).

4. The constraints of the conditions of lawful combatancy must not, however, be seen as binding on only one party to the conflict in Afghanistan. As the hostilities progressed, it became all too evident (again, thanks to the ubiquitous TV cameras) that some US combatants—CIA agents in the field, and conceivably others—were not wearing uniforms while in combat. It must be underscored that observance by even 99% of the armed forces of a party to a conflict of the seven conditions of lawful combatancy—including the condition relating to having a fixed distinctive emblem, such as a uniform (condition (ii))—does not absolve the remaining 1% from the unshakable obligation to conduct themselves pursuant to the same conditions. Consequently, had any US combatants in civilian clothing been captured by the enemy, they would not be any more entitled to prisoner of war status than Taliban and al Qaeda fighters in a similar situation.

5. Perhaps "the primary focus of debate and controversy" in this field has been the detention of al Qaeda terrorists transferred by the United States

---

82. On the principle of military objectives, see Yoram Dinstein, *Legitimate Military Objectives Under the Current Jus in Bello*, LEGAL AND ETHICAL LESSONS OF NATO'S KOSOVO CAMPAIGN, (Andru Wall ed., 2003) (Vol 79, US Naval War College International Law Studies).

from Afghanistan to Guantanamo Bay (on the island of Cuba).[83] Since unlawful combatants are not entitled to prisoners of war status, most criticisms against conditions of detention in Guantanamo are beside the point. However, it must be understood that—assuming that the detainees are not charged with any crime in judicial proceedings—detention (as a purely administrative measure) cannot go on beyond the termination of hostilities: hostilities in Afghanistan as regards Taliban personnel; hostilities in which al Qaeda is involved in the case of its incarcerated fighters.

Conclusion

Unlawful combatancy is a matter of great practical significance in present-day international law. Unlawful combatants may be tried for violations of ordinary domestic laws and they may also be detained without trial (as long as the hostilities by the force to whom they belong go on). The seven cumulative conditions of lawful combatancy are no doubt stringent. But as the Afghanistan case amply demonstrates, the need for maintaining the distinction between lawful and unlawful combatants is as imperative as ever. Otherwise, compliance with the basic rule of distinction between civilians and combatants would be in jeopardy.

---

83. Anderson, *supra* note 80, at 621.

VIII

The Laws of War in the War on Terror[1]

Adam Roberts[2]

Introduction

The laws of war—the parts of international law explicitly applicable in armed conflict—have a major bearing on the "war on terror" proclaimed and initiated by the United States following the attacks of 11 September 2001. They address a range of critical issues that perennially arise in campaigns against terrorist movements, including discrimination in targeting, protection of civilians, and status and treatment of prisoners. However, the application of the laws of war in counter-terrorist operations has always been particularly problematical. Because of the character of such operations, different in

---

1. Copyright © Adam Roberts, 2002, 2003. This is a revised version of *Counter-terrorism, Armed Force and the Laws of War*, 44 SURVIVAL 1 (Spring 2002), 7–32. It incorporates information available up to 15 December 2002. I am grateful for help received from a large number of people who read drafts, including particularly Dr. Dana Allin, Dr. Kenneth Anderson, Dr. Mary-Jane Fox, Colonel Charles Garraway, Richard Guelff, Commander Steven Haines, and Professor Mike Schmitt; participants at the Carr Centre conference on "Humanitarian Issues in Military Targeting," Washington DC, 7–8 March 2002; and participants at the US Naval War College conference on "International Law & the War on Terrorism," Newport, RI, 26–28 June 2002. Versions of this paper have also appeared on the website of the Social Science Research Council, New York, *at* http://www.ssrc.org.
2. Sir Adam Roberts is Montague Burton Professor of International Relations at Oxford University and Fellow of Balliol College. He is co-editor, with Richard Guelff (District of Columbia Bar), of DOCUMENTS ON THE LAWS OF WAR (Oxford and New York: Oxford University Press, 2000).

important respects from what was originally envisaged in the treaties embodying the laws of war, a key issue in any analysis is not just whether or how the law is applied by the belligerents, but also its relevance to the particular circumstances of the operations. It is not just the conduct of the parties that merits examination, but also the adequacy of the law itself. Thus there is a need to look at the actual events of wars involving a terrorist adversary, and at the many ways in which, rightly or wrongly, the law is considered to have a bearing on them.

The present survey critically examines not only certain statements and actions of the US administration, but also those of the International Committee of the Red Cross (ICRC) and certain other bodies concerned with humanitarian and human rights issues. While touching on many ways in which the laws of war impinge on policy, the main focus is on the following four core questions.

1. Are the laws of war, according to their specific terms, applicable to counter-terrorist military operations?

2. In the event that counter-terrorist military operations involve situations different from those envisaged in international agreements on the laws of war, should the attempt still be made to apply that body of law to such situations?

3. Are captured personnel who are suspected of involvement in terrorist organizations entitled to prisoner-of-war (POW) status? If they are not considered to be POWs, does the law recognize a different status, and what international standards apply to their treatment?

4. Is there a case for a revision of the laws of war to take into account the special circumstances of contemporary counter-terrorist operations?

The answers to these questions may vary in different circumstances. The US-led "war on terror" involves action in many countries, with different legal and factual contexts. By no means does all action against terrorism, even if part of the "war on terror," involve military action in any form, let alone armed conflict of the kind in which the laws of war are formally applicable. The war's most prominent military manifestation to date, and the focus of this survey, is the coalition military action in Afghanistan that commenced on 7 October 2001 and still continues. While certain phases and aspects of Operation ENDURING FREEDOM involved an international armed conflict, unquestionably bringing the laws of war into play, other phases and aspects are more debatable with respect to the application of this body of law.

The laws of war are not the only body of law potentially relevant to the consideration of terrorist and counter-terrorist actions. For example, in many cases terrorists acts would indeed be violations of the laws of war if they were conducted in the course of an international or an internal armed conflict. However, because they frequently occur in what is widely viewed as peacetime, the illegality of such acts has to be established first and foremost by reference to the national law of states; international treaties on terrorism and related matters;[3] and other relevant parts of international law (including parts of the laws of war) that apply in peacetime as well as wartime, for example the rules relating to genocide, crimes against humanity and certain rules relating to human rights. All of these legal categories are relevant to consideration of the attacks of 11 September. For example, the attacks constitute murder under the domestic law of states, and at the same time can be regarded as "crimes against humanity," a category which encompasses widespread or systematic murder committed against any civilian population.[4]

---

3. For texts of treaties and other international documents on terrorism, and useful discussion thereof, see TERRORISM AND INTERNATIONAL LAW (Rosalyn Higgins and Maurice Flory eds., 1997). For more recent treaties and UN resolutions see the information on terrorism on the UN website, at http://www.un.org.

4. Crimes against humanity, defined in the Charter and Judgment of the International Military Tribunal at Nuremburg in 1945–46, are more fully defined in Article 7 of the 1998 Rome Statute of the International Criminal Court, which entered into force on 1 July 2002. These crimes include any of the following acts when committed as part of a widespread or systematic attack directed against any civilian population, with knowledge of the attack:

(a) Murder;

(b) Extermination;

(c) Enslavement;

(d) Deportation or forcible transfer of population;

(e) Imprisonment or other severe deprivation of physical liberty in violation of fundamental rules of international law;

(f) Torture;

(g) Rape, sexual slavery, enforced prostitution, forced pregnancy, enforced sterilization, or any other form of sexual violence of comparable gravity;

(h) Persecution against any identifiable group or collectivity on political, racial, national, ethnic, cultural, religious, gender . . . or other grounds that are universally recognized as impermissible under international law, in connection with any act referred to in this paragraph or any crime within the jurisdiction of the Court;

(i) Enforced disappearance of persons;

(j) The crime of apartheid.

U.N. Diplomatic Conference of Plenipotentiaries on the Establishment of an International Criminal Court, Rome Statute of the International Criminal Court, U.N. Doc. No. A/CONF.183/9 (1998) [hereinafter Rome Statute]. The Rome Statute does not apply retroactively and the United States

In an effort to answer the questions posed in this introduction, this survey is divided into six parts.

	page
1. The Laws of War	178
2. Counter-Terrorist Military Operations	184
3. War in Afghanistan	191
4. Prisoners	208
5. Further Development of International Law	225
6. Conclusions	227

The Laws of War

The laws of war (also referred to as "jus in bello" and "international humanitarian law applicable in armed conflict") are embodied and interpreted in a variety of sources: treaties, customary law, judicial decisions, writings of legal specialists, military manuals and resolutions of international organizations. Although some of the law is immensely detailed, its basic principles are simple: the wounded and sick, POWs and civilians are to be protected; military targets must be attacked in such a manner as to keep civilian casualties and damage to a minimum; humanitarian and peacekeeping personnel must be respected; neutral or non-belligerent states have certain rights and duties; and the use of certain weapons (including chemical weapons) is prohibited, as also are certain other means and methods of warfare. The four 1949 Geneva Conventions—the treaties that form the keystone of the modern laws of war—are concerned largely with the protection of victims of war who have fallen into the hands of an adversary, as distinct from the conduct of military operations.[5]

---

has stated its intent to not become a party to this treaty. For a detailed treatment of US opposition to the ICC, see John Bolton, *The Risks and Weaknesses of the International Criminal Court from America's Perspective*, 41 VA. J. INT'L L. 186 (2000); Michael Newton, *Comparative Complementarity: Domestic Jurisdiction Consistent with Rome Statute of the International Criminal Court*, 167 MIL. L. REV. 20 (2001).

5. See Convention for the Amelioration of the Condition of the Wounded and Sick in Armed Forces in the Field, Aug. 12, 1949, Art. 2, 6 U.S.T. 3114, T.I.A.S. No. 3362, 75 U.N.T.S. 31; Convention for the Amelioration of the Condition of the Wounded, Sick, and Shipwrecked Members of Armed Forces at Sea, Aug. 12, 1949, 6. U.S.T. 3217, T.I.A.S. No. 3363, 75 U.N.T.S. 85; Convention Relative to the Treatment of Prisoners of War, Aug. 12, 1949, 6 U.S.T. 3316, T.I.A.S. No. 3364, 75 U.N.T.S. 135 [hereinafter GC III]; Convention Relative to the Protection of Civilian Persons in Time of War, Aug. 12, 1949, 6 U.S.T. 3516, T.I.A.S. No. 3365, 75 U.N.T.S. 287 [hereinafter GC IV]. These four conventions are all *reprinted in* DOCUMENTS ON THE LAWS OF WAR (Adam Roberts and Richard Guelff eds., 3rd ed., 2000) [hereinafter DOCUMENTS ON THE LAWS OF WAR]; and in THE LAWS OF ARMED CONFLICTS: A COLLECTION OF CONVENTIONS, RESOLUTIONS AND OTHER DOCUMENTS (Dietrich Schindler and Jiri Toman eds., 3rd ed. 1988). Treaty texts are also available at the International Committee of the Red Cross website, *at* http://www.icrc.org/eng (Jan. 3, 2003).

Treaties on the laws of war are the product of negotiations between states, and reflect their experiences and interests, including those of their armed forces. For centuries these rules, albeit frequently the subject of controversy, have had an important function in the policies and practices of states engaged in military operations. With respect to international coalitions involved in combat, given the needs of the members to harmonize their actions on a range of practical issues, these rules have long had particular significance. Even in situations in which their formal applicability may be questionable, they have sometimes been accepted as relevant guidelines.

Scope of application

The laws of war have a scope of application that is not limited to wars between recognized states. They apply in a wide, but not infinitely wide, variety of situations. In the 1949 Geneva Conventions, Common Article 1 specifies that the parties "undertake to respect and to ensure respect for the present Convention in all circumstances."[6] Common Article 2, which deals directly with scope of application, specifies that the Conventions "apply to all cases of declared war or of any other armed conflict which may arise between two or more of the High Contracting Parties, even if the state of war is not recognized by one of them," indicating that the existence or non-existence of a declaration of war, or a formal state of war, is not necessary for the application of the Conventions. Common Article 3 contains certain minimum provisions to be applied in the case of armed conflict not of an international character, concentrating particularly on treatment of persons taking no active part in hostilities.[7] Certain other

---

6. For an authoritative account of the origins and meanings of Common Article 1, see Frits Kalshoven, *The Undertaking to Respect and Ensure Respect in All Circumstances: From Tiny Seed to Ripening Fruit*, 2 Y.B. INT'L HUM. L. 1999, at 3-61 (2000).

7. Common Article 3 of the Geneva Conventions provides in part that:

> In the case of armed conflict not of an international character occurring in the territory of one of the High Contracting Parties, each Party to the conflict shall be bound to apply, as a minimum, the following provisions:
>
> (1) Persons taking no active part in the hostilities, including members of armed forces who have laid down their arms and those placed hors de combat by sickness, wounds, detention, or any other cause, shall in all circumstances be treated humanely, without any adverse distinction founded on race, colour, religion or faith, sex, birth or wealth, or any other similar criteria.
>
> To this end, the following acts are and shall remain prohibited at any time and in any place whatsoever with respect to the above-mentioned persons:

agreements, especially those concluded since the early 1990s, apply in non-international as well as international armed conflicts.

The distinction that has traditionally been drawn in the laws of war between international and non-international armed conflict has come under challenge in the post-1945 era. This is not only because many wars have involved elements of both civil and international war, but also because of the nature of counter-terrorist operations. These have aspects that are similar to a civil war, particularly as they typically involve governmental forces combating non-governmental groups; but they may not meet all the criteria (such as the holding of territory by insurgents) required for the application of parts of the law governing non-international armed conflict; and they can also have aspects that are more closely akin to international war, especially if the terrorists operate in armed units outside their own countries.

Application of the law is not necessarily dependent on formal designation of a conflict as international or non-international. In some instances, as indicated below, the UN Security Council or particular belligerents have deemed the rules governing international armed conflict to be applicable even to a largely internal situation. The US armed forces have indicated their intention to observe the rules governing international armed conflicts, even in situations that may differ in certain respects from the classical model of an interstate war. The Standing Rules of Engagement issued by the US Joint Chiefs of Staff spell this out:

> U.S. forces will comply with the Law of War during military operations involving armed conflict, no matter how the conflict may be characterized under international law, and will comply with its principles and spirit during all other operations.[8]

(a) violence to life and person, in particular murder of all kinds, mutilation, cruel treatment and torture;

(b) taking of hostages;

(c) outrages upon personal dignity, in particular humiliating and degrading treatment;

(d) the passing of sentences and the carrying out of executions without previous judgment pronounced by a regularly constituted court, affording all the judicial guarantees which are recognized as indispensable by civilized peoples....

See GC III, *supra* note 5, art. 3; DOCUMENTS ON THE LAWS OF WAR, *supra* note 5, at 245.

8. CHAIRMAN JOINT CHIEFS OF STAFF INSTR 3121.01A STANDING RULES OF ENGAGEMENT FOR U.S. FORCES, ENCLOSURE (A) A-9 [hereinafter CJCS INSTR 3121.01A]. A similar but not identical statement had appeared in the Standing ROE of 1 October 1994, which this document replaces. *See* CJCS INSTR, 3121.01 STANDING RULES OF ENGAGEMENT FOR U.S. FORCES (1 OCT. 1994). A number of other US military-doctrinal statements are equally definite that US forces will always apply the law of armed conflict.

In certain inter-state conflicts, Western armed forces, engaging with adversaries showing at best limited respect for ethical and legal restraints, have managed to observe basic rules of the laws of war. This was the case in the 1991 Gulf War, in which Iraq mistreated prisoners, despoiled the environment and had to be warned in brutally clear terms not to engage in chemical or biological attacks and terrorist operations. The US-led Gulf coalition sought to observe the law not because of any guarantee of reciprocity, but because such conduct was important to the ethos of the armed forces; and because it contributed to the maintenance of internal discipline, and of domestic and international support. Similar conclusions could be drawn from the 1999 Kosovo War. In short, practice has provided some evidence in support of the legal position that reciprocity with one adversary in one particular conflict is far from being a necessary condition for observing the laws of war.

Whether all aspects of counter-terrorist operations fall within the scope of application of the laws of war will be explored further in Part 2 below.

Jus ad bellum and jus in bello

In any armed conflict, including one against terrorism, it is important to distinguish between the legality of resorting to force and the legality of the way in which such force is used. In strict legal terms, the law relating to the right to resort to the use of force (jus ad bellum) and the law governing the actual use of force in war (jus in bello) are separate. The jus in bello applies to the conduct of belligerents in international armed conflict irrespective of their right to resort to the use of force under the jus ad bellum. As regards the jus ad bellum issues raised after 11 September, my own views are in favor of the legality, and indeed overall moral justifiability, of the military action in Afghanistan. However, this survey's focus is on the jus in bello aspects of the US-led military operations.

Despite the lack of a formal connection between jus ad bellum and jus in bello, there are certain ways in which they interact in practice, especially in a war against terrorists. By observing jus in bello, a state or a coalition of states may contribute to perceptions of the justice of a cause in three related ways. First, in all military operations, whether or not against terrorists, the perception that a state or a coalition of states is observing recognized international standards may contribute to public support domestically and internationally. Second, if the coalition were to violate jus in bello in a major way, for example by the commission of atrocities, that would be likely to advance the cause of the adversary forces, arguably providing them a justification for their resort to force. Third, in counter-terrorist campaigns in particular, a basis for engaging in military operations is often a perception that there is a definite moral distinction between the types of actions engaged in by terrorists and those engaged in by their adversaries. Observance of jus in bello can form a part of that moral distinction.

However, the jus ad bellum rationale that armed hostilities have been initiated in response to major terrorist acts can raise issues relating to the application of certain jus in bello principles. Two such issues are explored here: first, whether there is scope for neutrality in relation to an armed conflict in which one side is fighting in the name of opposing terrorism; second, whether those responsible for terrorist campaigns can be viewed as exclusively responsible for all the death and destruction of an ensuing war.

The right of states to be neutral in an armed conflict is a long-standing principle of the laws of war. Events of the past century, especially the obligations imposed by membership of international organizations, have exposed problems in the traditional idea of strictly impartial neutrality and have led to its modification and even erosion. In many conflicts there were states which, even while not belligerents, pursued policies favoring one side, for example joining in sanctions against a state perceived to be an aggressor. The UN Charter, by providing for the Security Council to require all states to take certain actions against offending states, added to the erosion of traditional concepts of neutrality, at least in those cases in which the Security Council has been able to agree on a common course of action (e.g., sanctions). The importance of new forms of non-belligerence, distinct from traditional neutrality, may help to explain the emergence of terms such as "neutral or non-belligerent powers" in post-1945 treaties on the laws of war.[9] In many recent episodes, including the 1991 Gulf War and the 1999 Kosovo War, when the use of armed force by a coalition has been combined with the application of general UN sanctions against the adversary state, the scope for traditional (i.e., impartial) neutrality has indeed been limited, but certain forms of non-belligerence have survived. As outlined below in Part 3 on War in Afghanistan, the "war on terror" which began in 2001 with Operation ENDURING FREEDOM would confirm that in certain armed conflicts, particularly when the UN Security Council has given approval to one party, the scope for neutrality may be limited or non-existent.

---

9. See GC III, *supra* note 5, at articles 4(B)(2) and 122. *See also* the references to "neutral and other States not Parties to the conflict" in 1977 Geneva Protocol I Additional to the Geneva Conventions of 12 August 1949 and Relating to the Protection of Victims of International Armed Conflicts, Articles 9, 19, 31 *opened for signature* Dec. 12, 1977, 1125 U.N.T.S. 1 [hereinafter GP I], *reprinted in* DOCUMENTS ON THE LAWS OF WAR at 419, *supra* note 5.

Can those who initiated terrorist campaigns be held responsible for all the death and destruction of an ensuing war? When fighting terrorism is the basis for resorting to war under the jus ad bellum, there is sometimes a tendency for the general indignation caused by terrorist attacks to affect adversely the implementation of jus in bello. It is sometimes argued that because the terrorists started the war, they are responsible for all the subsequent horrors. In early December 2001, discussing civilian casualties, US Secretary of Defense Donald Rumsfeld said: "We did not start this war. So understand, responsibility for every single casualty in this war, whether they're innocent Afghans or innocent Americans, rests at the feet of the al Qaeda and the Taliban."[10] Such a view, if it implies that the peculiar circumstances involved in the jus ad bellum might override certain considerations of jus in bello in the war that follows, has no basis in the law.

Proportionality

"Proportionality" is a long-established principle that sets out criteria for limiting the use of force. One of its meanings relates to the proportionality of a military action compared to a grievance, and thus constitutes a further link between jus in bello and jus ad bellum. It involves a complex balance of considerations, and it would be incorrect to interpret this principle to imply a right of tit-for-tat retaliation. For example, it would be legally unjustified for a military response to a terrorist act to have the objective of killing the same number of people, and there was no suggestion or indication that this was a coalition objective in Afghanistan. Nor does this principle prevent a response from taking into account a range of issues not limited to the size of the initial attack.[11]

The other main meaning of proportionality relates to the actual conduct of ongoing hostilities. As a US Army manual succinctly interprets it, "the loss of life and damage to property incidental to attacks must not be excessive in relation to the concrete and direct military advantage expected to be gained."[12] This meaning of proportionality (which is not directly linked to jus ad bellum) is often difficult to apply in armed conflict, especially in counter-terrorist

---

10. Secretary of Defense Donald Rumsfeld, News Conference at the Pentagon (Dec. 4, 2001), *available at* http://www.defenselink.mil/news/Dec2001/t12042001_t1204sd.html (Nov. 6, 2002).
11. In an assessment of the events of 2001, Christopher Greenwood has argued that "proportionality in self-defence looks forward. The test is whether the force used is proportionate to the threat it is designed to meet, not to the events of the past." *See* Christopher Greenwood, *International Law and the "War Against Terrorism,"* 78 INT'L AFF'S 2, 313–314 (April 2002).
12. U.S. DEPT OF ARMY, FIELD MANUAL 27-10, THE LAW OF LAND WARFARE, para. 41 (July 1956) [hereinafter FM 27-10].

operations. It may, but does not necessarily, limit the use of force to the same level or amount of force as that employed by an adversary. It exists alongside the principle of military necessity, which is defined in the US Army manual as one that "justifies those measures not forbidden by international law which are indispensable for securing the complete submission of the enemy as soon as possible."[13] The principle of proportionality is therefore in tension, but not necessarily in conflict, with the current US military doctrine, which favors the overwhelming use of force in order to achieve decisive victory quickly and at minimum cost in terms of US casualties.[14]

Counter-Terrorist Military Operations

Counter-terrorism has been defined as "offensive military operations designed to prevent, deter and respond to terrorism."[15] Such operations, including those resulting from the events of 11 September, may involve inter-state armed conflict as principally envisaged in the laws of war: in such cases that body of law applies straightforwardly. However, such operations can also involve conflict with other characteristics—a fact that helps to explain why the laws of war have often proved difficult to apply in them. Six factors, all relating to the nature of the opposition, point to potential problems in the application of the laws of war in counter-terrorist operations:

- Neither all terrorist activities, nor all counter-terrorist military operations, even when they have some international dimension, necessarily constitute armed conflict between states. Terrorist movements themselves generally have a non-state character. Therefore, military operations between a state and such a movement, even if they involve the state's armed forces acting

---

13. *Id.* at para. 3. A subsequent official US exposition of the principle states: "Only that degree and kind of force, not otherwise prohibited by the law of armed conflict, required for the partial or complete submission of the enemy with a minimum expenditure of time, life and physical resources may be applied." ANNOTATED SUPPLEMENT TO THE COMMANDER'S HANDBOOK ON THE LAW OF NAVAL OPERATIONS, para. 5-2 (A. Thomas and J. Duncan eds., 1999) (Vol. 73, US Naval War College International Law Studies).
14. For a brief discussion of United States and NATO strategic doctrine, see pages 191-208 infra.
15. By contrast, "antiterrorism" has been defined as "defensive measures to reduce the vulnerability of individuals and property to terrorist attacks." *See* INTERNATIONAL AND OPERATIONAL LAW DEP'T, THE JUDGE ADVOCATE GENERAL'S SCHOOL, U.S. ARMY, JA-422, OPERATIONAL LAW HANDBOOK (2003), at 312-3 [hereinafter OPLAW HANDBOOK]. This annual publication is available at https://www.jagcnet.army.mil/JAGCNETInternet/Homepages/AC/CLAMO-Public.nsf (Nov. 14, 2002).

outside its own territory, are not necessarily such as to bring them within the scope of application of the full range of provisions regarding international armed conflict in the 1949 Geneva Conventions and the 1977 Geneva Protocol I.[16]

- Counter-terrorist operations may assume the form of actions by a government against forces operating within its own territory; or, more rarely, may be actions by opposition forces against a government perceived to be committing or supporting terrorist acts. In both these cases, the conflict may have more the character of non-international armed conflict (that is, civil war) as distinct from international war. Fewer laws-of-war rules have been formally applicable to civil as distinct from international war, although the situation is now changing in some respects.

- In many cases, the attributes and actions of a terrorist movement may not come within the field of application even of the modest body of rules relating to non-international armed conflict. Common Article 3 of the 1949 Geneva Conventions is the core of these rules, but says little about the scope of application. The principal subsequent agreement on non-international armed conflict, the 1977 Geneva Protocol II, is based on the assumption that there is a conflict between a state's armed forces and organized armed groups which, under responsible command, exercise control over a part of its territory, and carry out sustained and concerted military operations. The protocol expressly does not apply to situations of internal disturbance and tension, such as riots, and isolated and sporadic acts of violence.[17]

- Since terrorist forces often have little regard for internationally agreed rules of restraint, the resolve of the counter-terrorist forces to observe them may also be weakened, given the low expectation of reciprocity and the tendency of some part of the public under attack to overlook any breaches by their own forces.

- A basic principle of the laws of war is that attacks should be directed against the adversary's military forces, rather than against civilians. This principle, violated in terrorist attacks specifically directed against civilians, can

---

16. In ratifying the 1977 Geneva Protocol I in 1998, the United Kingdom made a statement that the term "armed conflict" denotes "a situation which is not constituted by the commission of ordinary crimes including acts of terrorism whether concerted or in isolation." *See* GP I, *supra* note 9, *reprinted in* DOCUMENTS ON THE LAWS OF WAR, at 510, *supra* note 5.

17. 1977 Geneva Protocol II Additional to the Geneva Conventions of 12 August 1949, and Relating to the Protection of Victims of Non-International Armed Conflicts, art. 1, *reprinted in* DOCUMENTS ON THE LAWS OF WAR, at 481, *supra* note 5 [hereinafter GP II].

be difficult to apply in counter-terrorist operations, because the terrorist movement may not be composed of defined military forces that are clearly distinguished from civilians.

- Some captured personnel who are members of a terrorist organization may not meet the criteria for POW status as set out in 1949 Geneva Convention III. (The question of prisoners is discussed in greater detail below.)

These six factors reflect the same underlying difficulty governments have in applying the laws of war to civil wars, namely, that the opponent tends to be viewed as criminals, without the right to engage in combat operations. This factor above all explains why, despite the progress of recent decades, many governments are doubtful about, or opposed to, applying the full range of rules applicable in international armed conflict to operations against rebels and terrorists.

For at least 25 years, the United States has expressed a concern, shared to some degree by certain other states, regarding the whole principle of thinking about terrorists and other irregular forces in a laws-of-war framework. To refer to such a framework, which recognizes rights and duties, might seem to imply a degree of moral acceptance of the right of any particular group to resort to acts of violence, at least against military targets.[18] Successive US administrations have objected to certain revisions to the laws of war on the grounds that they might actually favor guerrilla fighters and terrorists, affording them a status that the United States believes they do not deserve. The strongest expression of this view was a letter of 29 January 1987 explaining why the administration was not recommending Senate approval of 1977 Geneva Protocol I. The letter mentioned that granting combatant status to certain irregular forces "would endanger civilians among whom terrorists and other irregulars attempt to conceal themselves." It indicated a concern that the provisions would endanger US soldiers, and stated in very general terms that "the Joint Chiefs of Staff have also concluded that a number of the provisions of the protocol are militarily unacceptable." United States repudiation of the protocol would be an important move against "the intense efforts of terrorist organizations and their supporters to promote the legitimacy of their aims and

---

18. For fuller discussion, and evidence that the concern about the hazards of coping with terrorism in a laws-of-war framework is not new, see ADAM ROBERTS, TERRORISM AND INTERNATIONAL ORDER, 14–15 (Lawrence Freedman et al. eds., 1986).

practices."[19] Whether all this was based on a fair interpretation of 1977 Geneva Protocol I is the subject of impassioned debate that is beyond the scope of this survey. The key point is the US concern—which has not changed fundamentally in the years since 1987—that the laws of war might be misused by some in order to give an unwarranted degree of recognition to guerrillas and terrorists.

Application of the law in previous operations

In many counter-terrorist campaigns since 1945 issues relating to the observance or non-observance of basic rules of law, including the laws of war, have perennially been of considerable significance. This has been the case both when a counter-terrorist campaign has been part of an international armed conflict, and when such a campaign has been a largely internal matter, conducted by a government within its own territory, in a situation which may not cross the threshold to be considered an armed conflict. In such circumstances the laws of war may be of limited formal application, but their underlying principles, as well as other legal and prudential limits, are important. Within functioning states, terrorist campaigns have often been defeated through slow and patient police work (sometimes with military assistance) rather than major military campaigns; for example, the actions against the Red Army Faction in Germany and the Red Brigades in Italy in the 1970s.

The British military and police operation against "Communist Terrorists" in Malaya after 1948 is an example (in a colonial context) of a long-drawn-out and patient counter-terrorist campaign that was eventually successful. One of the key military figures involved in that campaign, Sir Robert Thompson, distilling five basic principles of counter-insurgency from this and other cases, wrote of the crucial importance of operating within a properly functioning domestic legal framework:

> *Second principle.* The government must function in accordance with law. There is a very strong temptation in dealing both with terrorism and with guerrilla actions for government forces to act outside the law, the excuses being that the processes of law are too cumbersome, that the normal safeguards in the law for the individual are not designed for an insurgency and that a terrorist deserves to

---

19. Letter of Transmittal from President Ronald Reagan, 1977 Geneva Protocol I Additional to the Geneva Conventions of 12 August 1949 and Relating to the Protection of Victims of International Armed Conflict, S. Treaty Doc. No. 2, 100th Cong., 1st Sess., at III (1987), *reprinted in* 81 AM J. INT'L L. 910–912 (1988).

be treated as an outlaw anyway. Not only is this morally wrong, but, over a period, it will create more practical difficulties for a government than it solves.[20]

The United Kingdom's long engagement against terrorism in Northern Ireland, although in an essentially internal situation, provides one precedent for affording treatment based on certain international rules to prisoners whose status is contested. This was one of many conflicts in which those deemed to be "terrorists" were aware of the value, including propaganda value, of making claims to POW status. While denying that there was an armed conflict whether international or otherwise, and strongly resisting any granting of POW status to detainees and convicted prisoners, the United Kingdom did come to accept that international standards had to apply to their treatment. The minority report of a UK Commission of Inquiry in 1972 which led to this conclusion is an interesting example of asserting the wider relevance, even in an internal conflict, of certain international legal standards, including some from the main body of the four 1949 Geneva Conventions.[21] The UK government's acceptance of this approach was only a decision, not a complete solution to a matter that continued to be contentious.

Questions about the status and treatment of prisoners, some of whom were considered as terrorists, also arose during the US involvement in Vietnam. In 1967–8, the United States took a judiciously inclusive approach to the matter when it issued directives to classify Viet Cong main force and local force personnel, and certain Viet Cong irregulars, as POWs. This was despite the existence of doubts and ambiguities as to whether these forces met all the criteria in Article 4 of 1949 Geneva Convention III. Viet Cong irregulars were to be classified as POWs if captured while engaging in combat or a belligerent act under arms, "other than an act of terrorism, sabotage, or spying." There was provision for establishing tribunals, in accordance with Article 5 of the Geneva Convention, to

---

20. ROBERT THOMPSON, DEFEATING COMMUNIST INSURGENCY: EXPERIENCES FROM MALAYA AND VIETNAM, 52 (1966). From 1957 to 1961 the author was successively Deputy Secretary and Secretary for Defense in Malaya. As his and other accounts make clear, in the course of the Malayan Emergency there were certain derogations from human rights standards, including detentions and compulsory relocations of villages.
21. Report of the Committee of Privy Counsellors Appointed to Consider Authorized Procedures for the Interrogation of Persons Suspected of Terrorism, Cmnd. 4901, Her Majesty's Stationery Office, London, 1972, at 1–2 and 11–23.

determine, in doubtful or contested cases, whether individual detainees were entitled to POW status.[22]

One example of a counter-terrorist military campaign, the 1982–2000 Israeli presence in Lebanon, shows the importance of legal restraints in counter-terrorist operations, and the hazards that can attend a failure to observe them. This episode has certain similarities to the case of Afghanistan in 2001–2002, as well as some obvious differences. Israel's June 1982 invasion of Lebanon was explicitly in response to "constant terrorist provocations," including, since July 1981, "150 acts of terrorism instigated by the PLO, originating in Lebanon, against Israelis and Jews in Israel and elsewhere: in Athens, Vienna, Paris and London." Israel said that if Lebanon was unwilling or unable to prevent the harboring, training and financing of terrorists, it must face the risk of counter-measures.[23] The invasion led to the attacks on the inhabitants of Sabra and Shatila refugee camps outside Beirut in September 1982 by Israel's local co-belligerents, the Lebanese Phalangists. At the lowest estimates, several hundred Palestinians in the camps, including many women and children, were killed. This event aroused strong opposition internationally, and also in Israel. The Israeli authorities established a Commission of Inquiry, which concluded that, while the Phalangist forces were directly responsible for the slaughter, Israel bore indirect responsibility.[24] During the whole period of Israeli military involvement in Lebanon, the treatment of alleged terrorist detainees also caused controversy. Israel opposed granting them POW status on the grounds that as terrorists they were not entitled to it. The detainees were held in very poor conditions in notorious camps, including al-Khiam (run by the Israeli-created South Lebanese Army) and al-Ansar (run by the Israel

---

22. Two key directives issued by US Military Assistance Command, Vietnam, on the question of eligibility for POW status are (1) Annex A, "Criteria for Classification and Disposition of Detainees," part of Directive no. 381-46 of 27 December 1967; and (2) Directive no. 20-5 of 15 March 1968, "Inspections and Investigations: Prisoners of War – Determination of Eligibility," *reprinted in* 62 AM. J. INT'L L. 755, at 766-75 (1968).

23. *See* Yehuda Blum, Permanent Representative of Israel to the United Nations, Speech before the Security Council, U.N. SCOR, 36th Sess., Supp. 21, U.N. Doc. S/PV.2292 (1981). The Security Council unanimously demanded an end to all military activities and a withdrawal of Israeli forces from Lebanon in Resolutions 508 and 509 of 5 and 6 June 1982 respectively. *See* S. C. Res. 508, U.N. SCOR, 37th Sess., U.N. Doc. S/508/(1982); and S. C. Res. 509, U.N. SCOR, 37th Sess., U.N. Doc. S/509/(1982).

24. *See* Commission of Inquiry into the Events at the Refugee Camps in Beirut, Final Report at 53-54 (1983) [hereinafter Kahan Report], *reprinted in* 22 I.L.M. 3, at 473 (1983).

Defense Forces).[25] The Israeli military presence in Lebanon received extensive criticism internationally and in Israel, and cost many lives among the Israel Defense Forces, their adversaries and the civilian population. It ended with a unilateral Israeli withdrawal in May 2000.

Past evidence suggests that while the application of the law may be particularly difficult in counter-terrorist operations, it cannot be neglected. Some failures to observe legal restraints in past campaigns have been instructive. In military operations with the purpose of stopping terrorist activities, there has been a tendency for counter-terrorist forces to violate basic legal restraints. There have been many instances in which prisoners were subjected to mistreatment or torture. In some cases, excesses by the government or by intervening forces supporting the government may have had the unintended effect of assisting a terrorist campaign. Applying pressure on a government or army to change its approach to counter-terrorism, to bring it more into line with the laws of war and human-rights law, can be a difficult task.

In a counter-terrorist war, as in other wars, there can be strong prudential considerations that militate in favor of observing legal standards, which are increasingly seen as consisting of not only domestic legal standards, but also international ones, including those embodied in the laws of war. These considerations include securing public and international support; ensuring that terrorists are not given the propaganda gift of atrocities or maltreatment by their adversaries; and maintaining discipline and high professional standards in the counter-terrorist forces; and assisting reconciliation and future peace. Such considerations may carry great weight even in conflicts, or particular episodes within them, which differ from what is envisaged in the formal provisions regarding scope of application of relevant treaties. These considerations in favor of observing the law may be important irrespective of whether there is reciprocity in such observance by all the parties to a particular war. However, it is not realistic to expect that the result of the application of such rules will be a sanitized form of war in which civilian suffering and death is eliminated.

---

25. In a case concerning detainees in Ansar Prison on which the Israeli Supreme Court issued a judgment on 11 May 1983, the Israeli authorities asserted that the prisoners were "hostile foreigners detained because they belong to the forces of terrorist organizations, or because of their connections or closeness to terrorist organizations." Israel, while refusing them POW status, claimed to observe "humanitarian guidelines" of the 1949 Geneva Convention IV on civilians. For details of the case see 13 ISR. Y.B. HUM. RTS. 360–64 (1983).

War in Afghanistan

In wars in Afghanistan over the centuries, conduct has differed markedly from that permitted by the written laws of war. These wars always had a civil war dimension, traditionally subject to fewer rules in the laws of war; and guerrilla warfare, already endemic in Afghanistan in the nineteenth century, notoriously blurs the traditional distinction between soldier and civilian that is at the heart of the laws of war. Some local customs, for example regarding the killing of prisoners and looting, are directly contrary to long-established principles of the law. Other customs are different from what is envisaged by the law, but are not necessarily a violation of it: for example, the practice of soldiers from the defeated side willingly joining their adversary rather than being taken prisoner. In some cases, conduct has been consistent with international norms: for example, the ICRC had access to some prisoners during the Soviet intervention. Overall, however, compliance with the laws of war has been limited.

From the start, the implementation of the laws of war posed a problem for Operation ENDURING FREEDOM.[26] Difficult practical issues facing the coalition included: the problem of conducting operations discriminately against elusive enemies; the possibility that adversary forces might mistreat or execute coalition prisoners; the possibility that some enemy personnel facing capture might be reluctant to surrender their weapons, and that they might not meet the criteria for POW status; the urgent need for humanitarian relief operations during ongoing war; and maintenance of order (and avoidance of looting and revenge killings) in liberated towns. These problems were exacerbated by the character of the coalition's local partner, the Northern Alliance.[27] The number of different forces involved, many of which were under the command

---

26. The name Operation ENDURING FREEDOM was announced by Donald Rumsfeld at a press conference on 25 September 2001. *See* Secretary of Defense Donald Rumsfeld News Conference at the Pentagon (Sep. 25, 2001), *available at* http://www.defenselink.mil/news/Sep2001/t09252001_t0925sd.html (Dec. 28, 2002). Operation ENDURING FREEDOM, he said, was not the "umbrella phrase" for the entire anti-terror campaign, but referred to a "broad, sustained multifaceted effort." It has been used to refer to the coalition military operations in and around Afghanistan that began on 7 October 2001. Operation ENDURING FREEDOM does not encompass the operations of the International Security Assistance Force in Afghanistan, mentioned below.
27. "Northern Alliance" is a colloquial term for the "United Islamic Front for the Salvation of Afghanistan." This organization was formed in 1996-7. *See Afghanistan and the United Nations* (Jan. 6, 2003), *available at* http://www.un.org/News/dh/latest/afghan/un-afghan-history.shtml (Jan. 6, 2003).

of local warlords, and the lack of clear structures of authority, decision-making and military discipline within them, militated against the implementation of international norms.

The active role of the media in this war ensured that many of these issues were heavily publicized. Reporters operated close to, and even in front of, the front lines, sending back reports and high-resolution pictures as events unfolded. Up to the end of January 2002, more reporters died while covering the war in Afghanistan than non-Afghan coalition military personnel.[28] As in other modern wars, the press played a critical role in repeatedly raising matters germane to the laws of war.

This part deals mainly with the war in Afghanistan after the beginning of major US military action there on 7 October 2001. It cannot explore all the issues relating to the laws of war that have cropped up in regard to Afghanistan. It considers the applicability of the laws of war to the various aspects of this armed conflict generally, glances at the limited scope for neutrality, and then surveys three specific issues that were raised in the war: bombing; gas; and humanitarian assistance and refugee matters. Prisoners are considered in Part 4.

Applicability of the laws of war to the armed conflict

An armed conflict in Afghanistan—principally between the Taliban and Northern Alliance forces—had been going on for many years before the events of 11 September 2001. The UN Security Council had called on both parties to comply with their obligations under international humanitarian law. Like a similar resolution on Bosnia six years earlier, a 1998 UN Security Council Resolution on Afghanistan reaffirmed:

> that all parties to the conflict are bound to comply with their obligations under international humanitarian law and in particular the Geneva Conventions of 12 August 1949 and that persons who commit or order the commission of grave breaches of the Conventions are individually responsible in respect of such breaches.[29]

---

28. Eight reporters died in the period October–December 2001, several of them due to banditry rather than military operations. Interview with Nik Gowing, BBC World Television Reporter (Jan. 26, 2002).
29. UN Security Council Resolution 1193 of 28 August 1998, passed unanimously. See S. C. Res. 1193, U.N. SCOR, 53d Sess., U.N. Doc. S/1193/(1998). Identical wording had been used in S. C. Res. 764 of 13 July 1992 on the war in Bosnia and Herzegovina. See S. C. Res. 764, U.N. SCOR, 47th Sess., U.N. Doc. S/764/(1992). This wording did not necessarily mean that the Security Council viewed these wars as international armed conflicts, but it did mean that international standards had to be observed in them. Nor did it indicate that the Council considered any prisoners taken in these wars to have the full status of prisoners of war; but it implied that they should receive humane treatment in accord with international standards.

The reference to grave breaches would appear to suggest that the Security Council viewed all the rules of the 1949 Geneva Conventions as applicable, and not just Common Article 3, which deals with civil war. Thus, three years before it became directly involved, the United States as well as other powers viewed the laws of war as applicable to the Afghan conflict.

Like the period of Soviet intervention of 1979–89, and indeed wars in many countries in the period since 1945, the armed conflict in Afghanistan from 7 October 2001 can perhaps be best characterized as "internationalized civil war." This is not a formal legal category, but an indication that the rules pertaining to both international and civil wars may be applicable in different aspects and phases of the conflict.[30]

Major aspects of the war in Afghanistan have been international in character. Following the attacks of 11 September 2001, the UN Security Council adopted Resolution 1368, recognizing the right of individual or collective self-defense and condemning international terrorism as a threat to international peace and security. This and the more detailed Resolution 1373 recognized the international dimensions of the struggle against terrorism.[31] During the period October–December 2001, there was an international armed conflict between the US-led coalition on the one side, and the Taliban and al Qaeda on the other. Following the fall of the Taliban regime, and the accession to power of the Afghan Interim Authority on 22 December 2001, the coalition's role was essentially that of aiding a government but in a struggle that was at least partly international. Even after the convening of the Loya Jirga in Kabul in June 2002 and the establishment of the Afghan Transitional Government on 19 June, coalition (including Afghan) forces were engaged not only against Taliban or other mainly Afghan forces, but also against certain non-Afghan forces, especially al Qaeda. Despite the fact that al Qaeda lacked the structure of a state, the continuing hostilities with it could still be understood as part of an international armed conflict. This coalition military action was separate from the assistance to the government in maintaining security in Kabul and surrounding areas through the International Security Assistance Force (ISAF).[32]

---

30. *See* Hans-Peter Gasser, *Internationalized Non-International Armed Conflicts: Case Studies of Afghanistan, Kampuchea and Lebanon*, 33 AM. U. L. REV. 1 at 145–61 (Fall, 1983).
31. S. C. Res. 1368, U.N. SCOR, 53d Sess., U.N. Doc. S/1368/(2001) and S. C. Res. 1373, U.N. SCOR, 53d Sess., U.N. Doc. S/1373/(2001).
32. ISAF was established in Afghanistan in January 2002 on the basis of UN Security Council Resolution 1386 of December 20, 2001, passed unanimously. *See* S. C. Res. 1386, U.N. SCOR, 53d Sess., U.N. Doc. S/1386/(2001). Details of the Military Technical Agreement between ISAF and the Interim Administration, plus annexes, are *available at* http://www.operations.mod.uk/isafmta.doc (Nov. 15, 2002).

On the technical legal question as to which of the main laws of war treaties were formally binding on the belligerents in the international armed conflict between the US-led coalition and the Taliban regime in Afghanistan in October–December 2001, the 1907 Hague Convention IV On Land Warfare applied because of its status as customary law, thereby being binding on all states whether or not parties to the treaty. In addition, Afghanistan and the main members of the international coalition were parties to the following agreements:

- the 1925 Geneva Protocol on Gas and Bacteriological Warfare;
- the 1948 Genocide Convention; and,
- the four 1949 Geneva Conventions.

Some of the states involved were, or later became, parties to certain additional agreements.[33] However, the above-named treaties provide the basic treaty framework for considering the application of the law in the armed conflict that commenced in October 2001. In addition, rules of customary international law applied. Apart from the provisions of customary law embodied in the agreements indicated above, certain provisions of some later agreements, including 1977 Geneva Protocol I, are accepted as having that status.

As regards civil-war aspects of the Afghan war, some but not all of the provisions of the agreements listed above apply. The 1907 Hague Land War Convention's Article 2 indicates that the convention and its annexed regulations apply only to wars between states. The 1925 Geneva Protocol is not formally applicable to civil wars.[34] The 1948 Genocide Convention is considered to apply to non-international as well as international armed conflict. In the 1949 Geneva Conventions, Common Article 3 lists certain minimum provisions for humane treatment of those taking no active part in hostilities that are to be applied in non-international armed conflict. However, the UN Security

---

33. On 11 September 2002, Afghanistan acceded to the Ottawa Convention on Anti-personnel Mines. See "UN Committed to Ridding World of Landmine Threat, Annan tells Treaty Meeting" (Sep. 16, 2002), *available at* http://www.un.org/apps/news/storyAr.asp?NewsID =4724&Cr=mines&Cr1= (Nov. 8, 2002).

34. Afghanistan is nonetheless bound by the complete prohibition on possession and use of biological weapons in the 1972 Biological Weapons Convention, which it ratified on 26 March 1975. *See* Convention on the Prohibition of the Development, Production and Stockpiling of Bacteriological (Biological) and Toxin Weapons and on their Destruction, Apr. 10, 1972, 26 U.S.T. 583, 1015 U.N.T.S. 163, *reprinted in* THE LAWS OF ARMED CONFLICTS, *supra* note 5, at 137. Afghanistan is not yet a party to the 1993 Chemical Weapons Convention, which it signed on 14 January 1993 but has not ratified. *See* The Convention on the Prohibition of the Development, Production, Stockpiling, and Use of Chemical Weapons and on Their Destruction, opened for signature January 13, 1993, 32 I.L.M. 800 (1993) [hereinafter Chemical Weapons Convention], *available at* http://www.opcw.org/html/db/members_frameset.html (Nov. 12, 2002).

Council's 1998 resolution had called for application of the Geneva Conventions more generally.

Following the events of 11 September 2001, when it was evident that an armed conflict between the coalition and the Taliban regime was likely, the ICRC, consistent with its general practice, sent messages to certain governments reminding them of their obligations under international humanitarian law. Unfortunately these messages contained some debatable interpretations of the law. They put less reliance on binding treaty law than on provisions of 1977 Geneva Protocol I, to which neither the United States nor Afghanistan was a party, and not all of the provisions of which that were cited can plausibly be claimed to be "recognized as binding on any Party to an armed conflict," as the messages optimistically asserted. Furthermore, in the first of what would be many clashes between humanitarian bodies and national governments in this crisis, the ICRC messages to the US and UK governments stated: "The use of nuclear weapons is incompatible with the provisions of International Humanitarian Law." Although beyond the scope of this survey, this was undoubtedly wrong as a statement of law. Following strong US objections a revised text was sent to the US government, in which the offending wording was changed to the bland formula: "On the subject of nuclear weapons, the ICRC confirms its position as expressed in its Commentary on the 1977 Additional Protocols."[35] In its message to the Afghan authorities the ICRC indicated that the civil war in Afghanistan was governed primarily by the provisions applicable to non-international armed conflicts.[36] This reflected the ICRC view that there were two conflicts in Afghanistan (Coalition v. Taliban; and Taliban v. Northern Alliance) to which two different branches of law applied. However, this was a surprising stance in view of the strong view about the application of the 1949 Geneva Conventions to the situation in Afghanistan that had been expressed by the UN Security Council in August 1998. The ICRC subsequently issued some public statements on the application of the laws of war in this crisis, reminding all the parties involved—the Taliban, the Northern Alliance and the US-led coalition—of their obligations to respect the law, and stating that the ICRC was continuing a wide range of activities inside Afghanistan. One ICRC statement was explicit that "combatants captured by enemy forces in the international armed conflict between the Taliban and the US-led

---

35. See Memorandum from ICRC to Governments of the US and the UK (Sep. 28, 2001). This memorandum was amended and corrected on October 5 by the ICRC. See Memorandum from ICRC to Governments of the US and the UK (Oct. 5, 2001).
36. See Memorandum from ICRC to Government of Afghanistan (Sep. 2001) (unpublished memorandum).

coalition must be treated in accordance with the Third Geneva Convention," implying that other aspects of the war in Afghanistan did not rise to the level of international armed conflict, and that captured personnel in that aspect of the war would have a different and perhaps lesser degree of protection.[37]

In November 2002, the ICRC communicated to concerned countries its conclusions that from 19 June 2002 onwards, the armed conflict in Afghanistan was no longer an international armed conflict but an internal one, covered by Common Article 3 of the 1949 Geneva Conventions rather than by the more comprehensive regime of the conventions as a whole. This conclusion was not persuasive. It appeared to ignore the continuing involvement of certain non-Afghan forces, especially al Qaeda, inside Afghanistan, and the possible continued involvement in terrorist attacks world-wide of that and other bodies operating in Afghanistan; it failed to note the implications in earlier UN Security Council Resolutions that the conflict was international, and/or that the Geneva Conventions were applicable to it; and its issuance marked a departure from previous ICRC practice of adopting a low profile approach to the legal characterization of situations with characteristics of both international and internal armed conflict.[38]

Lack of scope for neutrality

The circumstances of the war against al Qaeda and the Taliban were such that little or no room was left for states to adopt a policy of traditional (i.e., impartial) neutrality, the stresses on which in wars in the twentieth century were already noted above. The lack of scope for neutrality was especially marked because al Qaeda operates in numerous states, and all states have been required by the UN to take a range of measures against it. The resolution passed by the UN Security Council in 1999 on the subject of the Taliban regime in Afghanistan,

---

37. Press Release 01/47, ICRC, Afghanistan: ICRC calls on all parties to conflict to respect international humanitarian law (Oct. 24, 2001), *available at* http://www.icrc.org/Web/eng/siteeng0.nsf/iwpList74/0E80282C0A643B05C1256B6600607E00 (Nov. 12, 2002).

38. *See* ICRC, Aide-Memoire to US (Nov. 19, 2002) (Similar messages were addressed to Afghanistan and other concerned countries). This communication made no reference to UN Security Council Resolutions that might suggest the possibility of a different conclusion about the status of the conflict and the applicability of the 1949 Geneva Conventions. With questionable legal logic, it asserted that the Third and Fourth Geneva Conventions no longer provided a legal basis to continue holding without criminal charge persons who had been captured in Afghanistan between 7 October 2001 and 19 June 2002, and that if these persons are to be kept in captivity, criminal charges must be brought against them. On previous ICRC caution regarding the categorization of conflicts, see Gasser, *Internationalized Non-International Armed Conflicts, supra* note 30, at 157–159.

condemning its support of terrorism and its refusal to hand over Osama bin Laden, had already required all states to take action against the Taliban and against Osama bin Laden and associates.[39] The UN Security Council's resolutions of 12 and 28 September 2001 required all states to take a wide range of actions against terrorism.[40] In his 20 September address to Congress, President George W. Bush framed the obligations on states in blunter and more US centered terms:

> Every nation, in every region, now has a decision to make. Either you are with us, or you are with the terrorists. From this day forward, any nation that continues to harbor or support terrorism will be regarded by the United States as a hostile regime.[41]

It is evident that the scope for traditional neutrality was implicitly understood by the Security Council, and explicitly proclaimed by the United States, to be very limited in the overall counter-terrorist campaign. Naturally, some states, including Iran, proclaimed that they were "neither with Bush nor bin Laden"; and not all states were willing to assist the US-led military action directly. It would be absurd to claim that all forms of non-belligerence are dead, but the particular understanding of neutrality in the written laws of war is further called in question by the character of the "war on terror."

Bombing

The development by US and allied forces of techniques of bombing that are more accurate than in previous eras has improved the prospects of certain air campaigns being conducted in a manner that is compatible with the long-established

---

39. *See* S. C. Res. 1267, U.N. SCOR, 54th Sess., U.N. Doc. S/1267/(1999). *See also* S. C. Res. 1076, U.N. SCOR, 51st Sess., U.N. Doc. S/1076/(1996); and S. C. Res. 1193, U.N. SCOR, 53d Sess., U.N. Doc. S/1193/(1998), which, in addressing the ongoing conflict in Afghanistan, refer to the problem of terrorism and call upon states to take specific actions, most notably to end the supply of arms and ammunition to all parties to the conflict.
40. *See* S. C. Res. 1368, U.N. SCOR, 53d Sess., U.N. Doc. S/1368/(2001) and S. C. Res. 1373, U.N. SCOR, 53d Sess., U.N. Doc. S/1373/(2001).
41. President George W. Bush, Address to a Joint Session of Congress and the American People, 37 WEEKLY COMP. PRES. DOC 1347–1351 (Sep. 20, 2001), *available at* http://frwebgate.access.gpo.gov/cgi-bin/getdoc.cgi?dbname=2001_presidential_documents&docid=pd17se01_txt-15 (Nov. 12, 2002). The peroration added that God is not neutral between freedom and fear, justice and cruelty.

laws-of-war principle of discrimination;[42] and with the more specific rules about targeting—rules which themselves have changed, not least in 1977 Geneva Protocol I. This is a momentous development in the history of war, yet its effects, especially as regards operations against terrorists, should not be exaggerated, as it cannot guarantee either success or no deaths of innocents. Precision-guided weapons are generally better at hitting fixed objects, such as buildings, than moving objects that can be concealed, such as people and tanks. Civilian deaths will still occur, whether because certain dual-use targets are attacked, because of the close proximity of military targets to civilians, or because of faulty intelligence and human or mechanical errors. In addition, malevolence and callousness can still lead to attacks on the wrong places or people. A further problem with the new type of US bombing campaign is that, in the eyes of third parties, it can easily look as if the United States puts a lower value on the lives of Iraqis or Serbs or Afghans than it does on its own almost-invulnerable aircrews: a perception which can feed those hostile views of the United States that help to provide a background against which terrorism can flourish.

Announcing the start of military strikes against Afghanistan on 7 October 2001, President Bush stated: "[t]heir carefully targeted actions are designed to disrupt the use of Afghanistan as a terrorist base of operations and to attack the military capability of the Taliban regime."[43] The principle that the bombing of Afghanistan should be discriminate was frequently repeated. On 21 October, General Richard B. Myers, the Chairman of the Joint Chiefs of Staff, said:

> [t]he last thing we want are any civilian casualties. So we plan every military target with great care. We try to match the weapon to the target and the goal is, one, to destroy the target, and two, is to prevent any what we call "collateral damage" or damage to civilian structures or civilian population.[44]

From the start of the campaign in Afghanistan, the United States was particularly sensitive about accusations that it acted indiscriminately. In late

---

42. The principle of discrimination, which is about the selection of weaponry, methods and targets, includes the idea that non-combatants and those hors de combat should not be deliberately targeted.
43. President George W. Bush, Address to the Nation, 37 WEEKLY COMP. PRES. DOC 1432–1433 (Oct. 7, 2001) available at http://frwebgate.access.gpo.gov/cgi-in/getdoc.cgi?dbname=2001_presidential_documents&docid=pd15oc01_txt-9.pdf (Nov. 12, 2002).
44. Interview by George Stephanopoulos of Chairman of the Joint Chiefs of Staff Richard Myers (ABC This Week television broadcast, Oct. 21, 2001), available at http://www.defenselink.mil/news/Oct2001/t10222001_t1021jcs.html (Nov. 12, 2002).

October Rumsfeld accused the Taliban and al Qaeda leaders of both causing and faking civilian damage: "they are using mosques for command and control, for ammunition storage, and they're not taking journalists in to show that. What they do is when there's a bomb. . . they grab some children and some women and pretend that the bomb hit the women and the children."[45] What truth there was in all this remains difficult to determine.

About 60% of the 22,000 US bombs and missiles dropped in Afghanistan were precision-guided: the highest percentage in any major bombing campaign. If, as reported, only one in four bombs and missiles dropped by the United States on Afghanistan missed its target or malfunctioned in some way, the 75% success rate was higher than that achieved in the 1991 Gulf War and the 1999 Kosovo War.[46] This was a remarkable achievement.

The bombing aroused much international concern. There were reports of many attacks causing significant civilian casualties and damage. Accuracy in hitting the intended target area did not itself necessarily eliminate such problems. An ICRC warehouse in Kabul was hit twice, on 16 and 26 October, leading to serious questions about failure to ensure that target lists were properly prepared and, after the first well-publicized disaster, amended.[47] The episode was subsequently investigated by the Pentagon.[48] Some later incidents were even more serious. For example, according to press reports over a hundred villagers may have died in bombings on 1 December 2001 of Kama Ado and neighboring villages in eastern Afghanistan, not far from the cave

---

45. *Secretary of Defense Donald Rumsfeld, Remarks outside ABC TV Studio* (Oct. 28, 2001), *available at* http://www.defenselink.mil/news/Oct2001/t10292001_t1028sd3.html Oct. 28, 2001 (Nov. 12, 2002).
46. *See* Eric Schmitt, *A Nation Challenged: The Bombing; Improved US Accuracy Claimed in Afghan Air War*, N.Y. TIMES, Apr. 9, 2002, at A-16 (reporting on an uncited, detailed Pentagon assessment).
47. *See, e.g.,* Vernon Loeb & Rajiv Chandrasekaran, *Red Cross Compound Mistakenly bombed; Pentagon Cites "Human Error in the Targeting Process" After Second Mishap*, WASH. POST, Oct. 28, 2001, at A16.
48. *See* Vernon Loeb, *"Friendly Fire" Probed in Death; Airstrike May Have Hit Afghan Convoy*, WASH. POST, Mar. 30, 2002, at A14. *See also Breaking News* (CNN television broadcast, Mar. 19, 2002) in which CNN reported that a preliminary Pentagon investigation into the bombings of the ICRC warehouse indicated that numerous clerical errors had led to the mistaken bombings, that the US commander in charge of the air campaign, Lt. Gen. Charles Wald, had "exceeded his authority in ordering the strike" of 26 October, and that a key issue was that, while the target had been placed on a "No Strike List" at the Pentagon, it was inadvertently left off a separate "No Strike List" maintained by the US Central Command in Tampa, Florida.

complex at Tora Bora.[49] On 1 July 2002, during an operation to hunt Taliban leaders, US aircraft attacked four villages around the hamlet of Kakrak. According to reports, this episode followed the firing of guns at two wedding parties, and resulted in killing over 50 people and injuring over 100. This led to another Pentagon investigation.[50] In several cases, bombings led to casualties among coalition forces: while this is not a laws-of-war issue as such, and is not uncommon in armed conflicts, it further confirms the fact that precision bombing can produce terrible disasters if the intended target is incorrectly identified.[51]

It is difficult to arrive at a reliable estimate of the overall number of civilian deaths caused directly by the bombing in Afghanistan. As in the 1991 Gulf and 1999 Kosovo wars, the Pentagon has been reluctant to issue figures. Whereas Iraq in 1991 and Yugoslavia in 1999 had reasonably effective systems of official record-keeping in place, Afghanistan in 2001 did not. As a result of these factors, estimates of Afghan civilian deaths have been unofficial.

Controversy was caused by an estimate of 3,767 as of mid-December 2001 made by Professor Marc Herold of the University of New Hampshire.[52] There were substantial grounds for doubt about his methodology; and his figure, almost certainly a serious over-estimate, was later modified.[53] In response to

---

49. *See, e.g.*, Richard Lloyd Parry & Justin Huggler, *Village Air Raid: Error or an act of terror?*, THE INDEPENDENT, Dec. 2, 2001, *available at* http://www.independent.co.uk/story.jsp?story=107928, (Nov. 13, 2002).

50. Dexter Filkins, *Flaws in U.S. Air War Left Hundreds of Civilians Dead*, N.Y. TIMES, Jul. 21 2002, at Sec. 1, p. 1, col. 5, *available at* http://query.nytimes.com/search/abstract?res=F40813F83D5C0C728EDDAE0894DA404482 (Nov. 13, 2002).

51. On 13 September 2002 two US pilots who mistakenly bombed and killed Canadian troops in Afghanistan on 18 April 2002 were charged – the first criminal charges against US pilots in connection with the events in Afghanistan. Katy Kay & Richard Cleroux, *US pilots charged over "friendly fire" deaths*, THE TIMES, Sep. 14, 2002, at 16.

52. Marc W. Herold, *A Dossier on Civilian Victims of US Aerial Bombing of Afghanistan: A Comprehensive Accounting* (Dec. 19, 2001), *at* http://pubpages.unh.edu/~mwherold/AfghanDailyCount.xls (Nov. 13, 2002).

53. Criticisms of Herold's methodology included the following: (1) The calculations leading to the total figures were not transparent. The author has informed me that the December figure was not intended to suggest total accuracy. (2) Unavoidably, in view of time constraints, the study relied heavily on media reports, some of them extremely dubious. (3) Some incidents were counted twice in the December total, e.g., due to different place names being used in reports. (4) In some instances al Qaeda deaths, and possibly Taliban deaths, may have been reported as civilian deaths. On the other hand it is probable that some civilian casualties of bombing went unreported and were thus omitted from the report. For a strong critique, see Jeffrey C. Isaac, *Civilian Casualties in Afghanistan: The Limits of Herold's "Comprehensive Accounting"* (Jan. 10, 2002), *available at* http://www.indiana.edu/~iupolsci/docs/doc.htm, (Nov. 13, 2002). In August 2002 Herold stated that "the figure for the October to December period should have been

Herold's December estimate, Rumsfeld stated in an interview on 8 January 2002:

> there probably has never in the history of the world been a conflict that has been done as carefully, and with such measure, and care, and with such minimal collateral damage to buildings and infrastructure, and with such small numbers of unintended civilian casualties.[54]

In 2002 a number of reports based on on-site examinations gave a more authoritative, but incomplete, picture. In July the *New York Times* published the results of a review of eleven of the "principal places where Afghans and human rights groups claim that civilians have been killed." It found that at these sites "airstrikes killed as many as 400 civilians."[55] A principal cause was poor intelligence. In September a San Francisco-based human rights group, Global Exchange, estimated on the basis of a survey conducted in Afghanistan that "at least 824 Afghan civilians were killed between October 7 and January 2002 by the US-led bombing campaign."[56] A Human Rights Watch report on civilian casualties in Afghanistan is in preparation.

While even an approximate figure for civilian casualties of the bombing in Afghanistan may never be known, it appears certain that the number of civilian deaths in the period October–December 2001 was far more than the 500 in Yugoslavia during the war over Kosovo in 1999, and probable that it was over one thousand. The question then is how this was possible given that twice the percentage of precision-guided munitions was used and the overall number of weapons dropped was much less. Of the many possible factors meriting investigation, two were the imperfections of the intelligence/targeting

---

between 2,650 and 2,970 civilian deaths," and that "between 3,125 and 3,620 Afghan civilians were killed between October 7 and July 31." Marc Herold, *Counting the Dead*, THE GUARDIAN, Aug. 8, 2002, at 17.

54. *Interview of Secretary of Defense Donald Rumsfeld* (CSPAN television broadcast, Jan. 8, 2002), *available at* http://www.defenselink.mil/news/Jan2002/t01082002_t0108sd.html (Nov. 13, 2002).

55. Filkins, *supra* note 50. This included reference to the Masuda Sultan survey mentioned immediately *infra*.

56. *See* Masuda Sultan et al., AFGHAN PORTRAITS OF GRIEF: THE CIVILIAN/INNOCENT VICTIMS OF US BOMBING IN AFGHANISTAN (2002), at 3, *available at* http://www.globalexchange.org/september11/apogreport.pdf (Nov. 13, 2002). This short (16-page) report was based on a survey conducted by a 5-person team between March and June 2002. It emphasizes that "it was impossible for our survey to be exhaustive and comprehensive," and that the figure of 824 "represents only a portion of civilian casualties." Finally, the report called on the US Government to establish an Afghan Victims Fund. *Id.* at 3, 6.

process, and the uncertain identity of the combatants—both of which are generic problems in counter-terrorist operations.

In legal terms, the incidence of civilian deaths per se does not always constitute a violation, absent other factors regarding the circumstances of such deaths. Wilful killings and intentional attacks against the civilian population as such or against individual civilians not taking part in hostilities are clearly illegal. In addition, the 1977 Geneva Protocol I, Article 57, spells out a positive obligation on commanders to exercise care to spare civilians and civilian objects.[57]

There are strong reasons to believe US statements that civilian deaths in Afghanistan due to the US bombing were unintended. Some of the deaths appear to have resulted from errors of various kinds, and some may have been unavoidable "collateral damage." One cause of civilian casualties in October–December 2001 may have been the fact that, in a legacy from the period of Soviet involvement in Afghanistan, many Taliban military assets were located in towns, where they were less vulnerable to raids from rural-based guerrillas, but where they were of course closer to civilians who risked getting hit in bombing attacks. While much of the bombing has been discriminate, questions have been raised about whether all appropriate measures have been taken to reduce civilian casualties and damage. Even if much of the civilian death and destruction is not a violation of the law, the resulting adverse public perception risks harming the coalition cause.

The air campaign in Afghanistan confirmed the lesson of earlier campaigns, especially the war over Kosovo in 1999, that there is tension between current US and NATO strategic doctrine and certain international legal provisions on targeting. The 1977 Geneva Protocol I, Article 52(2), opens with the words: "[a]ttacks shall be limited strictly to military objectives." It goes on to indicate the types of objects that might constitute military objectives. This provision presents some difficulties, and has been the subject of interpretative declarations by a number of states.[58] The United States, although not bound by the Protocol, has indicated that it accepts this article.[59] However, even before the United States involvement in Afghanistan, a number of US legal experts had expressed serious concerns about the provision. For example, Major

---

57. GP I, *supra* note 9, at art. 57.
58. GP I, *supra* note 9, at art. 52(2) *reprinted in* DOCUMENTS ON THE LAWS OF WAR, *supra* note 5 at 450. Declarations made by states that have a bearing on their understanding of this article include those by Australia, Belgium, Canada, Germany, Ireland, Italy, Netherlands, Spain, and the United Kingdom. *Id.* at 500–511.
59. OPLAW HANDBOOK, *supra* note 15, at 11.

Jeanne Meyer, co-editor of the US Army's *Operational Law Handbook*, stated that this article "tries to constrict the use of air power to the specific tactical military effort at hand" and "ignores the reality that a nation's war effort is composed of more than just military components." While not suggesting total rejection of the provision, she urged the United States to "resist the pressure to accept restrictive interpretations of Article 52(2)."[60] In general, the United States is anxious to retain some legal justification for attacks on certain targets that may not themselves be purely military, but which may, for example, contribute to the military effort or constitute key parts of a regime's infrastructure.

Did the concern over civilian casualties undermine the US bombing effort in Afghanistan in its most intense phase in October–December 2001? Its success against the Taliban would suggest not, but there were indications that the concern had serious effects. It was reported that the United States had deliberately slowed the pace of the campaign, and increased the risk to the people executing it, because of legal restraints and moral values. It was also stated that war planners frequently chose not to hit particular targets, even if they were militarily important, and pilots allegedly complained of lost opportunities. Yet the planners could not reveal their reasoning for ruling out certain targets, as it would give the adversary "a recipe book for not being bombed." The issue of civilian casualties also became ammunition for inter-service battles, particularly for Army arguments in favor of "boots on the ground."[61]

In addition to the direct casualties, there were also, inevitably, indirect casualties of the bombing. These appear to have come into two categories. First, the bombing caused thousands of Afghan civilians to flee their homes.[62] Some died in the harsh conditions of flight and displacement. Second, the use of cluster bombs led to immediate and longer-term civilian casualties. Cluster bombs are air-dropped canisters containing numerous separate bomblets that disperse over a given area. The bomblets, which are meant to explode on impact or to self-deactivate after a specific period, can cause particularly severe problems if they fail to do so. There have been objections to their use, principally on the ground that they have a tendency, like anti-personnel landmines, to kill people long after the conflict is over. Reports from Kosovo and

---

60. Jeanne M. Meyer, *Tearing Down the Facade: A Critical Look at the Current Law on Targeting the Will of the Enemy and Air Force Doctrine*, 51 A.F. L. REV. 166, 181 (2001).
61. William M. Arkin, *Fear of Civilian Deaths May Have Undermined Effort*, L.A. TIMES, Jan. 16, 2002, at A12, *available at* http://www.latimes.com/news/nationworld/world/la-011602milmemo.story (Nov. 13, 2002).
62. On those who fled from the intense fighting and bombing in Afghanistan in October–November 2001, see notes 74-75 and accompanying text infra.

elsewhere have confirmed the general seriousness of the problem.[63] The UN's Mine Action Programme for Afghanistan (MAPA) estimates that 1,152 cluster bombs were dropped by the United States, leaving up to 14,000 unexploded bomblets as a result.[64] According to the US State Department in July 2002, "the clearance of cluster munitions is being achieved at a rate faster than anticipated. All known cluster munition strike sites have been surveyed where access is possible and are in the process of being cleared."[65] As the law stands, there has been no agreement to outlaw cluster bombs, and while they are not illegal *per se*, their use does raise questions regarding their compatibility with fundamental principles of the laws of war. They are certain to be the subject of further pressures to limit or stop their use, or to ensure more effective safeguards against later accidental detonations.

A further issue concerns the use of bombing in the hunt for Taliban and al Qaeda personnel following the fall of the Taliban regime in early December 2001. In the preceding phase, bombing had been used primarily in support of Northern Alliance frontal operations aimed at capturing the main Taliban-held cities. Once this was achieved, a good deal of the bombing was directed against remnant al Qaeda mountain redoubts. It was also directed against Taliban and al Qaeda forces and their leaders, but many incidents were reported in the press in which those killed were apparently neither. The reports drew attention to the difficulty of distinguishing between civilians and these forces. They also raised the question of broader significance in counter-terrorist wars: to what extent can bombing remain an appropriate form of enforcement once a state is, to a greater or lesser degree, under the control of a new government that is opposed to the terrorists? At that point, can the focus be transferred to other forms of police and military action that may be less likely than bombing to cause civilian casualties? Here, the legal argument for greater reliance on the discriminate use of ground force merges into a practical argument that only such means can prevent the escape of the forces being targeted. United States civilian and military officials are reported to have concluded that Osama bin Laden had been present at the battle for Tora

---

63. According to the ICRC, in the year after the NATO bombing campaign over Kosovo ended in June 1999, more than 400 people were killed or injured by unexploded bomblets. *See* Ragnhild Imerslund, *In Action, When Toys Kill, Another Challenge in Kosovo*, ICRC MAGAZINE, 2000 *available at* http://www.redcross.int/EN/mag/magazine2000_2/Kosovo.html (Nov. 13, 2002).

64. Richard Norton-Taylor, *Afghanistan Littered with 14,000 Unexploded Bomblets Says UN*, THE GUARDIAN, Mar. 23, 2002, at 18.

65. US Department of State, *Fact Sheet: U.S. Humanitarian Demining Assistance to Afghanistan* (Jul. 30, 2002), *available at* http://www.state.gov/t/pm/rls/fs/2002/12274.htm (Nov. 13, 2002).

Bora in December 2001, and that failure to commit ground troops against him in this mountain battle was the gravest error of the war.[66] Whether or not this conclusion is correct, it does appear that the reliance of the United States on bombing and its reluctance to put its own troops in harm's way may have enabled Taliban and al Qaeda leaders to escape.

Gas

One long-standing prohibition in warfare is the rule against use of gas and bacteriological methods of warfare. The United States repeatedly expressed concern that al Qaeda might be preparing to use such methods in terrorist attacks. In addition, there were a few situations in Afghanistan in which there could have been pressures for the United States to use gas. When, in 1975, the United States had ratified the 1925 Geneva Protocol, it had indicated that it considered that certain uses of riot-control agents in armed conflict did not violate the protocol.[67] In early December 2001, Rumsfeld was asked at a press conference if the United States might use gas in the hunt for Taliban and al Qaeda personnel in mountain caves in Afghanistan. Rumsfeld's response contained no denial:

> Well, I noticed that in Mazar, the way they finally got the dead-enders to come out was by flooding the tunnel. And finally they came up and surrendered, the last hard core al Qaeda elements. And I guess one will do whatever it is necessary to do. If people will not surrender, then they've made their choice.[68]

Humanitarian relief and refugee issues

Humanitarian relief and refugee issues impacted upon all phases of operations in Afghanistan. The need for humanitarian relief is particularly likely to arise in counter-terrorist operations against a weak or failed state, because such states breed conditions in which, simultaneously, terrorist movements can operate and large-scale human misery and refugee flows can occur. The fact of a war being against terrorists, while it may affect the mode of delivery (since land convoys may be vulnerable to seizure) does not affect the law applicable to the provision of relief. The basic obligations of the various parties to an armed

---

66. Barton Gellman and Thomas E. Ricks, *U.S. Concludes Bin Laden Escaped at Tora Bora Fight*, WASH. POST, Apr. 17, 2002, at A1.
67. OPLAW HANDBOOK, *supra* note 15, at 15–16.
68. *Interview by Tim Russert of Secretary of Defense Donald Rumsfeld* (NBC Meet the Press television broadcast, Dec. 2, 2001), *available at* http://www.defenselink.mil/news/Dec2001/t12022001_t1202mtp.html (Nov. 13, 2002).

conflict to assist in and protect humanitarian relief operations are embodied in 1949 Geneva Convention IV, on civilians.[69]

The US government put heavy emphasis on air-dropping of supplies. Announcing the start of Operation ENDURING FREEDOM, President Bush stated: "[a]s we strike military targets, we will also drop food, medicine and supplies to the starving and suffering men and women and children of Afghanistan."[70] United States forces air-dropped considerable quantities of aid at the same time as the major bombing operations took place. In the first twenty-five days of the campaign more than one million "humanitarian daily rations" were delivered.[71] Some human rights and humanitarian agencies expressed specific worries about the air-dropping of food. They were doubtful of the value of airdropping supplies compared to the previous deliveries overland, and were concerned that the yellow wrapping of the food packages could lead Afghans to mistake yellow cluster bomblets for them. More generally, they were resistant to the use of military assets for humanitarian purposes, be it the dropping of supplies from the air, or shipping goods in military convoys to distribution points. They tended to be critical of the bombing campaign generally, and concerned also about the aggravated risks and obstacles to their relief and development work that resulted from the military operations, especially in view of the onset of winter. The unrealistic call for a bombing pause issued by the UN High Commissioner for Refugees (UNHCR) in October was indicative of the tension between some agencies and the US government.[72] In any event, the collapse of the Taliban regime in early December 2001 and its replacement by the interim administration facilitated, but by no means guaranteed,

---

69. *See* GC IV, at arts. 13–26 *reprinted in* DOCUMENTS ON THE LAWS OF WAR, *supra* note 5, at 430–436. *See also* GP I arts. 69–71, *supra* note 9, *reprinted in* DOCUMENTS ON THE LAWS OF WAR, *supra* note 5 at 324–5; GP II art. 18, *supra* note 17, *reprinted in* DOCUMENTS ON THE LAWS OF WAR, *supra* note 5, at 491. The issue of humanitarian relief is only touched on briefly in this survey as, while of critical importance in Afghanistan, only to a limited extent does it raise problems specific to counter-terrorist military operations.
70. President George W. Bush, Address to the Nation, *supra* note 43.
71. Figures for humanitarian daily rations dropped in Afghanistan were given in many Pentagon news briefings. *See, e.g.,* Gerry Gilmore, *Air Campaign Continues Against Taliban, Terrorist Targets* (American Forces News Service, Oct. 8, 2001), *available at* http://www.defenselink.mil/news/Oct2001/n10082001_200110085.html (Nov. 14, 2002); and Kathleen T. Rhem, *Fighters, Bombers, Not Only Planes Flying in Afghanistan* (American Forces News Service, Oct. 31, 2001), *available at* http://www.defenselink.mil/news/Oct2001/n10312001_200110314.html (Nov. 14, 2002).
72. *Interview with UN High Commissioner for Refugees* (Irish radio broadcast, Oct. 12, 2001); *Interview with UN High Commissioner for Refugees* (BBC-1 Breakfast with Frost television broadcast, Oct. 14, 2001).

the secure delivery of aid by land routes. A wide range of countries and organizations took part in the provision of aid.[73]

The refugee problem was of massive proportions and could itself have constituted a possible ground for action over Afghanistan. As of the beginning of September 2001 there were about 3.5 million Afghan refugees in neighboring countries, mainly Pakistan and Iran. The intense hostilities and bombing in October–December led to an additional 200,000 or more fleeing from Afghanistan, as well as in an increase in the number of internally displaced persons (IDPs) by perhaps half a million.[74] Many of the internally displaced in, and refugees from, Afghanistan testified eloquently to the disastrous effects of the bombing on civilians and their property.[75]

The subsequent return of refugees to Afghanistan was on a colossal scale. It started in January 2002, when 3,000 per day began returning to Afghanistan.[76] Not all who returned in 2002 chose to stay. By December some 300,000 were reported to have returned to Pakistan, disappointed by insecurity and economic hardship.[77] However, a total of 1.8 million Afghans had returned, 1.54 million of whom had come from Pakistan and resettled in Afghanistan in 2002. Playing a major role, the UNHCR reported in September that this was the

---

73. On the delivery of humanitarian aid after the collapse of the Taliban regime, see, e.g., Secretary of Defense Donald Rumsfeld and General Tommy Franks, DOD News Briefing (Aug. 15, 2002), available at http://www.defenselink.mil/news/Aug2002/t08152002_t0815sd.html (Nov. 14, 2002); and, Jim Garamone, *Humanitarian Success Story In Afghanistan* (American Forces News Service, Jan. 18, 2002), available at http://www.defenselink.mil/news/Jan2002/n01182002_200201185.htm (Nov. 14, 2002).
74. Figures current to Dec. 31, 2001 in UN HIGH COMMISSIONER FOR REFUGEES 2001 ED. OF REFUGEES BY NUMBERS, available at http://www.unhcr.ch/cgi-bin/texis/vtx/home/ (Nov. 14, 2002).
75. *See, e.g.,* THE DISPOSSESED (documentary film by Taghi Amirani, Nov.–Dec. 2001). This television documentary is about the Makaki Camp in Nimruz Province near the Afghan–Iranian border. The camp was initially under Taliban and then Northern Alliance control.
76. *See* UNHCR Spokesman, UNHCR Press Briefing at Palais des Nations, Geneva (Jan. 25, 2002), available at http://wwww.reliefweb.int/w/rwb.nsf/ (Nov. 14, 2002); and *UN Office for the Coordination of Humanitarian Affairs Report No. 37* (Jan. 29, 2002), available at http://www.reliefweb.int/w/rwb.nsf/ (Nov. 14, 2002). At that time there were also movements of ethnic Pashtun from Afghanistan to Pakistan.
77. Deutsche Presse Agentur Report of December 12, 2002, available at http://wwww.reliefweb.int/w/rwb.nsf/ (Jan. 6, 2003).

largest refugee repatriation in 30 years—i.e., since the creation of Bangladesh.[78] Some non-governmental charities and NGOs were critical of the pressure to encourage refugees to return.[79] The principal improvements that created the conditions for this vast movement of people back to their country resulted from the conclusion of major hostilities, the end of the Taliban regime in December 2001, and the ending of a years-long drought. Observance of humanitarian norms during the war in Afghanistan may have played some part, especially insofar as it helped to limit the amount of destruction caused by the bombing.

Prisoners

From late November 2001, the status and treatment of prisoners taken in the "war on terror" (most but not all of whom had been captured in Afghanistan) became the subject of major international controversies. These centered on three inter-related issues: first, the extraordinary events relating to prisoners in Afghanistan in late 2001; second, the broader debate about the legal status and treatment of prisoners taken in the "war on terror" generally, including those held at Guantanamo; and third, the question of possible judicial proceedings against prisoners for pre-capture offenses. This part looks at these three issues in turn. (It does not look at the court cases in several countries in which related questions have been raised.)

Prison disasters in Afghanistan

Initially, international attention focused on one event: the killing of a large number of Taliban and al Qaeda prisoners who had been taken at Kunduz at around the time of its fall on 23–24 November 2001, and who were then involved in the revolt at Qala-e Jhangi Fort near Mazar-e-Sharif in the period 25 November–1 December. There had been very little sign of serious preparation for handling prisoners. The precise chain of events leading to the revolt has yet to be established, but the causes appear to include the following heavy mix: Some of the prisoners were fanatical soldiers, for whom the whole concept of surrender would be anathema; the arrangements for receiving, holding and

---

78. Ron Redmond, UNHCR Press Briefing at Palais des Nations, Geneva (Sep. 3, 2002), *available at* http://www.unhcr.ch/cgi-bin/texis/vtx/home/ (Nov. 14, 2002); Nigel Fisher, UN Assistance Mission in Afghanistan Press Briefing (Dec. 12, 2002) *available at* http://www.reliefweb.int/w/rwb.nsf.

79. *See, e.g.,* Jonathan Steele, *Going Home to Hunger and Death: Aid Agencies Fear for Families Persuaded to Leave Refugee Camps,* THE GUARDIAN, Apr. 4, 2002, at 17.

processing them were *ad hoc* and then casual; there was a failure to communicate to them that they would be treated in accord with international standards; a number of them had not surrendered all their weapons; they were held in a place where there was a large store of weapons, to which they gained access; some of them, according to reports, feared that they were about to be killed, so had nothing to lose by revolt; and some feared interrogation by those whom they understood to be CIA operatives, which changed the situation from an Afghan/Afghan equation.[80]

The revolt at Qala-e Jhangi Fort was a desperate struggle in which not only many prisoners, but also a number of Northern Alliance troops in charge of the fort, died. United States bombing, and sharp-shooting by UK special forces, played a part in the defeat of the uprising. Public discussion in the United Kingdom and elsewhere focused on the events at the fort, including the question of whether the force used to quell the rebellion was excessive. If the situation was as desperate and threatening as reports indicated, the use of force was hardly surprising. Public discussion could more usefully focus on how prisoners should be received and dealt with. The real causes of the disaster were in the period before the prisoners arrived at the fort. There were failures to think the issue through, to make proper preparations, and especially to disarm all prisoners. The mix of Afghan and outside involvement in the handling of the prisoners may have further contributed to the outbreak of the revolt.

Other reports about treatment of Taliban and al Qaeda prisoners, especially at Sebarghan in northern Afghanistan, confirm that the overall approach of the Northern Alliance was defective. By late December there had been numerous reports of prisoners dying in shipping containers and Afghan captors beating their detainees. The ICRC was reported as expressing concern that it had been able to register only 4,000 of the 7,000 prisoners that the United States said it and its Afghan allies had in custody.[81] Long after most of the prisoners

---

80. Much valuable evidence about the outbreak and course of the prison revolt at Qala-e Jhangi Fort has emerged, including particularly video records. *See, e.g.,* Carlotta Gall, *Traces of Terror; Prisoners; Video Vividly Captures Prelude to Fortress Revolt,* N.Y. TIMES (Jul. 16, 2002), at A15.
81. *See, e.g.,* Carlotta Gall, *Long Journey to Prison Ends in Taliban Deaths: Many Suffocated in Sealed Ship Containers,* INT'L HERALD TRIBUNE, Dec. 11, 2001, at 4; Babak Dehghanpisheh et al., *The Death Camp of Afghanistan,* NEWSWEEK, Aug. 26, 2002, at 16-25; and Rory Carroll, *Afghan jailers beat confessions from men,* THE GUARDIAN, Dec. 28, 2001, at 13.

had been taken, conditions remained shocking, in violation of international standards.[82] International inquiries into these events are ongoing.

Whether the United States and its coalition partners had any influence over Northern Alliance actions in such basic matters as protection of prisoners—and, if so, whether they used it—is open to question. Some US statements indicated that there could have been such influence. In his Pentagon press briefing on 30 November, Rumsfeld indicated—in general terms, not in connection with the prisoner question—that the United States does have influence with the forces with which it operated in Afghanistan:

> [w]e have a relationship with all of those elements on the ground. We have provided them food. We've provided them ammunition. We've provided air support. We've provided winter clothing. We've worked with them closely. We have troops embedded in their forces and have been assisting with overhead targeting and resupply of ammunition. It's a relationship.[83]

Legal status and treatment of prisoners generally

Within the Pentagon it was recognized as early as September 2001 that in the forthcoming military action questions relating to the legal status and treatment of prisoners could be difficult. An unpublished document circulated by the US Air Force's International and Operations Law Division contained the main outlines of an approach that would continue to be influential: terrorists were to be treated as "unlawful combatants;" it was "very unlikely that a captured terrorist will be legally entitled to POW status under the Geneva Conventions;" however, there was a "practical US interest in application of Law of Armed Conflict principles in the context of reciprocity of treatment of captured personnel." As regards treatment upon capture,

> if a terrorist is captured, Department of Defense members must at the very least comply with the principles and spirit of the Law of Armed Conflict . . . A

---

82. Dexter Filkins, *3,000 Forgotten Taliban, Dirty and Dying*, INT'L HERALD TRIBUNE, Mar. 15, 2002, at 1.

83. Secretary of Defense Donald Rumsfeld and General Peter Pace, DOD News Briefing (Nov. 30, 2001), *available at* http://www.defenselink.mil/news/Nov2001/t11302001_t1130sd.html (Nov. 14, 2002). Compare an earlier statement of British Prime Minister Tony Blair, who when asked on 13 November, also in general terms, "what sanctions do we have over the Northern Alliance?" replied "None." Prime Minister Tony Blair, Press Briefing on Afghanistan (Nov. 13, 2001), *available at* http://www.pm.gov.uk/output/page3852.asp (Nov. 14, 2002).

suspected terrorist captured by US military personnel will be given the protections of but not the status of a POW.[84]

Consideration of the legal status and treatment of prisoners taken by the US-led coalition must begin with the distinction that has been drawn between the two main groups: Taliban and al Qaeda. As indicated below, one key factor in determining the lawfulness of a combatant and therefore the entitlement to participate directly in hostilities, is the affiliation of the combatant to a party to the conflict. The Taliban had a material connection to a state (Afghanistan), whereas al Qaeda did not. A possible complicating factor is that in some cases non-Afghan units appear to have fought alongside Taliban forces and may have been under their control, which would strengthen a claim to POW status. In certain cases it may be difficult to determine whether an individual should be considered Taliban or al Qaeda, or belongs in some other possible category. At Guantanamo there has evidently been a tendency to classify only Afghan prisoners as Taliban. All non-Afghans (some of whom were arrested outside Afghanistan) appear to have been classified as al Qaeda. However, it may be doubted whether all foreigners drawn to support an Islamic cause in Afghanistan, Pakistan or elsewhere, and who ended up in Guantanamo, were necessarily members of al Qaeda.

The basic rules for determining who is a lawful combatant entitled to POW status are in Article 4 of 1949 Geneva Convention III (the POW Convention). This states, in part:

A. Prisoners of war, in the sense of the present Convention, are persons belonging to one of the following categories, who have fallen into the power of the enemy:

(1) Members of the armed forces of a Party to the conflict as well as members of militias and volunteer corps forming part of such armed forces.

(2) Members of other militias and members of other volunteer corps, including those of organized resistance movements, belonging to a Party to the conflict and operating in or outside their own territory, even if this territory is occupied, provided that such militias or volunteer corps, including such organized resistance movements, fulfil the following conditions:

---

84. Memorandum from the International and Operations Law Division of Headquarters, US Air Force on the Summary of Legal Issues Relevant to Terrorism Incidents of 11 Sep 01, at 5-6 (Sep. 21, 2001).

(a) that of being commanded by a person responsible for his subordinates;

(b) that of having a fixed distinctive sign recognizable at a distance;

(c) that of carrying arms openly;

(d) that of conducting their operations in accordance with laws and customs of war.

(3) Members of regular armed forces who profess allegiance to a government or an authority not recognized by the Detaining Power.

(4) Persons who accompany the armed forces without actually being members thereof... provided that they have received authorization from the armed forces which they accompany, who shall provide them for that purpose with an identity card.[85]

The question as to whether, in order to qualify for POW status, members of a state's regular armed forces all have to meet the four conditions listed in Article 4(A)(2) specifically in respect to members of militias and resistance movements is not pursued here. The general assumption has been that states' regular forces should as a matter of course observe these conditions.[86] Even if this general assumption could be challenged, it is widely agreed that members of a state's forces must meet certain criteria. For example, they should wear uniforms when involved in military action—a rule that the United States views as applying even to commando forces and airborne troops operating singly.[87] There is also an obligation on parties to a conflict to supply identity documents to all their personnel liable to become POWs.[88]

However the criteria for POW status are interpreted, states have often deployed certain personnel such as spies in a manner that does not meet the criteria, knowing that if they fall into enemy hands they are unlikely to be viewed or treated as POWs; and they have also deployed certain personnel whose

---

85. See GC III, *supra* note 5, at art. 4.
86. International Committee of the Red Cross, 3 GENEVA CONVENTION RELATIVE TO THE TREATMENT OF PRISONERS OF WAR, COMMENTARY 48 (Jean S. Pictet ed., 1960) [hereinafter Commentary III]; Howard S. Levie, PRISONERS OF WAR IN INTERNATIONAL ARMED CONFLICT 36–38 (Howard S Levie ed., 1978) (Vol. 59, US Naval War College International Law Studies).
87. FM 27-10, para 63, *supra* note 12.
88. See GC III, art 17 and art. 4(A)(4), *supra* note 5. Article 4(A)(4), quoted above, indicates that civilian contracted personnel (who played a significant part in the US operations in Afghanistan in 2001–2) would appear to qualify for POW status provided that they have formal authorization. There is not a requirement that they wear uniform.

conformity with the criteria is debatable. With respect to the operations in Afghanistan in 2001, an argument could possibly be made that some US or coalition personnel did not meet one of the conditions: for example, members of US forces (including special forces or forward air controllers), if not wearing a uniform or fixed sign and not carrying arms openly. Such possibilities give the United States a potential interest in avoiding restrictive approaches to the granting of POW status and treatment.

All lawful combatants, if captured, are entitled to POW status and all of the rights set forth in the Geneva Convention III. They cannot be punished for the mere fact of having participated directly in hostilities, but they can be tried for violations of the detaining power's law, or of international law (including the laws of war) that they may have committed.[89]

Questions regarding the status of a variety of detainees who may fail to meet one of the above criteria are not new. In previous wars, POW status was seldom given to those involved in resistance activities against occupation, or in cases of alleged terrorism. On the other hand, some captured personnel who arguably failed to meet one criterion or another applicable at the time were viewed as entitled to POW status.[90]

A procedure for determining who is a lawful combatant, entitled to POW status, is addressed directly in two treaties. The first of these, 1949 Geneva Convention III, provides in Article 5 that, in cases of doubt, prisoners shall be treated as POWs "until such time as their status has been determined by a competent tribunal." This Article does not specify who has to have the doubt, nor the nature of the "competent tribunal." However, the general principle is clear and is accepted in US official manuals. For example, the US Army manual states unequivocally: "When doubt exists as to whether captured enemy personnel warrant continued POW [prisoner of war] status, Art. 5 Tribunals must be convened."[91]

The second treaty to address the procedure for determining who is a lawful combatant is 1977 Geneva Protocol I. Article 45 contains elaborations of 1949 Convention III's provisions on the status of detained persons. It suggests

---

89. *Id.* at arts. 99–104. The separate subject of sanctions in respect of offenses against prison camp discipline is covered in Articles 89–98. As regards judicial proceedings against detainees who do not have POW status, see text at notes 113–122 infra.

90. Professor Howard Levie, who has written extensively on the law relating to POWs, suggests that being of a different nationality from that of the army in which they serve would not prevent combatants from having POW status, but he is more doubtful about spies and saboteurs when not operating openly and in uniform. *See* Levie, *supra* note 86, at 74–84.

91. OPLAW HANDBOOK, *supra* note 15, at 22; *see also* ANNOTATED SUPPLEMENT, *supra* note 13, at paras. 11.7 and 12.7.1.

that a detainee has "the right to assert his entitlement to prisoner-of-war status before a judicial tribunal," but allows for considerable leeway in the procedure by which a tribunal could reach a decision about POW status. The possibilities that the proceedings could take place *after* a trial for an offense, and also *in camera* in the interest of state security, are not excluded. This article recognizes in plain language that not all those who take part in hostilities are entitled to POW status, but they are entitled to certain fundamental guarantees discussed further below.

The uncertainties regarding the status and treatment of people who are involved in hostile activities in various ways, but who fail to meet the criteria for POW status, are reflected in muddled terminology. "Unlawful combatant," the most common term, is generally used in this paper. The treaties that implicitly create the category do not offer any satisfactory term to describe such persons. The US Supreme Court, in its judgment in the July 1942 case, *Ex Parte Quirin*, used the terms "unlawful combatant" and "unlawful belligerent," apparently interchangeably, to refer to one who, "having the status of an enemy belligerent enters or remains, with hostile purpose, upon the territory of the United States in time of war without uniform or other appropriate means of identification."[92] One term advanced in the early 1950s by a respected authority as the most appropriate to cover a wide range of combatants who do not meet the POW criteria is "unprivileged belligerents"—a term that carries the important implication that such persons while not meeting the criteria for POW status, have not necessarily committed a definite violation of the laws of war.[93] In current US military manuals four terms—"unprivileged belligerents," "detainees," "unlawful combatants" and "illegal combatants"—are used, again apparently interchangeably, to refer to those who are viewed as not being members of the armed forces of a party to the conflict and not having the right to engage in hostilities against an opposing party.[94] The variety of the terminology is not in itself a major problem. The key element of confusion in the debate was the tendency, especially marked in the press in late 2001 and early

---

92. Ex parte Quirin, 317 U.S. 1, 4–16 (1942) [hereinafter Quirin].
93. The classic article on the subject is by Richard Baxter. *See* Richard R. Baxter, *So-called "Unprivileged Belligerency": Spies, Guerrillas and Saboteurs*, 28 BRIT. Y.B. INT'L L. 323–45 (1951). His key conclusion is that this large category of hostile conduct is not *per se* violative of any positive prohibition of international law, but it does expose those engaging in it to trial and punishment by the enemy, for example under the enemy's own laws and regulations. In the years since he wrote this, many terrorist acts have been prohibited in international law, so the category is not necessarily appropriate for those suspected of involvement in terrorism.
94. OPLAW HANDBOOK, *supra* note 15, at 12, 22, *see also* ANNOTATED SUPPLEMENT, *supra* note 13, at para. 12.7.1.

2002, to refer to such terms as "unlawful combatants" and "battlefield detainees" as if they were entirely new, were freshly invented by the US government, and were completely outside the existing treaty framework.

The ICRC and others have argued that detained persons who do not qualify for POW status (i.e., those often called "unlawful combatants") should be viewed as civilians and treated in accord with the 1949 Geneva Convention IV. This view would appear to be in conformity with the first paragraph of Article 4 of the Convention:

> [p]ersons protected by the Convention are those who, at a given moment and in any manner whatsoever, find themselves, in case of a conflict or occupation, in the hands of a Party to the conflict or Occupying Power of which they are not nationals.[95]

Pictet's commentary on this Convention may appear to confirm that those who are not classified as POWs must be viewed as civilians when it refers to:

> a general principle which is embodied in all four Geneva Conventions of 1949. Every person in enemy hands must have some status under international law: he is either a prisoner of war and, as such, covered by the Third Convention, a civilian covered by the Fourth Convention, or again, a member of the medical personnel of the armed forces who is covered by the First Convention. There is no 'intermediate status'; nobody in enemy hands can be outside the law.[96]

Further ammunition for this view can be found in Article 50 of 1977 Geneva Protocol I. However, the view is open to several objections that are rooted in the terms of relevant treaties. *(1)* It is in tension with the specific terms of Article 4 of the 1949 Geneva Convention IV, which excludes from the Convention's protection certain persons, namely nationals of neutral and co-belligerent states; and it is likewise in tension with Pictet's statement that the Convention is basically about "on the one hand, persons of enemy nationality living in the territory of a belligerent State, and on the other, the

---

95. 1949 Geneva Convention IV, Article 4, first paragraph. For a strong assertion that enemy combatants, if denied POW status, must be considered as civilians, see Hans-Peter Gasser, 'Acts of Terror, "Terrorism" and International Humanitarian Law,' *International Review of the Red Cross*, vol. 84, no. 847, September 2002, at p. 568. He emphasizes that "civilian detainees suspected of having committed a serious crime can and must be put on trial."
96. International Committee of the Red Cross, 4 GENEVA CONVENTION RELATIVE TO THE PROTECTION OF CIVILIAN PERSONS IN TIME OF WAR TREATMENT OF PRISONERS OF WAR, COMMENTARY 51 (Jean S. Pictet ed. 1960) [hereinafter Commentary IV].

inhabitants of occupied territories."⁹⁷ *(2)* The four 1949 Geneva Conventions, Common Article 3, acknowledge that in civil wars detainees may have a different status from that of POW or civilian. *(3)* The 1977 Geneva Protocol I, Articles 45 and 75, acknowledges that even in international armed conflicts certain detainees may have a status that is distinct from those of POWs and civilians under the 1949 Geneva Conventions III and IV. *(4)* It risks eroding the key distinction between combatants and civilians that is fundamental to the laws of war, and is reflected in the 1977 Geneva Protocol I, Article 48.

The fact that certain detainees taken in the "war on terror" may be denied status as either a POW or a civilian does not mean that they have no legal rights. The provisions of Common Article 3 of the 1949 Geneva Conventions, although not specific to this category of person and formally applicable only in non-international armed conflict, may be viewed as minimum guarantees to be applied to all detainees.⁹⁸ In addition, Article 45 of 1977 Geneva Protocol I addresses the matter much more directly: "Any person who has taken part in hostilities, who is not entitled to prisoner-of-war status and who does not benefit from more favorable treatment . . . shall have the right at all times to the protection of Article 75 of this Protocol." The said Article 75 elaborates a range of fundamental guarantees that are intended to provide minimum rules of protection for all those who do not benefit from more favorable treatment under other rules.

Although neither the United States nor Afghanistan is a party to 1977 Geneva Protocol I, the rules in Articles 45 and 75 are relatively uncontroversial and it is long-standing US policy that they should be implemented.⁹⁹ However, US officials have repeatedly omitted to mention these articles in connection with the treatment of prisoners held in the "war on terror." The omission may reflect the US general sensitivity to the 1977 Geneva Protocol I or specific doubts about certain provisions of these articles. Nonetheless the failure to mention the articles appears odd: reference to Article 75 would have been an

---

97. *Id.* at 45.
98. On the broad scope of application of Common Article 3, see, e.g., Commentary IV, *supra* note 96, at 36, 40.
99. Articles 45 and 75 are among the many articles of GP I (*supra* note 9) that the United States views as "either legally binding as customary international law or acceptable practice though not legally binding." *See* OPLAW HANDBOOK, *supra* note 15, at 11.

obvious way of indicating that the treatment of the detainees was still within an international legal framework.[100]

After the status and treatment of prisoners taken in Afghanistan became urgent in November 2001, public statements of the US government were consistent and clear on one point. By referring to these prisoners generally as "battlefield detainees" and "unlawful combatants" the United States signalled its unwillingness to classify al Qaeda and Taliban prisoners as POWs. However, it was slow to give detailed reasoning, and to indicate the principles to be followed in the handling of the detainees. On 11 January 2002, when asked whether the ICRC would have any access to the prisoners who had just been taken to the US naval base at Guantanamo Bay in Cuba, Rumsfeld stated:

> I think that we're in the process of sorting through precisely the right way to handle them, and they will be handled in the right way. They will be handled not as prisoners of war, because they're not, but as unlawful combatants. The, as I understand it, technically unlawful combatants do not have any rights under the Geneva Convention. We have indicated that we do plan to, for the most part, treat them in a manner that is reasonably consistent with the Geneva Conventions, to the extent they are appropriate, and that is exactly what we have been doing.[101]

In the following weeks there were numerous expressions of concern in the United States and internationally about the status and treatment of detainees, and about the risk that US conduct would lead to a global weakening of the POW regime.[102] There were also intense disagreements within the US administration.[103] The situation was made worse by the Pentagon's seemingly inept issuance on 19 January 2002 of a photograph showing bound and shackled prisoners, heads and eyes covered, kneeling before US soldiers at Guantanamo. The photographs, which showed a transitional processing stage during the prisoners' arrival, became a misleading symbol of how the Guantanamo camp was being operated.

---

100. One of the few US publications to note the potential applicability and value of Article 75 was by Lee A. Casey, David Rivkin and Darin R. Bartram. See Casey et al., *Detention and Treatment of Combatants in the War on Terrorism* (Fed. Soc. L. & Pub. Pol. Studies, 2002). This article was published in early 2002, before the White House announcement of 7 February.
101. Secretary of Defense Donald Rumsfeld, DOD News Briefing (Jan. 11, 2002), *available at* http://www.defenselink.mil/news/Jan2002/t01112002_t0111sd.html (Nov. 14, 2002).
102. *See, e.g.,* Steven Erlanger, *Europeans Take Aim at U.S. on Detainees*, INT'L HERALD TRIBUNE, Jan. 24, 2002, at 4.
103. *See* Thom Shanker and Katharine Q. Seelye, *Behind-the-Scenes Clash Led Bush to Reverse Himself on Applying Geneva Conventions*, N.Y. TIMES, Feb. 22, 2002, at A12.

Certain conciliatory gestures were made by the US administration. International Committee of the Red Cross officials started interviewing detainees at Guantanamo on 18 January 2002, and were able to establish a permanent presence there. Rumsfeld's above-quoted suggestion that unlawful combatants have no rights under the Geneva Convention was modified when, on 22 January, he recognized that "under the Geneva Convention, an unlawful combatant is entitled to humane treatment."[104] On 7 February, the White House, in the first major policy statement on the issue, announced:

> [t]he United States is treating and will continue to treat all of the individuals detained at Guantanamo humanely and, to the extent appropriate and consistent with military necessity, in a manner consistent with the principles of the Third Geneva Convention of 1949.
>
> The President has determined that the Geneva Convention applies to the Taliban detainees, but not to the al Qaeda detainees.
>
> Al Qaeda is not a state party to the Geneva Convention; it is a foreign terrorist group. As such, its members are not entitled to POW status.
>
> Although we never recognized the Taliban as the legitimate Afghan government, Afghanistan is a party to the Convention, and the President has determined that the Taliban are covered by the Convention. Under the terms of the Geneva Convention, however, the Taliban detainees do not qualify as POWs.
>
> Therefore, neither the Taliban nor al Qaeda detainees are entitled to POW status.
>
> Even though the detainees are not entitled to POW privileges, they will be provided with many POW privileges as a matter of policy.[105]

The Fact Sheet, while containing numerous detailed assurances about the treatment of the detainees at Guantanamo, indicated that they would not receive certain specific privileges afforded to POWs by the Geneva Convention III, including:

---

104. Secretary of Defense Donald Rumsfeld, DOD News Briefing, (Jan. 22, 2002), *available at* http://www.defenselink.mil/news/Jan2002/t01222002_t0122sd.html (Nov. 14, 2002).
105. Office of the White House Press Secretary, *Fact Sheet: Status of Detainees at Guantanamo* (Feb. 7, 2002), *available at* http://www.whitehouse.gov/news/releases/2002/02/20020207-13.html (Nov. 14, 2002).

- access to a canteen to purchase food, soap and tobacco
- a monthly advance of pay
- the ability to have and consult personal financial accounts
- the ability to receive scientific equipment, musical instruments, or sports outfits.[106]

This United States refusal to grant these particular privileges was justified in terms of the security risk posed by many detainees at Guantanamo to their guards and to each other. A specific indication of this kind can be compatible with an overall approach of respect for a legal regime, and can also contribute to change in that regime. The refusal of these privileges caused no outcry, and parts of the 7 February statement reassured international opinion.

However, the earlier part of the statement was incoherent in certain respects. The recognition that the Geneva Convention III did apply to the Taliban, followed by the blanket statement that the Taliban did not qualify as POWs, had the confusing appearance of simultaneous admission and retraction. In his accompanying statement, the White House Press Secretary indicated the reason why the Taliban detainees failed to qualify as POWs:

> [t]o qualify as POWs under Article 4, al Qaeda and Taliban detainees would have to have satisfied four conditions. They would have to be part of a military hierarchy; they would have to have worn uniforms or other distinctive signs visible at a distance; they would have to have carried arms openly; and they would have to have conducted their military operations in accordance with the laws and customs of war.
>
> The Taliban have not effectively distinguished themselves from the civilian population of Afghanistan. Moreover, they have not conducted their operations in accordance with the laws and customs of war. Instead, they have knowingly adopted and provided support to the unlawful terrorist objectives of the al Qaeda.
>
> Al Qaeda is an international terrorist group and cannot be considered a state party to the Geneva Convention. Its members, therefore, are not covered by the Geneva Convention, and are not entitled to POW status under the treaty.[107]

---

106. *Id.* at 2. The privileges cited are outlined in GC III, *supra* note 5, arts. 28, 60, 64–5 and 72.
107. White House Press Secretary Ari Fleischer, Press Briefing at the White House (Feb. 7, 2002), at 1–2, *available at* Lexis, Federal News Service (Jan. 6, 2003).

The argument about the Taliban appears to assume that the four conditions which are listed in Article 4(A)(2) specifically in respect of members of "other militias" and resistance movements must necessarily apply to the Taliban; and it then proceeds to interpret the four conditions in such a way that support for "unlawful terrorist objectives" becomes one basis for denial of POW status. As for the al Qaeda detainees, although certain of the stated reasons for not applying the Convention to them are well founded, the particular argument that because al Qaeda is not a party to the Convention it cannot benefit from it is far from correct. There was a curiously legalistic streak in an approach which put such emphasis on the purported distinction between the Taliban and al Qaeda detainees yet saw no practical consequences: "No distinction will be made in the good treatment given to the al-Qaida or the Taliban."[108] A striking feature of the statement is its avoidance of any hint of doubt about status: none of the detainees, even the Taliban ones, could possibly qualify as POWs. In keeping with this, nothing was said about the tribunals provided for in Article 5 of 1949 Geneva Convention III and Article 45 of 1977 Geneva Protocol I. A further notable omission was the absence of reference to Article 75 of the 1977 Protocol. Despite certain merits, the US statement was less technically proficient, and less reassuring, than it could have been. Expressions of international concern regarding the status and treatment of detainees in Guantanamo and elsewhere continued.

In response to the White House statement of 7 February, the ICRC Press Office in Geneva maintained its position that "people in a situation of international conflict are considered to be prisoners of war unless a competent tribunal decides otherwise."[109] The ICRC emphasis on POW status contrasted with its statements in respect of prisoners in the wars in the former Yugoslavia in 1991–5: in these wars, which were partly internal but also had an international dimension, the ICRC generally avoided status questions, and variously used such terms as "captured combatants," "prisoners" and "detainees."[110] The ICRC statement in respect of prisoners taken in Afghanistan is arguably in accord with Article 45 of 1977 Geneva Protocol I, but went well beyond Article 5

---

108. *Id.* at 3.
109. *See* ICRC, Press Release, Geneva Convention of Prisoners of War (Feb. 9, 2002), *available at* http://www.icrc.org/ (Nov. 14, 2002).
110. *See* ICRC Compilation of Press Releases and Communications to the Press by the ICRC: Former Yugoslavia, Federal Republic of Yugoslavia, Republic of Croatia, Republic of Bosnia and Herzegovina, 2 July 1991 – 20 March 1998 (1998) (bound collection of photocopied texts on file with author).

of 1949 Geneva Convention III, which makes the more modest stipulation that *in cases of doubt* prisoners shall be *treated as* POWs. Presumably, there could be cases in which there is no doubt in the first place. In some statements ICRC press spokesmen went so far as to deny the existence of a legal category of unprivileged or illegal combatant. Since the category of unprivileged belligerent has a long history, is implicit in the criteria for POW status in 1949 Geneva Convention III, and is explicit in Article 45 of 1977 Geneva Protocol I, these statements were not well founded and they were modified in the course of 2002. The same basic stance, with the same weaknesses, was taken by Amnesty International in London and Human Rights Watch in New York.[111] These positions may have reinforced the reservations of the US administration about the advice they were receiving from outside bodies.

The fundamental US position that many of the detainees taken in Afghanistan should not be accorded the status of POWs appears to have been based on three main practical considerations: the first related to conditions of detention of prisoners, the second to their release, and the third to the conduct of judicial proceedings.

On conditions of detention, a main concern was that 1949 Geneva Convention III famously states that POWs are only obliged to give names, rank, date of birth and serial number.[112] The United States was anxious to obtain considerably more information from the detainees. There is nothing in the Convention that precludes questioning on other issues and whether a different classification actually improves the prospects of securing accurate information is debatable. The United States also wished to keep the detainees more segregated from each other, and with less access to means of committing harm, than full observance of all the POW Convention's articles would provide.

---

111. *See, e.g.*, Kenneth Roth, Executive Director of Human Rights Watch, *Bush Policy Endangers American and Allied Troops*, INT'L HERALD TRIBUNE, Mar. 5, 2002, at 7. *See also* Amnesty International Memorandum to US Government on the Rights of People in US Custody in Afghanistan and Guantanamo Bay (Apr. 15, 2002), *available at* http://www.amnesty.org.uk/ (Nov. 14, 2002).

112. GC III, *supra* note 5, art. 17. This rule does not mean that a POW cannot be asked other questions, nor does it prohibit the POW from providing other information. In March 2002, Jakob Kellenberger, President of ICRC, pointed out that there is nothing in humanitarian law to stop a prisoner being questioned, but that he could not be forced to answer. "If he does not want to answer, that is his right. Under any system, you cannot do anything to people to make them speak. It is a non-issue." Jakob Kellenberger, *ICRC Rejects Talk of Geneva Conventions Review*, Reuters-Geneva (Mar. 21, 2002).

As regards release of prisoners, Geneva Convention III codifies a practice that is normally pursued after a war—releasing and repatriating POWs. Any such release of all the detainees from the "war on terror" would pose three problems. First, there may not be a clear end of hostilities: while the war in Afghanistan may be concluded at a definite date, it may be decades before the United States or other states can declare that the "war on terror" is over. Second, unlike POWs in a "normal" inter-state war, some of the prisoners concerned might continue to be extremely dangerous after release, given their training, their motivation to commit acts of terrorism, and lack of governmental control over them. Third, their countries of origin might refuse to accept them back, except perhaps as prisoners.

Judicial proceedings
As regards judicial proceedings in respect of pre-capture offenses, from early on in the war the United States reportedly intended to prosecute a number of al Qaeda and Taliban leaders, including Osama bin Laden if captured. However, it is unclear that the point of detaining the prisoners in Guantanamo is to try them.[113] Insofar as the possibility of trials is envisaged, the United States appears reluctant to pursue the procedure laid down in Geneva Convention III, which specifies that any sentence of a POW must be "by the same courts according to the same procedure as in the case of members of the armed forces of the Detaining Power."[114] If, following this provision, cases were handled through the normal US military courts, there could be problems, especially regarding the normal US military procedures for appeals.[115] Moreover, if a pre-capture offense was of a type that would result in members of the armed forces of the detaining power appearing before a civil court, then it is implicit in the above-quoted terms of the Convention that a POW could appear before a civil

---

113. In a thorough and perceptive account of Camp Delta at Guantanamo datelined 10 October 2002, Joseph Lelyveld suggests that it is a holding camp for detainees who are not likely to be released or tried soon, and many of whom may be relatively minor figures who were in the wrong place at the wrong time. Joseph Lelyveld, *In Guantanamo*, 17 N.Y. REV. OF BOOKS (Nov. 7, 2002), at 62–68, *available at* http://www.nybooks.com/articles/15806 (Nov. 30, 2002).

114. GC III, *supra* note 5, at art. 102. This appears to be the relevant article of the Convention so far as trials for crimes committed before capture are concerned. (The distinct subject of POW discipline issues is addressed in Article 82.) Commentary III, *supra* note 86, at 406 and 470-1. Unfortunately, Pictet fails to consider pre-capture crimes other than war crimes.

115. The normal appeal procedure for US armed forces is through the appellate court of each service, then through the US Court of Appeals for the Armed Forces, and then on to the US Supreme Court. *See* MANUAL FOR COURTS-MARTIAL, UNITED STATES, RULES FOR COURT MARTIAL 1203–1205 (2000).

court. Such standard procedures, US officials feared, could provide opportunities for al Qaeda suspects and their lawyers to prolong legal processes and attract publicity. There was also concern that in cases involving defendants with no documents and no willingness to collaborate with any of the procedures, and where evidence might be largely based on intelligence sources, it could be difficult to provide evidence that met high standards of admissibility, and equally high standards of proof of direct personal involvement in terrorist activities. Further, al Qaeda might learn valuable information from evidence in open court, for example about its vulnerability to intelligence gathering.

It was because of such fears about normal judicial procedures that the administration made provision for trial by military commissions. There are numerous precedents for such provision: for example, President Roosevelt's Proclamation of 2 July 1942, bluntly entitled "Denying Certain Enemies Access to the Courts of the United States."[116] In its decision of 31 July 1942 in the case of *Ex Parte Quirin* the US Supreme Court ruled in favor of the lawfulness of the Proclamation.[117] The current status of such legal precedent is beyond the scope of this survey. President Bush's Military Order of 13 November 2001 provides for the option of trying certain accused terrorists by military commissions operating under special rules. It applies only to non-US citizens. It specifies that individual terrorists, including members of al Qaeda, can be detained and tried "for violations of the laws of war and other applicable laws," and that the military commissions would not be bound by "the principles of law and the rules of evidence generally recognized in the trial of criminal cases in the United States district courts." It also contains some extremely brief provisions for humane conditions of detention, and provides for the Secretary of Defense to issue detailed regulations on such matters as the conduct of proceedings of the military commissions.[118]

President Bush's Military Order was the subject of considerable legal and political debate in the United States and elsewhere as to its constitutionality, practicability and advisability. The controversy about the military

---

116. Denying Certain Enemies Access to the Courts of the United States, Proclamation No. 2561, 7 Fed. Reg. 5,103 (Jul. 2, 1942). On this and other cases of US established military commissions, *see* CONGRESSIONAL RESEARCH SERVICE, TERRORISM AND THE LAW OF WAR: TRYING TERRORISTS AS WAR CRIMINALS BEFORE MILITARY COMMISSIONS 18–26, 46–48 (updated Dec. 11, 2001), *available at* http://www.fpc.state.gov/documents/organization/7951.pdf (Nov. 14, 2002).
117. Quirin, *supra* note 92, at 6.
118. Military Order of 13 November 2001 - Detention, Treatment and Trial of Certain Non-Citizens in the War Against Terrorism, secs. 1(e), 1(f), 3, 4(b), 4(c), 66 Fed. Reg. 57,833 (Nov. 16, 2001), *available at* http://frwebgate.access.gpo.gov/cgi-bin/multidb.cgi (Nov. 14, 2002).

commissions was part of a larger debate about which particular approach to the prosecution and trial of alleged terrorists should be pursued. Possibilities that were raised in public discussion included US federal courts, foreign national courts, a UN ad hoc international criminal tribunal, a coalition-based criminal tribunal, and a special Islamic court.[119]

The controversy about the proposed military commissions abated somewhat over time. On 30 November 2001, the President's Counsel offered several assurances, including that military commissions are one option, but not the only option.[120] On 21 March 2002 the Pentagon issued the long-promised detailed regulations on the conduct of proceedings of the projected military commissions, the terms of which went some way to meet the expressions of concern regarding President Bush's Military Order of the previous November.[121] As far as the laws of war are concerned, a key issue (not explicitly addressed in the Pentagon document) is whether the provisions regarding the trial procedure conform with the ten recognized principles of regular judicial procedure outlined in 1977 Geneva Protocol I, Article 75, which relates to persons not entitled to POW status. The Pentagon's detailed regulations appear to conform with almost all these principles apart, arguably, from the final one, which is that "a convicted person shall be advised on conviction of his judicial and other remedies and of the time-limits within which they may be exercised."[122]

A problem regarding the prisoners held by the United States is the uncertainty regarding whether and when they will be tried, and whether they will be held indefinitely or released. Nearly 600 suspects of many different nationalities are held at Guantanamo, but at the time of this writing, there is no sign of

---

119. For a useful exploration of these and other possibilities, see DAVID SCHEFFER, OPTIONS FOR PROSECUTING INTERNATIONAL TERRORISTS (US Institute of Peace, Nov. 14, 2001).

120. President's Counsel Alberto Gonzalez, Address to American Bar Association Meeting, (Nov. 30, 2001) cited in AM. SOC. INT'L L. NEWSLETTER, at 12 (Nov–Dec 2001).

121. DOD Military Commission Order No.1 - Procedures for Trials by Military Commissions of Certain Non-United States Citizens In the War Against Terrorism (Mar. 21, 2002), available at http://www.defenselink.mil/news/Mar2002/d20020321ord.pdf (Nov. 14, 2002) [hereinafter DOD Military Commission]. For a response claiming that these procedures, if not per se violative of international law, are highly problematic, see Jordan J. Paust, Antiterrorism Military Commissions: The Ad Hoc DOD Rules of Procedure Courting Illegality, 23 MICH J. INT'L L. 677 (Spring 2002).

122. GP I, supra note 9, at art. 75(4)(j). The Pentagon's detailed regulations provide for a post-trial Review Panel to which the defense can make written submissions, not for a full-blown appeal procedure. A further reservation about the regulations concerns the role of the defense counsel, who would be excluded with the accused from closed sessions, at which only an "assigned" defense counsel would be present who would be forbidden to speak with the co-counsel or the accused. See DOD Military Commission, supra note 119, at 8, 14.

the military commissions becoming operational. The United States has indicated that the judicial process may have to wait until after "the war on terror is won," at which distant point the detainees may be tried or released.[123] Their indefinite detention, without any charge or trial, would violate fundamental standards of human rights and be hard to justify. Yet when the main problem with potential suicide bombers is not what they have done, but what they might do in the future, the resort to judicial procedures does not address the essence of the problem.

Further Development of the Law

The phenomena of global terrorism and the response thereto, while by no means wholly new, pose many challenges to existing legal provisions, from matters as large as the meaning of "armed conflict" to those as detailed as the conditions of detention. Thus it is not surprising that there were several suggestions that the existing laws of war might need to be revised, updated, supplemented or reinterpreted to take into account new forms of conflict. The case for such reconsideration, which basically arose in connection with the war in Afghanistan and the many related issues, may have been reinforced by events elsewhere, especially the numerous cases of Palestinian suicide bombings in 2001–2. In February 2002, following the furor over the detainees at Guantanamo, Pierre-Richard Prosper, the US Ambassador-at-Large for War Crimes Issues, stated: "[t]he war on terror is a new type of war not envisioned when the Geneva Conventions were negotiated and signed."[124] He also said at that time: "[w]e should look at all international documents to see whether they are compatible with this moment in history."[125]

Such suggestions that the law might need to be revised are vulnerable to four obvious lines of criticism. *(1)* In several statements on the matter, Ambassador Prosper gave little indication of what particular revisions might be made to the 1949 Geneva Conventions. *(2)* There was naturally a suspicion in certain humanitarian organizations that suggestions that existing law was out of date or irrelevant to the terrorist problem might be a way of trying to evade

---

123. War Crimes at Large Ambassador Richard Prosper Address in London (Sep. 20, 2002) *cited in* Owen Boycott, *Guantanamo Britons Still a Threat, says US*, THE GUARDIAN, Sep. 21, 2002, at 23.
124. War Crimes at Large Ambassador Richard Prosper Address at the Royal Institute of International Affairs in London (Feb. 20, 2002).
125. Kim Sengupta and Andrew Buncombe, *Change Geneva Convention Rules, Says Bush Envoy Rules of Warfare Legal Foundation for the Red Cross has Helped Maintain Humanity and Dignity in Combat for 140 Years*, THE INDEPENDENT, Feb. 22, 2002, at 1–2.

obligations to implement existing law fully. (3) Proponents of change failed to mention that the negotiators at Geneva in 1949 had addressed a closely related issue, namely the activities of resistance movements during the Second World War, and that Articles 4 and 5 of the Geneva Convention III are among the provisions that already reflect this. (4) There was also a failure to mention in this context the revisions that had already been made to the 1949 Geneva Conventions. Proponents of change were notably reluctant to mention even the title of 1977 Geneva Protocol I although it constitutes the most important actual updating of the 1949 conventions. It contains the clearest prohibitions in the laws of war of certain actions in which many terrorist movements engage, such as attacks on civilians. It also introduces some constructive provisions that are germane to the "war on terror." Such provisions that the United States has in principle accepted include those on targeting, and on the treatment of detainees who do not qualify as POWs.

Although such criticisms have considerable force, the fact is that the law is bound to evolve in response to the new problems of a new age. Much of that evolution may take the form, not of new conventions, but rather of evolving state practice some of which may have, or acquire, the status of customary law. However, some of the legal evolution may involve international conferences.

Of the many issues related to the "war on terror" that could come up in any exploratory process with a view to further change in the law, five of the candidates for consideration could be: *(a)* the conditions of application of the laws of war; *(b)* the classification and treatment of detainees; *(c)* legitimate means of responding to suicide bombers who by definition cannot be deterred by normal means, and whether reprisals can ever be justified in this context; *(d)* the interpretation of the rules on targeting in the light of the experience of recent wars in Afghanistan and elsewhere; and *(e)* remnants of war, a problem that includes but is by no means restricted to cluster bombs, and is in any case the subject of separate negotiation in a UN framework in Geneva.

Partly because of the salience of such issues, there continued to be some demand for an exploration of how the law relates to certain aspects of contemporary conflicts. In September 2002 the Swiss Foreign Ministry announced that it "wishes to support an informal process and provide a space for debate on the reaffirmation and development of international humanitarian law in light of the new and evolving realities of contemporary conflict situations." Representatives of certain governments and international bodies, as well as independent experts, were to be invited to contribute to an informal meeting to be held in January 2003. Cautiously, the Swiss note announcing this stated that one of the purposes of the exercise was "if necessary, the consideration of the development of new rules." The potential topics listed were at this stage general and imprecise.[126]

Conclusions

There are ample grounds for questioning whether military operations involving action against terrorists constitute either a new, or a wholly distinct, category of war. The coalition operations in Afghanistan, and the larger war against terrorism of which they are a part, are not completely unlike earlier wars. Many forms of military action and issues raised are similar to those in previous military operations, and concern issues already addressed by the laws of war.

Events in Afghanistan have confirmed that there are particular difficulties in applying the laws of war to counter-terrorist operations. A war that has as a purpose the pursuit of people deemed to be criminals involves many awkward issues for which the existing laws of war are not a perfect fit. In addition, the use of local forces as proxies (a common feature in counter-terrorist wars) risks creating a situation in which major powers fail to exercise responsible control over their local agents, whose commitment to the laws of war may be slight. More fundamentally, any war against a grand abstraction, as the "war on terror" undoubtedly is, risks creating a mentality in which adversaries are seen as dehumanized, and the cosmic importance of the struggle may be thought to outweigh mundane legal or humanitarian considerations.

However, treating, or appearing to treat, the law in a cavalier manner risks creating new problems. If a major power is perceived as ignoring certain basic norms, this may have a negative effect within a coalition, or on enemies. It may involve severe risks to any of its own nationals who may be taken prisoner. It may also affect the conduct of other states in other conflicts. In that wider sense, the principle of reciprocity in the observance of law retains its value.

In particular, the United States' handling of questions relating to the treatment and status of prisoners has caused widespread concern and criticism. As regards those under Northern Alliance control, practical arrangements, around the time of the rebellion at Mazar -e-Sharif and also subsequently, were inadequate. More generally, although many key US positions were defensible, especially that certain prisoners did not qualify for POW status, aspects of US policy and procedures were poorly presented, and in some cases did not appear to be fully thought-out. The prisoner issue—always sensitive

---

126. *See* Diplomatic Note, Switzerland-US, Sep. 13, 2002. *See also* Unknown Author, *Swiss Call a Meeting to Re-examine the Geneva Conventions,* N.Y. TIMES, Oct. 6, 2002, at sec. 1, 15.

anyway—was especially significant in this war: if the coalition were perceived to have treated prisoners inhumanely, or to have regarded their status and treatment as being in an international legal limbo, there would be risks of a general weakening of the prisoner regime, including for any coalition personnel taken prisoner in the ongoing war on terrorism. The handling of this issue was a potential threat to coalition unity. The controversies over the prisoner question had a special resonance because of the concern of other countries that the United States had been moving towards unilateralism generally, on a wide range of matters. In this perspective, fairly or unfairly, the United States reluctance to accept the full application of 1949 Geneva Convention III to those particular prisoners was seen as one more example of a selective approach to international law.

In the course of the first year of its "war on terror," and especially in the early handling of prisoner issues in Afghanistan and at Guantanamo, the Bush Administration's expression of policies on certain laws-of-war issues was at times hesitant and unskillful. It would be easy to attribute this to the administration's alleged general ideological hostility towards international agreements. However, some other explanations may carry more weight. The United States had a record of concern stretching back decades about the ways in which international humanitarian law has been developing, especially as regards terrorism, and also in regard to the rules on what is a legitimate target. The administration was right that certain aspects of the law, including aspects of the POW regime, were not appropriate for the treatment of alleged terrorists. Part of the explanation of the administration's failure to handle the particular question of the status of detainees effectively may lie quite simply in the fact that it was proceeding in a reactive manner. In addition, there appears to have been insufficient consultation with the military's own legal specialists.

Whatever the defects of the Bush Administration's response, the professionalism of the US armed forces, coupled with the effect of criticism within and beyond the United States, led to policy and practice on the prisoner issues evolving in a generally sensible direction. This evolution has been ad hoc and incomplete. In general, there have been no major public doctrinal statements from the US government on how the laws of war apply to the "war on terror"—perhaps because the application of those laws can indeed be complicated and policy-makers do not wish to foreclose options.

This war occasioned a greater degree of tension between the United States on the one hand, and international humanitarian and human rights bodies on the other, than any of the wars of the post-Cold War period. The handling of certain laws-of-war issues by the ICRC and various other humanitarian organizations left much to be desired. It was natural that they should be nervous about the US administration's view of international humanitarian law and that they should press for full implementation of that law, especially in relation to prisoners. However, they were on legally dubious ground when they pressed on the United States to view detainees as being entitled to be POWs, and in their insistence that if they were not given POW status then they must be classified as civilians. They missed a major opportunity to point out publicly the relevance of certain provisions of 1977 Protocol I to persons not entitled to POW status. It was odd and out of character for the ICRC to deny the applicability of the law governing international armed conflict to certain aspects of the Afghan conflict including the phase from June 2002 onwards. Overall, the stance of such bodies, while leading to certain useful clarifications of US policy, may also have had the regrettable effect of reinforcing US concerns (well publicized in debates about the International Criminal Court) about zealous international lawyers standing in unsympathetic judgement on the actions of US forces.

Returning to the four questions set out at the beginning of this survey, the foregoing account suggests these responses:

First, according to a strict interpretation of their terms, the main treaties relating to the conduct of international armed conflict are formally and fully applicable to counter-terrorist military operations only when those operations have an inter-state character. Where counter-terrorist operations are simply part of a civil war, the parties must apply, as a minimum, the rules applicable to civil wars. Where operations are simply part of a state's policing, and not part of an armed conflict such as to bring the laws of war into play, the laws of war are not formally in force.

Second, in counter-terrorist military operations, certain phases and situations may well be different from what was envisaged in the scope of application and other provisions of the main treaties on the laws of war. They may differ from the provisions for both international and non-international armed conflict. Recognizing that there are difficulties in applying international rules in the special circumstances of counter-terrorist war, the attempt can and should nevertheless be made to apply the law to the maximum extent possible. At the very least, it has considerable value as a blueprint or template that the principles embodied in the laws of war should be applied in a wide variety of situations. This conclusion is reinforced by decisions of commissions of inquiry, certain resolutions of the UN Security Council, some doctrine and practice of states (including the United States), and considerations of prudence. In the "war on terror," while there have been shortcomings in the interpretation and application of existing law by governments and by humanitarian organizations, much of what has been done has been within the framework of the law and has confirmed its relevance.

Third, although the great majority of prisoners taken in war are viewed as qualifying for POW status, in a counter-terrorist war, as in other armed conflicts, there are likely to be individuals and even whole classes of prisoners who do not meet the treaty-defined criteria for such status. A procedure outlined in the 1949 POW Convention and in US military manuals is that in case of doubt about their status such people should be accorded the treatment, but not the status, of a POW until a tribunal convened by the captor determines the status to which the individual is entitled. However, in a struggle involving an organization that plainly does not meet the criteria (and especially where, as with al Qaeda, it is not in any sense a state) it may be reasonable to proclaim that captured members cannot be considered for POW status. In cases where it is determined that certain detainees are not POWs, they may be considered to be "unlawful combatants." It is doubtful whether such persons should be classified as "civilians." However, there are certain fundamental rules applicable to their treatment, including those outlined in Article 75 of 1977 Geneva Protocol I; and there is a tradition of applying basic norms of the POW regime. Any prisoner, whether classified as a POW or not, can be tried for offenses, including those against international law.

Fourth, there is a case for consideration of further revision of the existing law. Suggestions that the existing laws of war are generally out of date in the face of the terrorist challenge are wide of the mark. However imperfect, the law has played, and will continue to play, an important part in influencing the conduct of the "war on terror." There has neither been a serious suggestion that the existing legal framework should be abandoned, nor substantial proposals for an alternative set of rules. However, some modest evolutionary changes in the law can be envisaged, for example regarding conditions of application, the classification and treatment of detainees, the difficult problem of how to respond to suicide bombers, the problems of targeting, and possible new rules regarding remnants of war. The application of the law to non-international armed conflicts is another area in which there has been much development since 1990 and more may be anticipated. Some changes in some of these areas may require a formal negotiating process. Some, however, may be achieved—indeed, may have been achieved—by the practice of states and international bodies, including through explicit and internationally accepted derogations from particular rules that are manifestly inappropriate to the circumstances at hand; and also through the application of rules in situations significantly different from inter-state war.

IX

Panel II
Commentary—Jus in Bello

Charles Garraway[1]

All new warfare operates to stress existing law. This is true for every war and every conflict occurring over the last several hundred years. The new type of warfare involved in "the war on terrorism" is no exception. Caution should be taken, however, not to throw out the existing regime but instead we should study and analyze these stresses for such stresses are not necessarily fatal.

There is always a danger, amply demonstrated over the last few months, of decisions being taken and then followed by legal justifications. This in itself creates further dangers as it may lead to conflicting reinterpretations of existing law. For example, we have discussed the differences between Europe and the United States. However, despite these differences, the end result is often exactly the same. The departing point is in how European countries arrive at their conclusions since they have different drivers, different legal regimes (both national and international), different cultures, and different populations. It follows occasionally then, that the European legal justifications for an action may be quite different from that of the United States. This of course

---

1. Colonel Charles Garraway is currently serving in the Ministry of Defence of the United Kingdom, advising on issues of international law.

itself creates some danger as there are then two, or more competing legal justifications. Undoubtedly, states on both sides of the Atlantic would benefit from more consultation and coordination before particular positions are adopted.

I agree with Professor Dinstein that existing law is adequate for the issues presented today. I also agree that the principle of distinction is fundamental and absolutely vital when determining combatant status. However, I do not agree with Professor Dinstein on everything. The law of armed conflict is designed to have a greater degree of flexibility than national law because law, in many respects, always focuses on the last conflict. Accordingly, there is a requirement for built in flexibility so that we can apply the law designed for the last conflict to the new situation.

The definition of armed forces has for generations been based on traditional forms of armies. I am talking here about regular armed forces. In some parts of the world today though, we are returning almost to the Middle Ages and seeing feudal types of armed forces with warlords raising their own forces in much the same way as the barons did against King John. Accordingly, the notion of a structured, disciplined armed force is not reflected in the militaries of some states today. The question regarding these forces then becomes one of status and treatment under the law of armed conflict.

Should these forces be treated as militias and therefore be defined as combatants under the Hauge Regulations, Geneva Conventions, and their Protocols or as something else? Must we re-interpret what is meant by the term "armed forces?" Professor Dinstein chooses a tried and true method in determining that the Taliban are not members of the armed forces of a high contracting party to the Geneva Conventions and are therefore not entitled to the protections and privileges of combatancy. I, however, believe that there is grave danger in the position that has been taken that no Taliban members are entitled to prisoner of war status once captured as this position may rebound on the developed countries of the world in future conflicts. It seems somewhat strange to have an armed conflict in which one side, by definition, is made up entirely of "unprivileged belligerents."

Regarding the presentation of Professor Adam Roberts, I agree that simply because a war is started by a state, that state does not become responsible for everything occurring during the course of the war. I further agree that force applied in the current "war on terror" must be proportionate in nature. Proportionate here is used in a different context to the way it is used when discussing pure jus in bello concepts of course.

Terrorism occupies the zone between criminal law and the law of armed conflict. Sometimes terrorism is solely within one or the other of these realms. However, the current situation is one where substantial overlap exists between the two competing and somewhat conflicting legal regimes. When such an overlap exists, there is also the very real danger of gaps in coverage between the two systems.

An ad hoc approach to interpreting treaty obligations is one method demonstrated lately. The danger with such an approach is that your standing to protest the treatment of your own service members is weakened when you do not apply the Geneva Conventions to those who seem to fall within them. A perfect example of this is the US position on the "detainees" held in Guantanamo Bay, Cuba. As we all know, prisoners of war are subject to the rules and regulations of the armed forces of the detaining party. This would ordinarily mean trial by courts-martial. However, in the same way that service personnel cannot ordinarily be tried by military courts for pre-enlistment offences, so prisoners of war will not be subject to court-martial jurisdiction for offences prior to their capture.[2] This principle seems to force states back to their civil courts for jurisdiction over detainees. However, the United States has clearly stated that it will use military commissions and not prosecutions in its federal courts. Using military commissions is entirely consistent with the law of armed conflict provided they apply to all who commit war crimes, of whatever nationality. It seems that this issue may have been misapprehended when the issue of the designation of Taliban members as prisoners of war or detainees initially surfaced.

Finally I would just like to quote from the US Joint Chiefs of Staff Standing Rules of Engagement, dated January 15th, 2000: "U.S. Forces will comply with the law of war during military operations involving armed conflict no matter how the conflict may be characterized under international law and will comply with its principles and spirit during all operations."[3] That is a simple and clear instruction to commanders and to soldiers. I think those instructions are sensible and that we move away from them at our own peril.

---

2. See *generally* Geneva Convention III Relative to the Treatment of Prisoners of War, Aug. 12, 1949, 6 U.S.T. 3316, T.I.A.S. No. 3364, 75 U.N.T.S. 135, Chap. III - Penal and Disciplinary Sanctions, *reprinted in* DOCUMENTS ON THE LAWS OF WAR (Adam Roberts and Richard Guelff eds., 3rd ed., 2000) at 243.
3. CHAIRMAN JOINT CHIEFS OF STAFF INSTR 3121.01A STANDING RULES OF ENGAGEMENT FOR U.S. FORCES, ENCLOSURE (A) A-9, (15 Jan 2000).

X

Panel II
Commentary—Jus in Bello

Leslie Green[1]

The first issue to be considered when examining the impact of the law of armed conflict on the war against terrorism is the nature of that war. Immediately after the September 11th attacks, President George W. Bush declared that we were now involved in a "war against terrorism—the first war of the twenty-first century."[2] Moreover, President Bush subsequently declared that those "who are not with us are against us," thus negating any possibility that those failing to see eye to eye with him could claim to be neutrals as would be the case if this were a traditional war.[3] Prima facie, the President's statement

---

1. Leslie Green is Professor Emeritus of International Law at the University of Alberta, Canada.
2. President George W. Bush, Remarks by The President Upon Returning to the White House (Sep. 16, 2001), *available at* http://www.whitehouse.gov/news/releases/2001/09/20010916-2.html, (Sep. 23, 2002).
3. President George W. Bush, Remarks by the President to the Employees of the Department of Labor (Oct. 4, 2001), *available at* http://www.whitehouse.gov/news/releases/2001/10/20011004-8.html (Sep. 23, 2002). Note that the concept of neutrality is markedly changed when dealing with a UN Security Council Resolution calling upon all member nations to use force to achieve a certain objective. In this instance, the traditional concept of neutrality does not apply.

implied that any state not supporting the United States would be considered an "enemy" of the United States.

A major difficulty with the President's approach is that the attacks of September 11th, organized by non-state actors, were not the acts of a state triggering the traditional notion of self-defense against an act of aggression or a breach of the peace as outlined in Article 51 of the UN Charter.[4] Traditionally, and in accordance with the normally understood rules of international law, war is an armed conflict conducted by the organized armed forces of two or more contesting states. After the events of September 11th, there was no opposing "state" upon which to declare "war." In other words, the President's statement that "we are at war" seemed more to be political rhetoric, possessing certain similarities to the language used in the past in relation to the "war against poverty" or the "war against drugs."

The fundamental difference in this case from these other "wars" though is the determination of the United States to resort to armed force and to pursue and destroy or bring to justice the offenders identified as members of the al Qaeda terrorist group led by Osama bin Laden. This group had its headquarters in Afghanistan, a state governed by a de facto administration known as the Taliban. The Taliban was not the actual government of Afghanistan but instead was a group in possession of much of the territory of Afghanistan. The only government of Afghanistan legitimately recognized by the UN was the Northern Alliance. In fact, the Taliban administration had achieved only minimal recognition as the government of the country, only gaining official recognition of such status by Pakistan and two other Muslim states.[5] Shortly after the United States began its operations, even those states recognizing the Taliban as the legitimate government of Afghanistan withdrew their recognition.[6]

When the Taliban authorities rejected a demand that they capture Osama bin Laden and his leading henchmen and hand them over to the United States for trial and punishment, the American authorities decided to engage

---

4. U.N. CHARTER art. 51.
5. The two other states recognizing the Taliban as the legitimate government of Afghanistan on September 11th were Saudi Arabia and the United Arab Emirates. Both Saudi Arabia and the United Arab Emirates severed ties with the Taliban very quickly after September 11th. Pakistan did not do so until November 22, 2001. See *Pakistan Shuts Down Taliban Embassy*, USA TODAY, Nov. 22, 2001, *available at* http://www.usatoday.com/news/attack/2001/11/22/taliban-embassy.htm#more (Sep. 23, 2002).
6. *Id.*
7. President George W. Bush, Presidential Address to the Nation (Oct. 7, 2001) (transcript *available at* http://www.whitehouse.gov/news/releases/2001/10/20011007-8.html) (Sep. 23, 2002).

in self-help, invading Afghanistan.[7] This action was undertaken without resort to the Security Council but did receive general international support from a variety of states, particularly after al Qaeda made it clear that their terror campaign was not necessarily restricted to American targets. Given that the United States decided to use force against not only al Qaeda but also the Taliban administration, it might have been presumed that the law of armed conflict regarding prisoners of war and the application of the principles of distinction and proportionality would come into play.

The attacks against the Pentagon and the World Trade Center were clear threats to the sovereignty and security of the United States. While it may be argued that the attack on the World Trade Center was primarily directed against private, non-governmental interests and thus not prima facie aimed at the state, this cannot be the case as regards the Pentagon. The attack on the Pentagon was clearly aimed at the very heart of American governmental processes, thus constituting a threat to the very existence of the state. Such an attack clearly entitled the United States to expect authorities of states in which the perpetrators or their supporters reside to cooperate in seeking them out. The failure of the Taliban administration to do so opened the way for the United States to engage in self-help. Such self-help, though, would be limited solely against al Qaeda bases and any Afghan organization clearly associated with al Qaeda or supporting al Qaeda. The authority to target the Taliban administration itself would require proof of a close relationship between the Taliban itself and al Qaeda.

At the same time that the United States was beginning its attacks, it was building a coalition of nations. Propaganda by al Qaeda and previous terrorist acts directed against US embassies as well as a US warship made it clear that the events of September 11th were part of a continuum. Intelligence reports suggested that similar attacks were likely to follow, making it easier for other states to support the US efforts. Such states based their efforts upon the principle of collective self-defense, including the right of preventive and even anticipatory self-defense. Within this coalition, however, some issues developed as to the application of the law of armed conflict to certain personnel.

While the United States never declared "war" as such, the bombing and subsequent land offensive by it and allies such as Canada and the United Kingdom amounted to an armed conflict within the terms of the Geneva

---

8. See Geneva Convention III Relative to the Treatment of Prisoners of War, Aug. 12, 1949, art. 2, 6 U.S.T. 3316, T.I.A.S. No. 3364, 75 U.N.T.S. 135 [hereinafter GC III] reprinted in DOCUMENTS ON THE LAWS OF WAR (Adam Roberts and Richard Guelff eds., 3rd ed., 2000) at 243 [hereinafter DOCUMENTS ON THE LAWS OF WAR].

Conventions of 1949.[8] This seems particularly to be the case regarding Taliban members and installations under the control of the Taliban. Once operations evolved to the point that they were directed at al Qaeda and at the replacement of the Taliban with the Northern Alliance, the Geneva Conventions became relevant. Despite the absence of a declaration of war, the actual fact of conflict was enough to invoke the fundamental principles of the law of armed conflict, particularly those of proportionality and distinction.

By Article 2, common to all four Conventions:

> the present Convention shall apply to all cases of declared war *or of any other armed conflict which may arise between two or more of the High Contracting Parties even if the state of war is not recognized by one of them. The Conventions shall also apply to all cases of total or partial occupation of the territory of a High Contracting Party,* even if the said occupation meets with no resistance. Although one of the Powers in conflict may not be a party to the present Convention, the Powers who are parties thereto shall remain bound by it in their mutual relations.[9]

In accordance with the normal law concerning treaties, the Taliban administration would be bound in the same way as the Northern Alliance, against which it would be considered a rebel authority, with its forces entitled to the same rights and subject to the same duties as the forces of the legitimate Afghan government, the Northern Alliance. It might have been expected that allies of the legally recognized authority capturing Taliban personnel would hand such captives over to the Northern Alliance for trial or detention, as was the customary practice of the United States in its participation in hostilities on behalf of the Republic of Vietnam. In this case, however, the United States treated all captives, whether supporters of the Taliban or al Qaeda, as potential terrorists.

This ignored the fact that while the Taliban authorities might, due to their failure to cooperate in seeking out al Qaeda personnel, constitute a legitimate target, it does not follow that every member of the Taliban forces falls within the same category. Ample evidence exists to indicate that many of the rank and file Taliban were orthodox, if not fundamentalist, followers of Islam who had taken up arms only against the Northern Alliance.

As a consequence of this policy, the United States announced that it was not going to treat any captive or detainee as a prisoner of war, nor apply to

---

9. *Id.* (italics added).
10. Ari Fleisher, Press Briefing, Office of the Press Secretary (Jan. 31, 2002), *available at* http://www.whitehouse.gov/news/releases/2002/01/20020128-11.html#prisoners%20down%20in%20Guantanamo%20Bay (Sep. 24, 2002).

them the protection of Geneva Convention III relating to the treatment of prisoners of war.[10] Not all coalition members of the US campaign favored this policy, as the United Kingdom, Australia, and Germany registered concerns about the lack of adherence to the Geneva Convention on Prisoners of War (GC III).[11] Despite these protests, the United States refused to consider any detainees as potential prisoners of war.

Article 4 of the Convention provides in part that:

[p]risoners of war . . . are persons belonging to one of the following categories, who have fallen into the power of the enemy:

(1) Members of the armed forces of a Party to the conflict as well as members of militias or volunteer corps forming part of such armed forces.

(2) Members of other militias and members of other volunteer corps, including those of organized resistance movements, belonging to a Party to the conflict and operating in or outside their own territory, even if this territory is occupied, provided that such militias or volunteer corps, including such organized resistance movements, fulfill the following conditions:

(a) that of being commanded by a person responsible for his subordinates;

(b) that of having a fixed distinctive sign recognizable at a distance;

(c) that of carrying arms openly;

(d) that of conducting their operations in accordance with the laws and customs of war.

(3) Members of regular armed forces who profess allegiance to a government or an authority not recognized by the Detaining Power.[12]

---

11. *See, e.g., Coalition at Odds over Cuban Camp*, THE SCOTSMAN, 1, Jan. 21, 2002, *available at* http://news.scotsman.com/archive.cfm?id=75162002&rware=HYRBHPXMUZMV&CQ_CUR_DOCUMENT=4 (Sep. 24, 2002); *Rocks, stones found in cells - War on Terror Letters to a Missing Son*, THE DAILY TELEGRAPH, Jan. 28, 2002, *available at* LexisNexis, Major World Newspapers (Sep. 24, 2002). The United States changed this initial approach on February 7, 2002 when the Office of the Press Secretary released a fact sheet stating that "[t]he President has determined that the Geneva Convention applies to the Taliban detainees, but not to the al Qaeda detainees" but that "[u]nder the terms of the Geneva Convention, however, the Taliban detainees do not qualify as POWs" and "therefore neither the Taliban nor al Qaeda detainees are entitled to POW status." Office of the Press Secretary, Fact Sheet - Status of Detainees at Guantanamo, February 7, 2002, *available at* http://www.whitehouse.gov/news/releases/2002/02/20020207-13.html (Sep. 24, 2002).
12. *See* GC III, *supra* note 8 at art. 4.

Note that this article makes no reference to parties to the Convention, but refers solely to parties to the conflict. Paragraph 3 is significant for those opposing the Taliban or seeking al Qaeda members since it expressly refers to the forces of an authority unrecognized by a captor. As to paragraph 2, it seems that various Taliban units were under a proper command and may have been wearing a distinctive insignia as they wore a black head-covering of a similar type. These Taliban supporters carried their arms openly and it is not known whether they complied with the laws and customs of war as there were no real land operations allowing for this to be studied.

Further coalition problems arose regarding the actions of the United States when studying other articles of this convention. Article 5 provides:

> [t]he present Convention shall apply to the persons referred to in Article 4 from the time they fall into the power of the enemy and until their final release and repatriation.
>
> Should any doubt arise as to whether persons, having committed a belligerent act and having fallen into the hands of the enemy, belong to any of the categories enumerated in Article 4, such persons shall enjoy the protection of the present Convention until such time as their status has been determined by a competent tribunal.[13]

To date, not a single Article 5 hearing has been undertaken by the United States, nor are such hearing likely to take place in the future. The United States has taken the position that such hearings are not required for Taliban or al Qaeda members as they fall so clearly outside the scope of Article 4 that there can be no question but that they are not entitled to the protection of the Convention.

Additionally, although the United States has announced it is establishing special military commissions for the trial of these "detainees," trials have yet to take place. In fact, no charges have even been made public. Finally, it is unclear what crimes, if any, the majority of Taliban members detained at Guantanamo Bay have actually committed.

---

13. See GC III, *supra* note 8 at art. 5.
14. This is particularly true for those allies who have ratified Additional Protocol I which increases the types of people considered to be lawful combatants and imposes additional obligation on holding powers. *See, e.g.,* 1977 Geneva Protocol I Additional to the Geneva Conventions of 12 August 1949, and Relating to the Protection of Victims of International Armed Conflicts, *reprinted in* DOCUMENTS ON THE LAWS OF WAR, *supra* note 8 at 419.

This policy of refusing to treat detainees as required by the Third Geneva Convention has caused problems for US allies such as Canada and the United Kingdom.[14] By way of example, though Canada has not declared war, its policy is that its forces will at all times observe the law of armed conflict as recognized by Canada.[15] As debate developed in Canada as to the application of the Third Geneva Convention to detainees, Taliban members captured by Canadian Forces were turned over to the United States.[16] Such transfer was clearly in breach of Canadian obligations in Article 12 of the Third Geneva Convention which provides that:

> [p]risoners of war may only be transferred by the Detaining Power to a Power which is a Party to the Convention and after the Detaining Power has satisfied itself of the willingness and ability of such transferee Power to apply the Convention. . . . [I]f that Power fails to carry out the provisions of the Convention in any important respect, the Power by whom the prisoners of war were transferred shall, upon being notified by the Protecting Power, take effective measures to correct the situation or shall request the return of the prisoners of war. Such requests must be complied with.[17]

Though no Protecting Power existed in this case, the United States had made it clear that it would not apply the protections of GC III to these detainees. Nevertheless, no Canadian request for the return of these prisoners was ever made,[18] causing an apparent breach of GC III by Canada.

A singular lesson exists from these problems. As situations like these develop where a need exists to take combined action outside the umbrella of the UN, great care should be taken as early as possible to agree upon policies that will effectively deal with these types of issues to the satisfaction of all coalition members.

---

15. *See* Code of Conduct for CF Personnel, Office of the Judge Advocate General, October 20, 1999, p. 2, *available at* http://www.dnd.ca/jag/jag_pdf_docs/codeconduct_ch1to3_e.pdf (Sep. 24, 2002).
16. *See* Tim Naumetz, *Prisoner Furor Dogs Grits*, CALGARY HERALD, p. A1 (Jan. 30, 2002), *available at* LexisNexis, Major World Newspapers (Sep. 24, 2002).
17. GC III, art. 12, *supra* note 8.
18. Interestingly, the United Kingdom transferred personnel falling into the hands of its forces operating in Afghanistan to the Northern Alliance, as the legitimate government of that country, which was entitled to treat such persons in accordance with its own laws, such as there might be.

XI

Panel II
Commentary—Jus in Bello

Tony Montgomery[1]

The principle of distinction is a fundamental component of the law of armed conflict. Attackers must adhere to this principle in selecting targets for destruction. What is not appropriately stressed in the literature and commentary is that this same principle applies to the defender as well as to the attacker. Routinely, the enemies of the United States—the Saddam Husseins, the Slobodan Milosevics, and the Taliban—place military equipment in the middle of protected areas containing civilians. As is well known, this is a violation of the law of armed conflict yet the United States constantly finds itself struggling with such difficult targeting issues because of these illegal acts by the enemy.[2]

Cloaking such targets behind civilians and in protected places does not, however, deprive the target of its military utility. Greater discussion of the responsibility of the defender to segregate such military targets from civilians

---

1. Lieutenant Colonel Tony Montgomery is the Deputy Staff Judge Advocate for the US Special Operations Command.
2. *See* 1977 Geneva Protocol I Additional to the Geneva Conventions of 12 August 1949, and Relating to the Protection of Victims of International Armed Conflicts, *opened for signature* Dec. 12, 1977, 1125 U.N.T.S. 1, art. 51(7), *reprinted in* DOCUMENTS ON THE LAWS OF WAR (Adam Roberts and Richard Guelff eds., 3rd ed., 2000) [hereinafter DOCUMENTS ON THE LAWS OF WAR] at 419.

and protected places would be helpful to those who engage in the business of targeting.

On September 11th, I was a member of the Office of the Staff Judge Advocate for the US Special Operations Command. Recognizing that the terrorist acts perpetrated on September 11th would quickly elicit a response from our nation, my office began searching for use of force parallels that might apply. One we found that proved to be of great utility was an article dealing with the use of force in guerilla warfare.[3] Many might denounce any sort of similarity between guerilla war and the Global War on Terrorism. I suggest, however, that the concepts are far more similar than dissimilar.

From an application of force perspective, my office came to several conclusions. Our first conclusion was that our forces should apply the law of armed conflict in the face of the events of September 11th. United States forces have familiarity with these laws; they train using these laws and are comfortable adhering to them. Secondly, US public support of military operations is stronger when our forces adhere to the law of armed conflict. Lastly, US adherence to the law of armed conflict also helps ensure the support of US allies. These were provided to our commander explaining why the US response to the attacks should comply with the law of armed conflict.

Another controversial area we have been facing is the requirement to wear uniforms while conducting military operations in Afghanistan. A critical component of receiving the privileges accorded a lawful combatant by the Geneva Conventions is that, amongst other things, the individual wears a "fixed distinctive sign recognizable at a distance."[4]

The mission of US special operations forces is to plan, prepare for, and when directed, deploy to conduct unconventional warfare, foreign internal defense, special reconnaissance and direct actions in support of US national policy objectives within designated areas of responsibility.[5] There are many types of forces within the US Special Operations Command and each force has a different focus and mission. Some of our forces are designed for large scale operations and will always be in uniform while conducting operations. Others, however, have mission profiles that require smaller groups to conduct

---

3. Ken Brown, *Counter-Guerilla Operations: Does the Law of War Proscribe Success?*, 44 NAV. L. REV. 123 (1997).
4. *See* Geneva Convention (III) Relative to the Treatment of Prisoners of War, Aug. 12, 1949, 6 U.S.T. 3316, T.I.A.S. No. 3364, 75 U.N.T.S. 135, art. 4(2)(b), *reprinted in* DOCUMENTS ON THE LAWS OF WAR, *supra* note 2, at 234.
5. 10 U.S.C. § 167 (2000).

more unconventional types of warfare. These sorts of operations often will require our forces to live with the indigenous force conducting the campaign.

In Afghanistan, this was the Northern Alliance. As was made clear in the photographs broadcast by the media, many US forces, to blend in and to gain credibility, adopted at least some parts of the uniform worn by members of the Northern Alliance. Our office provided advice within our command on the requirement for our forces to wear a fixed, distinctive insignia in compliance with the Geneva Conventions. Our advice was that although for good operational reasons our forces might need to adopt some of the uniform of the Northern Alliance, they must still have some type of insignia distinctive to the United States. Judging from the photographs displayed by the media, this is still an issue needing resolution. Our office continues to believe that wearing this fixed distinctive insignia is required by the Third Geneva Convention and operates to protect our forces more than it does to identify them as targets.

One final thought based on comments I have read and heard today has to do with the relevancy of the existing laws of armed conflict and the US commitment to comply with those laws. The United States has recently withdrawn from the Anti-Ballistic Missile Treaty; will not ratify the Rome Statute enacting the International Criminal Court; has interpreted the Third Geneva Convention to not require Article 5 tribunals for determining the status of detainees currently confined in Guantanamo Bay, Cuba; is reviewing our policy on the use of nuclear weapons; and has announced a policy of preemptive response to threats to our security. The events of September 11th truly did change things. And, I for one do not believe we yet understand the magnitude of that change. The basis for the modern laws of war was after a time of great horror and reflect the thinking of that time. Have times changed to the point that those rules, restrictions, inhibitions are no longer sufficient? Or, is it simply that the United States needs a set of rules for its activities, with everyone else following the old rules? Whatever the case, the United States will continue to protect its citizens and sovereignty.

XII

Panel II
Discussion—Jus in Bello

On the Overlap Between Jus ad Bellum and Jus in Bello

Yoram Dinstein

The jus as bellum and the jus in bello are two distinct bodies of law, and there is no overlap between them. First of all, the aggressor (pursuant to the jus ad bellum) may conduct hostilities in an impeccable way from the standpoint of the jus in bello, and the state resorting to self-defense (under the jus ad bellum) may conduct hostilities in a manner incompatible with the jus in bello. True, sometimes the same party is held accountable for flagrant aggression (under the jus ad bellum) and for the most horrendous war crimes (in violation of the jus in bello). The paradigmatic case is the Nazi record in World War II. But even here, let us not forget that the Nazis were not the only ones who disregarded the jus in bello. The Soviet march to Berlin in 1945 was regrettably accompanied by hundreds of thousands of cases of rape of German women.[1] These grave breaches of the jus in bello do not diminish one iota from the fact that it was Germany that invaded the USSR in Operation BARBAROSSA in June 1941. Consequently, responsibility for the war of aggression (in conformity with the jus ad bellum) was incurred exclusively by the Nazis.

Secondly, the issue of proportionality—which is of consequence both in the jus ad bellum and in the jus in bello—has a totally different meaning in each body of law. In the context of the jus in bello, proportionality denotes that collateral damage to civilians must not be excessive compared to the military

---

1. ANTHONY BEEVOR, THE FALL OF BERLIN, 1945 (2002)

advantage anticipated in the attack. This requires a balancing act between the expected casualties among combatants and civilians. Insofar as the jus ad bellum is concerned, there is also a balancing act between casualties sustained in an armed attack and in a defensive armed reprisal carried out in response. However, if we are talking about war of self-defense in response to an armed attack of a critical nature, no such balance is required. The best example is that of Pearl Harbor and the Pacific War. The Japanese attack of 7 December 1941 was of critical significance, since it altered the entire strategic situation in the Pacific. Hence, it justified the American declaration of war in self-defense. As we all know, by the time the Pacific War was over, there was no proportion between the number of American casualties sustained in Pearl Harbor (or for that matter thereafter) and the countless Japanese losses throughout the war and especially towards the end (when Japanese cities were pulverized by both conventional and unconventional weapons). The issue of proportionality in losses and counter-losses was irrelevant under the jus ad bellum. Once the Japanese attack in Pearl Harbor justified a war of self-defense on the part of the United States, that war could be fought—as it was—to the finish, irrespective of total numbers of casualties.

Adam Roberts

I believe there is some overlap between jus ad bellum and jus in bello when it comes to the impact that they have in public debate. They are not in entirely separate watertight compartments. Charles Garraway put it particularly clearly when he quoted from the US Standing Rules of Engagement that it remains crucially important that irrespective of the circumstances in which a war begins, irrespective of the jus ad bellum, the jus in bello be observed. It is not my position that these two areas be completely confused with each other, merely that there is some degree of overlap occurring inevitably in public debate.

On the Power of the Security Council

Yoram Dinstein

In accordance with the UN Charter, members of the organization are bound to carry out decisions of the Security Council, especially in matters affecting peace and security.[2] In practice, when the Security Council states in a resolution that it is acting under Chapter VII of the Charter,[3] this is understood to mean the

---

2. U.N. CHARTER, arts. 25, 48.
3. U.N. CHARTER, arts. 39-51.

text is binding. Moreover, Article 103 of the Charter proclaims that, in the event of a conflict between the obligations of member states under the Charter and their obligations under any other treaty, the Charter obligations prevail. The upshot is that, when the Security Council creates obligations for a member state thorough a legally binding decision, the state has to observe the Security Council decree irrespective of any other conflicting obligation. The conflicting obligation may be derived from the Geneva or Hague Conventions governing the law of armed conflict. Notwithstanding their venerated status, these instruments must give ground to any obligation based on the Charter. This actually happened in 1990, in the Gulf War with Iraq, when the Security Council imposed a blockade going beyond the general rules regulating blockade in armed conflict. The Security Council had the authority to do this by virtue of Article 103 of the Charter.

On the Nature of the Current Conflict in Afghanistan

Yoram Dinstein

Unlike pirates who operate on the high seas, terrorists always operate from within a state. They may mount their attack against targets in the same state or they can use their bases in that state for attacks against other states. International law obligates a state not to allow its territory to be used as a springboard for attacks by terrorists against another state. If the local state in unable to eliminate the terrorists, that does not mean that the aggrieved state must sit idly by. In the absence of effective action by the local state, the aggrieved foreign state may send an expeditionary force into the territory of the state where the terrorists have their bases, with a view to taking them out. But then all action must be directed against the terrorists, and not against the local government.

The question in Afghanistan was not simply whether the United States could enter its territory in order to eradicate al Qaeda. The question was whether the United States could target only al Qaeda fighters on Afghan soil or also members of the Taliban forces. In my opinion, the Taliban opened themselves up to an American use of force because the regime ratified the actions of al Qaeda of 11 September 2001. Between September 11th and October 7th, the United States tried to persuade the Taliban to extradite bin Laden and otherwise disassociate themselves from al Qaeda. The Taliban ignored this pressure and refused to cooperate with the United States despite the warnings by the United States and the strong language used in Security Council Resolution 1373.[4] Thereby the Taliban regime aligned itself with al Qaeda and turned its own forces into legitimate targets for American action in self-defense against the armed attacks of September 11th.

An analogy for this type of retroactive ratification by a government of the misdeeds of non-state actors can be found in Iran in 1979. The Ayatollah's regime in Iran in 1979—just like the Taliban regime in Afghanistan in 2001—endorsed unlawful action against the United States by non-state actors. In 1979, that unlawful action consisted of the takeover of the US embassy by militant students. In 2001, it was the al Qaeda outrages of September 11. In both instances, the original armed attack was carried out by fanatics without the apparent advance approval of the local government (the Ayatollah's and the Taliban, respectively). But in both instances, the local government assumed full responsibility for the armed attack, and exposed itself to counteraction by way of self-defense. In the case of Iran, the US counteraction was ineffective. In the case of Afghanistan, the US counteraction brought an end to the Taliban regime.

On Shielding Military Targets with Noncombatants

Yoram Dinstein
Using civilians to shield military targets is clearly a very serious violation of the jus in bello. the question is whether, in light of the presence of the human shields, the other belligerent party must abort an attack against the military target, bearing in mind the expected high number of civilian casualties which is likely to ensue. In my opinion, in such instances, the proportionality principle (which forbids excessive collateral damage to civilians) need not be applied in the usual manner. Much more latitude has to be given to the attack, because the high number of civilian casualties is deliberately induced by the enemy. That is to say, an attack that would otherwise be unlawful due to excessive collateral damage to civilians would be permissible when caused by the enemy's abuse of the law. When shielding a military target with civilians, the blood of the civilians will normally stain the hands of the defending rather than the attacking side.

---

4. Resolution 1373 required, amongst other things, that states shall "refrain from providing any type of support . . . to entities or persons involved in terrorist attacks." *See* S. C. Res. 1373, U.N. SCOR, 56th Sess., U.N. Doc. S/1373/(2001)

On the Currency of the Law of Armed Conflict

Adam Roberts

There currently exists a problem with certain areas of the law of armed conflict. This may partly be a problem of some international agreements concluded with considerable pressure from non-governmental organizations and international governmental organizations that have considerable support from legal reformers but about which major powers that may have to engage in war have strong reservations. There is a possible disjunction there that needs to be taken seriously. I am not suggesting that the existing body of law is perfect. For example, the UK's reservations to Geneva Protocol I are extremely long and comprehensive. And in my view, despite the recent movement by negotiators to attempt to limit reservations to treaties such as the International Criminal Court, it is preposterous to prohibit reservations. Any major military power should and will be able to make reservations in some form. However, suggesting that there is a need for completely new law dealing with terrorist operations may be too much; a more evolutionary kind of approach based on the practice of states in customary international law may be more appropriate.

Unprivileged Combatants

Yoram Dinstein

Civilians who choose to act as combatants without wearing uniforms (or other fixed distinctive emblems) do not commit war crimes. But they expose themselves to attack as combatants, and, most significantly, they are deemed unlawful (or unprivileged) combatants and therefore are not entitled to the status of prisoners of war. Absent that status, they can be detained or put on trial by domestic courts for ordinary crimes such as murder, assault, or arson. The same rule applies to combatants who fight out of uniform, do not carry their arms openly, etc. The latter rule determines the fate of Taliban and al Qaeda fighters (currently in Guantanamo Bay and other places of detention). But it is equally true of Central Intelligence Agency (CIA) operatives and other Americans who participated in hostilities in Afghanistan out of uniform. Had they been captured by the enemy, they would have not qualified for protection under the Geneva Convention (III) Relative to the Treatment of Prisoners of War.

The decision to forego protection pursuant to the jus in bello may be deliberate. There is a cost/benefit calculus, and the CIA probably reached the conclusion that it was willing to run the risk (especially since, in any event, the Afghan reputation in terms of compliance with the Geneva Convention in regards to prisoners of war leaves a lot to be desired). There are other instances in which risks are deliberately assumed in view of the constraints of the situation. For example, in some armed conflicts, the enemy is known to concentrate fire on members of the medical personnel in the field, who are wearing the distinctive armband of the Red Cross (or its equivalent). A number of armed forces therefore instruct their medical personnel to remove their armband. There is nothing wrong with such instructions, but it must be borne in mind that the consequence is liable to be loss of protection under the Geneva Conventions. Of course, once they remove their armbands and lose the protection afforded by the Conventions, members of the medical personnel may as well behave as full-fledged combatants (actively participating in hostilities), neither seeking nor dispensing any protection from attack.

Charles Garraway

I am not convinced that a medic can actually give up his protection. He may choose not to wear the armband that indicates that he is protected under the Geneva Conventions but the fact remains that if he is a medic engaged in full-time medical duties, he is entitled to the protections of the Geneva Conventions. The difficulty arising from not wearing an armband is one of distinction for the enemy. However, if the enemy knows he is a medic and he is acting as a medic, despite the fact that he is not wearing a Red Cross armband, he may not be targeted.

An issue related to this which causes much concern is that of the definition of combatants. As you know, combatants are by definition permitted to take a direct part in the hostilities and it seems that many states are taking a narrower and narrower view of what it means to take a direct part in hostilities in an effort to save costs by using civilians in positions historically filled by members of the armed forces. This issue is a fundamental one and should be further studied to determine what exactly is meant by taking a direct part in the hostilities.

Panel III

Thursday—June 27, 2002

8:30 AM–12:30 PM

Maritime & Coalition Operations

Moderator:
    Vice Admiral James Doyle
    US Navy (Ret.)

Presenters:
    Professor Wolff Von Heinegg
    University of Frankfurt-Oder

    Professor Ivan Shearer
    Challis Professor of International Law
    University of Sydney

Commentators:
    Commander Kenneth O'Rourke
    Judge Advocate, US Navy
    Chief, Operations Law Division
    United States Central Command

    Commander Neil Brown
    Royal Navy, United Kingdom
    Fleet Legal Advisor
    CINCFLEET, United Kingdom

    Wing Commander Paul Cronan
    Legal Advisor, Headquarters Australian Theatre
    Australian Defense Force

    Lieutenant Colonel Jean-Guy Perron
    Assistant Judge Advocate/Ottawa
    Canadian Forces

XIII

The Legality of Maritime Interception/Interdiction Operations Within the Framework of Operation ENDURING FREEDOM

Wolff von Heinegg[1]

Object and Purpose of Operation ENDURING FREEDOM

While Operation ENDURING FREEDOM covers a wide set of measures against international terrorism, the naval forces deployed to the Horn of Africa and in the sea areas around the Arab peninsula have a clear task to fulfil. Their assignment covers inter alia

- control of sea traffic in the area;
- guaranteeing the freedom and safety of navigation;
- protection of endangered vessels;
- disruption of supplies for terrorist groups, especially by preventing others from supporting and financing international terrorism;
  - elimination of terrorist command and training facilities; and
  - capture of international terrorists for the purpose of prosecuting them.

---
1. Wolff von Heinegg is a Professor of International Law at Europa-University in Frankfurt (Oder), Germany.

The tasks presuppose a sound knowledge of the geography and of those present in the sea area concerned. The naval units, therefore, have to precisely and comprehensively monitor sea and air traffic. Intelligence collection and surveillance by means of the electronic and other equipment on board such warships does not create any significant legal problems, since it does not interfere with the rights of other states. If such equipment is used during passage in the territorial sea of another state, in principle, the prohibitions found in Article 19 of the UN Convention on the Law of the Sea (hereinafter LOS Convention) must be observed.[2] Activities "prejudicial to the peace, order or security of the coastal state" are, however, to some extent modified by the inherent right of self-defense found in both Article 51 of the UN Charter and customary international law. As soon as there is reasonable grounds to believe a concrete threat against the vessel or its personnel exists, the warships are entitled to take all measures necessary to neutralize or eliminate the threat.

---

2. Article 19 of the UN Convention on the Law of the Sea provides that "[p]assage is innocent so long as it is not prejudicial to the peace, good order or security of the coastal State." Passage prejudicial to peace, good order or security of the coastal state includes a foreign ship engaging in any of the following activities:

(a) any threat or use of force against the sovereignty, territorial integrity or political independence of the coastal State, or in any other manner in violation of the principles of international law embodied in the Charter of the United Nations;

(b) any exercise or practice with weapons of any kind;

(c) any act aimed at collecting information to the prejudice of the defence or security of the coastal State;

(d) any act of propaganda aimed at affecting the defence or security of the coastal State;

(e) the launching, landing or taking on board of any aircraft;

(f) the launching, landing or taking on board of any military device;

(g) the loading or unloading of any commodity, currency or person contrary to the customs, fiscal, immigration or sanitary laws and regulations of the coastal State;

(h) any act of wilful and serious pollution contrary to this Convention;

(i) any fishing activities;

(j) the carrying out of research or survey activities;

(k) any act aimed at interfering with any systems of communication or any other facilities or installations of the coastal State;

(l) any other activity not having a direct bearing on passage.

See U.N. Convention on Law of the Sea, U.N. Doc. A/CONF.62/122 (1982), art. 19, *reprinted in* BARRY CARTER AND PHILLIP TRIMBLE, INTERNATIONAL LAW SELECTED DOCUMENTS (2001), at 553 [hereinafter INTERNATIONAL LAW SELECTED DOCUMENTS].

Within a foreign territorial sea, replenishment at sea would be contrary to Article 19(g) of the LOS Convention, unless the coastal state expressly authorized it. All other activities, not listed in Article 19 UNCLOS are permitted. Importantly, coastal states may not require warships to notify them of their passage in advance or to make that passage subject to prior consent.[3] This, *a fortiori*, holds true for transit passage through international straits, such as in the Strait of Bab el Mandeb.

The purpose of this article is not to analyze each of these issues, however. Instead, the emphasis of this article is on the basis for, and legality of, maritime interception/interdiction operations.

Legality of Maritime Interception/Interdiction Operations

Given that flag states exercise exclusive jurisdiction over "their" vessels in sea areas beyond the territorial sea of third states, the question arises as to whether coalition members in the Global War on Terror may interfere with such vessels if the flag state has not consented or has expressly objected. Moreover, even if the flag state is obliged to tolerate maritime interception/interdiction operations (MIO) against its shipping, the applicable legal regime must be understood for such operations. This is particularly true today as although MIO is currently being conducted by the United States and coalition members in Operation ENDURING FREEDOM, the UN Security Council has neither imposed such an obligation on flag states nor expressly authorized the United States and its coalition members to conduct such operations.

Legal Basis For MIO

What then is the legal basis for the United States and coalition members conduct of MIO in support of Operation ENDURING FREEDOM? It must first be emphasized that international law permits interference with foreign ships, their cargo and their crew/passengers only when:

---

3. In their joint statement agreed upon in Jackson Hole on 23 September 1989 the former Soviet Union and the United States emphasized that "the provisions of the 1982 United Nations Convention on the Law of the Sea, with respect to traditional uses of the oceans, generally constitute international law and practice and balance fairly the interests of all States." See 89 DEPT. STATE BULL. 25f. (December 1989), *reprinted in* 14 LAW OF THE SEA BULLETIN, at 12 (December 1989).

- a treaty rule exists that expressly provides for interference such as in the case of piracy[4] or severe pollution of the marine environment,[5] or

- the interfering state finds itself in a special situation, i.e., in an international armed conflict.[6]

In the latter situation the parties of the conflict are not limited to visit, search, and capture of only enemy vessels. Rather, according to the law of maritime neutrality,[7] each state party may also take measures against vessels flying the flags of third/neutral states to include visit and search, capture, and in exceptional circumstances, even to the destruction of those vessels.[8] As long as these measures conform with the law of naval warfare and with the law of maritime neutrality, flag states must tolerate them. The reason for this requirement stems from the merging in certain aspects of the law of peace and the law of war. Given the existence of the UN Charter, the following considerations are now decisive:

In the absence of a Security Council resolution affirmatively identifying the aggressor state, it remains essential, in view of the continuing object and purpose of international law to secure international peace and security, to prevent the escalation of an ongoing international armed conflict. This purpose

---

4. *See* LOS Convention, *supra* note 2, at art. 105, *reprinted in* INTERNATIONAL LAW SELECTED DOCUMENTS at 582. Note, however, that the customary definition of piracy is broader than that agreed upon in the LOS Convention. *See* A.P. Rubin, *The Law of Piracy*, 63 INT'L L. STUD 305, 337 (1988). For measures that may be taken against pirates, see S.P. Menefee, *Foreign Naval Intervention in Cases of Piracy: Problems and Strategies*, 14 INT'L J. MARINE AND COASTAL L. 353 (1999).

5. *See, e.g.*, LOS Convention, *supra* note 2, at art. 220, para. 6, *reprinted in* INTERNATIONAL LAW SELECTED DOCUMENTS at 621. *See also*, Myron H. Nordquist, UNITED NATIONS CONVENTION ON THE LAW OF THE SEA 1982, A COMMENTARY, Vol. IV, at 301 (Dordrecht et al. eds., 1991); T. Treves, *Intervention en haute-mer et navires étrangers*, XLI ANNUAIRE FRANÇAIS DE DROIT INTERNATIONAL 651 (1995).

6. For the measures that may be taken against (neutral) merchant vessels see SAN REMO MANUAL ON INTERNATIONAL LAW APPLICABLE TO ARMED CONFLICTS AT SEA, paras. 59, 67, 118, 146 (Cambridge Univ. Press, 1995) [hereinafter SAN REMO MANUAL]. *See also*, W. HEINTSCHEL v. HEINEGG, SEEKRIEGSRECHT UND NEUTRALITÄT IM SEEKRIEG, at 363, 483, 567, 582 (Berlin 1995) [hereinafter SEEKRIEGSRECHT UND NEUTRALITÄT IM SEEKRIEG].

7. The exact status of the traditional law of neutrality is far from clear. On the one hand, there are overlaps with political concepts of neutrality. On the other hand, the scope of applicability (only in a "war" *strictu sensu*?) is highly disputed. Still, with regard to the maritime aspects of the law of neutrality some rules and principles have developed that are met by wide agreement. *See, e.g.*, Helsinki Principles on the Law of Maritime Neutrality, *in* 68 INT'L L. ASSOC. REP. 497 (1998) [hereinafter Helsinki Principles].

8. *Cf.* SAN REMO MANUAL, *supra* note 6, at paras. 67, 118, 146. *See also*, SEEKRIEGSRECHT UND NEUTRALITÄT IM SEEKRIEG, *supra* note 6, at 567, 582.

includes limiting and preventing the involvement of third states and their nationals. This indeed is the main objective of the law of maritime neutrality. On the one hand, according to that law, the parties to the conflict are, in principle, obliged not to interfere with neutral vessels and aircraft. On the other hand, neutral vessels and aircraft are prohibited from contributing to the warfighting efforts of one party to the disadvantage of the other party to the conflict.[9] If neutral vessels and aircraft violate these rules designed to serve their protection, they lose their protected status.[10]

According to the law of maritime neutrality, the parties to the conflict are entitled to monitor neutral shipping and neutral aircraft in order to verify if they are abiding by the prohibitions on non-neutral service. Flag states must tolerate these measures[11] and possess very limited means to prevent the parties to the conflict from interference.

Importantly, the foregoing principles only apply in international armed conflicts. In cases of inner disturbances and of internal armed conflicts the parties may not, beyond their own territorial sea, interfere with foreign shipping and aviation, unless the measures taken are in conformity with the law of the sea or with other rules of international law.[12]

---

9. See generally Chap. 7, ANNOTATED SUPPLEMENT TO THE COMMANDER'S HANDBOOK ON THE LAW OF NAVAL OPERATIONS (A. R. Thomas and James Duncan eds., 1999) (Vol. 73, US Naval War College International Law Studies) [hereinafter ANNOTATED SUPPLEMENT].
10. In this context, two situations must be distinguished: Neutral vessels actively participating in the hostilities or being integrated into the enemy's command, control and information system are legitimate military objectives in the sense of Article 52, para. 2 of Additional Protocol I and the corresponding customary law. See 1977 Geneva Protocol I Additional to the Geneva Conventions of 12 August 1949, and Relating to the Protection of Victims of International Armed Conflicts, Articles 52(2), opened for signature Dec. 12, 1977, 1125 U.N.T.S. 1 [hereinafter GP I], reprinted in DOCUMENTS ON THE LAWS OF WAR (Adam Roberts and Richard Guelff eds., 3rd ed., 2000), at 419 [hereinafter DOCUMENTS ON THE LAWS OF WAR]. Thus, such vessels may be attacked and sunk without prior warning. If, however, neutral merchant vessels merely assist the enemy, by, e.g., transporting contraband, they may only be captured and, if further preconditions are fulfilled, seized according to the law of prize. If the latter vessels resist capture they may also be considered legitimate military objectives. See ANNOTATED SUPPLEMENT, supra note 9, at para. 7.10.
11. Such measures include the stopping, visit, search and diversion (for the purpose of search) of merchant vessels. See SAN REMO MANUAL, supra note 6, at para 118; Helsinki Principles, supra note 7 at 5.2.1.
12. Hence, the legality of measures taken by France during the Algerian crisis is at least doubtful. For an evaluation see L. Lucchini, Actes de contrainte exercés par la France en Haute Mer au cours des opérations en Algérie, XII ANNUAIRE FRANÇAIS DE DROIT INTERNATIONAL at 803–822 (1966).

The present situation of the war on terrorism can be characterized as neither an internal nor an international armed conflict *strictu sensu*. An international armed conflict presupposes that at least two states are involved and though the United States has been (and most probably is and will be) the victim of acts of international (transborder) terrorism that can be equated to an armed attack in the sense of Article 51 of the UN Charter, there (still) is no other state to whom these acts can be attributed. While it might have been possible to attribute certain terrorist activities to Afghanistan or the Taliban regime in the past, in view of the changed circumstances, this is no longer possible. Therefore, MIO directed against the shipping of third states seem to be prohibited if it is not based upon the consent of the flag state or if implemented against the express will of the flag state. Clearly, this is true as there is no treaty rule expressly providing for MIO.

Analogizing MIO to anti-piracy measures does not help either. If international terrorists could be considered pirates in the sense of the LOS Convention, every state would be entitled to take measures against them in sea areas beyond the sovereignty of their state. However, this would presuppose that terrorists have taken control over a respective ship, a rather rare scenario. More importantly, however, is the absence of such an established analogy in international law—insofar as there exist special rules explicitly dealing with international terrorism and it is impossible to detect an *opinio juris* of states that the rules on piracy are applicable to acts of international terrorism.[13]

However, such tortured constructions are not necessary in concluding that current MIO performed by the United States and its coalition partners in and around the Persian Gulf states is legal. Recall that by Resolution 1368 the Security Council:

> calls on all States to work together urgently to bring to justice the perpetrators, organizers and sponsors of these terrorist attacks and stresses that those responsible for aiding, supporting or harbouring the perpetrators, organizers and sponsors of these acts will be held accountable.[14]

---

13. An example of how that could be achieved is the 1937 Nyon Agreement—by which certain attacks by unidentified submarines were considered acts of piracy. *See* Nyon Agreement, 181 L.N.T.S. 137-40, 151, *reprinted in* THE LAWS OF ARMED CONFLICTS: A COLLECTION OF CONVENTIONS, RESOLUTIONS AND OTHER DOCUMENTS (Dietrich Schindler and Jiri Toman eds., 3rd ed. 1988) at 887, 889. For an analysis of the Nyon Agreements, *see* L.F.E. Goldie, *Commentary on the 1937 Nyon Agreements*, *in* THE LAW OF NAVAL WARFARE. A COLLECTION OF AGREEMENTS AND DOCUMENTS WITH COMMENTARIES, 489 (N. Ronzitti ed., 1988).
14. S. C. Res. 1368, U.N. SCOR, 56th Sess., U.N. Doc. S/1368/(2001).

In Resolution 1373 the Security Council is more precise by deciding that all states shall, inter alia,

> [p]rohibit their nationals or any persons and entities within their territories from making any funds, financial assets or economic resources or financial or other related services available, directly or indirectly, for the benefit of persons who commit or attempt to commit or facilitate or participate in the commission of terrorist acts, of entities owned or controlled, directly or indirectly, by such persons and of persons and entities acting on behalf of or at the direction of such persons; . . .
>
> (a) Refrain from providing any form of support, active or passive, to entities or persons involved in terrorist acts, including by suppressing recruitment of members of terrorist groups and eliminating the supply of weapons to terrorists;
>
> (b) Take the necessary steps to prevent the commission of terrorist acts, including by provision of early warning to other States by exchange of information;
>
> (c) Deny safe haven to those who finance, plan, support, or commit terrorist acts, or provide safe havens;
>
> (d) Prevent those who finance, plan, facilitate or commit terrorist acts from using their respective territories for those purposes against other States or their citizens;
>
> (e) Ensure that any person who participates in the financing, planning, preparation or perpetration of terrorist acts or in supporting terrorist acts is brought to justice and ensure that, in addition to any other measures against them, such terrorist acts are established as serious criminal offences in domestic laws and regulations and that the punishment duly reflects the seriousness of such terrorist acts; . . .
>
> (g) Prevent the movement of terrorists or terrorist groups by effective border controls and controls on issuance of identity papers and travel documents, and through measures for preventing counterfeiting, forgery or fraudulent use of identity papers and travel documents; . . .[15]

This implies, for example, that states may not (knowingly) allow their nationals or ships and aircraft to transport international terrorists and goods that are designed to further acts of international terrorism. If they obtain knowledge of such

---

15. S. C. Res. 1373, para. 1d, 2a, 2e, U.N. SCOR, 56th Sess., U.N. Doc. S/1373/(2001).

activities they must take the necessary preventive or suppressive measures. If they willingly abstain from such measures they are not only in breach of their obligations under the UN Charter but may also become legitimate targets of self-defense measures if abstention is equated to permitting the activities concerned.

But even if such private acts may not be attributed to another state or if the flag state is unable to take the necessary measures according to Resolution 1373, abstaining from action would still have to be considered a breach of international law. In such cases third states are entitled, in lieu of the state with primary responsibility for acting, to take the necessary measures to fulfill the requirements of Resolution 1373. It would be incompatible with Resolution 1373 to permit a flag state to object to MIO by claiming the right of the sovereignty or the lack of explicit consent. As the Security Council has made abundantly clear, international terrorism is a threat to international peace and security that must be eliminated.[16] Accordingly, if a vessel is on the high sea and is suspected of carrying international terrorists or weapons destined to international terrorists it is not necessary to inform the flag state in advance because requiring such notice would jeopardize the effectiveness of the international efforts against international terrorism in an intolerable way.

To this point, this article has dealt with situations in which all participants have knowledge of the presence of either terrorists or certain cargo on board a vessel or aircraft. The question remains whether measures seeking simply to verify whether there is some involvement in international terrorism can also be considered as in accordance with international law in cases where there is no state counterpart. Recall in this context that vessels and aircraft regularly operate at great distance from the territories of their respective flag states. National authorities are generally ignorant of the route, of the cargo and of the identity of passengers on these vessels and aircraft. Even if they are in possession of this information, the information may be inaccurate or false. Only in exceptional cases will the national authorities be in a position to control or otherwise verify the veracity of a described route or of a passenger or cargo manifest. If, however, a vessel with international terrorists on board reaches its point of destination, further attacks like those seen on September 11th could be expected. States other than the flag state are therefore entitled to prevent this as early as possible. This again is only feasible if the vehicles in question can be controlled. Hence, the flag state must tolerate such control measures because they merely serve the purpose of

---

16. *Id.* at preamble. *See also* S. C. Res. U.N. SCOR, 55th Sess., U.N. Doc. S/1269/(1999) in which the Security Council, inter alia, condemns "all acts of terrorism, irrespective of motive, wherever and by whomever committed."

countering international terrorism as effectively as necessary. If such control reveals that the vehicle in question is incorporated into the network of international terrorism or is otherwise assisting it, all further adequate measures, such as capture, may be taken.

As far as the transport of weapons to Somalia is concerned a special feature ensues from Resolution 1356.[17] In paragraph 1 of that resolution, the Security Council "reiterates to all States their obligation to comply with the measures imposed by Resolution 733 (1992), and urges each State to take the necessary steps to ensure full implementation and enforcement of the arms embargo." Although the second part of this paragraph speaks to measures states are obliged to take in the sphere of their national jurisdiction, it nonetheless follows from the first part that Resolution 733[18] continues to be fully in force and applicable. Paragraph 5 of this resolution states:

> that all States shall, for the purpose of establishing peace and stability in Somalia, immediately implement a general and complete embargo on all deliveries of weapons and military equipment to Somalia until the Council decides otherwise.[19]

One means of implementing this weapons embargo is through the national measures provided for in paragraph 5 of Resolution 733. After all, without such national measures an arms embargo would not make much sense. Still, in order to fully comply with Resolution 733, states need not merely confine themselves to national measures. According to Resolution 733 they are to implement a "complete" and "general" embargo. Hence, embargo measures must not only cover all arms, weapons and the like (complete), but must also be directed against all actual and potential suppliers (general). If a state complies with this obligation by controlling the sea and air traffic to Somalia, it is allowed to stop and search any vessel or aircraft that is reasonably suspected of being engaged in the transport of arms because only by such control can a "general" embargo be effectively implemented. A feasible understanding of Resolution 733, given the wide meaning of "implement" then, authorizes states to conduct MIO for weapons destined for Somalia. Accordingly, the United States and its coalition partners are not restricted only to measures against vehicles flying their own flags or bearing their own markings.

---

17. S. C. Res. 1356, U.N. SCOR, 56th Sess., U.N. Doc. S/1356/(2001).
18. *See* S. C. Res. 733, U.N. SCOR, 47th Sess., U.N. Doc. S/733/(1992).
19. *Id.* at para. 5.

Some commentators may not be inclined to subscribe to such an interpretation of Resolutions 1356 (in connection with Resolution 733) and 1373 as the Security Council has neither authorized MIO explicitly nor obligated member states to tolerate such interference with their merchant shipping and civil aviation. However, even if this position is not shared by the rest of the world, MIO by the United States and its coalition partners would continue to be legal provided it was done as part of the exercise of these states' rights to individual and collective self-defense.

Clearly, the UN Security Council, by expressly reaffirming the right of self-defense in the context of the terrorist attacks on the United States in its Resolutions 1368 and 1373, has acknowledged the so-called Anglo-American concept of self-defense,[20] i.e., a broad interpretation of Article 51 of the UN Charter and of the customary inherent right of self-defense. In his press statement of 8 October 2001 the President of the Security Council, Richard Ryan, declared:

> [t]he members of the Security Council took note of the letters that the representatives of the United States and of the United Kingdom sent yesterday to the President of the Security Council, in accordance with Article 51 of the United Nations Charter, in which they state that the action was taken in accordance with the inherent right of individual and collective self-defense following the terrorist attacks in the United States of 11 September 2001.
>
> The permanent representatives made it clear that the military action that commenced on 7 October was taken in self-defense and directed at terrorists and those who harboured them. They stressed that every effort was being made to avoid civilian casualties, and that the action was in no way a strike against the people of Afghanistan, Islam or the Muslim world.
>
> The members of the Council were appreciative of the presentation made by the United States and the United Kingdom.[21]

Hence, self-defense is permitted not only in situations where a state, either with its armed forces or in some other way attributable to it, attacks another state but also where armed force is used against a state from outside its borders even when that use of force cannot be attributed to another state.[22] This situation

---

20. *Cf.* Alberto Coll, *The Legal and Moral Adequacy of Military Responses to Terrorism*, 81 PROC AM. SOC. INT'L L. 297, at 305 (1987).
21. Ambassador to the UN Richard Ryan, President of the Security Council, Press Statement (Oct. 8, 2001).
22. The same position is taken by T. Bruha & M. Bortfeld, *Terrorismus und Selbstverteidigung*, 5 VEREINTE NATIONEN, 161, at 165 (2001).

can be labelled a self-defense situation in a material sense only. Although this interpretation might exceed the wording of Article 51 UN Charter, it does not exceed the inherent, i.e., customary, right of self-defense.

This is confirmed by the reactions of the international community in the aftermath of the September 11th attacks. On 12 September the North Atlantic Council stated:

> [t]he Council agreed that if it is determined that this attack was directed from abroad against the United States, it shall be regarded as an action covered by Article 5 of the Washington Treaty, which states that an armed attack against one or more of the Allies in Europe or North America shall be considered an attack against them all.[23]

Moreover, the Organization for Security and Cooperation in Europe (OSCE)[24] as well as the majority of states obviously consider the United States as the state most entitled, according to the right of self-defense, to combat international terrorism by all necessary means.

Resolutions 1368 and 1373 must be understood in this broad sense. In the wake of September 11th, the Security Council has not by chance twice reaffirmed the right of self-defense. Nor has it pursued some kind of stockpiling policy in case that in some distant or near future the direct involvement of a foreign state can be proved. The express reaffirmation of the right of self-defense is contingent on the character of the terrorist attacks themselves. This is not based on the amount of damage done or lives lost, but instead because the attacks did not originate from US territory and could be carried out only due to the transnational character of the terrorist network. This network not only operates world-wide but it is also able to evade control by the authorities of the state in which it resides.

It can not be excluded that in some cases, state authorities acquiesce in the planning, organizing and execution of terrorist acts. In view of the special character of the al Qaeda network, it was not necessary for the Security Council to identify a state against which self-defense measures could be taken, for this form of international terrorism is far different from the context of "state-sponsored" terrorism or of a "classical" armed attack. This does not mean that

---

23. NATO Press Release 124 (Sep. 12, 2001), *available at* http://www.nato.int/docu/pr/2001/p01-124e.htm (Nov. 21, 2002).
24. OSCE Ministerial Council Decision No. 1, *Combatting Terrorism* (MC(9).DEC/1, Dec. 4, 2001), *available at* http://www.osce.org/events/mc/romania2001/documents/files/mc_1007474752_o.pdf (Nov. 21, 2002).

criteria used in identifying and evaluating these are no longer of relevance. Armed attacks and sheltering terrorists may be very different and therefore may not necessarily trigger the right to self-defense.[25] However, there are clearly instances where acts of international terrorism can be attributed to another state.

Although no state currently exists against which the terrorist acts can be attributed and that therefore could be the legitimate object of measures taken in self-defense, the potential target states of international terrorism are not obliged to adopt a wait-and-see policy until there is sufficient evidence of the (direct) involvement of a foreign state or even until further terrorist attacks occur. To the contrary, the United States and its coalition partners are entitled to take all measures reasonably necessary to prevent such attacks as early and as effectively as possible. Such measures do not merely include the capture of international terrorists and of weapons or other goods destined for them. The United States and coalition partners may also control international shipping and aviation in order to verify the innocent status of such shipping and aviation. Of course, MIO are governed by the principle of proportionality.[26] Accordingly, they can be based upon the right of self-defense only if there are sufficient intelligence indicators of the integration of the affected vehicles into conspiracies to commit, or acts of, international terrorism. Indiscriminate implementation and enforcement of MIO covering vast sea areas would be disproportionate and not justified by the right of self-defense. If limitations such as these are observed, affected states are obligated to tolerate these measures. Moreover, there is no need for prior approval or consent of third states as it is neither feasible nor compatible with the right of self-defense. Were this the case, the inherent right to self-defense would be subjugated to the will of third states. Article 51 of the UN Charter provides no basis for such an understanding. Interestingly, no state has yet objected to the legality of MIO in the framework of Operation ENDURING FREEDOM.

The validity of the above findings is confirmed by the parallels between the given situation and an international armed conflict at sea. In such a conflict it is irrelevant whether one of the parties violated the jus ad bellum.[27] Instead, each

---

25. *See* Military and Paramilitary Activities in and against Nicaragua (Nicaragua v. US), 1986 I.C.J. 14, at 104 (1986), *available at* http://www.icj-cij.org/icjwww/icases/inus/inusframe.htm (Nov. 21, 2002) [hereinafter Nicaragua Case].
26. For the validity of the principle of proportionality in the context of self-defense and for further references, see A. Randelzhofer, *Article 51*, CHARTA DER VEREINTEN NATIONEN – KOMMENTAR, at note 37 (B. Simma ed., 1991).
27. *See* SEEKRIEGSRECHT UND NEUTRALITÄT IM SEEKRIEG, *supra* note 6, at 86.

party is entitled to verify by appropriate control measures, like visit and search, whether neutral merchant vessels and civil aircraft are contributing to the respective enemy's war-fighting efforts.[28] According to the law of maritime neutrality, neutral states are obligated to tolerate these measures in order to prevent an escalation of the conflict and in order to meet the interests of the parties to the conflict.[29] This also holds true if further measures are taken, such as when a neutral merchant vessel is incorporated into the enemy's intelligence system.[30] The flag state of the merchant vessel has no right to interfere or to otherwise prevent a belligerent from capturing or even sinking the vessel.

While the current situation differs from an international armed conflict insofar as there is no "enemy state," this is not sufficient grounds to remove the duty of third states to tolerate interference with their merchant shipping and civil aviation. In an international armed conflict that obligation exists for the mere reason that the parties to the conflict have decided to take such measures. As long as the Security Council has not authoritatively identified one of the belligerents as the aggressor, the duty of toleration persists. A *fortiori* this must hold true if the Security Council has expressly affirmed the existence of a self-defense situation even though there is no state to which the attacks can be attributed.

For these reasons the United States and its coalition partners are entitled to establish *maritime interdiction areas*, i.e., to restrict access to certain sea areas for the shipping and aviation of third states.[31] These areas should not be confused with safety zones[32] because they are not primarily designed to serve the safety of

---

28. See SAN REMO MANUAL, *supra* note 5, para. 118; Helsinki Principles, *supra* note 6, at 5.2.1.; G.P. POLITAKIS, MODERN ASPECTS OF THE LAWS OF NAVAL WARFARE AND MARITIME NEUTRALITY, at 529 (1998) [hereinafter MODERN ASPECTS].
29. SAN REMO MANUAL, *supra* note 5, para. 118; Helsinki Principles, *supra* note 6, at 5.2.1.; MODERN ASPECTS, *supra* note 28, at 529.
30. See SAN REMO MANUAL, *supra* note 6, para. 67; SEEKRIEGSRECHT UND NEUTRALITÄT IM SEEKRIEG, *supra* note 6, at 5.2.1.
31. For the equivalent of such zones in the law of naval warfare see SAN REMO MANUAL, *supra* note 5, para. 105.
32. Such safety zones are sometimes labelled "naval vessel protection zones." *See, e.g.,* Regulated Navigation Areas and Limited Access Areas, 33 C.F.R. § 165 (2002). *See also* ANNOTATED SUPPLEMENT, *supra* note 9, at 7.8, which provides that:

> [w]ithin the immediate area or vicinity of naval operations, a belligerent may establish special restrictions upon the activities of neutral vessels and aircraft and may prohibit altogether such vessels and aircraft from entering the area. The immediate area or vicinity of naval operations is that area within which hostilities are taking place or belligerent forces are actually operating.

The legality of such safety zones is undisputed. *See,* inter alia, D.P. O'CONNELL, THE INFLUENCE OF LAW ON SEA POWER at 168 (1975); G.P. POLITAKIS, MODERN ASPECTS, *supra* note 26, at 104.

a warship or unit but to instead facilitate the identification of vessels and aircraft or to prevent international terrorists or weapons destined for them from getting access to the area concerned. Hence, the legal basis of maritime interdiction areas is to be found in Resolution 1373 and in the right of individual and collective self-defense. Note also that according to customary international law they are entitled to temporarily make exclusive use of restricted sea areas for military and security purposes.[33] However, it follows from the principle of proportionality that the exact coordinates of the sea areas affected as well as the measures to be taken there have to be published in advance—e.g., by a Notice to Mariners/Airmen. Moreover, foreign ships and aircraft may only be prohibited from entering the area as long as doubts persist about their identity, their cargo, their crews, and their passengers. If they refuse to give the relevant information or if they continue their journey regardless of a prior warning all necessary measures may be taken against them.

Legal Restrictions

The United States and its coalition partners are limited by more than simply the principle of proportionality however. If the jus in bello and the law of maritime neutrality are understood as an order of necessity, international law provides for situations in which two or more states consider themselves unable to adhere to the prohibition on the use of force,[34] then the legal restrictions laid down in that order of necessity, *a fortiori*, must be observed in situations that do

---

33. *Cf.* J. Astley & Michael Schmitt, *The Law of the Sea and Naval Operations*, 42 AF. L. REV. 119 (1997); Ch. E. Pirtle, *Military Uses of Ocean Space and the Law of the Sea in the New Millennium*, 31 OCEAN DEVELOPMENT & INT'L L. 7 (2000); R. Wolfrum, *Military Activities on the High Seas: What are the Impacts of the U.N. Convention on the Law of the Sea?*, in THE LAW OF ARMED CONFLICT: INTO THE NEXT MILLENIUM at 501 (Michael Schmitt & Leslie Green eds., 1998) (Vol. 71, US Naval War College International Law Studies). It may be added that the list of high seas freedoms in Article 87, paragraph 1 of the LOS Convention is not exhaustive. Accordingly, these freedoms also include the use of the high seas and of EEZ areas for military purposes. Moreover it is clear from the second sentence of that paragraph that freedom of the high seas is not only "exercised under the conditions laid down by this Convention" but also "by other rules of international law." *See* LOS Convention, *supra* note 4, at art. 87. The military uses of high seas areas (including EEZ areas) is governed by customary international law, by the law of naval warfare and by the law of maritime neutrality. Accordingly, and since military exercises traditionally have been conducted in those sea areas, such uses are generally acknowledged to be part of customary international law.
34. For this characterization see W. Heintschel v. Heinegg, *The Current State of International Prize Law*, INTERNATIONAL ECONOMIC LAW AND ARMED CONFLICT, 5–34 (H.H.G. Post ed., 1994).

not yet amount to an international armed conflict *strictu sensu*.[35] Hence, when conducting MIO, states are obliged to comply with the international minimum legal requirements of the law of naval warfare and of the law of maritime neutrality.

To begin with, they have to distinguish between state vessels and aircraft on the one hand and other vehicles on the other hand. State vessels and aircraft enjoy sovereign immunity and may not be interfered with unless they pose an imminent threat. That immunity is extended to merchant vessels travelling under the convoy of a warship. Therefore these merchant vessels are, in principle, exempt from the exercise of the right of visit and search.[36] However, the commander of the accompanying warship is obliged to provide all information as to the character of the merchant vessel and its cargo.[37]

If not travelling under convoy, foreign merchant vessels may be required to provide all information necessary to verify their identity, their destination, their route, their crews, their passengers and their cargo. If they refuse to provide this information, or if they otherwise try to evade identification, all measures necessary to enforce the duty of identification and information may be taken against them. Here again, the principle of proportionality applies. Accordingly, the use of armed force is admissible only as an *ultima ratio* measure; weapons may only be employed if there are no other means to stop the vessel or to prevent it from escape. Regularly, a warning shot fired away from the vessel will suffice. If not, it may be forced to stop by a shot into the rudder.

---

35. The International Court of Justice, in the Corfu Channel and in the Nicaragua Case, referred to Hague Convention VIII of 1907 although in both cases there existed no international armed conflict. See Corfu Channel (Merits) (U.K. v. Alb.), 1949 I.C.J. 4 (Apr. 9, 1949) [hereinafter Corfu Channel]; Nicaragua Case, *supra* note 25 at 112. See also Convention Relative to the Laying of Automatic Submarine Contact Mines, Oct. 18, 1907, 36 Stat. 2332 [hereinafter Hague VIII]. The principles laid down in Hague VIII were characterized by the ICJ as "certain general and well recognized principles, namely: elementary considerations of humanity, even more exacting in peace than in war." See Corfu Channel at 22; Nicaragua Case at 112. Hence, the ICJ also seems to take the position that the rules and principles of the jus in bello mark the final limits of what is tolerable under international law.

36. ANNOTATED HANDBOOK, *supra* note 9, para. 7.6.; FEDERAL MINISTRY OF DEFENCE OF THE FEDERAL REPUBLIC OF GERMANY, HUMANITARIAN LAW IN ARMED CONFLICTS – MANUAL (ZDv 15/2), para. 1141 (Bonn, 1993); R. W. TUCKER, THE LAW OF WAR AND NEUTRALITY AT SEA, at 334 (1957); M. DONNER, DIE NEUTRALE HANDELSSCHIFFAHRT IM BEGRENZTEN MILITÄRISCHEN KONFLIKT, at 174 (Kehl A.R. et al., 1993); CH. ROUSSEAU, LE DROIT DES CONFLITS ARMES, at 431 (1983); SAN REMO MANUAL, *supra* note 6 at paras. 120, 127. "The right of neutrals to convoy is recognized. Consequently, neutral States have the right to accompany commercial ships flying their own or another neutral State's flag by their warships." Helsinki Principles, *supra* note 7, at 6.1.

37. SAN REMO MANUAL, *supra* note 6, at para. 120(d).

Stricter legal restrictions apply when it comes to the use of force against civil aircraft that are also obliged to identify themselves and to provide the said information. In view of the vulnerability of aircraft, the use of armed force must be limited to warning shots as long as there is no clear evidence of a terrorist activity. The only means available of using force is to require the aircraft to land.[38]

If, according to intelligence information, there are reasonable grounds to believe that a merchant vessel is transporting terrorists or goods destined to them, or if doubts persist as to the truth of the information provided by its master, a boarding team may be sent on board the merchant vessel that may take all measures necessary to clarify the circumstances (e.g., examination of documents and search of the vessel). The members of the boarding team may be armed in order to be able to defend themselves against attacks. If the initial suspicion proves true or if circumstances cannot be clarified to the satisfaction of the responsible commander, the vessel may be diverted to a port or sea area where a thorough search will be conducted. If the master refuses to obey the diversion order, the boarding team may capture the vessel by taking over command and control. Note that in the majority of cases, search on the high seas will be practically possible only with the master's consent, when the circumstances are easily clarified, and if no other difficulties are encountered. Absent these conditions, the vessel must either be diverted or allowed to continue its journey. In view of the considerable economic losses involved, a diversion must be in strict accordance with the principle of proportionality. Mere suspicion of involvement with terrorist activities will generally not suffice. Rather, the grounds for suspicion must be clear and reasonable which presupposes sufficient intelligence information. The same limitations apply with regard to capture. The legality of capture cannot be doubted if the merchant vessel resists visit and search because it is a means to enforce the obligation to tolerate these measures. If the master has complied with his obligations, however, capture, as a severe encroachment on the flag state's sovereignty, is justified only where there is strong suspicion of the commission of an offense.

With respect to individuals on board who are suspected of being international terrorists or who are suspected of having assisted international terrorism in some other way and with regard to cargo that is bound for groups of international terrorists, specific rules and principles must be observed. Terrorists may be taken prisoner to prosecute them for their illegal actions. They

---

38. For the special protection of civil aircraft against the use of armed force see Convention on International Civil Aviation, *opened for signature* Dec. 7, 1944, art. 3, ICAO Doc. 7300/6, 15 U.N.T.S. 6605 and SAN REMO MANUAL, *supra* note 6, at para. 153.

may be taken to a court of the capturing warship's flag state or to a court of one of its allies.[39] If Taliban members are captured, there is a presumption of their participation in the hostilities on behalf of, or with the consent of, the de-facto government of Afghanistan. They remain liable, of course, for all crimes they have committed. They may, however, not be prosecuted and tried for having taken part in the hostilities. Moreover, they are entitled to prisoner of war (POW) status.[40] The mere change in government does not nullify *ex tunc* the authorization or consent of the predecessor. If those taken prisoner are members of al Qaeda they are entitled to POW status only if they had been part of the Afghan armed forces or if they had otherwise "belonged" to Afghanistan as a party to the armed conflict. If neither of these conditions can be ruled out the presumption or rule of doubt laid down in Article 5(2) of Geneva Convention III comes into operation and an Article 5 tribunal must take place.[41] Nevertheless POW status does not preclude punishment for participation in, or commitment of, acts of international terrorism.[42]

---

39. Transfer of prisoners to an ally will, however, pose considerable problems if the states concerned are bound by different rules of international law, especially with regard to the legality of the death penalty.
40. According to Article 4A of Geneva Convention III of 12 August 1949 relative to the Treatment of Prisoners of War not only members of the regular armed forces are entitled to POW status but also members of militias and volunteer corps either "forming part of such armed forces" or "belonging to a Party to the conflict." Also protected are "members of regular armed forces who profess allegiance to a government or an authority not recognized by the Detaining Power." See Convention Relative to the Treatment of Prisoners of War, Aug. 12, art. 4, 1949, 6 U.S.T. 3316, T.I.A.S. No. 3364, 75 U.N.T.S. 135 [hereinafter GC III]. **Editor's Note**—The US Government has taken the position that the Taliban are not entitled to POW status since the Taliban was never the legitimate government of Afghanistan and Taliban members do not meet the four part test found in Article 4 of GC III. See GC III at art. 4; see Statement by White House Press Secretary Ari Fleischer (Feb. 7, 2002).
41. "Should any doubt arise as to whether persons, having committed a belligerent act and having fallen into the hands of the enemy, belong to any of the categories enumerated in Article 4, such persons shall enjoy the protection of the present Convention until such time as their status has been determined by a competent tribunal." *Id.* at art. 5. This provision is generally accepted as customary international law based, in part, on the reaction of the international community and the media to the treatment of the detainees in Guantanamo Bay. For states parties to Additional Protocol I of 1977 a further obligation applies. According to Article 45 of this protocol, "a person who . . . is not held as a prisoner of war and is to be tried . . . . for an offence arising out of the hostilities . . . shall have the right to assert the entitlement to prisoner-of-war status before a judicial tribunal and to have the question adjudicated." GPI, *supra* note 10, at art. 45.
42. However, according to Article 85, GC III "prisoners of war prosecuted under the laws of the Detaining Power for acts committed prior to capture shall retain, even if convicted, the benefits of the present Convention." GC III, *supra* note 40, at art. 85.

Weapons, ammunition and other military equipment destined for international terrorists or supply goods as well as everything serving for the financing of international terrorism, including drugs or other prohibited goods, may be captured and seized. Other objects and cargo have to be returned to the owner.

Captured vessels (and aircraft) may also be seized as soon as there exists sufficient proof that they are owned by al Qaeda or some other group of international terrorists. As for the rest it will depend on the respective national criminal law whether their confiscation is possible or not. International law provides no clear rule on that question unless the vessel or aircraft concerned had been used in a terrorist attack or had actively resisted visit and search or diversion. Therefore, in case of doubt, these vehicles should be returned to their respective owners if a participation in terrorist acts cannot be established.

If MIO are conducted beyond the territorial sea of third states—or within the territorial sea with the approval of the coastal state—their legal basis derives from the right of individual and collective self-defense as long as the legal restrictions referred to above are observed. Would a US warship or an allied warship also be entitled to enter the territorial sea if the coastal state did not consent and if a merchant vessel suspected of transporting international terrorists tried to evade capture by taking refuge, for example, in the territorial sea of Somalia? From the perspective of the law of the sea that operation, in view of the territorial sovereignty of Somalia, would be illegal unless exceptionally justified. Here again a plea of self-defense could serve as a justification. However, self-defense as traditionally understood might pose a problem insofar as the inactivity of Somali authorities would perhaps not be sufficient to establish the attributability necessary to legitimize actions taken against that state. Still, the legality of pursuing such a vessel into the territorial sea becomes evident if the law of maritime neutrality is again considered. According to that law neutral states are under an obligation to take the measures necessary to terminate any violation of the law by one of the belligerents, especially if that belligerent makes use of the neutral's territorial sea as a base of his military operations. If the neutral state fails to terminate the violation—be it because it is unable or unwilling to do so—the opposing belligerent, if certain preconditions are met, may use such force as is strictly necessary to respond to the threat posed by the violation.[43] Note that the behavior of the neutral coastal state need not amount

---

43. SAN REMO MANUAL, *supra* note 6, at para. 22; SEEKRIEGSRECHT UND NEUTRALITÄT IM SEEKRIEG, *supra* note 6, at 505.

to a direct and attributable contribution to the enemy's war fighting efforts. If that were the case that state would become a party to the conflict. The law of maritime neutrality would be replaced by the jus in bello.

In any event, the measures taken within neutral territorial seas must be restricted to the termination of the violation. Resolution 1373 obligates all states to prevent and suppress within their territories all acts of international terrorism as well as all activities in support of international terrorism. A state that is either unwilling or unable to comply with these obligations violates international law. This also holds true where, as in Somalia, the state has failed. Hence, there are good reasons that exceptional situations like the present limited actions taken within foreign territorial seas in order to capture international terrorists and weapons destined for them are justified by international law if the coastal state is unwilling or unable to take the measures necessary according to Resolution 1373.

Conclusion

As seen, MIO conducted within the framework of Operation ENDURING FREEDOM can be based upon the right of individual and collective self-defense and, additionally, on Resolution 1373 of the UN Security Council. Third states are obligated to tolerate the control measures taken against their shipping and aviation by the United States and its coalition partners. The UN Security Council has made sufficiently clear that self-defense is not restricted to armed attacks attributable to a given state. Rather, it has acknowledged that a self-defense paradigm can exist without a state being the potential object of armed countermeasures. This, however, does not mean that the United States and its coalition partners are free to interfere with foreign shipping and aviation at their will. They must observe the limitations imposed upon them by the law of naval warfare and by the law of maritime neutrality. This corpus of international law must be observed in spite of the fact that there exists no international armed conflict *strictu sensu*. Respect for these requirements is of utmost importance because only thus can the support of the international community in the fight against international terrorism be maintained.

Of course, in view of the varying treaty obligations and in view of different concepts of self-defense, a multinational operation like ENDURING FREEDOM is a difficult task. The most promising way to cope with these difficulties is to draw multinational rules of engagement in order to ensure that at least the common minimum legal denominator that is so important for international political support operates effectively.

XIV

The Limits of Coalition Cooperation in the War on Terrorism

Ivan Shearer[1]

The Wide Range of Issues

The events of September 11, 2001 revealed deep and widespread feelings of revulsion, even in unlikely quarters, against the indiscriminate use of violence to achieve political ends. National leaders throughout the world condemned the terrorist attacks in the United States and expressed their solidarity with the American government and people. The world's press and other media were equally condemnatory. The reaction of the United Nations was swift: resolutions of broad reach and specific content were passed directing measures to be taken by all states to suppress terrorism and to cooperate in bringing terrorists to justice.[2]

The military operations carried out by the United States and a number of its allies in Afghanistan were not specifically authorized by the United Nations Security Council. Although justifiable as an exercise of the right of self-defense, recognized by Article 51 of the Charter of the United Nations, the failure of the United States to seek such authorization retrospectively, as

---

1. Ivan Shearer is the Challis Professor of International Law, University of Sydney, Australia
2. *See, e.g.,* S. C. Res. 1368, U.N. SCOR, 56th Sess., U.N. Doc. S/1368/(2001); S. C. Res. 1373, U.N. SCOR, 56th Sess., U.N. Doc. S/1373/(2001); S. C. Res. 1377, U.N. SCOR, 56th Sess., U.N. Doc. S/1377/(2001).

envisaged by Article 51, raises both political and legal questions. This paper will not, however, be concerned with these issues—the jus ad bellum—since they are dealt with elsewhere in this publication.[3] Moreover, it is perhaps less probable that the future war against terrorism will be conducted in circumstances where a state has admitted its responsibility for harboring terrorists and has refused to take effective measures against them. As a consequence, traditional jus in bello issues will not frequently arise in the familiar context of battlefield conditions, such as in Afghanistan, where operations were conducted against regular forces as well as terrorists, but may call for application, if at all, rather by way of analogy.

The issues most likely to arise are those relating to the cooperation between states in the early warning, hunting down, and bringing to justice of terrorists. There is unlikely to be a clearly delineated battlefield where terrorists conduct open armed operations or hide in caves. Their shadowy operations will be directed under the cover of apparently innocuous business or other entities located in unsuspecting host countries. They will move easily between countries on valid or false documents. Financial transactions will take place under seemingly innocent cover, or through informal means. Intelligence and communications networks will operate using freely available public facilities.

Since there is nearly universal recognition of the threat to international peace and security posed by terrorists and of the need for cooperation in their suppression, it follows that an effective response must lie in the hands of the many nations comprising the international community. That response must be multilateral and multilayered. It must not be left entirely to the states directly affected by terrorism, still less to the most powerful among them, above all the United States. There must be a coalition of states. This coalition will no doubt consist of an inner circle of closely allied states, and a perimeter of others, more loosely—or not at all—allied, which acknowledge the dangers to themselves of failing to cooperate to meet the global challenge of terrorism. Differences in their policies, laws, human and material resources, and in the efficiency of the exercise of their governmental powers, will call for consideration. Whether these differences constitute impediments to the effectiveness of the war against terrorism, and thus call for elimination, or whether they constitute legitimate constraints or sensitivities, and thus call for respect, is the topic of this paper.

It is taken as a given that international law is an integral part of the planning process in any actions against terrorists and that it constitutes the only

---

3. *See* Chapters VIII-XIII *supra*.

yardstick the world has against which to measure the legitimacy of the actions taken. There is a tendency in some quarters to see international law as an undue restraining factor to be set aside in times of crisis.[4] Not only does this attitude strike at the heart of civilized values; it ignores the very real opportunities afforded by the concessive rules of international law to allow effective action to be taken against terrorists in a principled fashion which upholds world public order.

Particular reference will be made in this paper to the laws and policies of Australia, as an example of a close ally of the United States and a coalition partner in the war against terrorism.

National Laws With Respect To Terrorism

In the absence of a universally accepted definition of terrorism, states are presently free to adopt their own definitions for the purposes of their domestic law. Many have no defined crime of terrorism, as such, in their laws, but all have laws respecting most of the constituent elements of terrorism, such as murder, manslaughter, violence against the person, criminal damage to property, and threats and conspiracies to commit crimes of violence.

In enacting anti-terrorism laws, states will generally note the definitions of terrorism contained in international conventions to which they are parties or to agreed definitions adopted by authoritative international bodies. Unfortunately, a universal definition of terrorism has proved to be difficult to achieve as witnessed by the lack of consensus found in the attempted definition in the Draft International Convention on Terrorism, presently before the United Nations.[5] The core definition of the crime in that draft is, however, not in doubt as Article 2 of the Draft Convention provides:

1. Any person commits an offence within the meaning of this Convention if that person, by any means, unlawfully and intentionally, causes:

    (a) death or serious bodily injury to any person; or

---

4. Former Australian Permanent Representative to the UN and head of the UN Special Commission on Disarmament in Iraq Ambassador Richard Butler, quoted US Undersecretary of State John Bolton, as having said in 2000 when discussing the International Criminal Court that "[t]here is no such thing as international law, only national sovereignty." Richard Butler, *The supine leading the blind,*" THE AUSTRALIAN, June 14, 2002 at 13.
5. *See* Report of the Ad Hoc Committee Established by General Assembly Resolution 51/210 of 17 December 1996, U.N. GAOR, 57th Sess., Supp. No. 37, U.N. Doc A/57/33.(2002), *available at* http://ods-dds-ny.un.org/doc/UNDOC/GEN/N02/248/17/PDF/N0224817.pdf?OpenElement (Jan. 11, 2003) [hereinafter Draft International Convention on Terrorism].

(b) serious damage to public or private property, including a place of public use, a state or government facility, a public transportation system, an infrastructure facility, or the environment; or

(c) damage to property, places, facilities or systems referred to in paragraph 1 (b) of this article, resulting or likely to result in major economic loss,

when the purpose of the conduct, by its nature or context, is to intimidate a population, or to compel a government or an international organization to do or abstain from doing any act. [6]

The difficulty that has arisen, and that so far remains to be resolved through continuing negotiations, concerns the qualifying provisions of draft article 18 of this convention. In one version, that article would exempt from categorization as terrorism the activities of armed forces during armed conflict governed by international humanitarian law, and in the other version, proposed by the Member States of the Organization of the Islamic Conference, would exempt the activities of the parties to an armed conflict, "including in situations of foreign occupation."[7] The basis of the disagreement in the continuing conflict between Israel and the Palestinians is obvious.

Both the United Kingdom[8] and Australia[9] have already adopted a domestic law definition of terrorism with the Australian definition largely following the UK model. It requires as an element of the offense that the act be committed "for the purpose of advancing a political, religious or ideological cause." It also excludes from the definition acts that consist of advocacy, protest, dissent or labor disputes.

For the purposes of domestic law, an internationally accepted definition of terrorism, if and when it eventuates, will be of crucial importance. In the constitutional systems of some states, the definition in the Convention will operate directly as domestic law upon its ratification and promulgation by the state parties. In other constitutional systems, especially those of the English common law inheritance such as Australia, Canada, and the United Kingdom, the

---

6. *Id.* at art. 2. Note that the precise definitions of the property and institutions mentioned in Article 2, paragraphs 1(b) and 1(c) are contained in Article 1 of the Draft Convention.
7. *Id.* at art. 18.
8. *See* Anti-terrorism, Crime and Security Act, 2001, c. 11 § 1 (UK). The version of this Act printed in CURRENT LAW STATUTES, 2000 (Sweet & Maxwell eds., 2000) contains annotations which trace the history of the definition from the troubles in Northern Ireland, from the Diplock and Lloyd Commissions, to the present.
9. *See* Criminal Code Act, c. 1, pt. 5.3 d. 100 (Austl.).

Convention definition will require adoption and incorporation by statute, and possibly also adaptation to meet local circumstances.

In the meantime, in many countries, new laws are being introduced or drafted in order to give the police, or intelligence agencies, increased powers to detain and question not only those suspected of terrorism but also those who may be thought to have relevant information. Bills currently before the Australian Parliament, for example, would give to the Australian Security and Intelligence Organization (ASIO), an organization not previously invested with coercive powers, the power to obtain a warrant to secretly detain persons suspected of terrorism or those thought to possess information about terrorists.[10] It is also proposed that the Attorney-General be given power to proscribe certain organizations.[11] Members and supporters of those organizations could be jailed for up to 25 years.

The definition of terrorism in domestic law, or the applicability under domestic law of other denominations of offense to terrorist acts, will have particular implications for jurisdiction and extradition.

Jurisdiction

International law recognizes the jurisdiction of states to prescribe and enforce their criminal laws subject to certain conditions.[12] The very wide power to prescribe laws, seemingly allowed by the Permanent Court of International Justice in the *Case of the S.S. Lotus* (1927),[13] must now be regarded as somewhat narrower in extent, especially since the decision of the present International Court of Justice in the *Case of the Arrest Warrant of 11 April 2000* (Democratic Republic of Congo v. Belgium) (2002).[14] It must now be regarded as essential to prescriptive jurisdiction that there be some nexus or linking point between the legislating state and the reprehended activity that is supported by the positive

---

10. The Australian Security and Intelligence Organization Legislation Amendment (Terrorism) Bill after passing both the Australian House and Senate was not approved by Prime Minister John Howard. The Bill will be reconsidered in the 2003 Parliament. *See* Paul Sheehan, *PM's Doubled-dissolution Trigger Finger must be Itching over ASIO Bill*, SYDNEY MORNING HERALD, Dec. 16, 2002, at 13.
11. *See* Security Legislation Amendment (Terrorism) Bill, No 65, 2002 (Austl.).
12. *See generally* A.L.I. RESTATEMENT (THIRD) FOREIGN RELATIONS LAW OF THE UNITED STATES, § 432, at pgs. 232, 235–238 (1987).
13. S.S. Lotus Case (Fr. v. Turk.), 1927 P.C.I.J. (ser. A) No. 10 (Sep. 7, 1927).
14. *See* Case of the Arrest Warrant of 11 April 2000 (Democratic Republic of Congo v. Belgium), 41 I.L.M. 536 (2002), *available at* http://www.lawschool.cornell.edu/library/cijwww/icjwww/ipresscom/ipress2002/ipresscom2002-04_cobe_20020214.htm (Jan. 10, 2002).

practice of other states.[15] In any event, the power to enforce validly prescribed laws is dependent upon physical custody of the offender or upon the availability of extradition from another state having custody.

States have jurisdiction to prescribe the applicability of their criminal laws upon the following generally recognized bases:

(a) The territorial basis of jurisdiction. States have jurisdiction to prescribe laws governing activities occurring in their territory, or in places assimilated to their territory, such as ships and aircraft of their nationality. It is an accepted extension of this basis of jurisdiction that states also have jurisdiction over offenses, elements of which occur outside their territory but which are completed, or have effect, or are intended to have effect, within it.[16]

(b) The nationality basis of jurisdiction. States have jurisdiction to prescribe laws governing the activities of their citizens wherever they occur. Whether states are also justified in international law in asserting jurisdiction over those who commit offenses *against* their citizens (the "passive nationality" basis of jurisdiction) is disputable. State practice in the matter is not uniform.[17]

(c) The protective principle of jurisdiction. States have jurisdiction to prescribe laws governing the activities of those who would assault its existence or damage its essential interests.[18] Accepted examples include planning an invasion of the territory or the overthrow of its government, counterfeiting its currency, and breaching the fiscal, immigration, sanitary and customs laws applicable against inbound vessels in the contiguous zone under the international law of the sea. Extensions, however, to interests that are not shared by the international community, such as the protection of the national religion through blasphemy laws, or the reputation of national rulers ("slander against the state") will not be widely recognized.

(d) The universality principle of jurisdiction. States have jurisdiction to prescribe laws that correspond to offenses regarded by international law as

---

15. *See, e.g.,* Israel v. Adolf Eichmann, 36 I.L.R. Rep. 5 (D.C. Jm., 1961) [hereinafter Eichmann].
16. *See* Liangsiriprasert v. US, [1991] 1 A.C. 225 (P.C.).
17. United States law recognizes this basis of jurisdiction for certain purposes, e.g., hostage-taking. *See, e.g.,* Hostage Taking Act § 2001, 18 U.S.C. § 1203 (2002). On a more comprehensive basis a Bill has been introduced into the Australian Parliament: The Criminal Code Amendment. This bill has now been enacted as Division 104 of the Criminal Code Act, 1995, *available at* http://search.aph.gov.au/search/ParlInfo.ASP?action=browse&Path=Legislation/Current+Bills+by+Title/Criminal+Code+Amendment+(Offences+Against+Australians)+Bill+2002&Start=3&iGD#top (Jan. 10, 2003).
18. *See* Eichmann, *supra* note 15, at 5.

crimes by the law of nations. The historic instance is piracy. Beyond that there is doubt, because of the difficulty in establishing whether definitions have crystallized as customary international law. Strong candidates for inclusion in the category, however, are slavery, crimes against humanity, genocide, planning and conducting a war of aggression, and war crimes.

Instead of leaving the development of crimes against international law, and the concomitant universality of jurisdiction over them, to the evolutionary processes of customary law, the trend since 1948 has been to define offenses against international law in international conventions. There are a large number of these.[19] The jurisdiction prescribed by these conventions is not truly universal in the sense that any state may prosecute, as in the case of piracy. Instead they prescribe a variety of jurisdictional bases for prosecution and a duty on the state actually having custody of the offender to either prosecute the offender itself or extradite to another state having jurisdiction on one of the bases set out. This duty is described as *aut dedere aut judicare (punire)* (the duty to extradite or to prosecute). It might therefore be described as a "quasi-universality" basis of jurisdiction, because there must be a linking point between the offense and the prosecuting state, even though that might merely be the fortuitous presence of the offender in the territory of the state that first finds and detains the offender.

Note that many of the above conventions incorporating the *aut dedere aut judicare* formula are related to particular forms of terrorism. The latest of these, the International Convention for the Suppression of Terrorist Bombings, 1998, incorporates the same formula.[20]

The Draft Comprehensive International Convention on Terrorism, under negotiation in the United Nations, also incorporates the *aut dedere aut judicare*

---

19. *See, e.g,*. Convention for the Amelioration of the Condition of the Wounded and Sick in Armed Forces in the Field, Aug. 12, 1949, Art. 2, 6 U.S.T. 3114, T.I.A.S. No. 3362, 75 U.N.T.S. 31; Convention for the Amelioration of the Condition of the Wounded, Sick, and Shipwrecked Members of Armed Forces at Sea, Aug. 12, 1949, 6. U.S.T. 3217, T.I.A.S. No. 3363, 75 U.N.T.S. 85; Convention Relative to the Treatment of Prisoners of War, Aug. 12, 1949, 6 U.S.T. 3316, T.I.A.S. No. 3364, 75 U.N.T.S. 135 [hereinafter GC III]; Convention Relative to the Protection of Civilian Persons in Time of War, Aug. 12, 1949, 6 U.S.T. 3516, T.I.A.S. No. 3365, 75 U.N.T.S. 287 [hereinafter GC IV]; Hague Convention for the Suppression of Unlawful Seizure of Aircraft, Dec. 16, 1970, 22 U.S.T. 1641 (1971); Convention Against Torture and Other Cruel, Inhuman or Degrading Treatment or Punishment, Dec. 10, 1984, G.A. Res. 39/46, U.N. GAOR, 39th Sess., Supp. No. 51, U.N. Doc. A/39/51 (1984), *reprinted* in 23 I.L.M. 1027, and in 24 I.L.M. 535 (entry into force for United States on Nov. 20, 1994)
20. *See* International Convention for the Suppression of Terrorist Bombings, GA Res. 52/164 (Dec. 15, 1997), 37 I.L.M. 249 (1998) (ratified by the United States on Jun. 26, 2002) [hereinafter Terrorist Bombings Convention].

principle.[21] In addition to the states whose jurisdiction must be assured pursuant to the Convention—the territorial state, the state of nationality of a vessel or aircraft affected, and the state of nationality of the offender—the following optional bases of national jurisdiction are also prescribed:

(a) The offence is committed by a stateless person who has his or her habitual residence in the territory of that state; or

(b) The offence is committed wholly or partially outside its territory, if the effects of the conduct or its intended effects constitute or result in, within its territory, the commission of an offence set forth in article 2;

(c) The offence is committed against a national of that state; or

(d) The offence is committed against a state or government facility of that state abroad, including an embassy or other diplomatic or consular premises of that state; or

(e) The offence is committed in an attempt to compel that state to do or to abstain from doing any act; or

(f) The offence is committed on board an aircraft which is operated by the government of that state.[22]

The Relevance of International Norms of Human Rights

In the treatment of suspected terrorists after their detention, states are bound by the international norms of human rights. The provisions of the Universal Declaration of Human Rights, 1948 are regarded as declaratory of generally binding international law, as are—for the greater part—the provisions of the International Covenant on Civil and Political Rights of 1966. The United States and 147 other states are parties to the latter instrument and are thus bound by it also as a treaty instrument.[23]

The following provisions of the Universal Declaration are especially relevant to the treatment of suspected terrorists:

---

21. See Draft International Convention on Terrorism, *supra* note 5, at art. 11.
22. *Id.*, art. 6(2).
23. *See* Universal Declaration of Human Rights, Dec. 10, 1948, G.A. Res. 217A(III), U.N. Doc. A/810 (1948) [hereinafter Universal Declaration of Human Rights]; International Covenant on Civil and Political Rights, opened for signature Dec. 19, 1966, 1991 U.N.T.S. 171 (entered into force Mar. 23, 1976, ratified by the United States on June 8, 1992) [hereinafter ICCPR].

Article 5. "No one shall be subjected to torture or to cruel, inhuman or degrading treatment or punishment."[24]

Article 9. "No one shall be subjected to arbitrary arrest, detention or exile."[25]

Article 10. "Everyone is entitled in full equality to a fair and public hearing by an independent and impartial tribunal in the determination of his rights and obligations and of any criminal charge against him."[26]

Article 11. "(1) Everyone charged with a penal offence has the right to be presumed innocent until proved guilty according to law in a public trial at which he has had all the guarantees necessary for his defence."[27]

These provisions are confirmed and expanded in articles 7, 9, and 14 of the International Covenant on Civil and Political Rights.[28]

Do these provisions impose extraterritorial obligations on states? Article 2 (1) of the Covenant obliges each state party to respect and to ensure the rights recognized in the Covenant "to all individuals within its territory and subject to its jurisdiction." Is the word "and" to be read conjunctively or disjunctively? The latter appears to be the preferred reading. The Human Rights Committee established under the Covenant, has determined that this article "does not imply that the state party concerned cannot be held accountable for violations of rights under the Covenant which its agents commit upon the territory of another state, whether with the acquiescence of the government of that state or in opposition to it."[29] The Committee has also had occasion to address the same point in its observations on Belgium's periodic report:

> The Committee is concerned about the behaviour of Belgian soldiers in Somalia under the aegis of the United Nations Operation in Somalia (UNSOM II), and acknowledges that the State Party has recognized the applicability of the

---

24. See Universal Declaration of Human Rights, *supra* note 23, art. 5.
25. *Id.* at art. 9.
26. *Id.* at art. 10.
27. *Id.* at art. 11.
28. See ICCPR, *supra* note 23, arts. 7, 9, 14.
29. See Sergio Ruben Lopez Burgos v. Uruguay, Comm. no. 12/52, Report of the Human Rights Committee, U.N. GAOR, 36th Sess., Supp. No. 40, at 176, U.N. Doc. A/36/40 (1981); *digested in* THE INTERNATIONAL COVENANT ON CIVIL AND POLITICAL RIGHTS: CASES, MATERIALS AND COMMENTARY (S. Joseph et al. eds., 2000), at 59–60 [hereinafter INTERNATIONAL COVENANT]. As noted by these authors, the separate reasoning in this case of Committee Member Christian Tomuschat is most persuasive. A similar conclusion was reached by the Human Rights Committee in the case of Celiberti de Casariego v. Uruguay. *See* Comm' No. R. 13/56, Report of the Human Rights Committee, U.N. GAOR, 36th Sess., Supp. No. 40, at 185, U.N. Doc. A/36/40 (1981).

Covenant in this respect and opened 270 files for the purposes of investigation.[30]

It would thus appear to be the case that states, in their operations against terrorists, cannot avoid their obligations under international human rights law by detaining suspects in offshore facilities. "Jurisdiction" means effectively "within the power of." In battlefield conditions, where it is not immediately obvious who are lawful combatants and who are criminals, the law of the Geneva Conventions, 1949, must obviously apply as a *lex specialis*. But in cases not covered by the Geneva Conventions, international human rights law applies.

It may be argued that the international norms of human rights apply only in normal circumstances and not in relation to terrorists, whose very aim is the violation of the human rights of others and the destruction of institutions—in many cases, transparent and democratically accountable institutions. The Covenant recognizes this by the inclusion, in Article 4, of a right of derogation, but in strictly limited circumstances. Article 4 states:

1. In time of public emergency which threatens the life of the nation and the existence of which is officially proclaimed, the States Parties to the present Covenant may take measures derogating from their obligations under the present Covenant to the extent strictly required by the exigencies of the situation, provided that such measures are not inconsistent with their other obligations under international law and do not involve discrimination solely on the ground of race, colour, sex, language, religion or social origin.

2. No derogation from articles 6, 7, 8 (paragraphs 1 and 2), 11, 15, 16 and 18 may be made under this provision.

3. Any State Party to the present Covenant availing itself of the right of derogation shall immediately inform the other States Parties to the present Covenant, through the intermediary of the Secretary-General of the United Nations, of the provisions from which it has derogated and of the reasons by which it was actuated. A further communication shall be made, through the same intermediary, on the date on which it terminates such derogation.[31]

---

30. *See* Human Rights Committee, 64th Sess., Consideration of Reports Submitted by State Parties Under Article 40 of the Covenant, U.N. Doc. CCPR/C/79/Add.99 *available at* http://www.hri.ca/fortherecord1998/documentation/tbodies/ccpr-c-79-add99.htm (Jan. 11, 2003); *reprinted in* INTERNATIONAL COVENANT, *supra* note 29, at 62.
31. *See* ICCPR, *supra* note 23, art. 4.

The provisions of Article 4 have been the subject of considerable elaboration and interpretation. The Human Rights Committee itself issued a General Comment on the article in 2001;[32] in 1984 the International Law Association adopted the Paris Minimum Standards of Human Rights Norms in a State of Emergency;[33] and, in 1985 a group of experts in international law adopted the Siracusa Principles on the Limitation and Derogation Provisions in the ICCPR.[34] Common to these formulations is the invocation of the principle of proportionality of the measures in derogation, and the requirement that they be withdrawn as soon as the emergency has passed.

It will be seen that the threshold of justification is set high by the terms of paragraph 1. For countries such as the United States or Australia, there would be an understandable reluctance to declare a state of emergency, even after such catastrophic events as those of 11 September 2001, for fear of spreading panic in the community, or of appearing to confess the inability of the government to take effective measures against terrorists within the existing law. The danger should have manifested itself more widely and frequently to justify such a step.[35] Nevertheless, certain measures have been taken in relation to suspected terrorists arrested in the United States, and those detained in Afghanistan and other places, without a declaration so far of derogation under the Covenant. Special powers of arrest and detention in relation to suspected

---

32. *See* U.N. International Human Rights Instruments, Compilation of General Comments and General Recommendations Adopted by Human Rights Treaty Bodies, Addendum, General Comment No. 29, U.N. Doc. HRI/GEN/1/Rev.5/Add.1 (Apr. 18, 2002) *available at* http://www.unhchr.ch/pdf/Gen1rev5add1_E.pdf (Jan. 12, 2003).

33. *See* THE PARIS MINIMUM STANDARDS OF HUMAN RIGHTS NORMS IN A STATE OF EMERGENCY (1984), *reprinted in* 79 AM. J. INT'L L. 1072 (1985).

34. *See* The Siracusa Principles on the Limitation and Derogation Provisions in the International Covenant on Civil and Political Rights, arts. 29–32, *reprinted in* 7 HUMAN RIGHTS QUARTERLY 1 (1985).

35. The United Kingdom had availed itself in the past of the power of derogation under the Covenant, but only in respect of the territory of Northern Ireland, notwithstanding that sporadic terrorist acts were being committed elsewhere in the United Kingdom. On 18 December 2001, however, the United Kingdom gave notice of derogation for the whole of the United Kingdom by reason of a general public emergency following the events of September 11, 2001. The declaration referred to the enactment of the Anti-terrorism, Crime and Security Act, 2001, but was limited to a derogation from article 9 of the Covenant in relation to extended powers of arrest and detention of *foreign* nationals where there is an intention to deport. *See* Anti-terrorism, Crime and Security Act 2001, c. 24, 21–23 (Eng.) (detailing the new law of the United Kingdom for dealing with suspected international terrorists, through certification, deportation, and detention), *available at* http://www.legislation.hmso.gov.uk/acts/acts2001/20010024.htm (Jan. 12, 2003).

terrorists are currently being considered by the Australian Parliament.[36] There is a question therefore whether these measures are compatible with the Covenant, in the absence of a formal declaration of derogation.

Extradition of Terrorists

It has long been accepted that there is no duty in customary international law to grant extradition of accused or convicted criminals at the request of another state. A duty to extradite is imposed only by treaty. These treaties may be bilateral, or they may be contained in multilateral treaties, especially of the type described above in which the parties are bound to either extradite or prosecute (*aut dedere aut judicare*).

Existing extradition treaties, whether bilateral or multilateral, between many countries already cover in substance the offenses commonly regarded as pertaining to terrorism. There are gaps in that coverage, however, both geographically and substantively. For those countries whose power to grant extradition depends on the existence of an applicable treaty the treaty network may have become neglected or have fallen behind in its recognition of new types of offenses, such as terrorism. For those countries whose laws permit them to grant extradition without a treaty, on an ad hoc basis, and subject to a demonstration of criminality under the laws of both the requesting and the requested states (the rule of dual criminality), those laws may similarly have fallen behind current needs.

Two frequently encountered exceptions to extradition found in treaties and national laws are a prohibition of the extradition by a state of its own citizens, and the exception of politically motivated offenders.

The prohibition of extradition of citizens is a rule deeply entrenched in the legal systems of civil law countries. It derives from Roman Law and exchanges for the duty of obedience that the citizen owes to the state a duty of the state not to deliver up a citizen to a foreign jurisdiction. Countries of the common law tradition recognize no such restriction. In many extradition treaties between civil law and common law countries, therefore, the refusal to extradite citizens is made discretionary, so that the civil law position can be maintained while giving an opportunity to the common law country to refuse by way of reciprocity. The result is a mismatch. Civil law countries allow for prosecution of their own citizens for crimes committed anywhere in the world, as is recognized in international law by the nationality principle of jurisdiction. With few

---

36. *See* note 10 *supra* and accompanying text.

exceptions, the common law countries remain attached to the territorial principle of jurisdiction. This attachment goes back to the earliest days of the English common law and the institution of trial by jury; crime was local because it could be presented by a grand jury and judged by a petty jury, composed only of local citizens. The result can be that where a common law country refuses extradition of one of its citizens by way of reciprocity, there is no power to try the offender in the common law country, and a failure of justice may result.[37] There would appear to be no way around this difficulty. The non-extradition of citizens is a principle even embedded in the constitutions of some countries. It is unlikely that any international convention on terrorism would succeed in setting aside that principle. Perhaps only the United Nations Security Council could do so, as it did in relation to those charged with the Lockerbie incident.[38]

The exception from extradition of political offenses and of persons who, if extradited, might suffer prejudice at their trial on account of their race, religion, nationality or political opinion is almost universally recognized in extradition treaties and national extradition laws.[39] Terrorism is an example par excellence of a politically motivated offense. As far back as the 19th century, doubts began to be voiced about protecting individuals from extradition who had committed indiscriminate or cruel crimes for a political motive. Anarchists were held to be outside the rule and therefore extraditable. Attempts to exclude the rule against the extradition of such individuals failed in the Hague (1970) and Montreal (1971) Conventions on hijacking and sabotage of aircraft, respectively. However, the European Convention on the Suppression of Terrorism, 1977, expressly set aside the rule [40] and the current Draft

---

37. IVAN SHEARER, EXTRADITION IN INTERNATIONAL LAW 94–131 (1971) [hereinafter SHEARER].
38. *See* Case Concerning Questions of Interpretation and Application of the 1971 Montreal Convention Arising from the Aerial Incident at Lockerbie (Libya v. US; Libya v. UK) (Request for the Indication of Provisional Measures), 1992 I.C.J. 3. [hereinafter Lockerbie Case].
39. SHEARER, *supra* note 37, at 166–193.
40. *See* European Convention on the Suppression of Terrorism, Eur. T.S. No. 90 (Jan. 27, 1977), *available at* http://conventions.coe.int (Jan. 13, 2003). The Convention requires that none of the following offenses shall be regarded as political for the purposes of extradition: crimes under the international conventions regarding hijacking and sabotage of aircraft, hostage taking, attacks against internationally protected persons, or "an offense involving the use of a bomb, grenade, rocket, automatic firearm or letter or parcel bomb if this use endangers persons." Attempts or complicity in the above offenses are also excluded. Optionally, under article 2, states parties may regard any act of violence against the person, or any act against property if the act created a collective danger to persons, as not qualifying as a political offense. *Id.*

Comprehensive Terrorism Convention, being considered by the United Nations, does so also.

Within some states, the domestic law may be in advance of what the conventions require, as is the case of Australia. The extradition laws of Australia exclude from the application of the political offense exception offenses established under the international conventions concerning the hijacking of aircraft, sabotage of aircraft, genocide, internationally protected persons, hostage taking, and torture.[41] Regarding countries to which this provision is applied specifically by regulation, the exception may not be invoked in respect of the murder, kidnapping or attack on the person of a Head of State or Head of Government of a country, or the taking or endangering of life being an offense "committed in circumstances in which such conduct creates a collective danger, whether direct or indirect, to the lives of other persons."[42] However, a general exception of terrorism from the category of political offenses in Australia's extradition laws has not yet been effected.

It thus emerges that the non-extradition of citizens rule constitutes the greater continuing handicap to the surrender of a terrorist offender to a requesting state. The national state of the offender, not being the state where the act occurred or had its effects, is entitled to prosecute but might do so under evidentiary handicaps, or without diligence. That state might indeed be most reluctant to undertake the task of prosecution, where local sympathies lay with the offender, or where the state felt intimidated by the prospect of possible retaliation against itself by associates of the offender. In such cases, if the International Criminal Court were invested with jurisdiction over the offense, it would be a relief to be able to cede the case to that Court.

Resolution 1373 (2001), adopted unanimously by the United Nations Security Council on 28 September 2001, did not attempt to impose a duty of extradition as such, but laid down several important obligations ancillary to the extradition process. Paragraph 2 of the resolution, adopted under Chapter VII of the Charter and under the heading "Decides" (which triggers its binding effect for all Members of the UN, as prescribed in article 25 of the Charter of the UN), includes the following subparagraphs:

---

41. *See* Extradition Act, 1988, § 5 (Austl).
42. *Id.*

Decides also that all States shall . . .

(e) Ensure that any person who participates in the financing, planning, preparation or perpetration of terrorist acts or in supporting terrorist acts is brought to justice and ensure that, in addition to any other measures against them, such terrorist acts are established as serious criminal offences in domestic laws and regulations and that the punishment duly reflects the seriousness of such terrorist acts;

(f) Afford one another the greatest measure of assistance in connection with criminal investigations or criminal proceedings relating to the financing or support of terrorist acts, including assistance in obtaining evidence in their possession necessary for the proceedings.[43]

The phrase in subparagraph (e) "is brought to justice" seems to comprehend the *aut dedere aut judicare* principle without explicitly saying so. The injunction that domestic laws be enacted to make terrorist acts, as such, distinct offenses under national law serves as a necessary precondition to the full application of the dual criminality requirement of extradition law.

Paragraph three of the resolution, in which the Security Council "*Calls upon* all States to . . .", is not binding under article 25 of the Charter, not being a decision, but is nonetheless a directive that has weight. Subparagraph (g) of this paragraph calls upon states to ensure that "claims of political motivation are not recognized as grounds for refusing requests for the extradition of alleged terrorists."[44] This relatively weak provision reflects the failure of previous efforts in multilateral conventions, such as the hijacking and sabotage of aircraft conventions, to exclude the political offense exception to extradition altogether. On the other hand, the political offense exception has been explicitly excluded in the International Convention for the Suppression of Terrorist Bombings (1998)[45] and in the current Draft Comprehensive International Convention on Terrorism.[46]

Another aspect of extradition of terrorists is revealed by the case of three men accused of conspiracy with Osama bin Laden and the al Qaeda group to

---

43. *See* S. C. Res. 1373, *supra* note 2.
44. *Id.*
45. *See* Terrorist Bombing Convention, *supra* note 20, art. 11.
46. *See* Draft International Convention on Terrorism, *supra* note 5, art. 5, which provides that "[e]ach State Party shall adopt such measures as may be necessary, including, where appropriate, domestic legislation, to ensure that criminal acts within the scope of this Convention are under no circumstances justifiable by considerations of a political, philosophical, ideological, racial, ethnic, religious or other similar nature."

commit the bombings of the American Embassies in Nairobi, Kenya and Dar es Salaam, Tanzania. They were arrested in the United Kingdom and held for extradition to the United States. No point could have been taken that the offenses, being politically motivated, should have been excluded from extradition, because terrorism is expressly excepted from the category of political offenses for which extradition may not be given.[47] The point taken on behalf of the accused on appeal to the House of Lords was that the alleged crimes, having been committed in Kenya and Tanzania, were not committed "within the jurisdiction" of the United States, as required by the applicable bilateral treaty of extradition between the United Kingdom and the United States, and the UK Extradition Act, 1989. The House of Lords held unanimously that "jurisdiction" was a wide enough expression to comprehend extraterritorial jurisdiction of the kind asserted by both the United States and the United Kingdom in like cases.[48] Lord Hutton stated that:

> [m]y principal reason for forming this opinion is that in the modern world of international terrorism and crime proper effect would not be given to the extradition procedures agreed upon between states if a person accused in a requesting state of an offence over which that state had extra-territorial jurisdiction (it also being an offence over which the requested state would have jurisdiction) could avoid extradition on the ground that the offence was not committed within the territory of the requesting state.[49]

The Death Penalty

Still another impediment to extradition of terrorists is the difference in policies among even otherwise like-minded states as to the death penalty. The countries of the European Union, Australia, Canada and New Zealand have abolished the death penalty in their own laws, and will extradite to states, such as the United States, which retain the death penalty, only on condition that the death penalty, if imposed, will not be carried out.

In the case of *In re Fawwaz*, Lord Scott of Foscote in his separate opinion noted that the Act of 1989 contained certain safeguards for the fugitive criminal whose extradition is sought. Among these was:

---

47. Extradition Act, 1989, c. 33, § 24 (UK).
48. In re Al-Fawwaz [2002] 1 A.C. 556; 41 I.L.M. 1224 (2002).
49. *Id.* at para. 64.

[h]e will not be extradited unless the [UK] Secretary of State decides, as a matter of discretion, to order that the extradition may proceed. It has become the settled practice, as I understand it, for the Secretary of State, in a case where the law of the extraditing state might subject the extradited prisoner on conviction to the death penalty, to require a guarantee that a death sentence will not be imposed (see *Soering v. UK* (1989) 11 EHRR 439).[50]

If, as is to be expected, an increasing number of terrorists associated with the events of September 11, 2001 are arrested in countries outside the United States, these differences in policies raise serious legal and political questions. The legal questions will arise under the laws of the requested state and under the terms of the applicable extradition treaties with the United States. Where the death penalty is available under the laws of both requesting and requested states there will be no problem. But an increasing number of states have abolished the death penalty. This gives rise to the specter of discrimination: the imposition of the death penalty on a terrorist extradited from another country will depend upon whether conditions have been attached to the extradition, as in *Fawwaz*. Presumably the United States would be in a position to enforce those conditions, where terrorists are prosecuted under federal and not state laws.[51]

The political questions are obvious, but their answers are not. How can one explain to the people of New York City, or indeed the entire United States, that an extradited terrorist associated with the attack on the World Trade Center can get a maximum of life imprisonment, whereas an ordinary murderer faces the death penalty?

Fair Trial Safeguards in Extradition

Extradition treaties do not usually contain provisions requiring the parties to observe accepted standards of a fair trial after extradition. In the past, the very existence of a bilateral treaty, or a willingness to act on an ad hoc basis, have been regarded as tacit acknowledgment of the respect the parties have for one another's processes. Doubts have emerged, however, in recent years where multilateral treaties containing extradition clauses are open to all states to adhere. It may sometimes be the case that the internal situation in a bilateral

---

50. *Id.* at para 121.
51. *See* Case Concerning the Vienna Convention on Consular Relations (Paraguay v. US), 1998 I.C.J. 99, 37 I.L.M. 812 (1998); Breard v. Greene, 532 U.S. 371 (1998) *reprinted in* 37 I.L.M. 824; LaGrand Case (F.R.G. v. US), 1999 I.C.J. 9.

partner state, once of an acceptable order, has deteriorated. There is concern that under the laws of some states it is difficult or impossible to refuse extradition on the grounds that the human rights of the person extradited might be violated after return: the so-called "rule of non-inquiry."[52]

To some extent, the issue of fair trial safeguards overlaps with the protection accorded political offenders. The formula most often used is to the effect that the extradition of a requested person may be refused if the requested state has reason to believe that, if returned, the alleged offender may be punished, or suffer prejudice at his or her trial, on account of race, religion, nationality or political opinion. On the other hand, if the issue of a fair trial arises in the context of corruption or incompetence in the legal system of the requesting state, or of cruel or unusual punishments, it is likely to be dealt with through the exercise of the general discretion of requested states to refuse extradition in all the circumstances of the case. Where the exercise of that discretion is unreviewable by a court in the requested state, the outcome for the alleged offender can be unpredictable.

A more principled manner in which the executive discretion to refuse extradition in such circumstances could be exercised would be by reference, to Article 14 of the International Covenant on Civil and Political Rights, which sets out fair trial rights in detail. Article 14 provides, inter alia, that "everyone shall be entitled to a fair and public hearing by a competent, independent and impartial tribunal established by law."[53] There is an exception, however, of particular relevance in respect to the procedures proposed for the trial of terrorist suspects in the United States:

> [t]he press and the public may be excluded from all or part of a trial for reasons of morals, public order (*ordre public*) or national security in a democratic society, or where the interest of the private lives of the parties so requires, or to the extent strictly necessary in the opinion of the court in special circumstances where publicity would prejudice the interests of justice; but any judgment rendered in a criminal case or in a suit at law shall be made public except where the interest of juvenile persons otherwise requires or the proceedings concern matrimonial disputes or the guardianship of children.[54]

Parts of this provision (made somewhat turgid in its attempt at comprehensiveness) have obvious implications for the trial of terrorists.

---

52. On this question see John Dugard and Christine Van den Wyngaert, *Reconciling Extradition with Human Rights*, 92 AM. J. INT'L. L. (1998).
53. *See* ICCPR, *supra* note 23, art. 14.
54. *Id.*

In the case of *Fawwaz*, Lord Scott, after raising the question of the death penalty, proceeded to another matter of concern: trial before special courts,

> [t]he media have, over the past few weeks, carried reports of the intention of the President of the US, acting under emergency executive powers, to establish military tribunals to try non-US citizens who are accused of terrorist offences. The offences with which these appellants are charged might well fall within the category of offences proposed to be dealt with by military tribunals. It is reported that the proposed military tribunals will be presided over by military personnel, not judges, will be able to admit evidence that would not ordinarily be admissible before a criminal court of law, and will be able to conduct the trial behind closed doors. The charges against the appellants that have led to the extradition requests were laid before the US District Court for the Southern District of New York. If the appellants are to be extradited I imagine that they will be tried before that court or some other Federal Court and not before a military tribunal that will not need to sit in public and that need not observe the rules of evidence.[55]

Although another member of the House of Lords, Lord Hutton, expressly dissociated himself from the remarks of Lord Scott, observing that the issue had not been raised in argument,[56] this consideration could clearly arise on a future occasion.

The International Criminal Court

The opposition of the United States to the establishment and future operation of the International Criminal Court is well known. It stands in contrast to the attitude of many of its closest allies, including Australia, Canada, and the United Kingdom, which have all ratified the Rome Statute. It is not proposed to examine the differences in policies in this paper. There are, however, two points of relevance to the topic of terrorism.

In the first place, terrorism, as such, is not a crime within the jurisdiction of the International Criminal Court. At the Rome Conference, states urging that terrorism be designated a crime within the jurisdiction of the Court included Algeria, India, Israel, Libya, Russia, and Turkey. However, most delegations were opposed. As one commentator has remarked, "An essential reason behind the resistance to the inclusion of terrorism within the ICC's jurisdiction

---

55. See In re Al-Fawwaz, *supra* note 48, at para. 121.
56. *Id.* at para. 93.

is the fear of politicization of the ICC. The League of Arab States opposed the inclusion of international terrorism in the ICC Statute on the ground that the international community has not been able to define 'terrorism' in such a way as to be generally acceptable."[57]

However, it seems that certain acts of terrorism might constitute a crime against humanity, as defined in the Statute. On the face of it, the definition of murder in Article 7 of the Rome Statute would cover such acts as the destruction of the PanAm flight over Lockerbie, Scotland, in 1988, and the attack on the World Trade Center on September 11, 2001:

> 1. For the purposes of this Statute, 'crime against humanity' means any of the following acts when committed as part of a widespread or systematic attack directed against any civilian population, with knowledge of the attack:
>
> a) murder; ...
>
> 2. For the purpose of paragraph 1:
>
> a) 'attack directed against any civilian population' means a course of conduct involving the multiple commission of acts referred to in paragraph 1 against any civilian population, pursuant to or in furtherance of a State or organizational policy to commit such attack.[58]

In both cases there was a systematic[59] attack causing multiple deaths of civilians in furtherance of an organizational policy by terrorist groups.

Whether such cases would be brought before the International Criminal Court, and whether that Court would accept jurisdiction over them, remains to be seen. It may be that, if current negotiations in the United Nations succeed in producing a widely accepted and comprehensive convention on terrorism, a new category of crimes following the convention definition of terrorism might be added to the Rome Statute by way of the amendment mechanism included in that Statute. The existence of such a neutral forum for the prosecution of terrorist offenses would have several advantages over

---

57. KRIANGSAK KITTICHAISAREE, INTERNATIONAL CRIMINAL LAW (2001), 227.
58. See Rome Statute of the International Criminal Court, art. 7, U.N. Doc. A/CONF.183/9 (1998), available at http://www.un.org/law/icc/statute/romefra.htm (Jan. 13, 2003) [hereinafter Rome Statute].
59. While not defined in the Rome Statute, the term "systematic" is familiar to recent ad hoc tribunals and was discussed in Prosecutor v. Akayesu, Judgement, No. ICTR-96-4-T (Sep. 2, 1998), which stated that: "systematic" may be defined as thoroughly organized and following a regular pattern on the basis of a common policy involving substantial public or private resources." See Prosecutor v. Tadic, Opinion and Judgment, No. IT-94-1-T, para. 652 (May 7, 1997), excerpted in 36 I.L.M. 908, § 6.4.

prosecution before the courts of the states most closely affected. The most important of these are the transparency and international character of the Court's proceedings, and the credibility of its findings and sentences.

There is some force in the objections raised by the United States towards the ICC, or at least in so far as it might in future assert jurisdiction over US citizens. As the almost always indispensable leader of UN and other peace enforcement operations, US personnel are more likely than others to be exposed to the possibility of maliciously inspired prosecutions for alleged war crimes. The principle of complementarity, which gives primacy to the national courts of the alleged offender, goes a long way towards meeting that objection. This, of course, assumes that in such a case the United States would be willing at least to conduct an investigation into the allegations. A negative finding would be accepted by the Court as a bar to prosecution before it, unless the decision not to prosecute in the national jurisdiction "resulted from the unwillingness or the inability of the State concerned genuinely to prosecute."[60]

Another protection built into the Rome Statute is that where a request is made of a state for the surrender of an accused person to the Court, the requested state may not be required to "act inconsistently with its obligations under international agreements pursuant to which the consent of a sending state is required to surrender a person of that state to the Court, unless the Court can first obtain the cooperation of the sending state for the giving of consent to the surrender."[61] The term "sending state" is not defined, but it is a term of art used not only to refer to the state establishing a diplomatic or consular mission in another state ("the receiving state") but also the state which stations military personnel in another state under arrangements of the nature of a status of visiting forces agreement. Thus US military personnel stationed in Australia would not be surrendered by Australia to the Tribunal without the consent of the United States.

The United States introduced into the Security Council in June 2002 a draft resolution that would have the effect of excluding from the jurisdiction of the ICC the personnel of all missions, military and civilian, engaged in operations sanctioned by the United Nations.[62] This is understandable. A Security

---

60. *See* Rome Statute, *supra* note 58, art. 17.
61. *Id.* at art. 98(2).
62. **Editors note:** This draft resolution resulted in S. C. Res. 1422, U.N. SCOR, 57th Sess., U.N. Doc. S/1422/(2002), which provides that consistent with Article 16 of the Rome Statute, "the ICC, if a case arises involving current or former officials or personnel from a contributing State not a Party to the Rome Statute over acts or omissions relating to a United Nations established or authorized operations, shall for a twelve-month period starting 1 July 2002 not commence or proceed with investigation or prosecution of any such case, unless the Security Council decides otherwise."

Council resolution would, of course, "trump" the provisions of the Rome Statute.[63] Less understandable is a draft bill introduced into Congress, the American Servicemembers' Protection Act, which would authorize retaliatory measures in the event that a US citizen were ever placed before the Court.[64] This is the kind of reaction that dismays America's allies. A spirit of triumphalism, or American exceptionalism, serves to undermine the international goodwill and spirit of cooperation that alone can defeat the forces of terrorism.

Conclusion

The events of September 11th, 2001 have driven home the point that significant issues impacting coalition operations continue to exist. These issues, ranging from the lack of an internationally accepted definition of terrorism, to the problems associated with jurisdiction and extradition of terrorists, highlight that a truly effective response to terrorist acts must be through an effective, coherent multilateral and multistate effort. Clearly there is much still to be done in these areas to win the war on terrorism.

---

63. *See* Lockerbie Case, *supra* note 38.
64. **Editor's note:** The American Servicemembers' Protection Act of 2002, was signed into law by President George W. Bush on August 2, 2002. Section 7427 of the act authorizes the president to use all necessary means to free certain individuals from the jurisdiction of the ICC. *See* The American Servicemember's Protection Act of 2002, 22 U.S.C.S. § 7427 (2002).

XV

Panel III
Commentary—Maritime & Coalition Operations

Kenneth O'Rourke[1]

I well remember the day, during Operation ENDURING FREEDOM, that General Tommy Franks[2] called me into his office and stated that intelligence indicated there were four vessels containing al Qaeda members departing Pakistani waters on their way to Northern Africa. His question was, what are we authorized to do? My response was that we are within our rights to intercept them—with some quick coordination, maritime interception operations (MIO) were born. I based my response primarily on Article 51 of the UN Charter and articulated that we had the right to intercept vessels containing terrorist leaders who represented an immediate threat to our country. Since this initial intercept, I have heard many argue that maritime intercepts are nothing more than piracy and interference with freedom of the high seas. Piracy it is not. The coalition is not interdicting every vessel on the high seas, nor stopping every vessel at gunpoint. Interdiction measures are limited in nature and

---

1. Commander Kenneth O'Rourke is a US Navy judge advocate serving as the Deputy Staff Judge Advocate for US Central Command.
2. General Franks is the current commander of the US Central Command. The Central Command geographic area of responsibility includes Afghanistan.

designed to address a specific threat, including what is ultimately a threat even to maritime safety.

There are a number of legal authorities used by various nations to conduct these operations. Two of the legal justifications for conducting MIO used by many of the coalition partners are the consent of the master and/or the consent of the flag state to conduct a visit/search. In that regard, the United States has bilateral agreements with various countries permitting such boardings. The belligerent right of visit and search is yet another authority some nations rely on. Of course, however, Article 51 of the UN Charter has come to be accepted as the primary basis for undertaking such operations.

In this war on terror there is a nontraditional enemy. This war does not have many of the characteristic associated with a traditional war. There is an enemy that blends with civilians, a criminal enemy in the case of al Qaeda, operating with an unrecognized sovereign, the Taliban. Neither of these enemies operate within a recognized chain of command that conforms to the laws of armed conflict, nor do they have traditional target sets such as military infrastructure and armored vehicle formations to engage. This is a new kind of war. This "war" is unique in that it is a blend of fighting criminals and traditional combatants. A war fought applying international criminal law and the law of armed conflict. Nontraditional measures may be required to respond to this threat.

For the time being, Article 51 provides the coalition with the necessary authority to engage in maritime interception operations against both the criminal and combatant elements of our enemy. This right to conduct operations in "self-defense" may become attenuated over time, however, as Afghanistan becomes a legitimate state and al Qaeda goes into, no doubt temporary, hiding. As time passes, the question will loom larger and larger as to whether the immediacy of the threat exists and additional authority is needed. Perhaps the authority to continue maritime interception operations against terrorist elements already exists as a matter of custom under international law. Will the Article 51 justification fade and not provide adequate authority to continue maritime intercept operations against terrorists? Only time will tell.

As we all know, Article 110 of the UN Law of Sea Convention (LOS Convention) provides authority to exercise limited jurisdiction over foreign flag vessels. That is, to undertake the right of approach and visit in circumstances where it is suspected that a vessel is, among other things, engaged in piracy or slave trade, or when the vessel is flagless.[3] Does the international community need more authority than is provided by Article 51 of the Charter, similar to that contained in Article 110 of the LOS Convention, to counter the threat from terrorism? I suggest that the additional authority already exists in custom and needs to be explicitly recognized. Application of Article 51 has its natural limits - temporal limits and geographic limits that are viewed by many to preclude continuing maritime interception operations to thwart present and future terrorist threats. It may be time for the international community to recognize that "terrorism" is an internationally recognized crime that is equally as abhorrent as piracy and slavery and that additional authority is required to combat the threat.

Only the future holds the answer to a number of very important questions related to the war on terrorism in a maritime environment. It remains to be seen if the United States and coalition partners can continue to use Article 51 as the basis for maritime interception operations six months or a year from now. Will it work over the entire globe or only close to Afghanistan? Will we be able to approach vessels providing financial support to terrorist networks planning a strike six months from now? Will these actions be acceptable under an Article 51 self-defense concept or will new legal authority be required by the international community? Have new legal authorities already been established in custom and practice treating vessels playing a part in terrorism like vessels participating in slavery and piracy? Clearly, there are unknowns in the future of the war on terrorism. The international community must address these issues and provide the legal authorities necessary to continue to prosecute the war on terrorism in a maritime environment.

---

3. *See* U.N. Convention on Law of the Sea, U.N. Doc. A/CONF.62/122 (1982), *reprinted in* BARRY CARTER AND PHILLIP TRIMBLE, INTERNATIONAL LAW SELECTED DOCUMENTS (2001), at 553.

XVI

Panel III
Commentary—Maritime & Coalition Operations

Paul Cronan[1]

While Australia has not yet participated in maritime interception operations in support of the global war on terrorism, Australia has been involved in maritime interception operations in the Gulf of Arabia enforcing UN Security Council resolutions against Iraq for over ten years. Australia strongly supports the Security Council sanctions enforcement regime and its involvement in these operations is ongoing. Given our participation in such maritime interception operations, Australia has been perfectly positioned to closely observe the conduct of maritime interception operations in support of the global war on terrorism. In my view, Australia would have few legal difficulties supporting these operations which have their legal basis in Article 51 of the UN Charter. Ample legal authority exists for conducting such operations provided the essential elements of an Article 51 operation are met. While it is certainly preferable to have a United Nations Security Council Resolution authorizing these interception operations, such authority is not necessary given

---

1. Wing Commander Paul Cronan is the Chief Legal Officer at Headquarters, Australian Theatre.

the existence of Article 51 and the customary international law right preceding this codification of the inherent right of self-defense.

On the subject of significant coalition legal issues that confronted Australia in the lead-up to deploying troops in support of the US-led military response to international terrorism, host nation basing arrangements was near the top of the list. Notwithstanding Australia's early agreement to support the US-led coalition, it took some time for Australia to put in place the necessary international agreements to support the basing of Australian troops in the Middle East. Most Middle East countries supported the United States in its endeavors to root out international terrorism from the region but negotiating basing agreements takes time. What quickly became apparent was that these potential host countries were fielding requests from a variety of nations to base people, aircraft, ships, etc. in their territory. Unlike Australia, the United States and United Kingdom had pre-existing relationships with many of these countries and, accordingly had little difficulty activating existing or negotiating new basing agreements. Australia had few pre-existing agreements with regional Middle East nations and it took time to negotiate relevant basing rights. This directly impacted on the timing of the deployment of relevant Australian Defence Force elements. The lesson for Australia then, and one it seems the United States understands well, is that existing strategic relationships with countries throughout Australia's sphere of interest is preferable to trying to put such relationships in place only when the need arises.

From a legal planning perspective, Australia had difficulties deploying its military legal officers (Judge Advocates) to those locations where they could best value-add to the operation. When the number of personnel deploying on an operation are limited, it is often difficult identifying where and when legal officers should be involved in the planning and operations process. In Australia's case, legal officers deploying on operations is a relatively recent phenomena. As the audience recognizes however, early identification and resolution of key legal issues can save considerable time and frustration later on. Because of this inability to position legal officers as desired and get them involved early in the coalition legal planning process, Australia tended to coordinate its rules of engagement only with the United States (as opposed to the United Kingdom and Canada, for example) and only then very late in the ROE development process. Although these ROE seem to be working fine for Australia today, from a coalition legal planning perspective this approach is not recommended. Proper positioning of legal officers early and in the right locations is a lesson re-learned for Australia's military legal staff.

XVII

Panel III
Commentary—Maritime & Coalition Operations

Neil Brown[1]

The United Kingdom's participation in operations against al Qaeda and the Taliban (in support of Operation ENDURING FREEDOM) is, with the exception of the contribution to the International Security and Assistance Force (ISAF) in Afghanistan, pursuant to the right to self-defense codified in Article 51 of the UN Charter. In those operations, the United Kingdom is participating in an extensive, US-led, multi-national coalition. No single set of coalition rules of engagement (ROE) exists for all states participating in Operation ENDURING FREEDOM. Each nation operates under its own national ROE, for what are perfectly understandable reasons. After all, the ROE are produced specifically for each mission, taking into account the threat, and it is each nation's policy and its view of the relevant international law which will define its national mission. Whereas for other coalition and combined operations, ROE are routinely shared, it seems more than likely, for reasons I will explain, that nations will, for the foreseeable future, keep a fairly close hold on the

---

1. Commander Neil Brown is an judge advocate serving in the UK Royal Navy. During the initial phase of Operation ENDURING FREEDOM he was assigned as a liaison officer to US Central Command.

ROE applying to their forces undertaking missions in what is often referred to as the "global war on terrorism."

The history of the United Kingdom is one that speaks to our marked involvement in the Gulf of Arabia over a long period. After all, oil production in the Gulf region began in earnest to meet the need for oil to fuel the Royal Navy's ships. In recent years, the United Kingdom has routinely deployed warships to the Gulf, first to keep oil flowing through the Straits of Hormuz during the Iran–Iraq War, and (apart from initial operations against Iraq following the invasion of Kuwait) ever since then in support of UN Security Council Resolution 665.[2]

The Royal Navy's familiarity with the region has been a tremendous operational strength, as has working with many of the same coalition members while adjoined to the US Central Command. In the days following September 11th, this familiarity was also, I sense, something of a complication. It is perhaps inevitable that differences between missions not sharing the same legal bases would not be immediately obvious, particularly when set against the political and media background presenting a united front in the war on terrorism. The fact that operations against al Qaeda and the Taliban are conducted under Article 51 as "collective self-defence" did not appear to many (other than the lawyers) to be significant at the outset. This only became an issue when it manifested in practice when UK ROE reflecting the precise scope of the UK mission were compared to, for example, the US ROE reflecting the US mission. The call to service lawyers that "there is an ROE issue," did not necessarily mean then that there is an ROE issue of the sort usually capable of resolution between military commands, but represented instead a friction point between different national policies and law. In the area of our coalition maritime operations this has been the background to much important and interesting debate, especially in the area of terrorism.

The UK approach to operations against al Qaeda and the Taliban, both in terms of law and policy, has permitted participation both in operations in Afghanistan and in simultaneous coalition maritime operations aiming to capture, or deprive sea mobility, to terrorists on the high seas, the latter as part of a coalition of states all of whose armed forces and other government agencies have collaborated to ensure that the important issues have been coordinated

---

2. S. C. Res. 665, U.N. SCOR, 45th Sess., U.N. Doc S/665/(1990) calls on all member states to "halt inward and outward maritime shipping to inspect their cargos and to ensure strict implementation with the provisions" contained in UN Security Council Resolution 661. S. C. Res. 661, U.N. SCOR, 45th Sess., U.N. Doc S/661/(1990) calls upon member states essentially to cease all trade with Iraq.

and addressed. That is not the same as saying that maritime operations are conducted as part of a global war against terrorism.

Terrorism is not a new phenomena to the United Kingdom, indeed it has been a part of our everyday lives for several decades. Terrorism has traditionally been dealt with as a law enforcement issue (albeit with military support to civilian authorities) and is thought by many in Europe to be essentially a criminal problem. It is accepted of course that the scale and character of the events of September 11th set them apart and are properly assessed as amounting to an armed attack for the purposes of Article 51 of the UN Charter, permitting states on this occasion to respond in self-defense with military force. In the context of this operation, the law of armed conflict clearly overlaps with international and domestic criminal law and it is the effect of this which we have worked hard to understand and deconflict.

Defining terrorism as a universal crime is a laudable goal but problematic. As Professor Shearer properly points out, "terrorism" when defined is immediately susceptible to politicization. This has probably stifled attempts to agree to a definition before now. By way of example, I recently heard a Russian flag officer, on extending his condolences and sympathy to the people of the United States for September 11th, make clear that in his view the situation in Afghanistan was identical to that faced by Russia in Chechnya. Without falling back on the trite and all too easy phrase about "one man's terrorist being another man's freedom fighter," this is a relevant example of the difficulty which will be faced in developing an internationally acceptable definition that will not be susceptible to political abuse.

Notwithstanding that offensive UK operations in Afghanistan may be conducted under Article 51 of the Charter, acting in collective self-defense with the United States, and that in Afghanistan (given the way in which al Qaeda and the Taliban are inextricably linked) operations are conducted under the law of armed conflict, it has not appeared clear to me that the same could necessarily be said for the simultaneous maritime operations. There is no al Qaeda Navy, nor is there an Afghan Navy. The terrorists, if they are at sea, may be on the high seas or in the territorial seas of a third state, and if their vessels are flagged at all will be in vessels which are also of a third state. The prospect of exercising belligerent rights in the current circumstances seems to me therefore to be implausible. And so it is my view that we have a situation where operations under Article 51 may not avail themselves of the full range of rights usually available to belligerents in an international armed conflict. The effect of this would be to say, for example, that although maritime units may use force such as is necessary and proportional, they may be required to do so within the peacetime rules and conventions which apply at sea, a case in point being the United Kingdom's fairly conservative view of the doctrine of flag state consent. As an example, the Royal Navy recently boarded a merchant vessel in the English Channel on the basis of intelligence that the vessel was carrying terrorists who were armed with some sort of weapon which presented an imminent chemical or biological threat.[3] Recognizing that the boarding could have occurred under an Article 51 basis of self-defense, the United Kingdom nonetheless, and perhaps somewhat conservatively, requested and received the consent of the flag state to board and search the vessel. While Professor von Heinegg's concern that this approach might undermine the continuing right to stop and search a vessel pursuant to Article 51 is noted, I believe that the United Kingdom is simply not prepared to invoke the right of self-defense for such boardings without seeking flag state approval unless that is necessary and proportional in the operational circumstances, for example in circumstances where a flag state would be unwilling or unable to give it and the request would compromise the mission.

As noted earlier, the question arises as to how long coalition members can in good faith continue to rely upon Article 51 as the legal basis for their use of force. From a maritime perspective, existing peacetime law permitting warships to board third party vessels on the high seas is quite limited indeed. Article 110 of the UN Convention on the Law of the Sea (LOS Convention) provides only limited permission to board when such acts as suspected piracy, slave trading, and unauthorized broadcasting are taking place or the vessel is state-less.[4] This is somewhat unsatisfactory, and one wonders whether, had the LOS Convention been negotiated in 1992, Article 110 might have included powers to interdict drug traffickers, and whether in 2002 it might have been extended to include terrorism. Professor von Heinegg touched on this very important area of third party consent when he talked about it in terms of

---

3. Unknown Author, *Anti-Terror Teams Intercept Ship*, IRISH TIMES, Dec. 20, 2001, available at LexisNexis Major World Newspaper (Oct. 1, 2002).

4. *See* U.N. Convention on Law of the Sea, U.N. Doc. A/CONF.62/122 (1982), art. 110, *reprinted in* BARRY CARTER AND PHILLIP TRIMBLE, INTERNATIONAL LAW SELECTED DOCUMENTS (2001), at 553. Article 110 provides in relevant part that "[e]xcept where acts of interference derive from powers conferred by treaty, a warship which encounters on the high seas a foreign ship, other than a ship entitled to complete immunity in accordance with articles and, is not justified in boarding it unless there is reasonable ground for suspecting that:

(a) the ship is engaged in piracy; (b) the ship is engaged in the slave trade; (c) the ship is engaged in unauthorized broadcasting and the flag State of the warship has jurisdiction under article 109; (d) the ship is without nationality; or (e) though flying a foreign flag or refusing to show its flag, the ship is, in reality, of the same nationality as the warship."

tolerating the control which belligerents might exercise. To extend this right, available to belligerents where there are reasonable grounds to suspect that a neutral vessel is subject to capture, to member states of the UN acting in accordance with Charter rights (as verified by the UN Security Council in all of its subsequent resolutions), is one thing. Indeed, it is not unreasonable to expect and even require that third parties permit us to board their vessels when there is intelligence that Taliban or al Qaeda members are on board. To take that further, and suggest for example that there is a general right of visit and search of third party vessels without such intelligence, is quite another.

XVIII

Panel III
Commentary—Maritime & Coalition Operations

Jean-Guy Perron[1]

Canada has contributed a significant number of personnel and assets to the global war on terrorism. Over the last several years, Canadian warships have conducted maritime interdiction missions to interdict shipping in breach of the UN Security Council resolutions on Iraq. However, such resolutions do not apply in Operation ENDURING FREEDOM (OEF) and Canada deployed it ships to conduct maritime interdiction operations for this operation pursuant to the right of collective and individual self-defense contained in Article 51 of the UN Charter.

Canada is considered to be in armed conflict with the Taliban and al Qaeda and such conflict is not limited geographically to the territory of Afghanistan but extends to the international waters of the high seas. Canadian maritime operations searching for those who support the Taliban or al Qaeda, or who are themselves such, were termed "visit and search" operations. These

---

1. Lieutenant Colonel Jean-Guy Perron is currently the Assistant Judge Advocate General for the National Capital Region (Ottawa) in Canada. He was deployed to Tampa, Florida in November 2001 as the legal advisor to the Commander, Canadian Joint Task Force South West Asia.

visit and search operations were conducted pursuant to the principles found in the *San Remo Manual on International Law Applicable to Armed Conflicts at Sea*.[2]

Canadian warships could also intercept other vessels pursuant to Article 110 of the United Nations Convention on the Law of the Sea.[3] The point here is that while there are differing legal bases for conducting boarding operations, the facts surrounding each such boarding must be carefully studied so as to ensure a legitimate basis for boarding exists in international law.

Recognizing that each state in a coalition is truly the master of its own ROE, much effort must be spent to harmonize ROE throughout the coalition by sharing and deconflicting competing ROE and understanding the limitations and constraints each coalition member has on its missions. Still, harmonizing ROE in a coalition, although sometimes problematic, must remain a priority. Each state will have a different interpretation of the application of international law. Operational factors relating to coalition member forces must be considered and domestic and international policy considerations must be adhered to. Two weapons systems provide good examples of the challenges inherent in structuring ROE for coalition operations: anti-personnel landmines and riot control agents. Many states have different rules and restrictions based on policy reasons, domestic law, or international law that make the use of these systems sometimes quite difficult to synthesize. However, working through this process is important for commanders as it helps them understand the constraints and limitations on assigning certain tasks to certain coalitions units.

On a different matter, Canada too had difficulties getting its forces into the theater of operations for Operation ENDURING FREEDOM. This demonstrated the need for improving strategic partnerships with other states throughout the world to improve this situation.

Finally, it is interesting to note the efforts that Canada has undertaken since the events of September 11th unfolded. In the area of anti-terror and domestic legislation, the Canadian government passed federal legislation

---

2. *See generally*, SAN REMO MANUAL ON INTERNATIONAL LAW APPLICABLE TO ARMED CONFLICTS AT SEA (Louise Doswald-Beck ed., 1995), Section II Visit and Search of Neutral Vessels [hereinafter SAN REMO MANUAL].
3. UN Convention on Law of the Sea, UN Doc. A/CONF.62/122 (1982), art. 110, *reprinted in* BARRY CARTER AND PHILLIP TRIMBLE, INTERNATIONAL LAW SELECTED DOCUMENTS, (2001) at 553.
4. *See* Anti-Terrorism Act, R.S.C., C-36 (Dec. 18, 2001); *see also*, Unknown Author, *Highlights of Anti-Terrorism Act, available at* http://canada.justice.gc.ca/en/news/nr/2001/doc_27787.html (Oct. 1, 2002) [hereinafter Anti-Terrorism Act].

permitting it to better identify, prosecute, and convict terrorist groups.[4] This Anti-Terrorism Act permits Canada to ratify the two remaining counter terrorism conventions it has signed but has yet to ratify.[5] Finally, the Canadian Legislature has amended the Official Secrets Act[6] to address national security concerns pertaining to terrorist related activities as well as the Canada Evidence Act[7] to provide a new process for dealing with the disclosure of sensitive information in judicial proceedings. Clearly, Canada's response to the events of September 11th have been quite measured and serious.

---

5. These two conventions are: The International Convention for the Suppression of the Financing of Terrorism, G.A. Res. 109, U.N. GAOR 6th Comm., 54 Sess., 76th mtg., Agenda Item 160, U.N. Doc. A/54/109 (1999) and International Convention for the Suppression of Terrorism Bombings, G.A. Res. 165, U.N. GAOR, 52 Sess, U.N. Doc. A/52/164 (1998).
6. See Anti-Terrorism Act, *supra* note 4.
7. Id.

XIX

Panel III
Discussion—Maritime and Coalition Operations

On the Abduction or Extradition of Terrorists

Ivan Shearer

Countries throughout the common law world draw a distinction between obtaining jurisdiction over individuals through some type of government collusion which violates international law and obtaining jurisdiction through happenstance over an individual. In the former case, such jurisdiction over a person constitutes an abuse of process for the court to continue trial and the case should be dismissed and the individual discharged. When jurisdiction is obtained through happenstance, however, trial may proceed. This approach stands in marked contrast to that taken by the US Supreme Court in *United States v. Alvarez-Machain* where the Court held that it effectively does not matter how jurisdiction over the body of the defendant is obtained.[1]

---

1. **Editor's Note:** After being indicted in the United States for the kidnapping and murder of a DEA agent, Humberto Alvarez-Machain was kidnapped by the Mexican police and flown to the United States to be turned over to DEA agents. Defendant contested the jurisdiction of the federal district court and the Ninth Circuit Court of Appeals reversed the holding of the district court. Upon government appeal to the Supreme Court, that Court reversed and remanded the holding of the Circuit Court of Appeals holding that a criminal defendant, abducted to the United States from a nation with which it has an extradition treaty does not acquire a defense to the jurisdiction of US courts simply by virtue of the abduction itself when the treaty does not exclude that a party might resort to self-help for achieving the presence of an individual. 504 U.S. 655 (1992) at 662 [hereinafter Machain].

Wolff von Heinegg

I do not agree that the practice of irregular rendition has a proper place in international law. The violation of a nation's sovereignty by resort to self-help is unconscionable. Using armed force to conduct such an irregular rendition is clearly a violation of international law.

Kenneth O'Rourke

United States courts have, on occasion, suggested that a defendant may not be prosecuted if his presence is obtained in violation of specific terms of an extradition treaty prohibiting abduction.[2] Where, however, an extradition treaty is not violated and a defendant's presence is obtained through forcible abduction, (commonly known as irregular rendition) the US Supreme Court has consistently recognized that jurisdiction may nonetheless be properly exercised.[3] The propriety of irregular rendition is less clear, however, within the international community, prompting the United States, as a matter of policy not to resort to its use. Having said that, I believe irregular rendition continues to have its place, particularly in the war on terrorism.

As for international law, I do not agree that irregular rendition is absolutely prohibited and not a proper mechanism for addressing terrorism. For example, the proposition that Article 51 of the UN Charter would not permit the United States to enter a country to conduct a rendition, or renditions, as a matter of national self-defense is illogical. Certainly, if the United States could have snatched Osama bin Laden to remove the threat to its peace and security, instead of engaging in a full blown attack on al Qaeda and the Taliban, it would have done so and it would have been, if not more favorable as a means of self-defense, at least a less aggressive means authorized under Article 51. It seems incongruous to suggest that a state can resort to a full blown armed conflict, invade another state as a matter of self-defense, but could not use a lesser means of force, such as an irregular rendition, to remove the threat. Clearly, renditions to remedy criminal activity not amounting to a threat to the peace and security of a state raise issues of sovereignty that many believe are not supported by international law. However, renditions to remedy threats to the peace and security of an aggrieved state under Article 51 of the UN Charter would be much preferable to full blown military action. Unfortunately, in the case of addressing the terrorist network operating out of Afghanistan, the United States was unable to take this less severe course of action (snatch

---

2. *See, e.g.,* United States v. Rauscher, 119 U.S. 407 (1986).
3. *See, e.g.,* Ker v. Illinois, 119 U.S. 436 (1886); *see also* Machain, *supra* note 1, at 669.

Osama Bin Laden) and, as a result, needed to resort to armed hostilities against bin Laden and the Taliban who provided material support to al Qaeda.

Christopher Greenwood
Were the US government to be asked whether it were lawful for the British government to abduct Irish Republican Army suspects from America, the answer would be no. If this is true, then it must be equally true that it is not lawful for the United States to abduct offenders who are otherwise not extraditable to bring them to the United States. It is a clear violation of international law for a state to exercise its jurisdiction on the territory of another. The fact that domestic law supports the subsequent trial of such a person is entirely separate from the question of whether jurisdiction exists to seize that person from the territory of another state. There may perhaps be a self-defense exception to this in the case of someone such as bin Laden, but this is very much the exception.

The normal remedy it seems for such an irregular rendition would be the return of the person concerned as restoration of the status quo is the normal remedy required by law. History provides an example of this type of remedy where a group of British jailers from Gibraltar who were pursuing a suspect managed to arrest him on the wrong side of the border with Spain. The suspect was ultimately returned to Spain to rectify the violation of Spanish sovereignty.[4]

John Murphy
In *United States v. Alvarez-Machain*, the issue before the Supreme Court was the bilateral extradition treaty between the United States and Mexico.[5] The majority conclusion in this case was that given that the defendant's abduction was not in violation of the extradition treaty between the United States and Mexico, the rule of *Ker v. Illinois* did not prohibit the trial of *Machain* in a US court for violations of the criminal laws of the United States.[6] It is worth noting though, that if the majority had come to the conclusion that the extradition treaty barred this abduction, then the defendant would have been released and returned to Mexico. The *Machain* Court also parenthetically addressed the issue of customary international law, noting that such an abduction may well have been a violation of customary international law as a violation of the

---

4. *See In re* Patrick Lawler *in* 1 Lord McNair International Law Opinions (1956) at 77–78.
5. Machain, *supra* note 1 at 669–70.
6. *Id.* at 669–70; *citing* Ker v. Illinois, 119 U.S. 436 (1886).

sovereignty of Mexico but that such a violation must properly be considered by the executive branch and not the judicial branch.[7]

Two final points of interest merit mention about this case. First, the subsequent history of this case tells us that the government's case was ultimately dismissed pursuant to Machain's motion for summary judgment.[8] Secondly, Dr. Machain currently has civil litigation pending against the United States for damages.[9]

Yoram Dinstein

There is a risk of confusing two completely unrelated issues. One is whether or not an act of abduction from abroad constitutes a violation of the sovereignty of a foreign state. Undoubtedly, that is the case, if the abduction is carried out without the consent of the local government. A separate issue is whether the state which acquired custody over an individual through such abduction (in breach of the sovereignty of another state and therefore in breach of international law) may nevertheless exercise jurisdiction over the abductee. The answer is clear: jurisdiction exists.

On the one hand, since the act of abduction is in violation of international law, the abducting state incurs responsibility vis-à-vis the other state whose sovereignty has been encroached upon. On the other hand, the jurisdiction of the abducting state vis-à-vis the person in the dock is not affected by the inter-state clash. The paradigmatic case is that of Adolph Eichmann.[10] As is well known, Eichmann was abducted from Argentina, brought to Israel, tried there, convicted, and executed. The matter was brought by Argentina before the Security Council.[11] Interestingly enough, the Security Council,

---

7. Id. at 669–70.
8. See Machain, supra note 1, at 669–70, rev'd and remanded to United States v. Alvarez-Machain, 971 F.2d 310 (9th Cir. Ct. App. 1992), amended and remanded by sub nom. United States v. Zuno-Acre, 44 F. 3d (9th Cir. Cal. 1995), post conviction relief denied in part, dismissed in part 25 F. Supp 2d 1087 (C.D. Cal. 1988), aff'd by 209 F. 3d 1095 (9th Cir. Cal. 2000).
9. See Alvarez-Machain v. United States, 96 F.3d 1246 (9th Cir. Cal. 1996) amended by 107 F.3d 696 (9th Cir. Cal. 1997), cert denied sub nom. Berellez v. Alvarez-Machain, 522 U.S. 814 (1997) remanded by Alvarez-Machain v. United States, 266 F.3d 1045 (9th Cir. Cal. 2001).
10. Adolph Eichmann, one of the key architects of the Holocaust, fled to Argentina after World War II. Abducted by Israeli Mossad agents in 1960 (after a prolonged worldwide search), he was put on trial for genocide and related crimes. See generally J. Fawcett, The Eichmann Case, 38 BRIT. Y.B. INT'L L. 181 (1962); L.C. Green, The Eichmann Case, 23 MODERN L. REV. 507 (1960); F. Mann, Reflections on the Prosecution of Persons Abducted in Breach of International Law, in INTERNATIONAL LAW AT A TIME OF PERPLEXITY: ESSAYS IN HONOUR OF SHABATI ROSENNE 407-422, 414 (Yoram Dinstein & Mala Tabory eds., 1989).
11. See S. C. Res. 138, U.N. SCOR, 15th Sess., U.N. Doc. S/138/(1960).

while acknowledging the breach of Argentinian sovereignty, did not demand that Israel return Eichmann to Argentina. Eichmann's case is in many respects unique. But the view of the US Supreme Court on the underlying issue was consolidated already in the 19th century in *Ker v. Illinois*.[12] The Court held that personal jurisdiction is not affected by the improper manner in which a defendant is brought before a court.

Christopher Greenwood

Eichmann is far from a paradigmatic case on the abduction of individuals from the territory of another state. First, Eichmann is an egregious case and there is no real counterpart to it today. Secondly, the case was decided under an almost entirely different world order. Today, the idea that the only violation in the posited case is that of the territorial sovereignty of the state where the abduction occurs, simply does not ring true. There is also a violation by the abducting state of the international human rights of the abducted individual.[13] Indeed, the Human Rights Committee illustrated clearly this to be the case in 1981.[14] This international human right against abduction, is contained in another form in the prohibition against arbitrary arrest and detention contained in Article Nine of the International Covenant on Civil and Political Rights to which the United States is a party.[15]

International law today would not permit a state to exercise jurisdiction over someone illegally seized for two reasons. In a case like *Machain*, where unlike Eichmann, the state from whose territory the man was abducted protested throughout, the normal principles of state responsibility require the abducting state to make good its violation of the other state's sovereignty by

---

12. *See* Ker v. Illinois, 119 U.S. 436, 444 (1886). *Accord* Frisbie v. Collins, 342 U.S. 519, 523 (1952) (no Constitutional prohibition on finding of guilt when criminal defendant is forcibly abducted)
13. *See* Beverly Izes, *Drawing Lines in the Sand: When State Sponsored Abduction of War Criminals Should be Permitted*, 31 COLUM. J. L. & SOC. PROBS. 1 (1997) 12–14. *See also* Felice Morgenstern, *Jurisdiction in Seizures Effected in Violation of International Law*, 29 BRIT. Y.B. INT'L L. 265, 270 (1952).
14. *See* Views of the Human Rights Committee on the Complaint of Lopez, 36 U.N. GAOR, Supp. No. 40, at 176–84, U.N. Doc. A/36/40 (1981); *See also* M. Cherif Bassiouni, *Unlawful Seizures and Irregular Rendition Devices as Alternatives to Extradition*, 7 VAND. J. TRANSNAT'L L. 25, 59 (1979) (forcible abduction said to violate human right to liberty and freedom from arbitrary detention).
15. *See* International Covenant on Civil and Political Rights, ratified by the United States in 1992, 991 U.N.T.S. 171, 31 I.L.M. 645 (May 1992). Note that the United States does not consider Articles 1–27 of the covenant as self-executing. *See* 138 CONG. REC. S4784 (Apr. 2, 1992).

restoring the status quo. Secondly, under the international law in existence today, the abducted individual possesses rights under human rights treaties which, if taken seriously, operate to ensure that he is not abducted.

The events in Eichmann, are so peculiar to their own facts that to generalize from them is a great mistake. The *Machain* Court simply created bad law and happens to turn on a point of US law only. This case was argued and developed by the defense on the interpretation of a bilateral extradition treaty and not on the proper grounds of violations of customary international law. Accordingly, if someone is abducted from the United States by any other country, and put on trial in that other country the United States would demand his return. No remedy less than this under international law would be proper.

Yoram Dinstein

I disagree. I believe that it is very dangerous to apply to extradition law—which essentially governs the relations between states—concepts of human rights law. As far as the individual is concerned, assuming that the state has jurisdiction over him, he should appear before the court when summoned to do so. He has no human right to be a fugitive from justice. If bounty hunters were to capture and return him, the legality of the act would scarcely be challenged. Why should the position be different if the abduction was carried out by state agents? Evidently, all this is not relevant to the grievance to the state whose sovereignty has been disregarded by the abducting agents. The state carrying out the abduction may have to compensate or otherwise satisfy the aggrieved state. But let us not confuse the state with the individual.

Robert Turner

The Ninth Circuit Court of Appeals in the *Machain* case, quite simply was in error and it was proper for the Supreme Court to correct this error in the law and bring the decision into line with *Ker v. Illinois*.[16] The issue here is not whether the state has remedies or not but instead, whether the defendant should be able to deprive the US courts of jurisdiction simply because of his abduction from another state. One reason this line of reasoning remains important today is that in the global war on terrorism, there are sometimes states that may be willing to assist the United States with intelligence on individuals operating within their borders and may be willing to surreptitiously permit a "cover abduction." To avoid angering other terrorists, such states must retain their ability to protest

---

16. *See* Machain, *supra* note 1, at 946 F. 2d 1466 (1991).

publicly such alleged violations of their sovereignty. This is not to say, however, that such individuals should go free. Accordingly, international law continues to recognize that states may engage in the practice of irregular rendition.

Ivan Shearer

Our case study on irregular rendition would not be complete without a reference to the Second Circuit Court of Appeals case of *United States v. Toscanino*.[17] In this 1974 case, the Second Circuit stated that if the abduction was accompanied by more than just an abduction, in other words some violation of due process such as torture or other human rights violation, then the Second Circuit would refuse to grant jurisdiction over the abducted person.[18] Accordingly, whether the jurisdiction would stand in the event of some additional harm to the abducted individual, other than the abduction itself, in US courts is somewhat subject to debate.

On the Application of the Law of Armed Conflict

Neil Brown

Typically, the armed forces are taught that rules of engagement (ROE) are a combination of mission and threat. Clearly, the mission is defined by policy and law. Threat is based on intelligence indicators and often the state of the world order. Currently, the only mission in support of the global war on terror being conducted by the United Kingdom that does not explicitly rely upon Article 51 of the UN Charter as its basis for action is that of the UK troops participating in support of the International Security Assistance Force mission in Afghanistan pursuant to Security Council Resolution 1386.[19] Of course, notwithstanding any policy constraints imposed on our forces by ROE, they always possess the right to self-defense.

Paul Cronan

From an Australian perspective, we are also relying on Article 51 as the legal basis for our involvement in Operation ENDURING FREEDOM. The question

---

17. *See* United States v. Toscanino, 500 F.2d 267, 275 (1972).
18. *Id.*
19. *See* S. C. Res. 1386, U.N. SCOR, 56th Sess., U.N. Doc. S/1386/(2001). This resolution provides for the establishment of the "International Security Assistance Force to assist the Afghan Interim Authority in the maintenance of security in Kabul and its surrounding areas, so that the Afghan Interim Authority as well as the personnel of the United Nations can operate in a secure environment."

that must be asked though, is at what point does the authorization to use force in self-defense under Article 51 begin to wane? In other words, what happens if our respective countries are not attacked or threatened with attack by terrorists for the next several years? When does the inherent right to continue to use force in self-defense end? How long, for example, can maritime enforcement operations based on self-defense continue to be legitimately argued? This is a difficult question and while there exists today a continuing threat, it is conceivable that this threat will ultimately wane. What then will be the basis for these operations?

Jean-Guy Perron
Canadian participation in Operation ENDURING FREEDOM is also based on the collective self-defense provisions contained in Article 51 of the UN Charter and in customary international law. Clearly, our forces' operations are bounded and constrained by the law of armed conflict and so our commanders and forces must understand how these laws affect their ability to accomplish the given mission.

Terrorism as a Criminal or International Law Problem

Charles Garraway
Up until the last few years, the international community recognized terrorism as a matter of criminal law to be dealt with by each state independently. This is not to say that there were not efforts to prohibit broad categories of terrorist acts but rather that these acts once prohibited were typically enforced through the courts of the states affected by them. During the last few years, and definitely since the events of September 11th, the international view on terrorism has changed from that of a criminal law matter to that of a law of armed conflict matter. In many respects, we are now operating in a new paradigm which calls for the legal application of deadly force against such terrorists and not their capture and subsequent trial. Perhaps as Commander Brown indicated in his comments, it would be wise to develop an interagency approach to this matter and revise the existing criminal law tools to increase the powers available to address the difficult problem of global terrorism.

Panel IV

Thursday—June 27, 2002

2:00 PM–5:00 PM

Bringing Terrorists to Justice: The Proper Forum

Moderator:
    Professor Harvey Rishikof
    Roger Williams University School of Law

Presenters:
    Lieutenant Colonel Michael Newton
    Judge Advocate, US Army
    Office of War Crimes Issues
    US Department of State

    Professor Christopher Greenwood
    London School of Economics and
    Political Science

Commentators:
    Colonel Manuel Supervielle
    Judge Advocate, US Army
    Staff Judge Advocate
    US Southern Command

    Mr. Daniel Helle
    Deputy Head
    ICRC Delegation to the United Nations

XX

International Criminal Law Aspects of the War Against Terrorism

Michael Newton[1]

On March 4, 1801, Thomas Jefferson, the newly inaugurated President of the United States, took charge of a nation torn between the possibilities of the new century and the uncertainty caused by the changing face of warfare. America was a new republic very much aware of its vulnerability, yet facing the future with faith built on dedication to the dual pillars of peace through justice and peace through strength.[2] As President Jefferson rose to deliver his inaugural address, America faced a new century filled with new dangers and unfolding challenges that threatened to erode the very foundations of our liberty and collective peace. His inaugural message was rooted in our democratic values, yet articulated an American vision to propel us forward as a nation of purpose and principle in the international arena.

---

1. Lieutenant Colonel Newton is an Assistant Professor of Law at the US Military Academy at West Point. He may be reached at michael.newton@usma.edu. The opinions and conclusions of this paper, as well as its flaws, are solely attributable to the author. They do not necessarily reflect the views of the Judge Advocate General, the United States Military Academy, the United States Army, the United States Department of State, or any other federal entity.
2. Robert F. Turner, *State Sovereignty, International Law, and the Use of Force in Countering Low-Intensity Aggression in the Modern World*, in LEGAL AND MORAL CONSTRAINTS ON LOW-INTENSITY CONFLICT, 44 (Alberto R. Coll, et al. eds., 1995), (Vol. 67, US Naval War College International Law Studies).

Summarizing the themes that would guide America through the uncertainties of a new era, President Jefferson began his speech by asserting the foundational principle of seeking "[e]qual and exact justice to all men, of whatever state or persuasion, religious or political."[3] President Jefferson portrayed a "bright constellation" composed of nonnegotiable values that would combine to form the "creed of our political faith" and serve as the touchstone for the future.[4] He pointedly told the nation that "should we wander from them in moments of error or alarm, let us hasten to retrace our steps, and to regain the road which alone leads us to peace, liberty, and safety."[5] After over two hundred years, these remain in many ways the core objectives for which we strive, albeit in a much more complicated and changed world.

The shock of the events of September 11 was a visceral kick to the consciousness of the world. Similar to the September 1972 kidnapping and murder of nine Israeli athletes participating in the Munich Olympics,[6] these terrorist attacks were one of those rare galvanizing events that resonated across our globe. The attacks directed against America affected every culture, age group, religion, and corner of civilization. Though terrorism is not a new phenomenon, the September 11 attacks killed citizens of over 80 nations and stunned the world by their scope and savagery. In rallying the support of the American people for the campaign against the terrorist aggressors and explaining his vision for the strategic campaign against terrorism, President Bush

---

3. Thomas Jefferson, First Inaugural Address, March 4, 1801, *reprinted in* WILLIAM J. BENNETT, THE SPIRIT OF AMERICA 347 (1997).
4. *Id.* Among the other principles that Mr. Jefferson promulgated were,
> peace, commerce, and honest friendship, with all nations, entangling alliances with none; the support of state governments in all their rights, as the most competent administration for our domestic concerns, and the surest bulwarks against antirepublican tendencies: — the preservation of the general government in its whole constitutional vigour (sic), as the sheet anchor of our peace at home, and safety abroad ... the diffusion of information, and arraignment of all abuses at the bar of public reason: — freedom of religion; freedom of the press; and freedom of person, under the protection of the habeas corpus: — and trial by juries impartially selected.

5. *Id.*
6. This 1972 attack was in fact the catalyst for the creation of modern US counter-terrorism policy structures. Vincent Cannistraro and David C. Bresett, *The Terrorist Threat In America, in* ALEXANDER MUNSCH, 16 TERRORISM/DOCUMENTS OF INTERNATIONAL AND LOCAL CONTROL 3, 26 (1998).

returned perhaps unconsciously to the themes articulated by President Jefferson over two centuries before.[7]

On September 20, 2001, President Bush addressed a Joint Session of Congress, aware that the world—and perhaps the terrorist network—was listening. The President declared, "we are a country awakened to danger and called to defend freedom. Our grief has turned to anger, and anger to resolution. Whether we bring our enemies to justice, or bring justice to our enemies, justice will be done."[8] President Bush's declaration of this clear national goal was met by the thunderous applause of the assembled Congress and audience (which also included British Prime Minister Tony Blair). His words stirred citizens across America to strengthen a communal resolve and rededicate a mutual commitment to the goal of justice. President Bush further declared that the campaign against international terrorism[9] is more than just a fight to secure

---

7. In another interesting and perhaps ironic parallel, President Jefferson was selected as the third chief executive in the wake of one of the most bitterly contested and divisive presidential elections in US history. Article II, section 1, clause 3 of the US Constitution specifies that the House of Representatives shall select the President by ballot if more than one candidate amasses the same number of electoral votes. The House of Representatives did not select President Jefferson until after a lengthy debate and thirty-five ballots. C.B. TAYLOR, A UNIVERSAL HISTORY OF THE UNITED STATES OF AMERICA EMBRACING THE WHOLE PERIOD FROM THE EARLIEST DISCOVERIES TO THE PRESENT TIME 250 (1836).

8. President George W. Bush, Address to a Joint Session of Congress, September 30, 2001; *available at* http://www.whitehouse.gov/news/releases/2001/09/20010920-8.html (Jan. 30, 2003). Secretary of State Powell echoed a similar sentiment in his first public comments made from Lima, Peru:

> A terrible, terrible tragedy has befallen my nation, but . . . you can be sure that America will deal with this tragedy in a way that brings those responsible to justice. You can be sure that as terrible a day as this is for us, we will get through it because we are a strong nation, a nation that believes in itself.

BOB WOODWARD, BUSH AT WAR 10 (2002).

9. *See* 18 U.S.C. § 2331, providing that for the purposes of the federal criminal law, the term "international terrorism" means activities that

> (A) involve violent acts or acts dangerous to human life that are a violation of the criminal laws of the United States or of any State, or that would be a criminal violation if committed within the jurisdiction of the United States or of any State;
>
> (B) appear to be intended –
>
>> (i.) to intimidate or coerce a civilian population;
>>
>> (ii.) to influence the policy of a government by intimidation or coercion; or
>>
>> (iii.) to affect the conduct of a government by assassination or kidnapping; and
>
> (C) occur primarily outside the territory jurisdiction of the United States, or transcend national boundaries in terms of the means by which they are accomplished, the persons they appear intended to intimidate or coerce, or the locale in which the perpetrators operate or seek asylum.

American freedoms because it is "civilization's fight" in the sense that it will be waged on behalf of all the people who "believe in progress and pluralism, tolerance and freedom."[10]

Seeking to achieve the goal of justice, the Bush Administration has reshaped the machinery of government around the changed security environment. For example, the National Security Strategy of the United States focuses on attaining the goal of justice:

> [i]n pursuit of our goals, our first imperative is to clarify what we stand for: the United States must defend liberty and justice because these principles are right and true for all people everywhere. No nation owns these aspirations, and no nation is exempt from them. Fathers and mothers in all societies want their children to be educated and to live free from poverty and violence. No people on earth yearn to be oppressed, aspire to servitude, or eagerly await the midnight knock of the secret police. America must stand firmly for the nonnegotiable demands of human dignity: the rule of law; limits on the absolute power of the state; free speech; freedom of worship; equal justice; respect for women; religious and ethnic tolerance; and respect for private property.[11]

Though the concept of seeking "justice" to achieve core national security goals has been a thread of American political dialogue from the early days of our Republic, the concrete form of that pursuit in practice retains an elusive, often ephemeral, character. "Justice" as a component of US foreign policy is a valued but vague objective. In the post-September 11 security environment, there is no doubt that the inherent and sovereign right of self-defense permits the United States to mete out "justice" using its military power.[12] However, the holistic pursuit of justice embodies a parallel dimension of personal penal responsibility. Pursuing personal criminal accountability against international terrorists necessarily entails a complicated political dynamic because of the persistence of state sponsorship ranging from philosophical sympathy to active operational support in the form of funding and official sanction for planning and training within the territorial bounds of the state.

The threats to national security presently posed by international terrorism require a balance between personal punishment of criminal perpetrators and

---

10. Joint Session, *supra* note 8.
11. THE NATIONAL SECURITY STRATEGY OF THE UNITED STATES OF AMERICA 3 (September 2002), *available at* http://www.whitehouse.gov/nsc/nss.pdf (Dec. 1, 2002).
12. *See* Jack M. Beard, *America's New War on Terror: The Case for Self-Defense Under International Law*, 25 HARV. J. L. & PUB. POL'Y 559 (2002).

the use of military power to eliminate the threats posed by terrorists. International terrorism remains a national security problem because it is a unique form of transnational crime in which private actors seek to unravel the fabric of civilized society and thereby undermine state, regional, and global security. The simple term "international terrorism" belies the reality that the deep-seated ideological motives of participants in terrorist acts combine with political reality and the interplay of seemingly insoluble root causes to make it perhaps the most difficult of all the problems facing international society. President Bush's vision reshaped the paradigm for punishing terrorists from an exclusive reliance on judicial mechanisms to address criminal conduct into a war-fighting model. In that sense the war on terrorism is much more than a politically convenient phrase. It is a new paradigm which requires an interface between effective judicial mechanisms capable of prosecuting those perpetrators who are not eliminated or emasculated by the application of military power.

This essay will argue that international crimes of terrorism should be handled domestically by individual states using existing criminal law mechanisms. Rather than blindly heeding the siren's song of international institutionalization, the states of the world should rededicate themselves to decisively addressing terrorist crimes using their sovereign forums. Bound by a sense of unity arising from the ashes of the World Trade Center and the Pentagon, the nations of the world now have a propitious opportunity to reconsider the appropriate forums for addressing international crimes of terrorism. Calls for an international criminal process to address terrorism assume the existence of the discrete discipline termed international criminal law which in turn implies a normative superiority of internationalized mechanisms over domestic forums. However, the existence of transnational terrorism and the cooperation of nationals from a variety of nations in the planning and execution of terrorist attacks does not mean that those crimes are properly punished in a supranational penal forum.

This essay superimposes the established framework for addressing terrorist crimes against the arguments in favor of a newly created supranational judicial forum; because the problem of transnational terrorism does not raise any of the problems that have been previously addressed by the establishment of an internationalized process, such a supranational forum is unnecessary and could actually undermine the pursuit of justice. The current legal framework is a collage akin to a patchwork quilt of existing norms and conventions that seeks to prevent and punish specifically identified terrorist activities. The international community has come together to address the core problem of transnational terrorism by negotiating a web of occasionally overlapping multilateral conventions. Although this web of conventional law[13] is built on the cornerstone of sovereign enforcement of applicable norms, the persistence of transnational terrorism as a feature of the international community shows that the existing conventional framework is not a panacea.[14] This essay, nevertheless, concludes that the voluntary efforts of sovereign states to implement and enforce international norms would not be materially enhanced by the creation of a new superstructure of supranational justice.

The Prospects for an International Terrorist Tribunal

Modern international law embodies a significant body of law and practice that empowers domestic states to adjudicate terrorist crimes. Recent arguments, however, have postulated that an internationalized enforcement mechanism is warranted simply by virtue of the international nature of the problems posed by transnational terrorism. International law often evolves in response to perceived weaknesses in the normative structure that are highlighted by current events.[15] This is the pattern for the post-September 11 wave of thinking about the linkage between international terrorism and an internationalized trial process. Given the inability of domestic forums to eradicate transnational terrorism, it is understandable that the aftermath of September 11 saw a groundswell of support for the creation of an international judicial forum to prosecute such terrorists. Even as they acknowledge that national courts are the backbone for the systematic prosecution of international terrorists, some scholars have pointed out that an international forum would "symbolize global justice for global crimes."[16]

---

13. See infra notes 72 to 83.
14. M. CHERIF BASSIOUNI, INTERNATIONAL TERRORISM: MULTILATERAL CONVENTIONS (1937–2001)(2001); M. Cherif Bassiouni, *Legal Control of International Terrorism: A Policy Oriented Assessment*, 43 HARV. INT. L. J. 83, 90 (2001).
15. See generally GEOFFREY BEST, WAR & LAW SINCE 1945 (1994)(focusing on the historical development of the law of armed conflict in response to the stimuli of world events, changing technology, and the weaknesses of codified law as demonstrated by new types of conflicts); M. CHERIF BASSIOUNI, CRIMES AGAINST HUMANITY IN INTERNATIONAL CRIMINAL LAW 1–87 (2d ed. 1999)(explaining the development of the law regarding crimes against humanity as a logical progression in response to world affairs and the development of human rights law).
16. Luncheon Address: Rogue Regimes and the Individualization of International Law, Anne-Marie Slaughter, 36 NEW ENG. L. REV. 815, 820 (2002)(comments based on a more detailed explication found in Anne-Marie Slaughter & William Burke-White, *An International Constitutional Moment*, 43 HARV. INT. L. J. 1 (2002)).

However, this strain of thought is merely the current incarnation of an older set of discarded ideas. Despite nearly a century of discussion and debate, the nations of the world have not agreed on a comprehensive definition of terrorism,[17] which is the obvious cornerstone of any international forum with jurisdiction over transnational terrorist acts. States instead shifted from a universal and general approach towards cooperative efforts to define and criminalize specific manifestations of terrorism through specific multilateral treaties which bind signatory states to proscribe and punish such acts using domestic systems.

As a logical corollary, states have repeatedly rejected proposals for an overarching international tribunal charged with prosecuting crimes of transnational terrorism. The repeated formal rejections of terrorism as an international problem that should be addressed in supranational judicial forums date back to the League of Nations era.[18] In 1926, the International Congress of Penal Law recommended that the Permanent Court of International Justice "be competent to judge individual liabilities" incurred as a result of crimes considered as international offenses "which constitute a threat to world peace."[19] This proposal died on the vine of international diplomacy.

The assassination of King Alexander of Yugoslavia in Marseilles on October 9, 1934 prompted the French government to propose an international convention for the suppression of terrorism in a letter to the Secretary-General of the League of Nations.[20] The core of the French proposal was a suggestion that an international criminal court would be the most feasible forum for addressing political crimes of an international character, and the Council of the League responded by establishing a Committee of Experts to prepare a preliminary draft of "an international convention to assure the repression of

---

17. *See* W. Michael Reisman, *International Legal Responses to Terrorism*, 22 HOUS. J. INT'L. L. 3, 22 (1999); Consensus Eludes Legal Committee in Final Act of Session as it Recommends Blanket Condemnation of Terrorism, Press Release GA/L/3140, Nov. 23, 1999.
18. *Voeau of the International Congress of Penal Law Concerning an International Criminal Court* (Brussels, 1926), *reprinted in Historical Survey of the Question of International Criminal Jurisdiction, Memorandum Submitted by the Secretary-General* 74, U.N. Doc. A/CN.4/7Rev.1 (1949) (Translating the original French text found in *Premier congres international de droit penal*, Actes du congres 634).
19. *Id.* This strain of thought eventually led to the development of a draft statute for a criminal chamber of the Permanent International Court of Justice, 34th *Report of the International Law Association* 113–125 (1927).
20. *Historical Survey of the Question of International Criminal Jurisdiction, Memorandum Submitted by the Secretary General* 16, U.N. Doc. A/CN.4/7Rev.1 (1949).

conspiracies or crimes committed with a political and terrorist purpose."[21] From November 1–16, 1937, the International Conference for the Repression of Terrorism met in Geneva and adopted a Convention for the Creation of an International Criminal Court.[22] This effort at an international forum to respond to terrorism was implicitly rejected by the international community after only one state (Italy) ratified the multilateral treaty.

Although the proposed 1937 Convention never entered into force[23] it remains highly relevant to the current debate for two reasons. In the first place, the jurisdiction of the international court proposed in the 1937 treaty derived solely from the consent of the affected states,[24] and the court was limited to applying the "least severe" domestic law of either the state in which the crimes were committed or the state of the offender's nationality.[25] In effect, the 1937 Convention created an internationalized process for applying the substantive law of different domestic systems, which is the antithesis for modern arguments that an international forum is essential for applying the international norms against terrorism.

This model of the 1937 Convention is really the precursor for the *Lockerbie Court*[26] and stands in sharp contrast to current efforts to portray transnational terrorism as an international problem that requires a generalized international definition and jurisdiction. Secondly, it is important to note that every one of

---

21. *Id. See also* 15 LEAGUE OF NATIONS O.J. 1760 (1934) (containing the text of the full resolution passed by the Council).
22. Convention for the Prevention and Punishment of Terrorism, *opened for signature* Nov. 16, 1937, 19 LEAGUE OF NATIONS O.J. 23 (1938), League of Nations Doc. C.546(I).M.383(I)1937.V (1938), *reprinted in* M. CHERIF BASSIOUNI, INTERNATIONAL TERRORISM: MULTILATERAL CONVENTIONS (1937–2001) 71 (2001) [hereinafter 1937 Convention].
23. After the Convention was transmitted to all the members of the League of Nations, 24 states signed the Convention but only India actually ratified its text.
24. 1937 Convention, *supra* note 22, art. 21 (referring to the obligation of the domestic states to enact criminal legislation to punish the acts defined in the underlying multilateral treaty and empowering those same states to "commit the accused to trial" before the International Criminal Court). This provision is in stark contrast to the highly controversial jurisdictional provisions of the Rome Statute of the International Criminal Court which allow the ICC to bypass non-consenting states in establishing personal jurisdiction over their citizens. *Rome Statute of the International Criminal Court*, United Nations Diplomatic Conference of Plenipotentiaries on the Establishment of an International Criminal Court, July 17, 1998, U.N. Doc. A/CONF.183/9, arts. 12–19 *reprinted in* 37 I.L.M. 998 (1998) [hereinafter Rome Statute].
25. 1937 Convention, *supra* note 22, art. 21.
26. The Scottish Court in the Netherlands was an internationalized process applying Scottish law to prosecute the Libyan nationals responsible for the 1988 bombing of Pan Am Flight 103. *See* http://www.scotcourts.gov.uk/index1.asp?path=%2Fhtml%2Flockerbie%2Easp (Jan. 30, 2003).

the multilateral conventions in the sixty-five years of international dialogue since the 1937 Convention have adhered to its pattern by defining different terrorist acts as substantive violations of international law and specifically requiring sovereign states to enact domestic criminal legislation for the purpose of punishing those acts. This uniform historical pattern undercuts faddish arguments that the very nature of transnational terrorism requires an international forum and forces proponents of an internationalized process to bear the burden of overturning the customary practice of the international community.

Another persistent strain of thought after September 11 postulated that international prosecutions would appear more legitimate, particularly to Muslim states, than domestic prosecutions, which could be seen with some suspicion overseas. In the view of some commentators, the perceived illegitimacy of US domestic mechanisms, especially the Military Commissions authorized by President Bush,[27] mitigates towards the creation of an international supranational tribunal. For example, Justice Richard Goldstone, the first chief prosecutor for the International Tribunal for the Prosecution of Persons Responsible for Serious Violations of International Humanitarian Law Committed in the Territory of Former Yugoslavia since 1991 (ICTY), speculated that the perceived difficulty of obtaining a fair trial for terrorists in the United States would cause some countries to resist extraditions to domestic courts, whereas those same countries would be legally barred from resisting extradition to a forum created under the Chapter VII authority of the Security Council.[28]

---

27. *See* Military Order of November 13, 2001, *Detention, Treatment, and Trial of Certain Non-Citizens in the War Against Terrorism*, 66 FED. REG. 57,833 (Nov. 16, 2001) (while it is beyond the scope of this essay to completely assess the merits of the forthcoming military commissions, the order defines the class of persons subject to the jurisdiction of military commissions as "any individual who is not a United States citizen" with respect to whom the President determines in writing that there is reason to believe that such individual, at the relevant times (i) is or was a member of al Qaeda, or (ii) has engaged in, aided, or abetted or conspired to commit acts of international terrorism, or acts in preparation therefore, that have caused, threatened to cause, or have as their aim to cause, injury to or adverse effects on the United States, its citizens, national security, foreign policy or economy; or (iii) has knowingly harbored one or more individuals described in subparagraphs (i) or (ii).)

28. Henry Weinstein, *A Trial Too Big for the U.S.?*, LOS ANGELES TIMES, Oct. 26, 2001, A1; Ed Vulliamy, *US Dilemma Over Trials of bin Laden*, GUARDIAN UNLIMITED OBSERVER, Nov. 4, 2001 (quoting Justice Goldstone as favoring international tribunals for the prosecution of terrorists and speculating that he would be selected as the first chief prosecutor of the International Criminal Court), *available at* http://www.observer.uk.co/afghanistan/story/0,1501,587365,00.html (Jan. 30, 2003).

Additionally, in the words of one prominent international lawyer if "we're thinking in terms of a global war on terrorism in the long-term, it would be better to try [bin Laden] in an international forum where we could get the input, but also the condemnation of judges from all the world's legal systems under both national and international law."[29] In a similar vein, the current ICTY prosecutor, Carla Del Ponte, reported that "quite a few people" at United Nations headquarters revealed in private conversations that prosecuting terrorists in The Hague would be the "most valid solution."[30] This would of course require the Security Council to expand the mandate of the ICTY. Ms. Del Ponte perhaps revealed her agenda for suggesting such an expansion with the caveat that "[i]f the Security Council were to decide to pursue that path, it would have to increase the funding earmarked for the Hague Tribunal."[31]

The Military Order authorizing military commissions has been one of the most controversial aspects of the United States' efforts to bring justice to terrorists,[32] yet even its most vocal critics accept that such forums promulgated under the President's constitutional authority as commander-in-chief are

---

29. America's Legal War on Terrorism: Are These Rules for Hunting Terrorists; Could bin Laden be Brought to Trial (CNN Burden of Proof broadcast, Oct. 6, 2001), *cited in* David J. Scheffer, *The Future of Atrocity Law*, SUFFOLK TRANS. L. REV. 389, 390 n.3 (Summer, 2002). This view perhaps represents a modern incarnation of the views articulated by the then Secretary of State Thomas Jefferson in a letter dated April 18, 1793, 8 WRITINGS OF THOMAS JEFFERSON 11 (1904):

> Compacts ... between nation and nation, are obligatory on them by the same moral law which obliges individuals to observe their compacts. . . . It is true that nations are to be judges for themselves; since no one nation has a right to sit in judgment over another, but the tribunal of our conscience remains, and that also of the opinion of the world. These will review the sentence we pass in our own case, and as we respect these, we must see that in judging ourselves we have honestly done the part of impartial and rigorous judges.

30. Prosecutor Del Ponte Hopes to Try Bin Laden in The Hague, Interview with the Hague International War Crimes Tribunal Chief Prosecutor Carla Del Ponte, Rome L'Avvenire, Dec. 2, 2001 (copy on file with author).
31. *Id.*
32. James Podgers, ABA Tackles Tribunals Issue, 1 A.B.A. J. e-Report, Feb. 8, 2002, *available at* http://www.abamet.org/journal/ereport/f8midtribus.html (Jan. 30, 2003); DAVID J. SCHEFFER, OPTIONS FOR PROSECUTING INTERNATIONAL TERRORISTS, UNITED STATES INSTITUTE FOR PEACE SPECIAL REPORT (2001), *available at* http://www.usip.org/pubs/specialreports/sr78.html (Jan. 30, 2003).

"clearly authorized under international law."[33] From this perspective, rather than sanctioning a "multiplicity of trials in various countries" the creation of an overarching international tribunal that could perhaps include participation of Islamic judges is being packaged as a part of the international coalition against terrorism.[34] Nevertheless, allowing sovereign states to bypass their domestic enforcement mechanisms and abdicate their responsibilities to a newly spawned international mechanism is not likely to be an effective response in the long term.

The cries for an international tribunal imply that an international response is always appropriate for crimes grounded in international law that shock the conscience of mankind, which in turn implies an unseemly assertion that domestic prosecutions are always inappropriate and unfair. While terrorism is widespread, and may be impossible to eradicate, the compelling motivations that have required the formation of international forums in other contexts are notably absent.

In other words, despite the inherent difficulty of investigating and prosecuting international terrorists, there is no culture of impunity because one or several sovereign states will always have jurisdiction, political will, and a very strong motivation to prosecute that particular set of terrorists when there is available evidence sufficient to sustain conviction of persons who are within the substantive and personal jurisdiction of the sovereign state. Creation of an international forum specifically designed to respond to crimes of terrorism would be a wholly new development in the field of international criminal law because it would be the first time that an international forum was created solely due to the nature of the crimes committed. If the nations of the world are committed to combating the core problem of transnational terrorism, the best place is in the domestic forums of affected states. This approach will accomplish the most in the long term to ensure that the rule of law is strengthened and justice is done.

---

33. William Glaberson, *U.S. Faces Tough Choices If Bin Laden Is Captured*, N.Y. TIMES, B5, Oct. 22, 2001; Michael R. Belknap, *A Putrid Pedigree: the Bush Administration's Military Tribunals in Historical Perspective* 38 CAL. W. L. REV. 433, 441 (Spring, 2002). The Bush Administration has pointedly reminded the world that the procedures published that will govern the conduct of any Military Commissions authorized by the President are in full compliance with the international standards, Article 75, Protocol I. *See* Protocol Additional to the Geneva Conventions of 12 August 1949 and Relating to the Protection of Victims of International Armed Conflicts, 1125 U.N.T.S. 3, *reprinted in* 16 I.L.M. 1391 (1977).

34. Comments by Justice Richard Goldstone, Bringing International Criminals to Justice, John F. Kennedy Library and Foundation Responding to Terrorism Series, Nov. 12, 2001, *available at* http://www.jfklibrary.net.forum_goldstone.html (Jan. 30, 2003).

"International Criminal Law"

Similarly, an international terrorist tribunal is not warranted by the very existence of an emerging collection of concepts and processes termed "international criminal law." The concept of international criminal law springs from the intersection of two distinct legal planes; due to the nature of the international system, the criminal aspects of international law are necessarily implemented through the criminal justice systems of sovereign states. For the purposes of this essay, it is important to realize that the simple recognition of legal norms under international law in no way leads ineluctably to the conclusion that the most appropriate, or even most desirable forum, is an internationalized court.

Though some states cooperate to prescribe some norms in binding international obligations,[35] the domestic criminal systems of sovereign states present a competing set of pragmatic and practical challenges in implementing and enforcing those same norms. The criminal aspects of international law originate in the choices made by sovereign states who united to criminalize certain conduct under established international norms.[36] In other words, the mechanisms of diplomacy and state consent work together to define and proscribe certain conduct to the point that it ripens into a violation of substantive international norms. From the standpoint of developing binding norms of conduct through the evolution of international law, the twentieth century was a period of almost breathtaking development.

At the same time, the development of international forums lagged behind the substantive development of crimes defined and articulated as a matter of international law. Indeed, the principle that states are obligated to use domestic forums to punish violations of international law has roots that run back to the ideas of Hugo Grotius.[37] The very nature of sovereign power allows the domestic forums of a state to punish criminals whether their crimes derive from international norms or domestic prohibitions. As early as 1842, US Secretary

---

35. Professor Bassiouni has listed 24 categories of international crime generated from 274 international conventions that help guide the merger of international law with criminal law. M. CHERIF BASSIOUNI, INTERNATIONAL CRIMINAL LAW CONVENTIONS AND THEIR PENAL PROVISIONS 20–21 (1997).
36. M. Cherif Bassiouni, *The Penal Characteristics of Conventional International Criminal Law*, in INTERNATIONAL CRIMINAL LAW AND PROCEDURE 27 (John Dugard & Christine van den Wyngaert, eds. 1996)(summarizing some twenty different acts and types of conduct criminalized under binding international conventions and discussing the differing approaches to enforcing international criminal norms).
37. RICHARD TUCK, THE RIGHTS OF WAR AND PEACE: POLITICAL THOUGHT AND THE INTERNATIONAL ORDER FROM GROTIUS TO KANT (1999).

of State Daniel Webster articulated the idea that a nation's sovereignty also entails "the strict and faithful observance of all those principles, laws, and usages which have obtained currency among civilized states, and which have for their object the mitigation of the miseries of war."[38]

One way to envision the current state of international criminal law is to imagine that pure domestic enforcement of international norms and the refinement of new and more effective international forums are like two sliding tectonic plates. Even though the body of terrorist conventions followed the pattern of requiring domestic enforcement, there is an inherent tension at the fault line between domestic and international criminal forums because the jurisdictional allocation is a zero sum game with regard to a particular individual or criminal act.

The phrase "international criminal law" describes a deceptively simple concept that is not confined to the title of law review articles or the spines of library books. The expression obscures the reality that its genesis lies in the lawmaking processes of the international community, and cannot therefore be seen as a linear exercise of legislative mandate accompanied by international judicial enforcement. The field of "international criminal law" is an ambiguous concept with indistinct boundaries.[39]

Because no single class of crimes or isolated body of law forms an accurate and complete foundation for the currently existing tribunals created at the international level to punish individuals for violations of international law, one distinguished scholar and diplomat has proposed the unifying concept of "atrocity crimes."[40] In short, the concept of international criminal law is more than a mere aspiration to be attained yet falls short of being a constrained body of law with an empirical existence and definable contours. For the close observer of this dynamic field, it is not surprising that there is an undercurrent of debate challenging the very existence of a distinct discipline termed "international criminal law."[41]

---

38. JOHN BASSETT MOORE, 1 A DIGEST OF INTERNATIONAL LAW 5–6 (1906).
39. Though international criminal law certainly includes the body of law proscribing international terrorism, this concept also includes crimes against humanity (and its component parts of persecution of minority populations) torture, some human rights violations, war crimes (both in the classic sense of conflicts between nation states and in the growing body of law regulating conduct in the context of non-international armed conflicts), genocide, and other transnational crimes such as piracy, slavery, and drug trafficking.
40. David J. Scheffer, *The Future of Atrocity Law*, SUFFOLK TRANS. L. REV. 389, 398 (Summer, 2002).
41. *See, e.g.*, Leslie C. Green, *Is There an International Criminal Law?*, 21 ALBERTA L. REV. 251 (1983).

As a result of this ambiguity, during the negotiations of the Elements of Crimes required by Article 9 of the Rome Statute of the International Criminal Court (ICC),[42] some delegations vehemently voiced their view that the concept of "international criminal law" is too ill defined and vague to have any practical meaning. The Elements of Crimes are designed to "assist the Court in the interpretation and application" of the norms defined in the Rome Statute.[43] The Rome Statute also stipulates that the Court "shall apply" the Elements of Crimes during its decision-making.[44] After agreeing that the Elements of Crimes would be much more than a summarized, non-binding set of brief comments, the delegates negotiated a detailed list of the component parts for every one of the numerous offenses proscribed in the Rome Statute with the understanding that the prosecutor must prove each element beyond a reasonable doubt to sustain a conviction for that offense. A number of delegations felt that referencing a discrete body of "international criminal law" in the Elements of Crimes document would introduce exactly the kind of circular vagueness that would defeat the very purpose of negotiating elements for each offense.

After extensive debate, the nations of the world joined consensus on the Final Draft Elements of Crimes. The Elements of Crimes are enshrined in a single, accessible document that takes otherwise amorphous crimes and delineates the conduct, consequences, and circumstances for every offense, along with the mens rea that attaches to each component of each crime. This is an important development because it portends the possibility that nations around the world now have a unified, consensus document to consult when considering the normative content of the crimes of genocide, found in Article 6 of the Rome Statute, crimes against humanity, contained in Article 7, and the expansive list of war crimes contained in Article 8.

The Elements of Crimes are a crosscut of legal norms that are an off-the-shelf source of accessible detail to assist domestic jurisdictions throughout the world, in addition to serving as a resource for judicial activities in the international arena. Many states are using the agreed elements as a framework for implementing those crimes within their domestic enforcement mechanisms.

For the purposes of this essay, the Elements do embody consensus agreement on the concept of an autonomous legal field termed "international criminal law." The chapeau language to the Article 7 crimes states clearly that the

---

42. Elements of Crimes, Adopted September 10, 2002, *reprinted in* Report of the Assembly of States Parties to the Rome Statute of the International Criminal Court, 1st Sess., 108–155, U.N. Doc. ICC-ASP/1/3 (2002).
43. *Id.*, art. 9(1).
44. *Id.*, art. 21.

crimes against humanity provisions relate to "international criminal law" and accordingly "should be strictly construed."[45] This diplomatic result recognized the emergence of an interrelated system in which domestic forums are responsible for implementing international norms, but in no way elevated international forums to a de facto hierarchical supremacy.

The Internationalization of International Criminal Law

The development of a general body of legal norms along with the emergence of a system termed in shorthand "international criminal law" does not mean that international forums are the preferred judicial enforcement mechanism. The pursuit of accountability for international crimes is a notable aspect of President Bush's recent observation that the nations of the world are "joined in serious purpose—very serious purposes—on which the safety of our people and the fate of our freedom now rest. We build a world of justice, or we will live in a world of coercion."[46] Nevertheless, international forums have been the courts of last resort rather than the courts primarily charged as the optimal first response.

Although states cooperate together to define and proscribe crimes under international law, the domestic courts of the world have the primary role in punishing violations and securing the rule of law.[47] The debate over the phrase "international criminal law" described above reflected a continuing tension between the international respect for sovereign justice systems, and the transcendent importance of truth and accountability. Phrased another way, none of the international forums in recent history have been created to enforce international norms simply because the offenses were defined and proscribed by the power of international law. Rather, internationalized mechanisms have been created only as a necessary fallback when domestic forums have failed to enforce the transcendent norms of international law.

---

45. U.N. Doc. PCNICC/2000/INF/3/Add.2 (2000).
46. Remarks by the President to a Special Session of the Bundestag, May 23, 2002, *available at* http://www.whitehouse.gov/news/releases/2002/05/20020523-2.html (Nov. 20, 2002).
47. *See, e.g.,* Attorney Gen. of Israel v. Eichmann-Supreme Court Opinion, *reprinted in* 36 I.L.R. 18, 26, (Isr. Dist. Ct.-Jerusalem, 1961), *aff'd* 36 I.L.R. 277 (Isr. Sup. Ct., 1962) (international law is "in the absence of an International Court, in need of the judicial and legislative organs of every country to give effect to its criminal interdictions and to bring the criminals to trial").

For example, in responding to what President Roosevelt later described as the "blackest crimes in all history,"[48] the Allied Powers issued the Moscow Declaration on October 30, 1943.[49] German forces were able to commit almost unthinkable brutalities under the shield of Nazi sovereignty. Adolf Hitler imposed the *Fuehrerprinzip* (leadership principle) in order to exercise his will as supreme through the police, the courts, the military, and all the other institutions of organized German society.[50] The oath of the Nazi party stated: "I owe inviolable fidelity to Adolf Hitler; I vow absolute obedience to him and to the leaders he designates for me."[51] Accordingly, power resided in Hitler, from whom subordinates derived absolute authority in hierarchical order. This absolute and unconditional obedience to the superior in all areas of public and private life led in Justice Jackson's famous words to "a National Socialist despotism equaled only by the dynasties of the ancient East."[52]

Sheltered from international scrutiny by German sovereign prerogative, the domestic system was harnessed to prevent a judicial response to the horrendous crimes committed because the outcomes of prosecutions were predetermined to accord with the political guidance of the Fuehrer. The rule of law in Germany was therefore twisted to conform to the Nazi party rather than the principles of restraint and justice. In response, the Allied powers used the Moscow Declaration to make punishing those perpetrators[53] a key allied war goal.

In the context of the current debate over internationalizing justice, it is important to note that the Moscow Declaration specifically favored punishment through the national courts in the countries where the crimes were committed. The Declaration specifically stated that German criminals were to be "sent

---

48. Statement by the President, March 24, 1944, *reprinted in* REPORT OF ROBERT H. JACKSON UNITED STATES REPRESENTATIVE TO THE INTERNATIONAL CONFERENCE ON MILITARY TRIBUNALS 12, DEPARTMENT OF STATE PUBLICATION 3080, WASHINGTON D.C. (1945) [hereinafter Jackson Report].
49. IX Department of State Bulletin, No. 228, 310, *reprinted in* Jackson Report, *supra* note 48, at 11. The Moscow Declaration was actually issued to the Press on November 1, 1943. For an account of the political and legal maneuvering behind the effort to bring this stated war aim into actuality, see PETER MAGUIRE, LAW AND WAR: AN AMERICAN STORY 85–110 (2000).
50. DREXEL A. SPRECHER, INSIDE THE NUREMBERG TRIAL: A PROSECUTOR'S COMPREHENSIVE ACCOUNT 1037–38.
51. *Id.* at 157.
52. Opening Statement to the International Military Tribunal at Nuremberg, II TRIAL OF THE MAJOR WAR CRIMINALS BEFORE THE INTERNATIONAL MILITARY TRIBUNAL 100 (1947) [hereinafter TRIAL OF THE MAJOR WAR CRIMINALS].
53. After extensive debate over the relative merits of the terms "perpetrator" or "accused" the delegates to the Preparatory Commission (PrepCom) ultimately agreed to use the former in the finalized draft text of the Elements of Crimes for the International Criminal Court, U.N. Doc. PCNICC/2000/INF/3/Add.2 (2000).

back to the countries in which their abominable deeds were done in order that they may be judged and punished according to the laws of these liberated countries and of the free governments which will be erected therein."[54] The precedence was clearly stated for building the rule of law at the domestic level, even though the subject matter jurisdiction for horrific violations came from international law. Presaging the actual International Military Tribunal, the Declaration went on to proclaim that major criminals whose crimes had "no particular geographical localization" would be punished by joint decision of the Allied governments.[55]

Seen through the prism of international criminal law, the Moscow Declaration and the subsequent London Charter did not elevate the international forum to an automatic precedence and superiority. The international forum was limited only to those offenses where a single country had no greater grounds for claiming jurisdiction than another country. Justice Jackson recognized this reality in his famous opening statement. He accepted the fact that the International Military Tribunal was merely an alternative to domestic courts for prosecuting the "symbols of fierce nationalism and of militarism."[56] He further clarified that any defendants who succeeded in "escaping the condemnation of this Tribunal . . . will be delivered up to our continental Allies."[57]

Following the legacy of Nuremberg by nearly fifty years, the current ad hoc tribunals were both created in contexts where justice would not be achieved or even pursued in domestic forums. Instead of being driven by an abstract evaluation of the nature of the offenses as violations of international law, the international community focused on the need to prosecute offenders by filling the domestic enforcement void with an international tribunal. In the Former Republic of Yugoslavia, the Milosevic regime exercised dictatorial power over the Yugoslav judicial system that prevented any accountability for the widespread violations of international law. Thus, the "particular circumstances" of the impunity in the Former Yugoslavia warranted the creation of the international tribunal.[58]

Similarly, in the context of the genocide in Rwanda, the Security Council created the International Criminal Tribunal for Rwanda (ICTR) where there

---

54. Eichmann, *supra* note 47.
55. Id.
56. TRIAL OF THE MAJOR WAR CRIMINALS, *supra* note 52, at 99.
57. Id. at 100.
58. *Report of the Secretary General pursuant to paragraph 2 of Security Council Resolution 808* (1993), U.N. SCOR, 48th Sess., U.N. Doc. S/2-5704, para. 26 (1993).

would have otherwise been a prosecutorial void. The genocide ripped apart Rwandan society. All the judges fled and the judicial system was in total disarray. In the case of Rwanda, the problem was not a lack of political will, but a complete breakdown of the rule of law hampered by a judicial system deemed to be incapable of addressing the mass of violations.[59]

Both the ICTY and ICTR drew their lifeblood from the political process of the Security Council because the only viable system of justice would have been a newly created international forum. From the perspective of Charter legal authority, the ICTY and ICTR are best understood as enforcement measures of a judicial nature. In other words, the Security Council was forced by the circumstances at hand to assume a quasi-sovereign role to create subordinate judicial structures within the territorial bounds that would otherwise have been policed by responsible governmental structures.[60] Nations are legally obligated to accept the decisions of the Security Council.[61] Hence, the use of Chapter VII authority in this manner was both unprecedented and ingenious because the international tribunals were grounded on a Security Council determination that judicial accountability for crimes would facilitate the maintenance and restoration of international peace and security.[62] The edifice of internationalized justice that has become such a familiar landmark on the international scene in the past decade merely filled the void left by dysfunctional domestic systems.

In relation to the current debate over creating a supranational forum to respond to terrorism, the essential feature of the ad hoc tribunals is the reality that they were not created as an international response simply due to the nature of the crimes as substantive violations of international law. Although the ad hoc tribunals enjoyed legitimacy and authority over sovereign states immediately upon their inception by virtue of the plenary authority of the Security Council with respect to maintaining international peace and security,[63] they represent a limited response to specific enforcement gaps. The specific

---

59. *See generally* VIRGINIA MORRIS & MICHAEL P. SCHARF, THE INTERNATIONAL CRIMINAL COURT FOR RWANDA (1998).
60. U.N. CHARTER art. 29. *See also* Theodor Meron, *War Crimes in Yugoslavia and the Development of International Law*, 88 AM. J. INT'L L. 78 (1994).
61. U.N. CHARTER art. 25.
62. *See* Report of the Secretary General, *supra* note 58, paras. 18–30.
63. *See, e.g.*, Certain Expenses of the United Nations (Article 17, Paragraph 2, of the Charter), I.C.J. REPORTS 151 (1962), *reprinted in* 56 AM. J. INT'L L. 1053 (1962)(holding in part that the Security Council has plenary authority under the Charter to take decisions and order enforcement measures under the Charter regime).

conditions that warranted the creation of the ad hoc tribunals also led the Security Council to mandate a jurisdictional hierarchy in which each international tribunal has explicit jurisdictional "primacy" over national courts.[64] Therefore, the jurisdictional framework of the ad hoc tribunals in no way implies an "inherent supremacy" for international tribunals over domestic forums that derives simply from the nature of the underlying criminal offenses.

In the context of the war on terrorism, the formation of the ICTY and ICTR do not warrant the assumption that international mechanisms are always the appropriate response to international crimes. The specific contextual interests of eliminating the problem of impunity and restoring respect for the rule of law mitigated against relying on domestic enforcement, but in no way does that lead to the conclusion that an international forum is the appropriate response to international crimes. Unlike the situation in the Former Yugoslavia, international terrorists are private actors who act outside the constraints of civilized society, and are therefore in no position to block state enforcement mechanisms. In Rwanda, the international mechanism was an essential gap filler to provide support to a collapsed judicial system.

As noted above, the jurisdictional hierarchy was a logical corollary to the use of Chapter VII authority to establish the tribunals. As a legal matter, international efforts are hardly sufficient to be the sole source for dispensing justice.[65] As a practical matter, the gap between the victims and the courts remains yawning. An effort to create an international tribunal for prosecuting terrorism would be similarly ineffective as the focal point of effective and complete enforcement.

The newly established ICC is the culmination of recent efforts to create a superstructure of international accountability mechanisms to address impunity for international offenses. With respect to the proposal for an international

---

64. VIRGINIA MORRIS & MICHAEL P. SCHARF, AN INSIDER'S GUIDE TO THE INTERNATIONAL CRIMINAL TRIBUNAL FOR THE FORMER YUGOSLAVIA 126 n.378 (1995).
65. At the time of this writing, the ICTY has issued 79 current indictments; with 55 suspects in legal proceedings (of which 44 are in custody and 11 are provisionally released under strict terms issued by the Trial Chamber); 33 individuals are currently in various stages of trial while 30 cases have been completed (20 indictments were withdrawn and 10 indictees were deceased). The ICTR has issued 80 indictments of whom 60 persons are in custody while 20 remain at large; 8 persons have been sentenced, 1 acquitted; 22 are in trial and 29 are in custody.

mechanism to try terrorists, it is significant that the Rome Statute did not include terrorism within its jurisdictional crimes because delegates could not agree on the form of such an offense.[66] Despite the clear rejection of ICC jurisdiction over terrorist crimes during the drafting of the Rome Statute, some ICC proponents vocally maintained after September 11 that its provisions for punishing crimes against humanity should be twisted to cover terrorist acts as well.

Attempts to stretch the jurisdictional bounds of the ICC to cover crimes of terrorism would be the most blatant effort to superimpose international mechanisms over functioning domestic courts. As of its entry into force on July 1, 2002, the Rome Statute purports to establish a permanent supranational institution that enshrines the principle that state sovereignty can be subordinated to the goal of achieving accountability for violations of international humanitarian law.[67] Indeed, one commentator at the diplomatic conference in Rome argued that "outmoded notions of state sovereignty must not derail the forward movement" towards international peace and order.[68] Even the most ardent supporters of the ICC are careful not to portray its potential authority as a naked exercise of political power, and view its erosion of state sovereignty only as a necessary but limited incursion.

In other words, the creation of a supranational court empowered to override the unfettered discretion of some states is seen by the supporters of the ICC as an overdue step towards a uniform system of responsibility designed to "promote values fundamental to all democratic and peace-loving states."[69] Depending on their perspectives, commentators on the ICC see either principled leadership backed by the courage of deeply held convictions or stark hypocrisy and self-serving opportunism.

---

66. See Rome Statute, *supra* note 24, art 5.
67. See Rome Statute, *supra* note 24, arts 12–19. The extension of unchecked international prosecutorial and judicial power over sovereign concerns is one of the primary reasons causing the United States position to remain unwilling to go forward with the Rome Statute "in its present form." David J. Scheffer, *The United States and the International Criminal Court*, 93 AM. J. INT'L L. 14, 21 (1999) [hereinafter Scheffer]. The United States joined international consensus on the Final Draft Rules of Evidence and Procedure and the Final Draft Elements of Crimes on June 30, 2000.
68. Benjamin Ferencz, Address to the United Nations Diplomatic Conference of Plenipotentiaries on the Establishment of the International Criminal Court (June 16, 1998), *available at* http://www.un.org/icc/speeches/616ppc.htm (Jan. 30, 2003).
69. Michael A. Newton, *Comparative Complementarity: Domestic Jurisdiction Consistent with the Rome Statute of the International Criminal Court*, 167 MIL. L. REV. 20 (2001); Bartram S. Brown, *Primacy or Complementarity: Reconciling the Jurisdiction of National Courts and International Tribunals*, 23 YALE J. INT'L L. 383, 436 (1998).

Though its supporters approach the ICC as the penultimate development of international criminal justice at the dawn of a new century, the roots of its core jurisdictional limitation are intellectually identical to the Nuremberg Tribunal and the ad hoc tribunals. Article 1 of the Rome Statute promulgates in simple language that the court will "be a permanent institution and shall have the power to exercise its jurisdiction over persons for the most serious crimes of international concern . . . and shall be complementary to national criminal jurisdictions."[70] The plain text of Article 1 compels the conclusion that the ICC is intended to supplement sovereign punishment of international violations rather than supplant domestic enforcement of international norms.

Accordingly, a case is admissible before the ICC only where a domestic sovereign that would otherwise exercise jurisdiction is "unwilling or unable to genuinely" carry out the investigation or prosecution.[71] The principle of complementarity is a mandatory limitation even in a case in which the other jurisdictional criteria are met because the Trial Chamber "shall determine that a case is inadmissible" where the admissibility criteria are not met. After hitting a diplomatic dead-end for nearly 70 years, persistent attempts to expand (some would say warp) the ICC jurisdictional scope over crimes of terrorism due to their highly emotionalized nature and the rise of global concern would subvert the complementarity mechanism. Paradoxically, such an expansion would vindicate the stringent arguments of those who view the supranational ICC mechanism simply as an international effort to undermine sovereignty.

The Nuremberg Tribunal, the ICTR, the ICTY and now the ICC have erected a formidable edifice of internationalized justice. At the same time, it is absolutely clear that where domestic jurisdictions are functioning, the internationalized response is not warranted (and in the case of the ICC not permissible). Though the development of international institutions to enforce international norms has broken new ground in the past fifty years and helped to end impunity in some contexts, international mechanisms are not appropriate where domestic courts are complying with the rule of law and remain capable of dispensing justice. Consequently, arguments for an international terrorist court fall of their own weight unless they can demonstrate a gap that such a mechanism would fill.

---

70. Rome Statute, *supra* note 24, art 1. Article 1 echoes the preambular language of the Rome Statute in which the signatories affirm that effective prosecution of international crimes "must be ensured by taking measures at the national level and by enhancing international cooperation."
71. Rome Statute, *supra* note 24, art 17(1). For the negotiating history of the complementarity regime, see Newton, *supra* note 69, at 44–55.

An International Terrorist Court Has No Purpose

The heading just above would probably seem curious to a casual observer. However, in light of the extensive jurisdictional framework conveying an extensive punitive capacity to sovereign forums, proponents of an international terrorist tribunal bear the burden of establishing its usefulness on the international landscape. The creation of an international mechanism to prosecute terrorist crimes would be an inherently political exercise. It would cost a great deal of money, and require the expenditure of an enormous amount of political good will. One of the truths of international diplomacy is that international mechanisms are created by the international community to achieve international interests. A terrorist tribunal could actually encourage acts of terrorism if it replaced relatively efficient domestic mechanisms with a cumbersome, expensive, and slow process far removed from the realities of everyday prosecutorial and diplomatic practice.

There is no preexisting gap in enforcement mechanisms that would be filled by an internationalized process to address crimes of terrorism. As of now, the sovereign states of the world have cooperated together in using the United Nations structure to adopt twelve multilateral antiterrorist conventions (though there are a number of other international instruments that address criminal conduct that could be termed "terrorist" depending on the circumstances). The core body of international instruments includes the following: Convention on Offenses and Certain Other Acts Committed on Board Aircraft[72] (known as The Tokyo Convention, 1963); Convention for the Suppression of Unlawful Seizure of Aircraft[73] (known as the Hague Hijacking Convention, 1970); Convention for the Suppression of Unlawful Acts against the Safety of Civil Aviation[74] (known as the Montreal Convention, 1971); Convention on the Prevention and Punishment of Crimes against Internationally Protected Persons, including Diplomatic Agents[75] (1973); International Convention

---

72. Convention on Offences and Certain Other Acts Committed on Board Aircraft, Sep. 14, 1963, 20 U.S.T. 2941, 704 U.N.T.S. 219, *reprinted in* 2 I.L.M. 1042 (1963).
73. Convention for the Suppression of Unlawful Seizure of Aircraft, Dec. 16, 1970, 22 U.S.T. 1641, 860 U.N.T.S. 105, *reprinted in* 10 I.L.M. 1333 (1971), *available at* http://www1.umn.edu/humanrts/instree/hague1970.html (Jan. 30, 2003).
74. Convention for the Suppression of Unlawful Acts against the Safety of Civil Aviation, Sep. 23, 1971, 24 U.S.T. 564, 974 U.N.T.S. 177, *reprinted in* 10 I.L.M. 1151 (1971).
75. Convention on the Prevention and Punishment of Crimes against Internationally Protected Persons, including Diplomatic Agents, Dec. 14, 1973, 28 U.S.T. 1975, 1035 U.N.T.S. 167, *reprinted in* 13 I.L.M. 41 (1974), *available at* http://www1.umn.edu/humanrts/instree/inprotectedpersons.html (Jan. 30, 2003).

against the Taking of Hostages[76] (1979); Convention on the Physical Protection of Nuclear Material[77] (1979); Protocol for the Suppression of Unlawful Acts of Violence at Airports Serving International Civil Aviation, supplementary to the Convention for the Suppression of Unlawful Acts against the Safety of Civil Aviation[78] (known as the Montreal Protocol, 1988); Convention for the Suppression of Unlawful Acts against the Safety of Maritime Navigation[79] (1988); Protocol for the Suppression of Unlawful Acts against the Safety of Fixed Platforms Located on the Continental Shelf[80] (1988); Convention on the Marking of Plastic Explosives for the Purpose of Detection[81] (1991); International Convention for the Suppression of Terrorist Bombing[82] (1997); and International Convention for the Suppression of the Financing of Terrorism[83] (1999).

As noted above, the piecemeal approach to addressing terrorism resulted from the failure of the international community, in conjunction with the United Nations, to develop an overarching, comprehensive convention against terrorism, largely because of lingering dissension over how to define the scope of the international proscription against acts of terrorism. Taken together, the pile of terrorism treaties accomplishes several crucial purposes.

---

76. International Convention against the Taking of Hostages, Dec. 17, 1979, T.I.A.S. 11081, 1316 U.N.T.S. 205, *reprinted in* 18 I.L.M. 1456 (1980), *available at* http://www1.umn.edu/humanrts/instree/takinghostages.html (Jan. 30, 2003).
77. Convention on the Physical Protection of Nuclear Material, Mar. 3, 1980, T.I.A.S. 11080, 1456 U.N.T.S. 101, *reprinted in* 18 I.L.M. 1419 (1980).
78. Protocol for the Suppression of Unlawful Acts of Violence at Airports Serving International Civil Aviation Supplementary to the Convention for the Suppression of Unlawful Acts against the Safety of Civil Aviation, Feb. 24, 1988, 974 U.N.T.S. 178, *reprinted in* 27 I.L.M. 627 (1988).
79. Convention for the Suppression of Unlawful Acts Against the Safety of Maritime Navigation, Mar. 10, 1988, 1678 U.N.T.S. 221, *reprinted in* 27 I.L.M. 668 (1988).
80. Protocol for the Suppression of Unlawful Acts Against the Safety of Fixed Platforms Located on the Continental Shelf, Mar. 10, 1988, 1678 U.N.T.S. 304, *reprinted in* 27 I.L.M. 685 (1988).
81. Convention on the Marking of Plastic Explosives for the Purpose of Detection, Mar. 1, 1991, U.N. Doc. S/22393/Corr. 1, *reprinted in* 30 I.L.M. 721 (1991).
82. International Convention for the Suppression of Terrorist Bombings, G.A. Res. 52/164, U.N. GOAR, 52d Sess., U.N. Doc A/RES/52/164, Annex (1997), *reprinted in* M. CHERIF BASSIOUNI, INTERNATIONAL TERRORISM: MULTILATERAL CONVENTIONS (1937–2001) 183 (2001), *available at* http://www.un.org/documents/ga/res/52/a52r164.htm (Jan. 30, 2003).
83. International Convention for the Suppression of the Financing of Terrorism, G.A. Res. 54/109, 54th Sess., U.N. Doc. A/RES/54/109, Annex (2000), *entered into force* Apr. 10, 2002, *available at* http://www.un.org/documents/ga/res/54/a54r109.pdf (Jan. 30, 2003).

Each treaty lists the specific acts that states should proscribe under applicable domestic law.[84] It is fair to say that the international instruments addressing aspects of terrorism have been at the forefront of expanding the scope of permissible domestic jurisdiction. The terrorist conventions built on established principles of territorial and nationality jurisdiction through the development of passive personality jurisdiction. Thus, this body of international instruments allows a state party to establish personal jurisdiction over offenders who direct attacks against its nationals regardless of the situs of the attack.[85] This principle has been extended to the point that if a perpetrator even intends to intimidate the population or to compel a government to do or to abstain from taking a particular act, that government may establish its criminal jurisdiction.[86] The body of existing conventional law therefore gives sovereign states a robust ability to prosecute acts of international terrorism, and generally supports jurisdiction of several states over any particular act or attempted act of international terrorism.

In addition to establishing the norms and the clearly recognizable right for sovereign states to enforce those substantive norms through domestic legislation, the existing framework deliberately facilitates the cooperative efforts necessary to ensure the proper exercise of jurisdiction by one or more states. The underlying goal of the conventions is to facilitate the administration of justice in the state most able to prosecute the perpetrator. Thus, a recurring feature of the texts requires a state party that apprehends an alleged offender in its territory to submit that case "without exception whatsoever" to its competent authorities without "undue delay" for purposes of prosecution or to extradite to another willing state.[87] Furthermore, the treaties facilitate extradition between sovereign states by specifically providing a legal basis either through the text of the convention itself or by inclusion of the offenses mentioned in the convention into existing or future extradition treaties between the parties. Lastly, the existing framework of domestic enforcement incorporates measures to ensure "the greatest measure of assistance" between

---

84. *See, e.g.,* 18 U.S.C. 32, 2331–2332e, 2339A, 3286, 3592 (2002). *See also* 28 U.S.C.A. 1605 (framing issues of jurisdiction).
85. *See, e.g.,* Terrorist Bombing Convention, *supra* note 82, art. 6(2); Hostage Convention, *supra* note 76, art. 5. *See also* Draft Convention on the Suppression of Acts of Nuclear Terrorism, U.N. Doc. A/AC.252/L.3, *reprinted in* M. CHERIF BASSIOUNI, INTERNATIONAL TERRORISM: MULTILATERAL CONVENTIONS (1937–2001) 219 (2001).
86. *See, e.g.,* Terrorist Bombing Convention, *supra* note 82, art. 2; Financing of Terrorism Convention, *supra* note 83, art. 7(2)(c); Hostage Convention, *supra* note 76, art. 5(1)(c); Fixed Platforms Convention, *supra* note 80, art. 3(2)(c).
87. *See, e.g.,* Terrorist Bombing Convention, *supra* note 82, art. 8.

states in connection with investigations and prosecutions related to acts of international terrorism.[88]

The Convention on the Prevention and Punishment of Crimes against Internationally Protected Persons provides a representative sample of the operation of domestic mechanisms in responding to acts of international concern. Its provisions require states parties to cooperate in order to prevent, within their territories, preparations for attacks on diplomats within or outside their territories, to exchange information, and to coordinate administrative measure against such attacks.[89] If a perpetrator succeeds in attacking an internationally protected person, state parties are obligated to exchange available information concerning the circumstances of the crime and the alleged offender's identity and whereabouts.[90] Ultimately, the state in whose territory the perpetrator is located must either extradite back to another state with jurisdiction or "submit, without exception and without undue delay, the case to its competent authorities for the purpose of prosecution, through proceedings in accordance with the laws of that State."[91]

In short, for every terrorist crime committed or attempted, there will always be one or more sovereign states that have both an available basis for extending jurisdiction over the crimes and the motivation to do so. In relation to the prosecution of terrorist crimes, there is simply no remaining function that an internationalized process would serve. Nevertheless, if an internationalized terrorism tribunal generated a marked deterrent effect on those who would commit similar crimes in the future, the vast amount of dollars, yen, riyals, and euros spent could be a bargain.

Evaluating the potentiality of an internationalized process as an instrument of deterrence, it is worth noting that such an international forum would almost certainly be unable to administer capital punishment, and its deterrent value would therefore be limited to an undetermined degree. Furthermore, there is no empirical evidence whatsoever of any deterrent effect of international justice mechanisms on the actions of real perpetrators in the real world who inflict their crimes on real victims. As Justice Jackson famously pointed out in his opening statement at Nuremberg, "[w]ars are started only on the

---

88. See, e.g., Terrorist Bombing Convention, supra note 82, art. 10(1).
89. Convention on the Prevention and Punishment of Crimes against Internationally Protected Persons, including Diplomatic Agents, supra note 75, art. 4.
90. Id., art. 5.
91. Id., art. 7.

theory and in the confidence that they can be won. Personal punishment . . . will probably not be a sufficient deterrent to prevent a war where the war makers feels the chances of defeat to be negligible."[92]

Justice Jackson was just articulating the enduring truth that international relations theorists are familiar with—regime elites are risk averse actors. If they see a high probability of punishment and adverse consequences, human psychology will often prevent the undesirable conduct. In the field of enforcing international norms, this is what we have termed "ending the cycle of impunity." In the context of deterring violations of humanitarian law, criminal prosecutions by international tribunals have a theoretical effect, but good hopes and genuine aspirations cannot substitute for the power of genuine deterrence. Terrorist actors would presumably be even less susceptible to external coercion because their modus operandi is to operate beyond the constraints of the rule of law and organized international society.

The Kosovo experience is the best available case study on the deterrent effect of an internationalized process, and it served to demonstrate the need for genuine deterrence rather than idealistic assertions of legal proscription. The Security Council repeatedly affirmed ICTY jurisdiction in an ongoing effort to prevent abuses by the Milosevic regime inside Kosovo, and expressly ordered the Belgrade regime to cooperate with the investigative efforts of tribunal personnel.[93] The same resolution directed the ICTY prosecutor to "begin gathering information related to the violence in Kosovo that may fall within its jurisdiction."[94]

In the face of an existing international forum with clear jurisdiction and stated international support, Serbian forces massacred forty-five innocent civilians at Racak, Kosovo, crimes that ultimately contributed to the NATO intervention in Operation ALLIED FORCE.[95] While governments grumbled over

---

92. TRIAL OF THE MAJOR WAR CRIMINALS 153, *supra* note 52, at 153.
93. *See, e.g.,* S. C. Res. 1160, U.N. SCOR, 54th Sess., U.N. Doc. S/1160/(1998).
94. *Id.,* para. 17.
95. Even as the NATO nations gathered in Washington to observe the 50th anniversary of the alliance, operations in Kosovo threatened to unravel the international posture that NATO is a community of common values based on principles of sovereignty, individual liberty, and respect for the rule of law. Operation ALLIED FORCE represented the resolve of the world's strongest military/political alliance to take concrete action against despots who commit intolerable atrocities. By failing to take strong, if belated, action in the face of the crimes against humanity committed by the Belgrade regime, NATO would have looked cynical and irrelevant to the security and peace in Europe. THE ECONOMIST 15, Apr. 24, 1999.

the perceived slow pace of the ICTY investigations,[96] the Rambouillet document reiterated ICTY jurisdiction over events in Kosovo through an explicit provision that required the cooperation of Federal Republic of Yugoslavia (FRY) officials with the investigative efforts by ICTY.[97]

Despite the clear warnings of the international community, and express jurisdiction of a functioning international tribunal, Belgrade's forces expelled over 1.5 million Albanians from their homes, committed uncounted rapes, pillaged whole communities, destroyed tens of thousands of civilian homes in at least 1,200 communities, and murdered an estimated 10,000 Kosovar civilians.[98] The ICTY subsequently indicted Slobodan Milosevic and four of his senior officials for crimes against humanity and violations of the laws or customs of war committed in Kosovo,[99] one count of which specifically charged the Racak massacre. This indictment and the trials it will spawn continue to spark debate and keen interest in the law of armed conflict throughout the world. Nevertheless, the Milosevic indictment represented an unequivocal deterrence failure for the established legal codes and judicial framework and the best measure of the likely deterrent effect of an international terrorist tribunal.

---

96. Charles Truehart, A *New Kind of Justice*, THE ATLANTIC MONTHLY 80 (April 2000). In February, 1999, the Chairman-in-Office of the Organization for Security and Cooperation in Europe reported that there were at least 210,000 internally displaced Kosovars, and reported the lack of cooperation by FRY officials with the surviving relatives of the victims from the Racak massacre. U.N. Doc. S/1999/214/(1999). This unwavering Security Council support was ultimately expressed in the Chapter VII resolution authorizing the international military and civil presence in Kosovo, which "demanded" full cooperation by all parties with the pending investigative efforts in the wake of the humanitarian disaster in Kosovo in the first six months of 1999. S. C. Res. 1244, U.N. SCOR, 54th Sess., U.N. Doc. S/1244/para. 14/(1999).
97. *See* Rambouillet Accords: Interim Agreement for Peace and Self-Government in Kosovo, U.N. Doc. S/1999/648, annex, Art. II, para. 13 (1999).

All parties shall comply with their obligation to cooperate in the investigation and prosecution of serious violations of international humanitarian law.

a) As required by United Nations Security Council Resolution 827 (1993) and subsequent resolutions, the Parties shall fully cooperate with the International Criminal Tribunal for the Former Yugoslavia in its investigations and prosecutions, including complying with its requests for assistance and its orders.

b) The Parties shall also allow complete, unimpeded, and unfettered access to international experts—including forensics experts and investigators—to investigate allegations of serious violations of international humanitarian law.

98. ETHNIC CLEANSING IN KOSOVO: AN ACCOUNTING, U.S. DEP'T OF STATE 3 (Dec. 1999). An earlier version of the report was compiled by the State Department, which also issued a series of weekly ethnic cleansing reports, *available at* http://www.state.gov/www/regions/eur (Jan. 30, 2003).
99. Prosecutor v Milosevic, *et al*, Indictment, No. IT-99-37 (May 24, 1999), *available at* http://www.un.org/icty/indictment/english/mil-ii990524e.htm (Jan. 30, 2003).

Security Council Resolution 1373

On September 28, 2001, the Security Council, acting under Chapter VII of the Charter, adopted Resolution 1373, which on its face is an extraordinary statement of international unity and purpose.[100] In the post-September 11 tidal wave of international concern and cooperation, states had the opportunity to revisit the approach that has been developed in dealing with international terrorism. The patchwork quilt of conventional law, implemented and administered through sovereign systems, is clearly not a complete solution, but the Security Council unanimously elected to reinforce the existing framework. Rather than opting for an internationalized process, the Security Council precisely framed the language of Resolution 1373 to buttress the current approach.

Resolution 1373 uses sweeping language to impose a duty on states to enact legislation and to punish the crimes of terrorism. The operative paragraph directs every nation in the world to

> [e]nsure that any person who participates in the financing, planning, preparation or perpetration of terrorist acts or in supporting terrorist acts is brought to justice and ensure that, in addition to any other measures against them, such terrorist acts are established as serious criminal offences in domestic laws and regulations and that the punishment duly reflects the seriousness of such terrorist acts.[101]

Because transnational terrorism is an illegal and immoral epidemic that undermines the stability of world order, the Security Council employed its binding authority under Chapter VII to craft the most effective response possible. It is important that the Security Council focused on improving and implementing the sovereign enforcement of international norms rather than instituting an internationalized judicial response.

In its landmark statement outlining the international response to terrorism, the Security Council also established a number of additional steps that member states are *required* to take to combat terrorism. For example, the Council "[d]ecides that all States shall . . . [p]revent and suppress the financing of terrorist acts"[102] and then mandated other explicit steps that states are to take

---

100. S. C. Res. 1373, U.N. SCOR, 56th Sess., U.N. Doc. S/1373/(2001).
101. *Id.*, para. 2(c).
102. *Id.*, para. 1(a).

such as facilitating early warning to other states through the exchange of information,[103] denying safe haven to terrorists,[104] and preventing the movement of terrorists by effective border controls and controls on the issuance of identity papers and travel documents.[105] In the context of criminal investigations and prosecutions, states must "[a]fford one another the greatest measure of assistance in connection with criminal investigations or criminal proceedings relating to the financing or support of terrorist acts, including assistance in obtaining evidence in their possession necessary for the proceedings."[106]

Finally, the Security Council exhorted all sovereign states to take a number of cooperative actions to combat terrorism, including, among others, "intensifying and accelerating the exchange of operational information,"[107] becoming parties to the relevant antiterrorist conventions, including the International Convention for the Suppression of Financing of Terrorism,[108] and ensuring, "in conformity with international law," that refugee status is not abused by terrorists, and that "claims of political motivation are not recognized as grounds for refusing requests for the extradition of alleged terrorists."[109]

Conclusion

My view is that an international tribunal in the present circumstances is an inadvisable and unnecessary aspect of the response to transnational terrorism. The world will successfully combat terrorism by aggressively cooperating to engage, investigate, hunt down, and prosecute those terrorists who survive military action against them. We've already seen investigations in countries all around the world that have uncovered links to terrorism—and if the press is credible, have prevented some terrorist attacks. Abdicating state responsibility to an internationalized process would be the first step towards paralyzing politicization of the fight against terrorism and could pave the way towards ultimate failure in this critical global campaign.

In lieu of creating a superstructure of international enforcement, the Security Council used Resolution 1373 to take the revolutionary step of establishing

---

103. *Id.*, para. 2(b).
104. *Id.*, para. 2(c).
105. *Id.*, para. 2(g).
106. *Id.*, para. 2(f).
107. *Id.*, para. 3(a).
108. *Id.*, para. 3(d).
109. *Id.*, para. 3(g).

a committee (the Counter-Terrorism Committee) to monitor state implementation of its terms. The Security Council asked all states to report to the committee, no later than 90 days after the date of adoption of the resolution, on the steps they have taken to implement the various aspects of the resolution.[110] This is an important effort at identifying the gaps that can be addressed through international assistance in creating a more certain expectancy of justice for those terrorists and would be terrorists who ignore and undermine the international order. In addition to the subsequent Security Council statements on terrorism, the reports that sovereign states have delivered to the Counter-Terrorism Committee regarding the concrete steps and present status of international progress in prosecuting terrorist crimes are available on-line.[111] The pathway towards a more secure future for us all treads the terrain of a vibrant international cooperation and sovereign investigations and prosecution. An international terrorist tribunal would disrupt that vital process.

---

110. *Id.*, para. 6.
111. *See* http://www.un.org/Docs/sc/committees/1373/ (Jan. 30, 2003).

XXI

Terrorism:
The Proper Law and the Proper Forum

Christopher Greenwood[1]

Introduction

The horrific events of 11 September 2001 changed the whole concept of terrorism in the minds not only of Americans but of many other people throughout the world. The atrocities perpetrated by al Qaeda that day were on a scale that was hitherto (and, we must all hope, for ever after) unparalleled. It is obvious, however, that terrorism did not begin that day. It is also a mistake to conceive of terrorism as something exclusively, or even primarily, directed against the United States. It is almost certainly the case that more lives were lost to terrorism in Algeria during 2001 than were cut short by the murders committed at the World Trade Center and the Pentagon but the names of Algeria's terrorist victims are unlikely ever to be recorded. To see the events of 11 September 2001 as the worst case of a phenomenon which has afflicted most of the world for many years, rather than as something unique, is in no way to diminish their horror, still less to excuse the conduct or minimize the evil of those responsible. It is, however, an important step which needs to be taken in understanding terrorism and seeking to combat it. A successful strategy against terrorism has to be based on a recognition

---

1. Christopher Greenwood is Professor of International Law at the London School of Economics and Political Science.

that it is an international phenomenon, the fight against which requires international cooperation on a scale which is all too rare.

That is particularly the case with attempts to bring terrorists to justice. In some respects the record of international cooperation since September 2001 is encouraging—the unprecedented action taken by the United Nations Security Council, and the number of ratifications which the main anti-terrorism treaties are now attracting, the broad coalition which cooperated in destroying al Qaeda's presence in Afghanistan all demonstrate what can be achieved by the international community when it works cohesively. But that is only part of the picture. Serious differences remain about the law to be applied to acts of terrorism, attempts to characterize terrorists as combatants in a war, the forum before which terrorist acts can be tried and a host of other issues.

The purpose of this paper will be to examine two of these issues. First, what is the law applicable to international terrorism and the reaction to it? In particular, what is the relationship between the laws of war and international criminal law in this context? Secondly, what is the appropriate forum for the prosecution of the surviving perpetrators of the 11 September outrage? In this context, it is also necessary to ask how the machinery for bringing terrorists before the appropriate forum can be made more effective.

The Proper Law

The Laws of War

A threshold question which has been raised by the events of 11 September and the reaction they have provoked is whether terrorism falls to be appraised by reference to the criminal law or the laws of war. The day after the attacks on the World Trade Center and the Pentagon, the President told the National Security Team that "the deliberate and deadly attacks which were carried out against our country were more than acts of terror; they were acts of war."[2] Others have argued that what happened was a crime but it had nothing to do with war.

In approaching this issue, it is important to keep in mind that the categories of crime and act of war are not necessarily exclusive. International law is not composed of a series of watertight compartments, each insulated from the others. The fact that a particular act is a crime under international law (and under national law) does not mean that it cannot also be an act of sufficient gravity that it constitutes a *casus belli*. Thus the fact that the attacks on the

---

2. Remarks by the President in Photo Opportunity with the National Security Team, at the White House Cabinet Room (Sep. 12, 2001), *available at* http://www.whitehouse.gov/news/releases/2001/09/20010912-4.html# (Apr. 29, 2003).

World Trade Center and the Pentagon were crimes does not preclude them from also constituting an armed attack for the purposes of the right of self-defense in international law. That has not prevented a measure of academic controversy on this point. A number of scholars have argued that the concept of "armed attack" in Article 51 of the United Nations Charter is confined to acts imputable to a state. Others have suggested that there is a borderline between crime and armed attack which cannot be crossed.

Neither view has much to commend it and both are at odds with the practice of states and international institutions. Nothing in the text or the drafting history of the Charter suggests that "armed attack" is confined to the acts of states. Moreover, the *fons et origo* of the right of self-defense in international law, the famous *Caroline* incident in 1837, concerned an attack on the United Kingdom's territory in Canada by a group of what we would now call terrorists, operating from US territory but in no way supported by the United States. Neither the United States nor the United Kingdom seems to have considered that this fact made any difference to the application of the law on self-defense and the formulation of the right of self-defense in the correspondence between them concerning the *Caroline* has been quoted ever since.[3]

Nor has state practice or the jurisprudence of international tribunals since the adoption of the Charter espoused a formalistic distinction between acts of states and acts of terrorist and other groups in determining what constitutes an armed attack. The fact that the International Court of Justice, when it recognized in the *Nicaragua* case[4] that the covert use of force could amount to an armed attack, referred only to covert actions by a state should not be taken as a finding (or even an *obiter dictum*) that covert uses of force by anything other than a state could not constitute an armed attack. The simple fact is that it was only state conduct which was in issue in the *Nicaragua* proceedings and the Court neither needed nor attempted to address the status of violence perpetrated without the involvement of a state. Moreover, the Security Council has repeatedly recognized that international terrorism, whether or not state supported, can amount to a threat to international peace and security and in resolutions 1368 and 1373 (2001), adopted in the aftermath of the events of 11 September, it expressly recognized that the United States had the right of self-defense in terms that could only mean it considered that terrorist acts on a sufficient scale constituted armed attacks for the purposes of Article 51 irrespective of who perpetrated them, for it was already likely by then that the

---

3. R.Y. Jennings, *The Caroline and MacLeod Cases*, 32 AM. J. INT'L L. 82 (1938).
4. Military and Paramilitary Activities in and against Nicaragua (Nicaragua v. United States), 1986 I.C.J. 3 [hereinafter Nicaragua Case].

attacks on the World Trade Center and the Pentagon were the work of al Qaeda.[5] The same approach was taken by the North Atlantic Council on behalf of the North Atlantic Treaty Alliance (NATO)[6] and the Foreign Ministers of the Organization of American States (OAS).[7]

The suggestion by some commentators that international terrorism must be dealt with exclusively through the mode of criminal prosecution of the individual and not through an application of the use of force in self-defense is, if anything, even more remote from reality and logic. Arrest, prosecution and the ordinary process of the criminal law can occur only once a degree of law and order have been reimposed within a society after a shocking resort to violence. That reimposition of law and order may well entail the use of the military even within a state and is still more likely to do so in the context of international society. The prosecution of the Nazi leadership for the crimes they committed in waging World War II was not an alternative to the use of force in self-defense but something which was made possible precisely because the victims of Nazi aggression were able successfully to employ force and overcome those aggressors. This is also the approach that must be used in dealing with the problem of international terrorism. Terrorism on the scale of what happened on 11 September cannot be addressed through the medium of international criminal law or the law on the use of force alone. It requires a conscious and judicious application of both.

To that extent, therefore, it is meaningful to talk of terrorism in the context of the law relating to war, for terrorism may supply a justification for resort to force under the jus ad bellum. The extent to which the military response to the events of 11 September 2001 was justified under the United Nations Charter is discussed elsewhere in this volume.[8] The present writer is firmly of the view that the military action in Afghanistan was lawful under the jus ad bellum.[9]

---

5. *See generally*, S. C. Res. 1368, U.N. SCOR, 56th Sess., U.N. Doc. S/1368/(2001) and S. C. Res. 1373, U.N. SCOR, 56th Sess., U.N. Doc. S/1373/(2001).
6. *See* Press Release, NATO Reaffirms Treaty Commitments in Dealing with Terrorist Attacks Against the U.S. (Sep. 12, 2001), *available at* http://www.nato.int/docu/update/2001/0910/e0912a.htm (Apr. 29, 2003).
7. Terrorist Threat to the Americas, OAS Res. RC.24/RES.1/01 (Sep. 21, 2001), *reprinted in* 40 I.L.M. 1273 (2001).
8. *See generally*, Chapters II & III *supra*.
9. Christopher Greenwood, *International Law and the "War against Terrorism"*, 78 INT'L AFF. 301 (2002); Christopher Greenwood, *International Law and the Pre-emptive Use of Force: Afghanistan, Al-Qaida and Iraq*, 4 SAN DIEGO INT'L L. J. 7 (2003).

To apply the jus ad bellum in this way, however, is a very different matter from applying the jus in bello to terrorism and the response to terrorism. Of course, where the response to an act of terrorism involves the use of force by one state against another—as happened in Afghanistan—there will be an international armed conflict governed by the jus in bello. Moreover, to the extent that the members of a terrorist movement such as al Qaeda fight as part of, or alongside, the armed forces of a state in such a conflict, their activities will be subject to the jus in bello (although they will not qualify for the status of lawful combatants in such a case unless they are integrated into the armed forces of a state or form a militia or irregular group responsible to that state and meeting the other criteria of the law of armed conflict[10]).

That is a very different matter, however, from treating al Qaeda as a belligerent in its own right and characterizing its relationship with the United States as an armed conflict governed by the jus in bello as some commentators have suggested. Indeed, some have gone so far as to suggest that there has been an armed conflict, presumably of an international character, between the United States and al Qaeda that goes back at least to the attacks on the United States embassies in Kenya and Tanzania in 1998[11] and possibly to the early 1990s and the first World Trade Center attack. On this analysis, this armed conflict was already in being at the time of the 2001 attack on the World Trade Center with the result that this attack, against what was plainly a civilian object containing thousands of civilians, was a war crime. The attack on the Pentagon would also have constituted a war crime on this analysis, even though the Pentagon was itself a military objective, because the means of attack was a hijacked civil airliner.

This theory has the obvious attraction that, as happened in World War II, the crimes which were committed could be tried by military commission.[12] Moreover, since this theory means that the United States has been engaged in an armed conflict for many years, the use of the military on a war footing and under wartime rules of engagement would raise no legal difficulties. These are important considerations but there are several reasons why the temptation which they present is one which should be resisted.

---

10. Geneva Convention (III) Relative to the Treatment of Prisoners of War, Aug. 12, 1949, art. 4A, 6 U.S.T. 3316, 75 U.N.T.S. 135 [hereinafter GC III].
11. On August 7, 1998, the US embassies in Nairobi, Kenya and Dar es Salaam, Tanzania were bombed by powerful car bombs. Over 250 people died in these attacks with over 5,000 injured. Osama bin Laden claimed responsibility for the attacks on behalf of al Qaeda.
12. For practice in World War II, see United States v. Quirin, 317 US 1 (1942).

First, something does not become so merely because it is useful that it should be so. The question whether there is an armed conflict is one which has to be decided by reference to the objective criteria laid down in international law, not the convenience (or inconvenience) of the results which may follow.

Secondly, if one applies the criteria of international law, it is clear that al Qaeda has neither the right nor the capacity to be a belligerent and to wage war on the United States. The concept of an international armed conflict is one which presupposes the existence in all the parties to the conflict of the legal capacity to wage war, that is to say the capacity to be party to international agreements on war, to comply with those agreements in the conduct of hostilities and, most importantly, to engage in hostilities on a footing of legal equality with one's adversary. This last consideration is fundamental, for it is one of the cardinal principles of the law of armed conflict that its rules apply equally to all parties to the conflict irrespective of whether their resort to force was lawful or unlawful.[13] As Sir Hersch Lauterpacht put it, "it is impossible to visualize the conduct of hostilities in which one side would be bound by rules of warfare without benefiting from them and the other side would benefit from them without being bound by them."[14] That principle could not be applied to hostilities between the United States and al Qaeda.

State practice before 11 September 2001—including, in particular, the practice of the United States—was consistent in treating the concept of international armed conflict as something which could normally arise only between states. To the extent that there was a departure from this principle for conflicts involving national liberation movements,[15] that departure was strictly confined to entities which had a degree of international personality and recognition and which were required to undertake to abide by the relevant international agreements which comprise most of the jus in bello. Even then it was a controversial move and one opposed by the United States. There is no support in state practice or in the literature of international law prior to 11 September 2001 for treating the concept of international armed conflict as broad enough to encompass a relationship between a state on the one side and

---

13. *See, e.g.,* United States v. List, *in* TRIALS OF WAR CRIMINALS BEFORE THE NUREMBERG MILITARY TRIBUNALS UNDER CONTROL COUNCIL LAW NO. 10, vol. 11, at 1228 (1950), *reprinted in* 8 LAW REPS. TRIALS OF WAR CRIMINALS 59.
14. Hersch Lauterpacht, *The Limits of Operation of the Laws of War*, 30 BRIT. Y. BK. INT'L. L. 206, 212 (1953).
15. Protocol Additional (I) to the Geneva Convention of 12 August 1949, and Relating to the Protection of Victims of International Armed Conflicts, arts. 1(4) and 96(3), Dec. 12, 1977, 1125 U.N.T.S. 3, 16 I.L.M. 1391 (1977).

a group which has no legal personality, no territory, no capacity to comply with the laws of the armed conflict (even if it wished to do so), and no competence to wage war in the terms of traditional international law.

Nor is there any sign that the United States regarded itself as engaged in an armed conflict with al Qaeda prior to 11 September 2001. The response to earlier acts of terrorism by al Qaeda was not couched in terms of the law of armed conflict.[16] Consequently, the suggestion that there has been an armed conflict between the two dating back, perhaps, to 1993 and the first attack on the World Trade Center, requires us to accept that such a conflict existed even though the United States was apparently unaware of the fact for the better part of a decade.

Finally, while the disadvantages of characterizing the relationship with al Qaeda as an armed conflict can no more preclude that relationship from being an armed conflict than the advantages of so characterizing it can make it one, it is important to realize that the policy considerations are by no means one-sided. To treat al Qaeda as a belligerent is to confer upon it a status to which it is not entitled and does not deserve but which will inevitably suggest to many observers a degree of equality in its relations with the United States. It is worth recalling that in the 1980s one of the demands made by the Provisional Irish Republican Army (IRA) was that the United Kingdom should treat their members as combatants, not as common criminals. The United Kingdom rightly resisted this demand even when ten IRA and Irish National Liberation Army (INLA) members starved themselves to death in protest. Why, then, give al Qaeda precisely what was demanded by, and denied to, the IRA? To do so will inevitably be taken as conferring an element of legitimacy on acts of violence which can have no legitimate basis whatever.

In addition, if the United States is engaged in an international armed conflict with al Qaeda, then its operations must be conducted by members of the armed forces subject to military discipline and not by the members of agencies such as the Central Intelligence Agency or the Federal Bureau of Investigation. There may also be serious consequences in the application of the law of neutrality by states which choose to stand aside from the conflict (as the law of armed conflict gives them every right to do).

---

16. *See, e.g.,* Remarks by President William Clinton on Departure for Washington DC From Martha's Vineyard (Aug. 20, 1998), 34 WEEKLY COMP. PRES. DOC. 1642 (Aug. 20, 1998). In his remarks explaining the US response to the embassy attacks, President Clinton did not refer to the laws of armed conflict as the basis for the US response.

An earlier speaker[17] suggested that when the law interferes with a whole series of policy imperatives, the law should be "retooled." The present writer accepts that international terrorism poses new threats which call for new thinking but that does not mean that law built up with painstaking care over many years can or should be brushed aside in favor of the "policy imperatives" of the moment. This is so not least because conflict between law and policy often masks a hidden conflict between immediate short-term policy objectives and longer-term policy imperatives. In the long run, it is patently in the interests of the United States that the rule of international law should be upheld and, in particular, that the laws of war should be respected and that principles such as equal application and the proper treatment of prisoners of war of which the United States has long been the champion should not be undermined.

At the very least, therefore, a departure from these principles could be in the policy interests of the United States only if it was really necessary. Yet that is not the case. The claim that the United States is engaged in an armed conflict has nothing to do with the legality of using force under the jus ad bellum. That has to be judged by reference to the criteria of self-defense discussed above (and in other chapters of this volume) irrespective of whether the United States is engaged in an armed conflict with al Qaeda. Moreover, nothing in international law precludes the United States from using its armed forces in counter-terrorist operations unless the jus in bello is applicable. Nor does international law fetter the use of lethal force or the adoption of robust rules of engagement when military forces are engaged in counter-terrorist operations in a way that can be avoided by the expedient of declaring that an armed conflict exists. It is difficult, therefore, to see what can be gained in terms of international law by a distortion of the concept of armed conflict to make it fit the operations against al Qaeda. If US law creates difficulties for the US Government—because, for example, of the application of the Posse Comitatus Act[18]—then the remedy lies with the US Congress.

Terrorism and Criminal Law

Let us turn, therefore, to the other body of law which may be applicable, namely the criminal law (both national and international) on terrorist activity. It should be made clear that the brief analysis which follows is confined to terrorism of a clearly international character. The most obvious point about such

---

17. See Chapter XI *supra*.
18. 18 U.S.C. § 1385 (2003).

international terrorism is that the acts by which it is accomplished are, of course, crimes under domestic law. A striking (and profoundly depressing) feature of the debate discussing the crimes committed on September 11th is that the most obvious crime, murder, is often omitted. Murder does not cease to be murder simply because the victims are counted in thousands rather than ones and twos. It does not cease to be murder because it is carried out by flying hijacked aircraft into buildings rather than by more conventional means. The *Lockerbie* verdict is a vindication of the principle that terrorist killing—the deliberate taking of life by terrorists—can and should be prosecuted as murder.[19]

Other crimes may exist in cases where no deaths occurred or a sufficient link between the individual being prosecuted and the casualties sustained cannot be established. Such crimes include crimes committed on or against aircraft such as those identified in the Hague and Montreal Conventions.[20] These crimes are of course found in almost all domestic law systems as well. In common law countries such as the United States and the United Kingdom, the offense of conspiracy offers a valuable weapon against those who plan terrorist outrages, even if the offenses they scheme to perpetrate are not in the end committed (e.g., because of police intervention). Conspiracy is not necessarily as readily available, however, in civil law countries. Other offenses such as the possession of explosives, firearms and biological or chemical poisons would certainly also be available for charging terrorists. The striking thing about the vast majority of these offenses is that they are generally ordinary crimes covered by the ordinary principles of criminal law.

The fact that in this particular context such crimes are committed by people we would call terrorists may be important for other reasons. However, it does not alter the underlying truth which is that the terrorist is, at bottom, a criminal and nothing more. The dichotomy that society tends to create between the common criminal and the terrorist is not always desirable. Sometimes this dichotomy seems to be created to make the terrorist criminal look worse than he otherwise might. However, what often happens is that distinguishing between the ordinary criminal and the terrorist operates to make the terrorist criminal look somehow less than a criminal given the purpose of his

---

19. *See* Her Majesty's Advocate v. Megrahi and Fhimah, No. 1475/99, High Court of Justiciary at Camp Zeist, the Netherlands, *reprinted in* 40 I.L.M. 582 (2001). An appeal by Megrahi was recently denied on March 14, 2002.
20. *See* Hague Convention for the Suppression of Unlawful Seizure of Aircraft (Hijacking), Dec. 16, 1970, 22 U.S.T. 1641, 860 U.N.T.S. 105 (1970) [hereinafter Hague Convention]; Montreal Convention For the Suppression of Unlawful Acts Against the Safety of Civil Aviation, 24 U.S.T. 567, T.I.A.S. No. 7570, 10 I.L.M. 1150 (1971) [hereinafter Montreal Convention].

crimes, for the terrorist often attempts to cloak his actions in the guise of freedom fighting and thereby claims that his noble aims permit his ignoble acts. Nothing should be allowed to distract from the criminal character of all terrorist activity.

Given that terrorist acts almost always constitute domestic crimes, there are still substantive rules of public international law worth keeping in mind when discussing these crimes. Many would argue that the Hague and Montreal Conventions are relevant when discussing the events of September 11th. In one sense, this is not the case. Since all four of the aircraft which were hijacked and then destroyed were US registered, took off from US airports, and were flying to other US airports, what happened appears to fall outside the scope of both conventions.[21] Nevertheless, although the events of 11 September 2001 appear to fall outside the scope of both conventions, if a perpetrator of one of the offenses recognized in the Conventions was found in a state other than the United States, the obligation to extradite or prosecute laid down in the Conventions would apply.[22]

Another Convention, which would have been relevant had the United States been party to it on 11 September 2001, is the Convention for the Suppression of Terrorist Bombings (1997).[23] Article 2(1) of that Convention provides that:

> Any person commits an offense within the meaning of this Convention if that person unlawfully and intentionally delivers, places, discharges or detonates an

---

21. *See, e.g.,* Montreal Convention *supra* note 20, art. 4(2) which provides that the Convention shall apply only if:
   (a) the place of take-off or landing, actual or intended, of the aircraft is situated outside the territory of the State of Registration of that aircraft; or
   (b) the offense is committed in the territory of a State other than the State of registration of the aircraft.
See also the comparable provision in Article 3(3) of the Hague Convention, *supra* note 20.

22. *See, e.g.,* Montreal Convention, *supra* note 20, art. 4(3) which provides that the requirement that offenses occur outside the state of the registration of the aircraft does not apply when an "offender or the alleged offender is found in the territory of a State other than the State of registration of the aircraft." Finding such an offender then triggers a requirement for a state "if it does not extradite him ... to submit the case to its competent authorities for the purpose of prosecution." Montreal Convention, *supra* note 20, art. 7. *See also* Articles 3(5), 6 and 7 of the Hague Convention, *supra* note 20.

23. *See* International Convention for the Suppression of Terrorist Bombings, U.N. Doc. A/Res.52/164 (Dec. 15, 1997), 37 I.L.M. 249 (1998) (not ratified by the United States until Jun. 26, 2002) [hereinafter Terrorist Bombing Convention].

explosive or other lethal device in, into or against a place of public use, a state or government facility, a public transportation system or an infrastructure facility:

(a) with the intent to cause death or serious bodily injury; or

(b) with the intent to cause extensive destruction of such a place, facility or system, where such destruction results in or is likely to result in major economic loss.

While the draftsmen of this Convention did not have in mind an attack carried out by flying hijacked civil airliners into buildings, relying on the explosive force of the impact and the fuel carried by the aircraft to achieve the destructive effect, the language of the Convention is entirely apposite to cover what occurred on 11 September 2001. Indeed, it is an important reminder that, however unprecedented the events of 11 September may have been, the existing fabric of international law is capable of dealing with them and there is no need to create an entirely new body of law for that purpose.

Crimes against Humanity

In passing, it should also be recognized that the conduct of those who planned and perpetrated the atrocities of September 11th could also be charged with crimes against humanity. Crimes against humanity are generally considered to consist of murder (or certain other offenses) committed as part of a widespread or systematic attack directed against a civilian population.[24] There is no requirement that the attack occur in an armed conflict.[25] Nor are crimes against humanity offenses which may be committed only by the state and its agents; they are also perfectly capable of being committed by non-state actors.[26] While the present writer would prefer to deal with the surviving perpetrators of the attacks of 11 September 2001 under the ordinary criminal law, supplemented, where necessary, by the counter-terrorism treaties, if, for some reason, it proved useful to try them for a crime against humanity, it seems clear that the elements of such a crime were present. Murder was undoubtedly committed and even if

---

24. *See, e.g.,* Rome Statute of the International Criminal Court, art. 5, U.N. Doc. A/CONF.183/9 (1998).
25. The requirement of a nexus with armed conflict in Article 5 of the Statute of the International Criminal Tribunal for the Former Yugoslavia is a limitation on the jurisdiction of that Tribunal and not a requirement of the substantive law.
26. *See* W.A. SCHABAS, AN INTRODUCTION TO THE INTERNATIONAL CRIMINAL COURT (Cambridge, 2001), 37. To the surprise of the present writer, Professor Schabas argued, in a discussion with the present writer for the BBC Radio programme "Law in Action" on 5 October 2001, that the events of 11 September could not constitute a crime against humanity.

there was not a widespread attack (a matter for debate) there was certainly a systematic attack on the civilian population.

The Proper Forum

National and International Tribunals

The second question to consider is what is the appropriate forum for trying these offenses? Like Lieutenant Colonel Newton, the present writer starts from the premise that in most cases the appropriate forum is a national court and that the most appropriate national court will generally be found in the state where the offense was committed. So far as this writer is concerned, the proper forum in which to try those persons still alive who were responsible for the attacks of September 11th is the courts of competent jurisdiction in the United States. Although it has sometimes been suggested that a jury in the United States could not give a defendant a fair trial in a case as highly charged as, for example, one involving the attack on the World Trade Center, there is no basis for such a suggestion. While it needs to be recognized that outside the common law countries the jury is often viewed as a threat to the rights of the accused rather than the guarantee of those rights,[27] it is nonsense to say that a jury which had heard all of the evidence put before it in a trial with the constitutional and other safeguards of the United States system and which was properly directed by an experienced judge could not do justice in such a case. To accept the argument that a fair trial in the United States would be impossible comes perilously close to creating an atmosphere in which the more serious the crime, the less likely it is that the perpetrator will be brought to justice, because it is far from obvious that there is a court in any other state which would be able to offer a better guarantee of a fair and effective trial.

The only alternative to trial in a national court would be trial before an international tribunal. Currently there is, of course, no international tribunal in existence which could exercise jurisdiction over the crimes committed on 11 September 2001. Neither the International Criminal Tribunal for the Former Republic of Yugoslavia (ICTY) nor the International Criminal Tribunal for Rwanda (ICTR) has subject matter jurisdiction over the crimes of September 11th. The International Criminal Court (ICC) does not have retroactive jurisdiction, quite apart from the fact that neither the United States

---

27. It is noticeable that in the *Lockerbie* trial, *supra* note 19, it was the defendants and the Government of Libya who insisted on trial without a jury; see Anthony Aust, *Lockerbie: The Other Case,* 49 INT'L & COMP. L. Q. 278 (2000).

(as the state in whose territory the offenses were committed) nor the states of nationality of at least some of the perpetrators are parties to the statute of the ICC. An international trial would, therefore, require the creation by the Security Council of a new court or tribunal. Such a step seems both unlikely and unnecessary.

That is not to say, however, that international tribunals have no part to play in the fight against terrorism. The fact that an act of terrorism on the scale of 11 September 2001 could constitute a crime against humanity means that future acts of terrorism on that scale could fall within the jurisdiction of the ICC. Indeed, it is worth recalling that the possibility of an international court exercising jurisdiction over terrorist offenses in cases where there was no national court which was in a position to do so without imposing unreasonable burdens on the state concerned was one of the reasons for the original proposals for the creation of an international criminal court.

On the subject of the ICC, it is necessary to say a little about the current controversy between the United States and most of the European States. There is no doubt that the differences between the two on this subject run deep. That the United States has serious concerns about the ICC is something which the European governments have to recognize. Some of the criticism of the United States position is exaggerated, to say the least. The United States was under no obligation to become a party to the ICC Statute and its choice not to do so is one which has to be respected. At the same time, however, US critics of the court should bear in mind that their constant attacks on the court are at least as exaggerated and may well be counter-productive. To many states—probably a majority—the ICC is an important step forward in international cooperation against the most serious of crimes. For the United States to denigrate that step while demanding a range of other forms of international cooperation against terrorist crime is scarcely the most effective way to win hearts and minds.

Enhancing Effectiveness of National Mechanisms for Bringing Terrorists to Justice

Since domestic courts are generally the most appropriate forum in which those accused of acts of international terrorism can be brought to justice, it is a matter of the utmost importance that the machinery for cooperation between states in relation to extradition and mutual assistance in criminal matters should be made as effective as possible. Sadly, the present system is far from effective. Extradition is understandably subject to safeguards for the accused and those safeguards have been supplemented by the effect of various decisions regarding the scope of international human rights treaties. The need for fundamental safeguards for the accused is, however, an entirely different matter from some of the restrictions and limitations with which the extradition process has become hedged around. This is not the place for a detailed examination of these issues but five matters require brief comment.

First, extradition must ultimately be based upon trust. The requested state has to be willing to trust the requesting state. That trust is not, of course, blind trust. It is axiomatic that extradition should not occur without guarantees of a fair trial. However, all too often it seems that our approach to this notion of the right to a fair trial is laced with a somewhat parochial attitude in which we perceive as deficiencies in the legal systems of other states any difference between their legal systems and our own. For example, many US lawyers look askance at the absence in English law of a strict exclusionary rule for illegally obtained evidence. On the other hand, many in the United Kingdom are horrified by the sight of a US prosecutor standing on the steps of a courthouse claiming that the defendant has been indicted for the most serious crimes in terms which—to the British ear—perhaps fail to make entirely clear the difference between indicted and convicted and which, in the United Kingdom would amount to a criminal contempt of court because of the risk of influencing the jury. Lawyers in both countries (and indeed throughout the common law world) are amazed at the practice in some civil law states where the accused's previous convictions are disclosed to the court at the commencement of the hearing.

It is entirely appropriate and necessary that the fairness of the process to which the accused will be subject in the requesting state is scrutinized in the requested country. The process of scrutiny, however, has to be accompanied by a recognition that the fact that the courts of the requesting state may have different procedures from those of the requested does not mean that they do not offer a fair trial. The fact that a state has no provision for jury trial, does not automatically exclude evidence illegally obtained, permits press comment on evidence which will be seen by the jury, or that imposes limitations unfamiliar to (or unknown in) the requested state on the right of appeal do not in and of themselves make the trial process in the requesting state unfair.

Secondly, the fact that in international law there is no duty on a state to extradite a suspect in the absence of an extradition treaty between that state and the state which wants to try the suspect makes it a matter of great importance that gaps in the network of extradition treaties be closed wherever possible. The multilateral agreements on terrorism, such as the Hague and Montreal Conventions and the Terrorist Bombings Convention, are of great significance here, since these treaties serve as extradition treaties between those parties who do not already have bilateral extradition agreements.

This is particularly important, because the negotiation of new bilateral agreements can be a very slow process, as can the amendment of existing agreements. A case in point is the negotiation in the mid-1980s of the Supplementary Extradition Treaty between the United Kingdom and the United States, which was designed to facilitate the extradition of terrorists (at that time, primarily IRA suspects wanted by the United Kingdom).[28] This process was, to say the least, complex and met with stringent opposition from some senators, notwithstanding that the treaty was between allies in the fight against terrorism with legal systems that are closely similar.

One feature of the requirement of a treaty as the basis for extradition is that many requests for extradition in terrorist cases are governed by treaties of some antiquity. Those treaties frequently assume that the only bases for jurisdiction are that the offense was committed on the territory of a requesting state or that the accused was a national of that state. Such an approach is, however, far too restrictive in dealing with the phenomenon of international terrorism. This point was highlighted in the *Al-Fawaz* case decided by the House of Lords in England in 2002. The case concerned a request by the United States for the extradition of three suspects accused of involvement in the bombings of the US embassies in East Africa in 1998. It was common ground that under international law the United States had extraterritorial jurisdiction in respect of these offenses, because they had been directed against embassies and diplomatic personnel but a question was raised as to whether jurisdiction of this kind was sufficient to meet the requirements of a treaty concluded at a time when the concept of jurisdiction was essentially territorial. The Divisional Court concluded that it was not (although it held that the defendants could be extradited on the strength of acts performed in the United States).

The House of Lords rejected the Divisional Court's narrow approach to jurisdiction. As Lord Hutton (who, as a former Chief Justice of Northern Ireland, has extensive experience of terrorist trials) said in the *Al-Fawaz* case:

> in the modern world of international terrorism and crime, proper effect would not be given to the extradition procedures agreed upon between states if a person accused in a requesting state of an offense over which that state had extra-territorial jurisdiction (it also being an offense over which the requested

---

28. *See* Supplementary Treaty Concerning the Extradition Treaty, June 25, 1985, U.S.-U.K., Exec. Rep. 99-17, 99th Cong., 2d Sess., 16 (1986), *reprinted in* 24 I.L.M. 1104.

state would have extra-territorial jurisdiction) could avoid extradition on the ground that the offense was not committed within the territory of the requesting state.[29]

This broader approach to jurisdiction is obviously far more likely to provide an effective mechanism for international cooperation against forms of terrorism for which the traditional concept of territorial jurisdiction is wholly inadequate. Yet it must be open to question whether all courts faced with one of the older extradition treaties would be willing to give that treaty the broader interpretation which the House of Lords gave to the United Kingdom-United States Treaty.

Thirdly, there is the question of the political offender exception which appears in most extradition treaties. The notion that an accused will not be extradited for a political offense is well established in most national extradition laws and has traditionally been seen as an important safeguard of civil liberties. Yet the nature of a terrorist offense is that it is almost always committed for political motives. If extradition could be prevented because of those political motives, it would effectively be precluded as a means of bringing terrorists to justice. Fortunately, while the political offender exception was a serious obstacle to the extradition of terrorists at one time, it is of far less importance today. The more modern multilateral counter-terrorist treaties each provide that the offenses to which they apply are not to be regarded as political offenses.[30] Similarly, the European Convention for the Suppression of Terrorism (1977) provides that the crimes to which it applies may not be treated as political offenses and relies instead upon the safeguard that a defendant should not be extradited if there are substantial grounds for believing that he or she would be prejudiced at their trial by virtue of their political beliefs, race, religion or nationality.[31] This approach makes far better sense, offering a safeguard based on the nature of the process which a defendant would face if extradited, rather than a "get out of jail free" card based on the nature of the offense of which they are accused.

Finally, it needs to be borne in mind that some differences between legal systems create obstacles to extradition which cannot be brushed aside. The most important instance is probably the different attitudes toward the death

---

29. *Id.*, para. 64.
30. *See, e.g.,* Terrorist Bombings Convention, *supra* note 21, art. 11.
31. *See* European Convention on the Suppression of Terrorism (1977), art. 5, *reprinted in* INTERNATIONAL INSTRUMENTS RELATED TO THE PREVENTION AND SUPPRESSION OF INTERNATIONAL TERRORISM (UN, 2001).

penalty in democratic states. While some, noticeably the United States, retain the death penalty for murder, the majority do not. For the parties to the European Convention on Human Rights, this fact creates a serious obstacle to extradition in cases where the accused faces a death sentence in the requesting state if convicted. In *Soering v. United Kingdom*[32] the European Court of Human Rights held that it would be a violation of the prohibition of Article 3 of the Convention (prohibiting torture, inhuman or degrading treatment or punishment) to extradite a person to a non-Convention state if that person faced a serious risk of being sentenced to death in a state where there was a long period of delay between sentence and execution. More significantly, for states party to Protocol 6 to the Convention, there is a broader prohibition on the death penalty which will generally preclude extradition where a death sentence is a real possibility.[33] In those circumstances, effective international cooperation in bringing terrorists to justice is not compatible with the maintenance of capital punishment.

Conclusion

The title of this panel is bringing terrorists to justice. Bringing terrorists to justice means that they must be brought before a court where they receive a trial that is fair and is seen to be fair. This is an important part of the whole process as it is not enough to lock someone in prison, execute them, or simply make them disappear. Instead, to fight terrorism properly, public opinion must be convinced of the guilt of the accused and of the egregious nature of the crime that he has committed. If that is to be done in an effective manner, it requires a clear understanding of the law applicable to terrorist crimes and a high degree of international cooperation.

---

32. Soering v. United Kingdom, 11 Eur. Ct. H.R. 439 (1989).
33. *See* Protocol 6 to the European Convention for the Protection of Human Rights and Fundamental Freedoms, April 28, 1983 (entered into force Mar. 1, 1985), E.T.S. 114, *reprinted in* 22 I.L.M. 539 (1983).

XXII

Panel IV
Commentary—Bringing Terrorists to Justice

Manuel Supervielle[1]

As the Staff Judge Advocate for the US Southern Command, I am exposed to a number of international legal issues occurring in the international community. Interestingly, given my position, I am exposed to the Central and Latin America position on these issues which often causes me to delve deeply into the positions the US government takes.

Mike Newton's thesis is that the decision as to how and where crimes against international law are dealt with is a question of national political will. To date, this thesis echoes the US position that it has the requisite ability to prosecute the types of crimes that many other nations want the International Criminal Court (ICC) to have jurisdiction over. The United States has the Uniform Code of Military Justice, a fairly extensive federal criminal code, and supporting state subordinate criminal codes. The United States also has an effective, independent judiciary, which is certainly not true in many areas of the world. However, something I think that is occasionally missed by those

---

1. Colonel Manuel Supervielle, an Army Judge Advocate, is the Staff Judge Advocate for the US Southern Command. In this position, he provides legal advice on international and operational law issues to US military commands or operations throughout Central and South America.

Panel IV Commentary—Bringing Terrorists to Justice

advocating the US position is that there are many nations that recognize that they do not have the rich history of an independent and impartial judiciary, nor do they have the type of separation of powers to remove bias and corruption from the court systems like the United States does. For these countries, many seem to prefer the ICC in lieu of their own domestic courts as they simply do not trust their own judicial and political systems. Hope has turned to frustration which has turned to despair in such countries and it is accordingly, not surprising that such countries see the ICC as holding out hope for achieving on an international scale, what has proven unattainable on the domestic scale. Recognizing then that the United States does have the rich, independent infrastructure and a proven history of being able to deal with war criminals and the like as well as the political will to handle those accused of crimes against international law, it might nonetheless behoove the anti-ICC advocates to consider that other nations and their citizens do not have the luxury of the same rich history. There may be very logical reasons as to why other countries would sign and ratify the Rome Statute that have nothing to do with the US view on the statute.

Chris Greenwood's point that terrorism certainly did not begin on September 11th is exactly correct. While terrorism became of greater importance to many US citizens on that date, it certainly was not created on that date. Many countries in the region in which I work have long histories of terrorism within their borders. As an example, Colombia has lost some 200,000 people to various acts of terror by the Revolutionary Armed Forces of Colombia over the last 40 years.[2] Peru has had its share of problems with the Sendero Luminoso terrorist group.[3] These examples bring to mind the idea that other places in the world have been dealing with the problem of terrorism for many years. The United States must be prepared to do so as well.

Finally, against the backdrop of this panel about challenges in bringing terrorists to justice and the previous panel on coalition operations, the likely passage of the American Servicemembers' Protection Act (ASPA) gives me some

---

2. The Revolutionary Armed Forces of Colombia are also known as the FARC.
3. Sendero Luminoso is also known as the Shining Path.

concern.[4] While there is much to like about the contents of this bill, if signed by the President, it is likely to make working in coalition operations and with friend and allies much more difficult in some situations than ever before. Basically this bill, with the exception of NATO countries, prohibits the US government from providing any kind of security assistance to countries that are party to the ICC. Currently, every country in South America, except for Surinam, and every country in Central America, except El Salvador and Honduras, have signed or ratified the Rome Statute.[5]

The caveat to the ASPA is that such security assistance may be provided by the United States to such countries as have entered into an Article 98 agreement agreeing not to permit extradition of US service-members to the ICC

---

4. **Editor's note:** The American Servicemember's Protection Act became law when President Bush signed the Emergency Anti-Terror Bill on August 2, 2002. Notably, the ASPA finds that "the United States will not recognize the jurisdiction of the International Criminal Court over United States nationals," and provides that no United States court, and no agency or entity of any state or local government, including any court, may cooperate with the ICC in response to a request for cooperation submitted by the ICC pursuant to the Rome Statute. ASPA, § 2004(b). The ASPA also prohibits the extradition of permanent resident aliens or US citizens to the ICC; the use of appropriated funds to assist the ICC; the participation of US service-members in any chapter VI or VII operations, the creation of which is authorized by the UN on or after the date the Rome Statute enters into effect (unless the President certifies that the service-members will not risk criminal prosecution by the ICC); and the provision of "military assistance" to a country that is a party to the ICC (this prohibition does not apply to NATO countries or major non-NATO allies (Australia, Egypt, Israel, Japan, Jordan, Argentina, the Republic of Korea and New Zealand) and Taiwan); the President is authorized to waive this prohibition on military assistance if in the national interest of the United States. ASPA, §§ 2004–2007. Finally, the statute grants the President the prospective authority to "use all means necessary and appropriate to bring about the release of any (covered) person who is being detained or imprisoned by, or on behalf of, or at the request of the International Criminal Court." See ASPA, § 2008(a). Covered persons include "members of the Armed Forces of the United States, elected or appointed officials of the United States Government, and other persons employed by or working on behalf of the United States Government, for so long as the United States is not a party to the International Criminal Court." See ASPA, § 2013(4).

5. For a current update on signatories to the Rome Statute, *see* Country by Country Ratification Report, *accessible at* http://untreaty.un.org/ENGLISH/bible/englishinternetbible/partI/chapterXVIII/treaty10.asp (Oct. 23, 2002).

from their countries.[6] The US State Department is currently pursuing such agreements with nations throughout the world but is not having great success. Absent such agreements in our area of operations, it will become increasingly difficult to plan, fund, and conduct coalition operations with many of our long-term allies in the Southern Hemisphere.

---

6. Article 98 of the Rome Statute provides

   1. The Court may not proceed with a request for surrender or assistance which would require the requested State to act inconsistently with its obligations under international law with respect to the State or diplomatic immunity of a person or property of a third State, unless the Court can first obtain the cooperation of that third State for the waiver of the immunity.

   2. The Court may not proceed with a request for surrender which would require the requested State to act inconsistently with its obligations under international agreements pursuant to which the consent of a sending State is required to surrender a person of that State to the Court, unless the Court can first obtain the cooperation of the sending State for the giving of consent for the surrender.

XXIII

Panel IV
Commentary—Terrorism and the Problem of Different Legal Regimes

Daniel Helle[1]

The multi-faceted nature of "terrorism" along with the lack of a commonly agreed understanding of the term gives rise to numerous questions on how the problems should be tackled. Such questions include determining whether additional or different norms may be necessary (including deciding which acts should be considered as international crimes) and how to combat terrorism while respecting the requirements imposed by existing law.

The following observations essentially relate to the relationship between different legal regimes, in particular international human rights law, international humanitarian law (IHL) and international criminal law.[2] All three, but

---

1. Daniel Helle is the Deputy Head of the ICRC Delegation to the United Nations.
2. When discussing the relationship between IHL and international criminal law, I think of "international criminal law instruments" as encompassing those conventions which have been specifically aimed at preventing and repressing terrorism. I do not wish to label the Geneva Conventions or their Additional Protocols as "international criminal law instruments," in spite of the fact that these conventions contain obligations on all state parties to prosecute or extradite persons suspected of having committed "grave breaches," several of which can cover terrorist acts. This is because the primary aim of IHL instruments is to highlight the rights and obligations of the parties to a conflict; whereas the regulation of how cases of non-implementation should be dealt with is treated on a separate, "second" level.

also other branches of international law, are relevant when addressing various aspects of "terrorism." While they share the common aim of seeking to protect human dignity and security, each have their strengths and weaknesses, and thus should be reserved to address the areas for which they are most suited.

The concurrent application of different legal regimes in any given situation is normally an advantage, notably because it helps ensure that various manifestations of terrorism can be addressed, taking into account who has committed the act (was it a private individual, a member of a party to an armed conflict, a representative of a state); who the act was committed against (a civilian, a member of the armed forces); and the related question of the context in which the act was committed (was it committed during an armed conflict or in "peace-time").

In some cases, such a concurrence may help prevent the occurrence of "gaps" in the system. For instance, if during an armed conflict, individuals who do not belong to any of the parties to the conflict commit a terrorist act (whatever the motive), humanitarian law may not adequately address the issue at the penal level and there is a need for international criminal law to "kick in."[1]

It is not necessarily a significant drawback that different legal regimes apply to the same event, if they all point toward a similar result, or the protection provided by one legal regime is "subsumed" by the other. Such may be the case, for instance, with respect to fair trial guarantees provided in human rights and humanitarian law.

There are, however, instances where different legal regimes point to different results, so that their simultaneous application to the same subject matter is difficult to reconcile, or they are simply incompatible with each other. In such cases, to achieve an acceptable result, it may be necessary to draft or interpret the scope of application of the relevant instruments as mutually exclusive.

One potential problem arises when the logic of criminal repression encroaches excessively onto that of humanitarian action and/or humanitarian law. The preservation of the latter two is an important reason why the International Committee of the Red Cross (ICRC) has been attentively following the drafting of international criminal law instruments at the United Nations.

---

1. The parties do have a general responsibility to protect civilians under their control, but this duty of diligence cannot be taken so far as to impose a criminal liability for failing to prevent every single act of violence which may occur. In any event, there also remains the separate need to punish the direct perpetrators of such acts.

An illustration of this possible tension was seen during the drafting of the International Convention for the Suppression of the Financing of Terrorism.[2] The Convention covers more than just the transfer of "funds" as this term is normally understood, so as to include notably "assets of every kind, whether tangible or intangible, movable or immovable."[3] It criminalizes the provision of funds in the knowledge that they are to be used for a terrorist act.[4] In the context of an armed conflict, what then would be the possibility of an organization such as the ICRC to carry out a large-scale humanitarian assistance program, if it were to assume that even a small portion of the assistance might be diverted by rebel groups who are labelled as terrorists by the government? Could it, in so doing, be accused of committing an international crime? The ICRC raised its concerns with government representatives, who amended the text of the draft convention (by better qualifying the crime), so as to preserve the possibility of delivering humanitarian assistance in conflict situations.

As a second example, it may be that an act (such as killing a person) is labelled as a crime in an international criminal law instrument, whereas the same act (such as killing a soldier) is not considered unlawful per se under international humanitarian law. Unless these two situations are distinguished, there is a risk that members of one of the parties will be labelled as international criminals, for the mere fact of having participated in hostilities, which may in turn be a disincentive for them to comply with the demands of humanitarian law (such as respecting and protecting detainees under their control). If one side ceases to comply with its obligations, there is a further risk that the opposite side will soon cease to comply also. The potential consequences for all those finding themselves in the power of a party to the conflict and/or exposed to the dangers of military operations should be evident.

A part of the problem is that "one man's terrorist is another man's freedom fighter," as was observed several times during the conference proceedings. This challenge has been a recurring one; for more than a century, there have been divergent views between government representatives on who has the right to take up arms against one another. It must be recalled, in this connection, that disagreement in 1899 on the resistance movement's right to fight enemy occupation led to the adoption of the Martens Clause, a provision which in its contemporary version ensures that no person is ever left

---

2. *See* International Convention for the Suppression of the Financing of Terrorism, G.A. Res. 109, U.N. GAOR, 6th Comm., 54th Sess., 76th Mtg., Agenda Item 160, U.N. Doc. A/54/109 (1999), *reprinted in* 39 I.L.M. 270 (2000) [hereinafter Suppression of Financing Convention].
3. *Id.*, art. 1.
4. *Id.*, art. 2.

to the arbitrary treatment of authorities, but remains under the protection of the law.[5]

Excluding an issue from the scope of international criminal law and leaving it to the domain of IHL does not necessarily mean that it will be left unaddressed, but rather that a different set of rules takes over. It should be noted in this regard that numerous acts of "terrorism" are already squarely prohibited by IHL, whether as such or as acts subsumed under numerous other qualifications, such as hostage-taking, deliberate attacks against civilians, or indiscriminate attacks. However, as suggested above, it must be acknowledged when considering what falls within the notion of "terrorism," that some acts which are lawful under IHL are clearly unlawful in peacetime.

When the core characteristics of human rights law, humanitarian law and criminal law are put in contrast, there is often no real problem to distinguish their different nature and thus to assess which legal regime should be relied upon to guide how terrorism should be countered. There are some areas, however, where the delimitation between these branches of international law is imprecise or uncertain, in which case one must carefully seek to establish the boundaries of each legal regime. In this process, it can be useful sometimes to approach "the border" from both sides, considering for each those arguments that speak for inclusion and those that speak for exclusion of the regime being considered. In this regard, it should be noted that there are risks associated not only with an excessive scope of application of international criminal law, but also of international humanitarian law. Thus, if there is doubt as to whether various persons can be considered as taking an active/direct part in hostilities, it may be relevant to approach the matter not only from the angle of IHL, but also to analyze the question from the perspective of human rights (including the right to life) and international criminal law.

The question of bringing "terrorists" before the right tribunal may be a function of how one looks at the subject-matter rather than one of terminology. One example can be found in Article 5 of the Third Geneva Convention, where the drafters, according to the records of the proceedings, seemed to have treated broadly, as one issue, the question of how doubts as to the status of POWs were to be resolved. This issue masks the fact that there may be vastly different questions being considered. In one case it may be, for instance, that the detaining authorities consider whether the person concerned should be sent to a POW camp or to a camp for civilian internees. This question is not entirely without importance, since treatment provided by the Third

---

5. For a discussion of the Martens Clause, see Theodor Meron, *The Martens Clause, Principles of Humanity, and Dictates of Public Conscience*, 94 AM. J. INT'L L. 78 (2000).

Convention is not identical to that provided by the Fourth Convention. It is however an entirely different matter to decide whether the person concerned should be punished for having taken part in hostilities. In the event that the death penalty can be imposed, any absence of available fair trial guarantees—including with respect to the composition of the tribunal and the procedure adopted, and whether these originate from humanitarian law or from human rights law—opens up the possibility for arbitrary execution. Since the above two questions are of a quite different nature, they should also be dealt with as separate matters; notably so that any initial decision with respect to where the person should be detained should have no impact on the question of criminal liability and punishment.

Lastly, it is clear that terrorism must be countered through a multitude of means, including diplomatic efforts, international cooperation to exchange information and freeze assets, public debate and awareness-raising, to name but a few. In this regard, IHL neither should be asked to perform more than what it was made for, nor should it be discredited on erroneous grounds, such as allegedly opposing criminal repression simply because it mandates humane treatment and judicial guarantees. Conversely, IHL should be respected in all cases where armed conflict occurs, whether or not the purpose of the conflict is related to terrorism and in regard to all persons involved in or affected by the conflict.

According IHL its appropriate place will help secure, on the one hand, that various branches of international law have sufficient vitality to bring terrorists to justice, while at the same time preserving other approaches aimed at protecting human dignity and public safety.

XXIV

Panel IV
Discussion—Bringing Terrorists to Justice

On the Distinction Between Armed Conflict and Armed Attack

Yoram Dinstein
Care must be taken to distinguish between the two, markedly different phrases of "armed conflict" and "armed attack." The expression "armed attack" is derived from Article 51 of the UN Charter and it constitutes the trigger for the exercise of the individual or collective right of self-defense. "Armed conflict," on the other hand, is the term of art characteristic especially of the 1977 Protocol I Additional to the Geneva Convention, where it is used in the sense of war as well as hostilities short of war between states.[1]

September 11th—Armed Attack, Armed Conflict, Ordinary Criminal Acts

Michael Newton
The United States was in an armed conflict with al Qaeda at the very least by September 11th. There were, in fact, a long series of armed attacks against US personnel and facilities beginning arguably with the downing of the Blackhawk helicopters in Mogadishu, including the bombings of the Khobar towers, the attacks on the US embassies in Nairobi and Kenya, and the bombing of the USS *Cole* in the Yemeni port. These armed attacks were reinforced and called for by

---

1. *See generally* Protocol Additional (I) to the Geneva Convention of 12 August 1949, and Relating to the Protection of Victims of International Armed Conflicts, arts. 51.5(a) & 57.2(a)(iii) & (b), Dec. 12, 1977, 1125 U.N.T.S. 3, 16 I.L.M. 1391 (1977).

various al Qaeda members as well as by bin Laden himself. Each time one of these armed attacks occurred, the United States had the authority under Article 51 of the UN Charter to engage in self-defense against al Qaeda. The 1998 missile attacks in Afghanistan are one manifestation of the United States pursuing its lawful right to self-defense.

Christopher Greenwood

I disagree that an armed conflict existed before, or even after, the events of September 11th between the United States and al Qaeda. Al Qaeda does not have the capacity to make a declaration of war any more than an individual in a non-official governmental capacity has the ability to do so. Politicians and academics alike, within the United States and outside, did not take the position before September 11th that the United States was party to an armed conflict with al Qaeda. It is only subsequent to these horrible events that some have argued this to be the case. One reason some have taken this position is that it then makes the unlawful targeting of civilians a war crime which may be properly brought before a military commission. I believe this to be a perversion of the law and quite incorrect. In this respect, I agree with Yoram Dinstein. The events preceding and including those on September 11th were armed attacks within the meaning of Article 51 of the UN Charter. These acts were threats to international peace and security and the Security Council, nations, and alliances clearly identified them as such.[2]

Is there an armed conflict against Afghanistan? To be sure there is. The fighting between the United States and al Qaeda personnel alongside the Taliban is regulated and governed by the law of armed conflict but not because they are al Qaeda members but instead because they are fighting with a party to an armed conflict—Afghanistan. The fact that an al Qaeda member turns up in another country does not mean that they are automatic targets for they are not. By claiming to be in an armed conflict with al Qaeda, the United States is giving a degree of legitimacy to people who are really nothing more than horrible criminals. This is a terrible error. I believe this error will make it exceedingly difficult to proceed against al Qaeda members before military tribunals. The United States will have to try and fit what is essentially a terrorist crime into a framework of criminal offenses designed for crimes of war.

Michael Newton

It is doubtful that anyone at this conference would contest the statement that the attacks on the World Trade Center and the Pentagon on September 11th

---

2. *See* S. C. Res. 1368, U.N. SCOR, 56th Sess. U.N. Doc. S/1378/(2001).

were indeed armed attacks within the meaning of Article 51 of the UN Charter. This clearly means that the United States may properly invoke its right to self-defense under Article 51 as against al Qaeda members—since they were the threat that caused the events of September 11th. The right of self-defense allows the United States then to do what? Not to engage in intentional attacks on civilians but instead to attack those who have attacked you. This is done in the context of an armed conflict. Recall that the United States is not a signatory to Protocol I of the Geneva Conventions so as far as the United States is concerned, these al Qaeda members are not proper combatants within the meaning of Article 44 of this Protocol.[3] They are not civilians since they are taking an active part in hostilities. Nor are they proper combatants. Instead, they are unprivileged or unlawful combatants with none of the protections of

---

3. *See* Protocol I, *supra*, art. 44, which provides in relevant part:

Article 44 — Combatants and prisoners of war

1. Any combatant, as defined in Article 43, who falls into the power of an adverse Party shall be a prisoner of war.

2. While all combatants are obliged to comply with the rules of international law applicable in armed conflict, violations of these rules shall not deprive a combatant of his right to be a combatant or, if he falls into the power of an adverse Party, of his right to be a prisoner of war, except as provided in paragraphs 3 and 4.

3. In order to promote the protection of the civilian population from the effects of hostilities, combatants are obliged to distinguish themselves from the civilian population while they are engaged in an attack or in a military operation preparatory to an attack. Recognizing, however, that there are situations in armed conflicts where, owing to the nature of the hostilities an armed combatant cannot so distinguish himself, he shall retain his status as a combatant, provided that, in such situations, he carries his arms openly:

    a. during each military engagement, and

    b. during such time as he is visible to the adversary while he is engaged in a military deployment preceding the launching of an attack in which he is to participate.

    c. Acts which comply with the requirements of this paragraph shall not be considered as perfidious within the meaning of Article 37, paragraph 1 (c).

4. A combatant who falls into the power of an adverse Party while failing to meet the requirements set forth in the second sentence of paragraph 3 shall forfeit his right to be a prisoner of war, but he shall, nevertheless, be given protections equivalent in all respects to those accorded to prisoners of war by the Third Convention and by this Protocol. This protection includes protections equivalent to those accorded to prisoners of war by the Third Convention in the case where such a person is tried and punished for any offences he has committed.

the Geneva Conventions. As unlawful combatants, however, they are committing war crimes which is exactly what al Qaeda members did on September 11th.

Christopher Greenwood
Al Qaeda members are not unlawful, lawful, or any other type of combatants at all. Clearly, no one would suggest that they are lawful combatants, even under Article 44 of GP I. You continue to give al Qaeda members a status they do not deserve. I agree that al Qaeda members who are fighting alongside Taliban members in Afghanistan are entitled to be called combatants because that is truly an armed conflict. However, the attack on the World Trade Center was not perpetrated by unlawful, unprivileged, or any other sort of combatant or belligerent. It was perpetrated by common criminals. Do not pretend that what these people did was a war crime. It was simple murder. Murder under the ordinary criminal code of the United States and New York, nothing more, nothing less.

By bringing this notion of an existing armed conflict dating back into the middle of the 1990s, I believe you are undermining the very laws of armed conflict. Taking this position, that an armed conflict exists, will make it much more difficult for the United States to bring them to justice.

Michael Newton
Inasmuch as your position suggests that these types of crimes are best prosecuted by domestic tribunals, I agree. That is not to say, however, that I believe these people to be the same as the ordinary criminal on the streets of New York City. Terrorism clearly overlaps the boundaries between criminal law and the law of armed conflict. As practitioners, however, we must be careful not to rush to apply domestic criminal law restrictions to what are international law of armed conflict issues.

Manuel Supervielle
This is an excellent point given the authorizations typically contained in rules of engagement when an opposing force is designated hostile. As we all know, when this occurs, US soldiers may target the enemy on sight, regardless of enemy actions—except of course if they meet the requirements of effectively attempting to surrender. With that being said, when we apply a domestic law paradigm to these situations, does it mean that the US sniper on the rooftop who suddenly sees an al Qaeda member must attempt to first arrest him for prosecution through domestic courts, or alternatively, when al Qaeda forces

are declared hostile, should he not simply be able to target an al Qaeda member on sight? These are the very real types of issues that must be resolved so soldiers have clear guidance and instruction in such difficult situations.

Harvey Rishikof
The tension that exists between these two positions is the problem associated with the current classification schemes. Professor Greenwood would have conference participants believe that al Qaeda members who committed the attacks on September 11th are garden variety, ordinary criminals. If this is the case, then the correct domestic response would be to mobilize the Federal Bureau of Investigation and bring them all to trial in federal court. This would mean that the appropriate response would not be one using the military but instead one using available police. On the other hand, these same al Qaeda members do not fit neatly within the established classification system of combatants or noncombatants. Importantly for the future here, these conflicts between the classification systems must be resolved. In the future, groups that are likely to cause such problems are likely to be one part criminal, one part terrorist, and one part political. How then do we resolve the classification scheme to deal with each category independently as well as different categories when combined?

Michael Newton
Fortunately, the law of armed conflict has demonstrated its ability to evolve over time and that is exactly what is happening now. It is no longer enough to treat terrorism in general within the paradigm of ordinary criminal conduct. The United States has proven since September 11th that it is unwilling to continue to treat terrorists this way. So the paradigm must expand or shift and that shift is to treat such behavior as war crimes precisely because the United States is unwilling to recognize the right of a group to attack a sovereign state. So the United States will treat them as unlawful combatants, participants if you do not like the word combatant, in what is an organized armed conflict, war if you will, controlled, directed, and funded against the United States.

Christopher Greenwood
An armed conflict has always been defined as a war or conflict between two states or possibly, in more modern times, between a state and an entity such as a national liberation movement which may have many of the attributes of the state. Suggesting that the current conflict between al Qaeda and the United States is an armed conflict within the meaning of that term elevates al Qaeda to a status it does not deserve nor is it entitled to. On what basis does a terrorist

movement such as al Qaeda acquire the right to declare war on a sovereign state such as the United States? By suggesting that it has that ability, you confer upon it a status that it does not otherwise possess. In doing so, you are legitimizing its activities. Finally, I am concerned that this is simply a matter of convenience of the moment to refer to al Qaeda in this fashion. It is certainly inconsistent with US actions towards al Qaeda in the past.

Adam Roberts

It is important to remember that the Military Order's jurisdictional mandate is for violations of the laws of war and for other applicable laws.[4] As I understand it then, there has been no exclusion within that framework for trying people for murder exactly as Professor Greenwood suggested they should be.

On Military Commissions

Michael Newton

Military commissions are an ad hoc mechanism that have existed in history for many years. A perception exists that these commissions will somehow not live up to the requirements of international humanitarian law but if one takes the time to look at the Executive Order and the Secretary of Defense's Implementing Rules, it will be quickly noted that these commissions will in fact provide the required due process and substantial fairness, fairness not found in a number of domestic court systems spread throughout the world.[5] Additionally, military commissions are not the only option for the prosecution of those detainees who ultimately are prosecuted, they are merely one option available. The United States may also release some detainees to other nations' courts and or to its own federal courts.

Christopher Greenwood

The idea of military tribunals does not actually bother me. I do find objectionable, however, the specific provision of the military order which provides that when a trial before a tribunal is ordered closed, the defense counsel may not disclose what transpired during the closed session to his own client. I do not

---

4. See Executive Order, Detention, Treatment, and Trial of Non-Citizens in the War Against Terrorism, 13 November 2001, art. 1.(e), *available at* http://www.whitehouse.gov/news/releases/2001/11/20011113-27.html (Oct. 10, 2002).
5. See generally *id.* See also Department of Defense, Military Commission Order No. 1, March 21, 2002, *available at* http://www.defenselink.mil/news/Mar2002/d20020321ord.pdf (Oct. 10, 2002).

believe that practicing lawyers could be, nor should they be, required to work under such conditions. Many lawyers I know consider such a provision unethical.

Michael Newton

Some commentators have taken the position that when armed conflict occurs, people must either be combatants or non-combatants. When captured, the combatants become prisoners of war while the non-combatants are civilians and should be released. The problem with this approach is that it leaves out a whole third category of individuals. These are people who do not qualify for lawful combatant status but yet have taken part in the hostilities. For example, members of al Qaeda are not lawful combatants if for no other reason than they do not meet the four-part test for becoming a lawful combatant as set out in the Hague Regulations of 1907 or the Geneva Conventions of 1949.[6] This third category is one of an unprivileged combatant in an armed conflict. That is to say by virtue of taking a part in the hostilities, this combatant is properly a target but is not entitled to the protection of the Geneva Conventions as he is not a lawful combatant. The United States has taken the position that for so long as these combatants are unprivileged/unlawful, they may be punished.

On the Challenges Associated with Defining and Addressing Terrorism

Michael Newton

The underlying act of killing in a political context, killing to create fear as in terrorism, or killing in an armed conflict context from an actus reus view is essentially the same. That is to say, it is the taking of a life. The difficulty comes in defining when it is a lawful taking of life and when the taking of life is done outside the law. As Daniel Helle indicated, this is a significant challenge in defining the applicable substantive legal provisions that set out what is terrorism versus what is a political murder versus what is the act of a lawful combatant taking part in armed conflict. The conventions on terrorism correctly point out in a number of places that certain acts do not comprise terrorism when committed by a lawful combatant taking part in armed conflict. For example, Article 19(2) of the Convention for the Suppression of Terrorist Bombings specifically

---

6. *See* Hague Convention (IV) Respecting the Law and Customs of War on Land, Anx. 1, Ch. 1, Art. 1(1–4); Convention for the Amelioration of the Condition of the Wounded and Sick in Armed Forces in the Field, Aug. 12, 1949, Art. 4(2(a–d)), 6 U.S.T. 3114, T.I.A.S. No. 3362, 75 U.N.T.S. 31.

states that the activities of armed forces during an armed conflict are governed by international humanitarian law rather than the Convention.

Panel V

Friday—June 28, 2002

8:30 AM–11:30 AM

The Road Ahead

Moderator:
    Dr. Richard Nuccio
    Director, Pell Center for International
    Relations and Public Policy
    Salve Regina University

Presenters:
    Professor John Murphy
    Villanova University School of Law

    Dr. Nicholas Rostow
    General Counsel
    US Mission to the United Nations

Commentators:
    Mr. James Terry
    Deputy Assistant Secretary for Global Affairs
    US Department of State

    Dr. Michael Saalfeld
    Director, International Legal Affairs
    German Ministry of Defence

    Mr. Ronald Winfrey
    Attorney Advisor
    US Pacific Command

    Captain Jane Dalton
    Judge Advocate, US Navy
    Legal Counsel
    Chairman of the Joint Chiefs of Staff

XXV

International Law and the War on Terrorism: The Road Ahead[1]

John Murphy[2]

On this, the last panel of the conference, we have been asked to consider "The Road Ahead" or, more specifically, the "application of any legal lessons learned, review of the role of international conventions on terrorism, and future military operations against terrorism." This is not an easy task. As Yogi Berra reportedly once observed, "it's difficult to make predictions, especially about the future." This is particularly true given that, as Richard Posner has recently pointed out, so-called "public intellectuals" or the "experts" have a notoriously bad record when it comes to predictions.[3] Accordingly, in this, as in so many enterprises, caveat emptor.

Be that as it may, this chapter proceeds along the following lines. First, since any effort at "futurism" necessarily involves an analysis of present trends, it attempts to identify the most salient trends in international terrorism and

---

1. I would like to express my appreciation for the excellent research assistance of Andrew Kenis, a third year student at the Villanova University School of Law, Rita Young-Jones, former reference law librarian at the Villanova University School of Law, and Charles J. Kocher, a second year student at the Villanova University School of Law. I am also grateful for a summer 2002 research grant from the Villanova University School of Law that greatly facilitated my work on this chapter.
2. John Murphy is a Professor of Law at Villanova University School of Law.
3. RICHARD A. POSNER, PUBLIC INTELLECTUALS (2001).

their impact on efforts to combat terrorism. Next it turns to two kinds of responses employed in combating terrorism which have been the focus of considerable scrutiny already at this conference: the so-called antiterrorism conventions, at both the global and the regional levels, and the use of coercive measures, i.e., economic sanctions and the use of armed force. As to these measures, the effort will be to evaluate their strengths and weaknesses, especially in light of current trends, and to set forth some tentative proposals for improvement.

Trends

September 11th itself is a spectacular demonstration of a disquieting trend in international terrorism: the increased willingness of terrorists to kill large numbers of people and to make no distinction between military and civilian targets.[4] Until recently many commentators were of the view that terrorists had little interest in killing large numbers of people because it would undermine their efforts to gain sympathy for their cause. A major cause of this radical change in attitude has been aptly pinpointed by Jeffrey Simon:

> Al Qaeda . . . is representative of the emergence of the religious-inspired terrorist groups that have become the predominant form of terrorism in recent years. One of the key differences between religious-inspired terrorists and politically motivated ones is that the religious-inspired terrorists have fewer constraints in their minds about killing large numbers of people. All nonbelievers are viewed as the enemy, and the religious terrorists are less concerned than political terrorists about a possible backlash from their supporters if they kill large numbers of innocent people. The goal of the religious terrorist is transformation of all society to their religious beliefs, and they believe that killing infidels or nonbelievers will result in their being rewarded in the afterlife. Bin Laden and al Qaeda's goal was to drive US and Western influences out of the Middle East and help bring to power radical Islamic regimes around the world. In February 1998, bin Laden and allied groups under the name "World Islamic Front for Jihad Against the Jews and Crusaders" issued a fatwa, which is a Muslim religious order, stating that it was the religious duty of all Muslims to wage war on US citizens, military and civilian, anywhere in the world.[5]

---

4. It is worth noting that in 1998 bin Laden told ABC News that "he made no distinction between American military and civilian targets, despite the fact that the Koran itself is explicit about the protections offered to civilians." *See* Peter L. Bergen, *Excerpts from Holy War, Inc.*, 82 PHI KAPPA PHI FORUM 26, 28 (2002).
5. Jeffrey D. Simon, *The Global Terrorist Threat*, 82 PHI KAPPA PHI FORUM 10, 11 (2002).

It is important to note that there are other religious terrorist groups besides al Qaeda. Examples include Hizballah, a radical Shia Islamic group in Lebanon, Hamas (Islamic Resistance Movement), and the Palestine Islamic Jihad, all of whom use terrorism in the West Bank, Gaza Strip, and Israel to undermine Middle East peace negotiations and to establish a fundamentalist Islamic Palestinian state. There are also the Abu Sayyaf Group, a radical Islamic separatist group operating in the southern Philippines; Al Gama'a al–Islamiyya (Islamic Group), which is based in Egypt and seeks the overthrow of the Egyptian government; and the Armed Islamic Group, which is located in Algeria and plots the overthrow of the secular Algerian government and its replacement with an Islamic state.

September 11th may also demonstrate another trend: the emergence of smarter and more creative terrorists. The planning and carrying out of the terrorist operation on September 11th was diabolically clever, and the 19 hijackers were well educated and from middle to upper middle class backgrounds. Smarter and more creative terrorists, moreover, are better equipped to take advantage of the information on weapons—including weapons of mass destruction—targets, and resources necessary for a terrorist operation readily available on the Internet. Similarly, they are better able to take advantage of the various vulnerabilities of a technologically advanced society, including major networks of communications, electrical power, pipelines, and data.

Another major trend is the "globalization" of terrorism.[6] According to Joseph Nye, globalization is "the growth of worldwide networks of interdependence."[7] In particular, Nye suggests, over the last several decades, there has been a substantial increase in "social globalization," i.e., the spread of peoples, cultures, images, and ideas, and this has resulted in "new dimensions of military globalism: humanitarian intervention and terrorism."[8] Perhaps the most salient example of social globalization resulting in terrorist military globalization is the worldwide expansion of the al Qaeda network, said to operate in more than sixty countries.[9] It is not the only example, however. Hizballah reportedly has operations in six continents, and Hamas and the Sri Lankan

---

6. For further discussion *see* John F. Murphy, *The Impact of Terrorism on Globalization and Vice-Versa*, 36 THE INTERNATIONAL LAWYER 77(2002).
7. JOSEPH S. NYE, JR., THE PARADOX OF AMERICAN POWER: WHY THE WORLD'S ONLY SUPERPOWER CAN'T GO IT ALONE 78 (2002).
8. *Id.* at 86–87.
9. *See Seeing the World Anew*, ECONOMIST, October 27, 2001, at 19.

Tigers of Tamil Eelam are said to "maintain cells far from the lands where their goals and grievances are focused."[10]

An encouraging trend is the apparent decline in state sponsored terrorism. The breakup of the Soviet Union, and the emergence of the countries in central and eastern Europe from under the Soviet yoke, greatly reduced the sources of state support that terrorists could rely on. Even for those countries that remain on the US State Department's list of sponsors of terrorism—Cuba, Iran, Iraq, Libya, North Korea, Sudan, and Syria—there has been some movement away from state support of terrorism toward cooperation with the international community's campaign against terrorism.[11] The main problem area is the Middle East. Although Iran and Syria, for example, have taken action against al Qaeda, they continue their active support for terrorist groups, such as Hamas and Hizballah, that primarily target Israel and its citizens, on the ground that these groups are not terrorists but national liberation movements.

Let us reflect for a moment on possible reasons for the distinctions made by Iran and Syria. It should come as no surprise that Iran and Syria should be willing to cooperate, at least to a limited extent, in efforts to suppress al Qaeda. The kind of radical Islamic fundamentalism espoused by bin Laden and al Qaeda is a serious threat not only to the United States but also to Islamic governments in the Middle East. Even though they may themselves be regarded as having radical Islamic governments, Iran and Syria are nonetheless among those threatened by al Qaeda. In contrast, Hamas and Hizballah direct their attention toward Israel, long the target of Iranian and Syrian enmity. Here, one may speculate, the greater danger for Iran and Syria may lie in *not* supporting these movements in light of the general support they enjoy among the people of the Islamic countries in the Middle East.

Interestingly, according to the latest US Department of State report, Latin America had by far the largest number of international terrorist attacks in 2000 and 2001.[12] Latin America, too, was a major venue for the activities of Hizbollah, as well as other terrorist groups, "in the tri-border area of Argentina, Brazil, and Paraguay, where terrorists raise millions of dollars annually via criminal enterprises."[13] There was also evidence of Hizbollah members or sympathizers in Chile, Colombia, Venezuela, and Panama. But allegations of

---

10. Paul R. Pillar, *Terrorism Goes Global: Extremist Groups Extend Their Reach Worldwide*, 19 BROOKINGS REVIEW 34 (2001).
11. *See* US DEPARTMENT OF STATE PATTERNS OF GLOBAL TERRORISM 2001 (May 2002), at 63.
12. *Id.* at 172.
13. *Id.* at 44.

the presence of bin Laden or al Qaeda support cells in Latin America remained uncorroborated.

Colombia was a particular problem area. In response to greatly increased violence and terror unleashed by Colombia's largest terrorist organization, the 16,000 member Revolutionary Armed Forces of Colombia (FARC), Colombia's former President Andres Pastrana decided, in February 2002, to terminate the peace process that had been a hallmark of his presidency and to reassert control over the FARC's demilitarized zone. Three Irish Republican Army members, allegedly helping the FARC prepare for an urban terror campaign, were arrested as they departed the demilitarized zone, and there were media allegations of similar support by the terrorist group Basque Fatherland and Liberty, or ETA.[14]

These developments in Latin America, along with an apparent comeback of the Shining Path in Peru, may have contributed to the successful conclusion of a new Inter-American Convention Against Terrorism by the OAS General Assembly on June 3, 2002 (discussed in the next section).

Perhaps the primary impact of these trends, as well as of the severity of the September 11th attacks and of the subsequent use of military force by US and select NATO forces against the Taliban and al Qaeda in Afghanistan, has been to raise an issue as to the appropriate legal regime to apply to efforts to control international terrorism. Prior to September 11th international terrorism had been treated primarily as a criminal law matter, with emphasis placed on preventing the commission of the crime through intelligence or law enforcement means, or, if prevention failed, on the apprehension, prosecution and punishment of the perpetrators. To be sure, the United States had previously used armed force on occasion against terrorism. For example, in 1986, the United States bombed Tripoli, Libya in response to Libya's apparent involvement in the bombing of a West Berlin discotheque frequented by American soldiers and the terrorist attack by Libyan backed Abu Nidal on El Al airline counters that killed five Americans and wounded many others. Similarly, in 1993, the United States bombed Baghdad, Iraq, in response to an assassination plot by Saddam Hussein against former President George Bush, and in 1998, it engaged in missile strikes against Afghanistan and the Sudan in response to the East African embassy bombings. But none of these actions involved military force of the magnitude and duration of the actions in Afghanistan after September 11th. Hence after, and in many respects because of,

---

14. Id.

September 11th, the law of armed conflict assumed a much greater prominence than it had previously in efforts to combat international terrorism.

But the law of armed conflict has hardly occupied the field. On the contrary, as the fourth panel of this conference (Bringing Terrorists to Justice: The Proper Forum) demonstrated, the issue now may be whether the law of armed conflict or international criminal law applies. Also, it is important to note that in the wake of September 11th, various fields of law and methodologies for combating international terrorism have taken on a much greater significance. These include, among others, immigration and refugee law, international human rights law, international finance, US constitutional law, private remedies (especially civil lawsuits), cyberlaw, privacy, homeland security, arms control, disarmament, non-proliferation, intelligence gathering, and public health law.[15]

Given these developing trends, how has international law responded both before and after September 11th? This chapter now turns to a classic subject of international criminal law: the so-called antiterrorism conventions; it then addresses economic sanctions against state sponsors of terrorism; and, lastly, the jus ad bellum dimensions of the use of armed force against terrorists; and their sponsors.

Antiterrorism Conventions

Global Treaties and Conventions

At this writing the UN or its specialized agencies have adopted twelve global, multilateral antiterrorist conventions.[16] These include the: Convention on Offenses and Certain Other Acts Committed on Board Aircraft (1963); Convention for the Suppression of Unlawful Seizure of Aircraft (1970); Convention for the Suppression of Unlawful Acts against the Safety of Civil Aviation (1971); Convention on the Prevention and Punishment of Crimes against Internationally Protected Persons, including Diplomatic Agents (1973); International Convention against the Taking of Hostages (1979); Convention on the Physical Protection of Nuclear Material (1979); Protocol for the Suppression of Unlawful Acts of Violence at Airports Serving International Civil Aviation, supplementary to the Convention for the Suppression of Unlawful Acts against

---

15. For a sense of the breadth and depth of subjects now relevant to efforts to combat terrorism, see the series of articles contained in the lengthy symposium *in Law and the War on Terrorism*, 25 HARV. J. L. PUB. POL'Y ix–834 (2002).
16. The texts of these conventions may be found *in* INTERNATIONAL INSTRUMENTS RELATED TO THE PREVENTION AND SUPPRESSION OF INTERNATIONAL TERRORISM 2–131 (UN, 2001).

the Safety of Civil Aviation (1988); Convention for the Suppression of Unlawful Acts against the Safety of Maritime Navigation (1988); Protocol for the Suppression of Unlawful Acts against the Safety of Fixed Platforms Located on the Continental Shelf (1988); Convention on the Marking of Plastic Explosives for the Purpose of Detection (1991); International Convention for the Suppression of Terrorist Bombing (1997); and International Convention for the Suppression of the Financing of Terrorism (1999).

This plethora of conventions covering individual manifestations of terrorism has resulted due to the inability of the UN to develop a comprehensive convention against terrorism, largely because of disagreement on how terrorism should be defined. This so-called "piecemeal" approach has resolved the problem of defining terrorism by avoiding it. Although these treaty provisions are often loosely described as "antiterrorist," the acts they cover are criminalized regardless of whether, in a particular case, they could be described as "terrorism." Recently, however, there have been renewed efforts to reach agreement on a comprehensive text, a controversial exercise that is examined below.

The basic purpose of the individual conventions is to establish a framework for international cooperation among states to prevent and suppress international terrorism. To accomplish this goal, the Convention on the Prevention and Punishment of Crimes against Internationally Protected Persons, including Diplomatic Agents, for example, requires state parties to cooperate in order to prevent, within their territories, preparations for attacks on diplomats within or outside their territories, to exchange information, and to coordinate administrative measures against such attacks.[17] If an attack against an internationally protected person takes place, and an alleged offender has fled the country where the attack occurred, state parties are to cooperate in the exchange of information concerning the circumstances of the crime and the alleged offender's identity and whereabouts.[18] The state party where the alleged offender is found is obliged to take measures to ensure his presence for purposes of extradition or prosecution and to inform interested states and international organizations of the measures taken.[19] Finally, state parties are to cooperate in assisting criminal proceedings brought for attacks on

---

17. *See* Convention on the Prevention and Punishment of Crimes Against Internationally Protected Persons, Including Diplomatic Agents, G.A. Res. 3166, U.N. GAOR 6th Comm., 27th Sess., 2202d plen. mtg., Supp. No. 30, U.N. Doc. A/9407 (1973), art. 4, *available at* http://www.undcp.org/odccp/terrorism_convention_protected_persons.html (Jan. 21, 2003).
18. *Id.*, art. 5.
19. *Id.*, art. 6.

internationally protected persons, including supplying all relevant evidence at their disposal.[20]

The key feature of these conventions requires a state party that apprehends an alleged offender in its territory either to extradite him or to submit his case to its authorities for purposes of prosecution. Strictly speaking, none of these conventions alone creates an obligation to extradite. Rather, they contain an *inducement* to extradite by requiring the submission of alleged offenders for prosecution if extradition fails. Moreover, a legal *basis* for extradition is provided either in the convention, or through incorporation of the offenses mentioned in the convention into existing or future extradition treaties between the parties. To varying degrees, the conventions also obligate the parties to take the important practical step of attempting to apprehend the accused offender and hold him in custody.

The most important goal of these provisions is to ensure that the accused is prosecuted. To this end the alternative obligation to submit for prosecution is stated quite strongly in these conventions. The obligation, however, is not to *try* the accused, much less to punish him, but to submit the case to be considered for prosecution by the appropriate national prosecuting authority. If the criminal justice system lacks integrity, the risk of political intervention in the prosecution or at trial exists. Such intervention may prevent the trial, a conviction or the appropriate punishment of the accused. Such concerns were a major factor in the insistence of the United States and the United Kingdom that Libya "surrender" the two Libyan intelligence agents accused of the bombing of Pan Am Flight 103 over Lockerbie, Scotland and their rejection of Libya's insistence that it had the right, under Article 7 of the Convention for the Suppression of Unlawful Acts against the Safety of Civil Aviation, to submit the accused instead to "its competent authorities for the purpose of prosecution."[21]

Even if the criminal justice system functions with integrity, it may be very difficult to obtain the evidence necessary to convict when the alleged offense was committed in a foreign country. This very practical impediment can be removed between states of goodwill only by patient and sustained efforts to develop and expand "judicial assistance" and other forms of cooperation between the law enforcement and judicial systems of different countries. The

---

20. *Id.*, art. 10.
21. For an interesting exposition of the events leading to the Lockerbie trial, see Scott Evans, *Lockerbie Incident Cases: Libyan-Sponsored Terrorism, Judicial Review And The Political Question Doctrine*, 18 MD. J. INT'L L. & TRADE 21 (1994); Donna Azrt, *The Lockerbie "Extradition by Analogy" Agreement: "Exceptional Measure" or Template for Transnational Criminal Justice?*, 18 AM. U. INT'L L. REV. 163 (2002).

conventions create an obligation to cooperate in this respect but this obligation poses major problems for even good faith efforts among countries with different types of legal systems.[22]

Under the piecemeal approach, and with the passage of time, gaps in the coverage of terrorist crimes by the early conventions became apparent, and new conventions covering other international crimes were concluded. For example, the Tokyo, Hague and Montreal conventions on civil aviation did not cover attacks at airports, such as those at the Rome and Vienna airports during the 1980s. As a consequence, the International Civil Aviation Organization (ICAO) adopted a Protocol to the Montreal Convention on the Suppression of Unlawful Acts of Violence at Airports serving International Civil Aviation.[23] Similarly, the hijacking of the Italian cruise liner "Achille Lauro" exposed the vulnerability of maritime navigation and infrastructure to terrorist attack and led to the adoption of the Convention for the Suppression of Unlawful Acts against the Safety of Fixed Platforms Located on the Continental Shelf.[24]

It was in the 1990s, however, that UN member states sought to fill the largest gap in coverage of terrorist crimes.

International Convention for the Suppression of Terrorist Bombing
The 1990s was a decade of extraordinary developments. One of the most, if not the most, extraordinary developments was the collapse of the Soviet Union and the end of the Cold War. Also of great significance was the end of apartheid in South Africa and the coming into power of new governments in South Africa and Namibia. These and other developments led to a less confrontational atmosphere in the UN and a sharp decline in support for "wars of national liberation." This in turn helped lessen, if not entirely eliminate, the division between the Western member states and the non-aligned member states that had frustrated previous efforts to reach agreement on measures to combat terrorism. Indeed, because of the change of atmosphere, the General Assembly decided in

---

22. The problems become particularly acute in the event of a computer network attack by terrorists. See John F. Murphy, *Computer Network Attacks By Terrorists: Some Legal Dimensions*, COMPUTER NETWORK ATTACK AND INTERNATIONAL LAW 323, 340–43 (Michael N. Schmitt and Brian T. O'Donnell eds., 2002) (Vol. 76, US Naval War College International Law Studies).
23. *See* Protocol for the Suppression of Unlawful Acts of Violence Against Safety of Civil Aviation, 27 I.L.M. 628 (1988).
24. *See* Convention for the Suppression of Unlawful Acts against the Safety of Fixed Platforms Located on the Continental Shelf, 27 I.L.M. 668 (1988), *available at* http://www.imo.org/Conventions/contents.asp?topic_id=259&doc_id=686 (Jan. 21, 2003).

1997 to reincarnate the Ad-Hoc Committee on Measures to Eliminate International Terrorism (hereinafter Ad-Hoc Committee on Terrorism) to prepare as a matter of priority a draft international convention for the suppression of terrorist bombing and a subsequent international convention for the suppression of acts of nuclear terrorism.

It is worthwhile to pause for a moment at this point and consider the importance, in terms of combating international terrorism, of the General Assembly's decision to mandate the preparation of a convention against terrorist bombing. In an article published in 1990, I suggested:

> A more serious deficiency is that none of the antiterrorist conventions cover those tactics most often used by terrorists, most particularly the deliberate targeting, by bombs or other weapons, of the civilian population. To understand the reason for this it is necessary to briefly return to the problem of defining terrorism.
>
> A look at the primary components of most definitions of terrorism will help us to understand why it has proved impossible to reach agreement in the United Nations and other international organizations. These definitions almost invariably include a political purpose of motivation behind the violent act and a government as the primary target, factors that serve to distinguish terrorism from violent acts classified as common crimes. The political purpose of the violent act is to influence the policy of a government by intimidation or coercion. These same factors, however, may lead some governments to be not only unwilling to criminalize such behavior but prone to actively support it.

****

Nonetheless, there appears to be a growing recognition that even favored national liberation groups cannot be permitted to engage in certain acts of violence against certain targets. Moreover, under the law of armed conflict the deliberate targeting of the civilian population is a war crime. It should be impermissible as well when the targeting takes place under circumstances not covered by the law of armed conflict. This was the conclusion reached recently by a joint group of U.S. and Soviet experts on international terrorism who recommended to their respective governments that they support the conclusion of an international convention that would make the deliberate targeting of a civilian population an international crime.[25]

---

25. John F. Murphy, *The Need for International Cooperation in Combating Terrorism*, 13 TERRORISM: AN INTERNATIONAL JOURNAL 381 (1990).

The adoption by the General Assembly of the International Convention for the Suppression of Terrorist Bombing[26] on December 15, 1997, vividly illustrates the sea change in the attitudes of UN member states towards terrorist acts that various developments in the 1990s brought about, including, it should be noted, several major terrorist bombings directed against various states.[27]

Others have written about the terrorist bombing convention in some detail,[28] and no such effort will be undertaken here. There are a few innovative aspects about the convention, however, that deserve highlighting. In keeping with the "piecemeal" approach, the convention does not define "terrorism" but identifies and defines particular conduct that is to be condemned internationally, regardless of its motivation, and subject to criminal penalties. Article 2(1) of the convention provides:

> Any person commits an offense within the meaning of this Convention if that person unlawfully and intentionally delivers, places, discharges or detonates an explosive or other lethal device in, into or against a place of public use, a State or governmental facility, a public transportation system or an infrastructure facility: (a) with the intent to cause death or serious bodily injury; or (b) with the intent to cause extensive destruction of such a place, facility or system, where such destruction results in or is likely to result in major economic loss.[29]

To ensure that sympathy with the motivation behind the bombing will not serve as a legal justification of the act, Article 5 requires state parties to adopt any measures that may be necessary to ensure that criminal acts within the scope of the convention, especially when they are intended to create a state of terror, are "under no circumstances justifiable by considerations of a political, philosophical, ideological, racial, ethnic, religious or other similar nature and are punishable by penalties consistent with their grave nature."[30] None of the earlier antiterrorist conventions has a similar provision. Along somewhat similar lines, Article 11 expressly eliminates, for the first time in a UN antiterrorist

---

26. See International Convention for the Suppression of Terrorist Bombings, U.N. Doc. A/Res.52/164 (Dec. 15, 1997), 37 I.L.M. 249 (1998) (ratified by US on Jun. 26, 2002) [hereinafter Terrorist Bombings Convention].
27. These included, among others, the truck bombing attack on US military personnel in Dhahran, Saudi Arabia, the poison gas attacks in Tokyo's subways, a bombing in Colombo, Sri Lanka, bombings in Tel Aviv and Jerusalem, and a bombing in Manchester, England. See Samuel M. Witten, *Current Developments: The International Convention for the Suppression of Terrorist Bombings*, 92 AM. J. INT'L L. 774, note 3 (1998).
28. Id.
29. Terrorist Bombings Convention, *supra* note 26, at art. 2(1).
30. Id., art. 5.

convention, the political offense exception for purposes of extradition and mutual legal assistance.[31] Samuel Witten notes the impact this provision is likely to have on US law and practice:

> In the case of most modern U.S. bilateral extradition treaties, the political offense exception has been narrowed and is already unavailable for offenses covered under the 'prosecute or extradite' multilateral conventions such as this Convention. As a result, Article 11 will have the most significant practical effect with respect to U.S. treaty practice on mutual legal assistance treaties with political offense exceptions without excluding prosecute or extradite multilateral conventions.[32]

At the same time that it eliminates the political offense exception, the bombing convention adds a protection for the accused in Article 12, which provides that nothing in the convention shall be interpreted as imposing an obligation to extradite or to afford mutual legal assistance, if the requested state party has substantial grounds for believing that the request was made "for the purpose of prosecuting or punishing a person on account of that person's race, religion, nationality, ethnic origin or political opinion or that compliance with the request would cause prejudice to that person's position for any of these reasons."[33] Such a "humanitarian" provision is normally not present in the UN antiterrorist conventions, although there is a provision along similar lines in the International Convention against the Taking of Hostages.[34]

Article 12 does not specify who in the requested state is to decide whether "substantial grounds" exist. In the United States there has been considerable debate over whether this decision is to be made by the executive branch or by the judiciary.[35] Interestingly, Article 6, which sets forth the mandatory and discretionary bases of criminal jurisdiction over the offenses covered by the convention, establishes a truly universal system of jurisdiction in that it utilizes all five of the accepted bases of jurisdiction in international criminal

---

31. *Id.*, art. 11.
32. Witten, *supra* note 27, at 779.
33. Terrorist Bombings Convention, *supra* note 26, at art. 12.
34. *See* International Convention against the Taking of Hostages, G.A. Res. 34/146, U.N. GAOR 6th Comm., 34th Sess., 105th Mtg, Supp. No. 46, U.N. Doc. A/34/819 (1979, entered into force 1983), art. 9, 1316 U.N.T.S. No. 21931.
35. For discussion of this debate, see Christopher H. Pyle, EXTRADITION, POLITICS, AND HUMAN RIGHTS 118–29 (2001).

law—territorial, nationality, universal, passive personality, and protective jurisdiction.[36] As noted by Witten,

> [o]f particular interest to countries such as the United States that maintain many government facilities outside their territory is the Convention's unprecedented recognition of broad protective jurisdiction in Article 6(2)(b)[37] with respect to attacks using explosive or other lethal devices against a state or government facility of that state abroad, including an embassy or other diplomatic or consular premises. This provision would recognize the United States jurisdiction, for example, to prosecute in US courts the perpetrators of bombing attacks against all US government facilities abroad, including diplomatic and consular premises and military installations, e.g., the 1996 Al-Khobar Towers bombing in Dhahran.[38]

It may be noted parenthetically that a US court recently upheld its jurisdiction to consider various charges arising from the bombing of the US embassies in Kenya and Tanzania, including bombing allegedly committed by foreign nationals that resulted in the deaths of foreign nationals on foreign soil.[39] The coming into force of the bombing convention clearly confirms this exercise of jurisdiction.[40]

Another innovative provision of the bombing convention, not found in prior antiterrorism conventions, is Article 8(2), which provides for so-called conditional extradition.[41] That is, an accused person might be sent temporarily by her state of nationality to a requesting state for a trial or proceeding

---

36. Terrorist Bombings Convention, *supra* note 26, at art. 6.
37. Under Article 6(2)(b) of the Terrorists Bombings Convention, each state party has discretion to establish its jurisdiction over offenses set forth in Article 2 when: "The offence is committed against a State or government facility of that State abroad, including an embassy or other diplomatic premises of that State." In a footnote Witten points out that "the Convention will reach attacks on extraterritorial government facilities such as tourist centers, economic development offices and military facilities." He notes further that "[t]he provisions of the Bombing Convention regarding attacks on government facilities are . . . broader than those of the 1973 Internationally Protected Persons Convention, which addresses attacks only on "the official premises, the private accommodation or the means of transport of an internationally protected person likely to endanger his person or liberty." Witten, *supra* note 27, at 778, fn 24.
38. Witten, *supra* note 27, at 778.
39. United States v. Bin Laden, 92 F. Supp. 2d 189 (S.D. N.Y. 2000).
40. The Terrorist Bombings Convention entered into force on May 23, 2001. As of May 28, 2002, it had 62 parties. The United States became a party to the convention on April 19, 2002.
41. Article 8(2) of the Bombing Convention provides:
    Whenever a State Party is permitted under its domestic law to extradite or otherwise surrender one of its nationals only upon the condition that the person will be returned to that State to serve the sentence imposed as a result of the trial or proceeding for which the extradition or surrender of the person was sought, and this State and the

for an offense under the convention and, if convicted, would be returned to her state of nationality to serve any sentence imposed as a result of the trial or proceeding for which the extradition or surrender had been sought.

As noted above, only the sea change in the attitudes of member states of the UN toward terrorist bombing that took place during the 1990s permitted the successful conclusion of the bombing convention. At this writing, however, there are troubling developments in the Middle East that could seriously undermine the success of the convention as an antiterrorist measure. Specifically, the sudden increase in suicide bombings by Palestinians against Israeli civilians, and the celebration in some circles of the resulting carnage, risks a return to some of the divisions between Western member states and certain member states of the developing world that characterized the UN during the 1970s.

International Convention on the Suppression of Terrorist Financing
As Hans Corell, Under-Secretary-General for Legal Affairs and Legal Counsel of the UN, has noted, as early as 1996, the Secretary-General had recognized the need for an international convention dealing with terrorist fund-raising.[42] Similarly, in May 1998, the foreign ministers of the G-8 countries issued a statement on terrorism identifying as a "priority area for further action: Preventing terrorist fund-raising. . . ."[43] The President of France subsequently called for the negotiation without delay of a "universal convention against the financing of terrorism" and in December 1998, the General Assembly decided that the Ad Hoc Committee on Terrorism "should elaborate a draft international convention for the suppression of terrorist financing to supplement existing international instruments."[44] France introduced a draft convention that served as the basis of discussions in the committee and on December 9, 1999,

---

State seeking the extradition of the person agree with this option and other terms they may deem appropriate, such a conditional extradition or surrender shall be sufficient to discharge the obligation set forth in paragraph 1 of the present article.

See Terrorist Bombings Convention, *supra* note 26, art. 8.
42. Hans Corell, *Possibilities and Limitations of International Sanctions Against Terrorism*, in COUNTERING TERRORISM THROUGH INTERNATIONAL COOPERATION 243, 253 (Alex P. Schmid ed., 2001) [hereinafter COUNTERING TERRORISM].
43. *See* Clifton M. Johnson, *Introductory Note to the International Convention for the Suppression of the Financing of Terrorism*, 39 I.L.M. 268 (2000).
44. *Measures to Eliminate International Terrorism*, G.A. Res. 53/108, U.N. GAOR, 53d Sess., Agenda Item 155 (1998).

the General Assembly adopted a resolution opening for signature the International Convention for the Suppression of the Financing of Terrorism.[45]

Like its immediate predecessor, the bombing convention, the financing convention is a "model" antiterrorist convention that incorporates what Clifton Johnson, the chief US negotiator for the convention, has called:

> increasingly standard provisions of the recent counterterrorism conventions. These include provisions: 1) limiting the Convention's application to acts with an international element; 2) obligating States Parties to criminalize the covered offenses irrespective of the motivation of the perpetrators; 3) obligating States Parties to take into custody offenders found on their territory; 4) facilitating the extradition of offenders; 5) requiring States Parties to afford one another the greatest measure of assistance in connection with the criminal investigations or proceedings relating to the covered offenses; 6) prohibiting extradition or mutual legal assistance requests relating to a covered offense from being refused on political offense grounds; and 7) providing for the transfer of prisoners in order to assist the investigation or prosecution of covered offenses.[46]

Johnson goes on to point out that the financing convention adds "specific and unique provisions directed at terrorism financing." If adopted and effectively implemented, these provisions have the potential to constitute a major step forward in the effort to combat international terrorism.

Dealing with the financing of terrorism is a delicate matter. A major problem is that terrorists often operate through "front organizations" which appear on the surface to be engaged in legitimate activities or through organizations that in fact have charitable, social or cultural goals and engage in legitimate activities to further these goals. Moreover, in some states, such as the United States, action by the government to prevent or limit the financing of organizations with charitable or similar goals could raise serious constitutional issues. In an effort to avoid such difficulties, Article 2(1) carefully limits the scope of the convention:

> 1. Any person commits an offence within the meaning of this Convention if that person by any means, directly or indirectly, unlawfully and wilfully, provides or collects funds with the intention that they should be used or in the knowledge

---

45. *See* International Convention for the Suppression of the Financing of Terrorism, G.A. Res. 109, U.N. GAOR 6th Comm., 54th Sess., 76th Mtg., Agenda Item 160, U.N. Doc. A/54/109 (1999), *reprinted in* 39 I.L.M. 270 (2000) [hereinafter Suppression of Financing Convention].
46. Johnson, *supra* note 43, at 268.

that they are to be used, in full or in part, in order to carry out: (a) An act which constitutes an offense within the scope of and as defined in one of the treaties listed in the annex; or (b) Any other act intended to cause death or serious bodily injury to a civilian, or to any other person not taking an active part in the hostilities in a situation of armed conflict, when the purpose of such an act, by its nature or context, is to intimidate a population, or to compel a government or an international organization to do or abstain from doing any act.[47]

Under paragraph 1(a) of Article 2, the convention requires actual intention that funds should be used or knowledge that they will be used to carry out one of the offenses listed in an annex to the convention. Such an intention or knowledge of how the funds are to be used is also required by paragraph 1(b). The latter paragraph, moreover, sets forth a definition of terrorism, although the definition is not identified as such. It therefore establishes an important precedent that may be drawn upon in future antiterrorism conventions.

As in the case of its predecessor conventions, the principal objective of the financing convention is to require state parties to criminalize and establish jurisdiction over the offenses set forth in the convention and to extradite or submit for prosecution the persons accused of the commission of such offenses. The financing convention goes further than its predecessors, however, in the requirements it imposes on state parties to take steps to prevent the commission of covered offenses.[48] In particular, as aptly summarized by Rohan Perera, Chairman of the Ad-Hoc Committee on Terrorism, the convention requires state parties to consider the following measures:

> (i) Adopt regulations, prohibiting the opening of accounts, the holders or beneficiaries of which are unidentified or unidentifiable and measures to ensure that such institutions verify the real owner of such transactions.
>
> (ii) With respect to the identification of legal entities, financial institutions when necessary are required to take measures to verify the legal existence and structure of the customer by obtaining either from the public register or from the customer or both, proof of incorporation or other relevant information.
>
> (iii) Obligations on financial institutions to report promptly to the competent authorities all complex, unusual large transactions and unusual patterns of transactions which have no apparent economic or obviously lawful purpose.

---

47. Suppression of Financing Convention, *supra* note 45, art. 2.
48. *Id.*, art. 18.

(iv) Measures requiring financial institutions to maintain at least for 5 years, all records on transactions, both domestic or international.[49]

More generally, the convention provides an extensive list of measures, many drawn from the 40 recommendations of the multilateral Financial Action Task Force, for state parties to consider in identifying, tracking and blocking transactions involving terrorism financing.[50]

Another innovative provision in the convention is Article 5, which requires each state party to "take the necessary measures to enable a legal entity located in its territory organized under its laws to be held liable when a person responsible for the management or control of that legal entity" has committed an offense under the convention.[51] Normally, the antiterrorist conventions address only the issue of criminal and not civil liability.[52] The convention also enhances the deterrent effect of its provisions by providing for the seizure or freezing of funds and proceeds used for the commission of an offense[53] and by prohibiting state parties from claiming privileged communication, banking secrecy, or the fiscal nature of the offense to refuse a request for mutual assistance from another state party.[54]

As Clifton Johnson has suggested, the financing convention has the potential to have a considerable impact on efforts to combat terrorism.[55] Johnson notes further, however, that the impact the convention has in practice will depend in no small measure on "the degree to which investigators and prosecutors can establish the necessary link between the act of financing and the terrorist intention of the contributor or collector of the funds."[56] This may be a heavy evidentiary burden to bear, since the contributors and recipients of funds for the commission of terrorist acts are adept at using money laundering and other techniques to disguise their purpose. Moreover, relatively few member states of the UN currently have in place the legal infrastructure or the

---

49. Rohan Ferera, *International Legal Framework for Co-operation in Combating Terrorism—the Role of the UN Ad-Hoc Committee on Measures to Eliminate International Terrorism*, in COUNTERING TERRORISM, *supra* note 42, at 284.
50. Suppression of Financing Convention, *supra* note 45, at art. 18.
51. *Id.*, art. 5.
52. Elsewhere I have advocated a more extensive use of civil liability against those who commit or sponsor the commission of international crimes. *See* John F. Murphy, *Civil Liability for the Commission of International Crimes as an Alternative to Criminal Prosecution*, 12 HARV. HUM. RTS. J. 1 (1999).
53. Suppression of Financing Convention, *supra* note 45, at art. 8.
54. *Id.*, arts. 12 & 13.
55. Johnson, *supra* note 43, at 268.
56. *Id.* at 269.

trained personnel to cope with the techniques of terrorist financing. One may hope, however, that the cooperative arrangements called for by the financing convention will help to remedy this situation.

For the financing convention to be effective, of course, it will have to be widely ratified and implemented. At this writing there are 132 signatories and 34 parties (including the United States). The UN Security Council itself has given an enormous boost to the convention and to the effort to combat terrorist financing. On September 28, 2001, the Security Council, acting under Chapter VII of the Charter, adopted Resolution 1373,[57] which, by any measure, constitutes a landmark step by the Council. In this extraordinary resolution, the Council sets forth a plethora of steps that member states are *required* to take to combat terrorism. For example, the Council "[d]ecides that all States shall . . . [p]revent and suppress the financing of terrorist acts" and then sets forth explicit steps that states are to take to this end.[58] The Council also decides that all states shall take a large number of other steps to combat terrorism.[59] Among the most noteworthy of these, states are to deny safe haven to terrorists, to afford one another the greatest measure of assistance in criminal investigations or proceedings relating to the financing or support of terrorist acts, including assistance in obtaining evidence necessary for such proceedings, and to prevent the movement of terrorists by effective border controls and controls on the issuance of identity papers and travel documents.

Using terms of exhortation rather than command, in Resolution 1373, the Council "[c]alls upon all States" to take a number of actions in cooperation with other states to combat terrorism, including, among others, "intensifying and accelerating the exchange of operational information," becoming parties to the relevant antiterrorist conventions, including the International Convention for the Suppression of Financing of Terrorism, and ensuring, "in conformity with international law," that refugee status is not abused by terrorists, and that "claims of political motivation are not recognized as grounds for refusing requests for the extradition of alleged terrorists."[60]

In my view, the most significant step the Council has taken in Resolution 1373 is to establish a committee (the Counter-Terrorism Committee) to monitor implementation of the resolution and to call upon all states to report to the committee, no later than 90 days after the date of adoption of the

---

57. S. C. Res. 1373, U.N. SCOR, 56th Sess., U.N. Doc. S/1373/(2001).
58. *Id.*, para. 1(b), (c), and (d).
59. *Id.*, para. 2(a)–(g).
60. *Id.*, para. 3(a)–(g).

resolution, on the steps they have taken to implement the resolution.[61] The Council further "[e]xpresses its determination to take all necessary steps in order to ensure the full implementation of this resolution, in accordance with its responsibilities under the Charter."[62] Failure to establish such monitoring devices to ensure that antiterrorist measures adopted by the UN are effective in practice has been a major deficiency of past UN efforts.

A primary example of UN antiterrorist measures that have not been effectively monitored in the past as to their implementation is the antiterrorist conventions. As we have seen, a sea change in attitudes on the part of many (though not all) member states of the UN has resulted in the conclusion of "model" new antiterrorist conventions, especially the bombing and financing conventions. The conclusion of new, or even the ratification of old, antiterrorist conventions, however, is not the crucial issue. The crucial issue is the extent to which the global antiterrorist conventions have been or will be vigorously implemented. Conclusion of antiterrorist conventions is only the first step in the process. Unfortunately, many state parties seem to regard it as the last.

Vigorous implementation, moreover, encompasses more than merely ratifying the conventions, passing implementing legislation, and adopting the necessary administrative measures, i.e., creating an appropriate legal infrastructure to combat international terrorism. It requires the taking of active steps toward ensuring the primary goals of the conventions: the prevention of the crimes covered by the conventions and the prosecution and punishment of the perpetrators of the crimes. The record of the conventions in this respect is unclear.

A major part of the problem is the lack of adequate data on the extent of successful actions to prevent terrorist acts and of successful prosecutions of terrorists. Although there appears to be adequate data available on the extradition, prosecution and punishment of aircraft hijackers,[63] information regarding other manifestations of terrorism is quite sparse. Most of the antiterrorist conventions contain provisions requiring the state party where the alleged offender is prosecuted to communicate the final outcome of the proceedings to the Secretary-General of the UN (or to the Director-General of IAEA or the

---

61. *Id.*, para. 6.
62. *Id.*, para. 8.
63. At least this was the case around 1985 when I last examined the data. *See* JOHN F. MURPHY, PUNISHING INTERNATIONAL TERRORISTS: THE LEGAL FRAMEWORK FOR POLICY INITIATIVES, 110–15 (1985).

Council of ICAO),[64] and the Secretary-General has issued reports on "Measures to Eliminate International Terrorism."[65] But these reports focus primarily on the terrorist events that triggered the conventions and on a summary of the most important provisions of these conventions. There appears to be little information on the extent and success of efforts to prevent the acts the conventions cover or to prosecute the perpetrators of these acts.

Ambassador Jeremy Greenstock, Chairman of the Counter-Terrorism Committee established by Resolution 1373, has recently emphasized the importance of implementing antiterrorist measures. According to Ambassador Greenstock, "Governments were already familiar with what needed to be done. But few had done it. Resolution 1373 drew on the language negotiated by all UN members in the 12 Conventions against terrorism, but also delivered a strong operational message: get going on effective measures now."[66] He reports that, as of May 30, 2002, 155 reports had been submitted to the committee from member states and others. Member states who have not submitted reports are "almost without exception those with little experience of the subject and unsophisticated law and order systems."[67]

A cursory review of the reports submitted by some member states with sophisticated law and order systems (the United States, United Kingdom, Israel, Germany and Italy) that have had major problems with international terrorism reveals that the Counter-Terrorism Committee is gathering valuable information regarding the legislative, executive and judicial steps these countries are taking to combat international terrorism in general and the financing of international terrorism in particular. One of the questions that member states have been asked to respond to is: "What steps have been taken to establish terrorist acts as serious criminal offenses and to ensure that the punishment reflects the seriousness of such terrorist acts? Please supply examples of any convictions obtained and the sentence given." However, the examples of convictions and sentences supplied in these reports are either non-existent or very brief. The US report is the most forthcoming in this respect, noting that the United

---

64. *See, e.g.*, Article 19 of the Suppression of Financing Convention, *supra* note 45.
65. *See, e.g., Measures to Eliminate International Terrorism: Report of the Secretary-General*, U.N. GAOR, 51st Sess., Agenda Item 153, U.N. Doc. A./51/336 (Sep. 6, 1996); *Measures to Eliminate International Terrorism: Report of the Secretary-General*, U.N. GAOR, 55th Sess., Agenda Item 166, U.N. Doc. A/55/179 (Jul. 26, 2000).
66. Presentation by Ambassador Greenstock, Chairman of the Counter-Terrorism Committee (CTC) at the Symposium: *Combating International Terrorism: The Contribution of the United Nations*, held in Vienna on 3–4 June 2002, *available at* http://www.un.org/Docs/sc/committees/1373/viennaNotes.htm (Jun. 12, 2002).
67. *Id.* at 2.

States has prosecuted cases under US laws implementing the Montreal Convention (Aircraft Sabotage), the Hague Convention (Aircraft Hijacking), the Hostages Convention, and the Internationally Protected Persons Convention and giving, by way of footnotes, citations to cases involving the crimes covered by these conventions.[68] Even this information is skimpy, however, giving, for example, no information regarding how US law enforcement officials came to have custody of the accused.

This is a serious problem that should be resolved. It may be that the Counter-Terrorism Committee, in its future interactions with member states, could request more detailed information regarding the apprehension, rendition (where applicable), prosecution and punishment of persons who commit the crimes covered by the 12 antiterrorist conventions. Alternatively, the UN Terrorism Prevention Branch, which is part of the Centre for International Crime Prevention in Vienna, might be assigned the task of collecting such information with respect to the 11 other antiterrorist conventions.[69] Still other alternative approaches might be for the Security Council to establish a monitoring committee that would receive and evaluate reports from state parties to some of the major antiterrorist conventions or to draft a convention that would establish a monitoring committee for selected antiterrorist conventions and create an international obligation for state parties to submit reports to it. For any such monitoring committees, the Counter-Terrorism Committee, with its proactive approach,[70] could serve as an excellent model.

The Draft International Convention for the Suppression of Nuclear Terrorism
One of the tasks the newly reconstituted Ad-Hoc Committee on Terrorism was entrusted with by the General Assembly in 1996 was the preparation of a draft international convention for the suppression of acts of nuclear terrorism. The Committee began this task in 1998, immediately upon completion of the bombing convention.[71]

---

68. The US report is attached as an annex to the Letter dated 19 December 2001 from the Chairman of the Security Council Committee established pursuant to Resolution 1373 (2001) concerning counter-terrorism addressed to the President of the Security Council, S/2001/1220 (December 21, 2001), *available at* http://www.un.org/Docs/sc/committees/1373/ (Jan. 15, 2003). The information regarding US prosecutions appears at page 22.
69. In his presentation, Ambassador Greenstock suggested that the Centre for International Crime Prevention (CICP) might provide "model laws and guidance on implementation" for the 11 other antiterrorist conventions. *See* Presentation by Ambassador Greenstock, *supra* note 66.
70. *Id.* at 1.
71. Corell, *supra* note 42, at 254.

The Russian Federation has been the primary proponent of a convention to combat nuclear terrorism in order to fill gaps in coverage left by the 1979 Convention on the Physical Protection of Nuclear Material.[72] The Convention on Nuclear Material prohibits parties from exporting or importing or authorizing the export or import of nuclear material used for peaceful purposes, unless they give assurances that such materials will be protected at prescribed levels during international transport. The convention also provides a framework for international cooperation in the recovery and protection of stolen nuclear material, and requires that state parties make certain serious offenses involving nuclear material punishable, and that they extradite or prosecute offenders. It does not, however, apply to nuclear material used for military purposes.

At this writing the draft convention[73] under consideration by the Ad-Hoc Committee on Terrorism would expand the definition of "nuclear material" to include objects and materials for military use and provide a clearer definition of the crime of illegal acquisition for terrorist purposes. It would also cover terrorist acts against nuclear power plants, vessels with nuclear power sources and the use of automatic nuclear devices. As noted by Hans Corell, "[i]n this regard, the new convention could cover to the broadest possible extent the possible targets, forms and manifestations of acts of nuclear terrorism. Furthermore, unlike the 1980 [actually 1979] Convention, the proposed convention would draw a distinction between acts of nuclear terrorism from other criminal acts involving the use of nuclear material by referring to the purpose of such acts."[74]

To date, however, it has not proven possible to reach agreement on a final draft of the convention. The main sticking point seems to be that some members of the non-aligned movement want the convention to cover the activities of the military forces of a state. Article 4(2) of the present draft excludes acts of armed forces from the scope of the convention. Other member states have proposed extending the scope of the convention to include acts of state terrorism.[75]

In this commentator's view, such proposals have a political agenda behind them and are unacceptable to Western member states. Only if the

---

72. Convention on the Physical Protection of Nuclear Material, opened for signature March 3, 1980, entered into force on 8 February 1987, 1456 U.N.T.S. 101, *reprinted in* 18 I.L.M. 1419 (1979).
73. *See* Measures to Eliminate International Terrorism: Report of the Working Group, Sixth Committee, 53rd Sess., A/C. 6/53/L.4 (Oct. 22, 1998), at 4.
74. Corell, *supra* note 42, at 254.
75. *Id.* at 255.

convention's scope is limited to nuclear terrorism by private actors and not extended to the acts of state military forces or of government officials is there likely to be any prospect of reaching a consensus on a draft convention on the suppression of acts of nuclear terrorism.

One may also question whether the draft convention's focus on the possibility of nuclear terrorism is too narrow. Many observers, including this one, are of the view that the risk of so-called "catastrophic terrorism"[76] is greater from the possible use of chemical, biological, or radiological weapons than it is from the use of nuclear weapons. For this reason, a joint group of US and Soviet experts on international terrorism recommended that their governments initiate and sponsor a draft convention to cover terrorism involving weapons of mass destruction, including in particular nuclear, radiological, chemical and biological weapons.[77] To be sure, there is substantial debate as to how great a risk there is of terrorists employing weapons of mass destruction.[78] But Barry Kellman's observations may serve as a sensible middle of the road position:

> Assessing risk is difficult because catastrophic terrorism is a low probability threat which, if it occurs, could have exceptionally high casualties. Yet four points can be offered without serious contradiction. First, technical obstacles to catastrophic terrorism will decline with time. The capabilities for producing lethal devices will spread, and the choke points of human activity will become more concentrated, thereby unfortunately converging the ability to make a lethal weapon with an ability to use it to devastating effect. The necessary ramification is that whatever the technological barriers to accomplishing an act of catastrophic terrorism may or may not be, those barriers will be overcome, sooner or later. Even if the risks are not now realistic, they will be.[79]

---

76. As pointed out by Barry Kellman, *Catastrophic Terrorism—Thinking Fearfully, Acting Legally*, 20 MICH. J. INT'L L. 537, note 1 (1999):

> Catastrophic terrorism is an intentionally undefined term, reflecting the fact that terrorists who aspire to inflict catastrophic injuries have a long menu of options to employ, and reflecting the conclusion that debates over whether a particular technology is or is not within this category are, essentially, inconclusive. The definition of 'catastrophic terrorism,' as opposed to conventional terrorism, turns less on what type of device is used than on the magnitude of the effects.

77. *See* COMMON GROUND ON TERRORISM 176–77 (John Marks and Igor Beliaev eds., 1991).
78. *See, e.g.,* Judith Miller, *Threat of Unconventional Terrorism is Overstated Study Says*, N.Y. TIMES, October 26, 2000, at A24, col. 1. For a contrary view, see, e.g., Patrick L. Moore, *Is Catastrophic Terrorism Just Strategic 'Peanuts,'* American Bar Association Standing Committee on Law and National Security, NATIONAL SECURITY LAW REPORT, July–August 2000, at 1.
79. Kellman, *supra* note 76, at 538. *See also* Barry Kellman, *An International Criminal Law Approach to Bioterrorism*, 25 HARV. J. L. PUB. POL'Y 721 (2002).

With regard to the possibility of catastrophic terrorism, three other multilateral conventions, while not directed expressly against terrorism, should be noted at least parenthetically. The Convention on the Prohibition of the Development, Production, and Stockpiling of Bacteriological (Biological) and Toxic Weapons and on Their Destruction[80] prohibits the development, production, or stockpiling of microbiological and biological agents (weapons) that are of potential use to terrorists. It is generally agreed, however, that this convention has been ineffective because of a lack of enforcement provisions, and an effort to remedy this situation through a protocol has apparently foundered in the face of opposition from the United States.[81] After years of effort, in 1993 the UN adopted the Convention on the Prohibition of the Development, Production, Stockpiling and Use of Chemical Weapons.[82] In sharp contrast to the Biological Weapons Convention, the Chemical Weapons Convention has rigorous verification procedures implemented through a new Organization for the Prohibition of Chemical Weapons, which was established at the Hague and has been functioning since 1997. Under the Chemical Weapons Convention, state parties are prohibited from using, producing or stockpiling poison gas or lethal chemical weapons, and are obliged to dispose of existing chemical weapons by the year 2010 at the latest. Lastly, the Treaty on the Nonproliferation of Nuclear Weapons (NPT),[83] which has as its primary goal the prevention of the spread of nuclear weapons among states, may also serve to limit the access of individual terrorists to nuclear arms.[84]

Draft Comprehensive Convention on International Terrorism
At this writing the Ad-Hoc Committee on Terrorism has a draft comprehensive convention on international terrorism before it.[85] Progress on this agenda item, however, has been slow and, in the opinion of this observer, likely to

---

80. Convention on the Prohibition of the Development, Production and Stockpiling of Bacteriological (Biological) and Toxic Weapons and on Their Destruction, April 10, 1972, 1015 U.N.T.S. 1419, 26 U.S.T. 583.
81. *See* Elizabeth Olson, *US Rejects New Accord Covering Germ Warfare*, N.Y. TIMES, July 26, 2001, at A47, col. 1.
82. Convention on the Prohibition of the Development, Production, Stockpiling and Use of Chemical Weapons, January 13, 1993, 1974 U.N.T.S. 3, A/RES/47/391.
83. Treaty on the Nonproliferation of Nuclear Weapons, July 1, 1968, 729 U.N.T.S. 161.
84. For a brief discussion of the NPT, *see* John F. Murphy, *Force and Arms*, in THE UNITED NATIONS AND INTERNATIONAL LAW 97, 122–29 (Christopher C. Joyner ed., 1997).
85. *See* Report of the Ad Hoc Committee established by General Assembly Resolution 51/210 of 17 December 1996, 6th Sess. (28 January–1 February 2002), U.N. GAOR, 57th Sess., Supp. No. 37(A.57/37), at 4–16.

remain so. I hold with those who question the wisdom of such an exercise. The history of efforts to conclude a comprehensive convention on international terrorism—from the 1937 League of Nations Convention[86] to the 1972 draft convention introduced by the United States in the UN General Assembly[87]—has not been a happy one. Michael Reisman, an eminent authority in international law, has recently cautioned that,

> d]espite the relatively promising developments in the 1996 General Assembly resolution . . . and the 1998 Convention for the Suppression of Terrorist Bombing, the political positions which have retarded the development of an effective international legal regime in this regard have changed little. The Non-Aligned Movement's solidarity has been broken by a number of prominent defections, yet a substantial number of states still resist a definition of terrorism that might be applied to terrorist activities of groups that some wish to view as 'freedom fighters' or fighters in wars of 'national liberation.'[88]

Despite its limitations, the "piecemeal" approach has served the world community well. It should continue.

Convention against Transnational Organized Crime
Although the recently concluded Convention against Transnational Organized Crime[89] is not, strictly speaking, an antiterrorist convention, it deserves a brief mention, if only because it has extensive provisions on international cooperation that might serve as a model for the parties to the antiterrorist conventions. Moreover, as pointed out by Hans Corell, the General Assembly, in its resolution adopting the convention, recommends

> that the Ad Hoc Committee established by the General Assembly in its resolution 51/210 of 17 December 1996, which is beginning its deliberations with a view to developing a comprehensive convention on international terrorism, pursuant to

---

86. Convention for the Prevention and Punishment of Terrorism, 7 INTERNATIONAL LEGISLATION 862, 868 (Manley O. Hudson ed., 1941).
87. Draft Convention for the Prevention and Punishment of Certain Acts of International Terrorism, U.N. Doc. A/C. 6/L. 850 (1972).
88. W. Michael Reisman, *International Legal Responses to Terrorism*, 22 HOUS. J. INT'L L. 3, 58 (1999).
89. Convention Against Transnational Organized Crime, G.A. Res. 55/25, U.N. GAOR, 55th Sess., Supp. No. 49, U.N. Doc. A/45/49 (2001). The text of and information regarding the convention may be found at http://www.undcp.org/odccp/crime_cicp_convention.html (Jan. 15, 2003).

Assembly resolution 54/110 of 9 December 1999, should take into consideration the provisions of the UN Convention against Transnational Organized Crime.[90]

As noted above, I have grave doubts about the wisdom of trying to conclude a comprehensive convention on international terrorism, but provisions in the Convention against Transnational Organized Crime may well serve as a guide to future efforts to combat international terrorism.

Regional Treaties and Conventions
There are now at least eight antiterrorist conventions that have been adopted at the regional level.[91] It is unclear, however, the extent to which these conventions have had any operational significance. Five of these conventions have been adopted only very recently,[92] and it is therefore too early to evaluate them in terms of their operational efficiency. Some of these recently adopted regional conventions have noteworthy provisions, however, and these will be briefly explored below. The Organization of American States (OAS) Convention to Prevent and Punish the Acts of Terrorism Taking the Form of Crimes Against Persons and Related Extortion that are of International Significance, 1971, and the European Convention on the Suppression of Terrorism, 1977, are of earlier vintage and will be explored in somewhat greater detail. The terms of the South Asian Association for Regional Cooperation (SAARC) Regional Convention

---

90. Hans Corell, Statement by Mr. Hans Corell to the Security Council Briefing on International Terrorism, December 9, 2000, at 9 (copy on file with author).
91. The texts of and dates of entry into force and other information concerning seven of these treaties and conventions may be found in INTERNATIONAL INSTRUMENTS RELATED TO THE PREVENTION AND SUPPRESSION OF INTERNATIONAL TERRORISM, *supra* note 16, at 134–225. These include: the OAS Convention to Prevent and Punish the Acts of Terrorism Taking the Form of Crimes Against Persons and Related Extortion that are of International Significance; the European Convention on the Suppression of Terrorism; the South Asian Association for Regional Cooperation (SAARC) Regional Convention on Suppression of Terrorism; the Arab Convention on the Suppression of Terrorism; the Treaty on Cooperation among the States Members of the Commonwealth of Independent States in Combating International Terrorism; the Convention of the Organization of the Islamic Conference on Combating International Terrorism; and the OAU Convention on the Prevention and Combating of Terrorism. The text of the Inter-American Convention Against Terrorism, adopted on June 3, 2002, is available at http://www.oas.org/xxxiiga/english/docs_en/docs_items/AGres1840_02.htm (Jan. 17, 2003).
92. The five recently adopted antiterrorist conventions include the Arab Convention on Suppression of Terrorism, 1998; the Treaty on Cooperation among the States Members of the Commonwealth of Independent States in Combating Terrorism, 1999; the Convention of the Organization of the Islamic Conference on Combating International Terrorism, 1999; the OAU Convention on the Prevention and Combating of Terrorism, 1999; and the Inter-American Convention Against Terrorism, 2002.

on Suppression of Terrorism, 1987, will be briefly examined, but there appears to be insufficient data available to allow for an evaluation of its operational significance.

The Arab Convention on the Suppression of Terrorism

The Arab Convention on the Suppression of Terrorism (Arab Convention) has several noteworthy features. The first is that only member states of the League of Arab States can be parties to the convention.[93] The second is that, unlike most of the antiterrorist conventions, the Arab Convention defines terrorism as:

> [a]ny act or threat of violence, whatever its motives or purposes, that occurs for the advancement of an individual or collective criminal agenda, causing terror among people, causing fear by harming them, or placing their lives, liberty or security in danger, or aiming to cause damage to the environment or to public or private installations or property or to occupy or seize them, or aiming to jeopardize a national resource.[94]

The convention goes on to define "terrorist offence" as "[a]ny offence or attempted offence committed in furtherance of a terrorist objective in any of the Contracting States, or against their nationals, property or interests, that is punishable by their domestic law."[95] Also included within the definition of terrorist offense are offenses stipulated in several global antiterrorist conventions,[96] as well as the provisions of the UN Convention of 1982 on the Law of the Sea, relating to piracy on the high seas.[97]

Significantly, however, the Arab Convention also provides that "[a]ll cases of struggle by whatever means, including armed struggle, against foreign occupation and aggression for liberation and self-determination, in accordance with the principles of international law, shall not be regarded as an offence. This provision shall not apply to any act prejudicing the territorial integrity of

---

93. Arab Convention on Suppression of Terrorism, art. 1, *available at* http://www.al-bab.com/arab/docs/league/terrorism98.htm (Jan. 17, 2003) [hereinafter Arab Convention].
94. *Id.*, art. 2.
95. *Id.*, art. 3.
96. These include the Tokyo Convention on Offences and Certain Other Acts Committed on Board Aircraft; the Hague Convention for the Suppression of Unlawful Seizure of Aircraft; the Montreal Convention for the Suppression of Unlawful Acts against the Safety of Civil Aviation; the Convention on the Prevention and Punishment of Crimes against Internationally Protected Persons, including Diplomatic Agents; the International Convention against the Taking of Hostages; and the Arab Convention, *supra* note 93, at art. 3(a)–(e).
97. Arab Convention, *supra* note 93, at art. 3(f).

any Arab State."[98] To be blunt, this provision seeks to justify the commission of terrorist acts against Israel and reflects an attitude that prevented the Ad-Hoc Committee on Terrorism from adopting measures against terrorism during the early 1970s. There appears to be no data available on the operational significance of the convention, if any.

Treaty on Cooperation among the States Members of the Commonwealth of Independent States in Combating Terrorism
The Treaty on Cooperation among the States Members of the Commonwealth of Independent States in Combating Terrorism (Commonwealth Treaty), like the Arab Convention, has a definition of terrorism, but, unlike the Arab Convention, has no provisions providing exceptions for "wars of national liberation." Under the Commonwealth Treaty terrorism is defined as "an illegal act punishable under criminal law committed for the purpose of undermining public safety, influencing decision-making by the authorities or terrorizing the population, and taking the form of: [there follows a listing of various manifestations of violence or threats of violence against persons or property]."[99] The Commonwealth Treaty also contains an elaborate definition of "technological terrorism" involving the use or threat of use of nuclear, radiological, chemical or bacteriological (biological) weapons or their components—a provision not found in the other antiterrorist conventions.[100] Also noteworthy are the Commonwealth Treaty's many detailed provisions on cooperative measures to prevent and punish terrorism, including provisions that envision the possibility of an antiterrorist unit of one state party crossing the borders of another state party in order to render assistance to the latter state in the event of a terrorist incident.[101] Again though, there appears to be little data on the operational significance, if any, of the Commonwealth Treaty.

---

98. *Id.*, art. 2(a).
99. Treaty on Cooperation among the States Members of the Commonwealth of Independent States in Combating Terrorism, art. 1 (1999).
100. *Id.*
101. Article 12(1) of the Treaty, for example, provides: "The parties may, at the request or with the consent of the Party concerned, send representatives of their competent authorities, including special anti-terrorist units, to provide procedural, advisory or practical aid in accordance with this Treaty." *Id.* at art. 12.

OAU Convention on the Prevention and Combating of Terrorism
At this writing the current status of the OAU Convention on the Prevention and Combating of Terrorism is most uncertain because of the dissolution of the Organization of African Unity and the establishment of the African Union.[102] Assuming that the new organization adopts the OAU Convention, however, the convention deserves some brief comment.

Like the other recently adopted regional conventions, the OAU Convention contains a detailed definition of a "terrorist act,"[103] as well as extensive provisions calling for cooperation among state parties in preventing and combating terrorism. Unfortunately, like the Arab Convention, as well as the Convention of the Organization of the Islamic Conference on Combating International Terrorism,[104] the OAU Convention also includes a provision that "the struggle waged by peoples in accordance with the principles of international law for their liberation or self-determination, including armed struggle against colonialism, occupation, aggression and domination by foreign forces shall not be considered as terrorist acts."[105] It is worth noting that such provisions are incompatible with the approach taken by Article 5 of the UN Terrorist Bombing Convention, which provides that terrorist bombings are "under no circumstances justifiable by consideration of a political, philosophical, ideological, racial, religious or other similar nature and are punishable by penalties consistent with their grave nature."

Inter-American Convention Against Terrorism
The Inter-American Convention Against Terrorism,[106] adopted on June 3, 2002, came about in response to the events of September 11th. The Organization of American States was the first organization to condemn the September 11th attacks, and ten days thereafter the OAS Foreign Ministers meeting in Washington instructed the OAS Permanent Council to prepare a draft text of an Inter-American Convention Against Terrorism in time for the meeting of

---

102. *See* Corinne A. Packer and Donald Rukare, *The New African Union and Its Constitutive Act*, 96 AM J. INT'L L. 365 (2002).
103. OAU Convention on the Prevention and Combating of Terrorism, art. 1(3), *available at* http://www.fidh.org/intgouv/ua/rapport/1999/antiterroconvention.pdf (Jan. 17, 2003).
104. *See* Convention of the Organization of the Islamic Conference on Combating International Terrorism, art. 2, *available at* http://www.oic-un.org/26icfm/c.html (Jan. 17, 2003).
105. OAU Convention, *supra* note 103, at art. 3(1).
106. *See* Inter-American Convention Against Terrorism, *supra* note 77.

the OAS General Assembly on June 3.[107] By any measure the convention is an extraordinary instrument.

Previously, the only antiterrorist convention adopted in the Inter-American context was the OAS Convention to Prevent and Punish the Acts of Terrorism Taking the Form of Crimes Against Persons and Related Extortion that are of International Significance (OAS Convention).[108] The OAS Convention, however, is focused narrowly on the kidnaping of diplomats, despite efforts to broaden the scope of the convention, contains many ambiguities, and fails to deal with crucial problems. Moreover, it has a total of only nine parties, including the United States, and has not been an effective international instrument for the protection of diplomats. In practice it has in effect been superceded by the UN Convention on the Prevention and Punishment of Crimes against Internationally Protected Persons, including Diplomatic Agents.[109]

By contrast, 30 of the 33 nations present at the meeting of the OAS General Assembly signed the Inter-American Convention Against Terrorism.[110] And there is nothing narrow about the focus of the Inter-American Convention. On the contrary, among other things, the convention defines "offenses" within the scope of its coverage as including the offenses covered by the UN antiterrorist conventions and requires state parties to the Inter-American Convention to make a declaration upon ratification that they are not parties to one or the other of the UN antiterrorist conventions if they wish these conventions to be inapplicable to them, thus creating a strong inducement on OAS member states to sign and ratify the UN antiterrorist conventions.[111] Also, under Article 3 of the convention, state parties "shall endeavor" to become parties to the UN antiterrorist conventions and "to adopt the necessary measures to effectively implement such instruments. . . ."[112] The convention further requires state parties to use the recommendations of the Financial Action Task Force and other specialized entities as guidelines for measures

---

107. *See* Secretary of State Colin L. Powell, *Opening Remarks and Q&A With the Press Following OAS General Assembly*, June 3, 2002, http://www.state.gov/secretary/rm/2002/10670.htm (Jun. 4, 2002).
108. This convention was signed by the United States on Feb. 2, 1971 and entered into force for the United States on Oct. 8, 1976. T.I.A.S. No. 8413, *available at* http://untreaty.un.org/English/Terrorism/Conv16.pdf (Jan. 17, 2003).
109. For further discussion of the OAS Convention, *see* John F. Murphy, *Protected Persons and Diplomatic Facilities*, in LEGAL ASPECTS OF INTERNATIONAL TERRORISM 277, 299–303 (Alona E. Evans and John F. Murphy eds., 1977).
110. *See* Powell, *supra* note 107, at 2.
111. *See* Inter-American Convention Against Terrorism, *supra* note 91, at art. 2.
112. *Id.*, art. 3.

combating the financing of terrorism,[113] to deny safe haven to persons suspected of terrorism, as either refugees,[114] or asylum seekers,[115] and to reject application of the political offense exception to requests for extradition or mutual legal assistance.[116] On the other hand the convention permits a state party to refuse to provide mutual legal assistance if it "has substantial grounds for believing that the request has been made for the purpose of prosecuting or punishing a person on account of that person's race, religion, nationality, ethnic origin, or political opinion, or that compliance with the request would cause prejudice to that person's position for any of these reasons."[117]

By way of affirmative steps, the convention requires state parties to adopt domestic law measures to provide for the identification and seizure of funds used to finance terrorism,[118] to promote cooperation and the exchange of information in order to improve border and customs control measures necessary to prevent the international movement of terrorists and trafficking in arms, without prejudicing applicable international commitments regarding the free movement of people and the facilitation of commerce,[119] to enhance channels of communication between their law enforcement authorities,[120] to "afford one another the greatest measure of expeditious mutual legal assistance with respect to the prevention, investigation, and prosecution of the offenses established [in the UN antiterrorist conventions],"[121] and to promote technical cooperation and training programs.[122]

Significantly, Article 18 of the convention requires the state parties to hold periodic meetings of consultation, with a view to "[t]he full implementation of this Convention. . . ."[123] The Secretary General of the OAS is to convene a meeting of consultation of the state parties after receiving the 10th instrument of ratification (under Article 22 the convention is to enter into force on the 30th day following the date of deposit of the sixth instrument of ratification). Also, the Inter-American Committee against Terrorism, established in 1998, has been revitalized and become active.

---

113. *Id.*, art. 4(2).
114. *Id.*, art. 12.
115. *Id.*, art. 13.
116. *Id.*, art. 11.
117. *Id.*, art. 14.
118. *Id.*, art. 5.
119. *Id.*, art. 7.
120. *Id.*, art. 8.
121. *Id.*, art. 9.
122. *Id.*, art. 16.
123. *Id.*, art. 18.

The Inter-American Convention Against Terrorism, then, has the potential to become an important instrument for the effective implementation, at least on a regional basis, of the UN antiterrorist conventions. Whether it will do so remains to be seen. It might be useful to this end for the OAS to establish a liaison with the UN's Counter-Terrorism Committee.

European Convention on the Suppression of Terrorism
The European Convention on the Suppression of Terrorism (European Convention)[124] was an early attempt to deal with a primary obstacle, especially during the 1970s, in the way of efforts to combat terrorism, the political offense exception to international extradition. To this end, Article 1 of the convention lists a series of offenses, none of which "for the purposes of extradition between Contracting States" are to be regarded "as a political offense or as an offense connected with a political motive or as an offense inspired by political motives."[125] Under Article 2, the convention invites state parties to exclude additional acts of violence against persons or property from the political offense exception.[126] At the same time, Article 13 of the convention allows a state party to register a reservation permitting it to reject a request for extradition on the ground that the offense is of a political character—notwithstanding that a listed offense is involved:

> provided that it undertakes to take into consideration when evaluating the character of the offense any particularly serious aspects of the offense including: (a) that it created a collective danger to the life, physical integrity or liberty of persons; or (b) that it affected persons foreign to the motives behind it; or (c) that cruel or vicious means had been used in the commission of the offense.[127]

Under Article 5 of the Convention a requested state may refuse to extradite an accused if it:

> has substantial grounds for believing that the request for extradition for an offense mentioned in Article 1 or 2 has been made for the purpose of prosecuting or punishing a person on account of his race, religion, nationality,

---

124. *See* European Convention on the Suppression of Terrorism (1977), *reprinted in* INTERNATIONAL INSTRUMENTS RELATED TO THE PREVENTION AND SUPPRESSION OF INTERNATIONAL TERRORISM, *supra* note 16, at 139, *available at* http://conventions.coe.int/Treaty/EN/Treaties/Html/090.htm (Jan. 17, 2003).
125. This description of the European Convention is taken largely from Murphy, *supra* note 52, at 13–15.
126. European Convention, *supra* note 124, art. 2.
127. *Id.*, art. 13.

or political opinion, or that the person's position may be prejudiced for any of these reasons.[128]

Should a state party decide not to extradite an offender covered by the convention, under Article 7 it must "submit the case, without exception whatsoever and without undue delay to its competent authorities for the purpose of prosecution."[129]

Although the convention is an antiterrorism initiative, it nowhere attempts to define terrorism. In attempting to exclude a variety of common crimes as well as "terrorism" from the political offense exception to extradition, the convention may have attempted too much, because many states, upon signing or ratifying the convention, reserved the right to refuse to extradite for an offense which they consider as political.[130] This defect, if such it be, has largely been cured, at least among state parties who are members of the European Union, by the EU's 1996 Convention relating to the Extradition between Member States.[131] Article 5 of the EU Convention eliminates the political offense exception in extradition between state parties and paragraph 4 of that article provides that reservations to the European Convention shall not apply to extradition between member states.[132] However, a member state may limit the ambit of Article 5 of the EU Convention to the violent crimes listed in Articles 1 and 2 of the European Convention.[133] Moreover, paragraph 3 of Article 5 preserves the right to refuse extradition if the fugitive might be persecuted or punished on account of his race, religion, nationality or political opinion.[134]

Adoption of the EU Convention, then, would appear to have removed, at least partially, the "internal inconsistency" of the European Convention that raised serious doubts as to its effectiveness in practice.[135] Moreover, some early hold outs, such as Ireland and France, have become parties to the

---

128. *Id.*, art. 5.
129. *Id.*, art. 7.
130. Murphy, *supra* note 52, 14–15.
131. *See* Convention relating to the Extradition between Member States, OJ 96 C 313/02 of 27 September 1996.
132. *Id.*, art. 5.
133. *Id.*
134. *Id.*
135. *See* Geoff Gilbert, *The "Law" and "Transnational Terrorism,"* 26 NETHERLANDS Y.B. INT'L L. 3, 21 (1995).

European Convention,[136] and English and French courts have applied it when surrendering fugitives.[137] Hence, although one could wish there was more of it, there is some evidence that the European Convention has been of some use to European efforts to combat terrorism.

SAARC Regional Convention on Suppression of Terrorism
Like the European Convention, the SAARC Regional Convention on Suppression of Terrorism (SAARC Convention),[138] in Article I, lists a number of offenses and provides that, for the purpose of extradition, they shall not be regarded as political offenses. Further, under Article II, any two or more state parties may agree among themselves for purposes of extradition to include any other offenses involving violence, in which case this offense, too, shall not be regarded as a political offense.[139] Unlike the European Convention, the SAARC Convention contains no provision for reservations to the requirement that the listed offenses be regarded as nonpolitical offenses. Article VII, however, provides for an exception to extradition requirements:

> if it appears to the requested State that by reason of the trivial nature of the case or by reason of the request for the surrender or return of a fugitive offender not being made in good faith or in the interests of justice or for any reason it is unjust or inexpedient to surrender or return the fugitive offender.[140]

Although all seven members of SAARC (Bangladesh, Bhutan, India, Maldives, Nepal, Pakistan and Sri Lanka) are parties to the convention, it is unclear the extent to which it has had operational significance. As of 1993 it appeared that some member states of SAARC had not yet enacted the enabling legislation required to give effect to the convention.[141]

---

136. Initially, Ireland did not even sign the convention, claiming that to ratify it would violate its constitution, and France, while an initial signatory, did not ratify because of opposition from the French Left, which had traditionally opposed the extradition of political offenders. See Murphy, *supra* note 52, at 14–15.
137. *See* Gilbert, *supra* note 135, at 21.
138. *See* SAARC Regional Convention on Suppression of Terrorism (1987), *reprinted in* INTERNATIONAL INSTRUMENTS RELATED TO THE PREVENTION AND SUPPRESSION OF INTERNATIONAL TERRORISM, *supra* note 16, at 147, *available at* http://untreaty.un.org/English/Terrorism/Conv18.pdf (Jan. 17, 2003).
139. *Id.*, art. II.
140. *Id.*, art. VII.
141. *See* Report of the Secretary-General, *Measures to Eliminate International Terrorism*, U.N. Doc A/51/336, Sep. 6, 1996, at 42.

Coercive Measures Against Terrorists And State Sponsors Of Terrorists

Economic Sanctions

As briefly noted above, the primary goal of the International Convention for the Suppression of the Financing of Terrorism and a primary goal of the just concluded Inter-American Convention Against Terrorism is to impose economic sanctions against terrorists by denying them financing as well as against private organizations who support them by seizing and freezing their funds. A detailed discussion of United States and other countries' efforts to block the financing of international terrorism is beyond the scope of this chapter. It is worth noting parenthetically, however, that, according to recent newspaper reports, members of al Qaeda may be turning to trade in gold, diamonds, and gems to finance their terrorist network in response to the freezing of their bank accounts.[142] Also, al Qaeda reportedly increasingly relies heavily on the Internet and on an informal money transfer system, known as "hawala" in Arabic, to move its funds. Hawala relies on trust and networks of friends and family to move its funds and leaves no paper or electronic trails. It is, of course, impossible to monitor or freeze an account if there is no bank account or electronic movement of money. Lastly, again according to recent newspaper reports, the United States is beginning to face growing resistance among its European allies over how it identifies terrorists and their financiers. European officials are reportedly questioning the listing of several individuals and organizations whose links to extremist causes are less clear than those of al Qaeda or the Taliban.[143]

The focus of this section of the chapter is on economic sanctions against state sponsors of terrorism and, more specifically, mandatory economic sanctions imposed by the UN Security Council under Chapter VII of the UN Charter. Economic sanctions imposed unilaterally by the United States, or in concert with like minded states, not pursuant to Security Council mandate, are outside the scope of this chapter.

Although it was its invasion of Kuwait rather than its sponsorship of terrorism that precipitated Security Council action against Iraq, in its famous Resolution 687,[144] the Council "[r]equires Iraq to inform the Security Council that

---

142. *See, e.g.,* Sengupta, *U.N. Report Says al Qaeda May be Diversifying Its Finances,* N.Y. TIMES, May 23, 2002, at A15, col. 1.
143. *See* Johnson et al., *Bush Faces Widening Gap With Europe,* WALL ST. J., May 21, 2002, at A 15, col. 6.
144. S. C. Res. 687, U.N. SCOR 46th Sess., U.N. Doc. S/687/(1991).

it will not commit or support any act of international terrorism or allow any organization directed toward commission of such acts to operate within its territory and to condemn unequivocally and renounce all acts, methods and practices of terrorism."[145] Evidence that Iraq has failed to carry out this requirement is considerable.[146]

Economic sanctions imposed by the Security Council against Iraq have become a highly contentious issue, with critics contending that they hurt the people but not the government of Iraq and that the Security Council actions are lacking in legitimacy because of dominance by the permanent members.[147] To meet these criticisms and to ensure the continuance of economic sanctions against Iraq, the Security Council recently agreed to a major revision of the sanctions, including the adoption of new so-called "smart sanctions."[148] Under the new sanctions regime, UN export controls on purely civilian goods purchased by Iraq are lifted. Indeed, all contracts for export of goods to Iraq under the oil for food program are presumed approved unless found to contain items on a "Goods Review List" (GRL).[149] The GRL consists of so-called "dual use" items that may have both a legitimate civilian use and a potential military use in a prohibited nuclear, chemical, biological, ballistic missile or conventional military program. These items will be subjected to additional scrutiny by the Iraq Sanctions Committee established by the Security Council. Perhaps most important, Resolution 687 remains in force, with its requirements that Iraq destroy its nuclear, chemical and biological weapons programs, and limit its ballistic missiles range to 150 km.

It remains to be seen, however, whether the new "smart" sanctions will be any more effective than the old "dumb" sanctions were in inducing Iraq to fulfill its obligations under Resolution 687. This commentator, for one, remains skeptical. We will return to this issue when we turn to the use of military force to combat terrorism later in this chapter.

Prior to its recent actions with respect to al Qaeda and the Taliban, the most elaborate set of actions that the Security Council had undertaken with respect to international terrorism was with respect to Libya. In response to evidence of Libyan complicity in the destruction of Pan Am flight 103 over Lockerbie, Scotland and of *Union de transports aeriens* (UTA) flight 772, the

---

145. *Id.*, para. 32.
146. *See, e.g.*, PATTERNS OF GLOBAL TERRORISM 2001, *supra* note 11, at 65.
147. *See, e.g.*, Jose E. Alvarez, *The Once and Future Security Council*, 18 WASH. QTRL'Y 3 (1995).
148. *See* S. C. Res. 1409, U.N. SCOR, 57th Sess., U.N. Doc. S/1409/(2002) and S. C. Res. 1382, U.N. SCOR, 56th Sess., U.N. Doc. S/1382/(2001).
149. S. C. Res. 1382, *supra* note 148.

Council adopted a resolution urging the Libyan Government to provide "full and effective" responses to requests made by the French, the UK, and the US Governments concerning these catastrophes.[150] When the Libyan Government failed to do so, the Council decided that this failure constituted a threat to international peace and security.[151] Acting under Chapter VII of the Charter, the Council decided that states should adopt various sanctions against Libya unless it responded to the requests for cooperation. To avoid these measures Libya also had to commit itself "definitely to cease all forms of terrorist action and all assistance to terrorist groups and . . . promptly, by concrete actions, demonstrate its renunciation of terrorism."[152] In a third resolution the Council applied further comprehensive sanctions against Libya in 1993.[153]

Although they had previously strongly resisted a proposal along these lines, in 1998, the United States and the United Kingdom agreed to a trial of the two persons charged with the bombing of Pan Am flight 103 before a Scottish Court siting in the Netherlands. The Security Council welcomed this initiative,[154] and decided that the Libyan Government was to ensure the appearance in the Netherlands of the two accused persons.[155] The Council also decided that it would suspend the sanctions it had imposed against Libya once the Secretary-General had reported to the Council that the two accused persons had arrived in the Netherlands for trial and the Libyan Government had satisfied the French judicial authorities with regard to the bombing of UTA flight 772.

On April 5, 1999, the Secretary-General reported to the Council that the two accused persons had arrived in the Netherlands for trial and that the French authorities had informed him that the Libyan Government had satisfied the Council's demands with respect to the bombing of UTA flight 772. Accordingly, the President of the Council announced that the sanctions against Libya had been suspended.[156]

On January 31, 2001, a three judge Scottish Court, sitting at Camp Zeist, the Netherlands, convicted Abdelbaset Ali Mohmed al Megrahi, a Libyan intelligence agent, of murdering 270 people in the 1988 bombing of Pan Am flight 103. The second Libyan defendant, Al Amin Khalifa Fhiman, former

---

150. S. C. Res. 731, U.N. SCOR, 47th Sess., U.N. Doc. S/731/(1992).
151. S. C. Res. 748, U.N. SCOR, 47th Sess., U.N. Doc. S/748/(1992).
152. Id.
153. S. C. Res. 883, U.N. SCOR, 48th Sess., U.N. Doc. S/883/(1993).
154. S. C. Res. 1192, U.N. SCOR, 53d Sess., U.N. Doc. S/1192/(1998).
155. Id., at para. 4.
156. Statement of the President of the Council, April 8, 1999, S/PRST/1999/10.

manager of the Libyan Arab Airlines in Malta where the bomb originated, was acquitted.[157] The court sentenced Megrahi to life in prison, and his conviction was upheld on appeal.[158]

The Council's actions against Libya, then, have had a quite extraordinary denouement. Less successful were the Council's measures against Afghanistan prior to September 11th and against Sudan. With respect to Afghanistan, the Council, acting under Chapter VII of the Charter, demanded that the Taliban hand over Osama bin Laden, who had been indicted by the United States for the August 7, 1998 bombings of the US embassies in Kenya and Tanzania, to "appropriate authorities in a country where he has been indicted, or to appropriate authorities in a country where he will be returned to such a country, or to appropriate authorities in a country where he will be arrested and effectively brought to justice."[159] By the same resolution the Council decided to impose economic sanctions against the Taliban as of November 14, 1999, if they failed to accede to this demand. When the Taliban had not turned Osama bin Laden over by November 14, 1999, the Council announced on November 15, 1999, that the sanctions were to come into effect.

As to the Sudan, the Security Council became involved in response to a Sudan backed assassination attempt on the life of the President of Egypt in Addis Ababa, Ethiopia on June 26, 1995. In a resolution adopted on January 31, 1996, the Council declared that "those responsible for that act must be brought to justice," called upon the Government of the Sudan immediately to "extradite to Ethiopia for prosecution the three suspects sheltering in the Sudan and wanted in connection with the assassination attempt. . . ." and further called upon the Sudan to "[d]esist from engaging in the activities of assisting, supporting and facilitating terrorist elements and act in its relations with its neighbors and with others in full conformity with the Charter of the UN and with the Charter of the Organization of African Unity."[160] When the Government of the Sudan did not comply with this request, the Council, acting under Chapter VII of the Charter, decided to impose certain economic sanctions against the Sudan.[161]

---

157. *See* Peter Finn, *Libyan Convicted of Lockerbie Bombing: Second Man acquitted in Attack*, WASH. POST, Feb. 1, 2001, at A 1.
158. Al Megrahi v. Her Majesty's Advocate, Appeal No. C104/01 (J.C. 2002) (Scot.), *available at* http://www.scotcourts.gov.uk/download/lockerbieappealjudgement.pdf (Jan. 17, 2003).
159. S. C. Res. 1267, U.N. SCOR, 54th Sess., U.N. Doc. S/1267/(1999), para. 2.
160. S. C. Res. 1044, U.N. SCOR, 51st Sess., U.N. Doc. S/1044/(1996), para. 4.
161. S. C. Res. 1070, U.N. SCOR, 51st Sess., U.N. Doc. S/1070/(1996).

Economic sanctions imposed by the Security Council are often regarded as an alternative to the use of force in dealing with state sponsors of terrorism. When the Council declines to impose economic sanctions, or when sanctions imposed by the Security Council fail to induce a target state to cease its sponsorship or support of international terrorism, however, the controversial issue of what measures of self-help may be taken by states acting without Council authorization may arise. It is to this issue that we turn in the next section of this chapter.

Use of Armed Force

Other participants in this conference have addressed the jus ad bellum aspects of the war on terrorism, and I will try to minimize overlap with the presentations of these other participants. To this end I will largely limit my comments to the possible future use of armed force against terrorists in countries other than Afghanistan and against their state sponsors. As to the use of armed force against al Qaeda and the Taliban, I will just state my view that it has been fully consonant with the jus ad bellum limitations of the UN Charter.[162] I will not address any of the jus in bello issues.

At this writing there are numerous newspaper reports that the Bush administration is developing a doctrine of preemptive action against states and terrorist groups trying to develop weapons of mass destruction.[163] United States Vice President Dick Cheney reportedly has given as the rationale for such a doctrine the inadequacy of the Cold War approaches of arms control treaties and the policy of deterrence for present circumstances. One newspaper report quoted Cheney as saying: "In terror, we have enemies with nothing to defend. A group like al-Qaeda cannot be deterred or reasoned with. This struggle will not end in a treaty or accommodation with terrorists—it can only end in their complete and utter destruction."[164]

It seems clear that al Qaeda cannot be deterred or reasoned with. But all indications are that the likely first target of the new doctrine is Iraq and most particularly the regime of Saddam Hussein.[165] It is at least debatable whether

---

162. Besides the presentations at the conference, for an analysis of the jus ad bellum dimensions of the use of armed force in Afghanistan, see, e.g., Thomas M. Franck, *Terrorism and the Right of Self-Defense*, 95 AM. J. INT'L L. 839 (2001); Jack M. Beard, *America's New War on Terror: The Case for Self-Defense under International Law*, 25 HARV. J. L. PUB. POL'Y 559 (2002).
163. *See, e.g.*, David E. Sanger, *Bush to Formalize a Defense Policy of Hitting First*, N.Y. TIMES, June 17, 2002, at A1, col. 1; Lydia Adetunji, *Bush to lay out first-strike policy against terrorism*, FINANCIAL TIMES, June 11, 2002, at 3, col. 1; and Thom Shanker, *Defense Secretary Tells NATO to Beat Terrorists to Punch*, N.Y. TIMES, June 7, 2002, at A8, col. 3.
164. Adetunji, *supra* note 163.
165. *See, e.g.*, Sanger, *supra* note 163.

Saddam Hussein can be deterred or reasoned with. There is substantial evidence that, unlike al Qaeda or Palestinian suicide bombers, Saddam Hussein cares greatly about his own survival and the survival of his regime.

To be sure, there is no question of the evil nature of Saddam Hussein and his regime. He is, after all, a man who used chemical weapons against both his own people and in the war with Iran. Because of this history and Iraq's invasion of Kuwait, Security Council Resolution 687 demands that Iraq renounce terrorism and eliminate its weapons of mass destruction under international inspection. For the last three years, however, Iraq has barred the UN inspectors,[166] and it is widely assumed that it has been developing its capacity for chemical and biological weapons during this time. Margaret Thatcher, the former British Prime Minister known as the "Iron Lady," has recently come out strongly in favor of the removal of Saddam Hussein:

> Saddam must go. His continued survival after comprehensively losing the Gulf War has done untold damage to the West's standing in a region where the only unforgivable sin is weakness. His flouting of the terms on which hostilities ceased has made a laughingstock of the international community. His appalling mistreatment of his own countrymen continues unabated. It is clear to anyone willing to face reality that the only reason Saddam took the risk of refusing to submit his activities to U.N. inspection was that he is exerting every muscle to build WMD [weapons of mass destruction]. We do not know exactly what stage that has reached. But to allow this process to continue because the risks of action to arrest it seem too great would be foolish in the extreme.[167]

There is a great variety of views on the issue of whether, as a *policy* matter, Saddam should be removed. One alternative view is that he can be contained, and the appropriate policy is to ensure the destruction or degradation of Saddam's weapons of mass destruction, if necessary by the use of armed force.[168] A variant of this view is that there should be a new "Bush doctrine" that would eschew the use of force to overthrow Saddam under present circumstances but state explicitly that certain actions or "triggers" would result

---

166. **Editor's Note:** UN weapons inspectors returned to Iraq in November 2003, pursuant to Security Council Resolution 1441. U.N. SCOR 58th Sess., U.N. Doc. S/1441/(2002).
167. Margaret Thatcher, *Don't Go Wobbly*, WALL ST. J., June 17, 2002, at A18, col. 4. For another strong statement favoring the removal of Saddam Hussein, see Lawrence F. Kaplan, *Why the Bush Administration will go after Iraq*, THE NEW REPUBLIC, Dec. 10, 2001, at 21.
168. For an article setting forth this view, although the author of the article rejects it, see Kaplan, *supra* note 167.

in military action and the overthrow of the Saddam regime. Examples of such "triggers" might include further evidence about Saddam's links with al Qaeda,

> any transfer of weapons of mass destruction to al Qaeda or similar groups; direct complicity in the September 11th attacks or any such attacks in the future; involvement in the September–October 2001 anthrax attacks; or the harboring of groups that carry out terrorism against the United States. Bush could also make clear that a range of other Iraqi actions unrelated to terrorism—significant progress toward the acquisition of a nuclear weapon; another attempted invasion of Kuwait; an attack on Israel; or the use of force against American troops—would also be considered redlines that would produce a policy of overthrow.[169]

This chapter does not examine the detailed policy arguments that have been advanced in favor of and against a policy of removal of the Saddam Hussein regime. Rather, for present purposes, it assumes that the policy decision has been made to remove Saddam and that the use of armed force will be required to do so. The question then arises whether this policy can be implemented in a manner consistent with US international legal obligations, especially those set forth in the UN Charter. Time and space limitations require that this chapter examine this question only briefly.[170]

The examination starts from the basic proposition that, under the UN Charter, the use of military force is permitted in only two instances: in individual or collective self-defense under Article 51 of the Charter or pursuant to a Security Council resolution adopted by the Council under Chapter VII of the

---

169. *See* Philip H. Gordon and Michael E. O'Hanlon, *Should the War on Terrorism Target Iraq? Implementing a Bush Doctrine on Deterrence*, THE BROOKINGS INSTITUTION, Policy Brief 93, at 8 (2002).
170. Because of the recent nature of its formulation, there has been relatively little legal commentary on the Bush Administration's announced intention to remove Saddam Hussein from power, if necessary by force. An exception is Anthony Clark Arend, *Iraq: First Make the Case*, WASH. POST, Apr. 17, 2002, at A15. Also, there are a number of writings on the use of force against terrorism that are relevant to the Bush Administration's plans. *See* especially Reisman, *supra* note 88. Some other writings of note include Christine Gray, *From Unity to Polarization: International Law and the Use of Force against Iraq*, 13 EUR. J. INT'L L. 1 (2002); Michael Byers, *The Shifting Foundations of International Law: A Decade of Forceful Measures against Iraq*, 13 EUR. J. INT'L L. 21 (2002); Nigel White and Robert Cryer, *Unilateral Enforcement of Resolution 687: A Treaty Too Far?*, 29 CAL. W. L. REV. 243 (1999); Jules Lobel, *The Use of Force to Respond to Terrorist Attacks: The Bombing of Sudan and Afghanistan*, 24 YALE J. INT'L L. 537 (1999); and Ruth Wedgwood, *Responding To Terrorism: The Strikes Against Bin Laden*, 24 YALE J. INT'L L. 559 (1999).

Charter.[171] I am not among those who favor a doctrine of "humanitarian intervention," either as *lex lata* or as *de lege feranda*.

Let us consider the second exception first. There is little doubt that the Security Council could adopt a resolution authorizing member states to use armed force to remove Saddam Hussein from power. Indeed, a good argument could be made that Security Council Resolution 678,[172] which authorized the use of force against Iraq in the Gulf War, would have permitted the removal of Saddam Hussein if, as a policy matter, a decision was made to do so.[173] Assuming arguendo that the Council will not adopt a new resolution explicitly authorizing Saddam's removal, the issue arises whether any previous Security Council resolutions adopted with reference to Iraq implicitly provide such authorization.

The United States and the United Kingdom have, in the past, argued that Security Council resolutions have implicitly authorized the use of force against Iraq. For example, the United States, the United Kingdom, and France relied on Resolution 688[174] as support for the establishment by armed force of refugee camps in Northern Iraq in 1991, and later in Southern Iraq, as well as the creation of "no-fly" zones in both parts of the country. But this was a highly tenuous argument.[175] As noted by Christine Gray,

> Security Council Resolution 688 was not passed under Chapter VII and it did not authorize the use of force: it demanded that Iraq end the repression of its civilian population and allow access to international humanitarian organizations. This did not stop the USA and the UK from claiming that their actions in the continuing clashes with Iraq over the no-fly zones were 'consistent with', 'supportive of', 'in implementation of' and 'pursuant to' Resolution 688.[176]

Reliance on implied Security Council authorization was also used by the United States and the United Kingdom to justify military actions against Iraq for non-cooperation with UN weapons inspectors under the Resolution 687 ceasefire regime. Both countries also added another justification for their use of armed force against Iraq. Christine Gray has aptly summarized the circumstances. She is worth quoting at some length:

---

171. For further discussion of the Charter paradigm, see Murphy, *supra* note 84.
172. S. C. Res. 678, U.N. SCOR, 45th Sess., U.N. Doc S/678/(1990).
173. For a brief discussion of this point, see John F. Murphy, *Force and Arms*, in 1 UNITED NATIONS LEGAL ORDER 247, 287–288 (Oscar Schachter and Christopher C. Joyner eds., 1995).
174. S. C. Res. 688, U.N. SCOR, 46th Sess., U.N. Doc S/688/(1991).
175. For my view of this argument, see Murphy, *supra* note 68, at 290–91.
176. Gray, *supra* note 170, at 9.

Thus in December 1998 the USA and UK undertook *Operation Desert Fox* in response to the withdrawal by Iraq of cooperation with the UN weapons inspectors; this was a major operation lasting four days and nights and involving more missiles than used in the entire 1991 conflict. The USA and UK referred to Security Council Resolutions 1154 and 1205 as providing the legal basis for their use of force; these resolutions had been passed under Chapter VII, but had not made express provision for the use of force. The first said that Iraq must, under Resolution 687, accord immediate and unrestricted access to UNSCOM and IAEA inspectors and that any violation would have "the severest consequences for Iraq." The second resolution condemned the decision by Iraq to stop cooperation with UNSCOM and demanded that Iraq rescind its decision. Although these resolutions did not explicitly authorize force, the UK argued that they provided a clear basis for military action; by Resolution 1205 the Security Council had implicitly revived the authority to use force given in Resolution 678. The USA also said that its forces were acting under the authority provided by the Security Council resolutions. But this argument of implied authorization was not accepted by other states; in the Security Council debate following the operation only Japan spoke out clearly in its favor. . . .

The argument of implied authorization was not used on its own by the USA and the UK; this justification was supplemented by the claim that the use of force was a lawful response to a breach by Iraq of the ceasefire. Thus the USA argued that Iraq had repeatedly taken actions which constituted flagrant, material breaches of its obligations: following these breaches of its obligations . . . the "coalition" had exercised the authority given by Security Council Resolution 678 for Member States to employ all necessary means to secure compliance with the Council's resolutions and restore international peace and security in the area. The UK, in the Security Council debate, said that Resolution 687 made it a condition of the ceasefire that Iraq destroy its weapons of mass destruction and agree to the monitoring of its obligations to destroy such weapons. By Iraq's flagrant violation of the ceasefire resolution the Security Council implicitly revived the authority to use force given in Resolution 678 (1990).[177]

In my view Gray has convincingly responded to the US and UK arguments:

the argument of material breach has been criticized by commentators because it arrogates to individual states power that properly resides with the Security Council. It is for the Security Council to determine not only the existence of a breach of the ceasefire, but also the consequences of such a breach in cases where there is a binding ceasefire imposed by the Security Council. Moreover, it seems doubtful whether any breach of Resolution 687 not itself involving the

---

177. *Id.* at 11–12.

use of force can justify the USA and UK in turning to force in response. Those who support this doctrine of material breach seem impatient of disagreement within the Security Council; they revive Cold War arguments that when the Security Council is unable to act because of a permanent member then the USA and the UK can go ahead to use force, if there has been a breach of a prior resolution passed under Chapter VII, even in the absence of express authorization. But this has dangers for the Security Council: it discounts the words of the resolutions reserving the Security Council's right to consider further action; it also discounts statements in debates that it is for the Security Council to take further action. This undermines the authority of the Security Council and ignores the careful negotiations between states attempting to reach agreement on controversial issues. . . .[178]

It might also be noted that, as discussed above, the Security Council has recently adopted a resolution[179] that establishes a new system of "smart sanctions" to induce Iraq to fulfill its responsibilities under Resolution 687. Arguably, implicit in this resolution is a requirement that member states give these sanctions a chance to work. If so, the use of armed force now would seem incompatible with this resolution.

Assuming, again arguendo, that existing Security Council resolutions would not authorize the use of force to remove Saddam's regime from power, the issue arises whether such an action could be justified as an exercise of individual or collective self-defense under Article 51 of the UN Charter. In pertinent part, Article 51 provides: "Nothing in the present Charter shall impair the inherent right of individual or collective self-defense if an armed attack occurs against a Member of the United Nations . . . ." This and other language in Article 51 has been the subject of much critical analysis and debate.[180] Professor Michael Glennon has recently argued that Article 51 is "incoherent," that indeed "international 'rules' concerning use of force are no longer considered obligatory by states," and that therefore "Article 51, as authoritatively interpreted by the International Court of Justice, cannot guide responsible US policy-makers in the US war against terrorism in Afghanistan or elsewhere."[181]

---

178. Id. at 12–13.
179. See S. C. Resolution 1409, U.N. SCOR, 57th Sess., U.N. Doc. S/1409/(2002).
180. For discussion and citations, see LORI F. DAMROSCH ET AL, INTERNATIONAL LAW 955–73 (4th ed. 2001).
181. Michael J. Glennon, *The Fog of Law: Self-Defense, Inherence, and Incoherence in Article 51 of the UN Charter*, 25 HARV. J. L. PUB. POL'Y 539, 540, and 541 (2002). See also MICHAEL J. GLENNON, LIMITS OF LAW, PREROGATIVES OF POWER: INTERVENTION AFTER KOSOVO (2001); Michael J. Glennon, *The Case for Anticipatory Self-Defense*, WEEKLY STANDARD, Jan. 28, 2002, at 24.

This is not the place or time to address Glennon's views, except to say that, in my view, they are seriously wrongheaded.[182] It suffices for present purposes to note that, if Glennon is right, and Article 51 and indeed all of the UN Charter norms on the use of force are inoperative, we are largely wasting our time at this conference. Interestingly, Glennon himself states that he has "attempted merely to suggest what the rules are *not*, not what the rules *should be*."[183] Apparently he believes that, with rules of the UN Charter on the use of force inoperative, we should simply make up the rules as we go along—a sure prescription for a return to the "law of the jungle" in my view.

Be that as it may, let us return for present purposes to the text of Article 51 of the UN Charter. By its terms Article 51 seems to require the presence of an "armed attack" as a condition precedent for the use of force in individual or collective self-defense. To demonstrate that Iraq had committed an armed attack on the United States, it would appear necessary, at a minimum, that some evidence be forthcoming that Iraq was involved in some direct way with the planning of, or otherwise directly supported, al Qaeda's September 11th attack. Such support was at least part of the case in favor of the legitimacy as an act of self-defense of the use of armed force against the Taliban in Afghanistan. There is some evidence of contact between Iraqi intelligence agents and al Qaeda members prior to September 11th,[184] but, at least to my knowledge, there is no evidence at this point of Iraq's involvement in the September 11th attack.

One of the hotly debated issues over Article 51 is whether it permits an exercise of anticipatory self-defense, i.e., the use of armed force to prevent an armed attack, not just to respond to a completed armed attack.[185] A literal reading of Article 51 would seem to bar anticipatory self-defense, but many have argued, focusing on the term "inherent" in Article 51 and citing an ambiguous drafting history of that article, that Article 51 is a savings clause,

---

182. Some, but by no means all, of the problems with Glennon's views are identified in Charles H. Tiefer's review of Glennon's book, *Limits of Law, Prerogatives of Power: Interventionism After Kosovo*, 96 AM J. INT'L L. 489 (2002).
183. Glennon, *The Fog of Law: Self-Defense, Inherence, and Incoherence in Article 51 of the UN Charter*, *supra* note 181, at 557.
184. According to Lawrence Kaplan, "Czech Prime Minister Milos Zeman announced on November 9 that, in the months preceding the attacks in New York and Washington, September 11th ringmaster Mohammed Atta met twice in Prague with senior Iraqi intelligence agent Ahmed Khalil Ibrahim Samir Al-Ani. . . . According to Zeman, the two men explicitly discussed an attack on Radio Free Europe's headquarters in Prague." Kaplan, *supra* note 167, at 123.
185. For discussion of the debate over anticipatory self-defense and additional citations, see DAMROSCH ET AL, *supra* note 180, at 968–72.

preserving the right to self-defense under customary international law as it existed prior to the adoption of the UN Charter. Assuming arguendo that Article 51 permits an exercise of anticipatory self-defense, at least a colorable argument can be made that the use of force to remove Saddam would fall within the scope of that doctrine. There is considerable evidence that al Qaeda has actively sought the possession of weapons of mass destruction. Iraq's meetings with al Qaeda members, and its provision of bases to various Middle Eastern terrorist groups,[186] raise the possibility that Iraq might supply al Qaeda or other terrorist groups with weapons of mass destruction, especially biological weapons. Iraq's past use of chemical weapons makes such a scenario plausible. A key element of the customary international law of self-defense, as formulated by US Secretary of State Daniel Webster in a diplomatic note to the British in 1842 during the *Caroline* incident, was that self-defense must be limited to cases in which "the necessity of that self-defence is instant, overwhelming, and leaving no choice of means, and no moment for deliberation."[187] This requirement of an imminent armed attack is at first blush clearly lacking in the case of Iraq. But the concept of imminence arguably takes on a new meaning when al Qaeda or other terrorist groups may be supplied biological weapons. Under such circumstances it will often be impossible to know when an attack is imminent, since the terrorist group will decide when it will be launched with no forewarning.

When Israel destroyed the Iraqi nuclear reactor near Baghdad in a preemptive attack in 1981, there was general outrage expressed in the UN, and the Security Council adopted a resolution[188] that condemned the attack. Michael Reisman has suggested that "now the general consensus is that it [the attack] was a lawful and justified resort to unilateral preemptive action."[189] Perhaps. But in any event the situation has changed dramatically from 1981. Now the threat from Iraq is not nuclear weapons but chemical and biological weapons. Moreover, now the threat is not so much that Iraq will use such weapons but rather that it will make such weapons available to terrorist groups that will not be deterred by the threat of massive retaliation. Under these circumstances, it may be argued, it would be suicidal to wait for clear evidence of an imminent attack. As Dean Acheson once said in a different context, "the law is not a suicide pact."

---

186. *See* PATTERNS OF GLOBAL TERRORISM 2001, *supra* note 11, at 65.
187. 2 MOORE, DIGEST OF INTERNATIONAL LAW 412 (1906).
188. S. C. Res. 487, U.N. SCOR, 36th Sess., U.N. Doc. S/487/(1981).
189. Reisman, *supra* note 88, at 18.

Many, perhaps most, will not find this argument convincing. As part of an advocate's brief, however, it perhaps has a measure of cogency. At this writing, the Bush administration has reportedly concluded that military support to opposition forces or fomenting a coup should be tried over the next few months to dislodge Saddam before any decision is made to engage in an all out military assault.[190] President Bush has reportedly not yet decided on a single cause of action, but there are "some indications" that he "may give the covert strategy and international sanctions time to run their course."[191] Such an approach would be less problematic from an international law standpoint than an all out military assault and likely to engender much less negative reaction. Condoleezza Rice, President Bush's National Security Adviser, has reportedly stated that a "critical component" of the administration's new military strategy is establishing "a common security framework for the great powers," in which the United States, Russia, China, Japan and Europe "share a common security agenda" in which they work together to keep terrorists and rogue states from challenging that system.[192] Avoiding precipitous action on Iraq and working as closely as possible with the other great powers would seem the best way to build such a common security framework and to develop a common security agenda.[193]

---

190. *See* Christopher Marquis, *Bush Officials Differ on Way to Force Out Iraqi Leader*, N.Y. TIMES, June 19, 2002, at A7, col. 1.

191. *Id.*

192. *Id.* at A6.

193. As this article is being reviewed in the page proof stage, the United States, the United Kingdom and other member states of a "coalition of the willing" are bringing to a successful conclusion the armed conflict stage of Operation IRAQI FREEDOM. Time does not permit the revision of this article to include a detailed analysis of the legal basis for the launching of the armed attack against Iraq. A few preliminary observation may be in order, however. First, In its report to the Security Council on the commencement of hostilities, the United States relies on previously adopted Security Council resolutions, including Resolution 1441 (November 8, 2002), as the legal basis for its resort to armed force. *See* Letter dated 20 March 2003 from the Permanent Representative of the United States of America to the United Nations Addressed to the President of the Security Council (Mar. 21, 2003), U.N. Doc. S/351/(2003). The British justification for the attack also stresses the argument that previous Security Council resolutions, including Resolution 1441, authorize the use of armed force against Iraq. *See* Statement by the Attorney General Lord Goldsmith in Answer to a Parliamentary Question (regarding the legal basis for the use of force against Iraq), *at* (Apr. 30, 2003). It is noteworthy that neither the US nor the British statements cite self-defense and Article 51 of the UN Charter as a justification.

Resolution 1441 adds a substantial complexity to the mix, in that it constitutes what I would call a "masterpiece of deliberate diplomatic ambiguity" that masked real differences of view between the United States and the United Kingdom, on the one hand, and France, Germany and Russia, on the other, on how Iraq's failure to fulfill its obligations under Security Council Resolution 687 should be handled. To the United States, for example, the words "serious

At this juncture it would seem fruitless to speculate about possible military action against other state sponsors of terrorism, including the other two members of the "axis of evil," Iran and North Korea, except to suggest that in current circumstances neither case would seem to call for the use of armed force.[194] The use of US military force against al Qaeda cells or other terrorist groups is likely to be undertaken with the consent and indeed active participation of the host country, as at present in the Philippines or possibly in the future in Indonesia. The goal should be to continue to develop an understanding on the part of all states that terrorism is a common action that can be defeated only through a common effort.

---

consequences" were code words for the use of armed force, but this was not the interpretation favored by France, Germany, and Russia. See Bob Sherwood, *Military force: pre-emptive defence of breach of international law?*, FINANCIAL TIMES, Mar. 11, 2003, at 11, col. 2. Lord Goldsmith's statement argues that the absence of an explicit requirement in Resolution 1441 of a further decision of the Security Council before resort to force may take place shows that no requirement was intended by the Council. To the contrary, however, the drafting history of Resolution 1441 demonstrates that France, Russia and Germany viewed the absence of an explicit authorization in the resolution as precluding the use of armed force without a further decision of the Security Council. *See, e.g., World Urges Iraq to Comply with U.N.* CNN International at (Apr. 28, 2003).

Assuming arguendo that, on balance, existing Security Council resolutions, including Resolution 1441, do not authorize the use of force against Iraq because of its failure to eliminate its weapons of mass destruction as required by Resolution 1441, this should not be the end of the analysis. There is considerable evidence, and more is likely to be disclosed in the near future, that, far from helping to enforce Resolution 687, France and Russia engaged in deals with the Saddam Hussein government that undermined its enforcement. Moreover, in refusing to accept a US and UK proposal that the Security Council adopt a resolution explicitly authorizing the use of force if Iraq failed to carry out its obligations to disarm, France, Germany and Russia arguable failed to fulfill their obligation as members of the Council to allow the Council to perform its collective security functions to maintain international peace and security. As Edward Luck, a long time observer and commentator on the United Nations, recently noted: "The United Nations, sadly, has drifted far from its founding vision. Its Charter neither calls for a democratic council nor relegates the collective use of force to a last resort. It was a wartime document of a military alliance, not a universal peace platform." Edward C. Luck, *Making the World Safe for Hypocrisy*, N.Y. TIMES, Mar. 22, 2003, at A11, col. 1.

Further, as Jacques de Lisle has recently suggested, there may be a virtue in acting in an "almost legal" manner and, if so, the United States and other members of the coalition cannot justly be accused of engaging in lawless behavior. Jacques de Lisle, *Illegal? Yes. Lawless? Not so Fast: The United States, International Law, & the War in Iraq*, Foreign Policy Research Institute (Mar. 28, 2003). Professor de Lisle also suggests that, if after the armed conflict in Iraq is over, there is substantial evidence uncovered of weapons of mass destruction and plans to use them as well as of the heinous nature of the Iraq regime, this would "greatly strengthen the US and its partners' arguments for the near-legality and, thus, the legitimacy of their war in Iraq." *Id.* at 9.
194. It is worth noting that even the "Iron Lady" has not called for the use of military force against either Iran or North Korea. Thatcher, *supra* note 167.

The Road Ahead: Conclusions and Recommendations

Most of my conclusions and recommendations are set forth in previous sections of this chapter. In this, the concluding section of the chapter, I hope to highlight a few especially important points and, with trepidation, speculate a bit about the future.

A general observation is that we have reached the stage where *implementing* the legal regime that has been developed to combat terrorism is of paramount importance. We now have in place an impressive array of antiterrorist conventions, at both the global and regional levels, that covers almost all possible manifestations of terrorism. To be sure it might be useful to develop a convention directed toward the possible use of weapons of mass destruction by terrorists but otherwise coverage is impressive. Until recently, however, there has been little effort to ensure that these conventions constitute an operative system for combating terrorism. In contrast, establishment of the Counter-Terrorism Committee by the Security Council to oversee efforts to combat terrorism, especially the financing of terrorism, and adoption of the Inter-American Convention Against Terrorism are significant steps to this end.

The "catastrophic terrorism" of September 11th may so "concentrate the mind wonderfully"[195] that we will finally give the problem of terrorism the kind of attention it deserves. The unprecedented cooperation among states, inside and outside of the UN, that followed September 11th is a prime example of the high priority efforts to combat terrorism currently enjoy. But the risk of becoming complacent is always present, and may become greater if, as time goes on, no new examples of catastrophic terrorism occur. In this connection it is worth noting that in the past al Qaeda has demonstrated great patience in its planning of terrorist attacks, with such attacks coming at three year intervals.

Moreover, we are still engaged in a struggle to establish the proposition that the acts of terrorism covered by the antiterrorist conventions are illegitimate at all times and under all circumstances whatever the political motivation of the terrorist. The support, explicit or tacit, given by many states to the Palestinian suicide bombings in Israel and on the West Bank graphically illustrates the problem. Although this is a subject outside the scope of this conference, it is crucially important to efforts to combat terrorism that a peaceful resolution of the conflict between Israel and the Palestinians be found.

---

195. This paraphrases, of course, the famous quote from Samuel Johnson, "Depend upon it, Sir, when a man knows he is to be hanged in a fortnight, it concentrates his mind wonderfully." Respectfully Quoted: A Dictionary Of Quotations Requested From The Congressional Research Service 74 (Suzy Platt ed., 1989).

Besides the antiterrorist conventions we need to use other tools at our disposal more effectively if we are to succeed in this "war on terrorism." As indicated previously in this chapter, the record of economic sanctions applied against state sponsors of terrorism is spotty at best. The record of economic sanctions against Iraq has been egregiously bad. We need to work further on "smart sanctions" that will have a real impact on the governments of state sponsors of terrorism while sparing the general population of the targeted country.

Finally, I return to Ms. Rice's reported comment calling for the establishment of "a common security framework for the great powers" within which they "share a common security agenda" and work together to keep terrorists and rogue states from challenging the system. With respect I would suggest that we already have such a common security framework: the UN Security Council and Chapter VII of the UN Charter. Contrary to Professor Glennon's fulminations, in the face of numerous obstacles, this common security framework has from time to time served us well. It is now time for the great powers to recommit themselves to making the collective security system of the UN work as envisaged by its founders. Such a pledge is long overdue.

XXVI

Al Qaeda And Taliban Detainees—An Examination Of Legal Rights And Appropriate Treatment

James Terry[1]

Introduction

The war against the terrorists who attacked the United States on September 11, 2001, is a new kind of international conflict. It does not represent traditional warfare between states adhering to the law of armed conflict. Rather, it reflects non-traditional violence against states and innocent civilians by individuals or groups for political ends without regard to the civilized behavior on the battlefield that underpins the four 1949 Geneva Conventions, including the Convention Relative to the Treatment of Prisoners of War (Geneva Convention III).[2]

---

1. James Terry is a retired Marine Colonel currently serving as the Deputy Assistant Secretary of State for Regional, Global and Functional Affairs in the Bureau of Legislative Affairs within the US Department of State. The views expressed in this paper are the views of the author alone.
2. *See* Convention for the Amelioration of the Condition of the Wounded and Sick in Armed Forces in the Field, Aug. 12, 1949, Art. 2, 6 U.S.T. 3114, T.I.A.S. No. 3362, 75 U.N.T.S. 31; Convention for the Amelioration of the Condition of the Wounded, Sick, and Shipwrecked Members of Armed Forces at Sea, Aug. 12, 1949, 6. U.S.T. 3217, T.I.A.S. No. 3363, 75 U.N.T.S. 85; Convention Relative to the Treatment of Prisoners of War, Aug. 12, 1949, 6 U.S.T. 3316, T.I.A.S. No. 3364, 75 U.N.T.S. 135 [hereinafter GC III]; Convention Relative to the Protection

The perpetrators of the September 11th violence, the al Qaeda organization, were protected and given safe haven in Afghanistan by the Pushtun Taliban militia. Although the Taliban was the strongest of the ethnic militias in Afghanistan by mid-2001, it was unable to conduct normal foreign relations or to fulfill its international legal obligations. Because the Taliban militia consistently refused to comply with UN Security Council Resolutions 1333 (2000), 1267 (1999) and 1214 (1998),[3] independent press reports concluded that it had become so subject to the domination and control of al Qaeda that it could not pursue independent policies with respect to other states.[4]

While the US–led coalition together with Afghan Northern Alliance forces were successful in crushing al Qaeda and the Taliban in Operation ENDURING FREEDOM, the detainees captured in Afghanistan and transported to Guantanamo Bay, Cuba for post conflict disposition raised issues not addressed since the Vietnam Conflict when Viet Cong forces were captured in South Vietnam. Although entitled only to Common Article 3 status under

---

of Civilian Persons in Time of War, Aug. 12, 1949, 6 U.S.T. 3516, T.I.A.S. No. 3365, 75 U.N.T.S. 287 [hereinafter GC IV]. These four conventions are all reprinted in DOCUMENTS ON THE LAWS OF WAR (Adam Roberts and Richard Guelff eds., 3rd ed., 2000) [hereinafter DOCUMENTS ON THE LAWS OF WAR]; and in THE LAWS OF ARMED CONFLICTS: A COLLECTION OF CONVENTIONS, RESOLUTIONS AND OTHER DOCUMENTS, Dietrich Schindler and Jiri Toman eds., 3rd ed. 1988). Treaty texts are also available at the International Committee of the Red Cross website *at* http://www.icrc.org/eng (Jan. 3, 2003).

3. Security Council Resolution 1333 "strongly condemn[ed]" the Taliban for the "sheltering and training of terrorists and [the] planning of terrorist acts," and "deplor[ed] the fact that the Taliban continues to provide a safe haven to Usama bin Laden and to allow him and others associated with him to operate a network of terrorist training camps from Taliban controlled territory and to use Afghanistan as a base from which to sponsor international terrorist operations." U.N. SCOR 55th Sess., U.N. Doc. S/1333/(2000). In its preamble, Resolution 1267 found that the Taliban's failure to comply with the Council's 1998 demand in Resolution 1214 to terminate the use of Afghanistan as a base from which to sponsor international terrorism constituted a threat to the peace. U.N. SCOR 54th Sess., U.N. Doc. S/1267/(1999). Paragraph 13 of Resolution 1214 enjoined the Taliban from providing a sanctuary and training for terrorists. U.N. SCOR 53d Sess., U.N. Doc. S/1214/(1998).

4. *See, e.g.*, Michael Dobbs and Vernon Loeb, *2 U.S. Targets Bound By Fate*, WASH. POST, Nov. 14, 2001, at A22.

each of the four Geneva Conventions,[5] the Viet Cong prisoners were nevertheless treated as prisoners of war (POWs).[6]

Simply stated, the issues presented US officials in Afghanistan required (1) a determination whether the 1949 Geneva Conventions applied to the conflict represented by Operation ENDURING FREEDOM and Operation ANACONDA; and (2), if so, whether members of al Qaeda as a group and the Taliban individually or as a group are entitled to POW status under Geneva Convention III.

The Application of the Laws of War in Afghanistan

Following the post-World War II review of serious breaches of customary international law and the Hague Conventions of 1899 and 1907 by the Axis Powers, a diplomatic conference invested nearly three years writing the four Geneva Conventions designed to regulate treatment of those individuals who become victims of warfare. These four conventions, like other treaties, establish legal relationships between nations, not between nations and groups or nations and subnational organizations.[7] The United States and Afghanistan are both High Contracting Parties to the Conventions,[8] including Geneva Convention III, and are thus bound by their terms and provisions.

Under Geneva Convention III, individuals entitled to POW status upon capture include members of the regular armed forces of a party, the militia, and those volunteers and volunteer units fighting with the regular armed forces of a party.[9] Irregular forces, including militia and volunteers, fighting apart from the regular armed forces, can also qualify for POW status when captured, provided they are serving under an authority responsible for their conduct, are in uniform or are wearing a distinctive sign recognizable at a

---

5. Common Article 3 appears in each of the four 1949 Geneva Conventions and addresses individuals and groups who do not represent a government or state but rather an insurgency or opposition group to the recognized regime. Unlike the Viet Cong, however, neither the Taliban nor al Qaeda were factions within a state with a recognized central government. Like the Viet Cong, however, they were fighting an international coalition of the willing within the recognized borders of a nation, despite its lack of central government, which was a high contracting party to the Geneva Conventions.
6. See *Contemporary Practice of the United States*, 62 AM. J. INT'L L. 766–768 (1968) *citing* MACV, Annex A of Directive No. 381-46, December 27, 1967.
7. See U.S. ex rel Saroop v. Garcia, 109 F.3d 165, 167 (3d Cir. 1997) where the court stated that "[T]reaties are agreements between nations."
8. The United States became a party on July 14, 1955 while Afghanistan acceded on Sep. 26, 1956.
9. GC III, *supra* note 2, art. 4(A)(1) & 4(A)(4).

distance, carry their arms openly, and conduct operations in a manner consistent with the laws of war.[10]

When a captive's status as a POW is challenged because a party believes the individual did not meet the criteria set forth above, that individual is to be accorded POW treatment until a tribunal convened by the captor state reviews the facts and makes a determination.[11] Similarly, when an individual's belligerent status is not clear upon falling into the hands of the enemy, that individual enjoys the protection of Geneva Convention III until such time as his status can be determined by an appropriate tribunal.[12]

The Administration Position

On February 7, 2002, Ari Fleischer, White House Press Secretary, gave the Administration view of the status of Taliban and al Qaeda detainees captured in Afghanistan.

> President Bush today has decided that the Geneva Convention will apply to the Taliban detainees, but not to the al Qaeda international terrorists.
>
> Afghanistan is a party to the Geneva Convention. Although the United States does not recognize the Taliban as a legitimate Afghani government, the President determined that the Taliban members are covered under the treaty because Afghanistan is a party to the Convention.
>
> Under Article 4 of the Geneva Convention, however, Taliban detainees are not entitled to POW status. To qualify as POWs under Article 4, al Qaeda and Taliban detainees would have to have satisfied four conditions: They would have to be part of a military hierarchy; they would have to have worn uniforms or other distinctive signs visible at a distance; they would have to have carried arms openly; and they would have to have conducted their military operations in accordance with the laws and customs of war.
>
> The Taliban have not effectively distinguished themselves from the civilian population of Afghanistan. Moreover, they have not conducted their military operations in accordance with the laws and customs of war. Instead, they have knowingly adopted and provided support to the unlawful terrorist objectives of the al Qaeda.

---

10. *Id.*, art 4(A)(2); *see also* 1907 Hague Convention IV Respecting the Laws and Customs of War on Land, Oct. 18, 1907, 36 Stat. 2227, Annex.
11. GC III, *supra* note 2, art. 5(2).
12. *Id.*

Al Qaeda is an international terrorist group and cannot be considered a state party to the Geneva Convention. Its members, therefore, are not covered by the Geneva Convention, and are not entitled to POW status under the treaty.[13]

What the White House was clearly implying, if not saying, was that this war on terrorism was not a war envisaged when Geneva Convention III was signed in 1949. In this war, global terrorists transcend national boundaries and internationally target the innocent. In the February 7 White House statement, the Bush Administration committed the United States to the principles of Geneva Convention III, while recognizing that the Convention does not cover every situation in which people may be captured or detained by military forces.

Effect of Not Applying Geneva Convention III to al Qaeda

The language of the four Geneva Conventions applies to international conflicts first[14] and only then does it address the status of those involved. It is clear, however, that all international conflicts are covered. The Bush Administration position of not applying the Convention to al Qaeda appears to be at odds with these principles. More importantly, it overlooks the very fabric of the Convention which is designed to address all combatant actors in a conflict. Specifically, the Convention divides all combatants into the category of lawful combatant, or alternatively, that of unlawful combatant.

By decrying the application of Geneva Convention III to al Qaeda fighters, the US decision deprives the United States of its strongest legal rationale for jurisdiction both in US federal court and internationally. More specifically, absent the authority to act under Geneva Convention III, the authority to detain al Qaeda fighters, to remove them from Afghanistan, to try them before military commissions for war crimes, to provide them no more than humane treatment, and to send them to third countries could be challenged. Without the authority of Geneva Convention III to rely upon, the detainees could be

---

13. White House Press Secretary Ari Fleischer, Press Briefing at the White House (Feb. 7, 2002), at 1–2, *available at* Lexis, Federal News Service (Jan. 6, 2003).
14. *See, e.g.,* GC III, *supra* note 2, art. 2. Article 2, common to all four Geneva Conventions, provides in relevant part that the conventions shall "apply to all cases of declared war or of any other armed conflict which may arise between two or more of the High Contracting Parties. . . ."

entitled to rights either enshrined in the US Constitution or the International Covenant on Civil and Political Rights (ICCPR)[15] as the ICCPR is generally believed to apply to those situations in which Geneva Convention III does not apply.

The Taliban and Al Qaeda Fighters Must Be Viewed as One for Purposes of Application of International Law

During the period that Taliban authorities controlled the political machinery of state in Kabul, they constituted the de facto government of Afghanistan. Afghanistan continued to have the essential elements of statehood, and was called upon by the international community to comply with its obligations, as reflected in Security Council Resolutions 1267 (1999) and 1333 (2000) (which called upon the Taliban to take specific actions), and the international agreements prior Afghan governments had signed (even if it was unable or unwilling to comply with their terms).[16] The close relationship between the Taliban and al Qaeda political and military elements was obvious. As Resolution 1333 recognized, "the Taliban continue[d] to provide a safe haven to Usama bin Laden and to allow him and others associated with him to operate a network of terrorist training camps from Taliban-controlled territory and to use Afghanistan as a base from which to sponsor international terrorist operations."[17]

Professor Robert Turner of the University of Virginia explained that when "bin Laden masterminded the attacks on New York and Washington, Afghanistan [was] in breach of its state responsibility to take reasonable measures to prevent its territory from being used to launch attacks against other states."[18] Prior to September 11, 2001, al Qaeda supplied the Taliban with the money, material, and personnel to help it gain the upper hand with the Northern Alliance.[19]

---

15. International Covenant on Civil and Political Rights, opened for signature Dec. 19, 1966, 1992 U.N.T.S. 171 (entered into force Mar. 23, 1976, signed by the United States Oct. 5, 1977) [hereinafter ICCPR]. The ICCPR provides the same protections, in article 14, that the President has provided to the detainees here.
16. No Security Council document exists claiming that Afghanistan had lost its right to nationhood or that it had ceased to exist as a viable state.
17. S. C. Res. 1333, *supra* note 3.
18. Robert F. Turner, *International Law and the Use of Force in Response to the World Trade Center Pentagon Attacks*, JURIST ONLINE, *available at* http://jurist.law.pitt.edu/forum/forumnew34.htm (Jan. 23, 2003).
19. Michael Jansen, *U.S. Focused Initially on bin Laden Mercenaries*, IRISH TIMES, Oct. 30, 2001 *available at* NEXIS, Major World Newspapers (Jan. 23, 2003).

Thus Afghanistan, as a sovereign state, under the leadership of Taliban authorities, had thoroughly aligned itself with al Qaeda forces prior to September 11. As the President stated on November 13, 2001, "[i]nternational terrorists, *including members of al Qaeda*, have carried out attacks on United States diplomatic and military personnel and facilities abroad and on citizens and property within the United States on a scale that has created a state of armed conflict that requires the use of the United States Armed Forces."[20] This statement reflects recognition that the Taliban and al Qaeda are closely aligned and that the Taliban provided the safe haven in which al Qaeda could function.[21] In light of the support and safe haven provided al Qaeda by the Taliban leadership, it must be concluded that the Taliban fighters and al Qaeda members who were together when fighting US and Northern Alliance forces when captured must be viewed as one when determining the application of Article 4(A)(1) of Geneva Convention III.

Geneva Convention III is Applicable to al Qaeda and the Taliban

Geneva Convention III applies to the detention and trial of the regular and irregular forces of a state party whose militia has been engaged in an international armed conflict.[22] Article 2 of the Convention provides that it shall apply to armed conflict which "may arise between two or more of the High Contracting Parties." As stated previously, Afghanistan has been a state party to the 1949 Geneva Conventions since 1956, the United States since 1955. The Taliban, with its al Qaeda allies, effectively controlled nearly 90 percent of Afghan territory, while exercising governmental functions therein, to include operating a system of taxation, administering Islamic courts, appointing and confirming regional governors, district leaders, mayors, and other regional and local officials, and imposing law and order.

The fact that the United States and its coalition partners did not recognize the Taliban government is immaterial to the treatment of its fighters and

---

20. Military Order of President of the United States, Detention, Treatment, and Trial of Certain Non-Citizens in the War Against Terrorism, November 13, 2001, *available at* http://www.whitehouse.gov/news/releases/2001/11/20011113-27.html (Jan. 23, 2003) (emphasis supplied).
21. *See, e.g.,* S. C. Res. 1267, U.N. SCOR, 54th Sess., U.N. Doc. S/1267/(1999) which provides: "[d]eploring the fact that the Taliban continues to provide safe haven to Usama bin Laden and to allow him and others associated with him to operate a network of terrorist training camps from Taliban-controlled territory and to use Afghanistan as a base from which to sponsor international terrorist operations. . . . "
22. *See* GC III, *supra* note 3, arts. 4 & 5.

those of the allied al Qaeda under Geneva Convention III. Article 4(3) of the Convention is clear on this point. That provision extends coverage to forces who profess allegiance to a government or an authority "*not recognized* by the Detaining Power." This interpretation is supported by the Article 4(3) negotiating history.[23] Because the Taliban, with its al Qaeda supporters, exercised actual control over the greater part of Afghanistan prior to and after September 11, 2001, and clearly opposed the coalition's use of force in Operation ENDURING FREEDOM, it must be concluded that an armed conflict did exist between two High Contracting Parties to Geneva Convention III.

Taliban and al Qaeda Forces Do Not Qualify for POW Status

The fact that the Convention applies to an international armed conflict and its opposing forces does not mean that these forces will be accorded POW status under the Convention, however. Article 4(A) sets forth in pertinent detail the basic categories of persons entitled to protection as POWs. As noted earlier, these include: (1) armed forces of a party and militias and volunteer corps forming part of such armed forces; (2) members of other militia and volunteer corps who meet the four basic requirements; and (3) members of regular armed forces who profess allegiance to an authority not recognized.

Neither the Taliban nor al Qaeda forces qualify for protection under the Convention as the "armed forces of a Party," or the "militias and volunteer corps forming part of such armed forces." This results from their failure to fulfill the basic requirements applicable to any armed force, militia, or volunteer corps under Article 4(A) of the Convention. Neither al Qaeda nor the Taliban satisfied the requirement of wearing uniforms or other distinctive insignia;[24] neither were subject to a command structure that enforced the laws

---

23. *See* INTERNATIONAL COMMITTEE OF THE RED CROSS, 3 GENEVA CONVENTION RELATIVE TO THE TREATMENT OF PRISONERS OF WAR, COMMENTARY 63 (Jean S. Pictet ed. 1960) (noting that Article 4(A)(3) is written to bring an end to the practice of refusing to give POW status to unrecognized but otherwise deserving combatants).
24. The White House and Department of Defense stated publicly that the Taliban and al Qaeda did not distinguish themselves from the civilian population. *See* Press Briefing at the White House, *supra* note 13.

and customs of warfare,[25] and neither in their operations adhered to the laws and customs of warfare.[26]

As one independent observer has reported with regard to the lack of respect shown to the laws of war:

> These non-Afghan fighters, along with the Taliban army, have not only broken the traditional norms of Afghan civil societies, they have also committed massive crimes against humanity by beheading and killing prisoners of war (POWs) and massacring thousands of civilians in different parts of the Country. In 1998 and 1999, the International Red Cross reported that the Taliban and their non-Afghan army killed thousands of civilians in Bamyan and set fire to 8,000 houses and shops.[27]

This wanton violence has continued until quite recently. The Department of State has reported that the Taliban "massacred hundreds of Afghan civilians, including women and children, in Yakaoloang, Mazar -e-Sharif, Bamayan, Qezelbad, and other towns."[28] The Taliban routinely failed in its attacks to discriminate between military objectives and civilians, as required under the law of armed conflict. For example, "[t]here are reports that as many as 5,000 persons, mostly ethnic Hazara civilians, were massacred by the Taliban after the takeover of Mazar -e-Sharif."[29]

---

25. Article 4 of GC III requires that forces be "commanded by a person responsible for his subordinates." This military command requirement is intended to ensure widespread compliance with the laws and customs of war. According to the US Department of Defense, these forces "are not commanded by any person responsible for his subordinates." *US Department of Defense Memorandum: Why Taliban are Unlawful Combatants*, at 1 (Oct. 19, 2001) (copy on file with author).

26. The Taliban and al Qaeda as a whole ignored the laws and customs of war. According to the laws and customs of warfare, parties must take precautions to protect civilians, for example, by verifying the military nature of targets, respecting the principles of proportionality and necessity, and minimizing incidental loss of civilian life. *See generally*, GC IV, *supra* note 2; *see also*, 1977 Geneva Protocol I Additional to the Geneva Conventions of 12 August 1949, and Relating to the Protection of Victims of International Armed Conflicts, Part IV - Civilian Population, *opened for signature* Dec. 12, 1977, 1125 U.N.T.S. 1 [hereinafter GP I], *reprinted in* DOCUMENTS ON THE LAWS OF WAR at 419, *supra* note 2.

27. NEAMATOLLAH NOJUMI, THE RISE OF THE TALIBAN IN AFGHANISTAN, 229 (2002). *See also*, Lee A. Casey et. al, *By the Laws of War, They aren't POWs*, WASH. POST, Mar. 3, 2002, at A3.

28. US Department of State, *Fact Sheet: Taliban Actions Imperil Afghan Civilians*, November 2, 2001, at 1, *available at* http://usembassy.state.gov/islamabad/wwwh01110301.html (Jan. 23, 2003).

29. US DEPARTMENT OF STATE COUNTRY REPORTS ON HUMAN RIGHTS PRACTICES, 2000–Afghanistan, at §1(g) (Feb. 2001).

The State Department also reported in November 2001 that the Taliban were using the entire populations of villages as human shields to protect their stockpiles of ammunition and weapons, that they were relocating the police ministry in Kandahar to mosques, that they had taken over humanitarian relief organization buildings, and that they were discovered transporting tanks and mortar shells in the guise of humanitarian relief.[30] These and other similar reports provide strong support for the President's conclusion that the Taliban (and al Qaeda) forces flagrantly violated the laws and customs of war, failed to exhibit insignia or otherwise distinguish themselves from civilians, and were not subject to responsible military command. Under these circumstances, the Taliban and al Qaeda do not meet the Article 4 criteria for groups entitled to POW status.

A Group Determination of Status Does Not Violate the Convention

Article 5 of Geneva Convention III provides that where doubt arises as to the proper status of an individual or individuals, "such persons shall enjoy the protection of the present convention until such time as their status has been determined by a competent tribunal." For the reasons set forth above, there can be no doubt that the Taliban and al Qaeda do not qualify for POW status, a decision the President came to after consulting with his most senior advisors, and undertaking a careful and reasoned analysis.

The process of group determination exercised by the Executive Branch was consistent with the drafters' intent that questions of status are given serious consideration by responsible leaders.[31] It was also consistent with US and allied decisions on POWs in Korea and Vietnam, although Article 5 Tribunals were established in Vietnam to address individual cases where doubt existed.[32] Nevertheless, the President determined that the detainees would continue to enjoy the protections of the present convention as long as they are held.

The protections to be accorded all prisoners of war are contained in Part II of Geneva Convention III. Those protections, which the President has determined applicable to all al Qaeda and Taliban detainees, even though these individuals do not warrant designation as POWs, require humane treatment

---

30. US Department of State, *Fact Sheet: The Taliban's Betrayal of the Afghan People*, November 6, 2001, *available at* http://usembassy.state.gov/islamabad/wwwh01110702.html (Jan. 23, 2003).
31. *See, e.g.*, FRITZ KALSHOVEN AND LIESBETH ZEBVELD, CONSTRAINTS ON THE WAGING OF WAR 53 (2001).
32. *See, e.g.*, Roberts, *supra* Chapter VII, note 22 and accompanying text.

and protection from insults, reprisals, and public curiosity.[33] Part II also requires free "maintenance" and medical attention. The detainees are being provided meals that reflect their Muslim culture and religion, and clothing, shelter, pads for sleeping, blankets, and medical care.[34] They are also receiving additional privileges, including the ability to send and receive mail, the right to visit individually with the ICRC, and the opportunity to worship with the assistance of a Muslim chaplain provided by the US Navy.

While the detainees at Guantanamo are being accorded all protections due POWs under Part II of Geneva Convention III, they are not subject to the privileges and benefits accorded POWs under the Convention. These benefits include respect for rank,[35] pay,[36] and traditional courtesies accorded military personnel by others in the profession of arms.[37]

The Trial of Detainees before Military Commissions

When President Bush issued his Military Order of November 13, 2001, the trial of non-citizens before military tribunals had not been contemplated since World War II, and then not specifically for terrorist defendants. In this case, the use of military commissions to try these defendants for war crimes provides important advantages over civilian trials. As White House Counsel Alberto Gonzales stated,

> [t]hey spare American jurors, judges and courts the grave risks associated with terrorist trials. They allow the government to use classified information as evidence without compromising intelligence or military efforts. They can dispense justice swiftly, close to where our forces may be fighting, without years of pretrial proceedings or post-trial appeals.
>
> And they can consider the broadest range of relevant evidence to reach their verdicts. For example, circumstances in a war zone often make it impossible to meet the authentication requirements for documents in a civilian court, yet

---

33. GC III, *supra* note 2, art. 13.
34. *Id.*, arts. 15–16. The rights announced by President Bush in his Military Order of November 13, 2001, *supra* note 19, at 2, are consistent with the provisions of these two articles.
35. *Id.*, arts. 44–45.
36. *Id.*, arts. 54, 62.
37. *See, e.g.*, GC III, *supra* note 2, art. 18, which provides, in pertinent part, that "badges of rank and nationality, decorations, and articles having above all a personal or sentimental value may not be taken from prisoners of war."

documents from al Qaeda safe houses in Kabul might be essential to accurately determine the guilt of al Qaeda cell members hiding in the West.[38]

The procedures for trials by military commission are carefully set forth in Department of Defense Military Commission Order No. 1, signed by Secretary Rumsfeld on March 21, 2002.[39] As the Order makes clear, "[t]hese procedures (discussed in detail below) shall be implemented and construed so as to ensure that any such individual receives a full and fair trial before a military commission...."[40]

Military commissions do not gain their authority from Article III of the Constitution which underlies our federal court system. Rather, these tribunals operate as a function of the President's Commander–in–Chief authorities under Article I and have been specifically approved by the US Supreme Court.[41] The nature of the proceedings and the nature of the evidence are shaped by the law of armed conflict. That body of law has very different premises than our domestic criminal law. Under domestic law, the killing of another person is presumed unlawful unless justified or excused by a specific defense (e.g., self-defense) or condition (e.g., mental defect). Under the law of armed conflict, there is a presumption that the killing of another combatant is lawful unless some other norm is violated, such as the status of the aggressor as an unlawful combatant. In such cases, the individual had no combatant immunity to engage in belligerent acts.

It is also important to note that the purpose of holding the detainees at Guantanamo is not specifically in anticipation of trial, but rather as a traditional function of the US war effort. This is based on a common-sense recognition that if released, detainees would quickly rejoin the hostilities. For this reason, trials—if any are held—will not begin until the conflict is over. At the end of hostilities, the equation, of course, could change. Continued detention at that point would have to be based on a legitimate judicial or law

---

38. Alberto R. Gonzales, *Military Justice, Full and Fair*, N.Y. TIMES, Nov. 30, 2001, at A18.
39. DOD Military Commission Order number 1 – Procedures for Trials by Military Commissions of Certain Non-United States Citizens In the War Against Terrorism (Mar. 21, 2002), *available at* http://www.defenselink.mil/news/Mar2002/d20020321ord.pdf (Jan. 23, 2003) [hereinafter DOD Military Commission Order].
40. *Id.*, at 1.
41. *See* Ex parte Quirin, 317 U.S. 1, 30–31 (1942). This case involved the trial by military commission of unlawful combatants who were German soldiers smuggled into the United States by submarine who discarded their uniforms upon entry, but were captured prior to committing acts of sabotage.

enforcement need. It is premature at this point to determine to whom the need might apply.

At the conclusion of hostilities, those individuals for whom investigations have revealed violations of the law of war could be charged with offenses before a military commission. Under the provisions of Military Commission Order No. 1: (1) the accused will be furnished a copy of the charges sufficiently in advance of trial to prepare a defense; (2) a presumption of innocence will apply; (3) the standard of proof is beyond a reasonable doubt; (4) at least one defense counsel shall be provided; (5) the accused shall not be required to testify; (6) the accused and his counsel shall have access to the prosecution's evidence, including exculpatory evidence, in advance of trial; (7) defense witnesses and evidence may be presented; and (8) the accused shall be present at all phases of the proceeding.[42]

Within this construct, commission membership shall include between 3 and 7 members who shall be commissioned officers of the US armed forces.[43] The presiding officer shall be a judge advocate.[44] This official shall ensure the expeditious conduct of the trial as well as its fairness.[45] Prosecutors shall either be judge advocates from the US armed forces or special trial counsel from the Department of Justice made available by the Attorney General.[46]

The conduct of each trial before a commission follows the federal model and is precisely set forth in Article 6(E) of DOD Order No. 1. Post-trial procedures include a formal review process by a three officer review panel, with one of the officers experienced as a judge.[47] The Secretary of Defense will then review each record of trial and the recommendation of the review panel. Finally, after review by the Secretary, the record of trial and all recommendations will be forwarded to the President for review and final decision.[49]

Conclusion

The Bush Administration has embarked upon a careful process of identification and detention of al Qaeda and Taliban combatants, investigation of

---

42. DOD Military Commission Order, *supra* note 39, art. 5.
43. *Id.*, art. 4A(2), (3).
44. *Id.*, art. 4A(4).
45. *Id.*, art. 4A(5)(a), (c).
46. *Id.*, art. 4B(2).
47. *Id.*, art. 6H(4).
48. *Id.*, art. 6H(5).
49. *Id.*, art. 6H(6).

offenses, and the development of a thorough and fair adjudicative process. While differences may exist in terms of how al Qaeda members are characterized in terms of Geneva Convention III, the regime established to examine the conduct of their actions and the actions of the Taliban fighters will likely result in a mere "distinction without a difference."

The President has stated that he will only try foreign enemy war criminals before military commissions, and then only if they are chargeable with offenses against the international laws of war. Trials before military commissions will be as open as possible, consistent with the urgent needs of national security. Each defendant before a military commission will know the charges against him, be represented by qualified counsel and be allowed to present a robust defense.

The President's Military Order of November 13, 2001, like the Secretary of Defense's Military Commission Order No. 1 of March 21, 2002, is designed to ensure that individuals subject thereto receive a full and fair trial. The military commissions that are authorized will not undermine the constitutional values of any American nor violate the civil liberties of any non-US national appearing before them. Rather, the regime created draws a delicate balance between the President's obligation to defend the nation and the desire of all Americans that any commission established under the President's Constitutional authorities provide the same procedural and substantive protections evident in the domestic courts of this country.

XXVII

Panel V
Commentary—The Road Ahead in Afghanistan

James Terry[1]

Today I will offer a series of observations on actions we must consider as the United States moves to the road ahead in Afghanistan. Winning the war on terrorism requires that we approach this complex problem in a multifaceted way. We must cultivate counter-terrorism cooperation on a regional basis as well as on an individual state basis for it is only through such cooperation that we can be successful.

Using all instruments of power available, we must stimulate an increased political will to act on the part of states on the front lines in this war on terrorism. We must enhance our public diplomacy efforts and economic support to stimulate religious and social institutions, especially educational institutions, to be more responsive and responsible in the education of their future citizens. We must further, across the reaches of the US Government, enhance our image and our relationship with the Muslim population, at home and abroad.

---

1. James Terry, a retired Marine Colonel, serves as the Deputy Assistant Secretary of State for Regional, Global and Functional Affairs in the Bureau of Legislative Affairs within the US Department of State. The views expressed in these remarks are the views of the author alone.

Of critical importance in these efforts is our focus on non heavy-handed, American aid to countries struggling with the difficulty of dealing with the conditions that foster the development of terrorism. In these efforts, we can not be seen as unilateralists but instead must be seen as partners in the global effort to address these issues. We must foster the development of greater cooperative action, including the effective exchange of information, especially among Muslim states. This has occurred most recently with Morocco, a country with which the United States did not have as developed a relationship before the events of September 11th.

We must share the best counter-terrorism laws, regulations, and treaties we can develop with these states in an effort to aid them in the development of similar laws. We must create effective agreements between states for law enforcement operations so as to ensure that terrorists captured abroad are subject to extradition. And we must enhance cooperation in our nation's intelligence gathering and sharing, much as has been done since September 11th, with countries like Uzbekistan and Turkmenistan.

Regional training programs and bilateral programs designed to enhance forensic law enforcement and legal methodology, as are currently being pursued with Pakistan, must be undertaken. At the same time, it is critical that we guard against the imposition of those US laws and policies which alienate us from those we wish to influence. As an example, recent Arab bashing legislation proposed in the House of Representatives and the Senate does not necessarily serve our interests well. These efforts may well be called for but they do not help us in our efforts to appear even handed to different groups.

Operationally, it is important to understand that capacity building in such front line states must focus on the ultimate goal of individual state responsibility in dealing with the problems of terrorism. In working towards this goal, the United States must overcome the view that it has a bias against institutions such as the United Nations. It is important that we not be seen as UN bashing in either our legislation or our voice. In that regard, for the last nine months I have been the head of a working group addressing the American Servicemembers Protection Act.[2] Our focus has been on ensuring that this act does not deprive the president of the flexibility he needs to support the International Criminal Court when it is in our national interest to do so. That this work is occurring should be shared with coalition and allied partners to ensure they understand that while our principled objections to the problems

---

2. American Servicemembers' Protection Act of 2002, Pub. L. No. 107–206, 116 Stat 899 (2002).

inherent in the Rome Statute remain very real, our government recognizes that there may be a time, if certain changes are made to the Rome Statute, when the United States will agree to become a member of the International Criminal Court.

The long-term goal of these operational considerations must be the internal sustainability of this process region-wide and world-wide. Our main goal must be to create national counter-terrorism systems that really do work. In support of this goal, we must focus on programs like our International Military Education and Training Program and ensure that funds for these programs support those countries working alongside us in pursuit of our goal. Such training assistance must account for the stated needs of the host and not just our perceived view of what would make them more effective. In this regard, a phased approach to engaging these countries would be useful.

Phasing our cooperation and operations with countries in such a way that we move from training to policy and then to operations may well allow us to gauge the will of these participants at each step; building trust and debunking myths about US objectives that are simply not true. On the diplomacy side, we must work with states to harness their desire to increase their regional counter-terrorism role. An example of how this can be successful is the regional counter-terrorism operations center for Southeast Asia, recently created by Indonesia, Malaysia, Singapore, and the United States. This new center promises real opportunities to work alongside and support our allies in the war on terrorism. Obviously, the regional combatant commanders and their respective staff judge advocates must play an important role in the development and working of these centers as consultation on the desired training, policy development and operations for such centers is critical for their success. Finally, useful agreements must be developed between the United States and other states which tie cooperation on counter-terrorism efforts to US assistance. Such agreements may, by necessity, need to be confidential in the early stages of cooperation but they are nonetheless necessary.

From a governmental process perspective, this will not be easy. In Southeast Asia for example, Congress must provide the authority to overcome restrictions on aid to countries such as Burma, Cambodia, Laos, and Indonesia. Necessarily, such legislation will be required to be drafted in such a way that US assistance is contingent upon the particular country's participation in the global war on terrorism. At the same time, over-reaching congressional mandates must be avoided. We must avoid the traditional "litmus test report" language as a condition for aid and we must ensure that the entire range of foreign military financing, economic support funding and international military and education training funding is used.

Not surprisingly, we have invoked each of these strategies in our efforts in Afghanistan. Our goals for the road ahead in Afghanistan have focused on security, infrastructure support, nation building—and by that I include political development, education and woman's rights—and reconstruction (including the revitalization of the agricultural sector). In the security area, continued steps to destroy the al Qaeda network include the success of Operation ANACONDA and the other follow-on operations to ENDURING FREEDOM that have been complemented by the provision of stability by the International Security Assistance Force (ISAF) in Kabul.

The initial steps to train an Afghan Army and police force are key elements of the US and German efforts to build a more secure Afghanistan. In this task, the Germans are doing a superb job in developing a police organization that understands and respects fundamental human rights. An effort to build consensus among the different war lords has been pursued through their inclusion in the political process, most recently in the Loya Jirga electoral process; a process that resulted in the election of Hamed Karzai to head the transitional governing authority for the next two years. The inclusion of the war lords in this process has helped ease ethnic tensions existing in such cities as Mazar -e- Sharif, Kandahar, and Jalabad.

This is a great start but it is not enough. We must focus now on honing the instruments of power in the Afghan government. By that I mean the legal, economic, political, and military instruments. In that regard, the Bonn Agreement[3] that established this process eight months ago is holding. As an example, woman's rights have been emphasized through the naming of two women to major cabinet posts within Karzai's transitional authority. In the reconstruction area, three successful conferences in Washington, in Brussels, and in Tokyo have produced pledges of some 4.5 billion dollars in aid, and additional conferences are scheduled. Money is starting to flow to the transitional authority through UN development programs, bilateral donors and the accessing of assets frozen during the Taliban regime. Importantly also, refugees and displaced persons by the hundreds of thousands are returning to their homes, and schools have reopened for millions of Afghan children.

---

3. Agreement on Provisional Arrangements in Afghanistan Pending the Re-Establishment of Permanent Government Institutions, Dec. 5, 2001, pmbl., *at* http://www.uno.de/frieden/afghanistan/talks/agreement.htm (Apr. 26, 2003).

To achieve these goals of political stability, economic development and effective reconstruction of Afghanistan's infrastructure, we must ensure that a broad based government at the working level—not just the cabinet level—is established. We must ensure that security forces are trained to respect and protect human rights. We must ensure that peaceful and cooperative relations are fostered between Afghanistan and its neighbors, especially Pakistan and Iran. We must ensure that major drug production and trafficking is eliminated.

Within the next two years, we must help Afghanistan move toward increased stability and prosperity; a stability and prosperity marked by a transitional authority beginning to provide important social services to its twenty-five million citizens. We must help Afghanistan develop into an emerging economy through agricultural development and small scale industry. We must facilitate the establishment of a national military and police force capable of assuming responsibility for internal security. And perhaps most importantly, we must be prepared to overcome the inevitable backlash which will result when this struggle proves to be long and hard. The road ahead in Afghanistan is surely a difficult one to traverse, but one that our country, working together with others, can do so with success.

XXVIII

Panel V
Commentary—The Road Ahead

Nicholas Rostow[1]

I will begin by saying a few words about the United Nations and terrorism before September 11, 2001, the impact of September 11th, and where the United Nations seems to be headed.[2] UN Member States have always had, at best, an ambivalent relationship with terrorism. Some delegates have preferred to see it as a social phenomenon, not as a criminal instrument for advancing a political or other agenda. Indeed, at a UN terrorism symposium in Vienna in 2002, over fifty delegates spoke, and almost all of them talked about terrorism as a social phenomenon; only one speaker addressed terrorism as a weapon. Part of the difficulty arises from the fact that wars of independence often involved acts of terrorism. It is difficult for participants in such struggles to admit

---

1. Nicholas Rostow is currently the General Counsel to the United States Mission to the United Nations. He held the Stockton Chair in International Law at the U.S. Naval War College in 2001, prior to September 11 and being called to the U.S. Mission to the United Nations. He has served in a number of senior Federal government positions, including Legal Adviser to the National Security Council, 1987–1993, and Staff Director of the Senate Select Committee on Intelligence, 1999–2000. The views expressed are his own and do not necessarily reflect the positions of the U.S. Government.
2. See my *Before and After: The Changed UN Response to Terrorism since September 11th*, 35 CORNELL INT'L L.J. 476 (2002) and Eric Rosand, *Security Council Resolution 1373, the Counter-Terrorism Committee, and the Fight against Terrorism*, 97 AM. J. INT'L L. 333 (2003).

to having used terrorist tactics. And, of course, in the debates about the Arab-Israeli conflict and the Pakistani-Indian conflict over Kashmir, Arabs and Pakistanis and others deprecate the use of the term "terrorist" to describe any acts undertaken against "foreign occupation."[3] In contrast, there is substantial evidence, including in the Arab-Israeli warfare since September 2000, that terrorism is a weapon. The evidence of terrorism's political effectiveness with many governments, inter-governmental institutions, and commentators has been accumulating for decades; as UN Secretary General Kofi Annan has said on many occasions, terrorism, although itself unjustifiable under any circumstances, does not invalidate legitimate grievances.[4]

Prior to September 11th, UN Member States addressed the issue of terrorism chiefly through the General Assembly and the Sixth (Legal) Committee in particular. The Sixth Committee and other UN bodies have provided the principal forum for negotiating the twelve conventions elaborating particular terrorist acts: handling of nuclear material,[5] hostage taking,[6] maritime navigation,[7] and the like.[8]

---

3. *See, e.g.,* Rostow, *supra* note 1, at 475 n. 4 (Pakistani and Syrian positions). Pakistan's UN Mission website states that "a comprehensive legal definition of terrorism should not only draw a clear distinction between terrorism and people's legitimate struggle for right of self-determination but must also take into account all forms of terrorism including state-sponsored terrorism." *Available at* http://www.un.int/pakistan/terrorism.html (last visited June 16, 2003). In addition, on June 4, 2002, Pakistan's UN Ambassador told a meeting of the Organization of the Islamic Conference (OIC) at the UN that, "After the events of 11 September 2001, India has sought to take undue advantage of the opportunity to portray the Kashmir liberation struggle as terrorism, and to delegitimize the struggle, disregarding the fact that the right of self-determination is a crucial principle of the UN Charter, as is also the people's right to defend themselves, including by armed resistance. This is true of liberation struggles everywhere including Palestine." *Available at* http://www.un.int/pakistan/20020604.html (last visited June 16, 2003).
4. *See* Statement of Secretary-General Kofi Annan to the 20 January Security Council ministerial meeting on terrorism, S/PV.4688 (2003), ("Just as terrorism must never be excused, so must genuine grievances never be ignored. True, it tarnishes a cause when a few wicked men commit murder in its name. But it does not make it any less urgent that the cause be addressed, the grievance heard and the wrong put right. Otherwise, we risk losing the contest for the hearts and minds of much of mankind.")
5. *See* Convention on the Physical Protection of Nuclear Material, 1929, 1456 U.N.T.S. 24631.
6. *See* International Convention Against the Taking of Hostages, Dec. 17, 1979, 1361 U.N.T.S. 206.
7. *See* Convention for the Suppression of Unlawful Acts against the Safety of Maritime Navigation, Mar. 10, 1988, S. Treaty Doc. No. 101-1 (1988), *reprinted in* 27 I.L.M. 672 (1988).
8. All the Conventions, including in addition some regional conventions, are reprinted in a UN publication, INTERNATIONAL INSTRUMENTS RELATED TO THE PREVENTION AND SUPPRESSION OF INTERNATIONAL TERRORISM (2001).

The United Nations first began to look seriously at terrorism after the massacre of the Israeli athletes at the 1972 Munich Olympics. On the initiative of the then–Secretary General, the General Assembly began attempting to negotiate a comprehensive convention on terrorism. The fact that, thirty years later, such a convention still does not exist highlights the fundamental problems the international community confronts in terms of reaching consensus on how to define terrorism and whether it is unacceptable in all circumstances. The Security Council did not begin dealing with terrorism until the end of the twentieth century. When Russia held the presidency of the Security Council in October 1999, the Russian UN delegation proposed Resolution 1269, a strong condemnation of terrorist attacks as threats to international peace and security.[9] At the same time, the General Assembly's Sixth Committee continued its work on outlawing specific terrorist acts such as terrorist bombings and the financing of terrorism.[10] The events of September 11th changed the Security Council's focus, making terrorism one of the Council's central concerns.

The Security Council's immediate response was the adoption of Resolution 1368, a severe condemnation of the attacks recognizing that such attacks give rise to the inherent right to use force in self-defense.[11] The Resolution does not include any language about the causes of terrorism. That was a sign that the attacks of September 11, 2001, had shaken everyone. Secondly, without much ado, the Resolution uses the word "terror" instead of the phrase "acts of terrorism." September 11 thus caused delegates to put to one side their usual use of the subject of terrorism in order to engage in political warfare over the Arab-Israeli and India-Pakistan conflicts. Then, on September 28, 2001, the Security Council adopted Resolution 1373.

Resolution 1373 is one of the most far reaching Security Council resolutions ever adopted. It calls on all member states to take the kind of action normally set forth in multilateral conventions. Indeed, a number of paragraphs dealing with the financing of terrorism mirror provisions of the Terrorist Financing Convention.[12] Without defining terrorism, the Resolution requires all

---

9. See S.C. Res. 1269, U.N. SCOR 54th Sess., U.N. Doc. S/1269 (1999).
10. See e.g. International Convention for the Suppression of Terrorism Bombings, G.A. Res. 165, U.N. GAOR, 52d Sess, U.N. Doc. A/52/164 (1998); International Convention for the Suppression of the Financing of Terrorism, G.A. Res. 109, U.N. GAOR 6th Comm., 54 Sess., 76th mtg., Agenda Item 160, U.N. Doc. A/54/109 (1999).
11. See S. C. Res. 1368, U.N. SCOR, 56th Sess., U.N. Doc. S/1368/(2001).
12. International Convention for the Suppression of the Financing of Terrorism, Dec. 9, 1999, 37 ILM 249 (1998).

states to cease active and passive assistance to terrorists, including by prohibiting the harboring of terrorists. States are to make criminal the transit of their territory by terrorists as well as financial transactions on behalf of terrorists. The Resolution requires States to freeze assets of terrorists and their collaborators. It calls on States to strengthen border controls, take measures to make the forging of identity documents more difficult than it is, and cooperate internationally against terrorism, including through sharing information. In addition, the Resolution notes with concern the connection between terrorism and other criminal activity such as narcotics trafficking.

Security Council Resolution 1373 established the Counter-Terrorism Committee (CTC) to monitor implementation. Membership is the whole Security Council. The Committee named itself and established its own procedures for carrying out its mandate. It also has developed relations with the UN membership that have been path-breaking in Security Council terms. Both the first Chairman, the British Permanent Representative, and his successor, the Spanish Permanent Representative, have reported at least once a month to all Member State delegations on the activities of the CTC. This practice of transparency has enhanced Member States' understanding and acceptance of the CTC.[13] One result is that the CTC has received more than 300 self-evaluations by Member States of their implementation of Resolution 1373. The CTC responds to each such report, continuing an open-ended dialogue with Member States that has made the CTC the center of world-wide efforts to build counter-terrorist capacity. As part of its work, the CTC has forged relations with international, regional, and sub-regional organizations, encouraging them to establish counter-terrorist priorities for their members and to assist their members in improving their counter-terrorist capabilities. The work focuses on infrastructure, rather than operations, but it is infrastructure that permits successful counter-terrorism operations.

The CTC, like other Security Council committees, operates by consensus. Each member therefore has a veto. As a result, the CTC has not yet been able to overcome the political differences about terrorism, including how to define terrorism, among its members. Nevertheless, the Committee has progressed from engaging in a paper dialogue with UN Members to consideration of site visits to determine if States are doing what they claim. And, in the

---

13. A refrain at the United Nations is the complaint that the Security Council does not act with "transparency." The CTC has avoided this criticism through the device of frequent Chairman's briefings. The CTC thus has created a model other committees and, indeed, the Security Council itself may follow.

future, the CTC may conclude that it has to refer recalcitrant Members to the Security Council.

Terrorist sanctions constitute another prong of the Security Council's attack on terrorism. The original sanctions regime on terrorism in Afghanistan was established in Resolution 1267.[14] This resolution was aimed at that part of Afghanistan under the control of the Taliban, Osama bin Laden and al Qaeda and demanded that bin Laden be turned over to "appropriate authorities." After the collapse of the Taliban regime, the Security Council removed the territorial focus from the Resolution.[15] This change also constituted a Security Council innovation. Hitherto, the Council had adopted sanctions as a means to influencing a government. Resolution 1390 (2002) and its successor Resolution 1455 (2003) target Taliban and al Qaeda personnel in whatever form they may take in whatever location they may be. Members provide the Security Council Committee charged with monitoring terrorist sanctions—the 1267 Committee—with names of persons and entities identified as engaged in terrorism or terrorism-related activities to be adopted so that the entire international community can take action against them. While this system raises some procedural and due process concerns, it has resulted in worldwide action against al Qaeda members and collaborators.[16]

The attacks of September 11, 2001, have had a transforming effect. Americans see the world differently as a result. Other countries have been slower to change their perceptions; some have yet to do so. The United Nations, as an organization and as a collectivity of independent States, has changed its habits. Some of the changes have enhanced the international community's capacity to combat terrorism, and some have enhanced the international community's ability to undertake anti-terrorist operations. All have increased the role of the United Nations in counter-terrorism, including in relation to other international organizations. All also have increased in UN institutional expertise on terrorism. These actions are not the solution to the terrorism crisis; they are important and useful steps in the international struggle to combat terrorism.

---

14. *See* S. C. Res. 1267, U.N. SCOR, 54th Sess., U.N. Doc. S/1267/(1999).
15. *See* S. C. Res. 1390, U.N. SCOR, 57th Sess., U.N. Doc. S/1390/(2002).
16. *See* the discussion of these issues in the Proceedings of the American Society of International Law annual meeting, April 3, 2003, panel entitled "An Imperial Security Council? Implementing Security Council Resolutions 1373 and 1390."

XXIX

Panel V
Commentary—The Road Ahead

Michael Saalfeld[1]

Our discussions have revealed again the extent to which this situation has confronted us with complex new questions and challenges from an international legal perspective. We must respond to them with joint efforts, with determination and solidarity but in doing so we must keep our heads.

The answers we are looking for in the legal field will be decisive for the future guidelines on countering international terrorism. And we should be well aware of the fact that the shape of these guidelines will be decisive for the effectiveness and stability of the long-term cooperation between the states forming the international coalition against terrorism.

The NATO Alliance as a consequence of the attacks of September 11th considered the attacks to be an act covered by Article 5 of the North Atlantic

---

1. Michael Saalfeld is the Director of International Legal Affairs for the Federal Ministry of Defense in Germany.

Treaty, which states that an armed attack on one or more of the Allies in Europe or North America shall be considered an attack against them all.[2] On that basis the European NATO Allies are providing substantial military contributions to combating terrorism.

Germany, for instance, has a third of its naval assets operating in the Gulf of Aden area in support of Operation ENDURING FREEDOM. In Afghanistan, German special operations forces are employed alongside US forces, fulfilling Germany's obligations under Security Council Resolution 1373 which requires that all states "take the necessary steps to prevent the commission of terrorist acts . . . (and to) ensure that any person who participates in the financing, planning, preparation and perpetration of terrorist acts or in supporting terrorist acts is brought to justice. . . ."[3]

The requirement for close cooperation among nations in fulfilling this political mandate, often with military means, calls for some creativity and innovative thinking in the legal arena as well. There seems to be consensus on at least one point, the longer the war on terrorism lasts, the more importance the aspect of acceptance of the use of these means will gain. In Europe recently, the discussion has been characterized by the aim to harmonize as far as possible the military need to prevent further terrorist acts with the legal need to preserve the standards of human rights and humanitarian law which have been well established over the last 50 years.

Regarding Operation ENDURING FREEDOM, there seems to be a clear understanding between all coalition partners that the inherent right of collective and individual self-defense as embodied in Article 51 of the UN Charter provides the authorization to take all necessary measures to accomplish the tasks set out in Security Council Resolutions 1368 and 1373. Accordingly, there is no doubt that military forces in the areas of operation are entitled to target persons suspected of perpetrating or supporting acts of international terrorism. Similarly, there is no doubt that military forces have the authority to seize and detain such personnel in order to bring them before the courts. On the

---

2. *See* North Atlantic Treaty, 4 April 1949, 34 U.N.T.S. 243, art. 5, *available at* http://www.nato.int/docu/basictxt/treaty.htm (Oct. 29, 2002), which provides:

> The Parties agree that an armed attack against one or more of them in Europe or North America shall be considered an attack against them all and consequently they agree that, if such an armed attack occurs, each of them, in exercise of the right of individual or collective self-defence recognised by Article 51 of the U.N. Charter, will assist the Party or Parties so attacked by taking forthwith, individually and in concert with the other Parties, such action as it deems necessary, including the use of armed force, to restore and maintain the security of the North Atlantic area.

3. *See* S. C. Res 1373, U.N. SCOR 56th Sess., U.N. Doc. S/1373/(2001).

other hand it is also clear from these two resolutions that self-defense is legitimate only when performed in accordance with the Charter, which tries to balance the protection of human rights against the aim of maintaining international peace and security. The crucial question then becomes, what does the Charter require?

The fight against international terrorism has to be fought on multiple fronts with multiple means. Three questions have been debated in Europe regarding the post September 11th behavior of nations. These questions are:

1. To what extent does humanitarian law, applicable in armed conflict, apply to detainees in the "War on Terrorism"?

2. To what extent does common human rights law apply?

3. What effect does the prohibition on the death penalty found in the European Convention on Human Rights have on US-European military cooperation within the coalition for Operation ENDURING FREEDOM (OEF)?[4]

I will discuss each of these questions briefly.

Regarding the first question, the UN High Commissioner for Human Rights, Mary Robinson, in her speech at the Commonwealth Institute in London on 6 June of this year stated:

> There has been a tendency to ride roughshod over—or at least to set aside—established principles of international human rights and humanitarian law. There has been confusion about what is and what is not subject to the Geneva Conventions of 1949. There have been suggestions that the terrorist acts of 11 September and their aftermath in the conflict in Afghanistan demonstrated that the Geneva Conventions were out of date.

In that context the President of the ICRC, Jakob Kellenberger, has given an answer which appears as simple as it is to the point:

> International humanitarian law is, quite distinctly, the body of rules that regulates the protection of persons and conduct of hostilities during an armed conflict. . . . Inasmuch as the fight against terrorism takes the form of armed conflict, the position is uncontroversial: international humanitarian law is applicable. Factually, if there exists an armed conflict, whatever the causes,

---

4. *See* Sixth Protocol to the Convention for the Protection of Human Rights and Fundamental Freedoms Concerning the Abolition of the Death Penalty, art. 1, Apr. 28, 1983, Europ. T.S. No. 114, 32, *available at* http://ccbh.ba/en/econv/protocol6.asp (Oct. 29, 2002).

whatever the aim, whatever the name, it is regulated by international humanitarian law.[5]

While there is an ongoing international discussion as to whether the fighting in Afghanistan was or is an armed conflict, in my view there are good reasons for believing that an international armed conflict exists between the United States and its allies on the one hand and the Taliban as the de facto government of Afghanistan on the other. This view also seems to be shared by a number of US legal experts.[6] If this is the case, the law of armed conflict started to apply no later than October 7, 2001, the day Operation ENDURING FREEDOM commenced.

Given that the law of armed conflict applied then in October 2001, Article 4 of the Third Geneva Convention would require that Taliban and Al Qaeda personnel integrated into the Taliban fighter force be treated as Prisoners of War (POWs). As POWs, these personnel could not be punished for the mere participation in hostilities in Afghanistan as they were privileged combatants. These individuals could, however, be held liable for violations of the law of armed conflict and for crimes unrelated to the hostilities. For these crimes, they would, of course, be subject to prosecution. This view seems to be shared throughout the European Union. By way of example, none other than Javier Solano, the European Union Foreign Policy Chief, called for the recognition by the United States of the right of the detainees held in Guantanamo Bay to be treated as prisoners of war. Mr. Solano further argued Article 5 tribunals should be held for those personnel whose status is uncertain.[7]

What does that mean for international cooperation in meeting the aims set by Security Council Resolution 1373, especially that of bringing terrorists to justice? Article 12 of the Third Geneva Convention stipulates that POWs may only be transferred to a power that is a party to the Convention and only after the detaining power has satisfied itself of the willingness and ability of the transferee power to apply the Convention.[8] If it is agreed that the Geneva

---

5. Jakob Kellenberger, Address at the 26th Round Table in San Remo on Current Problems in International Humanitarian Law, "The two Additional Protocols to the Geneva Conventions: 25 years later – challenges and prospects." (Sep. 5, 2002), *available at* http://www.icrc.org/Web/eng/siteeng0.nsf/iwpList99/EFC5A1C8D8DD70B9C1256C36002EFC1E (Oct. 30, 2002).
6. *See, e.g.,* Curtis Bradley & Jack Goldsmith, *The Constitutional Validity of Military Commissions,* 5 GREEN BAG 2d 249, 256 (2002); Robert Goldman, *Certain Legal Questions and Issues Raised by the September 11th Attacks,* 9 HUM. RTS. BR. 2 (2001).
7. *See* David Lee, *Al Qaeda Britons have no Complaints,* THE SCOTSMAN, Jan. 22, 2002.
8. *See* Geneva Convention Relative to the Treatment of Prisoners of War, *opened for signature* Aug. 12, 1949, 6 U.S.T. 3316, 75 U.N.T.S. 134, Art. 12 (1949).

Conventions apply to those personnel currently held in Guantanamo Bay, then Article 12 must be adhered to in the event of exchanges of detainees between coalition partners.

Certainly, however, not every person captured in Operation ENDURING FREEDOM is entitled to POW status. There might be al Qaeda members who have never participated in the fighting in Afghanistan but who have taken part in the preparation or perpetration of terrorist acts someplace else in the world. Those criminals cannot be POWs but should be granted the minimum standards of human rights which are non-abrogable for each person detained by a state authority. These non-abrogable minimum standards are quite similar both according to common human rights law and international humanitarian law of armed conflict. Protocol I to the Geneva Conventions provides a set of minimum standards in Article 75 for all persons in the power of a party to a conflict who do not benefit from more favorable treatment under the Geneva Conventions or Protocol I.[9] Under the assumption that Article 75 of Protocol I codifies—more or less—customary law, this article could form the set of minimum rights to which each suspect is entitled. Accordingly, those detainees who are not entitled to POW recognition and protection, should be treated at a minimum in compliance with Article 75 of Protocol I.

Finally, I would like to address the European prohibition on the death penalty as established in the 6th Protocol to the European Convention on Human Rights.[10] With its Resolution 1271 (2002), "Combating Terrorism and Respect for Human Rights," on January 24, 2002, the Parliamentary Assembly of the Council of Europe called upon all Council member states "to refuse to extradite suspected terrorists to countries that continue to apply the death sentence . . . unless assurances are given that the death penalty will not be sought." Similarly, section 8 of the German International Legal Assistance Act stipulates that the extradition of a person to a requesting state whose laws provide for the death penalty for the criminal offense committed is only acceptable if the requesting state guarantees that the death penalty will either not be imposed or enforced.

Clearly, significant differences exist among "War on Terrorism" coalition members with respect to the death penalty. Moreover, with the recent ratification of the Rome Statute and the subsequent creation of the International

---

9. *See* Protocol Additional to the Geneva Conventions of 12 August 1949, and Relating to the Protection of Victims of International Armed Conflicts (Protocol I), *adopted* June 8, 1977, 1125 U.N.T.S. 3, 40-41. Article 75 identifies certain acts that are prohibited regardless of the status of a conflict. Such prohibitions include murder, the taking of hostages, and torture, among others.
10. *Supra* note 3.

Criminal Court on 1 July 2002, different obligations with respect to rights standards may seriously affect the ability of coalition members to cooperate militarily in the "War on Terrorism." This is particularly the case where personnel of a state bound by the Rome Statute are required to work with personnel of a state not a party to the Rome Statute, for these personnel will have less far-reaching human rights obligations than those personnel from the ratifying state.

Panel V
Commentary—The Road Ahead

Ronald Winfrey[1]

Jim Terry spoke about pursuing regional cooperation in the fight against terrorism, about the effective exchange of information, about intelligence gathering and sharing. I too shall touch on a few of those points momentarily, as well as a new framework within the structure of the US Pacific Command that is being used to promote such cooperation.

There is quite clearly, a pervasive global threat when you talk about addressing international terrorism. As the twenty-first century progresses, it is marked by increased interdependence and an increasingly multilateral response to these threats. Interagency coordination is currently a buzzword within the US Government but this term is somewhat lacking as it misses a vital part of what is necessary in this global war on terrorism. Interagency coordination is simply part of the solution. It must be coupled with intergovernment coordination on a scale never seen before. With this must come cooperative efforts with nongovernmental organizations as well.

A framework that I would suggest as a potential starting point for promoting regional cooperation on terrorism is that used by the Pacific Command's

---

1. Ronald Winfrey currently serves as Attorney-Advisor for International Law and Homeland Defense and as the foreign engagement coordinator for the Office of the Staff Judge Advocate, US Pacific Command.

joint interagency coordination group for counter-terrorism. This particular organization was formed at Pacific Command in Honolulu immediately after the events of September 11th. It was formed in Pacific Command's Operations Directorate and it is a permanent part of that organization.

Generally, we know that terrorists have and will continue to exploit legal seams between nations, such as nations where passports are easily obtained, as well as the inherent seams between law enforcement agencies and immigration agencies. Indeed as we now know, the perpetrators of the September 11th attacks were using legally obtained US visas. Acknowledging that some of these seams may never be closed, there is still much that can be done. As with many other aspects of this War on Terrorism, the effort to close the seams will not be the domain of any single agency, department or ministry. Accordingly, new forms of governmental and international cooperation are required.

The new counter-terrorism group at Pacific Command is designed to emphasize capabilities. While coordination is imperative, it is not the means to defeat terrorism—improved capabilities are. Actionable intelligence is pivotal and a collaborative interagency team is the optimum tool to obtain such intelligence. Once this intelligence is obtained, interagency options include theater security cooperation with allies in the Pacific, information operations, public affairs or public diplomacy initiatives, and finally, military options. The point to leave you with on this is that as terrorist cells become more adaptable and flexible, so too must governments in their methods of responding. The starting point is great intelligence collection and analysis followed by coordination across multiple agencies, multiple governments, and nongovernmental organizations.

Still another area highlighted by the events of September 11th is the difficulty in synchronizing a response plan that not only cuts across multiple agencies but multiple time zones and countries. There was a real need after 9/11 to ensure security not only in the immediate area of Hawaii but also across our area of responsibility including Japan, Korea, Alaska and Guam. To facilitate this, the Pacific Command uses a Joint Rear Area Coordinator (JRAC) organization. The Joint Rear Coordinator Organization is the central hub for antiterrorism efforts in the Pacific Command regarding homeland defense. This organization coordinates the contributions of approximately thirty thousand law enforcement officials (local, state, and federal first responders) to a terrorist incident. These officials include fire fighters, paramedics, civil defense officials, public utility officials, and others. This organization provides the framework for coordinated information sharing and planning to protect not only Department of Defense installations but also critical civilian infrastructure within our area. With homeland defense preparations have come a number of very unique legal issues dealing with the use of Department of Defense personnel in response to terrorist attacks—that arena being the primary area of responsibility of civilian law enforcement agencies such as the FBI and others. Here Pacific Command must be careful not to run afoul of the Posse Comitatus Act which, as you know, limits the ability of the Department of Defense to undertake certain actions in the United States.[2]

Jim Terry also spoke of a phased approach to regional cooperation. In the Pacific Command, we use and believe in this phased approach, much like any developmental process. Initially, we might begin furthering cooperation with a certain country through workshops, seminars, and war games. Thereafter, we might build practical modules into existing exercises—such as our annual Cobra Gold exercise. Finally, we might transition to a Team Challenge series of exercises.

In closing, the scope of cooperation in the current war on terrorism, as you know, is truly remarkable worldwide. Many of the security challenges we face not only in the Pacific but throughout the world will require new partnerships, relationships and agreements to begin our effective coordination. There is a lot more to be done but I believe that our initial efforts have proven fruitful and we are moving in the right direction.

---

2. 18 U.S.C. § 1385 (2003).

XXXI

Panel V
Commentary—The Road Ahead

Jane Dalton[1]

I believe that September 11th proved beyond any reasonable doubt that international treaties and other negotiated documents are not sufficient, by themselves, to win the War on Terrorism. I was in the Pentagon when the attack came and there is no doubt in my mind that the Pentagon and the United States were attacked with weapons of mass effects. Some 3,200 people from more than 90 countries throughout the world died on that day.[2] This was an attack on democracy, on liberty and on religious freedom. This was not the first armed attack by these terrorists on these core American values either. This was one of a continuing series of attacks, beginning in 1993, if not before, with the first World Trade Center bombing. These armed attacks included the 1998 embassy attacks in Kenya and Tanzania and continued with the tragic attack on USS *Cole* in 2000.

For me then, it is interesting to consider the concept of preemption or anticipatory self-defense while in the middle of an armed conflict as these two concepts do not seem well juxtaposed at times. In World War II and the Gulf

---

1. Navy Captain Jane Dalton is currently the Legal Advisor to the Chairman of the Joint Chiefs of Staff.
2. *See Fact Sheet: September 11th, 2001 Basic Facts*, Department of State (Aug. 25, 2002), *available at* http://www.state.gov/coalition/cr/fs/12701.htm (Oct. 30, 2002).

War, enemy forces were declared hostile. No hostile intent was necessary before striking enemy forces. Being engaged in armed conflict, the United States appropriately took the fight to the enemy, not waiting for the enemy to come to us, nor waiting for some indication of hostile intent or hostile act. Looking at the series of events occurring since 1993, it is clear that the United States is currently involved in an armed conflict, an ongoing conflict where preemptive or anticipatory self-defense is not an issue.

If one were to ask leaders of al Qaeda this instant, whether or not they were involved in an armed conflict with the United States, they would assuredly answer yes. Their actions have made this clear as have their words. I believe that they are at this very moment planning more attacks on the Unites States for the very next possible instant that they can accomplish these attacks.

I concur with John Murphy that imminence takes on a new meaning when you are talking about weapons of mass destruction. Perhaps the new paradigm regarding such imminence or immediacy is not that used in World War II or in Iraq when forces were massing on borders or scud missiles were flying. Perhaps instead the new paradigm must consider that at the next possible opportunity the United States will have to act decisively to prevent an attack on the United States. The intelligence indicators found in past conflicts do not apply in this one; we will not see armored units massing on an opposing border. What may be found, however, is the constituent components necessary to build weapons of mass destruction (WMD) being transferred from a country to a terrorist group. The indicators of the future may be the assembly of components and the conducting of tests. This point in time may now be the United States last possible opportunity to prevent an attack. For if the threat is not eliminated then, it may be impossible to eliminate it later. This, to me, is the new concept of imminence that scholars and practitioners must understand.

One reason the UN condemned the Israel attack on the Osiraq reactor was because the threat caused by the reactor, providing enriched uranium for Iraqi nuclear weapons development, was foreseeable but not imminent.[2] Today the situation may well be reversed. That is, we know that an attack is imminent, but it is difficult to foresee exactly where or when the attack will occur. Given this case, the United States must strike now while it has the enemy and their weapons in its sites and it is within US capabilities to strike. Delaying such a strike may cause the opportunity to evaporate forever.

---

2. *See* G.A. Res. 36/27 (Nov. 13, 1981), *available at* http://www.un.org/Depts/dhl/res/resa36.htm (Oct. 30, 2002). *See generally*, Mallison & Mallison, *The Israeli Aerial Attack of June 7, 1981, Upon the Iraqi Nuclear Reactor: Aggression or Self-Defense?*, 15 VAND J. TRANSNAT'L L. 417 (1982).

I agree with the idea that there are self-defense criteria that should be studied before acts in self-defense are undertaken. These four criteria are: do objective indicators that an attack is imminent exist; does past conduct or hostile declarations reasonably lead to the conclusion that an attack is probable; do the nature of the weapons available support a likely attack; and are there no other practicable means than the use of force to mitigate/eliminate the threat. Regarding objective intelligence indicators, although I cannot reveal classified intelligence here, I believe that there are substantial objective indicators that an attack is imminent. On the second criterion, the past conduct of al Qaeda from 1993 to the present coupled with present declarations are nothing short of hostile and indicate that other attacks are planned. As to the third criterion, al Qaeda has proven its ability to be extremely flexible and agile, making civilian airliners as well as simple pleasure boats into weapons. Finally, are there other options short of using force to mitigate/eliminate the threat—there do not seem to be such options available. When people are willing to martyr themselves, there is very little deterrence that you can use. When terrorists belong to no territory, when they have no population which they are trying to protect, when their goal is to destroy innocent civilians, then the concept of deterrence becomes an entirely new challenge. Traditional deterrence as we know it does not seem to apply to such zealots.

Yoram Dinstein's position on interceptive self-defense also intrigues me.[3] This notion of an irreversible course of action commencing might merit further study. I am uncertain as to what metrics we might develop for measuring what is truly an irreversible course of action other than by studying exactly the things that we have previously discussed, the history of a group, its stated intent, the weapons available, alternative courses of action, etc. Clearly, even using interceptive self-defense, actions of the United States would still be bound by proportionality and discrimination.

Recall also that the use of military force is only one of the many instruments of national power at our disposal. We must continue to use all available sources to achieve our objectives. The conventions that John Murphy spoke of, as well as diplomacy, economic and other sanctions, law enforcement, are all available instruments of power. These instruments of power should be used relentlessly, on all fronts, as appropriate. The joint rear area coordination

---

3. Professor Dinstein argues that "[i]nterceptive, unlike anticipatory, self-defense takes place after the other side has committed itself to an armed attack in an ostensibly irrevocable way. Whereas a preventive strike anticipates an armed attack, an interceptive strike counters an armed attack which is 'imminent' and practically 'unavoidable.'" See YORAM DINSTEIN, WAR, AGGRESSION AND SELF-DEFENSE (3d ed. 2001) 172–173.

Panel V Commentary—The Road Ahead

group that Ron Winfrey spoke about in the Pacific Command area of operations also exists in the Southern Command, European Command and the Central Command. These different exercises of US instruments of power are all absolutely critical. Having said this, the United States should not hesitate to use military force to accomplish "involuntary disarmament" of its enemies when necessary.

As Ron Winfrey indicated, the greatest current need is for actionable intelligence. The United States must improve its ability to conduct intelligence gathering, surveillance, and reconnaissance. We are working towards this. As an example, Germany has been an exceptional ally in support of our intelligence gathering efforts to support our maritime interdiction operations in the Central and European Commands' areas of responsibility. Similarly, the Philippine Armed Forces have increased dramatically both their intelligence gathering and counter-terrorism forces in the last 12 months.

Still another point to be made though is that an increase in US capabilities is not, by itself, enough. Other states must also step to the forefront and take action. The United States is available to assist such states as Yemen and Georgia, but we cannot do it for them. The United States should not be required to be the world's protector. Other states must also accept responsibility for their own safety. The United States will certainly be willing and able to continue to advise and assist in this respect as we are doing in the Philippines and Georgia and Yemen.

Similarly, if we wish to expand regional cooperation, we must expand the funding available for such cooperation. As you well know, the Department of Defense is constrained in its ability to conduct security assistance missions since it receives no direct funding for such missions. Instead, the Department of State, as the Security Assistance Program Manager, receives funding for security assistance and then determines how this funding will be spent. If we wish to improve our coordination and cooperation with our allies, we must pursue alternative and additional funding to increase our ability to train alongside and conduct exercises with our allies. A significant challenge to accomplishing these missions is the restriction on expenditure of funds that constrains the Department of Defense.

Finally, the coming years offer many challenges as we deconflict jurisdiction in the homeland defense arena. The United States has significant challenges facing it that must be overcome so as to ensure that the Department of Defense, the Federal Bureau of Investigation, the Central Intelligence Agency, the Coast Guard, the Bureau of Alcohol, Tobacco, and Firearms, the Secret Service and other agencies understand who has primary control over what specific types of operations and in response to what specific threats occurring in the homeland of the United States.

XXXII

Panel V
Discussion—The Road Ahead

On Iraq

Yoram Dinstein

The road ahead must surely go through Iraq, given recent statements issued by the administration in Washington and—even more significantly—Saddam Hussein's continued breaches of Iraq's undertakings under the cease-fire agreement of 1991. At the present moment, however, this is not a question of self-defense. Self-defense as an issue vis-à-vis Iraq arose—and was resolved—on 2 August 1990, when Iraq invaded Kuwait. At that point in time, the Security Council determined—in a binding resolution—that Iraq had committed a breach of the peace.[1] Ultimately, the Security Council did not directly impose military sanctions on Iraq, in accordance with Article 42 of the UN Charter, because the Security Council (which has no standing army) cannot activate Article 42 unless and until special agreements are included with states, as per Article 43. What the Security Council did instead was give its blessing to the use of force, in the exercise of collective self-defense (pursuant to Article 51 of the Charter), by an Amercian-led coalition of states who came to the aid of Kuwait.[2] Legally speaking, the coalition invoking the collective right to self-defense could have acted on its own, without the blessing of the Security

---

1. S. C. Res. 660, U.N. SCOR, 45th Sess., U.N. Doc S./660/(1990).
2. *Id.*; S. C. Res. 678 para. 2 authorized, in relevant part all "Member States co-operating with the Government of Kuwait... to use all necessary means to restore international peace and security in the area." U.N. SCOR, 45th Sess., U.N. Doc. S/678/(1990).

Council (which is not envisaged as necessary by Article 51). However, from a practical-political standpoint, the blessing of the Security Council proved beneficent both domestically (in the United States) and internationally (in cementing the unusual coalition which emerged).

From a jus ad bellum viewpoint, the respective positions of Iraq (as the aggressor) and the coalition (fighting in collective self-defense) was fixed for the duration of the war on 2 August 1990. Contrary to what many laymen and even lawyers believe, that war has not yet come to an end. Hostilities were suspended in 1991 following a cease-fire concluded with the consent of all the parties, based on Security Council Resolution 687.[3] The cease-fire has since been punctuated by thousands of acts of hostilities, the latest of which occurred only last week (when Amercian and British warplanes attacked Iraqi radar stations which tried to lock on to coalition aviation). There have been other, and more serious, rounds of hostilities in 1998 and 1999.

By dint of Iraq's continued violations of the 1991 cease-fire—especially, albeit not exclusively, insofar as the disarmament of weapons of mass destruction is concerned—if the United States opts to resume hostilities against Iraq tomorrow or the day after, it would not need a Security Council resolution. The fact that Iraq has systematically violated the cease-fire terms is indisputable, and it suffices to justify unilateral forcible action by the United States against Iraq. Should anyone wish to stop the United States, let him go to the Security Council and seek such a resolution (which would certainly be vetoed by the United States). Forcible action against Iraq at the present juncture does not commence a new armed conflict. It represents, purely and simply, a continuation of the ongoing armed conlict that began when Iraq invaded Kuwait on 2 August 1990. Therefore, the question of the imminence of any threat posed by Iraq today is irrelevant. All that need be said is that Iraq is in clear material breach of the cease-fire agreement. Under Article 60 of the 1969 Vienna Convention on the Law of Treaties, a material breach of any treaty (including a cease-fire agreement) justifies termination of the treaty by the aggrieved party.[4]

John Murphy

Yoram Dinstein in his inimitable fashion has set forth a marvelous advocate's brief for further military action against Iraq. However, I do not quite see it as

---

3. S. C. Res. 687, U.N. SCOR, 46th Sess., U.N. Doc. S/687/(1991).
4. Vienna Convention on the Laws of Treaties, art. 30, 1155 U.N.T.S. 331, 8 I.L.M. 679 (entered into force Jan. 27, 1980).

iron tight. There are other positions to be considered, particularly since this is a very complex question. Clearly, the Security Council authorized the use of individual and collective self-defense in its Resolution 678.[5] It is also clear that this right existed in any event under the terms of Article 51 of the UN Charter. However, this right to self-defense was to drive Iraq out of Kuwait, not necessarily to re-engage Iraq more than a decade after the ceasefire was signed.

Security Council Resolution 687 recognizes the restoration of the territorial integrity of Kuwait and imposes a number of significant obligations upon Iraq. These obligations include everything from desisting from the practice of terrorism, the involuntary disarmament of weapons of mass destruction, and the accompanying inspectors to prove this disarmament.[6] Clearly, Saddam Hussein and his regime supporting thugs have violated this resolution. The key question though is who gets to decide what happens about these violations? Who decides whether the cease-fire has been broken? Who decides, if there has been a material breach, whether this breach is justification for the continuing use of force? It strikes me that such a decision is properly taken before the same organization that authorized the initial use of force, the Security Council. Accepting Yoram Dinstein's argument that no additional authority is needed from the Security Council to re-engage Iraq stretches the very nature of the previous resolutions. I believe there is language in these resolutions to the contrary and I also believe that there is negotiating history to the contrary. Yoram Dinstein's case is a nice work of advocacy. But there is at least as strong an argument on the other side of his position.

James Terry
President George Herbert Walker Bush was very clear in his view that Resolution 678 provided the authority to do very specific things. This essentially was to remove Iraqi forces from Kuwait and restore the territorial integrity of Kuwait, nothing more. To take the position now that Resolution 687, which interprets the original authority of Resolution 678, would allow the United States to do such things as Yoram Dinstein suggests must be studied very carefully. Pragmatic action must prevail as we consider the world community, the other permanent members of the Security Council, and our friends and allies. It would be dangerous, in my view, to act on the position advocated by Yoram Dinstein.

---

5. S. C. Res 678, *supra* note 2.
6. S. C. Res. 687, *supra* note 4.

On Terrorism

Chris Greenwood

It is very important to recognize that terrorism is a habit and that one of the most serious of the many moral and practical arguments against terrorism is that it becomes rapidly endemic and has done so in many parts of the world in the course of the twentieth century. Because the major problem of terrorism is that it is endemic, it is important not to have illusions that the complete elimination of terrorism can be achieved in any short measure of time for as soon as one proclaims terrorism has been eliminated, every subsequent terrorist bomb becomes a victory for the terrorists and a defeat for those claiming elimination. Accordingly, there is a need in pursing this campaign against terrorism to keep the rhetoric careful and limited and not to raise false expectations.

Secondly, there is a need for humility and caution in the matter of military operations in response to terrorist acts. Sometimes they may be extremely effective as they have been so far in Afghanistan. In other cases, they may not be. It is sobering to remember that World War I began as an Austrian attempt to wipe out what Vienna perceived as the hornet's nest of terrorists in Serbia. The most difficult issue in dealing with terrorism is not the legal basis for action but the prudential judgment as to whether a particular course of action is wise and will be supported by the international community. This must be a continuing criterion, discussed and analyzed, before action is taken. A large part of this battle as has been reflected by numerous conference participants, is for that of ideas. For in many respects, this is a battle to de-legitimize terrorism and to gain international support, recognizing that gaining such support on the international stage often requires a large number of compromises.

Finally, it is important to study how terrorist campaigns end. Sometimes they run out of steam, sometimes because of the very extreme character of their actions—and this may well be true ultimately of al Qaeda—they become discredited. Sometimes as we all know, compromises, political compromises of various kinds are reached with terrorist groups. We must remember that some terrorists sometimes do act in the name of a larger public cause. Such public causes may have serious elements of legitimacy that must be considered even if the means by which they are pursued cannot be defended. Often, very difficult decisions have to be made as we see that have occurred in Israel regarding Palestine. In other words, there is no substitute in the whole of the campaign against terrorism for the continuous exercise of historically informed political judgment.

Nick Rostow

The United States has long based its national security policy on the validity of anticipatory self-defense. Perhaps not articulated quite as sharply as President George Walker Bush articulated it but anticipatory self-defense nonetheless. I do not believe that President Bush changed much in his policy from the US historical approach to protecting itself and its citizens.

APPENDIX A

Contributors

Contributors

Commander Neil Brown, United Kingdom Royal Navy, is currently assigned to the UK Joint Force Headquarters and deployed as Legal Adviser to the UK National Contingent Commander for Operation TELIC. In this position, he provides legal advice on all aspects of the UK contribution to Operation Iraqi Freedom. Previously, CDR Brown has served aboard HM Ship's ROTHESAY, LIVERPOOL, YORK, and ILLUSTRIOUS. He has been the Assistant to the Chief Naval Judge Advocate; Legal Adviser to the Flag Officer Surface Flotilla; and most recently, Legal Adviser to Commander in Chief Fleet (augmenting the staff of the UK Permanent Joint Headquarters during Operation ORACLE (UK contribution to Operation Enduring Freedom). CDR Brown has multiple deployments including to the Persian Gulf, Barents Sea, South China Seas, Sierra Leone, and in support of counter-drug operations.

Wing Commander Paul Cronan, Royal Australian Air Force. Wing Group Commander Cronan was commissioned in the Royal Australian Air Force as a Flight Lieutenant Legal Officer in 1985 and is currently serving as the Chief Legal Advisor for Headquarters Australian Theatre. In this capacity, he is responsible for providing advice to the Commander and Staff of the Australian Theatre on all legal aspects of the planning and conduct of theatre campaigns and operations. Previously, he has held various legal positions at the Defence Legal Office in Canberra and Headquarters Air Command, with the US Air Force Judge Advocate General's Department in Washington D.C., with the Directorate of Air Force Legal Services in Canberra and in RMA Butterworth, Malaysia.

Captain Jane Dalton, JAGC, US Navy is currently the Legal Counsel to the Chairman of the Joint Chiefs of Staff. She provides legal advice to the senior military official responsible for advising the President on military operations. Other career highlights include Commander, Naval Legal Service Office North Central, Washington D.C. (1998-2000); Deputy Legal Counsel to the Chairman of the Joint Chiefs of Staff, Washington D.C. (1996-98); Staff Judge Advocate, Third Fleet, San Diego, CA (1994–96); and Oceans

Law & Policy Specialist, Strategic Plans & Policy Directorate, Joint Staff, Washington, D.C. (1992–94). Before attending law school at Georgetown University Law Center, Captain Dalton was a Surface Warfare Officer in the US Navy.

Captain William H. Dalton, JAGC, US Navy (Ret.) is currently assigned to the Department of Defense Office of General Counsel as Associate Deputy General Counsel (Intelligence). From 1965 to 1995, he served as a judge advocate in the US Navy. His assignments included service as the Executive Officer, Naval Legal Service Officer, Pearl Harbor, Hawaii; the Deputy Assistant Judge Advocate General, Department of the Navy; the Staff Judge Advocate, US Pacific Command in Hawaii; and as the Inspector General, Naval Sea Systems Command, Washington, D.C. Captain Dalton also served on the faculty of the US Naval War College as the first Deputy Director, Oceans Law and Policy Department.

Professor Yoram Dinstein is currently the Charles H. Stockton Professor of International Law as the US Naval War College, an appointment he also filled from 1999–2000. Previously, he served as a Humboldt Fellow at the Max Planck Institute of Foreign, Comparative and International Law in Heidelberg, Germany (2000–01) and as Professor of International Law, Yanowicz Professor of Human Rights, President (1991–98), Rector (1980–85) and Dean of the Faculty of Law (1978–80) at Tel Aviv University. Professor Dinstein started his career in Israel's Foreign Service and served as Consul of Israel in New York and a member of Israel's Permanent Mission to the United Nations (1966–70). Professor Dinstein was among a group of international lawyers and naval experts who produced the San Remo Manual on International Law Applicable to Armed Conflicts at Sea. He is a member of the Institute of International Law and the Council of the International Institute of Humanitarian Law in San Remo. Professor Dinstein is the editor of the Israel Yearbook of Human Rights, the author of War, Aggression and Self-Defence, and has written extensively on subjects relating to international law, human rights, and the law of armed conflict.

Vice Admiral James H. Doyle, Jr., US Navy (Ret.). Vice Admiral Doyle graduated from the US Naval Academy in 1946. From 1950–1953, Vice Admiral Doyle attended George Washington University Law School. As a junior officer, he served in USS Chicago and USS, John W. Thomason. He was the executive officer of USS Bulwark, USS John S. McCain and USS Newport News. Vice Admiral Doyle was subsequent the commander of USS Ruff, USS Redstart, USS John R. Craig, and USS Bainbridge. As a flag officer, Admiral Doyle was Chief, International Negotiations Division, Joint Chiefs of Staff where his work involved him in SALT 1 and Incidents at Sea negotiations with the Soviet Union. Admiral Doyle also represented the Joint Chiefs of Staff on the US Delegation to the Law of the Sea Conference. Admiral Doyle also commanded Cruiser-Destroyer Group TWELVE, Attack Carrier Striking Group Two, and Third Fleet (1974–75) Admiral Doyle's final active duty position was as the Deputy Chief of Naval Operations for Surface Warfare (1975–80). Since retiring from active duty, Admiral Doyle has been advising the Johns Hopkins University Applied Physics Laboratory on various aspects of Anti-Air Warfare and Fleet Air Defense. He is also the Vice Chairman of the Strike, Land Attack and Air Defense Committee for the National Defense Industrial Association and serves on the Board of Directors for the Center for Oceans Law and Policy, University of Virginia and the International Law Department of the US Naval War College.

Colonel Charles H. B. Garraway, United Kingdom Army is currently serving in the UK Ministry of Defence in London where he is a principal advisor on issues relating to international law. Colonel Garraway's tours of duty have included Cyprus, Germany, Belgium (SHAPE) and Hong Kong as well as various tours throughout the United Kingdom. Colonel Garraway served as the senior Army Legal Service officer during the Gulf Ware where he dealt extensively with prisoner of war issues. Currently, Colonel Garraway is the Army consultant on the draft Tri-Service Manual on the Law of Armed Conflict and has contributed to a number of academic publications and published a number of articles on issues relating to international law. He has lectured extensively on issues associated with the law of armed conflict and international humanitarian law in both the United Kingdom and abroad and has taught at the International Institute of Humanitarian Law in San Remo since 1994. Colonel Garraway is a member of the Managing Board and the Board of Directors of the International Society for Military Law and the Law of War and is a General Rapporteur for its 2003 Congress in Rome as well as the Chairman of the General Affairs Committee. He is a visiting professor at the School of Law, King's College, University of London.

Colonel David E. Graham, JAGC, US Army (Ret.) retired from the US Army in 2002. Prior to his retirement, Colonel Graham was the Chief, International and Operational Law Division within the Office of the Judge Advocate General, Department of the Army and the Director, Center for Law and Military Operations, the Judge Advocate General's School of the Army, Charlottesville, Virginia. In a career spanning from 1971 to 2002, Colonel Graham's other assignments have included Chief, Strategic Planning, Office of the Judge Advocate General; Staff Judge Advocate, US Southern command;

Legal Advisor, Multinational Forces and Observers: Peacekeeping Force, Sinai; Attorney-Advisor, International Law, Office of the Staff Judge Advocate, Headquarters, US Army Europe and Seventh Army, and Professor, International and Operational Law Department, The Judge Advocate General's School of the Army.

Professor Leslie C. Green is a former Charles H. Stockton Professor of International Law at the US Naval War College (1996–98). After serving in the British Army during World War II, he held university appointment at the University of London; University of Singapore; University of Alberta, where he is University Professor Emeritus; Kyung Hee University, Seoul Korea; University of Colorado; and the University of Denver. Professor Green's many government appointments include Member and Legal Advisor to the Canadian delegation to the Geneva Conference on Humanitarian Law in Armed Conflict (1975–77) and special consultant to the Judge Advocate General, National Defence Headquarters. In the latter capacity, he wrote the Canadian Manual on Armed Conflict Law. Professor Green is the author of numerous books including The Contemporary Law of Armed Conflict and over 300 papers and articles.

Professor Christopher Greenwood is Professor of International Law at the London School of Economics and Political Science. He is a Barrister, practicing from Essex Court Chambers in London, and has represented the United Kingdom before the International Court of Justice in the Nuclear Weapons and Lockerbie cases, as well as appearing regularly in the UK courts where his cases have included Pinochet and the Guantanamo Bay detainees cases. Professor Greenwood was formerly a Fellow and Lecturer at Magdalene College, Cambridge, had been a Visiting Professor at the Universities of Marburg, West Virginia, and Mississippi, and Director of Studies and Lecturer at the Academy of International Law in The Hague. He is a regular lecturer at military colleges, has published a number of articles on international law, and is the author of a forthcoming book, The Modern Law of Armed Conflict.

Professor Wolff Heintschel von Heinegg is Professor of Public International Law at the University of Frankfurt-Oder and former Professor of Law at the University of Augsburg, Germany. He was the Rapporteur of the International Law Association Committee on Maritime Neutrality and is currently the Vice-President of the German Society of Military Law and the Law of War. Professor Heintschel von Heinegg was among a group of international lawyers and naval experts who produced the San Remo Manual on International Law Applicable to Armed Conflicts at Sea. He is a widely published author of articles and books on the law of the sea and naval warfare.

Mr. Daniel Helle has been the Deputy Head of the ICRC Delegation to the United Nations since 2000. A native of Norway, Mr. Helle's previous experience includes Legal Adviser, Legal Division, ICRC, Geneva, Switzerland (1998–2000) where he provided institutional support on questions related to the status of the ICRC, forced displacements, and women and children in armed conflict; Associate Expert/Junior Professional Officer, UN Centre for Human Rights/Office of the High Commissioner for Human Rights, Geneva, Switzerland (1994–98) where he worked extensively on internally displaced persons and human rights and mass exoduses; and as Legal Adviser for the Norwegian Institute for Human Rights, Oslo Norway.

Lieutenant Colonel Tony E. Montgomery, US Air Force is the Deputy Staff Judge Advocate, US Special Operations Command, MacDill Air Force Base, Florida. During his career which began in 1983, his assignments have included service as the Area Defense Counsel for Florennes Air Base, Belgium; Chief of Military Justice at Hill Air Force Base, Utah; Staff Judge Advocate for Goodfellow Air Force Base, Texas; Chief, Operations and International Law for Headquarters Air Combat Command, Langley Air Force Base, Virginia; and from 1998–2001, Deputy Judge Advocate and Chief, Operational Law for the US European Command. During the summer of 1996, Lieutenant Colonel Montgomery served as the Staff Judge Advocate to the Commander, Joint Task Force Southwest Asia.

Professor Rein Müllerson is Professor and Chair of International Law at King's College of London University where he is also the Director of the Master of Arts Program on International Peace & Security. From 1992–1994, he was visiting Centennial Professor of the London School of Economics and Political Science. He served as the First Deputy Foreign Minister of Estonia during 1991–1992 and from 1988–1992, Professor Müllerson was a Member of the United Nations Human Rights Committee. He is a member of the Institut de Droit International and is the author of six books on international law and politics as well as more than 150 articles and reviews. His latest books are Human Rights Diplomacy (1997) and Ordering Anarchy: International Law in International Society (2000).

Professor John F. Murphy is Professor of Law at Villanova University School of Law. In addition to teaching, his career has included a year in India on a Ford Foundation Fellowship, private practice in New York and Washington D.C., and service in the Office of the Assistant Legal Adviser for United Nations Affairs, US Department of State. He was previously on the law faculty at the University of Kansas, and has been a visiting professor at Cornell University and Georgetown University. From 1980–81, Professor Murphy was the Charles H. Stockton Professor of International Law at the US Naval War College. He is the author or editor of numerous books and monographs and has authored numerous articles, comments, and reviews on international law and relations. Professor Murphy has served as a consultant to the US Departments of State and Justice, the ABA standing Committee on Law and National Security, and the United Nations Crime Bureaus. He has testified before Congress on multiple occasions and is currently the American Bar Association's Alternate Observer at the US Mission to the United Nations.

Lieutenant Colonel Michael A. Newton, JAGC, US Army, is currently an Assistant Professor of Law at the United States Military Academy at West Point, New York. Prior to this position, Lieutenant Colonel Newton was the Senior Advisor to the US Ambassador-at-Large for War Crimes Issues (2001–02) where he was involved in a wide range of issues related to the formation of US policy regarding law of armed conflict issued to include support to accountability mechanisms worldwide. In this capacity, Lieutenant Colonel Newton served as the US representative on the UN Planning Mission for the Sierra Leone Special Court. Lieutenant Colonel Newton has also served as a Special Advisor in the Office of War Crimes Issues (1999–2000) and helped negotiate the Elements of Crimes document for the International Criminal Court. Lieutenant Colonel Newton's other military assignments include as a Professor of International and Operational Law at the Judge Advocate General's School of the Army, Charlottesville, VA (1996–98), Brigade Judge Advocate, 194th Armored Brigade (Separate) Fort Knox, KY (1993–96); and Group Judge Advocate, 7th Special Force Group, Fort Bragg, NC 1990–92). Lieutenant Colonel Newton has deployed in support of both Operation Provide Comfort and Operation Uphold Democracy. He is published in multiple journals to include the Military Law Review, The Virginia Journal of International Law, and the Army Lawyer.

Dr. Richard A. Nuccio is the Founding Director of the Pell Center at Salve-Regina University. Prior to assuming his position as director, he served in a number of senior foreign policy position in the US Government. From 1995–1996, he was special advisor to the President and the Secretary of State for Cuba. After leaving the White House, he returned to the State Department as senior policy adviser to Assistant Secretary of State for Inter-American Affairs. From 1997–1998, Dr. Nuccio was the senior foreign policy adviser to Senator Robert G. Torricelli (D-NJ) and from 1998–1999, he was an adviser on civil society to the director of the UN Development Program's Latin American and Caribbean Bureau, a consultant to the Rand Corporation and the

Peace Research Institute of Oslo. Dr. Nuccio has taught numerous courses as multiple colleges and universities to include Williams College, Bennington College, Georgetown University and the School of Advanced International Studies of Johns Hopkins University.

Lieutenant Colonel Jean-Guy Perron, Canadian Forces, is presently the Assistant Judge Advocate General for the National Capital Region (Ottawa), Canada. Prior assignments have included as Legal Adviser to the Commander of Canadian Joint Task Force South West Asia, Tampa, FL (2001–02); Prosecutor, Office of the Director of Military Prosecutions (1998–2001); Legal Adviser to Commander, Canadian Contingent Implementation Forces in Bosnia-Herzegovina (1996) and Legal Adviser to the Commander, Canadian Contingent Central Africa (1996) in support of Operation Assurance in both Rwanda and Uganda. Prior to joining the office of the JAG, Lieutenant Colonel was an infantry officer (Royal 22e Regiment).

Rear Admiral Rodney P. Rempt, US Navy, is the 48th President of the US Naval War College. Read Admiral Rempt graduated from the U.S. Naval Academy in 1966 and holds Masters Degrees in Systems Analysis from Stanford University and in National Security and Strategic Studies from the Naval War College. He has commanded USS Callaghan (DDG 994) and USS Bunker Hill (CG 52). From 1996–1998, Rear Admiral Rempt was the Program Executive Officer, Theater Air Defense (PEO TAD), additionally serving as the U.S. Steering Committee Member for the NATO Seasparrow and Rolling Airframe Missile multi national programs. From 1998–2000, Rear Admiral Rempt was the first Deputy Assistant Secretary of the Navy for Theater Combat Systems where he was the principle advisor on the introduction of Naval TBMD and the development of advanced shipboard combat systems. In 2000, Rear Admiral Rempt became the first Assistant Chief of Naval Operations for Missile Defense.

Professor Harvey Rishikof is Professor of Law at Roger Williams University School of Law. Professor Rishikof has a long history of public service, having worked as the Legal Counsel for the Deputy Director for the Federal Bureau of Investigation, Washington D.C. (1997–99) where he was involved in issues affecting the Deputy Director's Office on general policy and legal matters; Administrative Assistant to the Chief Justice of the US Supreme Court, Washington D.C. (1994–96) where he was responsible for both internal Supreme Court and external judicial administrative matters including acting as a liaison for the Executive Branch and Congress; and as a Judicial Fellow in the Administrative Office of the US Courts, Washington D.C. (1993–94). Professor Rishikof lectures extensively and has been published numerous times to include in the Journal of Policy Analysis and Management, the Valparaiso Law Review, and the Social Science Research Council.

Professor Sir Adam Roberts is the Montague Burton Professor of International Relations at Oxford University and a Fellow of Balliol College. He has been a lecturer in International Relations at the London School of Economics and Political Science and was the Alastair Buchan Reader in International Relations and Fellow of St. Antony's College, Oxford from 1981–1986. He has a three-year Leverhumle Major research Fellowship for 2000–2003. He is the author of numerous articles and books including Nations in Arms: The Theory and Practice of Territorial Defence and he co-edited Documents on the Laws of War.

Professor Nicholas Rostow is General Counsel, US Mission to the United Nations. Prior to that appointment, he was the Charles H. Stockton Professor of International Law at the US Naval War College. Professor Rostow has served in senior positions in both the legislative and executive branches of the US Government. These include Staff Director of the Senate Select Committee on Intelligence; Deputy Staff Director and Counsel of the House Select Committee on US National Security and Military /Commercial Concerns with the People Republic of China (more familiarly known as the Cox Committee); Special Assistant to the State Department's Legal Adviser; as a Special Assistant to President Reagan and President George H. Bush; and Legal Adviser to the National Security Council. In addition to government service, Professor Rostow has taught law and history at the University of Tulsa and the Fletcher School of Law and Diplomacy. His publications are in the fields of international law and diplomatic history.

Dr. Michael Saalfeld is the Director, International Legal Affairs for the German Ministry of Defense. Dr. Saalfeld began his tour as a legal advisor in the Federal Armed Forces (Corps level) in 1982. He then became Deputy Director, International Legal Affairs in 1987 and held that position for the next seven years. Subsequently, he served for three years in the Personnel Office of the Ministry of Defenses' State Secretary for Personnel and Budget Affairs. In 1999, during the Kosovo Campaign, Dr. Saalfeld was the Head of the Personal Office of Minster Rudolf Scharping.

Professor Michael N. Schmitt is Professor of International Law at the George C. Marshall European Center for Security Studies, Garmisch-Partenkirchen, Germany. Prior to arriving at the Marshall Center, Professor Schmitt enjoyed a career in the US Air Force. During that career, he specialized in operational and international law, and was senior legal adviser to multiple Air Force units, including units conducting combat operations over

Northern Iraq. Professor Schmitt has been on the faculty of the Air Force Academy where he was Deputy Head of the Department of Law, and was Assistant Director for Aerial Warfare in the International Law Department of the Naval War College. He has been a Visiting Scholar at Yale Law School and lectures and teaches regularly at the International Institute of Humanitarian Law and the NATO School. He is the author of many scholarly articles on law and military affairs and a contributing editor for multiple volumes of the International Law Studies.

Professor Ivan Shearer is the Challis Professor of International Law at the University of Sydney. He was formerly Professor of Law and Dean of the Faculty of Law at the University of New South Wales, where he was awarded Emeritus status in 1993. He has been a Visiting Fellow at All Souls College, Oxford, and held visiting appointments at universities in Germany and Greece. Professor Shearer is the Vice President of the Australian International Law Association and is on the editorial board of three professional journals. He is a member of the International Institute of Humanitarian Law, San Remo, and was among a group of international lawyers and naval expert that produced the San Remo Manual on International Law Applicable to Armed Conflicts at Sea. He holds the rank of Captain (retired) in the Royal Australian Naval Reserve, and in that capacity gives advice within the Department of Defence and frequent lectures on the law of the sea and international law to various service bodies. For his services to legal education in the Australian Defence Force he was made a Member of the Order of Australia in 1995. In 2000 he was elected to a four-year term as a Member of the Human Rights Committee of the United Nations. During 2000–2001, Professor Shearer was the Charles H. Stockton Professor of International Law at the US Naval War College.

Colonel Manuel E. Supervielle, US Army, is currently the Staff Judge Advocate for the US Southern Command. Colonel Supervielle's prior assignments include: Chair & Professor, International and Operational Law Department, The Judge Advocate General's School of the Army (1998–2000); Staff Judge Advocate, US Army South, Republic of panama (1996–98); Chief, International Law Branch, International and Operational Law Division, US Army, Office of the Judge Advocate General (1993–95) and Deputy Chief of the Division (1995–96) and Assistant Staff Judge Advocate, US Pacific Command Honolulu, Hawaii (1990–1992). Colonel Supervielle has deployed twice as the Staff Judge Advocate for Joint Task Forces performing disaster assistance missions in Western Samoa (1990) and Bangladesh (1991). He is the author of numerous articles on both international law and military justice and serves as the President of the Military Law Committee of the Inter-American Bar Association.

Colonel James P. Terry, US Marine Corp (Ret.) currently serves as Deputy Assistant Secretary of State for Global, Functional and Regional Affairs in the Bureau of Legislative Affairs of the US Department of State. Following service as an infantry officer in Vietnam, he served as Commanding Officer of the Marine Detachment aboard the USS Ticonderoga and in Judge Advocate billets as trial and defense counsel, military judge, Division Staff Judge Advocate, Marine Expeditionary Force Staff Judge Advocate, and as Legal Adviser to the Chairman of the Joint Chiefs of Staff from 1992–1995. After retiring from the US Marine Corps, Colonel Terry served in the Senior Executive Service in the Department of the Interior, serving first as Deputy Director of the Office of hearings and Appeals and then as an Administrative Judge on the Board of Land Appeals. He joined the Department of State in 2001.

Professor Robert F. Turner holds his doctorates from the University of Virginia School of Law, where in 1981, he co-founded the Center for National Security Law. He continues to serve as the Center's Associate Director. A former three-term chairman of the ABA Standing Committee on Law and National Security, and Editor of the ABA *National Security Law Report* for many years, he previously served as a Principal Deputy Assistant Secretary of State and as the first President of the congressionally-established US Institute of peace in Washington D.C. The author or editor of more than a dozen books and numerous articles, Professor Turner has testified before more than a dozen congressional committees and was the Charles H. Stockton Chair of International Law at the Naval War College during 1994–1995.

Captain Ronald R. Winfrey, JAGC, US Navy (Ret.) is the Attorney-Advisor for International Law and Homeland Defense and the Foreign Engagement Coordinator for the Office of the Staff Judge Advocate of the US Pacific Command. In this capacity, Captain Winfrey provides legal advice to the Staff Judge Advocate for the Commander, US Pacific Command on legal issues affecting international law and homeland defense. Captain Winfrey served in the US Navy's Judge Advocate Generals Corps from 1976–1998. His duty assignments included Naval Legal Service Office, Treasure Island, San Francisco, CA; USS Coral Sea; Office of the Judge Advocate General (Litigation /Personnel Division), Washington D.C.; Staff Judge Advocate, Joint Task Force Middle East; Staff Judge Advocate, US Third Fleet, and Deputy Staff Judge Advocate, US Pacific Fleet and Commanding Officer, Trial Service Office Pacific.

Index

A

abduction of terrorists, 312–319
Abu Nidal, 395
Abu Sayyaf Group, 393
Acheson, Dean, 436
Achille Lauro hijacking, 399
ACLU (American Civil Liberties Union), 92 n. 44
Afghanistan, xxi, 2, 3 (*see also* Operation ENDURING FREEDOM; Taliban)
    coalition operations in, *see* coalition operations
    cross-border counter-terrorist attacks in pursuit of non-state entities, 38–47
    East African US Embassy bombings, retaliation for, *see* East African US Embassy bombings, 1998
    economic aid efforts, 455–456, 458–459
    economic sanctions, 425, 428
    future operations in, 455–459
    government by Taliban, legitimacy of, 69, 129–135, 139, 140–141, 143, 446
    history of war in, 191
    humanitarian intervention as grounds for use of force against, 130, 144
    humanitarian relief in, 205–208
    ISAF (International Security Assistance Force), 16, 111, 193, 319, 458
    MAPA (Mine Action Program for Afghanistan), 204
    Northern Alliance, 191, 192, 209–210, 227, 236, 238
    police force training, 458
    POW status of Taliban and al Qaeda prisoners, 171–174, 441–454, 468–471 (*see also* unlawful/lawful combatancy and POW status)
    raids on terrorist facilities following 1998 US Embassy bombings, 42, 395
    refugees, 207–208
    self-defense as reason for invasion of, *see* self-defense
    UN Security Council statements pre-9/11, 22–23
Africa, 41, 65, 106 n. 87, 419 (*see also* individual countries)
African National Congress (ANC), 41, 106 n. 87
Ago, Robert, 109
aid efforts, 455–456, 458–459
air-dropping supplies, 206
airlines and aircraft
    El Al Airline counters, Libyan-backed attacks on, 395
    Hague Convention for the Suppression of Unlawful Seizures of Aircraft, 35, 287, 361, 366, 399, 411
    International Civil Aviation Organization (ICAO), 399, 410
    Pan Am Flight 103 (Lockerbie), 21, 64, 294, 426–428
    Tokyo Convention on Offenses and Certain Other Acts Committed on Board Aircraft, 35, 399
    UTA Flight 722, 21, 426–428
Al-Fawwaz case, 290–291, 293, 367

Index

al-Islamiyya, 393
al Qaeda, ix, xiii, xiv, xvi, xvii, xx (*see also* September 11 attacks)
    armed conflict between United States and, existence of, 357–360, 381–386, 470, 478
    continuing viability of, 37
    criminal enforcement against, impossibility of, 36
    detainees held in Guantanamo Bay, Cuba, *see* unlawful/lawful combatancy and POW status
    distinguishing from Taliban, 139, 140
    East African bombings of 1988, *see* East African US Embassy bombings, 1998
    economic sanctions, 425, 428
    Iraqi/Hussein, links with, 431, 436
    judicial proceedings against Taliban/al Qaeda detainees, 222–225
    Latin American cells, 394–395
    POW status of Taliban and al Qaeda prisoners, 171–174, 441–454, 468–471 (*see also* unlawful/lawful combatancy and POW status)
    raids on terrorist facilities following 1998 US Embassy bombings, 42
    responsibility for September 11 attacks, 10–11
    self-defense against, 33–47
    state sponsorship, 394
    Taliban, connections to, 12–13, 40, 47–48, 53, 138, 442, 446–447
    terrorist threat posed by, 10–12
    weapons of mass destruction (WMD), 91, 116, 146, 430, 433, 436
Albania (*Corfu Channel* case), xiv, 49–51
Alcohol, Tobacco, and Firearms (ATF), 480
Alexander of Yugoslavia (prince), assassination of (1934), 329
Algeria, 293, 353
alternatives to use of force
    antiterrorism conventions, *see* treaties and conventions
    economic sanctions, 425–429, 440
    future developments, 479–480
    proper law and proper forum for terrorism, 356
    self-defense, 34–36
Alvarez-Machain case (*United States v. Alvarez-Machain*), 312, 315–316, 317–318
American Civil Liberties Union (ACLU), 92 n. 44
American Servicemembers' Protection Act (ASPA), 372–374, 456
Amnesty International, 92
An-Na'im, Abdullahi Ahmed, 107 n. 88
anarchists, extraditability of, 287
ANC (African National Congress), 41, 106 n. 87
Angola, 112, 113
Annan, Kofi, 101–102
anticipatory use of force, *see* preemptive use of force
antiterrorism conventions, *see* treaties and conventions
Aquinas, Thomas of (saint), 76
Arab Convention on the Suppression of Terrorism, 417–418
Arab States, League of, 65, 294
Argentina, 316–317, 394

Index

armed attacks
   defining, 21 n. 46, 25–27, 33, 66–67, 112–115
   differentiating from armed conflicts, 381–386
   jus ad bellum, 112–115, 117–119, 131–132
   non-state entities, state responsibility for armed attacks by, 38–47, 68–70, 110, 141–142
   proper law and proper forum, 355
   "scale and effects" as to what constitutes, 21 n. 46, 25–27, 33
   self-defense, 66–67
armed conflict
   Canada and al Qaeda, existence of armed conflict between, 309
   differentiating armed attack from armed conflict, 381–386
   MIO, 258–260
   United States and al Qaeda, existence of armed conflict between, 357–360, 381–386, 470, 478
Armed Islamic Group, 393
Arrest Warrant of 11 April 2000 (Democratic Republic of Congo v. Belgium), case of, 279
Article 51 of United Nations Charter, xiv, xviii (*see also* United Nations for other articles of UN Charter)
   authorization, failure to seek, 275–276
   coalition operations relying on, 319–320
   future developments and adequacy of, 431–438, 468–469
   irregular rendition, 314
   jus ad bellum, 132
   MIO, 256, 260, 264, 265, 266, 297–299, 301–302, 306
   proper law and proper forum, 355
   self-defense exception, 14, 20, 33–34, 305, 306
Ashburton, Lord, 43, 77
Asia-Pacific Economic Cooperation Forum, 18
ASPA (American Servicemembers' Protection Act), 372–374, 456
assassination and assassination attempts
   Alexander of Yugoslavia (prince), 1934, 329
   Bush, President George H.W., 62, 395
   Sudanese-backed attempt to assassinate president of Egypt, 428
ATF (Bureau of Alcohol, Tobacco, and Firearms), 480
Athens, 75–76
Augustine of Hippo (saint), 76
Australia
   coalition operations, 277–279, 285–286, 288, 290, 295, 302, 319–320
   death penalty, 290
   extradition, 288, 290
   Guantanamo detainees, concerns regarding, 239
   human rights law and arrest of terrorists, 285–286
   ICC jurisdiction, 295
   MIO, 301–302
   Operation ENDURING FREEDOM, 277–279, 285–286, 288, 290, 295, 301–302
   self-defense issues, 17, 18, 65
   terrorism laws, national, 278, 279

Index

authorization of use of force by United Nations, 16, 24, 143, 145, 275–276, 432
"axis of evil," 438 (*see also* Iran, Iraq/Sadam Hussein, North Korea)

B

Barak, Ehud, 93
Belgium, 279, 283
Berra, Yogi, 391
bin Laden, Osama (*see also* al Qaeda)
    abduction or extradition of terrorists, 315
    future developments and, 394, 395, 428
    judicial proceedings against, 222–225
    jus ad bellum and, 113, 134
    self-defense issues, 10, 15, 37, 44, 64
    Tora Bora, presence at, 204–205
biological weapons
    Biological Weapons Convention, 414
    Iraq/Hussein's experiments with, 146
"Blue Book" series, ix
bombing
    Convention for the Suppression of Terrorist Bombings, 35, 281, 289, 362–363, 366, 387
    humanitarian relief, call for pause in bombing for, 206
    jus in bello and modern bombing techniques, 197–205
Bosnia, *see* Yugoslavia, Bosnia, Serbia, and Kosovo
Brazil, 394
Brown, Chris, 98, 126
Brown, Commander Neil, xix, 303–307, 319, 491
Brownlie, Ian, 80, 85–86
Bureau of Alcohol, Tobacco, and Firearms (ATF), 480
Burke-White, William, 104, 116
Burma, 457
Burundi, 98
Bush, President George H.W., 62, 395, 485, 487
Bush, President George W., and administration, 197, 218–219, 235–236, 325–326, 337, 430, 437, 444–445, 487
Byford, Granville, 106 n. 87

C

Cambodia, 41, 457
Canada, 18, 237, 241, 278, 290, 309–311, 320
capital punishment, 290–291, 368–369, 379, 471–472
Caroline case, 27, 30, 31, 42–44, 77, 108–109, 133, 138, 355, 436
Carr, Caleb, 108
case law
    Al-Fawwaz case, 290–291, 293, 367
    Arrest Warrant of 11 April 2000 (Democratic Republic of Congo v. Belgium), case of, 279

Index

Caroline case, 27, 30, 31, 42–44, 77, 108–109, 133, 138, 355, 436
Corfu Channel case, xiv, 49–51
Diplomatic and Consular Staff case, 52–53
Kassem case, 162–163
Kei case, 164, 166
Ker v. Illinois, 315, 318
Lockerbie (Pan Am Flight 103), 21, 64, 294, 426–428
Lotus case, 39, 141
Machain case (*United States v. Alvarez-Machain*), 312, 315–316, 317–318
Mohamed Ali case, 159–160, 166
Nicaragua case, 26, 51–52, 54–56, 70, 117, 119–120, 133, 135, 355
Nuclear Weapons opinion, International Court of Justice, 28
Prosecutor v. Tadic/Dusco Tadic case, 24 n. 56, 56–57, 120, 294 n. 59
Quirin case, 154, 160, 214
Toscanino case (*United States v. Toscanino*), 319
Cassese, Antonio, 117
Central Intelligence Agency (CIA), 3, 173, 251, 359, 480
Centre for International Crime Prevention, Vienna, 411
Chapultepec, Act of, 132
characteristics of terrorist attacks and responses, 111–119
Charney, Jonathan, 71–72
Chechnya, 140, 305
chemical weapons
    Afghanistan's potential for using gas, 205
    Iraq/Hussein's experiments with, 436
Chemical Weapons Convention, 414
Cheney, Vice-president Dick, 429
Chile, 394
China, 18, 61, 63, 437
Christianity, 76–77, 124
CIA (Central Intelligence Agency), 3, 173, 251, 359, 480
CIS (Commonwealth of Independent States) antiterrorism convention, 418
citizens
    extradition prohibitions, 286–287, 288
    jurisdiction, nationality basis for, 280, 282, 286–287
    lawful/unlawful combatancy and POW status, 163–164, 173
civil aviation, *see* airlines and aircraft
civil law countries, 286
civil wars, 194
civilians
    distinguished from combatants, 151–153, 170, 197–205, 198, 232, 243–245
    shields, used as, 243–245, 250
clear and convincing standard of evidence, validation of counter-terrorist strikes, 70–72
coalition operations, xviii–xix, 275–296
    Article 51 of UN Charter, reliance on, 319–320
    Australia, 277–279, 285–286, 288, 290, 295, 302, 319–320
    Canada, 309–311, 320

Index

  death penalty issues, 290–291
  extradition, 286–293
  human rights law, international, 282–286
  ICC, 293–296
  international law, role of, 276–277
  jurisdiction, 279–282, 286–287
  national laws on terrorism, 277–279
  Operation ENDURING FREEDOM, 235–241
  pre-existing strategic relationships, importance of, 302
  self-defense, 319–320
  United Kingdom, 303–307, 319
  unlawful/lawful combatancy and POW status of Taliban/al Qaeda detainees, 227–228, 238–241
Coast Guard, 480
Cold War, 58–59, 62, 79, 83, 86–88, 91, 106, 120, 399, 434
Cole (US vessel), attack on, 477
collateral damage, 18, 29–30, 197–205
Colombia, xx, 372, 394, 395
combatants
  civilians distinguished from, 151–153, 170, 197–205, 198, 232, 243–245
  lawful/unlawful, *see* unlawful/lawful combatancy and POW status
common law countries, 278, 286
common security framework, need for, 437, 440, 473–475
Commonwealth of Independent States (CIS) antiterrorism convention, 418
community values regarding self-defense, evolving standard of, 57–72
Comprehensive Convention on International Terrorism (Draft), 277–278, 281–282, 288, 289, 414–415
Congo (Democratic Republic), 42, 279
conservatives *vs.* liberals, 91–96, 126–127
Constitution, U.S., 446
Continental Shelf, Convention for the Suppression of Unlawful Acts against the Safety of Fixed Platforms Located on, 399
conventions, *see* treaties and conventions; specific titles
Convention against Transnational Organized Crime, 415–416
Convention for the Suppression of Terrorist Bombings, 35, 281, 289, 362–363, 366, 387
Convention for the Suppression of Unlawful Acts against the Safety of Fixed Platforms Located on the Continental Shelf, 399
Convention on the Physical Protection of Nuclear Material, 412
Convention on the Prevention and Punishment of Crimes against Internationally Protected Persons, 397, 411
Cooper, Richard, 97, 99, 100, 101
Corell, Hans, 404, 415
Corfu Channel case, xiv, 49–51
Counter-Terrorism Committee (CTC), United Nations, 464–465
counter-terrorist military operations, 184–190 (*see also* specific operations)
  cross-border attacks in pursuit of non-state entities, 38–47, 68, 141–142
  defining, 184

Index

potential problems in applying jus in bello to, 184–186
previous operations, applicability of jus in bello in, 187–190
crimes against humanity, 177, 363–364, 365
criminal law
    armed attack, armed conflict, and ordinary criminal acts, 381–386
    international, *see* international criminal law; international terrorist tribunals
    murder, terrorism as, 361, 363–364
    national enforcement, *see* national courts as forum for terrorist trials
    self-defense actions, criminal law enforcement as alternative to, 34–36, 356
    terrorism, proper law for, 320, 360–363, 395–396
    training in law enforcement, 456
Cronan, Wing Commander Paul, xix, 301–302, 319–320, 491
Cronin, Audrey, 89–90, 95
cross-border counter-terrorist attacks in pursuit of non-state entities, 38–47, 68, 141–142
CTC (Counter-Terrorism Committee), United Nations, 464–465
Cuba, 394
Cuellar, Javier Perez de, 61
Czech Republic, 18

D

Dalton, Capt. Jane, xxii, 477–481, 491–492
Dalton, Capt. William H., xv, 137–138, 492
Dar es-Salaam US Embassy bombings, *see* East African US Embassy bombings, 1998
De Gaulle, Charles, 171
de Lisle, Jacques, 438 n. 193
de Vattel, Emerich, 77
death penalty, 290–291, 368–369, 379, 471–472
Declaration of Paris, 152
Declaration on the Strengthening of International Security, 48
definition of terrorism, xviii, 277–279, 305, 387
Del Ponte, Carla, 332
Democratic Republic of Congo, 42, 279
Department of Defense (DOD), 480
detainees held in Guantanamo Bay, Cuba, *see* unlawful/lawful combatancy and POW status
deterrence
    international terrorist tribunal as instrument of, 347–349
    preemptive strikes against groups that cannot be deterred or reasoned with, 429–438
dichotomy of responses to terrorism, 91–96
Dilhorne, Viscount, 159
Dinstein, Yoram, xv, 112–113, 147, 151–174, 232, 247–252, 316–318, 381, 479, 483–485, 492
Diplomatic and Consular Staff case, 52–53
diplomatic efforts, 455, 457
discrimination as cause of terrorism, 95
discrimination/distinction principle (between civilians and armed combatants), 151–153, 170, 197–205, 198, 232, 243–245

Djibouti, 63
DOD (Department of Defense), 480
Doyle, Vice Admiral James H., Jr., 492–493
Draft Comprehensive Convention on International Terrorism, 277–278, 281–282, 288, 289, 414–415
Draft International Convention for the Suppression of Nuclear Terrorism, 411–414
Dupuy, Pierre-Marie, 112
Dusco Tadic case (*Prosecutor v. Tadic*), 24 n. 56, 56–57, 120, 294 n. 59
Dworkin, Ronald, 106

E

East African US Embassy bombings, 1998
    coalition operations, 289–290
    extradition and jurisdiction, 289–290
    proper law and proper forum for terrorism, 357, 367
    self-defense, 22, 36, 42, 45, 64–66, 68, 70
economic aid efforts, 455–456, 458–459
economic sanctions, 425–429, 440
Egypt, 18, 63, 393
Eichmann, Adolph, 316–317
El Al Airline counters, Libyan-backed attacks on, 395
el Qadhafi, Muammar, 60
El Salvador, *see Nicaragua* case
Elements of Crimes, Rome Statute of the International Criminal Court (ICC), 336
Emergency, Paris Minimum Standards of Human Rights Norms in a State of, 285
Enayat, Hamid, 124
Entebbe Raid of 1976, 110
environmental law, 81, 82
Europe and European Union, 18, 90, 96–102, 231, 265, 290, 437, 469
European Convention on Human Rights, 369, 469–472
European Convention on the Suppression of Terrorism, 368, 416, 422–424
evidence as validation of counter-terrorist strikes, 70–72
extradition, xix, 286–293, 312–319, 365–369, 398

F

failed states, intervention in, 91
fair trial concerns, 291–293, 331–333, 366
Falk, Richard, 95
FARC (Revolutionary Armed Forces of Colombia), xx, 395
Al-Fawwaz case, 290–291, 293, 367
Federal Bureau of Investigation (FBI), 3, 359, 475, 480
financing counter-terrorism, 480
Financing of Terrorism, International Convention for the Suppression of, xxi, 345, 351, 377, 397, 404–411, 405, 408, 425
Finland, 98

Fisk, Robert, 126
Fixed Platforms Located on the Continental Shelf, Convention for the Suppression of Unlawful Acts against the Safety of, 399
flag states and jurisdiction over maritime vessels, 257, 260, 298–299
flagless vessels, 299
"flatland" thinking, 91–96
"for us or against us" argument, 47, 91–96, 197, 235
force, use of, *see* jus ad bellum
forum, xix–xx, 364–369
    armed attack, armed conflict, and ordinary criminal acts, 381–386
    humanitarian, human rights, and criminal law, international, 375–379
    international forum, *see* international terrorist tribunal
    jurisdiction over international terrorist acts, 333, 337–342
    military commissions used to try terrorists, 222–225, 233, 331–332, 357, 386–387, 451–453
    national courts, *see* national courts as forum for terrorist trials
fragmentation, 87
France, 65, 329, 404, 427, 432, 438 n. 193
Franks, General Tommy, 297
"Free France" forces (WWII partisans), lawful combatancy status, 164–165, 171
Freedman, Lawrence, 93
French Foreign Legion, 163–164
French Revolution, 165
Friedman, Thomas, 94
Friendly Relations Declaration, 48
Fukuyama, Francis, 124
fundamentalism, 98, 100 n. 68, 103, 124–127
funding
    counter-terrorism, 480
    International Convention for the Suppression of Financing of Terrorism, xxi, 345, 351, 377, 397, 404–411, 405, 408, 425
future attacks, anticipatory actions in self-defense against, 32, 38, 116–119, 133, 134–135, 435–437
future "trends" in terrorism, xx, 391–396

G

Garraway, Col. Charles H. B., xvii, 231–233, 248, 252, 320, 493
gas, *see* entries at chemical weapons
Gaulle, Charles De, 171
Gellner, Ernest, 125
Geneva Conventions, xvii, xxi, 2, 441 (*see also* unlawful/lawful combatancy and POW status)
    Afghanistan as party to, 194
    coalition operations, 284
    detention of POWs, rules for, 153
    different legal regimes, 378–379
    entitlement to POW status, 157–167, 211–212, 215–216, 443–444, 471
    judicial proceedings against detainees, 222–225

jus ad bellum, 81, 83
major concerns of, 178
Protocol I, 167–170, 186–187, 213–216
release of POWs, 222
scope of application, 179
specific applicability of GC III to Taliban and al Qaeda prisoners, 444–445, 447–448, 470
US concerns over thinking about terrorism in laws of war framework, 186–187
Vietnamese prisoners, 188–189
Georgia (nation), 18, 480
Germany
French Foreign Legion, German national in, 163–164
future developments, 410, 438 n. 193, 458
Guantanamo detainees, concerns regarding, 239
jus ad bellum issues, 77, 123, 135
La Belle disco bombing, Berlin, 60–61, 63, 395
Nazis, 123, 247, 316–317, 338–339 (*see also* Nuremberg Trials)
Operation ENDURING FREEDOM, 468
proper law and proper forum, 338–339
Red Army Faction, 187
self-defense issues, 18, 63, 65
Glennon, Michael, 58, 104, 135, 434–435
global antiterrorist conventions, 396–416
Global Exchange, 201
Global War on Terrorism (GWOT), 3, 8, 137, 140, 244, 257, 473
globalization, 87, 393
Goldstone, Justice Richard, 331
Gonzales, Alberto, 451
Goods Review List (GRL), economic sanctions, 426
Graham, Col. David E., 493–494
gravity of aggressive act, 54–55, 117–119
Gray, Christine, 432–434
Greece, classical, 75–76, 77
Green, Leslie C., xvii, 139–140, 235–241, 494
Greenstock, Jeremy, 410
Greenwood, Christopher, xix, xx, 143, 315, 317–318, 353–369, 372, 382, 384, 385–387, 486, 494
GRL (Goods Review List), economic sanctions, 426
Grotius, Hugo, 334
Group of African States, 65
Group of Islamic States, 65
Guam, 474
Guantanamo Bay, Cuba detainees, *see* unlawful/lawful combatancy and POW status
Gulf War (*see also* Iraq/Sadam Hussein; Kuwait)
bombings, 199, 200
coalition operations and MIO, 304
future developments and, 477–478, 483
jus ad bellum, 115, 134

Index

neutrality issues, 182
reasons for observing jus in bello, 180
UN Security Council blockade, 249
GWOT (Global War on Terrorism), 3, 8, 137, 140, 244, 257, 473

H

habit, terrorism as, 486
Hague Convention for the Suppression of Unlawful Seizures of Aircraft, 35, 287, 361, 366, 399, 411
Hague Regulations, 156–167, 194, 232
The Hague Tribunal, 332
Haiti, 100
Hamas, 93, 393, 394
Heinegg, Wolff Heintschel von, xvii–xviii, 143, 144, 255–273, 306, 314, 494
Helle, Daniel, xx, 375–379, 387, 495
Herold, Marc, 200–201
History of the Peloponnesian War (Thucydides), 75
Hitler, Adolph, 135, 338
Hizballah, 393, 394
Hobbes, Thomas, 97, 100
hors de combat, 153
human rights
    European Convention on Human Rights, 369, 469–472
    Guantanamo detainees, 217, 220–222, 445–446, 470–471
    international human rights law, 282–286, 317–318, 375–379, 469–471
    Paris Minimum Standards of Human Rights Norms in a State of Emergency, 285
    Universal Declaration of Human Rights, xviii–xix, 282–283
humanitarian intervention, use of force for, 20, 79, 91, 114, 123, 130, 144, 432
humanitarian law, international (IHL), 375–379, 469–471
humanitarian relief, 205–208, 455–456, 458–459
humanity, crimes against, 177, 363–364, 365
Hussein, Sadam, *see* Iraq/Sadam Hussein
Hutton, Lord, 290, 293, 367

I

ICAO (International Civil Aviation Organization), 399, 410
ICC, *see* International Criminal Court (ICC)
ICCPR (International Covenant on Civil and Political Rights), 103, 282, 284–286, 292, 317, 446
ICRC (International Committee of the Red Cross), 176, 195–196, 215, 217–218, 220–221, 228–229, 376–377, 469
ICTR (International Criminal Tribunal for Rwanda), 339–340, 343, 364
ICTY (International Criminal Tribunal for the Former Yugoslavia), 120–121, 331–332, 339–340, 343, 349, 364
IHL (international humanitarian law), 375–379, 469–471
ILC, *see* International Law Commission (ILC)

Index

imminency principle, self-defense, 30–31, 38, 66–67, 115–116, 138, 436, 478
India, 18, 293, 462
indirect aggression, acts of, 114
Indo-China War, 163–164
Indonesia, 23, 159–160, 457
inequality and terrorism, 95
intelligence collection and intelligence services, 100, 256, 270, 279, 311, 480–481
Inter-American Convention Against Terrorism, 395, 419–422, 425
International Civil Aviation Organization (ICAO), 399, 410
International Committee of the Red Cross (ICRC), 176, 195–196, 215, 217–218, 220–221, 228–229, 376–377, 469
International Congress for the Repression of Terrorism (1937), 330–331
International Congress of Penal Law, 1926, 329
International Convention for the Suppression of Nuclear Terrorism (Draft), 411–414
International Convention for the Suppression of Terrorist Bombing, 35, 281, 289, 345, 362, 387, 397, 399–404, 415
International Convention for the Suppression of the Financing of Terrorism, xxi, 345, 351, 377, 397, 404–411, 405, 408, 425
International Court of Justice, 25–26, 28, 52, 105, 119–120, 133, 355
International Covenant on Civil and Political Rights (ICCPR), 103, 282, 284–286, 292, 317, 446
International Criminal Court (ICC), xix
    coalition operations, 293–296
    future developments, 456–457
    jurisdiction, 293–296
    proper law and proper forum, 336, 341–343, 364–365, 372, 373–374
    Rome Statute, 293–296, 336, 342, 357
international criminal law
    armed attack, armed conflict, and ordinary criminal acts, 381–386
    "atrocity crimes" proposed as unifying concept behind, 335
    concept and status of, 334–337
    Elements of Crimes, Rome Statute of the International Criminal Court (ICC), 336
    global antiterrorist conventions, goals of, 397–399
    historical ad hoc tribunals, basis for, 338–341
    jurisdiction based on failure of domestic forums, 337–342
    multilateral antiterrorist conventions, 344–347, 350–351, 362–363, 365–366
    relationship to international human rights law and international humanitarian law, 375–379
    terrorism, proper law for, 320, 360–363, 375–379, 395–396
    UN Security Council Resolution 1373 reinforcing current framework, 251–352
International Criminal Tribunal for Rwanda (ICTR), 339–340, 343, 364
International Criminal Tribunal for the Former Yugoslavia (ICTY), 120–121, 331–332, 339–340, 343, 349, 364
international human rights law, 282–286, 317–318, 375–379, 469–471
international humanitarian law (IHL), 375–379, 469–471
international law
    coalition operations, role in, 276–277
    crimes against humanity, 363–364, 365
    criminal law, *see* international criminal law

relationship between different branches of, 375–379
terrorism, proper law for, 320, 360–363, 375–379, 395–396
Westphalian international system as basis for, 83
International Law Association, 285
International Law Commission (ILC)
    Articles on State Responsibility, 49–52, 121
    Caroline case, 108–109
International Military Tribunal at Nuremberg, xv, xix, 338–339, 343
international/multilateral antiterrorist conventions, 344–347, 350–351, 362–363, 365–366
international phenomenon, terrorism as, 353–354
International Security Assistance Force (ISAF), 16, 111, 193, 319, 458
International Terrorism, Draft Comprehensive Convention on, 277–278, 281–282, 288, 289, 414–415
international terrorist tribunals, xix–xx, 364–369 (*see also* specific tribunals)
    armed attack, armed conflict, and ordinary criminal acts, 381–386
    deterrence, as instrument of, 347–349
    historical ad hoc tribunals as model for, 338–341
    history of attempts at establishing, 328–331
    ICC as, 341–343
    national courts, Newton's critique in favor of, 323–352
    prospects for establishment of, 328–333
    UN Security Council Resolution 1373 reinforcing current framework, 251–352
    usefulness and purpose, problems with establishing, 344–349
Internationally Protected Persons, Convention on the Prevention and Punishment of Crimes against, 397, 411
Internet, terrorist use of, 393
IRA (Irish Republican Army), xx, 188, 315, 359, 395
Iran, 52–53, 63, 65, 394, 438
Iran hostages, 52–53
Iraq/Sadam Hussein (*see also* Gulf War)
    al Qaeda, links with, 431, 436
    antiterrorism conventions, 394, 395
    economic sanctions, 425–426
    Israel's destruction of Baghdad reactor, 436, 478
    jus ad bellum, 101, 115, 133, 134–135, 146
    Operation IRAQI FREEDOM, 436–438 n. 193
    preemptive use of force against, 429–438, 483–485
    regime change, 146–147, 429–437, 483–485
    self-defense as argument for attacking, 2, 41–42, 62, 63, 65, 434–436, 483–485
    weapons of mass destruction (WMD), 430, 433, 484
Irish Republican Army (IRA), xx, 188, 315, 359, 395
irregular rendition, 312–319
irreversible course of action, 479
ISAF (International Security Assistance Force), 16, 111, 193, 319, 458
Islam, 76–77, 124–125
Islamic Conference, Organization of, 18, 278
Islamic Jihad, 393

Index

Islamic States, Group of, 65
al-Islamiyya, 393
Israel (*see also* Palestine)
    Baghdad reactor, destruction of, 436, 478
    Eichmann trial, 316–317
    El Al Airline counters, Libyan-backed attacks on, 395
    future developments, 393, 410
    ICC, 293
    jus ad bellum, 92–94, 106 n. 87, 110, 146
    Lebanon, invasion of, 189–190
    proper law and proper forum, 324
    self-defense issues, 41, 61, 63
    suicide bombings, 225, 439
    terrorism, definition of, 278
    terrorist tactics, Palestinian admission of use of, 462
    unlawful combatants, law on, 155–156, 162–163
Italy, 18, 63, 187, 410

J

Jackson, Justice (Nuremberg trials), 338, 339, 347–348
Japan, 18, 63, 65, 123, 248, 437, 474
Jefferson, Thomas, 323–324
Jennings, Judge Sir Robert, 120
Johnson, Clifton, 405, 407
Jordan, 63, 162
Judaism, 76, 124
judicial decisions, *see* case law
judicial proceedings against Taliban/al Qaeda detainees, 222–225
jurisdiction
    coalition operations, 279–282, 286–287
    extradition treaties, 367–368
    ICC, 293–296
    international terrorism, proper forum for, 337–342, 364–365
    maritime vessels, 257, 298–299
    multilateral antiterrorist conventions establishing grounds for domestic jurisdiction and prosecution, 344–347, 350–351, 362–363, 365–366
    national courts, 333, 337–342, 346–347, 364
    nationality basis, 280, 282, 286–287
    POW status, effect of denying, 445–446
    territorial basis, 280, 286–287
    treaties and conventions, 281–282
    universality principle, 280–281
    U.S. homeland defense issues, 480–481
jus ad bellum, xiii–xv, 356–357
    alternatives to, 34–36, 356, 479–480
    defined, 9 n. 6

Index

    dichotomy of responses to terrorism, 91–96
    evolving concept of, 79–91, 232–233
    future use of armed force against terrorists, 429–438
    geopolitical changes, effect of, 80–91, 122–126
    historical background, 75–80
    historical figures' violations, acceptance of, 106 n. 87
    jus in bello and, 181–183, 247–248
    non-state entities, *see* non-state entities
    normative framework for use of force, 19–24
    panel, 5
    positivism, normativism, and normative positivism, 75–80
    proportionality, 183–184, 247–248
    "scale and effects" as to what constitutes an armed attack, 21 n. 46, 25–27, 33
    self-defense, *see* self-defense
    terrorism as issue of, 106–108
    terrorism's difference from other traditional wars, 90–91
    UN Charter, intent and interpretation of, 102–106
jus cogens norm, UN Charter's prohibition on use of force as, 103
jus in bello, xiii, xv–xvii, 357
    armed attack, armed conflict, and ordinary criminal acts, 381–386
    bombing techniques, 197–205
    cassus belli, what constitutes, 354–355
    civilians deliberately used as shields, 243–245
    combatants, lawful/unlawful, *see* unlawful/lawful combatancy and POW status
    counter-terrorist military operations, 184–190
    distinguishing combatants and civilians, 151–153, 170, 197–205, 198, 232, 243–245
    existence of armed conflict between al Qaeda and United States, 357–360, 381–386
    formal applicability to counter-terrorist operations, xvi–xvii, 175–230 (*see also* more specific entries)
    ICRC statements regarding, 195–196
    jus ad bellum and, 181–183, 247–248
    Operation ENDURING FREEDOM, 191–208, 249–250
    potential problems in applying to counter-terrorist operations, 184–186
    POWs, 208–225 (*see also* unlawful/lawful combatancy and POW status)
    previous counter-terrorist operations, applicability in, 187–190
    proportionality, 183–184, 247–248
    reasons for adhering to, 181, 190, 231–233, 244
    revision of law in light of present developments, 225–227, 230, 251
    scope of application, 179–181, 229–230
    terrorism as issue of, 106–108, 354–360, 395–396
justice as sovereign principle, 324–326, 328, 352
justifications for terrorism, 114–115, 377, 439, 462

K

Kagan, Robert, 90, 96–100
Kant, Immanuel, 97, 101

Index

Karadjic, Radovan, 99
Karzai, Hamed, 458
Kashmir, 462
Kassem case, 162–163
Kei case, 164, 166
Kellenberger, Jakob, 469
Kellman, Barry, 413
Kellogg-Briand Pact of 1928, 78, 83, 132, 141
Kenyan US Embassy bombings, *see* East African US Embassy bombings, 1998
Ker v. Illinois, 315, 318
Kim Il Sung, 135
Korea
   North Korea, 135, 394, 438
   South Korea, 18, 63, 135, 474
Kosovo, *see* Yugoslavia, Bosnia, Serbia, and Kosovo
Kurds, 41–42
Kuwait, 23, 62, 115, 304, 425, 430, 483, 485 (*see also* Gulf War)

L

La Belle disco bombing, Berlin, 60–61, 63, 395
Laden, Osama bin, *see* bin Laden, Osama
Laos, 457
Latin America (*see also* individual countries)
   incidence of terrorist attacks in, 394–395
   OAS (Organization of American States), 17, 355, 395, 416, 419–422
law
   conservative nature of, 80–82
   crimes against humanity, 363–364, 365
   international, *see* international law
   policy imperatives and retooling, 360
   reactive nature of, 9–10
   terrorism, proper law for, 320, 360–363, 375–379, 395–396
   training in law enforcement, 456, 458
laws of war, *see* jus in bello
League of Arab States, 65, 294
League of Nations, 78, 83, 329, 415
Lebanon, 189–190
levée en masse, 155–156, 165
Lewis, Bernard, 88, 94
lex ferenda and *lex lata*, 19
liberals *vs.* conservatives, 91–96, 126–127
Libya, 21, 24, 60–61, 63–65, 293, 394, 395, 426–428
Lisle, Jacques de, 438 n. 193
Lockerbie, *see* Pan Am Flight 103 (Lockerbie)
Lockerbie (Pan Am Flight 103), 21, 64, 294, 426–428
London Charter, Nuremberg Trials, 339

Index

LOS (law of the sea) convention, 81, 82, 256–257, 298, 299, 417
Lotus case, 39, 141

M

Machain case (*United States v. Alvarez-Machain*), 312, 315–316, 317–318
Malaysia, 160, 187, 457
Mandela, Nelson, 106 n. 87
MAPA (Mine Action Program for Afghanistan), 204
maritime interception and interdiction operations (MIO), xvii–xviii, 255–273
    areas of maritime interdiction, right to establish, 267–268
    Australia, 301–302
    Canada, 309–311
    cargo, seizure of, 270, 272
    goals and objectives, 255–257
    legal basis for, 257–268, 297–299, 301–302
    legal restrictions on, 268–273
    non-state entities, 260, 267, 305
    piracy law, 260, 297, 298
    POW status of individuals taken, 271
    proportionality principle, 266, 268
    self-defense, 255–257, 264–266, 272
    state sponsorship of terrorist groups, 265–266
    state *vs.* merchant vessels and civil aircraft, distinguishing, 269–270
    United Kingdom, 304, 305–306
    vessels, confiscation of, 272
Martens Clause, 377
Mayer, Ann Elisabeth, 77
media
    Guantanamo detainees, photographs of processing of, 217
    role in Operation ENDURING FREEDOM, 192
medical personnel as targets, removal of identifying markers by, 252
Mexico, 41, 77, 312, 315–316
militarist fallacy, 91–96
military attacks in response to terrorism, *see* counter-terrorist military operations
military commissions used to try terrorists, 222–225, 233, 331–332, 357, 386–387, 451–453
Milosevic, Slobodan, 99, 243, 339, 348, 349
Mine Action Program for Afghanistan (MAPA), 204
MIO, *see* maritime interception and interdiction operations (MIO)
mission and threat, ROE defined by, 319
Mladic, General, 99
Mohamed Ali case, 159–160, 166
Montgomery, Lt. Col. Tony E., xvii, 243–245, 495
Montreal Convention for the Suppression of Unlawful Acts against the Safety of Civil Aviation, 35, 287, 361, 366, 399, 411
Moore, John Basset, 39
moral reasons for use of force, 20, 79–80

Morocco, 63
Moscow Declaration, 338–339
Müllerson, Rein, xiv–xv, 75–127, 134, 140, 495
multilateral antiterrorist conventions, 344–347, 350–351, 362–363, 365–366
Munich Olympics, 1972, 324, 463
murder/killing and terrorism, 361, 363–364, 377, 387–388
Murphy, John F., xx–xxi, 315–316, 391–440, 478, 479, 484–485, 495–496
Murphy, Sean, 104–105
Myers, General Richard B., 198
Myjer, Eric, 87, 111 n. 99, 112

N

An-Na'im, Abdullahi Ahmed, 107 n. 88
Nairobi US Embassy bombings, *see* East African US Embassy bombings, 1998
Napoleonic Wars, 83
national courts as forum for terrorist trials, xix–xx, 323–328, 364–369
    armed attack, armed conflict, and ordinary criminal acts, 381–386
    extradition, xix, 365–369
    international criminal law based on national norms and domestic crimes, 334–335, 361, 362
    jurisdiction of sovereign states, 333, 337–342, 346–347, 364
    legitimacy and fairness, perception of, 291–293, 331–333, 366
    multilateral antiterrorist conventions establishing grounds for domestic jurisdiction and prosecution, 344–347, 350–351, 362–363, 365–366
    political will of sovereign states, 333, 337–342, 371–372
    self-defense actions, criminal law enforcement as alternative to, 34–36, 356
    UN Security Council Resolution 1373 reinforcing current framework, 251–352
national laws on terrorism and coalition operations, 277–279
national security
    Canadian legislation, 311
    justice used to achieve goals of, 326–327
nationality, *see* citizens
NATO, *see* North Atlantic Treaty Organization (NATO)
Nazis, 123, 247, 316–317, 338–339 (*see also* Nuremberg Trials)
necessity principle, self-defense, 27–28, 34–36, 67, 108–111
Netanyahu, Benjamin, 92, 94
Netherlands, 18, 101, 427–428
neutrality
    erosion of concept of, 182
    "for us or against us" argument, 47, 91–96, 197, 235
    maritime neutrality, 258–259, 269, 272–273
    Operation ENDURING FREEDOM'S lack of scope for, 196–197
    tight of states to be neutral, 182
New Zealand, 18, 290
Newton, Lt. Col. Michael A., xix–xx, 323–352, 364, 371, 381–388, 496
Nicaragua case, 26, 51–52, 54–56, 70, 117, 119–120, 133, 135, 355

Index

no-fly zones, 23
non-state entities, xiv–xv, xx, 17, 355
    community consensus regarding, 66–67, 112–115
    MIO, 260, 267, 304
    piracy laws, 134, 260
    self-defense against, 33–34, 38–47, 48–54, 66–67, 355–356
    state responsibility for armed attacks by, 38–47, 68–70, 110, 141–142
    state sponsorship of non-state terrorist entities, 54–57, 68–70, 119–120
normativism, positivism, and normative positivism, 75–80
North Atlantic Treaty Organization (NATO)
    future developments, 467–468
    jus ad bellum, 113
    MIO, 265
    proper law and proper forum for terrorism, 467–468
    self-defense, 16–17, 20, 23, 24, 34, 71, 72
North Korea, 135, 394, 438
Northern Alliance, 191, 192, 209–210, 227, 236, 238, 245
Northern Ireland, xx, 188, 315, 359, 395
Nuccio, Richard A., 496–497
nuclear weapons
    Convention on the Physical Protection of Nuclear Material, 412
    Draft International Convention for the Suppression of Nuclear Terrorism, 411–414
    ICRC statement regarding, 195
    International Court of Justice *Nuclear Weapons* opinion, 28
    Iraq/ Hussein's attempts to obtain, 146
Nuremberg Trials, xv, xix, 338–339, 343
Nye, Joseph, 393

O

OAS (Organization of American States), 17, 355, 395, 416, 419–422
OAU (Organization of African Unity) Convention on the Prevention and Combating of Terrorism, 419
O'Connell, Mary Ellen, 70–71
Office of Homeland Security/Homeland Security Council, 12
Oman, 18
Operation ALLIED FORCE, 23, 348
Operation ANACONDA, 458
Operation BARBAROSSA, 247
Operation DENY FLIGHT, 23
Operation DESERT STORM, 115, 123
Operation EL DORADO CANYON, 60–61, 68, 72
Operation ENDURING FREEDOM, xvii, 14–18, 458 (*see also* Afghanistan)
    applicability of jus in bello to, 192–196
    Australia, 277–279, 285–286, 288, 290, 295, 301–302
    bombing pause, call for, 206
    bombing techniques, 197–205

Canada, 309–311
chemical weapons, 205
coalition operations, 235–241 (*see also* coalition operations)
humanitarian and human rights law, 468–471
humanitarian relief, 205–208
jus in bello issues, 191–208, 249–250
media role in, 192
MIO, *see* maritime interception and interdiction operations (MIO)
neutrality, lack of scope for, 196–197
neutrality, scope for, 182
nontraditional nature of enemy, 298
Northern Alliance, 191, 192, 209–210, 227, 238
POW disasters in Afghanistan, 208–210
POW status of Taliban and al Qaeda prisoners, 171–174, 211–222, 441–454, 468–471 (*see also* unlawful/lawful combatancy and POW status)
refugees, 207–208
self-defense, 13
United Kingdom, 237, 303–307
Operation IRAQI FREEDOM, 436–438 n. 193
opinio juris, 78
Organization for Security and Cooperation in Europe (OSCE), 265
Organization of African Unity (OAU) Convention on the Prevention and Combating of Terrorism, 419
Organization of American States (OAS), 17, 355, 395, 416, 419–422
Organization of the Islamic Conference, 18, 278
Organized Crime, Convention against Transnational, 415–416
O'Rourke, Commander Kevin, xix, 297–299, 314–315
OSCE (Organization for Security and Cooperation in Europe), 265

P

Pacific Command coordination group framework, 473–475, 480
Pacific theater, WWII, 248
pacifist fallacy, 91–96
Pakistan, 18, 63, 65, 69, 129, 236, 297, 456, 462
Palestine (*see also* Israel)
    future developments, 462
    Islamic Jihad, 393
    jus ad bellum, 115
    PLO (Palestine Liberation Organization), 41, 189
    Popular Front for the Liberation of Palestine, 162–163
    suicide bombings, 225, 439
    terrorism, definition of, 278
Pan Am Flight 103 (Lockerbie), 21, 64, 294, 426–428
Panama, 394
Paraguay, 394
Paris, Declaration of, 152

Index

Paris Minimum Standards of Human Rights Norms in a State of Emergency, 285
partisans of WWII, lawful combatancy status of, 164–165, 171
Pastrana, Andres, 395
Pearl Harbor, 248
Peloponnesian War, 75
penal law, International Congress of (1936), 329 (*see also* criminal law)
Pentagon, 9/11 attack on, *see* September 11 attacks
Perera, Rohan, 406
Perez de Cuellar, Javier, 61
Perron, Lt. Col. Jean-Guy, xix, 309–311, 320, 497
Pershing, General John, 41
Peru, 372, 395
Phalangists, 189
Philippines, 2, 393, 438
Pictet, Jean, 215
piracy, 134, 249, 260, 297, 298
PLO (Palestine Liberation Organization), 41, 189
police force training, 456, 458
political correctness, 126–127
political offender exception to extradition agreements, 286–288, 292, 368
political will of sovereign states to prosecute terrorists, 333, 337–342, 371–372, 455–459
Ponte, Carla Del, 332
Popular Front for the Liberation of Palestine, 162–163
Portugal, 113
positivism, normativism, and normative positivism, 75–80
Posner, Richard, 391
poverty and terrorism, 95
POWs, *see* prisoners of war (POWs)
pre-modern *vs.* post-modern societies, 96–102, 122–126, 134
preemptive use of force
    "axis of evil," against, 438
    Iraq/Sadam Hussein, against, 429–438, 483–485
    self-defense, anticipatory, 32, 38, 116–119, 133, 134–135, 435–437, 487
prisoners of war (POWs)
    Afghanistani POW disasters, 208–210
    release of, 222
    status as, *see* unlawful/lawful combatancy and POW status
proper forum, *see* forum
proper law for terrorism and terrorists, 320, 360–363, 375–379, 395–396
proportionality principle
    jus in bello/jus ad bellum, 183–184, 247–248
    MIO, 266, 268
    self-defense, 28–30, 36–38, 67
Prosper, Pierre-Richard, 225
Protocol I, Geneva Conventions, 167–170, 186–187, 213–216

Q

el Qadhafi, Muammar, 60
al Qaeda, *see* al Qaeda, under a
Qala-e Jhangi Fort, POW revolt at, 208–209
Qatar, 18
Quirin case, 154, 160, 214

R

Raslam, Karim, 125
Red Brigade, 187
Red Cross (International Committee, ICRC), 176, 195–196, 215, 217–218, 220–221, 228–229, 376–377, 469
refugees, 207–208
regime change in Iraq, 146–147
regional agreements
    antiterrorist conventions, 416–424
    counter-terrorism programs, 456, 457, 473–475, 480
Reisman, Michael, 59 n. 150, 60 n. 151, 66, 118, 415, 436
religion, 76–77, 94–95, 124–127
Rempt, Rear Admiral Rodney P., 1–3, 137, 497
rendition, irregular, 312–319
replenishment at sea, 257
repression and terrorism, 95
reprisals, defensive, 116–119
Resolution 1373, United Nations Security Council, xiii, xiv, xviii (*see also* other Resolutions under United Nations Security Council Resolutions)
    extradition, 288–289
    future developments, 408, 463–464, 470
    international dimensions of Afghan conflict, recognition of, 193
    jus ad bellum, 110, 145
    maritime interception and interdiction operations (MIO), 260–262, 264, 265, 273
    MIO, 260–262
    proper forum and proper law for terrorism, 350–352, 355
    self-defense, 15, 34
Rhodesia, 112
Rice, Condoleezza, 437, 440
Richard, Ryan, 264
Rio Treaty, 17
Rishikof, Harvey, 385, 497–498
Roberts, Sir Adam, xvi–xvii, 175–230, 232, 248, 251, 386, 498
Robinson, Mary, 469
ROE (rules of engagement), 180, 233, 248, 302, 303–304, 310, 319
"rogue" nations, 91
Rome Statute of the International Criminal Court (ICC), 293–296, 336, 342, 357
Roosevelt, President Franklin D., 323, 338

Index

Rostow, Nicholas, xx, xxii, 461–465, 487, 498
rules of engagement (ROE), 180, 233, 248, 302, 303–304, 310, 319
Rumsfeld, Donald, 183, 199, 201, 205, 217
Russia
    future developments, 394, 418, 437, 438 n. 193
    ICC, 293
    jus ad bellum, 89 n. 35, 140, 247
    self-defense, 18, 61, 63, 65
    terrorism, defining, 305
Rwanda, 98, 100, 339–340, 343, 364

S

Saalfeld, Michael, xxii, 467–472, 498
SAARC (South Asian Association for Regional Cooperation) Regional Convention on Suppression of Terrorism, 416–417, 424
Saint Augustine of Hippo, 76
Saint Thomas Aquinas, 76
San Remo Manual, 310
Sandinistas, *see Nicaragua* case
Saudi Arabia, 18, 69
Schmitt, Michael N., xiv, 7–73, 105, 129–134, 141, 142, 145, 147, 498–499
Schwarzenberger, Georg, 162
Schwebel, Judge Stephen, 55, 120
Scott of Foscote, Lord, 290, 293
sea, law of the (LOS Convention), 81, 82, 256–257, 298, 299, 417
Secret Service, 480
self-defense, xiv, 7–73
    abduction of terrorists, 315
    al Qaeda, US actions in self-defense against, 33–47
    basic principles of, 25–32
    characteristics of terrorist attacks and responses, 111–119
    civilians carrying light arms for purposes of, 164–165
    coalition operations, 319–320
    criminal law enforcement as alternative, 34–36
    criteria for, 479
    cross-border counter-terrorist attacks in pursuit of non-state entities, 38–47, 68, 141–142
    evidence requirement, 70–72
    evolving standard of, 57–72
    future attacks, anticipatory responses to, 32, 38, 116–119, 133, 134–135, 435–437, 487
    geopolitical circumstances, change in, 122–123
    imminency principle, 30–31, 38, 66–67, 115–116, 138, 436, 478
    Iraq/Sadam Hussein, 2, 41–42, 62, 63, 65, 434–436, 483–485
    irreversible course of action, 479
    MIO, 255–257, 264–266, 272
    necessity principle, 27–28, 34–36, 67, 108–111
    non-state entities, 33–34, 38–47, 48–54, 66–67, 355–356

Index

normative UN framework for use of force, 19–24, 131–134, 143–145
Operation ENDURING FREEDOM, 468–469
pre-combat (unconditional) demands, sufficiency of, 44–46
proportionality principle, 28–30, 36–38, 67
purpose of, 68
regime change in Iraq, 146–147
"scale and effects" as to what constitutes an armed attack, 21 n. 46, 25–27, 33
September 11 attacks and aftermath, 9–19
state responsibility for actions of non-state entity within its borders, 48–54, 142, 145
state sponsorship of terrorists, 54–57, 68–70
Taliban, US actions in self-defense against, 47–57
United Kingdom and coalition operations, 304
September 11 attacks, xi, xiii–xv, xx, xxii (*see also* al Qaeda; more specific topics)
armed conflict between al Qaeda and United States, existence of, 357–360, 381–386
conduct in accordance with jus in bello and POW status of al Qaeda detainees, 172–173
cost of, 130–131
impact of, 84, 87, 91, 353, 439, 461–465
justice as goal following, 324–325
qualitative/quantitative distinctiveness of, 7–8
statement of facts and aftermath, 9–19
threat to sovereignty of US from, 232
"trend" in terrorism, as, 392, 393
Serbia, *see* Yugoslavia, Bosnia, Serbia, and Kosovo
Shaltut, Sheikh, 77
Shearer, Ivan, xviii–xix, 275–296, 312, 319, 499
Shehada, Sheikh Salah, 93
Shining Path, 395
Simon, Jeffrey, 392
Singapore, 160, 457
Siracusa Principles on the Limitation and Derogation Provisions in the ICCPR, 285
Slaughter, Anne-Marie, 104, 116
slave trade, vessels engaged in, 299
smallpox, 146
Smith, Ian, 112
social phenomenon, terrorism viewed as, 461–462
Somalia, 23, 100, 140, 263, 272, 283
South Africa, 41
South America, *see* Latin America
South Asian Association for Regional Cooperation (SAARC) Regional Convention on Suppression of Terrorism, 416–417, 424
South Korea, 18, 63, 135, 474
Soviet Union, *see* Russia
space law, 81, 82
Spain, 65
Sparta, 75
special operations forces, US, 244–245
Sri Lankan Tigers of Tamil Eelan, 393–394

Index

state responsibility for armed attacks by terrorist groups, 38–47, 68–70, 110, 141–142, 145, 456–457
state sponsorship of terrorist groups, 54–57, 68–70, 119–122, 265–266, 394
Stone, Chief Justice, 154
Sudan, 24, 42, 64, 65, 70, 394, 395, 428
suicide bombings, Palestinian, 225, 439
Sun Tzu, 134
Supervielle, Col. Manuel E. F., xx, 371–374, 384–385, 499–500
Sweden, 98
Syria, 394

T

Tadic, Dusco (*Prosecutor v. Tadic/Dusco Tadic* case), 24 n. 56, 56–57, 120, 294 n. 59
Tajikistan, 18
Taliban, ix, xiii, xiv, xvi, xvii, 2 (*see also* Afghanistan)
    al Qaeda connections, 12–13, 40, 47–48, 53, 138, 442, 446–447
    detainees held in Guantanamo Bay, Cuba, *see* unlawful/lawful combatancy and POW status
    distinguishing from al Qaeda, 139, 140
    economic sanctions, 425, 428
    judicial proceedings against Taliban/al Qaeda detainees, 222–225
    legitimacy of government by, 69, 129–135, 139, 140–141, 143, 446
    POW status of Taliban and al Qaeda prisoners, 171–174, 441–454, 468–471 (*see also* unlawful/lawful combatancy and POW status)
    self-defense against, US actions in, 47–57
    state sponsorship of al Qaeda, 54–57, 68–70
Tamil Tigers, 393–394
Tanzanian US Embassy bombings, *see* East African US Embassy bombings, 1998
technology, terrorists' use of, 100
territorial basis for jurisdiction, 280, 286–287
terrorism and terrorists (*see also* more specific entries)
    cassus belli, what constitutes, 354–355
    casual/indiscriminate use of term, 139–140, 377
    characteristics of terrorist attacks and responses, 111–119
    crimes against humanity, terrorism as, 363–364, 365
    defining, xviii, 277–279, 305, 387
    dichotomy of responses to, 91–96
    habit, terrorism as, 486
    international phenomenon, terrorism as, 353–354
    jus ad bellum and jus in bello, applicability of, 106–108, 354–360, 395–396
    justifications for terrorism, 114–115, 377, 439, 462
    national laws on terrorism and coalition operations, 277–279
    proper law for, 320, 360–363, 375–379, 395–396
    social phenomenon *vs.* weapon, 461–462
    traditional wars, terrorism's difference from, 90–91
    "trends" in terrorism, xx, 391–296
Terry, Col. James P., xx, xxi–xxii, 441–459, 473, 475, 485, 500

Thatcher, Margaret, 430
third states' maritime vessels, interception and interdiction of, *see* maritime interception and interdiction operations (MIO)
Thirty Years War, 83
Thomas Aquinas (saint), 76
Thompson, Sir Robert, 187
threat and mission, ROE defined by, 319
Thucydides, 75
Tibi, Bassam, 88, 100 n. 68, 124, 125
Tigers of Tamil Eelam, 393–394
Tokyo Convention on Offenses and Certain Other Acts Committed on Board Aircraft, 35, 399
Tora Bora, 200, 204–205
Toscanino case *(United States v. Toscanino)*, 319
training in law enforcement, 456, 458
Transnational Organized Crime, Convention against, 415–416
Travalio, Gregory, 116, 122
treaties and conventions, 396–424 (*see also* specific titles)
    effectiveness of, 84–86, 396–399, 477
    extradition treaties, 286, 291, 365–369
    global conventions, 396–416
    implementation of, 439
    jurisdiction, 281–282
    jus in bello, 179, 229, 233
    MIO, 258
    multilateral antiterrorist conventions, 344–347, 350–351, 362–363, 365–366
    piecemeal *vs.* comprehensive approach, 397–399
    regional conventions, 416–424
Treaty on Cooperation among the States Members of the Commonwealth of Independent States in Combating Terrorism, 418
"trends" in terrorism, xx, 391–296
Trenin, Dmitri, 123
Tunisia, 41
Turkey, 18, 41–42, 293
Turkmenistan, 456
Turner, Robert F., xv, 129–135, 140–142, 143–144, 318–319, 446, 500

U

Uganda, 110
unconditional demands, 44–46
uniforms, requirement that lawful combatants wear, 160–162, 170, 171–172, 244–245
unilateral use of force, 59
UNITA, 112
United Arab Emirates, 18, 69
United Kingdom
    coalition operations, 303–307, 319
    counter-terrorist military operations, application of jus in bello to, 187–188

Index

East African 1988 US Embassy bombings, extradition and jurisdiction issues, 290
future developments, 410, 427, 432
Guantanamo detainees, concerns regarding, 239, 241
Gulf region, historic involvement in, 304
IRA (Irish Republican Army), xx, 188, 315, 359, 395
jus ad bellum, 77
MIO, 304, 305–306
mission and threat, ROE defined by, 319
Operation ENDURING FREEDOM, 237, 303–307
Operation IRAQI FREEDOM, 436–438 n. 193
proper law and proper forum for terrorists, 359, 367
self-defense, 14–15, 18, 61, 63, 65
terrorism, definition of, 278
United Nations
    antiterrorism conventions, xx–xxi, 396–397 (*see also* specific conventions)
    "armed attacks," what constitute, 21 n. 46, 25–27, 33, 66–67, 112–115
    Article 2(4) of Charter, 19–24, 33, 38, 131
    Article 39 of Charter, 23, 33–34
    Article 42 of Charter, 16, 19, 483
    Article 51 of Charter, *see* Article 51 of United Nations Charter
    Article 103 of Charter, 249
    Article 110 of Charter, 306
    authorization of use of force, 16, 24, 143, 145, 275–276, 432
    common security framework, regarded as, 440
    Counter-Terrorism Committee (CTC), 464–465
    economic sanctions, 425–429
    effect of 9/11 attacks on, xxii, 461–465
    enforcement operations, 19, 23–24
    General Assembly Resolution 2131, 48
    geo-political changes, effect of, 80–91, 122–126
    intent and interpretation of Charter, 102–106, 134, 137–138
    Iraq and Saddam Hussein's violations of Security Council Resolutions, 146
    law of the sea (LOS) convention, 81, 82, 256–257, 298, 299, 417
    multilateral antiterrorist conventions, 344–347, 350–351, 362–363, 365–366
    non-state *vs.* state entities, self-defense against, 33–34
    normative framework for use of force, 19–24
    normative positivism of Charter, movement away from, 79–80
    notification requirements, 14, 25, 64
    powers of Security Council, 248–249
    September 11 attacks, response to, 15–16, 23–24
    Terrorism Prevention Branch, 411
United Nations Security Council Resolutions
    Resolution 678, 433, 485
    Resolution 687, 430, 438 n. 193, 484, 485
    Resolution 688, 432
    Resolution 733, 263
    Resolution 1154, 433

Resolution 1193, 192
Resolution 1205, 433
Resolution 1214, 442
Resolution 1267, 196–197, 442, 446, 465
Resolution 1269, 22
Resolution 1333, 45, 442, 446
Resolution 1356, 263, 264
Resolution 1368, 15, 34, 110, 145, 193, 197, 260, 265, 355, 463
Resolution 1373, *see* Resolution 1373, United Nations Security Council
Resolution 1377, 23
Resolution 1378, 15
Resolution 1386, 15, 119
Resolution 1441, 437–438 n. 193
Resolution 1445, 465
United States (*see also* more specific entries)
    armed conflict between al Qaeda and, existence of, 357–360, 381–386, 470, 478
    concerns over thinking about terrorism in laws of war framework, 186–187
    Constitution, 446
    European concepts as to war on terrorism *vs.*, 96–102
    extradition agreement with United Kingdom, 367
    hyperpower following Cold War, 79–80
    ICC, opposition to, *see* International Criminal Court (ICC)
    Iraq, regime change in, 429–430, 437
    special operations forces, 244–245
    Standing Rules of Engagement, 180, 233, 248
United States v. Alvarez-Machain, 312, 315–316, 317–318
United States v. Toscanino, 319
Universal Declaration of Human Rights, xviii–xix, 282–283
universality principle of jurisdiction, 280–281
unlawful/lawful combatancy and POW status, xv–xvi, xvii, 151–174, 210–222, 378–379, 441–454 (*see also* Geneva Conventions)
    Afghanistan war, specific applicability to, 171–174, 211–222, 441–454, 468–471
    allegiance/non-allegiance to the detaining power, 163–164, 173
    belonging to a party in the conflict, 162–163
    Bush Administration's position as to al Qaeda and Taliban prisoners, 444–445
    carrying arms openly, 162, 169–170, 171, 172
    coalition operations threatened by, 227–228, 238–241
    concerns regarding treatment of Guantanamo detainees, 217–219
    conduct in accordance with jus in bello, 162, 169, 172–173
    distinguishing combatants and civilians, 151–153, 170
    distinguishing lawful and unlawful combatants, 153–156, 211–217
    distinguishing (or not distinguishing) al Qaeda from Taliban fighters, 172–173, 211, 445–447
    distinguishing war criminals from unlawful combatants, 155
    doubt as to status, 172, 230
    eligibility for POW status, 448–450, 451
    entitlement to POW status, 156–167, 211–217, 443–444, 471

Index

group *vs.* individual determination of status, 450–451
group *vs.* individual observance of laws regarding, 166–167
Hague Regulations, 156–167
human rights and humanitarian law, 217, 220–222, 445–446, 470–471
Israeli special legislation on detention of unlawful combatants, 155–156
judicial effects of denying POW status to al Qaeda detainees, 445–446
judicial proceedings against detainees, 222–225
jus in bello, 210–222
Lebanon, Israel's invasion of, 189
levée en masse, 155–156, 165
maritime interception and interdiction operations (MIO), 271
medical personnel as targets, removal of identifying markers by, 252
military commissions, trial of detainees before, 222–225, 233, 451–453
Northern Ireland/IRA, 188
organizational requirements for lawful combatants, 162
Protocol I, 167–170, 186–187, 213–216
purpose of taking prisoners of war, 153
recognition of Taliban government, 447–448
regular *vs.* irregular forces, 159–167
release of prisoners, 222
rights of detainees, 445–446
self-defense issues, 2–3, 19
subordination to a responsible commander, 160, 172
terminological problems regarding, 214–215
UN Charter paradigm and, 137–138
uniform or fixed distinct emblem recognizable at a distance, 160–162, 170, 171–172, 244–245
US combatants not conforming to requirements, 173, 213, 244–245, 251–252
US elucidation of position, 217–222, 227–228
Vietnam, 188–189, 442–443
wounded combatants, 153
UNSCOM, 433
USS Cole, attack on, 477
UTA Flight 722, 21, 426–428
Uzbekistan, 18, 456

V

Vattel, Emerich de, 77
Venezuela, 77, 394
Vera Cruz incident, 77
Victoria, Franciscus, 76
Vienna Centre for International Crime Prevention, 411
Vienna Convention on the Law of Treaties, 484
Vietnam, 41, 100, 188–189, 442–443
Villa, Pancho, 41
von Heinegg, Wolff Heintschel, xvii–xviii, 143, 144, 255–273, 306, 314, 494

Index

W

war criminals distinguished from unlawful combatants, 155
war, laws of, *see* jus in bello
Warner, Daniel, 94
weapon, terrorism viewed as, 461–462
weapons of mass destruction (WMD), 91, 116, 146, 430, 433, 436, 478, 484 (*see also* biological weapons; chemical weapons; nuclear weapons)
Webster, Daniel, 27, 43, 77, 138, 335, 436
White, Nigel, 87, 111 n. 99, 112
Wilber, Ken, 91
Winfrey, Capt. Ronald R., xxii, 473–475, 480, 500
WMD (weapons of mass destruction), 91, 116, 146, 430, 433, 436, 478, 484 (*see also* biological weapons; chemical weapons; nuclear weapons)
World Trade Center
1993 bombing, 11, 294
September 11 attack on, *see* September 11 attacks
World War I and World War II, influence of, 2, 58, 83–85, 123, 132, 247–248, 477–478
World War II partisans, lawful combatancy status, 164–165, 171
wounded combatants, 153

Y-Z

Yemen, 65, 480
Yugoslavia, Bosnia, Serbia, and Kosovo
  Alexander of Yugoslavia (prince), assassination of (1934), 329
  bombings, 199, 201 203–204
  ICRC statements on detainees, 220
  International Criminal Tribunal for the Former Yugoslavia (ICTY), 120–121, 331–332, 339–340, 343, 349, 364
  jus ad bellum, 84, 101, 102, 112, 120
  jus in bello, observance of, 181
  neutrality, erosion of concept of, 182
  proper forum and proper law for terrorism, 329, 339, 348–349
  self-defense, 23, 56
Zimbabwe, 112